# ARAGON
# ISSUES IN
# PHILOSOPHY

# PARAGON ISSUES IN PHILOSOPHY

# THE PARAGON ISSUES IN PHILOSOPHY SERIES

**A** t colleges and universities, interest in the traditional areas of philosophy remains strong. Many new currents flow within them, too, but until recently many of these—the rise of cognitive science, for example, or feminist philosophy—often went largely unnoticed in undergraduate philosophy courses. The Paragon Issues in Philosophy Series responds to both perennial and newly influential concerns by bringing together a team of able philosophers to address the fundamental issues in philosophy today and to outline the state of contemporary discussion about them.

More than twenty volumes are scheduled; they are organized into three major categories. The first covers the standard topics—metaphysics, theory of knowledge, ethics, and political philosophy—stressing innovative developments in those disciplines. The second focuses on more specialized but still vital concerns in the philosophies of science, religion, history, sport, and other areas. The third category explores new work that relates philosophy and fields such as feminist criticism, medicine, economics, technology, and literature.

The level of writing is aimed at undergraduate students who have little previous experience studying philosophy. The books provide brief but accurate introductions that appraise the state of the art in their fields and show how the history of thought about their topics has developed. Each volume is complete in itself but also aims to complement others in the series.

Traumatic change characterized the twentieth century and the twenty-first will be no different in that regard. All of its pivotal issues will involve philosophical questions. As the editors at Paragon House continue to work with us, we hope that this series will help to encourage the understanding needed in a new millennium whose times will be as complicated and problematic as they are promising.

John K. Roth
Claremont McKenna College

Frederick Sontag
Pomona College

# GLOBAL JUSTICE: SEMINAL ESSAYS

# THOMAS POGGE
# DARREL MOELLENDORF

# GLOBAL JUSTICE: SEMINAL ESSAYS

## Global Responsibilities
## Volume I

ARAGON
ISSUES IN
PHILOSOPHY

**PARAGON HOUSE ✦ ST. PAUL**

First Edition 2008

Published in the United States by
Paragon House
1925 Oakcrest Avenue Ste 7
St. Paul, MN 55113-2619

Paragon Issues in Philosophy Series
    Global Responsibilities
      Volume I: Global Justice: Seminal Essays
      Volume II: Global Ethics: Seminal Essays

Library of Congress Cataloging-in-Publication Data

Pogge, Thomas Winfried Menko.
  Global justice : seminal essays / Thomas Pogge, Darrel Moellendorf. -- 1st
ed.
     p. cm. -- (Paragon issues in philosophy series)
  Summary: "Carefully selected papers by political philosophers and
political theorists on global justice"--Provided by publisher.
  Includes bibliographical references and index.
  ISBN 978-1-55778-869-6 (pbk. : alk. paper)
  1. Justice. 2. Political science--Philosophy. I. Moellendorf, Darrel.
II. Title.
  JC578.P62 2008
  320.01'1--dc22
                        2007043694

Manufactured in the United States of America

10 9 8 7 6 5 4 3

For current information about all releases from Paragon House,
visit the web site at http://www.paragonhouse.com

# CONTENTS

## VOLUME I: GLOBAL JUSTICE

# VOLUME II: GLOBAL ETHICS

# Preface:

# INTRODUCTION TO THE
# TWO-VOLUME COLLECTION

For centuries, moral reflection on international relations was focused on matters of war and peace. These issues are still important and much discussed. Since World War II, however, other themes have become more prominent due to increasing global interdependence and an erosion of sovereignty. The United Nations and the Universal Declaration of Human Rights reflect efforts to establish globally uniform minimum standards for the treatment of citizens within their own countries. The Bretton Woods institutions and later the World Trade Organization powerfully shape the economic prospects of countries and their citizens. Global and regional organizations, most notably the UN Security Council and the European Union, have acquired political functions and powers that were traditionally thought to belong to national governments.

These developments are in part a response to the horrors of World War II. But they are also fueled by technological innovations that limit the control governments can exert within their jurisdictions. Thus, industrialization has massive transnational effects that no country can avoid—effects on culture and expectations, on biodiversity, climate, oceans, and atmosphere. New communications technologies make it much harder to control the information available to a national population. And many of the goods demanded by more affluent consumers everywhere require ingredients imported from many foreign lands. The traditional concerns with the just internal organization of societies and the moral rules governing warfare leave out some highly consequential features of the modern world.

After some delay, academic moral reflection has responded to these developments. Beginning in the early 1970s, philosophers and others have asked probing questions about how the emergence of a post-Westphalian world modifies and enlarges the moral responsibilities of governments, corporations, and individuals. These debates were driven also by the realization that world poverty has overtaken war as the greatest source of avoidable human misery. Many more people—some 300 million—have died from hunger and remediable diseases in peacetime in the seventeen years since the end of the Cold War than have perished from wars, civil wars, and government repression over the entire twentieth century. And poverty continues unabated, with some 830 million human beings chronically undernourished, 1100 million lacking access to safe water, and 2600 million lacking access to basic sanitation;[1] 2000 million lacking access to essential drugs;[2] 1000 million lacking adequate shelter and 2000 million lacking electricity;[3] 774 million adults being illiterate,[4] and 218 million children between five and seventeen doing wage work outside their household.[5] Such severe deficits in the fulfillment of social and economic human rights also bring further deficits in civil and political human rights in their wake. Very poor people—often physically and mentally stunted due to malnutrition in infancy, illiterate due to lack of schooling, and much preoccupied with their family's survival—can cause little harm or benefit to the politicians and officials who rule them. Such rulers have far greater incentive to attend to the interests of agents more capable of reciprocation: the interests of affluent compatriots and foreigners, of domestic and multinational corporations, and of foreign governments.

The great catastrophe of human poverty is ongoing, as is the annual toll of 18 million deaths from poverty-related causes, roughly one-third of all human deaths.[6] Three facts make such poverty deeply problematic,

---

1. UNDP (United Nations Development Program), *Human Development Report 2006* (Houndsmills: Palgrave Macmillan, 2006), 33 and 174. Also at hdr.undp.org/hdr2006.
2. See www.fic.nih.gov/about/plan/exec_summary.htm.
3. UNDP, *Human Development Report 1998* (New York: Oxford University Press, 1998), 49, http://hdr.undp.org/reports/global/1998/en/pdf/hdr_1998_ch3.pdf.
4. See www.uis.unesco.org.
5. See ILO (International Labour Office), *The End of Child Labour: Within Reach* (Geneva: ILO 2006), Table 1.1. Also at www.ilo.org/public/english/standards/relm/ilc/ilc95/pdf/rep-i-b.pdf.
6. See WHO (World Health Organisation), *The World Health Report 2004* (Geneva: WHO Publications 2004), 120-25. Also at www.who.int/whr/2004.

morally. First, it occurs in the context of unprecedented global affluence that is easily sufficient to eradicate all life-threatening poverty. Although 2735 million human beings are reported to be living below the World Bank's $2/day poverty line,[7] and 42 percent below it on average,[8] their collective shortfall from this line amounts to less than 1 percent of the national incomes of the high-income countries with their 1 billion people.[9] A shift in the global income distribution involving only 0.7 percent of global income would wholly eradicate the severe poverty that currently blights the lives of over 40 percent of the human population. While the income inequality between the top and bottom tenth of the human population is a staggering 320:1,[10] the wealth inequality is nine times greater still. In 2000 the bottom 50 percent of the world's adults together had 1.1 percent of global wealth with the bottom 10 percent having only 0.03 percent, while the top 10 percent had 85.1 percent and the top 1 percent had 39.9 percent.[11] Severe poverty today is avoidable at a cost that is tiny in relation to the incomes and fortunes of the

7. See Shaohua Chen and Martin Ravallion, "How Have the World's Poorest Fared since the Early 1980s?" *World Bank Research Observer* 19 (2004), 141–69, 153. Also at wbro.oupjournals.org/cgi/content/abstract/19/2/141.

8. Ibid., 152 and 158, dividing the poverty gap index by the headcount index.

9. To count as poor by the $2/day standard, a person in the US must in 2007 live on less than $1120. (This figure is based on the official definition of the poverty line in terms of the purchasing power that $2.15 had in the US in 1993 as updated via the US consumer price index at www.bls.gov/cpi/home.htm). Ascribing much greater purchasing power to the currencies of poor countries than market exchange rates would suggest, the World Bank assumes that about one-quarter of this amount, $280 per person per year, is sufficient to escape poverty in typical poor countries. The 2735 million global poor live, then, on approximately $444 billion annually and lack roughly $322 billion annually relative to the $2/day poverty line. This $322 billion is less than one percent of the gross national incomes of the high-income countries which, in 2005, summed to $35,529 billion. See World Bank, *World Development Report, 2007* (New York: Oxford University Press, 2006), 289.

10. Branko Milanovic, *Worlds Apart: Measuring International and Global Inequality* (Princeton: Princeton University Press, 2005), 108.

11. James B. Davies, Susanna Sandstrom, Anthony Shorrocks, and Edward N. Wolff, *The World Distribution of Household Wealth*, World Institute for Development Economics Research (WIDER), December 5, 2006 (www.wider.unu.edu/research/2006-2007/2006-2007-1/wider-wdhw-launch-5-12-2006/wider-wdhw-report-5-12-2006.pdf), Table 10a.

affluent—very much smaller, for instance, than the Allies' sacrifice in blood and treasure for victory in World War II.

Second, the enormous global inequalities just described are increasing relentlessly. Branko Milanovic reports that real incomes of the poorest 5 percent of world population declined 20 percent in the 1988–93 period and another 23 percent during 1993–98, while real global per capita income increased by 5.2 percent and 4.8 percent respectively.[12] For the 1988–98 period he finds that, assessed in terms of purchasing power parities (PPPs), the Gini measure of inequality among persons worldwide increased from 62.2 to 64.1, and the Theil from 72.7 to 78.9.[13] We can confirm and update his findings with other, more intuitive data. The World Bank reports that, in the high-income Organisation for Economic Co-operation and Development (OECD) countries, household final consumption expenditure per capita (constant 2000 US Dollars) rose 56.3 percent in real terms over the 1984-2004 globalization period: from $11,582 in 1984 to $18,103 in 2004.[14] World Bank interactive software can be used to calculate how the poorer half of humankind have fared, in terms of their real (inflation/PPP adjusted) consumption expenditure, during this same period.[15] Here are the gains for various percentiles of world population labeled from poorest to richest:

| | | | |
|---|---|---|---|
| 48.62% | gain for the | 50th | percentile (median) |
| 47.18% | gain for the | 40th | percentile |
| 42.20% | gain for the | 30th | percentile |
| 36.16% | gain for the | 20th | percentile |
| 33.72% | gain for the | 15th | percentile |
| 32.61% | gain for the | 10th | percentile |
| 31.92% | gain for the | 7th | percentile |
| 30.86% | gain for the | 5th | percentile |
| 30.44% | gain for the | 3rd | percentile |
| 22.87% | gain for the | 2nd | percentile |
| 9.64% | gain for the | 1st | percentile |

12. Milanovic, *Worlds Apart*, 108.
13. Ibid.
14. See devdata.worldbank.org/dataonline; last accessed 10 June 2007
15. See iresearch.worldbank.org/PovcalNet/jsp/index.jsp. Full calculations are on file with the author. Unfortunately, this database excludes the populations of the high-income countries and therefore permits no similarly detailed calculations for the top half of the human population.

Because economic inequality is increasing also within the high-income countries—in the US, for example, households in the top one percent of the income hierarchy have expanded their share of national pre-tax income from 9 percent to 16 percent since 1979[16]—we can conclude that global inequality is rising across the entire income spectrum. The shares of the most affluent percentiles of the human population are growing faster than the average, the shares of poorer percentiles are growing slower, and the shares of the poorest percentiles are growing the least.

Third, conditions of life anywhere on earth are today deeply affected by international interactions of many kinds and by the rules that shape such interactions. In the modern world, the traffic of international and even intranational economic transactions is profoundly influenced by an elaborate system of treaties and conventions about trade, investments, loans, patents, copyrights, trademarks, double taxation, labor standards, environmental protection, use of seabed resources, and much else. Insofar as we participate in this system and share some responsibility for its design, we are morally implicated in any contribution it makes to ever-increasing global economic inequality and to the consequent persistence of severe poverty.

These plain facts about the contemporary world render obsolete the traditional sharp distinction between *intra*national and *inter*national relations. Until the twentieth century, these were seen as constituting distinct worlds, the former inhabited by persons, households, corporations and associations within one territorially bounded society, the latter inhabited by a small number of actors: sovereign states. National governments provided the link between these two worlds. On the inside such a government was a uniquely important actor within the state, interacting with persons, households, corporations and associations, and dominating these other actors by virtue of its special power and authority—its *internal sovereignty*. On the outside, the government *was* the state, recognized as entitled to act in its name, to make binding agreements on its behalf, and so on—its *external sovereignty*. Though linked in this way, the two worlds were seen as separate, and normative assessments unquestioningly took this separation for granted, sharply distinguishing two separate domains of moral theorizing.

---

16. David Leonhardt: "Larry Summers's Evolution," *New York Times Magazine*, 10 June 2007.

Today, very much more is happening across national borders than merely interactions and relations among governments. For one thing, there are many additional important actors on the international scene: international agencies, such as the United Nations, the European Union, the World Trade Organization, the World Bank, and the International Monetary Fund, as well as multinational corporations and international non-governmental organizations (NGOs). Interactions and relations among states and these new actors are structured through highly complex systems of rules and practices, some with associated adjudication and enforcement mechanisms. Those actors and these rules powerfully influence the domestic life of national societies: through their impact on pollution and climate change, invasive diseases, culture, and information technology, and (most profoundly) through market forces that condition access to capital and raw materials, export opportunities, domestic tax bases and tax rates, prices, wages, labor standards, and much else.

This double transformation of the traditional realm of international relations—the proliferation of transnational actors and the profound influence of the systematic activities of these actors deep into the domestic life of national societies—is part of what is often meant by the vague term *globalization*. It helps explain why "global" is displacing "international" in both explanatory and moral theorizing. This terminological shift reflects that much more is happening across national borders than merely interactions and relations among states. It also reflects that the very distinction between the national and international realms is dissolving. With national borders losing their causal and explanatory significance, it appears increasingly incongruous and dogmatic to insist on their traditional role as moral watersheds.

To complete the picture, let us now attend to the distinction that underlies the division of this work into two volumes. There are distinct ways of looking at the events of our social world. On the one hand, we can see such events interactionally: as actions, and effects of actions performed by individual and collective agents. On the other hand, we can see them institutionally: as effects of how our social world is structured and organized—of our laws and conventions, practices and social institutions. These two ways of viewing entail different descriptions and explanations of social phenomena, and they also lead to two distinct kinds of moral analysis or moral diagnostics.

Take some morally salient event, for example the fact that some particular child suffers from malnutrition, that some woman is unemployed, or that a man was hurt in a traffic accident. We can causally trace such events back to the conduct of individual and collective agents, including the person who is suffering the harm. Doing so involves making counterfactual statements about how things would or might have gone differently if this or that agent had acted in some other way. We can then sort through these counterfactual statements in order to determine whether any of the causally relevant agents ought to have acted differently and thus is partly or wholly at fault for the regrettable event. This will involve us in examining whether any such agents could have foreseen that their conduct would lead to the regrettable event and could also reasonably have averted the harm without causing substantial costs to themselves or third parties. Inquiries of this kind might be referred to as *interactional* moral analysis or *interactional* moral diagnostics.

Often, regrettable events can also be traced back to standing features of the social system in which they occur: to its culture, for example, or to its institutional order. In this vein, one might causally trace child malnutrition back to high import duties on foodstuffs, unemployment to a restrictive monetary policy, and traffic accidents to the lack of regular motor vehicle safety inspections. Doing so involves making counterfactual statements about how things would or might have gone differently if this or that set of social rules had been different. We can then sort through these counterfactual statements in order to determine whether the causally relevant rules ought to have been different and whether anyone is responsible for defects in these rules that are partly or wholly to blame for the regrettable events. This will involve us in examining whether those responsible for the design of the relevant rules—for instance, members of parliament—could have foreseen that they would lead to harm and could reasonably have reformulated the rules without causing substantial harm elsewhere. We might refer to inquiries of this kind as *institutional* moral analysis or *institutional* moral diagnostics.

Interactional moral analysis emerged quite early in the evolution of moral thought. Institutional moral analysis is more demanding, presupposing an understanding of the conventional (rather than natural or divine) nature of social rules as well as of their, often statistical, comparative effects. Even a mere eighty years ago, the poor and unemployed were still often seen as lazy and delinquent merely on the ground that others of equally humble origins had risen from dishwasher to millionaire. Many people then did not understand the *structural* constraints on social mobility: that the pathways to riches are limited and that the structure of prevailing markets for capital and labor unavoidably produce certain basic rates of ("structural") unemployment and poverty. Nor did they understand that existing rates of unemployment and poverty could be influenced through intelligent redesign of the rules. Today, after Keynes, the US New Deal, and various similar national transformations, these matters are well understood, and governments are held responsible for their decisions regarding institutional design and for the effects of such decisions on the fulfillment or frustration of human needs. This understanding has been—belatedly, yet very admirably—articulated in philosophy through John Rawls's classic *A Theory of Justice*. Through this grand work, Rawls has firmly established social institutions as a distinct domain of moral assessment and has marked this domain terminologically by associating it with the term *(social) justice*. This terminological innovation has taken hold, by and large, at least in Anglophone philosophy. So the term *justice* is now predominant in the moral assessment of social rules (laws, practices, social conventions, and institutions) and used only rarely in the moral assessment of the conduct and character of individual and collective agents. In the wake of Rawls the distinction between institutional and interactional moral analysis has come to be marked as a distinction between *justice* and *ethics*.

We are quite familiar today with the focus of Rawls's book: with institutional moral analysis applied to the internal organization of one state. Still in its infancy, however, is institutional moral analysis applied beyond the state. This time lag is hardly surprising, seeing that the realm of international relations is traditionally conceived as so much smaller and more surveyable than the vast and highly complex inner workings of a modern national society. We don't need institutional moral analysis, it seems, for a world of a few dozen relevant actors in which, when bad things happen, it is usually pretty clear whose conduct is at fault. And Rawls himself, in his late work *The Law of Peoples*, explicitly shunned such analysis and confined himself to developing and defending a set of rules of good conduct for states.

The phenomena of globalization, described above, show such an account to be deeply inadequate to the world in which we live. It ignores the increasingly important transnational actors other than states as well as the increasingly profound effects transnational rules, practices, and actors have on the domestic life of national societies. Shaping the environment (e.g., global markets) in which national societies exist, such transnational rules and practices deeply shape these societies themselves: how they govern and tax themselves, how they organize education, health care, agriculture, and defense, and how they regulate foreign investment, intellectual property rights, foreign trade. Some of this influence is due to competitive pressures and transnational bargaining. Some of it works by affecting domestic incentives and power distributions: International rules that recognize any person or group exercising effective power in a less developed country as entitled to sell its natural resources, to borrow, and to import weapons in its name make it extremely tempting in resource-rich such countries to attempt to take power by force. These countries are therefore very likely to experience coup attempts, civil wars, and repressive (often military) rule. Such foreseeable effects of transnational institutional arrangements are surely relevant to their moral assessment, but other factors may be relevant as well: the way such arrangements were created or emerged, for example, and the judgments and interests of present participants in these institutional arrangements. The discourse about global justice is about this question, how to assess transnational institutional arrangements.

Justice assessment of transnational institutional arrangements can have important implications for the conduct of individual and collective actors participating in such arrangements: for governments, corporations, associations, and individuals. Insofar as transnational arrangements are just, their participants have moral reason to support them and to comply with them. Insofar as such arrangements are unjust, their participants have moral reason to seek their reform and possibly also to help protect some of their victims. Such duties must, however, be integrated into a larger account of moral responsibilities. Victims of unjust transnational arrangements in which we are participants are not the only ones who have a claim to our moral attention as individuals. We also face victims of natural calamities, victims of historical or contemporary wrongs (wrongs of colonialism, slavery, and genocide, some perhaps committed by our own country), and victims of domestic injustice (associated with race, gender, ethnic identity, religion or social class). We confront global threats and dangers (proliferation of weapons of mass destruction, climate change, new infectious diseases) as well as personal responsibilities toward our family, friends, and professional associates. And we have projects, ambitions, needs, and desires of our own that militate against devoting our whole lives to our various moral responsibilities. The situation of collective agents is characterized by a similarly diverse and confusing array of conflicting claims. Governments must balance their special responsibilities toward their own citizens against their general responsibilities toward foreign nationals who may need refuge, protection, or assistance. A corporation must analogously balance its special responsibilities toward its shareholders, customers, and those who work for it directly or indirectly against its more general responsibilities toward the communities in which it operates and toward outsiders who may be affected by its activities in multifarious ways. Religious organizations and NGOs must similarly integrate such more general and increasingly global responsibilities with their special responsibilities toward members and contributors as well as with their defining missions. For all these actors, gaining a clear moral orientation is becoming more difficult as the world in which they operate becomes larger and more interdependent. The discourse about global ethics is about how such actors should take into account and fulfill their increasingly complex and increasingly transnational moral responsibilities.

The two-volume collection before you brings together a representative sampling of the most significant, most original, most influential writings moral thinkers have composed on these issues in the three decades following 1971. These essays are of continuing importance because they have developed the terms in which these issues are debated today. These essays have sharpened the concepts that dominate our current discussions, have created the fault lines dividing present intellectual camps, and have inspired or revolted thousands of later writers, students, and ordinary citizens.

To be sure, there is other work from these three decades that could plausibly have been included, as additions or substitutions. But we wanted a manageable and affordable collection of uncut essays and have worked hard to put together a set of writings that, together, optimally reflect the formative debates. The division of the essays into two volumes follows the distinction just drawn between the two moral responsibilities of governments, corporations, and individuals. The *Global Justice* volume features essays about their political responsibilities relating to institutional design. The *Global Ethics* volume features essays about their ethical responsibilities within the context of the international order as it is. Evidently, not all the selected writings fall squarely on one or the other side of this divide. In hard cases, we were guided by the aim of making each volume as unified and self-contained as possible.

After much experimentation, we concluded that, within each volume, the essays are best presented in straight chronological order of their first publication. This ordering causes thematic leaps occasionally, but the essays do not display sufficient uniformities of scope to sustain any other arrangement. Moreover, a chronological reading is surprisingly illuminating about how the moral debate about international relations gradually took on its present shape and structure. In any case, readers and teachers will find their own selection and ordering of the materials.

For ease of use, we have inserted, in brackets, cross references within and across the two volumes. Cross references within a volume use "herein" and cross references to the companion volume use its full title or its acronym (*GJSE* or *GESE*).

From the beginning, it has been a central concern of the editors to make these texts available at an affordable price. We want our collection to be widely accessible—not merely in the affluent regions, but especially also to students in the poorer countries who are hugely interested in these issues and all too often lack electronic access to journals. It has not been easy. But in the end we have achieved an incredibly low sales price for volumes of this size. For this, the editors and readers have to thank, first and foremost, the Centre for Applied Philosophy and Public Ethics which, funded by the Australian Research Council, spans three institutions: Charles Sturt University, the University of Melbourne, and the Australian National University. CAPPE has absorbed all the permission fees as an ethical and highly cost-effective way of promoting its own mission and has also funded the crucial assistance we received from David Mollica, Matt Peterson, Tamara Shanley, and Ling Tong who competently and cheerfully converted our tables of contents into two neatly formatted volumes of text with introductory summaries and index. We must further thank Gordon Anderson and Rosemary Yokoi of Paragon House who were ready to share our vision and work with us while other publishers declared the project economically unviable. While some publishers have made extortionate demands for their copyrights, forcing us to make substitutions for some essays (though not authors), most copyright holders have been willing to waive, or greatly to reduce, their usual commercial reprinting rates. We have gratefully received cost-free permissions from Bilingual Press, from Mary Malin (Elsevier), from the *Journal of Philosophy* with authors Charles Beitz, Avishai Margalit and Joseph Raz, from the *New York Review of Books*, from Erica Wetter (New York University Press), from Peter Ohlin (Oxford University Press, US), from Dennis Moran *(Review of Politics)*, from Richard Rorty, from Springer, from the United Nations University's World Institute for Development Economics Research (UNU-WIDER), and from Utah University Press. To underscore the noncommercial character of this collection, the editors have assigned all royalties to Oxfam.

Thomas Pogge

# INTRODUCTION

*Global Justice* is part of a two-volume set of seminal essays on global justice and ethics. This volume comprises essays on persons' moral entitlements and duties in relation to global and international institutional arrangements. The claims of justice, or social justice, are a part of morality, not the whole of it. The companion volume, called *Global Ethics*, is devoted to other important matters of individual and state conduct. One source of this distinction between justice and ethics is in the writings of John Rawls. Rawls limits the subject of justice to the basic structure of the social system as a whole, "the way in which the major social institutions distribute fundamental rights and duties and determine the division of advantages from social cooperation."[1] He takes an institution to be "a public system of rules which defines offices and positions with their rights and duties, powers and immunities, and the like."[2] An institution exists, Rawls maintains, "when the actions specified by it are regularly carried out in accordance with a public understanding that the system of rules defining the institution is to be followed."[3] Among the examples of institutions that might be identified at particular times and places Rawls includes "parliaments, markets, and systems of property."[4] The guiding idea of this volume is that matters of global justice are moral matters that concern how global and international institutions should be structured so as to ensure that persons' justified claims are met.

Each of the twenty-two essays of this volume takes up the morality of the distribution of fundamental entitlements and duties by major global and international institutions, for example, the distribution of entitlements to income by the global market and of political membership by state borders and policies. The range of specific topics discussed is very broad. The volume includes discussions of, inter alia, the following questions: What are persons owed as a matter of fundamental human rights? What are the bases, if any, of duties of global justice? Does justice require global institutions that would distribute wealth and income in ways that are to some extent contrary to market distributions? If so, which principles should form the basis of such a redistribution? Which goods should be the focus of global distributive justice? Who is entitled to own and control the world's natural resources? What sort of restrictions, if any, on immigration are just? What should be the scope of governing institutions? What rules should govern in cases in which persons want to secede from an existing state? What role should the interests of persons and corporate bodies, such as states, nations, or peoples, play in theorizing about global justice? Which duties, if any, are owed only to compatriots or conationals? What is the basis of state sovereignty and what are its limits? How democratic ought global institutions to be?

We have chosen the particular essays included, not because they are the last word on theses issues, nor even the first, but because typically they have served to clarify and refine the concepts, and to develop the arguments, that are central to contemporary debates among political philosophers and theorists concerning global justice, and because they represent many of the most influential intellectual camps in present debates.

The richness of the essays frustrated our attempts to present the papers neatly according to theme. So, we have elected to present them in chronological order, even though this is not particularly satisfying intellectually. Although a thematic organization might be useful for the purposes of clarifying the development of debates, it is impossible to organize the chapters thematically without multiple listings. To further the purpose of clarifying thematic relations between the papers, we offer the following example of a grouping of chapters according to themes (chronologically ordered within each group):

Poverty and Hunger[5]
"Lifeboat Earth," Onora O'Neill
"Poverty and Food: Why Charity Is Not Enough," Thomas Nagel
"Humanity and Justice in Global Perspective," Brian Barry

Distributive Justice[6]
"Justice and International Relations," Charles R. Beitz
"Poverty and Food: Why Charity Is Not Enough," Thomas Nagel
"Equality of What?" Amartya Sen
Excerpts from Basic Rights: chapter 1, "Security and Subsistence" and chapter 2, "Correlative Duties," Henry Shue

"Humanity and Justice in Global Perspective," Brian Barry
"An Egalitarian Law of Peoples," Thomas Pogge
"Human Capabilities, Female Human Beings," Martha C. Nussbaum
"Just Taxation and International Redistribution," Hillel Steiner
"Distributive Justice, State Coercion, and Autonomy," Michael Blake

The Scope of Duties of Justice[7]
"What Is So Special about Our Fellow Countrymen," Robert E.
    Goodin
"The Ethical Significance of Nationality," David Miller
"Special Ties and Natural Duties," Jeremy Waldron
"The Law of Peoples," John Rawls
"Constructing the Law of Peoples," Darrel Moellendorf
"Distributive Justice, State Coercion, and Autonomy," Michael Blake

Immigration[8]
"The Distribution of Membership," Michael Walzer
"Aliens and Citizens: The Case for Open Borders," Joseph H. Carens
"Citizenship and National Identity: Some Reflections on the Future of
    Europe," Jürgen Habermas

Sovereignty and Institutional Scope[9]
"Democracy: From City-States to a Cosmopolitan Order?" David
    Held
"Cosmopolitanism and Sovereignty," Thomas Pogge
"The Law of Peoples," John Rawls
"Constructing the Law of Peoples," Darrel Moellendorf
"Theories of Secession," Allen Buchanan
"Liberal Toleration in Rawls's Law of Peoples," Kok-Chor Tan

Nationality and Cultural Pluralism[10]
"The Ethical Significance of Nationality," David Miller
"Citizenship and National Identity: Some Reflections on the Future
    of Europe," Jürgen Habermas
"The Law of Peoples," John Rawls
"Liberal Toleration in Rawls's Law of Peoples," Kok-Chor Tan

There are, of course, alternative ways to group the chapters for purposes of studying them thematically. We are confident that teachers will find useful alternative groupings for instructional purposes.

The field of global justice is young; none of these seminal essays is very old. The questions that they address are of obvious practical relevance. A good deal of what makes study and work in this field so engaging is the combination of the freshness and the importance of the debates. We trust that students who study these seminal papers will also come to enliven the field and advance it appropriately.

## NOTES

1. John Rawls, *A Theory of Justice* (Cambridge, MA: Harvard University Press, 1971), 7.

2. Ibid., 55.

3. Ibid.

4. Ibid.

5. The following chapters from the companion volume *Global Ethics: Seminal Essays* are also relevant to this theme: 1, 2, 8, 9, 15, 16, 19, 22, and 23.

6. The following chapters from *Global Ethics: Seminal Essays* are also relevant to this theme: 6, 19, 22, and 23.

7. The following chapters from *Global Ethics: Seminal Essays* are also relevant to this theme: 6, 19, 23, and 24.

8. Chapter 6 from *Global Ethics: Seminal Essays* is also relevant to this theme.

9. Chapters 4 and 10 from *Global Ethics: Seminal Essays* are also relevant to this theme.

10. The following chapters from *Global Ethics: Seminal Essays* are also relevant to this theme: 6, 7, 10, 12, 17, 22, and 24.

# 1. ONORA O'NEILL

Beginning from the assumption that people have a right not to be killed unjustifiably, O'Neill argues that those in a position to prevent or postpone famine deaths have a duty to do so, and further, that if they fail to do so, they will bear some of the blame for those deaths. O'Neill concedes that not all killings are unjustifiable; in particular, unavoidable killings and killing in self-defense do not fit into this category. She then conducts a thought experiment involving six survivors on a lifeboat, and considers various sorts of killings that may be perpetrated in that situation, in addition to some of the justifications that may be advanced for those killings. On a lifeboat equipped with adequate supplies, all killings are avoidable, but the self-defense justification would apply under certain conditions. Conversely, on an underequipped lifeboat, some deaths are unavoidable, but sometimes the death of any particular person is avoidable. The underequipped lifeboat is, of course, a metaphor for planet Earth. As things stand, it is as if some occupants of the lifeboat (citizens of rich countries) have accumulated more than a fair share of the available resources and thereby deprived others (the world's poor) of the essential supplies they need to live decently. O'Neill argues that, at some time in the past, the plight of the distant poor might not have implied obligations on the part of the citizens of rich countries, but that today's global technological and economic interconnectedness has changed that. People in affluent countries sometimes, through their activities, violate not only the mooted right of the distant poor not to be allowed to die, but also their more firmly established right not to be killed.

## Lifeboat Earth

*First published in* Philosophy and Public Affairs *4:3 (spring 1975): 273–92.*

If in the fairly near future millions of people die of starvation, will those who survive be in any way to blame for those deaths? Is there anything that people ought to do now, and from now on, if they are to be able to avoid responsibility for unjustifiable deaths in famine years? I shall argue from the assumption that persons have a right not to be killed unjustifiably to the claim that we have a duty to try to prevent and postpone famine deaths. A corollary of this claim is that if we do nothing we shall bear some blame for some deaths.

## JUSTIFIABLE KILLING

I shall assume that persons have a right not to be killed and a corresponding duty not to kill. I shall make no assumptions about the other rights persons may have. In particular, I shall not assume that persons have a right not to be allowed to die by those who could prevent it or a duty to prevent others' deaths whenever they could do so. Nor will I assume that persons lack this right.

Even if persons have no rights other than a right not to be killed, this right can justifiably be overridden in certain circumstances. Not all killings are unjustifiable. I shall be particularly concerned with two sorts of circumstances in which the right not to be killed is justifiably overridden. The first of these is the case of unavoidable killings; the second is the case of self-defense.

Unavoidable killings occur in situations where a person doing some act causes some death or deaths he could not avoid. Often such deaths will be unavoidable because of the killer's ignorance of some relevant circumstance at the time of his decision to act. If $B$ is driving a train, and $A$ blunders onto the track and is either unnoticed by $B$ or noticed too late for $B$ to stop the train, and $B$ kills $A$, then $B$ could not have avoided killing $A$, given his decision to drive the train. Another sort of case of unavoidable killing occurs when $B$ could avoid killing $A$ or could avoid killing $C$, but cannot avoid killing one of the two. For example, if $B$ is the carrier of a highly contagious and invariably fatal illness, he might find himself so placed that he cannot avoid meeting and so killing either $A$ or $C$, though he can choose which of them to meet. In this case the unavoidability of $B$'s killing someone is not relative to some prior decision $B$ made. The cases of unavoidable killings with which I want to deal here are of the latter sort, and I shall argue that in such cases $B$ kills justifiably if certain further conditions are met.

A killing may also be justifiable if it is undertaken in self-defense. I shall not argue here that persons have a right of self-defense that is independent of their right not to be killed, but rather that a minimal right of self-defense is a corollary of a right not to be killed. Hence the notion of self-defense on which I shall rely is in some ways different from, and narrower than, other interpretations of the right of self-defense. I shall also assume that if *A* has a right to defend himself against *B*, then third parties ought to defend *A*'s right. If we take seriously the right not to be killed and its corollaries, then we ought to enforce others' rights not to be killed.

The right of self-defense that is a corollary of the right not to be killed is a right to take action to prevent killings. If I have a right not to be killed, then I have a right to prevent others from endangering my life, though I may endanger their lives in so doing only if that is the only available way to prevent the danger to my own life. Similarly, if another has the right not to be killed, then I should, if possible, do something to prevent others from endangering his life, but I may endanger their lives in so doing only if that is the only available way to prevent the danger to his life. This duty to defend others is *not* a general duty of beneficence, but a very restricted duty to enforce others' rights not to be killed.

The right to self-defense so construed is quite narrow. It includes no right of action against those who, though they cause or are likely to cause us harm, clearly do not endanger our lives. (However, specific cases are often unclear. The shopkeeper who shoots a person who holds him up with a toy gun was not endangered, but it may have been very reasonable of him to suppose that he was endangered.) And it includes no right to greater than minimal preventive action against a person who endangers one's life. If *B* is chasing *A* with a gun, and *A* could save his life either by closing a bulletproof door or by shooting *B*, then if people have only a right not to be killed and a minimal corollary right of self-defense, *A* would have no right to shoot *B*. (Again, such cases are often unclear—*A* may not know that the door is bulletproof or not think of it or may simply reason that shooting *B* is a better guarantee of prevention.) A right of proportionate self-defense that might justify *A* in shooting *B*, even were it clear that closing the door would have been enough to prevent *B*, is not a corollary of the right not to be killed. Perhaps a right of proportionate retaliation might be justified by some claim such as that aggressors lose certain rights, but I shall take no position on this issue.

In one respect the narrow right of self-defense, which is the corollary of a right not to be killed, is more extensive than some other interpretations of the right of self-defense. For it is a right to take action against others who endanger our lives whether or not they do so intentionally. *A*'s right not to be killed entitles him to take action not only against aggressors but also against those "innocent threats"[1] who endanger lives without being aggressors. If *B* is likely to cause *A*'s death inadvertently or involuntarily, then *A* has, if he has a right not to be killed, a right to take whatever steps are necessary to prevent *B* from doing so, provided that these do not infringe *B*'s right not to be killed unnecessarily. If *B* approaches *A* with a highly contagious and invariably lethal illness, then *A* may try to prevent *B* from getting near him even if *B* knows nothing about the danger he brings. If other means fail, *A* may kill *B* in self-defense, even though *B* was no aggressor.

This construal of the right of self-defense severs the link between aggression and self-defense. When we defend ourselves against innocent threats there is no aggressor, only somebody who endangers life. But it would be misleading to call this right a right of self-preservation. For self-preservation is commonly construed (as by Locke) as including a right to subsistence, and so a right to engage in a large variety of activities whether or not anybody endangers us. But the right which is the corollary of the right not to be killed is a right only to prevent others from endangering our lives, whether or not they intend to do so, and to do so with minimal danger to their lives. Only if one takes a Hobbesian view of human nature and sees others' acts as always completely threatening will the rights of self-defense and self-preservation tend to merge and everything done to maintain life be done to prevent its destruction. Without Hobbesian assumptions the contexts where the minimal right of self-defense can be invoked are fairly special, yet not, I shall argue, rare.

There may be various other circumstances in which persons' rights not to be killed may be overridden. Perhaps, for example, we may justifiably kill those who consent to us doing so. I shall take no position on whether persons can waive their rights not to be killed or on any further situations in which killings might be justifiable.

## JUSTIFIABLE KILLINGS ON LIFEBOATS

The time has come to start imagining lurid situations, which is the standard operating procedure for this type of discussion. I shall begin by looking at some sorts of killings that might occur on a lifeboat and shall consider the sorts of justifications that they might be given.

Let us imagine six survivors on a lifeboat. There are two possible levels of provisions:

(1)  Provisions are on all reasonable calculations sufficient to last until rescue. Either the boat is near land, or it is amply provisioned or it has gear for distilling water, catching fish, etc.

(2)  Provisions are on all reasonable calculations unlikely to be sufficient for all six to survive until rescue.

We can call situation (1) *the well-equipped lifeboat situation*; situation (2) *the underequipped lifeboat situation*. There may, of course, be cases where the six survivors are unsure which situation they are in, but for simplicity I shall disregard those here.

On a well-equipped lifeboat it is possible for all to survive until rescue. No killing could be justified as unavoidable, and if someone is killed, then the justification could only be self-defense in special situations. Consider the following examples:

(1A) On a well-equipped lifeboat with six persons, *A* threatens to jettison the fresh water, without which some or all would not survive till rescue. *A* may be either hostile or deranged. *B* reasons with *A*, but when this fails, shoots him. *B* can appeal to his own and the others' right of self-defense to justify the killing. "It was him or us," he may reasonably say, "for he would have placed us in an underequipped lifeboat situation." He may say this both when *A* acts to harm the others and when *A* acts as an innocent threat.

(1B) On a well-equipped lifeboat with six persons, *B*, *C*, *D*, *E*, and *F* decide to withhold food from *A*, who consequently dies. In this case they cannot appeal to self-defense—for all could have survived. Nor can they claim that they merely let *A* die—"We didn't *do* anything"—for *A* would not otherwise have died. This was not a case of violating the problematic right not to be allowed to die but of violating the right not to be killed, and the violation is without justification of self-defense or of unavoidability.

On an underequipped lifeboat it is not possible for all to survive until rescue. Some deaths are unavoidable, but sometimes there is no particular person whose death is unavoidable. Consider the following examples:

(2A) On an underequipped lifeboat with six persons, *A* is very ill and needs extra water, which is already scarce. The others decide not to let him have any water, and *A* dies of thirst. If *A* drinks, then not all will survive. On the other hand it is clear that *A* was killed rather than allowed to die. If he had received water he might have survived. Though some death was unavoidable, *A*'s was not, and selecting him as the victim requires justification.

(2B) On an underequipped lifeboat with six persons, water is so scarce that only four can survive (perhaps the distillation unit is designed for supplying four people). But who should go without? Suppose two are chosen to go without, either by lot or by some other method, and consequently die. The others cannot claim that all they did was to allow the two who were deprived of water to die—for these two might otherwise have been among the survivors. Nobody had a greater right to be a survivor, but given that not all could survive, those who did not survive were killed justifiably if the method by which they were chosen was fair. (Of course, a lot needs to be said about what would make a selection procedure fair.)

(2C) The same situation as in (2B) holds, but the two who are not to drink ask to be shot to ease their deaths. Again the survivors cannot claim that they did not kill but at most that they killed justifiably. Whether they did so is not affected by their shooting rather than dehydrating the victims, but only by the unavoidability of some deaths and the fairness of procedures for selecting victims.

(2D) Again the basic situation is as in (2B). But the two who are not to drink rebel. The others shoot them and so keep control of the water. Here it is all too clear that those who died were killed, but they too may have been justifiably killed. Whether the survivors kill justifiably depends neither on the method of killing nor on the victims' cooperation, except insofar as cooperation is relevant to the fairness of selection procedures.

Lifeboat situations do not occur very frequently. We are not often confronted starkly with the choice between killing or being killed by the application of a decision to distribute scarce rations in a certain way. Yet this is becoming the situation of the human species on this globe. The current metaphor "spaceship Earth" suggests more drama and less danger; if we are feeling sober about the situation, "lifeboat Earth" may be more suggestive.

Some may object to the metaphor "lifeboat Earth." A lifeboat is small; all aboard have equal claims to be there and to share equally in the provisions. Whereas the earth is vast, and while all may have equal rights to be there, some also have property rights which give them special rights to consume, while others do not. The starving millions are far away and have no right to what is owned by affluent individuals or nations, even if it could prevent their deaths. If they die, it will be said, this is a violation at most of their right not to be allowed to die. And this I have not established or assumed.

I think that this could reasonably have been said in times past. The poverty and consequent deaths of far-off persons was something the affluent might perhaps have done something to prevent, but which they had (often) done nothing to bring about. Hence they had not violated the right not to be killed of those living far off. But the economic and technological interdependence of today alters this situation.[2] Sometimes deaths are produced by some persons or groups of persons in distant, usually affluent, nations. Sometimes such persons and groups of persons violate not only some persons' alleged right not to be allowed to die but also their more fundamental right not to be killed.

We tend to imagine violations of the right not to be killed in terms of the killings so frequently discussed in the United States today: confrontations between individuals where one directly, violently, and intentionally brings about the other's death. As the lifeboat situations have shown, there are other ways in which we can kill one another. In any case, we do not restrict our vision to the typical mugger or murderer context. $B$ may violate $A$'s right not to be killed even when

(a) $B$ does not act alone.

(b) $A$'s death is not immediate.

(c) It is not certain whether $A$ or another will die in consequence of $B$'s action.

(d) $B$ does not intend $A$'s death.

The following set of examples illustrates these points about killings:

(aa)  $A$ is beaten by a gang consisting of $B$, $C$, $D$, etc. No one assailant single-handedly killed him, yet his right not to be killed was violated by all who took part.

(bb)  $A$ is poisoned slowly by daily doses. The final dose, like earlier ones, was not, by itself, lethal. But the poisoner still violated $A$'s right not to be killed.

(cc)  $B$ plays Russian roulette with $A$, $C$, $D$, $E$, $F$, and $G$, firing a revolver at each once, when he knows that one firing in six will be lethal. If $A$ is shot and dies, then $B$ has violated his right not to be killed.

(dd)  Henry II asks who will rid him of the turbulent priest, and his supporters kill Becket. It is reasonably clear that Henry did not intend Becket's death, even though he in part brought it about, as he later admitted.

These explications of the right not to be killed are not too controversial taken individually, and I would suggest that their conjunction is also uncontroversial. Even when $A$'s death is the result of the acts of many persons and is not an immediate consequence of their deeds, nor even a certain consequence, and is not intended by them, $A$'s right not to be killed may be violated.

# FIRST CLASS VERSUS STEERAGE ON LIFEBOAT EARTH

If we imagine a lifeboat in which special quarters are provided for the (recently) first-class passengers, and on which the food and water for all passengers are stowed in those quarters, then we have a fair, if crude, model of the present human situation on lifeboat Earth. For even on the assumption that there is at present sufficient for all to survive, some have control over the means of survival and so, indirectly, over others' survival. Sometimes the exercise of control can lead, even on a well-equipped lifeboat, to the starvation and death of some of those who lack control. On an ill-equipped lifeboat some must die in any case and, as we have already seen, though some of these deaths may be killings, some of them may be justifiable killings. Corresponding situations can, do, and will arise on lifeboat earth, and it is to these that we should turn our attention, covering both the presumed present situation of global sufficiency of the means of survival and the expected future situation of global insufficiency.

## SUFFICIENCY SITUATIONS

Aboard a well-equipped lifeboat, any distribution of food and water that leads to a death is a killing and not just a case of permitting a death. For the acts of those who distribute the food and water are the causes of a death that would not have occurred had those agents either had no causal influence or done other acts. By contrast, a person whom they leave in the water to drown is merely allowed to die, for his death would have taken place (other things being equal) had those agents had no causal influence, though it could have been prevented had they rescued him.[3] The distinction between killing and allowing to die, as here construed, does not depend on any claims about the other rights of persons who are killed. The death of the shortchanged passenger of example (1B) violated his property rights as well as his right not to be killed, but the reason the death was classifiable as a killing depended on the part which the acts of the other passengers had in causing it. If we suppose that a stowaway on a lifeboat has no right to food and water and is denied them, then clearly his property rights have not been violated. Even so, by the above definitions he is killed rather than allowed to die. For if the other passengers had either had no causal influence or done otherwise, his death would not have occurred. Their actions—in this case distributing food only to those entitled to it—caused the stowaway's death. Their acts would be justifiable only if property rights can sometimes override the right not to be killed.

Many would claim that the situation on lifeboat Earth is not analogous to that on ordinary lifeboats, since it is not evident that we all have a claim, let alone an equal claim, on the earth's resources. Perhaps some of us are stowaways. I shall not here assume that we do all have some claim on the earth's resources, even though I think it plausible to suppose that we do. I shall assume that even if persons have unequal property rights and some people own nothing, it does not follow that $B$'s exercise of his property rights can override $A$'s right not to be killed.[4] Where our activities lead to others' deaths that would not have occurred had we either done something else or had no causal influence, no claim that the activities were within our economic rights would suffice to show that we did not kill.

It is not far-fetched to think that at present the economic activity of some groups of persons leads to others' deaths. I shall choose a couple of examples of the sort of activity that can do so, but I do not think that these examples do more than begin a list of cases of killing by economic activities. Neither of these examples depends on questioning the existence of unequal property rights; they assume only that such rights do not override a right not to be killed. Neither example is one for which it is plausible to think that the killing could be justified as undertaken in self-defense.

Case one might be called the *foreign investment* situation. A group of investors may form a company that invests abroad—perhaps in a plantation or in a mine—and so manage their affairs that a high level of profits is repatriated, while the wages for the laborers are so minimal that their survival rate is lowered, that is, their expectation of life is lower than it might have been had the company not invested there. In such a case the investors and company management do not act alone, do not cause immediate deaths, and do not know in advance who will die; it is also likely that they intend no deaths. But by their involvement in the economy of an underdeveloped area they cannot claim, as can another company that has no investments there, that they are "doing nothing." On the contrary, they are setting the policies that determine the living standards that determine the survival rate. When persons die because of the lowered standard of living established by a firm or a number of firms that dominate a local economy and either limit persons to employment on their terms or lower the other prospects for employment by damaging traditional economic structures, and these firms could either pay higher wages or stay out of the area altogether, then those who establish these policies are violating some persons' rights not to be killed. Foreign investment that *raises* living standards, even to a still abysmal level, could not be held to kill, for it causes no additional deaths, unless there are special circumstances, as in the following example.

Even when a company investing in an underdeveloped country establishes high wages and benefits and raises the expectation of life for its workers, it often manages to combine these payments with high profitability only by having achieved a tax-exempt status. In such cases the company is being subsidized by the general tax revenue of the underdeveloped economy. It makes no contribution to the infrastructure—for example, roads and harbors and airports—from which it benefits. In this way many underdeveloped economies have come to include developed enclaves whose development is achieved in part at the expense of the poorer majority.[5] In such cases, government and company policy combine to produce a high wage sector at the expense of a low wage sector; in consequence, some of the persons in the low wage sector, who would not otherwise have died, may die; these persons, whoever they may be, are killed and not merely allowed to die. Such killings may sometimes be justifiable—perhaps, if they are outnumbered by lives saved through having a developed sector—but they are killings nonetheless, since the victims might have survived if not burdened by transfer payments to the developed sector.

But, one may say, the management of such a corporation and its investors should be distinguished more sharply. Even if the management may choose a level of wages, and consequently of survival, the investors usually know nothing of this. But the investors, even if ignorant, are responsible for company policy. They may often fail to exercise control, but by law they have control. They choose to invest in a company with certain foreign investments; they profit from it; they can, and others cannot, affect company policy in fundamental ways. To be sure the investors are not murderers—they do not intend to bring about the deaths of any persons; nor do the company managers usually intend any of the deaths company policies cause. Even so, investors and management acting together with the sorts of results just described do violate some persons' rights not to be killed and usually cannot justify such killings either as required for self-defense or as unavoidable.

Case two, where even under sufficiency conditions some persons' economic activities result in the deaths of other persons, might be called the *commodity pricing* case. Underdeveloped countries often depend heavily on the price level of a few commodities. So a sharp drop in the world price of coffee or sugar or cocoa may spell ruin and lowered survival rates for whole regions. Yet such drops in price levels are not in all cases due to factors beyond human control. Where they are the result of action by investors, brokers, or government agencies, these persons and bodies are choosing policies that will kill some people. Once again, to be sure, the killing is not single-handed, it is not instantaneous, the killers cannot foresee exactly who will die, and they may not intend anybody to die.

Because of the economic interdependence of different countries, deaths can also be caused by rises in the prices of various commodities. For example, the present near-famine in the Sahelian region of Africa and in the Indian subcontinent is attributed by agronomists partly to climatic shifts and partly to the increased prices of oil and hence of fertilizer, wheat, and other grains.

> The recent doubling in international prices of essential foodstuffs will, of necessity, be reflected in higher death rates among the world's lowest income groups, who lack the income to increase their food expenditures proportionately, but live on diets near the subsistence level to begin with.[6]

Of course, not all of those who die will be killed. Those who die of drought will merely be allowed to die, and some of those who die because less has been grown with less fertilizer will also die because of forces beyond the control of any human agency. But to the extent that the raising of oil prices is an achievement of Arab diplomacy and oil company management rather than a windfall, the consequent deaths are killings. Some of them may perhaps be justifiable killings (perhaps if outnumbered by lives saved within the Arab world by industrialization), but killings nonetheless.

Even on a sufficiently equipped earth some persons are killed by others' distribution decisions. The causal chains leading to death-producing distributions are often extremely complex. Where they can be perceived with reasonable clarity, we ought, if we take seriously the right not to be killed and seek not merely to avoid killing others but to prevent third parties from doing so, to support policies that reduce deaths. For example—and these are only examples—we should support certain sorts of aid policies rather than others; we should oppose certain sorts of foreign investment; we should oppose certain sorts of commodity speculation, and perhaps support certain sorts of price support agreements for some commodities (e.g., those that try to maintain high prices for products on whose sale poverty-stricken economies depend).

If we take the view that we have no duty to enforce the rights of others, then we cannot draw so general a conclusion about our duty to support various economic policies that might avoid some unjustifiable killings. But we might still find that we should take action of certain sorts either because our own lives are threatened by certain economic activities of others or because our own economic activities threaten others' lives. Only if we knew that we were not part of any system of activities causing unjustifiable deaths could we have no duties to support policies that seek to avoid such deaths. Modern economic causal chains are so complex that it is likely that only those who are economically isolated and self-sufficient could know that they are part of no such systems of activities. Persons who believe that they are involved in some death-producing activities will have some of the same duties as those who think they have a duty to enforce others' rights not to be killed.

## Scarcity Situations

The last section showed that sometimes, even in sufficiency situations, some might be killed by the way in which others arranged the distribution of the means of subsistence. Of far more importance in the long run is the true lifeboat situation—the situation of scarcity. We face a situation in which not everyone who is born can live out the normal span of human life and, further, in which we must expect today's normal life span to be shortened. The date at which serious scarcity will begin is not generally agreed upon, but even the more optimistic prophets place it no more than decades away.[7] Its arrival will depend on factors such as the rate of technological invention and innovation, especially in agriculture and pollution control, and the success of programs to limit human fertility.

Such predictions may be viewed as exonerating us from complicity in famine deaths. If famine is inevitable, then—while we may have to choose whom to save—the deaths of those whom we do not or cannot save cannot be seen as killings for which we bear any responsibility. For these deaths would have occurred even if we had no causal influence. The decisions to be made may be excruciatingly difficult, but at least we can comfort ourselves that we did not produce or contribute to the famine.

However, this comforting view of famine predictions neglects the fact that these predictions are contingent upon certain assumptions about what people will do in the prefamine period. Famine is said to be inevitable *if* people do not curb their fertility, alter their consumption patterns, and avoid pollution and consequent ecological catastrophes. It is the policies of the present that will produce, defer, or avoid famine. Hence if famine comes, the deaths that occur will be results of decisions made earlier. Only if we take no part in systems of activities that lead to famine situations can we view ourselves as choosing whom to save rather than whom to kill when famine comes. In an economically inter-dependent world, there are few people who can look on the approach of famine as a natural disaster from which they may kindly rescue some, but for whose arrival they bear no responsibility. We cannot stoically regard particular famine deaths as unavoidable if we have contributed to the emergence and extent of famine.

If we bear some responsibility for the advent of famine, then any decision on distributing the risk of famine is a decision whom to kill. Even a decision to rely on natural selection as a famine policy is choosing a policy for killing—for under a different famine policy different persons might have survived, and under different prefamine policies there might have been no famine or a less severe famine. The choice of a particular famine policy may be justifiable on the grounds that once we have let it get to that point there is not enough to go around, and somebody must go, as on an ill-equipped lifeboat. Even so, the famine policy chosen will not be a policy of saving some but not all persons from an unavoidable predicament.

Persons cannot, of course, make famine policies individually. Famine and prefamine policies are and will be made by governments individually and collectively and perhaps also by some voluntary organizations. It may even prove politically impossible to have a coherent famine or prefamine policy for the whole world; if so, we shall have to settle for partial and piecemeal policies. But each person who is in a position to support or oppose such policies, whether global or local, has to decide which to support and which to oppose. Even for individual persons, inaction and inattention are often a decision—a decision to support the famine and prefamine policies, which are the status quo whether or not they are "hands off" policies. There are large numbers of ways in which private citizens may affect such policies. They do so in supporting or opposing legislation affecting aid and foreign investment, in supporting or opposing certain sorts of charities or groups such as Zero Population Growth, in promoting or opposing ecologically conservative technology and lifestyles. Hence we have individually the onus of avoiding killing. For even though we

(a)   do not kill single-handedly those who die of famine

(b)   do not kill instantaneously those who die of famine

(c)   do not know which individuals will die as the result of the prefamine and famine policies we support (unless we support something like a genocidal famine policy)

(d)   do not intend any famine deaths

we nonetheless kill and do not merely allow to die. For as the result of our actions in concert with others, some will die who might have survived had we either acted otherwise or had no causal influence.

## FAMINE POLICIES AND PREFAMINE POLICIES

Various principles can be suggested on which famine and prefamine policies might reasonably be based. I shall list some of these, more with the aim of setting out the range of possible decisions than with the aim of stating a justification for selecting some people for survival. One very general policy might be that of adopting whichever more specific policies will lead to the fewest deaths. An example would be going along with the consequences of natural selection in the way in which the allocation of medical care in situations of great shortage does, that is, the criteria for relief would be a high chance of survival if relief is given and a low chance otherwise—the worst risks would be abandoned. (This decision is analogous to picking the ill man as the victim on the lifeboat in 2A.) However, the policy of minimizing deaths is indeterminate, unless a certain time horizon is specified. For the policies that maximize survival in the short run—e.g., preventive medicine and minimal living standards—may also maximize population increase and lead to greater ultimate catastrophe.[8]

Another general policy would be to try to find further grounds that can justify overriding a person's right not to be killed. Famine policies adopted on these grounds might permit others to kill those who will forgo their right not to be killed (voluntary euthanasia, including healthy would-be suicides) or to kill those whom others find dependent and exceptionally burdensome, for example, the unwanted sick or aged or unborn or newborn (involuntary euthanasia, abortion, and infanticide). Such policies might be justified by claims that the right not to be killed may be overridden in famine situations if the owner of the right consents or if securing the right is exceptionally burdensome.

Any combination of such policies is a policy of killing some and protecting others. Those who are killed may not have their right not to be killed violated without reason; those who set and support famine policies and prefamine policies will not be able to claim that they do not kill, but if they reason carefully they may be able to claim that they do not do so without justification.

From this vantage point it can be seen why it is not relevant to restrict the right of self-defense to a right to defend oneself against those who threaten one's life but do not do so innocently. Such a restriction may make a great difference to one's view of abortion in cases where the mother's life is threatened, but it does not make much difference when famine is the issue. Those who might be chosen as likely victims of any famine policy will probably be innocent of contributing to the famine, or at least no more guilty than others; hence the innocence of the victims is an insufficient ground for rejecting a policy. Indeed it is hard to point a finger at the guilty in famine situations. Are they the hoarders of grain? The parents of large families? Inefficient farmers? Our own generation?

In a sense we are all innocent threats to one another's safety in scarcity situations, for the bread one person eats might save another's life. If there were fewer people competing for resources, commodity prices would fall and starvation deaths be reduced. Hence famine deaths in scarcity situations might be justified on grounds of the minimal right of self-defense as well as on grounds of the unavoidability of some deaths and the reasonableness of the policies for selecting victims. For each famine death leaves fewer survivors competing for whatever resources there are, and the most endangered among the survivors might have died—had not others done so. So a policy that kills some may be justified on the grounds that the most endangered survivors could have been defended in no other way.

Global scarcity is not here yet. But its imminence has certain implications for today. If all persons have a right not to be killed and a corollary duty not to kill others, then we are bound to adopt prefamine policies that ensure that famine is postponed as long as possible and is minimized. And a duty to try to postpone the advent and minimize the severity of famine is a duty on the one hand to minimize the number of persons there will be and on the other to maximize the means of subsistence.[9] For if we do not adopt prefamine policies with these aims, we shall have to adopt more drastic famine policies sooner.

So if we take the right not to be killed seriously, we should consider and support not only some famine policy for future use but also a population and resources policy for present use. There has been a certain amount of philosophical discussion of population policies.[10] From the point of view of the present argument it has two defects. First, it is for the most part conducted within a utilitarian framework and focuses on problems such as the different population policies required by maximizing the total and the average utility of a population. Second, this literature tends to look at a scarcity of resources as affecting the quality of lives but not their very possibility. It is more concerned with the question, How many people should we add? than with the question, How few people could we lose? There are, of course, many interesting questions about population policies that are not relevant to famine. But here I shall consider only population and resource policies determined on the principle of postponing and minimizing famine, for these are policies that might be based on the claim that persons have a right not to be killed, so that we have a duty to avoid or postpone situations in which we shall have to override this right.

Such population policies might, depending upon judgments about the likely degree of scarcity, range from the mild to the draconian. I list some examples. A mild population policy might emphasize family planning, perhaps moving in the direction of fiscal incentives or measures that stress not people's rights, but their duties to control their bodies. Even a mild policy would require a lot both in terms of invention (e.g., the development of contraceptives suitable for use in poverty-stricken conditions) and innovation (e.g., social policies that reduce the incentives and pressures to have a large family).[11] More draconian policies would enforce population limitation—for example, by mandatory sterilization after a certain number of children were born or by reducing public health expenditures in places with high net reproduction rates to prevent death rates from declining until birth rates do so. A policy of completely eliminating all further births (e.g., by universal sterilization) is also one that would meet the requirement of postponing famine, since extinct species do not suffer famine. I have not in this argument used any premises which show that a complete elimination of births would be wrong, but other premises might give reasons for thinking that it is wrong to enforce sterilization or better to have some persons rather than no persons. In any case, the political aspects of introducing famine policies make it likely that this most austere of population policies would not be considered.

There is a corresponding range of resource policies. At the milder end are the various conservation and pollution control measures now being practiced or discussed. At the tougher end of the spectrum are complete rationing of energy and materials consumption. If the aim of a resources policy is to avoid killing those who are born, and adequate policy may require both invention (e.g., solar energy technology and better waste retrieval techniques) and innovation (e.g., introducing new technology in such a way that its benefits are not quickly absorbed by increasing population, as has happened with the green revolution in some places).

At all events, if we think that people have a right not to be killed, we cannot fail to face up to its long-range implications. This one right by itself provides ground for activism on many fronts. In scarcity situations that we help produce, the defeasibility of the right not to be killed is important, for there cannot be any absolute duty not to kill persons in such situations but only a commitment to kill only for reasons. Such a commitment requires consideration of the condition or quality of life that is to qualify for survival. Moral philosophers are reluctant to face up to this problem; soon it will be staring us in the face.

# NOTES

1. Cf. Robert Nozick, *Anarchy State and Utopia* (New York, 1974), p. 34. Nozick defines an innocent threat as "someone who is innocently a causal agent in a process such that he would be an aggressor had he chosen to become such an agent."

2. Cf. Peter Singer, "Famine, Affluence, and Morality," *Philosophy & Public Affairs* 1, no. 3 (spring 1972): 229–43, 232 [reprinted in *Global Ethics: Seminal Essays*, 1–14, 4]. I am in agreement with many of the points that Singer makes, but am interested in arguing that we must have some famine policy from a much weaker set of premises. Singer uses some consequentialist premises: Starvation is bad; we ought to prevent bad things when we can do so without worse consequences; hence we ought to prevent starvation whether it is nearby or far off and whether others are doing so or not. The argument of this article does not depend on a particular theory about the grounds of obligation, but should be a corollary of any nonbizarre ethical theory that has any room for a notion of rights.

3. This way of distinguishing killing from allowing to die does not rely on distinguishing "negative" from "positive" acts. Such attempts seem unpromising since any act has multiple descriptions of which some will be negative and others positive. If a clear distinction is to be made between killing and letting die, it must hinge on the *difference* that an act makes for a person's survival, rather than on the description under which the agent acts.

4. The point may appear rather arbitrary, given that I have not rested my case on one theory of the grounds of obligation. But I believe that almost any such theory will show a right not to be killed to override a property right. Perhaps this is why Locke's theory can seem so odd—in moving from a right of self-preservation to a justification of unequal property rights, he finds himself gradually having to reinterpret all rights as property rights, thus coming to see us as the owners of our persons.

5. Cf. P. A. Baron, *The Political Economy of Growth* (New York, 1957), especially chapter 5, "On the Roots of Backwardness"; or A. G. Frank, *Capitalism and Underdevelopment in Latin America* (New York, 1967). Both works argue that underdeveloped economies are among the products of developed ones.

6. Lester R. Brown and Erik P. Eckholm, "The Empty Breadbasket," *Ceres* (F.A.O. Review on Development), March–April 1974, p. 59. See also N. Borlaug and R. Ewell, "The Shrinking Margin," in the same issue.

7. For discussions of the time and extent of famine see, for example, P. R. Ehrlich, *The Population Bomb*, rev. ed. (New York, 1971); R. L. Heilbroner, *An Inquiry into the Human Prospect* (New York, 1974); *Scientific American*, September 1974, especially R. Freedman and B. Berelson, "The Human Population"; P. Demeny, "The Populations of the Underdeveloped Countries"; R. Revelle, "Food and Population."

8. See *Scientific American*, September 1974, especially A. J. Coale, "The History of the Human Population."

9. The failure of "right to life" groups to pursue these goals seriously casts doubt upon their commitment to the preservation of human lives. Why are they active in so few of the contexts where human lives are endangered?

10. For example, J. C. C. Smart, *An Outline of a System of Utilitarian Ethics* (Melbourne, 1961), pp. 18, 44ff.; Jan Narveson, "Moral Problems of Population," *Monist* 57 (1973): 62–86; "Utilitarianism and New Generations," *Mind* 76 (1967): 62–72.

11. Cf. Mahmood Mamdani, *The Myth of Population Control* (New York, 1972), for evidence that high fertility can be based on rational choice rather than ignorance or incompetence.

# 2. CHARLES R. BEITZ

Beitz argues that Rawls's theory of justice pays insufficient attention to two problems in international relations. The first is whether states have exclusive rights to their natural resource endowments. The second is whether states are subject to an international distributive principle such as the difference principle that Rawls defends as appropriate domestically. With respect to the first problem, Beitz argues that the answer is negative within Rawls's assumptions about international relations. This renders states subject to a resource redistribution principle. With respect to the second problem, Beitz argues for a positive answer by appeal to a modified original position that excludes knowledge of citizenship. The moral importance of international economic interdependence justifies extending Rawlsian distributive principles to the world at large.

## Justice and International Relations

*First published in* Philosophy and Public Affairs *4:4 (summer 1975): 360–89.*

> Current events have brought into sharp focus the realization
> that...there is a close inter-relationship between the prosperity of
> the developed countries and the growth and development of the
> developing countries....International cooperation for development
> is the shared goal and common duty of all countries.[1]

Do citizens of relatively affluent countries have obligations founded on justice to share their wealth with poorer people elsewhere? Certainly they have some redistributive obligations, founded on humanitarian principles requiring those who are able to help those who, without help, would surely perish. But obligations of justice might be thought to be more demanding than this, to require greater sacrifices on the part of the relatively well off, and perhaps sacrifices of a different kind as well. Obligations of justice, unlike those of humanitarian aid, might also require efforts at large-scale institutional reform. The rhetoric of the United Nations General Assembly's "Declaration on the Establishment of a New International Economic Order" suggests that it is this sort of obligation that requires wealthy countries to substantially increase their contributions to less developed countries and to radically restructure the world economic system. Do such obligations exist?

This question does not pose special theoretical problems for the utilitarian, for whom the distinction between obligations of humanitarian aid and obligations of social justice is a second-order distinction. Since utility-maximizing calculations need not respect national boundaries, there is a method of decision available when different kinds of obligations conflict. Contractarian political theories, on the other hand, might be expected to encounter problems in application to questions of global distributive justice. Contractarian principles usually rest on the relations in which people stand in a national community united by common acceptance of a conception of justice. It is not obvious that contractarian principles with such a justification underwrite any redistributive obligations between persons situated in different national societies.

This feature of contractarian principles has motivated several criticisms of Rawls's theory of justice.[2] These criticisms hold, roughly, that it is wrong to take the nation-state as the foundation of contractarian principles, that, instead, such principles ought to apply globally.[3] I want to pursue this theme here, in part because it raises interesting problems for Rawls's theory, but also because it illuminates several important features of the question of global justice, a question to which too little attention has been paid by political philosophers. In view of increasingly visible global distributive inequalities, famine, and environmental deterioration, it can hardly be denied that this question poses a main political challenge for the foreseeable future.

My discussion has four parts. I begin by reviewing Rawls's brief remarks on international justice and show that these make sense only on the empirical assumption that nation-states are self-sufficient. Even if this assumption is correct, I then claim, Rawls's discussion of international justice is importantly incomplete, for it neglects certain problems about natural resources. In part 3, I go on to question the empirical foundation of the self-sufficiency assumption and sketch the consequences for Rawlsian ideal theory of abandoning the assumption. In conclusion, I explore the relation of an ideal theory of international justice to some representative problems of politics in the nonideal world.

This is a large agenda, despite the absence of any extended consideration of the most familiar problems of international ethics, those concerning the morality of war, which I take up only briefly. While these are hardly insignificant questions, it seems to me that preoccupation with them has too often diverted attention from more pressing distributive issues. Inevitably, I must leave some problems undeveloped, and merely suggest some possible solutions for others. The question of global distributive justice is both complicated and new, and I have not been able to formulate my conclusions as a complete theory of global justice. My main concern has been to see what such a theory might involve.

# I

Justice, Rawls says, is the first virtue of social institutions. Its "primary subject" is "the basic structure of society, or more exactly, the way in which the major social institutions distribute fundamental rights and duties and determine the division of advantages from social cooperation" (7). The central problem for a theory of justice is to identify principles by which the basic structure of society can be appraised.

Rawls's two principles characterize "a special case of the problem of justice." They do not characterize "the justice of the law of nations and of relations between states" (7–8) because they rest on morally significant features of an ongoing scheme of social cooperation. If national boundaries are thought to set off discrete schemes of social cooperation, as Rawls assumes (457), then the relations of persons situated in different nation-states cannot be regulated by principles of social justice. As Rawls develops the theory, it is only after principles of social justice and principles for individuals (the "natural duties") are chosen that principles for international relations are considered, and then only in the most perfunctory manner.

Rawls assumes that "the boundaries" of the cooperative schemes to which the two principles apply "are given by the notion of a self-contained national community" (457). This assumption "is not relaxed until the derivation of the principles of justice for the law of nations" (457). In other words, the assumption that national communities are self-contained is relaxed when international justice is considered. What does this mean? If the societies of the world are now to be conceived as open, fully interdependent systems, the world as a whole would fit the description of a scheme of social cooperation and the arguments for the two principles would apply, a fortiori, at the global level. The principles of justice for international politics would be the two principles for domestic society writ large, and their application would have a very radical result, given the tendency to equality of the difference principle. On the other hand, if societies are thought to be *entirely* self-contained—that is, if they are to have no relations of any kind with persons, groups, or societies beyond their borders—then why consider international justice at all? Principles of justice are supposed to regulate conduct, but if, ex hypothesi, there is no possibility of international conduct, it is difficult to see why principles of justice for the law of nations should be of any interest whatsoever. Rawls's discussion of justice among nations suggests that neither of these alternatives describes his intention in the passage quoted. Some intermediate assumption is required. Apparently, nation-states are now to be conceived as largely self-sufficient, but not entirely self-contained. Probably he imagines a world of nation-states that interact only in marginal ways; perhaps they maintain diplomatic relations, participate in a postal union, maintain limited cultural exchanges, and so on. Certainly the self-sufficiency assumption requires that societies have no significant trade or economic relations.

Why, in such a world, are principles of international justice of interest? Rawls says that the restriction to ideal theory has the consequence that each society's external behavior is controlled by its principles of justice and of individual right, which prevent unjust wars and interference with human rights abroad (379). So it cannot be the need to prohibit unjust wars that prompts his worries about the law of nations. The most plausible motivation for considering principles of justice for the law of nations is suggested by an aside regarding the difficulties of disarmament (336), in which Rawls suggests that state relations are inherently unstable despite each one's commitment to its own principles of justice. Agreement on regulative principles would then be a source of security for each state concerning each other's external behavior, and would represent the minimum conditions of peaceful coexistence.

For the purpose of justifying principles for nations, Rawls reinterprets the original position as a sort of international conference:

> One may extend the interpretation of the original position and think of the parties as representatives of different nations who must choose together the fundamental principles to adjudicate conflicting claims among states. Following out the conception of the

initial situation, I assume that these representatives are deprived of various kinds of information. While they know that they represent different nations each living under the normal circumstances of human life, they know nothing about the particular circumstances of their own society.... Once again the contracting parties, in this case representatives of states, are allowed only enough knowledge to make a rational choice to protect their interests but not so much that the more fortunate among them can take advantage of their special situation. This original position is fair between nations; it nullifies the contingencies and biases of historical fate [378].

While he does not actually present arguments for any particular principles for nations, he claims that "there would be no surprises, since the principles chosen would, I think, be familiar ones" (378). The examples given are indeed familiar; they include principles of self-determination, nonintervention, the *pacta sunt servanda* rule, a principle of justifiable self-defense, and principles defining *jus ad bellum* and *jus in bello*.[4] These are supposed to be consequences of a basic principle of equality among nations, to which the parties in the reinterpreted original position would agree in order to protect and uphold their interests in successfully operating their respective societies and in securing compliance with the principles for individuals that protect human life (378, 115).

One objection to such reasoning might be that there is no guarantee that all of the world's states are internally just, or if they are, that they are just in the sense specified by the two principles. If some societies are unjust according to the two principles, some familiar and serious problems arise. In a world including South Africa or Chile, for example, one can easily imagine situations in which the principle of nonintervention would prevent other nations from intervening in support of an oppressed minority fighting to establish a more just regime, and this might seem implausible. More generally, one might ask why a principle that defends a state's ability to pursue an immoral end is to count as a moral principle imposing a requirement of justice on other states.

Such an objection, while indicating a serious problem in the real world, would be inappropriate in this context because the law of nations, in Rawls, applies to a world of just states. Nothing in Rawls's theory specifically requires this assumption, but it seems consonant with the restriction to ideal theory and parallels the assumption of "strict compliance" that plays a role in arguments for the two principles in domestic societies. It is important to see, however, that the suggested justification of these traditional rules of international law rests on an ideal assumption not present in most discussions of this subject. It does not self-evidently follow that these rules ought to hold in the nonideal world; at a minimum, an additional condition would be required, limiting the scope of the traditional rules to cases in which their observance would promote the development of just institutions in presently unjust societies while observing the basic protections of human rights expressed by the natural duties and preserving a stable international order in which just societies can exist.

Someone might think that other principles would be acknowledged, for example, regarding population control and regulation of the environment. Or perhaps, as Barry suggests, the parties would agree to form some sort of permanent international organization with consultative, diplomatic, and even collective security functions.[5] However, there is no obvious reason why such agreements would emerge from an international original position, at least so long as the constituent societies are assumed to be largely self-sufficient. Probably the parties, if confronted with these possibilities, would reason that fundamental questions of justice are not raised by them, and such issues of policy as arise from time to time in the real world could be handled with traditional treaty mechanisms underwritten by the rule, already acknowledged, that treaties are to be observed. Other issues that are today subjects of international negotiation—those relating to international regulation of common areas such as the sea and outer space—are of a different sort. They call for a kind of regulation that requires substantive cooperation among peoples in the use of areas not presently within the boundaries of any society. A cooperative scheme must be evolved that would create new wealth to which no national society could have a legitimate claim. These issues would be excluded from consideration on the ground that the parties are assumed not to be concerned with devising such a scheme. As representatives of separate social schemes, their attention is turned inward, not outward. In coming together in an international original position, they are moved by considerations of equality between "independent peoples organized as states" (378). Their main interest is in providing conditions in which just domestic social orders might flourish.

## II

Thus far, the ideal theory of international justice bears a striking resemblance to that proposed in the Definitive Articles of Kant's *Perpetual Peace.*[6] Accepting for the time being the assumption of national self-sufficiency, Rawls's choice of principles seems unexceptionable. But would this list of principles exhaust those to which the parties would agree? Probably not. At least one kind of consideration, involving natural resources, might give rise to moral conflict among states and thus be a matter of concern in the international original position. The principles given so far do not take account of these considerations.

We can appreciate the moral importance of conflicting resource claims by distinguishing two elements that contribute to the material advancement of societies. One is human cooperative activity itself, which can be thought of as the human component of material advancement. The other is what Sidgwick called "the utilities derived from any portion of the earth's surface," the natural component.[7] While the first is the subject of the domestic principles of justice, the second is morally relevant even in the absence of a functioning scheme of international social cooperation. The parties to the international original position would know that natural resources are distributed unevenly over the earth's surface. Some areas are rich in resources, and societies established in such areas can be expected to exploit their natural riches and to prosper. Other societies do not fare so well, and despite the best efforts of their members, they may attain only a meager level of well-being due to resource scarcities.

The parties would view the distribution of resources much as Rawls says the parties to the domestic original position deliberations view the distribution of natural talents. In that context, he says that natural endowments are "neither just nor unjust; nor is it unjust that men are born into society at any particular position. These are simply natural facts. What is just or unjust is the way that institutions deal with these facts" (102). A caste society, for example, is unjust because it distributes the benefits of social cooperation according to a rule that rests on morally arbitrary factors. Rawls's objection is that those who are less advantaged for reasons beyond their control cannot be asked to suffer the pains of inequality when their sacrifices cannot be shown to advance their position in comparison with an initial position of equality.

Reasoning analogously, the parties to the international original position, viewing the natural distribution of resources as morally arbitrary, would think that they should be subject to redistribution under a resource redistribution principle. This view is subject to the immediate objection that Rawls's treatment of natural talents is troublesome. It seems vulnerable in at least two ways. First, it is not clear what it means to say that the distribution of talents is "arbitrary from a moral point of view" (72). While the distribution of natural talents is arbitrary in the sense that one cannot deserve to be born with the capacity, say, to play like Rubinstein, it does not obviously follow that the possession of such a talent needs any justification. On the contrary, simply having a talent seems to furnish prima facie warrant for making use of it in ways that are, for the possessor, possible and desirable. A person need not justify his possession of talents, despite the fact that he cannot be said to deserve them, because they are already *his*; the prima facie right to use and control talents is fixed by natural fact.

The other point of vulnerability is that natural capacities are parts of the self, in the development of which a person might take a special kind of pride. A person's decision to develop one talent, not to develop another, as well as his choice as to how the talent is to be formed and the uses to which it is to be put, are likely to be important elements of his effort to shape an identity. The complex of developed talents might even be said to constitute the self; their exercise is a principal form of self-expression. Because the development of talents is so closely linked with the shaping of personal identity, it might seem that one's claim to one's talents is protected by considerations of personal liberty. To interfere with the development and use of talents is to interfere with a self. Or so, at least, it might be argued.

While I believe that Rawls's discussion of talents can be defended against objections like these, that is not my concern here. I want to argue only that objections of this sort do not apply to the parallel claim that the distribution of natural resources is similarly arbitrary. Like talents, resource endowments are arbitrary in the sense that they are not deserved. But unlike talents, resources are not naturally attached to persons. Resources are found "out there," available to the first taker. Resources must be appropriated before they can be used, whereas, in the talents case, the "appropriation" is a fait accompli of nature over which persons have no direct control. Thus, while we feel that the possession of talents confers a right to control and benefit from their use, we may feel differently about resources. Appropriation may not always need a justification; if the resources taken are of limited value, or if, as

Locke imagined, their appropriation leaves "enough and as good" for everyone else, justification may not present a problem. In a world of scarcity, however, the situation is different. The appropriation of valuable resources by some will leave others comparatively, and perhaps fatally, disadvantaged. Those deprived without justification of scarce resources needed to sustain and enhance their lives might well press claims to equitable shares.

Furthermore, resources do not stand in the same relation to personal identity as do talents. It would be inappropriate to take the sort of pride in the diamond deposits in one's back yard that one takes in the ability to play the *Appassionata*. This is because natural resources come into the development of personality (when they come in at all) in a more casual way than do talents. As I have said, talents, in some sense, are what the self is; they help constitute personality. The resources under one's feet, because they lack this natural connection with the self, seem to be more contingent than necessary elements of the development of personality. Like talents, resources are used in this process; they are worked on, shaped, and benefited from. But they are not there, as parts of the self, to begin with. They must first be appropriated, and prior to their appropriation, no one has any special natural claim on them. Considerations of personal liberty do not protect a right to appropriate and use resources in the same way as they protect the right to develop and use talents as one sees fit. There is no parallel, initial presumption against interference with the use of resources, since no one is initially placed in a naturally privileged relationship with them.

I conclude that the natural distribution of resources is a purer case of something's being "arbitrary from a moral point of view" than the distribution of talents. Not only can one not be said to deserve the resources under one's feet; the other grounds on which one might assert an initial claim to talents are absent in the case of resources as well.

The fact that national societies are assumed to be self-sufficient does not make the distribution of natural resources any less arbitrary. Citizens of a nation that finds itself on top of a gold mine do not gain a right to the wealth that might be derived from it *simply* because their nation is self-sufficient. But someone might argue that self-sufficiency, nevertheless, removes any possible grounds on which citizens of other nations might press claims to equitable shares. A possible view is that no justification for resource appropriation is necessary in the global state of nature. If, so to speak, social cooperation is the root of all social obligations, as it is on some versions of contract theory, then the view is correct. All rights would be "special rights" applying only when certain conditions of cooperation obtain.[8]

I believe that this is wrong. It seems plausible in most discussions of distributive justice because their subject is the distribution of the benefits of social cooperation. Appropriate distributive principles compensate those who are relatively disadvantaged by the cooperative scheme for their participation in it. Where there is no social cooperation, there are no benefits of cooperation, and hence no problem of compensation for relative disadvantage. (This is why a world of self-sufficient national societies is not subject to something like a global difference principle.) But there is nothing in this reasoning to suggest that our *only* moral ties are to those with whom we share membership in a cooperative scheme. It is possible that other sorts of considerations might come into the justification of moral principles. Rawls himself recognizes this in the case of the natural duties, which are said to "apply to us without regard to our voluntary acts" (114) and, apparently, without regard to our institutional memberships.

In the case of natural resources, the parties to the international original position would know that resources are unevenly distributed with respect to population, that adequate access to resources is a prerequisite for successful operation of (domestic) cooperative schemes, and that resource supplies are scarce. They would view the natural distribution of resources as arbitrary in the sense that no one has a natural prima facie claim to the resources that happen to be under his feet. The appropriation of scarce resources by some requires a justification against the competing claims of others and the needs of future generations. Not knowing the resource endowments of their own societies, the parties would agree on a resource redistribution principle that would give each national society a fair chance to develop just political institutions and an economy capable of satisfying its members' basic needs.

There is no intuitively obvious standard of equity for such matters; perhaps the standard would be population size, or perhaps it would be more complicated, rewarding nations for their efforts in extracting resources and taking account of the differential resource needs of nations with differing economies. The underlying principle is that each person has an equal prima facie claim to a share of the total available resources, but departures from this initial standard could be justified (analogously to the operation of the difference principle) if the resulting inequalities were to the greatest benefit of those least advantaged by the inequality (cf. 151). In any event, the resource redistribution principle would function in international society as the difference principle functions in domestic society. It provides assurance to resource-poor nations that their adverse fate will not prevent them from realizing economic conditions sufficient to support just social institutions and protect human rights guaranteed by the principles for individuals. In the absence of this assurance, these nations might resort to war as a means of securing the resources necessary to establish domestic justice, and it is not obvious that wars fought for this purpose would be unjust.[9]

Before turning to other issues, I must note two complications of which I cannot give a fully satisfactory account. The international original position parties are prevented by the veil of ignorance from knowing their generation; they would be concerned to minimize the risk that, when the veil is lifted, they might find themselves living in a world where resource supplies have been largely depleted. Thus, part of the resource redistribution principle would set some standard for conservation against this possibility. The difficulties in formulating a standard of conservation are at least as formidable as those of defining the "just savings rate" in Rawls's discussion of justifiable rates of capital accumulation. I shall not pursue them here, except to point out that some provision for conservation as a matter of justice to future generations would be necessary (cf. 284–93).

The other complication concerns the definition of "natural resources." To what extent is food to be considered a resource? Social factors enter into the production of food in a way that they do not in the extraction of raw resources, so it may be that no plausible resource principle would require redistribution of food. A nation might claim that it deserves its abundant food supplies because of its large investments in agriculture or the high productivity of its farmers. On the other hand, arable land is a precondition of food production and a nation's supply of good land seems to be as morally arbitrary as its supply of, say, oil.[10] A further complication is that arable land, unlike iron ore or oil, cannot be physically redistributed to those nations with insufficient land, while food grown on the land is easily transportable. These dilemmas might be resolved by requiring redistribution of a portion of a country's food production depending on the ratio of its arable land to its total production; but the calculations involved would be complex and probably controversial. In the absence of a broader agreement to regard international society as a unified scheme of social cooperation, formulation of an acceptable food redistribution rule might prove impossible.

In failing to recognize resource problems, Rawls follows other writers who have extended the social contract idea to international relations.[11] Perhaps this is because they have attributed a greater symmetry to the domestic and international contracts than is in fact appropriate. Resource problems do not arise as distinct questions in the domestic case because their distribution and conservation are implicitly covered by the difference principle and the just savings principle. When the scope of social cooperation is coextensive with the territorial boundaries of a society, it is unnecessary to distinguish natural and social contributions to the society's level of well-being. But when justice is considered internationally, we must face the likelihood of moral claims being pressed by members of the various social schemes that are arbitrarily placed with respect to the natural distribution of resources. My suggestion of a resource redistribution principle recognizes the fundamental character of these claims viewed from the perspective of the parties' interests in securing fair conditions for the development of their respective schemes.

# III

Everything that I have said so far is consistent with the assumption that nations are self-sufficient cooperative schemes. However, there are strong empirical reasons for thinking that this assumption is no longer valid. As Kant notes in the concluding pages of *The Metaphysical Elements of Justice*, international economic cooperation creates a new basis for international morality.[12]

The main features of contemporary international interdependence relevant to questions of justice are the result of the progressive removal of restrictions on international trade and investment. Capital surpluses are no longer confined to reinvestment in the societies where they are produced, but instead are reinvested wherever conditions promise the highest yield without unacceptable risks. It is well known, for example, that large American corporations have systematically transferred significant portions of their capitalization to European, Latin American, and East Asian societies where labor costs are lower, markets are better, and profits are higher. A related development is the rise of an international division of labor whereby products are manufactured in areas having cheap, unorganized labor and are marketed in more affluent areas. Because multinational businesses, rather than the producing countries themselves, play the leading role in setting prices and wages, the international division of labor results in a system of world trade in which value created in one society (usually poor) is used to benefit members of other societies (usually rich).[13] It is also important to note that the world economy has evolved its own financial and monetary institutions that set exchange rates, regulate the money supply, influence capital flows, and enforce rules of international economic conduct.

The system of interdependence imposes burdens on poor and economically weak countries that they cannot practically avoid. Industrial economies have become reliant on raw materials that can only be obtained in sufficient quantities from developing countries. In the present structure of world prices, poor countries are often forced by adverse balances of payments to sell resources to more wealthy countries when those resources could be more efficiently used to promote development of the poor countries' domestic economies.[14] Also, private foreign investment imposes on poor countries patterns of political and economic development that may not be optimal from the point of view of the poor countries themselves. Participation in the global economy on the only terms available involves a loss of political autonomy.[15] Third, the global monetary system allows disturbances (e.g., price inflation) in some national economies to be exported to others that may be less able to cope with their potentially disastrous effects.[16]

Economic interdependence, then, involves a pattern of relationships that are largely nonvoluntary from the point of view of the worse-off participants, and that produce benefits for some while imposing burdens on others. These facts, by now part of the conventional wisdom of international relations, describe a world in which national boundaries can no longer be regarded as the outer limits of social cooperation. Note that this conclusion does not require that national societies should have become entirely superfluous or that the global economy should be completely integrated.[17] It is enough, for setting the limits of cooperative schemes, that some societies are able to increase their level of well-being via global trade and investment while others with whom they have economic relations continue to exist at low levels of development.[18]

In view of these empirical considerations, Rawls's passing concern for the law of nations seems to miss the point of international justice altogether. In an interdependent world, confining principles of social justice to national societies has the effect of taxing poor nations so that others may benefit from living in "just" regimes. The two principles, so construed, might justify a wealthy nation's denying aid to needy peoples if the aid could be used domestically to promote a more nearly just regime. If the self-sufficiency assumption were empirically acceptable, such a result might be plausible, if controversial on other grounds.[19] But if participation in economic relations with the needy society has contributed to the wealth of the "nearly just" regime, its domestic "justice" seems to lose moral significance. In such situations, the principles of domestic "justice" will be genuine principles of justice only if they are consistent with principles of justice for the entire global scheme of social cooperation.

How should we formulate global principles? As several others have suggested, Rawls's own two principles, suitably reinterpreted, could themselves be applied globally.[20] The reasoning is as follows: If evidence of global economic and political interdependence shows the existence of a global scheme of social cooperation, we should not view national boundaries as having fundamental moral significance. Since boundaries are not coextensive with the scope of social cooperation, they do not mark the limits of social obligations. Thus, the parties to the original position cannot be assumed to know that they are members of a particular national society, choosing principles of justice primarily for that society. The veil of ignorance must extend to all matters of national citizenship. As Barry points out, a global interpretation of the original position is insensitive to the choice of principles.[21] Assuming that the arguments for the two principles are successful as set out in Rawls's book, there is no reason to think that the content of the principles would change as a result of enlarging the scope of the original position so that the principles would apply to the world as a whole.[22]

Rawls's two principles are a special case of the "general conception" of social justice.[23] The two principles hold when a cooperative scheme has reached a level of material well-being at which everyone's basic needs can be met. The world, conceived as a single cooperative scheme, probably has not yet reached this threshold. Assuming that this is the case, on Rawls's reasoning, we should take the general conception, which does not differentiate the basic liberties from other primary goods, as the relevant standard for assessing global economic institutions. In conditions of underdevelopment or low-average levels of well-being, he argues, rational people might opt for a principle allowing rapid growth at the expense of some personal liberties, provided that the benefits of growth and the sacrifices of liberty are fairly shared and that the bases of self-respect relevant to such background conditions are not undermined (see 152, 298–303). The argument is that the prospects of the least advantaged would be less advanced, all things considered, by observing the lexical priority of liberty than by following the general conception of social justice.[24]

The globalization of the two principles (or of the general conception, if appropriate) has the consequence that principles of justice for national societies can no longer be viewed as ultimate. The basic structure of national societies continues to be governed by the two principles (or by the general conception), but their application is derivative and hence their requirements are not absolute. A possible view is that the global principles and the principles applied to national societies are to be satisfied in lexical order. But this view has the consequence, which one might find implausible, that national policies that maximize the welfare of the least-advantaged group within the society cannot be justified if other policies would be more optimal from the point of view of the lesser advantaged elsewhere. Furthermore, no society could justify the additional costs involved in moving from the general to the special conception (for example, in reduced productivity) until every society had, at least, attained a level of well-being sufficient to sustain the general conception.

These features of the global interpretation of Rawlsian principles suggest that its implications are quite radical—considerably more so even than their application to national societies. While I am not now prepared to argue positively that the best theory of global justice consists simply of Rawls's principles interpreted globally, it seems to me that the most obvious objections to such a theory are not valid. In the remainder of this section, I consider what is perhaps the leading type of objection and suggest some difficulties in giving it theoretically compelling form.

Objections of the type I have in mind hold that considerations of social cooperation at the national level justify distributive claims capable of overriding the requirements of a global difference principle. Typically, members of a wealthy nation might claim that they deserve a larger share than that provided by a global difference principle because of their superior technology, economic organization, and efficiency.

Objections of this general sort might take several forms. First, it might be argued that even in an interdependent world, national society remains the primary locus of one's political identifications. If one is moved to contribute to aggregate social welfare at any level, this level is most likely to be the national level. Therefore, differential rates of national contribution to the global welfare ought to be rewarded proportionally. This is a plausible form of the objection; the problem is that, in this form, it may not be an objection at all. The difference principle itself recognizes the probability that differential rates of reward may be needed as incentives for contribution; it requires only that distributive inequalities that arise in such a system be to the greatest benefit of the world's least-advantaged group. To the extent that incentives of the kind demanded by this version of the objection actually do raise the economic expectations of the least advantaged without harming them in other ways, they would not be inconsistent with the difference principle.

Such objections count against a global difference principle only if they hold that a relatively wealthy nation could claim more than its share under the difference principle. That is, the objection must hold that some distributive inequalities are justified even though they are not to the greatest benefit of the world's least-advantaged group. How could such claims be justified? One justification is on grounds of personal merit, appealing to the intuition that value created by someone's unaided labor is properly his, assuming that the initial distribution was just.[25] This sort of argument yields an extreme form of the objection. It holds that a nation is entitled to its relative wealth because each of its citizens has complied with the relevant rules of justice in acquiring raw materials and transforming them into products of value. These rules might require, respectively, that an equitable resource redistribution principle has been implemented and that no one's rights have been violated (for example, by imperial plunder) in the process of acquisition and production leading to a nation's current economic position. (Note that my arguments for a resource principle are not touched by this sort of objection and would impose some global distributive obligations even if the personal merit view were correct in ruling out broader global principles.)

This interpretation of the objection is strictly analogous to the conception of distributive justice that Rawls calls the "system of natural liberty." He objects to such views that they allow people to compete for available positions on the basis of their talents, making no attempt to compensate for deprivations that some suffer due to natural chance and social contingency. These things, as I have said, are held to be morally arbitrary and hence unacceptable as standards for distribution (cf. 66–72). I shall not rehearse this argument further here. But two things should be noted. First, the argument seems even more plausible from the global point of view since the disparity of possible starting points in world society is so much greater. The balance between "arbitrary" and "personal" contributions to my present well-being seems decisively tipped toward the "arbitrary" ones by the realization that, no matter what my talents, education, life goals, etc., I would have been virtually precluded from attaining my present level of well-being if I had been born in a less developed society. Second, if Rawls's counterargument counts against natural liberty views in the domestic case, then it defeats the objection to a global difference principle as well. A nation cannot base its claim to a larger distributive share than that warranted by the difference principle on factors that are morally arbitrary.

A third, and probably the most plausible, form of this objection holds that a wealthy nation may retain more than its share under a global difference principle, provided that some compensation for the benefits of global social cooperation is paid to less fortunate nations, and that the amount retained by the producing nation is used to promote domestic justice, for example, by increasing the prospects of the nation's own least favored group. The underlying intuition is that citizens owe some sort of special obligation to the less fortunate members of their own society that is capable of overriding their general obligation to improve the prospects of lesser advantaged groups elsewhere. This intuition is distinct from the intuition in the personal desert case, for it does not refer to any putative individual right to the value created by one's labor. Instead, we are concerned here with supposedly conflicting rights and obligations that arise from membership in overlapping schemes of social cooperation, one embedded in the other.

An argument along these lines needs an account of how obligations to the sectional association arise. One might say that the greater degree or extent of social cooperation in national societies (compared with that in international society) underwrites stronger intranational principles of justice. To see this objection in its strongest form, imagine a world of two self-sufficient and internally just societies, *A* and *B*. Assume that this world satisfies the appropriate resource redistribution principle. Imagine also that the least-advantaged representative person in society *A* is considerably better off than his counterpart in society *B*. While the members of $A$ may owe duties of mutual aid to the members of $B$, it is clear that they do not have parallel duties of justice, because the two societies, being individually self-sufficient, do not share membership in a cooperative scheme. Now suppose that the walls of self-sufficiency are breached very slightly; $A$ trades its apples for $B$'s pears. Does this mean that the difference principle suddenly applies to the world that comprises $A$ and $B$, requiring $A$ to share all of its wealth with $B$, even though almost all of its wealth is attributable to economic interaction within $A$? It seems not; one might say that an international difference principle can only command redistribution of the benefits derived from international social cooperation or economic interaction. It cannot touch the benefits of domestic cooperation.

It may be that some such objection will turn out to produce modifications on a global difference principle. But there are reasons for doubting this. Roughly, it seems that there is a threshold of interdependence above which distributive requirements such as a global difference principle are valid, but below which significantly weaker principles hold. I cannot give a systematic account of this view here, but perhaps some intuitive considerations will demonstrate its force.

Consider another hypothetical case. Suppose that, *within* a society, there are closely knit local regions with higher levels of internal cooperation than the level of cooperation in society as a whole. Certainly there are many such regions within a society such as the United States. The argument rehearsed above, applied to closely knit localities within national societies, would seem to give members of the localities special claims on portions of their wealth. This seems implausible, especially since such closely knit enclaves might well turn out to contain disproportionate numbers of the society's most advantaged classes. Why does this conclusion seem less plausible than that in the apples and pears case? It seems to me that the answer has to do with the fact that the apples and pears case looks like a case of voluntary, free-market bargaining that has only a marginal effect on the welfare of the members of each society, whereas we assume in the intranational case that there is a nonvoluntary society-wide system of economic institutions that defines starting positions and assigns economic rights and duties. It is these institutions—what Rawls calls "the basic structure" (7–11)—that stand in need of justification, because, by defining the terms of cooperation, they have such deep and pervasive effects on the welfare of people to whom they apply regardless of consent.

The apples and pears case, of course, is hardly a faithful model of the contemporary world economy. Suppose that we add to the story to make it resemble the real world more closely. As my review of the current situation (above, pp. 373–75 [herein 32-34]) makes clear, we would have to add just those features of the contemporary world economy that find their domestic analogues in the basic structure to which principles of justice apply. As the web of transactions grows more complex, the resulting structure of economic and political institutions acquires great influence over the welfare of the participants, regardless of the extent to which any particular one makes use of the institutions. These features make the real-world situation seem more like the case of subnational, closely knit regions.

These considerations suggest that the amount of social and economic interaction in a cooperative scheme does not provide a straightforward index of the strength of the distributive principle appropriate to it. The existence of a powerful, nonvoluntary institutional structure, and its pervasive effects on the welfare of the cooperators, seems to provide a better indication of the strength of the appropriate distributive requirements. This sort of consideration would not necessarily support a global difference principle in the apples and pears case; but it does explain why, above a threshold measure of social cooperation, the full force of the difference principle may come into play despite regional variations in the amount of cooperation.[26]

Proponents of this objection to a global difference principle might have one last resort. They might appeal to noneconomic features of national societies to justify the special obligations that citizens owe to the less fortunate members of their own societies. On this basis, they could claim that the difference principle applies to national societies despite regional variations in cooperation but not to international society. Probably the plausibility of this sort of argument will depend on the degree to which it psychologizes the ties that bind the members of social institutions.[27] There are problems, however. First, it needs to be shown that psychological ties such as national loyalty are of sufficient moral importance to balance the international economic ties that underwrite a global difference principle. Second, even if this could be persuasively argued, any account of how institutional obligations arise that is sufficiently psychological to make plausible a general conflict of global and sectional loyalties will probably be too psychological to apply to the large modern state (cf. 477).

Perhaps this line of objection can be made good in some way other than those canvassed here. If this could be done, it would not follow that there are no global distributive obligations but only that some portion of a nation's gross product would be exempt from the requirements of the global standard provided that it were used domestically in appropriate ways. The question would not be whether there are global distributive obligations founded on justice, but rather to what extent considerations relevant to the special features of cooperation within national societies modify the egalitarian tendencies of the global standard.

## IV

We have now reached two main conclusions. First, assuming national self-sufficiency, Rawls's derivation of the principles of justice for the law of nations is correct but incomplete. He importantly neglects resource redistribution, a subject that would surely be on the minds of the parties to the international original position. But second, the self-sufficiency assumption, upon which Rawls's entire consideration of the law of nations rests, is not justified by the facts of contemporary international relations. The state-centered image of the world has lost its normative relevance because of the rise of global economic interdependence. Hence, principles of distributive justice must apply in the first instance to the world as a whole, then derivatively to nation-states. The appropriate global principle is probably something like Rawls's general conception of justice, perhaps modified by some provision for intranational redistribution in relatively wealthy states once a threshold level of international redistributive obligations has been met. Rawls's two principles become more relevant as global distributive inequalities are reduced and a higher average level of well-being is attained. In conclusion, I would like to consider the implications of this ideal theory for international politics and global change in the nonideal world. In what respects does this interpretation of the social contract doctrine shed light on problems of world order change?

We might begin by asking, in general, what relevance social ideals have for politics in the real world. Their most obvious function is to describe a goal toward which efforts at political change should aim. In Rawls's theory, a very important natural duty is the natural duty of justice, which "requires us to support and to comply with just institutions that exist and . . . constrains us to further just arrangements not yet established, at least if this can be done without too much cost to ourselves" (115). By supplying a description of the nature and aims of a just world order, ideal theory "provides . . . the only basis for the systematic grasp of these more pressing problems" (9). Ideal theory, then, supplies a set of criteria for the formulation and criticism of strategies of political action in the nonideal world, at least when the consequences of political action can be predicted with sufficient confidence to establish their relationship to the social ideal. Clearly, this task would not be easy, given the complexities of social change and the uncertainties of prediction in political affairs. There is the additional complication that social change is often wrongly conceived as a progressive approximation of actual institutions to ideal prescriptions in which people's welfare steadily improves. An adequate social theory must avoid the pitfalls of a false incrementalism as well as what economists call the problem of the second best.[28] But a coherent social ideal is a necessary condition of any attempt to conquer these difficulties.

Ideal justice, in other words, comes into nonideal politics by way of the natural duty to secure just institutions where none presently exist. The moral problem posed by distinguishing ideal from nonideal theory is that, in the nonideal world, the natural duty of justice is likely to conflict with other natural duties, while the theory provides no mechanism for resolving such conflicts. For example, it is possible that a political decision that is likely to make institutions more just is equally likely to involve violations of other natural duties, such as the duty of mutual aid or the duty not to harm the innocent. Perhaps reforming some unjust institution will require us to disappoint legitimate expectations formed under the old order. The principles of natural duty in the nonideal world are relatively unsystematic, and we have no way of knowing which should win out in case of conflict. Rawls recognizes the inevitability of irresolvable conflicts in some situations (303), but, as Feinberg has suggested, he underestimates the role that an intuitive balancing of conflicting duties must play in nonideal circumstances.[29] Rawls says that problems of political change in radically unjust situations must rely on a utilitarian calculation of costs and benefits (352–53). If this is true, then political change in conditions of great injustice marks one kind of limit of the contract doctrine, for in these cases the principles of justice collapse into utilitarianism. It seems to me, however, that this conclusion is too broad. At least in some cases of global justice, nonideal theory, while teleological, is not utilitarian. I shall try to show this briefly with respect to questions of food and development aid, the principle of nonintervention, and the obligation to participate in war on behalf of a nation-state.

The duty to secure just institutions where none exist endows certain political claims made in the nonideal world with a moral seriousness that does not derive merely from the obligations that bind people regardless of the existence of cooperative ties. When the contract doctrine is interpreted globally, the claims of the less advantaged in today's nonideal world—claims principally for food aid, development assistance, and world monetary and trade reform—rest on principles of global justice as well as on the weaker duty of mutual aid. Those who are in a position to respond to these claims, despite the absence of effective global political mechanisms, must take account of the stronger reasons provided by the principles of justice in weighing their response. Furthermore, by interpreting the principles globally, we remove a major source of justifying reasons for not responding more fully to such claims. These reasons derive from statist concerns, for example, a supposed right to reinvest domestic surpluses in national societies that are already relatively favored from a global point of view. The natural duties still require us to help members of our own society who are in need, and a wealthy nation would be justified on this account in using some of its resources to support domestic welfare programs. What cannot be argued is that a wealthy nation's general right to retain its domestic product always overrides its obligation to advance the welfare of lesser-advantaged groups elsewhere.

An ideal theory of global justice has implications for traditional doctrines of international law as well. Consider, as a representative example, the rule of nonintervention. It is often remarked that this rule, which is prominently displayed in a number of recent authoritative documents of international law, seems inconsistent with the international community's growing rhetorical commitment to the protection of human rights, which is also prominently displayed in many of the same documents.[30] The conflict can be illustrated with reference to South Africa: The doctrine of nonintervention seems to prevent other states from giving aid to local insurgent forces explicitly committed to attaining recognition of basic human rights for the vast bulk of the South African population. Ordinarily, such conflicts are regarded as simple matters of utilitarian balancing, but the global interpretation of social contract theory shows that more can be said. The global interpretation introduces an asymmetry into the justification of the rules of international law. These rules impose different obligations depending on whether their observance in particular cases would contribute to or detract from a movement toward more just institutions.

The nonintervention rule is to be interpreted in this light. When it would demonstrably operate to advance or protect just arrangements, it furnishes a strong reason not to intervene. In the absence of compelling reasons to the contrary, it imposes a duty to comply. This is typically the case when intervention would interfere with a people's right of self-determination, a right that protects the fair exercise of political liberty. Thus, American intervention in Allende's Chile certainly violated a basic requirement of global justice. But sometimes, as in South Africa, observing the nonintervention rule cannot be justified in this way. Rather than resting on considerations of justice, which give strong reasons for compliance, it rests on considerations of natural duty—such as protection of the innocent against harms that might be suffered if large-scale military intervention occurred—and of international stability. These are certainly not negligible reasons for nonintervention, but, from the standpoint of global justice, they are weaker reasons than those provided by global justice itself. Obviously, peaceful resolution of cases such as that of South Africa is to be preferred. But when this goal cannot be attained, or when insurgent forces fighting for human rights request foreign assistance, intervention cannot be opposed as a matter of justice (as it could be on the traditional interpretation of this international rule, preserved in Rawls's own brief discussion), for its effect would be to help secure rights, including the right of self-determination, protected by the global principles. Again, in the absence of compelling reasons to the contrary (of which, certainly, a great number can be imagined), there might be an international duty to intervene in support of insurgent forces. I say that there may be an *international* duty because it seems clear that unilateral intervention can almost always be successfully opposed on grounds of international stability. But a decision by the international community to enforce principles of justice would be less susceptible to this sort of objection. Here I note what has too often been overlooked (except, perhaps, by American multinationals), that intervention in another country's internal affairs can take many nonviolent forms, including economic blockades, nonmilitary aid to insurgent forces, diplomatic pressure, and so on. While such forms of intervention obviously carry no guarantee of success, it is fair to say that their potential effectiveness has been widely underestimated.[31]

Finally, what are the implications of global justice for participation in a nation's military forces? From what I have said thus far, it should be clear that the global interpretation supplies reasons for acting or not acting that are capable of overriding the reasons provided by traditional rules of international law. These reasons are also capable of overriding the rule that demands compliance with internally just domestic regimes. One important consequence is that conscientious refusal to participate in a nation's armed forces would have far broader possible justifications than on the account given in Rawls (cf. 377–82), assuming for the moment that, given the great destructiveness of modern weapons and war strategies, participation in national armed forces could ever be justified at all. For instance, in some circumstances, a war of self-defense fought by an affluent nation against a poorer nation pressing legitimate claims under the global principles (for example, for increased food aid) might be unjustifiable, giving rise to a justified refusal to participate in the affluent nation's armed forces.

These three examples show that the contract doctrine, despite limitations noted here, sheds light on the distinctive normative problems of the shift from statist to global images of world order. The extension of economic and cultural relationships beyond national borders has often been thought to undermine the moral legitimacy of the state; the extension of the contract doctrine gives a systematic account of why this is so, and of its consequences for problems of justice in the nonideal world, by emphasizing the role of social cooperation as the foundation of just social arrangements. When, as now, national boundaries do not set off discrete, self-sufficient societies, we may not regard them as morally decisive features of the earth's social geography. For purposes of moral choice, we must, instead, regard the world from the perspective of an original position from which matters of national citizenship are excluded by an extended veil of ignorance.

I do not believe that Rawls's failure to take account of these questions marks a pivotal weakness of his theory; on the contrary, the theory provides a way of determining the consequences of changing empirical circumstances (such as the assumption of national self-sufficiency) for the concept of justice. The global interpretation is the result of recognizing an important empirical change in the structure of world political and social life. In this way the theory allows us to apply generalizations derived from our considered judgments regarding familiar situations to situations that are new and which demand that we form intelligent moral views and act on them when action is possible and appropriate. This is no small achievement for a moral theory. Some might think, however, that our moral intuitions are too weak or unreliable to support such an extension of the theory. I doubt that this is true; rather, it often seems to be a convenient way to beg off from unpleasant moral requirements. But if I am wrong about this—if we cannot expect moral theory to provide a firm guide for action in new situations—one might wonder whether moral theory has any practical point at all.

## NOTES

I am grateful to Huntington Terrell, who stimulated my interest in questions of international ethics, for comments and criticisms on an earlier version and to Thomas Scanlon, Richard Falk, and Dennis Thompson for many helpful discussions of earlier drafts.

1. "Declaration on the Establishment of a New International Economic Order," Resolution No. 3201 (S-VI), 1 May 1974, United Nations General Assembly, *Official Records: Sixth Special Session*, Supp. No. 1 (A/9559) (New York, 1974), p. 3.

2. John Rawls, *A Theory of Justice* (Cambridge, MA, 1972). Page references are given parenthetically in the text.

3. Such criticisms have appeared in several places. For example, Brian Barry, *The Liberal Theory of Justice* (Oxford, 1973), pp. 128–33; Peter Danielson, "Theories, Intuitions and the Problem of World-Wide Distributive Justice," *Philosophy of the Social Sciences* 3 (1973), pp. 331–40; Thomas M. Scanlon Jr., "Rawls' Theory of Justice," *University of Pennsylvania Law Review* 121, no. 5 (May 1973), pp. 1066–67.

4. These principles form the basis of traditional international law. See the discussion, on which Rawls relies, in J. L. Brierly, *The Law of Nations*, 6th ed. (New York, 1963), especially chapters 3 and 4.

5. Barry, *The Liberal Theory of Justice*, p. 132.

6. Trans. and ed. Lewis White Beck (Indianapolis, 1957), pp. 10–23.

7. Henry Sidgwick, *The Elements of Politics* (London, 1891), p. 242; quoted in S. I. Benn and R. S. Peters, *The Principles of Political Thought* (New York, 1959), p. 430. Sidgwick's entire discussion of putative national rights to land and resources is relevant here—see *Elements*, pp. 239–244.

8. William N. Nelson construes Rawlsian rights in this way in "Special Rights, General Rights, and Social Justice," *Philosophy & Public Affairs* 3, no. 4 (summer 1974): 410–30.

9. On this account, United Nations General Assembly Resolution 1803 (XVII), which purports to establish "permanent sovereignty over natural

resources," would be prima facie unjust. However, there are important mitigating factors. This resolution, as the text and the debates make clear, was adopted to defend developing nations against resource exploitation by foreign-owned businesses, and to underwrite a national right of expropriation (with compensation) of foreign-owned mining and processing facilities in some circumstances. While the "permanent sovereignty" doctrine may be extreme, sovereignty-for-time-being might not be, if it can be shown (as I think it can) that resource-consuming nations have taken more than their fair share without returning adequate compensation. United Nations General Assembly, *Official Records: Seventeenth Session*, Supp. No. 17 (A/5217) (New York, 1963), pp. 15–16.

10. This statement needs qualification. After a certain point in economic development, a society could make good much of its apparently nonarable land, for example, by clearing and draining or irrigating. So we ought not regard the total amount of arable land as fixed in the same sense as the total of other resources like oil. This was pointed out to me by Huntington Terrell.

11. Two classical examples are Pufendorf and Wolff. See Walter Schiffer, *The Legal Community of Mankind* (New York, 1954), pp. 49–79.

12. Trans. John Ladd (Indianapolis, 1965), pp. 125ff.

13. Cf. Richard J. Barnet and Ronald E. Müller, *Global Reach* (New York, 1975), chapters 2, 6, and passim. See also Stephen Hymer, "The Multinational Corporation and the Law of Uneven Development," in *Economics and World Order*, ed. J. N. Bhagwati (New York, 1972), pp. 113–41.

14. Suzanne Bodenheimer gives an account of the role of foreign investment in exploiting the resources of Latin American countries in "Dependency and Imperialism: The Roots of Latin American Underdevelopment," *Politics and Society* I (1971): 327–57.

15. Peter B. Evans, "National Autonomy and Economic Development," in *Transnational Relations and World Politics*, ed. Robert O. Keohane and Joseph S. Nye (Cambridge, MA, 1972), pp. 325–42.

16. See Richard N. Cooper, "Economic Interdependence and Foreign Policy in the Seventies," *World Politics* 24, no. 2 (January 1972): 159–81.

17. This conclusion would hold even if it were true that wealthy nations such as the United States continue to be economically self-sufficient, as Kenneth Waltz has (mistakenly, I think) argued. A nation might be self-sufficient in the sense that its income from trade is marginal compared with total national income, and yet still participate in economic relations with less developed countries that impose great burdens on the latter. (See fn. 18, below.) To refute the claim I make in the text, it would be necessary to show that all, or almost all, nations are self-sufficient in the sense given above. This, plainly, is not the case. Waltz argues his view in "The Myth of National Interdependence," *The International Corporation*, ed. Charles P. Kindleberger (Cambridge, MA, 1970), pp. 205–26; he is effectively refuted by Richard Cooper, "Economic Interdependence ..." and Edward L. Morse, "Transnational Economic Processes," in *Transnational Relations and World Politics*, pp. 23–47.

18. The situation is probably worse than this. A more plausible view is that the poor countries' economic relations with the rich have actually worsened economic conditions among the poor. Global trade widens rather than narrows the rich-poor gap and harms rather than aids the poor countries' efforts at economic development. See André Gunder Frank, "The Development of Underdevelopment," in James D. Cockcroft et al., *Dependence and Underdevelopment* (Garden City, NY, 1972), pp. 3–18. This raises the question of whether interdependence must actually benefit everyone involved to give rise to questions of justice. I think the answer is clearly negative; countries *A* and *B* are involved in social cooperation even if *A* (a rich country) could get along without *B* (a poor country), but instead exploits it, while *B* gets nothing out of its "cooperation" but exacerbated class divisions and Coca-Cola factories. If this is true, then Rawls's characterization of a society as "a cooperative venture for mutual advantage" (4) may be misleading, since everyone need not be advantaged by the cooperative scheme in order for requirements of justice to apply. It would be better to say that such requirements apply to systems of economic and social interaction that are nonvoluntary from the point of view of those least advantaged (or most disadvantaged) by them, and in which some benefit as a result of the relative or absolute sacrifices of others.

19. For example, on utilitarian grounds. See Peter Singer, "Famine, Affluence, and Morality," *Philosophy & Public Affairs* 1, no. 3 (spring 1972): 229–43 [reprinted in *Global Ethics: Seminal Essays*, 1–14].

20. For example, Barry, *The Liberal Theory of Justice*, pp. 128–33; and Scanlon, "Rawls' Theory of Justice," pp. 1066–67.

21. Barry, *The Liberal Theory of Justice*, p. 129.

22. David Richards also argues that the principles apply globally. But he fails to notice the relationship between distributive justice and the morally relevant features of social cooperation on which its requirements rest. It is this relationship, and not the simpler, blanket assertion that the original position parties are ignorant of their nationalities, which explains why Rawlsian principles of social justice should be thought to apply globally. See David A. J. Richards, *A Theory of Reasons for Action* (Oxford, 1971), pp. 137–41.

23. The general conception reads as follows: "All social primary goods—liberty and opportunity, income and wealth, and the bases of self-respect—are to be distributed equally unless an unequal distribution of any or all of these goods is to the advantage of the least favored" (303).

24. It must be noted that the question whether the general conception is more appropriate to developing societies turns heavily on empirical considerations. In particular, it needs to be shown that sacrifices of liberty, equally shared, really do promote more rapid advances in average levels of well-being than any other possible development strategy not involving such sacrifices. After considering the evidence, it might seem that an altogether different conception of justice is more appropriate to such societies than either of Rawls's conceptions. Perhaps, in the end, the general conception will turn out

to be the best that can be advanced, but it would be interesting to canvass the alternatives. See Norman Bowie's attempt to do this in *Towards a New Theory of Distributive Justice* (Amherst, MA, 1971), pp. 114ff.

25. This, roughly, is Robert Nozick's view in *Anarchy, State, and Utopia* (New York, 1974), chapter 7.

26. I do not claim to have resolved the problem that underlies this objection, although I believe that my remarks point in the right direction. It should be noticed, however, that what is at issue here is really a general problem for any theory that addresses itself to institutional structures rather than to particular transactions. One can always ask why institutional requirements should apply in full force to persons who make minimal use of the institutions they find themselves in. This point emerged from discussions I have had with Thomas Scanlon.

27. For a suggestive account of a similar problem, see Michael Walzer, "The Obligation to Disobey," *Obligations: Essays on Disobedience, War, and Citizenship* (Cambridge, MA, 1970), pp. 3–23.

28. On the problem of the second best, see Brian Barry, *Political Argument* (London, 1965), pp. 261–62.

29. Joel Feinberg, "Duty and Obligation in the Nonideal World, "*Journal of Philosophy* 70 (10 May 1973): 263–75.

30. For example, the UN Charter, articles 2(4) and 1(3), and article 1 of the "Declaration of Principles of International Cooperation..." approved by the General Assembly on 24 October 1970. Both are reprinted in *Basic Documents in International Law*, ed. Ian Brownlie, 2nd ed. (Oxford, 1972), pp. 1–31 and 32–40.

31. See Gene Sharp, *The Politics of Nonviolent Action* (Boston, 1973).

# 3. THOMAS NAGEL

Nagel defines "radical inequality" as characteristic of situations in which the poorest party is in direst need (i.e., lacking in even the barest essential goods), and claims that this kind of inequality raises issues beyond those posed by inequality per se. His concern is to develop an argument for why radical inequality between the world's affluent and its starving multitudes is unjust—an argument that is independent of the claim that the affluent have, through colonization for instance, played a role in causing the relevant poverty. For Nagel, the mere existence of radical inequality in the world is a mark of continuing injustice: Even if the rich countries (and their citizens) have done nothing wrong, the global political and economic system that allows radical inequality to persist is morally objectionable.

## Poverty and Food: Why Charity Is Not Enough

*First published in* Food Policy: The Responsibility of the United States in the Life and Death Choices, *ed. Peter G. Brown and Henry Shue (New York: The Free Press, 1977), 54–62. Reprinted with the permission of The Free Press, a Division of Simon & Schuster Adult Publishing Group. Copyright © 1977 by The Free Press. All rights reserved.*

Although the world food situation raises acute problems of distributive justice, they are not comparable to problems about how to distribute a definite quantity of food that is already on hand to numerous hungry victims of a natural calamity. Because of the significant effects of distribution on production, and the impossibility of separating the distribution of food from that of wealth in general, there is no isolable question of justice about redistribution of food from the haves to the have-nots. In a sense, therefore, the ethical aspects of this topic can be discussed only as part of the general problem of global economic inequality. In a money economy, anything can be exchanged for anything else, and the issue of the distribution of food is inseparable from that of the distribution of transistors or power plants.

Nevertheless there is a reason for thinking about the larger question in terms of food. Food is basic. It is the last thing an individual can afford to give up, if he can afford nothing else, and this means that in the current world situation we are not dealing with an abstract problem of inequality, but with something more specific and acute. If everyone in the world had at least a minimally adequate standard of living, there would still be ethical problems about the justice of big differences in wealth above that minimum—as there are, for example, about the distribution of wealth within the United States. But whatever may be said about this general problem, the inequalities that appear in the distribution of food on a worldwide scale are of a very different kind, and raise a different issue. They are, to be sure, basically inequalities in wealth rather than in food; but inequalities in wealth and income that result in starvation or severe malnutrition for some are in a different moral class from those inequalities higher on the scale that result in luxuries and multiple dwellings for some and marginal poverty for others. When the subject is enough to eat rather than a yacht, the difference between haves and have-nots goes beyond the general problem of equality and distributive justice. It is an extreme case, involving extreme needs.

I shall use the term "radical inequality" to describe this situation. A radical inequality exists when the bottom level is one of direst need, the top level one of great comfort or even luxury, and the total supply is large enough to raise the bottom above the level of extreme need without bringing significant deprivation to those above—specifically, without reducing most people to a place somewhat above the current bottom, or otherwise radically reducing their standard of living. The term therefore describes not merely the size of the gap between top and bottom but also the available total and the level of the bottom. The distribution of the world's food supply is a case of radical inequality because in a situation of adequate productive capacity for the world's population over the predictable short term, economic inequalities mean that under a market system millions of people will be undernourished from infancy and their health and life expectancy severely damaged.

The point of separating out this kind of case for special treatment is to forestall or at least weaken the force of a question that tends to arise whenever the rectification of inequalities is discussed: the question

"Where do you draw the line?" When it is observed that people in the U.S. and Northern Europe have a high standard of living and people in South Asia are starving or malnourished, and that there is something wrong with this, one reaction is anxiety about the prospect of bringing everyone to a common level only a bit higher than that of an Indian peasant. Now there may be an argument that justice requires such a solution, but it is not one that I am prepared to endorse, and the issue does not have to be decided in order to deal with situations of radical inequality. It does not take a strongly egalitarian principle to indicate that something is wrong in these cases, and that it would be an improvement to raise the bottom even if the resulting distribution were still very unequal.

But even if one decides that radical inequality is unacceptable, that does not tell us what to do about it. If those who are well off had *stolen* their riches from those who are poor, then redistribution would be nothing more than the uncontroversial rectification of past wrongs. But it is not so simple as that. To be sure, there has been substantial colonial exploitation of poor countries by rich ones, in trade, in labor, and in development. But a great deal of the difference in wealth between developed and underdeveloped countries is independent of this and depends on a big head start in technology, organization, and capital accumulation, which would have existed even without colonialism. While this claim may be disputed, it seems important to arrive at a view of the situation on the assumption that it is true. One would concede too much if one tried to base an argument for the injustice of radical inequality entirely on the claim that the inequality arose through wrongdoing. Even if it did not, there is still something wrong with the result, and with the system that allows it to continue. There is something wrong, in other words, with an international market economy in which many people are malnourished while many others live high, when there is enough productive capacity to feed everyone adequately. There is something wrong even if nobody is stealing from anyone else, and even if the inequalities result automatically from the influence of supply and demand, which can produce inequalities of wealth that result in inequalities of distribution.

Such a view challenges the idea that individuals, companies, or nations have a basic right to accumulate wealth and property and to trade with others on whatever terms are mutually acceptable, letting the chips fall where they may. It challenges the idea that if, by industrial and other development, the U.S., the USSR, Europe, and Japan become wealthy enough so that competition between them bids the price of grain up out of the range that India and other poor countries can afford, then there is no moral objection to this outcome because no one has done anything wrong. The position I want to defend is that even if it doesn't involve anyone's *doing* anything wrong, the system that permits this outcome is still morally objectionable. It is true that the moral principles that tell us not to harm other people, by killing or injuring them or stealing the food out of their mouths, are extremely important. But they do not exhaust the moral conditions on personal interaction.

It may seem that the natural suggestion to make at this point is that the worst effects of market inequalities should be dealt with by charity: charity of the rich nations toward the poor. This is a familiar remedy, and seems particularly appropriate when the inequality of wealth is paralleled by an inequality of power. In such circumstances the only motive available for parting the wealthy from their possessions seems to be generosity, if indeed that is available. Perhaps appeal can even be made to something stronger, a *duty* of charity, which comes into force when one can help others in serious distress without excessive cost to oneself. Certainly most people would acknowledge an obligation to throw a life preserver to a drowning man, even if they wouldn't risk their lives to save someone from a burning building. Where in between these extremes the duty of aid to others gives out is not clear. Peter Singer[1] has advocated rectification of inequality along these lines. Governments and individuals are sometimes motivated in varying degrees to engage in charitable aid, and such policies are worth encouraging.

Nevertheless I think it is important to reject charity as a satisfactory solution to the problem. It is important to reject it in this context, not only because of the limits on what it can achieve but because of what it presupposes. Until recently voluntary charity was the major instrument of redistribution *within* countries, and it still has its advocates. It is not threatening to those asked to give, for two reasons. First, it is left to them to determine when the sacrifice they are making for others has reached a point at which any further sacrifice would be supererogatory. Second, it does not question their basic entitlement to what they are asked to donate. The legitimacy of their ownership, and of the processes by which it came about, is not challenged. It is merely urged that, because of the severe need of others, those who are well off should voluntarily part with some of the wealth to which they are morally quite entitled. For this reason people are especially happy to donate help to the victims of a flood, tornado, or earthquake, since the needs created by such natural disasters cannot possibly be taken to cast doubt on the legitimacy of possession of those who have not suffered a comparable calamity. The inequality in these cases, however radical, has not in any sense been produced by a set of social institutions, and a request for rectification by charity cannot therefore be construed as an implicit criticism of the legitimacy of existing wealth.

Radical economic inequalities, however, are not like the results of natural catastrophes. When they persist and tend to reproduce themselves over generations, then the system of political and economic institutions that provides a vehicle for their operation needs to be examined critically. An appeal to charity as a solution, with its implied refusal to challenge the legitimacy of the system of property under which the donors of charity hold title to their possessions, tends to obscure this need. That is why charity has been largely superseded in domestic political arrangements, at least for the most basic requirements of life, by various schemes of redistributive taxation, public benefits, and mandatory social insurance.

The central claim I want to make is that any system of property, national or international, is an institution with moral characteristics: claims of right or entitlement made under it, claims as to what is ours to use as we wish, carry only as much moral weight as the legitimacy of the institution will bear. An institution of property is defined by the mechanisms of acquisition, exchange, inheritance, taxation, and transfer that determine when someone has, loses, or acquires title to something. Moral criticism of these mechanisms may cast doubt on the moral importance of the fact that something belongs to someone under that institution of property—without challenging the claim that it does so belong.[2]

The possibility of such criticism is not limited to any particular point of view. A welfare state will be found illegitimate by a libertarian because it expropriates the well off in order to support those who have not earned or been given enough to live adequately. A laissez-faire system will be found illegitimate by someone of more egalitarian sympathies, because it permits prosperity to depend too much on the fortunes of birth, background, and talent. My own views are of this second kind. I believe that the provision by sovereign states of a social minimum for their citizens is justified by the fact that morally arbitrary factors can exert so powerful a negative influence on people's lives in the absence of such a policy. For this reason a procedurally orderly system in which no one cheats, coerces, or steals from anyone else can still be morally objectionable because of radical inequalities that systematically arise under it, caused in part by morally arbitrary differences between people in natural endowments, family influence, or access to resources. A society that fails to combat these influences permits the existence of an illegitimate system of property, whose legal conditions of entitlement are morally questionable. The appropriate remedy is not an exhortation to charity, but a revision of the system of property rights to remove its objectionable features. There are more and less radical ways of accomplishing this, but some form of redistributive social welfare is generally accepted as a built-in feature of the operation of modern national economies. It then defines new conditions for legitimate ownership, acquisition, and exchange.

A redistributive tax may be regarded by some libertarians as a form of enforced charity. (Others would call it theft.) But from the point of view I am advocating it is an attempt to build into the conditions of exchange, accumulation, and possession certain safeguards that prevent them from being unjust. Within the United States, for example, a system that permitted one-fourth of the population to starve while the rest were well off would be regarded as unacceptable even if this result arose without coercion or theft, by nonfraudulent economic transactions. The possibility of such a result would generally be taken to undermine the legitimacy of the system, and therefore indirectly the legitimacy of possessions held under it. It wouldn't mean that they were not legal possessions, but only that they were not morally legitimate. Property, in other words, is not a value-free institution. Like political institutions (systems of voting, authority, representation), or judicial institutions, it can possess or lack legitimacy, depending on how it is organized. And the pure workings of market exchange, governed entirely by supply and demand, do not constitute a legitimate institution of property if they permit certain kinds of outcomes. (Just as a system of majority rule would be illegitimate, no matter how impartially applied, if it contained no safeguards against the persecution of unpopular minorities.)

Despite the vast differences in scale and in the political form of the problem, I think these considerations can be applied to the assessment of the international economic order as well. One question about the application of this view is what constitutes a single institution of property in the relevant sense. Why are all the inhabitants of the US, for example, participants in one system that can therefore be criticized if it allows excessive inequalities? And what would it mean to call the world economy such a system? If the world contained countries that could not trade or interact with one another, inequalities between them could not be used to criticize the "world economic system." But when a set of institutions governs and authorizes the economic transactions of even a very large population, they become to that extent a community and the effects of the institutions require scrutiny. If the institutions are economic, they govern the lives and require the adherence of practically everyone in their geographical range, and if they play an essential part in creating great wealth in some areas but not in others, then they can be said to contribute to the production of radical inequality even if they do not produce the poverty that is its other aspect. If there are possible alternative arrangements that would reduce the inequality without drastically harming productivity, then such a system is illegitimate.

It seems fairly clear that there is a world economy and that it is illegitimate in this way. Internationally, it is essentially a market economy, with conspicuous deviation toward monopoly in some areas but no significant international taxation, certainly none designed to ensure distributive justice. That kind of thing goes on, to varying degrees, within the boundaries of states. But internationally there is no check to the development of astronomical differences in purchasing power, with disastrous results for the poor countries when the rich countries compete in the market for a limited world grain crop and drive prices out of reach of the poor. These inequalities are largely due to factors of development, resources, population, and history that are morally arbitrary as far as the people involved are concerned. To a limited extent the situation can be mitigated by charity in the form of foreign aid, but it is not an ideal solution. Some internal conditions on the international economy and international markets, to make the whole system of property more legitimate, would be far preferable.[3]

The problem, of course, is that no one is in a position to impose such conditions. It will not be done unless the wealthy countries decide that an improvement in the economic condition of the rest of the world is to their advantage, or at least that it will not cost them much. This is a risky proposition. While redistributive systems do not simply take away from the top what they give to the bottom—since the economy is not like a jar of already baked cookies—still, there is likely to be some effect on the position of the wealthy from any reform that raises the buying power of the poor. Where there are serious problems of scarcity in resources, these effects are likely to be adverse. Moreover, even if it were generally recognized that an international system of taxation would benefit everyone, it would still require forcible imposition because otherwise no nation could be confident that others would contribute if they did. This is the standard problem of coordination and sovereignty familiar since Hobbes analyzed it in the *Leviathan*.

But even though nothing of this kind is likely to occur without a strong international system, it provides a different view of the problem. One cannot take as beyond challenge the fact that each nation owns what it produces and what it can buy on the open market, and that therefore what we have is ours to decide what to do with. Legally this is true, and even if we are moved by the plight of the poor to transfer some of our wealth to them, it is entirely a matter of decision for us, about how to allocate our wealth. Until another system of property is developed, moreover, this will be the main method of combating radical inequality at the international level. But it is useful to keep the illegitimacy of the system in mind, if only for the force it adds to the charitable arguments for foreign aid.

One consequence of the view that radical inequality is an injustice arising from the economic system is that aid should be truly humanitarian. By this I mean that it should be directed at the impoverished purely in virtue of their humanity and not in virtue of their special relation to the donor. Everyone at the bottom deserves help. Perhaps some forms of aid are appropriately influenced by such factors. But aid that simply lifts people off the absolute bottom and helps them to a minimally adequate diet addresses a need so general and basic that it is an inappropriate vehicle for the expression of political preference. Therefore a feature of recent U.S. aid policy that has caused controversy seems clearly objectionable: the preference given to military allies in the allocation of direct aid under P.L. 480. Congress was understandably motivated to impose a requirement that at least 70 percent of food aid under Title I of P.L. 480 go to the most seriously affected countries, independently of their alliances with us. Actually, if the program were truly humanitarian, it would disregard politics entirely. This is not because the somewhat better-off countries that are our allies do not need food aid and cannot use it to serve basic human needs. It is just that the inhabitants of the most seriously affected countries need it more, and if a policy is to be purely humanitarian it must be directed at people in virtue of their humanity alone, and not in virtue of their politics. A humanitarian food aid policy would therefore base allocation solely on nutritional needs.

The trouble is that no aid can be entirely nonpolitical in its *effects*. Aid of any kind permits the transfer of resources from that sector to another and is therefore equivalent to monetary aid. Food aid to either a friendly or an unfriendly nation permits it to spend more on arms than it could otherwise. There is no aid without some side effects of this sort. Nevertheless, the provision of certain basic human needs can be given priority over political and even strategic considerations, as it is in warfare. The laws of war[4] prohibit attacks on medical personnel and hospitals, destruction of crops, and blockades aimed at starving out the enemy population. Such measures might be militarily useful, but they are prohibited as inhumane. I suggest that the reverse side of this coin is that positive aid, if it is to be fully humane, should not be influenced by political factors when it concerns basic and universal human needs—even when, as is almost inevitable, it has politically relevant effects.

A final point to consider is the one raised by Garrett Hardin in support of what he calls the "lifeboat ethic."[5] He argues that food aid to the poorest countries will do harm rather than good, because by reducing the death rate without altering the birth rate it will result in larger populations and ensure a larger-scale collapse at a later date, when the world's productive capacities are exhausted. This means that the most beneficial policy toward the poor countries coincides remarkably with the interest of the rich—namely not to give any aid at all.

We should be suspicious of a result that coincides so perfectly with our economic self-interest. Certainly population control and internal agricultural development are the most important factors in improving the situation of the poorest countries over the long term. But the immediate problem still exists, and transfers are the only way of preventing starvation and malnutrition for millions of people over the next ten years. Those people have already been born, and a very powerful reason would be needed to deny them food resources that are definitely available. The reason offered by Hardin is not powerful enough, for it depends on a conjecture about what will happen in the future. We are therefore weighing the certainty of a present disaster against the possibility of a greater future disaster—a possibility to which no definite likelihood can be assigned. While the determinants of birth rate are complex and not uniform, population growth often diminishes following a rise in the standard of living, for good reason. Since the catastrophic results predicted by Hardin are not inevitable, and can be combated directly, it would be wrong to refuse to avert certain disaster in the present on the assumption that this was the only way to prevent greater and equally certain disaster in the future. Sometimes a present sacrifice must be made to forestall even the uncertain prospect of a far greater evil in the future. But this is true only if the two evils are of different orders of magnitude. In the case at hand, the present sacrifice is too great to be subject to such calculations.

While foreign aid is not the best method of dealing with radical inequality—being comparable to private charity on the domestic scene—it is the only method now available. It does not require a strongly egalitarian moral position to feel that the U.S., with a gross national product of a trillion dollars and a defense budget which is 9 percent of that, should be spending more than its current two-fifths of 1 percent of GNP on nonmilitary foreign aid, given the world as it is. The worst-off countries are so poor and unable to compete in the world commodity market that without transfers millions of individuals in them will grow up malnourished, with short and wretched life spans. We can afford to give substantially more than we do without reducing ourselves to starvation.

Whether the rich should give more than is needed to combat *radical* inequality—whether they should take a more general equality as their goal—is a question I shall not address. It seems in any case that charity is a poor instrument for the achievement of substantial equality, and that alternative institutional arrangements would be required. It is moreover unrealistic to ask the well-off to make substantial sacrifices voluntarily in order to improve the standard of living of others who are merely much less well off, without being wretchedly poor. Redistribution of this kind requires a universal involuntary system that can be enforced, and that does not depend on the sum of individual decisions. Perhaps someday such a system will exist. But till then, there is much to be done to ameliorate the worst effects of those radical inequalities that are produced by the unimpeded operation of the international market economy.

## NOTES

1. "Famine, Affluence, and Morality," *Philosophy and Public Affairs*, 1 (spring, 1972), pp. 229–43 [reprinted in *Global Ethics: Seminal Essays*, 1–14]. Also see Peter Singer's "Reconsidering the Famine Relief Argument" in *Food Policy: The Responsibility of the United States in the Life and Death Choices*, ed. Peter G. Brown and Henry Shue (New York: The Free Press, 1977).

2. My remarks are influenced by Thomas M. Scanlon, "Liberty, Contract and Contribution," in *Markets and Morals*, ed. by G. Dworkin, G. Bermant. and P. Brown (Washington, DC: Hemisphere Press, 1977).

3. For a penetrating discussion of this topic, see Charles R. Beitz, "Justice and International Relations," *Philosophy and Public Affairs*, 4 (summer 1975), pp. 360–89, esp. pp. 381–82, [reprinted herein, pp. 21–48, esp. pp. 38–39], at which he discusses the conditions of social cooperation and institutional unification that makes requirements of distributive justice apply.

4. The Hague Convention on Land Warfare, of 1907, and the Geneva Convention on the Law of War, of 1949.

5. See "Living on a Lifeboat," *Bioscience* 24 (October 1974), pp. 561–68 [expanded from "Lifeboat Ethics: The Case against Helping the Poor," first published in *Psychology Today* 8: 4, (September 1974): 38–43, 123–126 and reprinted in *Global Ethics: Seminal Essays*, 15–27].

# 4. AMARTYA SEN

Sen rejects three much-discussed views concerning the proper object of egalitarian distributive justice, namely, equal marginal utility, equal welfare, and equal Rawlsian primary goods. In contrast to these three he defends the ideal of basic capability equality. He cites instances of morally relevant inequality that arguably are not captured by the other three views, but are captured by basic capability equality. The capability approach has been employed extensively in discussions of development and justice and informs the methodology of the Human Development Index employed by the United Nations Development Programme (UNDP).

## Equality of What?

*First published in* The Tanner Lectures on Human Values, *Volume I, ed. Sterling M. McMurrin (Salt Lake City and Cambridge: University of Utah Press and Cambridge University Press, 1980), 197-220.*

Discussions in moral philosophy have offered us a wide menu in answer to the question: equality of what? In this lecture I shall concentrate on three particular types of equality, viz., (i) utilitarian equality, (ii) total utility equality, and (iii) Rawlsian equality. I shall argue that all three have serious limitations, and that while they fail in rather different and contrasting ways, an adequate theory cannot be constructed even on the *combined* grounds of the three. Toward the end I shall try to present an alternative formulation of equality that seems to me to deserve a good deal more attention than it has received, and I shall not desist from doing some propaganda on its behalf.

First a methodological question. When it is claimed that a certain moral principle has shortcomings, what can be the basis of such an allegation? There seem to be at least two different ways of grounding such a criticism, aside from just checking its *direct* appeal to moral intuition. One is to check the *implications* of the principle by taking up particular cases in which the results of employing that principle can be seen in a rather stark way, and then to examine these implications against our intuition. I shall call such a critique a *case-implication critique*. The other is to move not from the general to the particular, but from the general to the *more* general. One can examine the consistency of the principle with another principle that is acknowledged to be more fundamental. Such prior principles are usually formulated at a rather abstract level and frequently take the form of congruence with some very general procedures. For example, what could be reasonably assumed to have been chosen under the *as if* ignorance of the Rawlsian "original position," a hypothetical primordial state in which people decide on what rules to adopt without knowing who they are going to be—as if they could end up being any one of the persons in the community.[1] Or what rules would satisfy Richard Hare's requirement of "universalizability" and be consistent with "giving equal weights to the equal interests of the occupants of all the roles."[2] I shall call a critique based on such an approach a *prior-principle critique*. Both approaches can be used in assessing the moral claims of each type of equality, and will indeed be used here.

## 1. UTILITARIAN EQUALITY

Utilitarian equality is the equality that can be derived from the utilitarian concept of goodness applied to problems of distribution. Perhaps the simplest case is the "pure distribution problem": the problem of dividing a given homogeneous cake among a group of persons.[3] Each person gets more utility the larger his share of the cake, and gets utility *only* from his share of the cake; his utility increases at a diminishing rate as the amount of his share goes up. The utilitarian objective is to maximize the sum-total of utility irrespective of distribution, but that requires the *equality* of the *marginal* utility of everyone—marginal utility being the incremental utility each person would get from an additional unit of cake.[4] According to one interpretation, this equality of marginal utility embodies equal treatment of everyone's interests.[5]

The position is a bit more complicated when the total size of the cake is not independent of its distribution. But even then maximization of the total utility sum requires that transfers be carried to the point at which the marginal utility gain of the gainers equals the marginal utility loss of the losers, after taking into account the effect of the transfer on the size and distribution of the cake.[6] It is in this wider context that the special type of equality insisted upon by utilitarianism becomes assertively distinguished. Richard Hare has claimed that "giving equal weight to the equal interests of all the parties" would "lead to utilitarianism"—thus satisfying the prior-principle requirement of universalizability.[7] Similarly, John Harsanyi shoots down the nonutilitarians (including this lecturer, I hasten to add), by claiming for utilitarianism an exclusive ability to avoid "unfair discrimination" between "one person's and another person's equally urgent human needs."[8]

The moral importance of needs, on this interpretation, is based exclusively on the notion of utility. This is disputable, and having had several occasions to dispute it in the past,[9] I shall not shy away from disputing it in this particular context. But while I will get on to this issue later, I want first to examine the nature of utilitarian equality without—for the time being—questioning the grounding of moral importance entirely on utility. Even when utility is the sole basis of importance there is still the question as to whether the size of *marginal* utility, irrespective of *total* utility enjoyed by the person, is an adequate index of moral importance. It is, of course, possible to define a metric on utility characteristics such that each person's utility scale is coordinated with everyone else's in a way that equal social importance is simply "scaled" as equal marginal utility. If interpersonal comparisons of utility are taken to have no descriptive content, then this can indeed be thought to be a natural approach. No matter how the relative social importances are arrived at, the marginal utilities attributed to each person would then simply reflect these values. This can be done explicitly by appropriate interpersonal scaling,[10] or implicitly through making the utility numbering reflect choices in situations of *as if* uncertainty associated with the "original position" under the additional assumption that ignorance be interpreted as equal probability of being anyone.[11] This is not the occasion to go into the technical details of this type of exercise, but the essence of it consists in using a scaling procedure such that marginal utility measures are automatically identified as indicators of social importance.

This route to utilitarianism may meet with little resistance, but it is noncontroversial mainly because it says so little. A problem arises the moment utilities and interpersonal comparisons thereof are taken to have some independent descriptive content, as utilitarians have traditionally insisted that they do. There could then be conflicts between these descriptive utilities and the appropriately scaled, essentially normative, utilities in terms of which one is "forced" to be a utilitarian. In what follows I shall have nothing more to say on utilitarianism through appropriate interpersonal scaling, and return to examining the traditional utilitarian position, which takes utilities to have interpersonally comparable descriptive content. How moral importance should relate to these descriptive features must, then, be explicitly faced.

The position can be examined from the prior-principle perspective as well as from the case-implication angle. John Rawls's criticism as a preliminary to presenting his own alternative conception of justice took mostly the prior-principle form. This was chiefly in terms of acceptability in the "original position," arguing that in the postulated situation of *as if* ignorance people would not choose to maximize the utility sum. But Rawls also discussed the violence that utilitarianism does to our notions of liberty and equality. Some replies to Rawls's arguments have reasserted the necessity to be a utilitarian by taking the "scaling" route, which was discussed earlier, and which—I think—is inappropriate in meeting Rawls's critique. But I must confess that I find the lure of the "original position" distinctly resistible since it seems very unclear what precisely would be chosen in such a situation. It is also far from obvious that prudential choice under *as if* uncertainty provides an adequate basis for moral judgment in *un*original, that is, real-life, positions.[12] But I believe Rawls's more direct critiques in terms of liberty and equality do remain powerful.

Insofar as one is concerned with the *distribution* of utilities, it follows immediately that utilitarianism would in general give one little comfort. Even the minutest gain in total utility *sum* would be taken to outweigh distributional inequalities of the most blatant kind. This problem would be avoidable under certain assumptions, notably the case in which everyone has the *same* utility function. In the pure distribution problem, with this assumption the utilitarian best would require absolute equality of everyone's total utilities.[13] This is because when the marginal utilities are equated, so would be the total utilities if everyone has the same utility function. This is, however, egalitarianism by serendipity: just the accidental result of the marginal tail wagging the total dog. More important, the assumption would be very frequently violated, since there are obvious and well-discussed variations between human beings. John may be easy to please, but Jeremy not. If it is taken to be an acceptable prior-principle that the equality of the distribution of total utilities has some value, then the utilitarian conception of equality—marginal as it is—must stand condemned.

The recognition of the fundamental diversity of human beings does, in fact, have very deep consequences, affecting not merely the utilitarian conception of social good, but others as well, including (as I shall argue presently) even the Rawlsian conception of equality. If human beings are identical, then the application of the prior-principle of universalizability in the form of "giving equal weight to the equal interest of all parties" simplifies enormously. Equal marginal utilities of all—reflecting one interpretation of the equal treatment of needs—coincides with equal total utilities—reflecting one interpretation of serving their overall interests equally well. With diversity, the two can pull in opposite directions, and it is far from clear that "giving equal weight to the equal interest of all parties" would require us to concentrate only on one of the two parameters—taking no note of the other.

The case-implication perspective can also be used to develop a related critique, and I have tried to present such a critique elsewhere.[14] For example, if person A as a cripple gets half the utility that the pleasure-wizard person B does from any given level of income, then in the pure distribution problem between A and B the utilitarian would end up giving the pleasure-wizard B more income than the cripple A. The cripple would then be doubly worse off: both since he gets less utility from the same level of income, *and* since he will also get less income. Utilitarianism must lead to this thanks to its single-minded concern with maximizing the utility sum. The pleasure-wizard's superior efficiency in producing utility would pull income away from the less efficient cripple.

Since this example has been discussed a certain amount,[15] I should perhaps explain what is being asserted and what is not. First, it is *not* being claimed that anyone who has lower total utility (e.g., the cripple) at any given level of income must of necessity have lower marginal utility also. This must be true for some levels of income, but need not be true everywhere. Indeed, the opposite could be the case when incomes are equally distributed. If that were so, then of course even utilitarianism would give the cripple more income than the noncripple, since at that point the cripple would be the more efficient producer of utility. My point is that there is no guarantee that this will be the case, and more particularly, if it were the case that the cripple were not only worse off in terms of total utility but could convert income into utility less efficiently everywhere (or even just at the point of equal income division), then utilitarianism would compound his disadvantage by settling him with less income on top of lower efficiency in making utility out of income. The point, of course, is not about cripples in general, nor about all people with total utility disadvantage, but concerns people—including cripples—with disadvantage in terms of both total *and* marginal utility at the relevant points.

Second, the descriptive content of utility is rather important in this context. Obviously, if utilities were scaled to reflect moral importance, then wishing to give priority to income for the cripple would simply amount to attributing a higher "marginal utility" to the cripple's income; but this—as we have already discussed—is a very special sense of utility—quite devoid of descriptive content. In terms of descriptive features, what is being assumed in our example is that the cripple can be helped by giving him income, but the increase in his utility as a consequence of a marginal increase in income is less—in terms of the accepted descriptive criteria—than giving that unit of income to the pleasure-wizard, when both have initially the same income.

Finally, the problem for utilitarianism in this case-implication argument is not dependent on an implicit assumption that the claim to more income arising from disadvantage must dominate over the claim arising from high marginal utility.[16] A system that gives some weight to both claims would still fail to meet the utilitarian formula of social good, which demands an exclusive concern with the latter claim. It is this narrowness that makes the utilitarian conception of equality such a limited one. Even when utility is accepted as the only basis of moral importance, utilitarianism fails to capture the relevance of overall advantage for the requirements of equality. The prior-principle critiques can be supplemented by case-implication critiques using this utilitarian lack of concern with distributional questions except at the entirely marginal level.

## 2. TOTAL UTILITY EQUALITY

Welfarism is the view that the goodness of a state of affairs can be judged entirely by the goodness of the utilities in that state.[17] This is a less demanding view than utilitarianism in that it does not demand—in addition—that the goodness of the utilities must be judged by their sum-total. Utilitarianism is, in this sense, a special case of welfarism, and provides one illustration of it. Another distinguished case is the criterion of judging the goodness of a state by the utility level of the worst-off person in that state—a criterion often attributed to John Rawls. (*Except* by John Rawls! He uses social primary goods rather than utility as the index of advantage, as we shall presently discuss.) One can also take some other function of the utilities—other than the sum-total or the minimal element.

Utilitarian equality is one type of welfarist equality. There are others, notably the equality of total utility. It is tempting to think of this as some kind of an analogue of utilitarianism shifting the focus from marginal utility to total utility. This correspondence is, however, rather less close than it might first appear. First of all, while we economists often tend to treat the marginal and the total as belonging to the same plane of discourse, there is an important difference between them. Marginal is an essentially *counterfactual* notion: Marginal utility is the additional utility that *would be* generated if the person had one more unit of income. It contrasts what is observed with what allegedly would be observed if something else were different: in this case if the income had been one unit greater. Total is not, however, an inherently counterfactual concept; whether it is or is not would depend on the variable that is being totaled. In case of utilities, if they are taken to be observed facts, total utility will not be counterfactual. Thus total utility equality is a matter for direct observation, whereas utilitarian equality is not so, since the latter requires hypotheses as to what things would have been under different postulated circumstances. The contrast can be easily traced to the fact that utilitarian equality is essentially a consequence of sum *maximization,* which is itself a counterfactual notion, whereas total utility equality is an equality of some directly observed magnitudes.

Second, utilitarianism provides a complete ordering of all utility distributions—the ranking reflecting the order of the sums of individual utilities—but as specified so far, total utility equality does not do more than just point to the case of absolute equality. In dealing with two cases of nonequal distributions, something more has to be said so that they could be ranked. The ranking can be completed in many different ways.

One way to such a complete ranking is provided by the lexicographic version of the maximin rule, which is associated with the Rawlsian difference principle, but interpreted in terms of utilities as opposed to primary goods. Here the goodness of the state of affairs is judged by the level of utility of the worst-off person in that state; but if the worst-off persons in two states respectively have the same level of utility, then the states are ranked according to the utility levels of the second worst-off. If they too tie, then by the utility levels of the third worst-off, and so on. And if two utility distributions are matched at each rank all the way from the worst off to the best off, then the two distributions are equally good. Following a convention established in social choice theory, I shall call this *leximin*.

In what way does total utility equality lead to the leximin? It does this when combined with some other axioms, and in fact the analysis closely parallels the recent axiomatic derivations of the difference principle by several authors.[18] Consider four utility levels *a, b, c, d*, in decreasing order of magnitude. One can argue that in an obvious sense the pair of extreme points *(a, d)* displays greater inequality than the pair of intermediate points *(b, c)*. Note that this is a purely *ordinal* comparison based on ranking only, and the exact magnitudes of *a, b, c,* and *d* make no difference to the comparison in question. If one were *solely* concerned with equality, then it could be argued that *(b, c)* is superior—or at least noninferior—to *(a, d)*. This requirement may be seen as a strong version of preferring equality of utility distributions, and may be called "utility equality preference." It is possible to combine this with an axiom due to Patrick Suppes that captures the notion of *dominance* of one utility distribution over another, in the sense of each element of one distribution being at least as large as the corresponding element in the other distribution.[19] In the two-person case this requires that state *x* must be regarded as at least as good as *y, either* if each person in state *x* has at least as much utility as himself in state *y, or* if each person in state *x* has at least as much utility as the *other* person in state *y. If,* in addition, at least one of them has strictly more, then of course *x* could be declared to be strictly better (and not merely at least as good). If this Suppes principle and the "utility equality preference" are combined, then we are pushed in the direction of leximin. Indeed, leximin can be fully derived from these two principles by requiring that the approach must provide a complete ordering of all possible states no matter what the interpersonally comparable individual utilities happen to be (called "unrestricted domain"), and that the ranking of any two states must depend on utility information concerning *those* states only (called "independence").

Insofar as the requirements other than utility equality preference (i.e., the Suppes principle, unrestricted domain, and independence) are regarded as acceptable—and they have indeed been widely used in the social choice literature—leximin can be seen as the natural concomitant of giving priority to the conception of equality focusing on total utility.

It should be obvious, however, that leximin can be fairly easily criticized from the prior-principle perspective as well as the case-implication perspective. Just as utilitarianism pays no attention to the force of one's claim arising from one's disadvantage, leximin ignores claims arising from the *intensity* of one's needs. The *ordinal* characteristic that was pointed out while presenting the axiom of utility equality preference makes the approach insensitive to the magnitudes of potential utility gains and losses. While in the critique of utilitarianism that was presented earlier I argued against treating these potential gains and losses as the only basis of moral judgment, it was *not* of course alleged that these have no moral relevance at all. Take the comparison of *(a, d)* vis-à-vis *(b, c)*, discussed earlier, and let *(b, c)* stand for (3, 2). Utility equality preference would assert the superiority of (3, 2) over (10, 1) as well as (4, 1). Indeed, it would not distinguish between the two cases at all. It is this lack of concern with "how much" questions that makes leximin rather easy to criticize *either* by showing its failure to comply with such prior-principles as "giving equal weight to the equal interest of all parties," *or* by spelling out its rather austere implications in specific cases.

Aside from its indifference to "how much" questions, leximin also has little interest in "how many" questions—paying no attention at all to the number of people whose interests are overridden in the pursuit of the interests of the worst off. The worst-off position rules the roost, and it does not matter whether this goes against the interests of one other person, or against those of a million or a billion other persons. It is sometimes claimed that leximin would not be such an extreme criterion if it could be modified so that this innumeracy were avoided, and if the interests of *one* worse-off position were given priority over the interests of exactly *one* better-off position, but not necessarily against the interests of *more than one* better-off position. In fact, one can define a less demanding version of leximin, which can be called leximin-2, which takes the form of applying the leximin principle *if* all persons other than two are indifferent between the alternatives, but not necessarily otherwise. Leximin-2, as a compromise, will be still unconcerned with "how much" questions on the magnitudes of utilities of the two non-indifferent persons, but need not be blinkered about "how many" questions dealing with numbers of people: The priority applies to one person over exactly one other.[20]

Interestingly enough, a consistency problem intervenes here. It can be proved that given the regularity conditions, viz., unrestricted domain and independence, leximin-2 logically entails leximin in general.[21] That is, given these regularity conditions, there is no way of retaining moral sensitivity to the number of people on each side by choosing the limited requirement of leximin-2 without going all the way to leximin itself. It appears that indifference to *how much* questions concerning utilities implies indifference to *how many* questions concerning the number of people on different sides. One innumeracy begets another.

Given the nature of these critiques of utilitarian equality and total utility equality respectively, it is natural to ask whether some *combination* of the two should not meet both sets of objections. If utilitarianism is attacked for its unconcern with inequalities of the utility distribution, and leximin is criticized for its lack of interest in the magnitudes of utility gains and losses, and even in the numbers involved, then isn't the right solution to choose some mixture of the two? It is at this point that the long-postponed question of the relation between utility and moral worth becomes crucial. While utilitarianism and leximin differ sharply from each other in the use that they respectively make of the utility information, both share an exclusive concern with utility data. If nonutility considerations have any role in either approach, this arises from the part they play in the determination of utilities, or possibly as surrogates for utility information in the absence of adequate utility data. A combination of utilitarianism and leximin would still be confined to the box of welfarism, and it remains to be examined whether welfarism as a general approach is *itself* adequate.

One aspect of the obtuseness of welfarism was discussed clearly by John Rawls.

> In calculating the greatest balance of satisfaction it does not matter, except indirectly, what the desires are for. We are to arrange institutions so as to obtain the greatest sum of satisfactions; we

ask no questions about their source or quality but only how their satisfaction would affect the total of well-being. . . . Thus if men take a certain pleasure in discriminating against one another, in subjecting others to a lesser liberty as a means of enhancing their self-respect, then the satisfaction of these desires must be weighed in our deliberations according to their intensity, or whatever, along with other desires. . . . In justice as fairness, on the other hand, persons accept in advance a principle of equal liberty and they do this without a knowledge of their more particular ends. . . . An individual who finds that he enjoys seeing others in positions of lesser liberty understands that he has no claim whatever to this enjoyment. The pleasure he takes in other's deprivation is wrong in itself: it is a satisfaction which requires the violation of a principle to which he would agree in the original position.[22]

It is easily seen that this is an argument not merely against utilitarianism, but against the adequacy of utility information for moral judgments of states of affairs, and is, thus, an attack on welfarism in general. Second, it is clear that as a criticism of welfarism—and a fortiori as a critique of utilitarianism—the argument uses a principle that is unnecessarily strong. If it were the case that pleasures taken "in other's deprivation" were not taken to be wrong in itself, but simply *disregarded,* even then the rejection of welfarism would stand. Furthermore, even if such pleasures were regarded as valuable, but *less* valuable than pleasures arising from other sources (e.g., enjoying food, work, or leisure), welfarism would still stand rejected. The issue—as John Stuart Mill had noted—is the lack of "parity" between one source of utility and another.[23] Welfarism requires the endorsement not merely of the widely shared intuition that any pleasure has some value—and one would have to be a bit of a killjoy to dissent from this—but also the much more dubious proposition that pleasures must be relatively weighed *only* according to their respective intensities, irrespective of the source of the pleasure and the nature of the activity that goes with it. Finally, Rawls's argument takes the form of an appeal to the prior-principle of equating moral rightness with prudential acceptability in the original position. Even those who do not accept that prior principle could reject the welfarist no-nonsense counting of utility irrespective of all other information by reference to other prior principles, for example, the irreducible value of liberty.

The relevance of nonutility information to moral judgments is the central issue involved in disputing welfarism. Libertarian considerations point toward a particular class of nonutility information, and I have argued elsewhere that this may require even the rejection of the so-called Pareto principle based on utility dominance.[24] But there are also other types of nonutility information that have been thought to be intrinsically important. Tim Scanlon has recently discussed the contrast between "urgency" and utility (or intensity of preference). He has also argued that "the criteria of well-being that we actually employ in making moral judgments are objective," and a person's level of well-being is taken to be "independent of that person's tastes and interests."[25] These moral judgments could thus conflict with utilitarian—and more generally (Scanlon could have argued) with welfarist—moralities, no matter whether utility is interpreted as pleasure, or—as is increasingly common recently—as desire-fulfillment.

However, acknowledging the relevance of objective factors does not require that well-being be taken to be independent of tastes, and Scanlon's categories are *too* pure. For example, a lack of "parity" between utility from self-regarding actions and that from other-regarding actions will go beyond utility as an index of well-being and will be fatal to welfarism, but the contrast is not, of course, independent of tastes and subjective features. "Objective" considerations can count along with a person's tastes. What is required is the denial that a person's well-being be judged *exclusively* in terms of his or her utilities. If such judgments take into account a person's pleasures and desire-fulfillments, but also certain objective factors, for example, whether he or she is hungry, cold, or oppressed, the resulting calculus would still be nonwelfarist. Welfarism is an extremist position, and its denial can take many different forms—pure and mixed—so long as totally ignoring nonutility information is avoided.

Second, it is also clear that the notion of urgency need not work only *through* the determinants of personal well-being—however broadly conceived. For example, the claim that one should not be *exploited* at work is not based on making exploitation an additional parameter in the specification of well-being on top of such factors as income and effort, but on the moral view that a person deserves to get what he—according to one way of characterizing production—has produced. Similarly, the urgency deriving from principles such as "equal pay for equal work" hits directly at discrimination without having to redefine the notion of personal well-being to take note of such discriminations. One could, for example, say: "She must be paid just as much as the men working in that job, not primarily because she would otherwise have a lower level of well-being than the others, but simply because she is doing the *same* work as the men there, and why should she be paid less?" These moral claims, based on nonwelfarist conceptions of equality, have played important parts in social movements, and it seems difficult to sustain the hypothesis that they are purely "instrumental" claims—ultimately justified by their indirect impact on the fulfillment of welfarist, or other well-being-based, objectives.

Thus the dissociation of urgency from utility can arise from two different sources. One disentangles the notion of personal well-being from utility, and the other makes urgency not a function only of well-being. But, at the same time, the former does not require that well-being be independent of utility, and the latter does not necessitate a notion of urgency that is independent of personal well-being. Welfarism is a purist position and must avoid any contamination from either of these sources.

## 3. RAWLSIAN EQUALITY

Rawls's "two principles of justice" characterize the need for equality in terms of—what he has called—"primary social goods."[26] These are "things that every rational man is presumed to want," including "rights, liberties and opportunities, income and wealth, and the social bases of self-respect." Basic liberties are separated out as having priority over other primary goods, and thus priority is given to the principle of liberty which demands that "each person is to have an equal right to the most extensive basic liberty compatible with a similar liberty for others." The second principle supplements this, demanding efficiency and equality, judging advantage in terms of an index of primary goods. Inequalities are condemned unless they work out to everyone's advantage. This incorporates the "difference principle" in which priority is given to furthering the interests of the worst-off. And that leads to maximin, or to leximin, defined not on individual utilities but on the index of primary goods. But given the priority of the liberty principle, no trade-offs are permitted between basic liberties and economic and social gain.

Herbert Hart has persuasively disputed Rawls's arguments for the priority of liberty,[27] but with that question I shall not be concerned in this lecture. What is crucial for the problem under discussion is the concentration on bundles of primary social goods. Some of the difficulties with welfarism that I tried to discuss will not apply to the pursuit of Rawlsian equality. Objective criteria of well-being can be directly accommodated within the index of primary goods. So can be Mill's denial of the parity between pleasures from different sources, since the sources can be discriminated on the basis of the nature of the goods. Furthermore, while the difference principle is egalitarian in a way similar to leximin, it avoids the much-criticized feature of leximin of giving more income to people who are hard to please and who have to be deluged in champagne and buried in caviar to bring them to a normal level of utility, which you and I get from a sandwich and beer. Since advantage is judged not in terms of utilities at all, but through the index of primary goods, expensive tastes cease to provide a ground for getting more income. Rawls justifies this in terms of a person's responsibility for his own ends.

But what about the cripple with utility disadvantage, whom we discussed earlier? Leximin will give him more income in a pure distribution problem. Utilitarianism, I had complained, will give him *less*. The difference principle will give him neither more nor less on grounds of his being a cripple. His utility disadvantage will be irrelevant to the difference principle. This may seem hard, and I think it is. Rawls justifies this by pointing out that "hard cases" can "distract our moral perception by leading us to think of people distant from us whose fate arouses pity and anxiety."[28] This can be so, but hard cases do exist, and to take disabilities, or special health needs, or physical or mental defects as morally irrelevant, or to leave them out for fear of making a mistake, may guarantee that the *opposite* mistake will be made.

And the problem does not end with hard cases. The primary goods approach seems to take little note of the diversity of human beings. In the context of assessing utilitarian equality, it was argued that if people were fundamentally similar in terms of utility functions, then the utilitarian concern with maximizing the sum-total of utilities would push us simultaneously also in the direction of equality of utility levels. Thus utilitarianism could be rendered vastly more attractive if people really were similar. A corresponding remark can be made about the Rawlsian difference principle. If people were basically very similar, then an index of primary goods might be quite a good way of judging advantage. But, in fact, people seem to have very different needs varying with health, longevity, climatic conditions, location, work conditions, temperament, and even body size (affecting food and clothing requirements). So what is involved is not merely ignoring a few hard cases, but overlooking very widespread and real differences. Judging advantage purely in terms of primary goods leads to a partially blind morality.

Indeed, it can be argued that there is, in fact, an element of "fetishism" in the Rawlsian framework. Rawls takes primary goods as the embodiment of advantage, rather than taking advantage to be a *relationship* between persons and goods. Utilitarianism, or leximin, or—more generally—welfarism does not have this fetishism, since utilities are reflections of one type of relation between persons and goods. For example, income and wealth are not valued under utilitarianism as physical units, but in terms of their capacity to create human happiness or to satisfy human desires. Even if utility is not thought to be the right focus for the person-good relationship, to have an entirely good-oriented framework provides a peculiar way of judging advantage.

It can also be argued that while utility in the form of happiness or desire-fulfillment may be an *inadequate* guide to urgency, the Rawlsian framework asserts it to be *irrelevant* to urgency, which is, of course, a much stronger claim. The distinction was discussed earlier in the context of assessing welfarism, and it was pointed out that a rejection of welfarism need not take us to the point in which utility is given no role whatsoever. That a person's interest should have nothing directly to do with his happiness or desire-fulfillment seems difficult to justify. Even in terms of the prior-principle of prudential acceptability in the "original position," it is not at all clear why people in that primordial state should be taken to be so indifferent to the joys and sufferings in occupying particular positions, or if they are not, why their concern about these joys and sufferings should be taken to be morally irrelevant.

## 4. BASIC CAPABILITY EQUALITY

This leads to the further question: Can we not construct an adequate theory of equality on the *combined* grounds of Rawlsian equality and equality under the two welfarist conceptions, with some trade-offs among them? I would now like to argue briefly why I believe this too may prove to be informationally short. This can, of course, easily be asserted *if* claims arising from considerations other than well-being were acknowledged to be legitimate. Nonexploitation, or nondiscrimination, requires the use of information not fully captured either by utility or by primary goods. Other conceptions of entitlements can also be brought in going beyond concern with personal well-being only. But in what follows I shall not introduce these concepts. My contention is that *even* the concept of *needs* does not get adequate coverage through the information on primary goods and utility.

I shall use a case-implication argument. Take the cripple again with marginal utility disadvantage. We saw that utilitarianism would do nothing for him; in fact it will give him *less* income than to the physically fit. Nor would the difference principle help him; it will leave his physical disadvantage severely alone. He did, however, get preferential treatment under leximin, and more generally, under criteria fostering total equality. His low level of total utility was the basis of his claim. But now suppose that he is no worse off than others in utility terms despite his physical handicap because of certain other utility features. This could be because he has a jolly disposition. Or because he has a low aspiration level and his heart leaps up whenever he sees a rainbow in the sky. Or because he is religious and feels that he will be rewarded in afterlife, or cheerfully accepts what he takes to be just penalty for misdeeds in a past incarnation. The important point is that despite his marginal utility disadvantage, he has no longer a total utility deprivation. Now not even leximin—or any other notion of equality focusing on total utility—will do much for him. If we still think that he has needs as a cripple that should be catered to, then the basis of that claim clearly rests neither in high marginal utility, nor in low total utility, nor—of course—in deprivation in terms of primary goods.

It is arguable that what is missing in all this framework is some notion of "basic capabilities": a person being able to do certain basic things. The ability to move about is the relevant one here, but one can consider others, for example, the ability to meet one's nutritional requirements, the wherewithal to be clothed and sheltered, the power to participate in the social life of the community. The notion of urgency related to this is not fully captured by either utility or primary goods, or any combination of the two. Primary goods suffers from fetishist handicap in being concerned with goods, and even though the list of goods is specified in a broad and inclusive way, encompassing rights, liberties, opportunities, income, wealth, and the social basis of self-respect, it still is concerned with good things rather than with what these good things *do* to human beings. Utility, on the other hand, *is* concerned with what these things do to human beings, but uses a metric that focuses not on the person's capabilities but on his mental reaction. There is something still missing in the combined list of primary goods and utilities. If it is argued that resources should be devoted to remove or substantially reduce the handicap of the cripple despite there being no marginal utility argument (because it is expensive), despite there being no total utility argument (because he is so contented), and despite there being no primary goods deprivation (because he has the goods that others have), the case must rest on something else. I believe what is at issue is the interpretation of needs in the form of basic capabilities. This interpretation of needs and interests is often implicit in the demand for equality. This type of equality I shall call "basic capability equality."

The focus on basic capabilities can be seen as a natural extension of Rawls's concern with primary goods, shifting attention from goods to what goods do to human beings. Rawls himself motivates judging advantage in terms of primary goods by referring to capabilities, even though his criteria end up focusing on goods as such: on income rather than on what income does, on the "social bases of self-respect" rather than on self-respect itself, and so on. If human beings were very like each other, this would not have mattered a great deal, but there is evidence that the conversion of goods to capabilities varies from person to person substantially, and the equality of the former may still be far from the equality of the latter.

There are, of course, many difficulties with the notion of "basic capability equality." In particular, the problem of indexing the basic capability bundles is a serious one. It is, in many ways, a problem comparable with the indexing of primary good bundles in the context of Rawlsian equality. This is not the occasion to go into the technical issues involved in such an indexing, but it is clear that whatever partial ordering can be done on the basis of broad uniformity of personal preferences must be supplemented by certain established conventions of relative importance.

The ideas of relative importance are, of course, conditional on the nature of the society. The notion of the equality of basic capabilities is a very general one, but any application of it must be rather culture-dependent, especially in the weighting of different capabilities. While Rawlsian equality has the characteristic of being both culture-dependent and fetishist, basic capability equality avoids fetishism, but remains culture-dependent. Indeed, basic capability equality can be seen as essentially an extension of the Rawlsian approach in a non-fetishist direction.

## 5. CONCLUDING REMARKS

I end with three final remarks. First, it is not my contention that basic capability equality can be the sole guide to the moral good. For one thing morality is not concerned only with equality. For another, while it is my contention that basic capability equality has certain clear advantages over other types of equality, I did not argue that the others were morally irrelevant. Basic capability equality is a partial guide to the part of moral goodness that is associated with the idea of equality. I have tried to argue that as a partial guide it has virtues that the other characterizations of equality do not possess.

Second, the index of basic capabilities, like utility, can be used in many different ways. Basic capability equality corresponds to total utility equality, and it can be extended in different directions, for example, to leximin of basic capabilities. On the other hand, the index can be used also in a way similar to utilitarianism, judging the strength of a claim in terms of incremental contribution to *enhancing* the index value. The main departure is in focusing on a *magnitude* different from utility as well as the primary goods index. The new dimension can be utilized in different ways, of which basic capability equality is only one.

Last, the bulk of this lecture has been concerned with rejecting the claims of utilitarian equality, total utility equality, and Rawlsian equality to provide a sufficient basis for the equality-aspect of morality—indeed, even for that part of it which is concerned with needs rather than deserts. I have argued that none of these three is sufficient, nor is any combination of the three.

This is my main thesis. I have also made the constructive claim that this gap can be narrowed by the idea of basic capability equality, and more generally by the use of basic capability as a morally relevant dimension taking us beyond utility and primary goods. I should end by pointing out that the validity of the main thesis is not conditional on the acceptance of this constructive claim.

# NOTES

For helpful comments I am most grateful to Derek Parfit, Jim Griffin, and John Perry.

1. J. Rawls, *A Theory of Justice* (Cambridge: Harvard University Press, 1971), pp. 17–22. See also W. Vickrey, "Measuring Marginal Utility by Reactions to Risk," *Econometrica* 13 (1945), and J. C. Harsanyi, "Cardinal Welfare, Individualistic Ethics, and Interpersonal Comparisons of Utility," *Journal of Political Economy* 63 (1955).

2. R. M. Hare, *The Language of Morals* (Oxford: Clarendon Press, 1952); "Ethical Theory and Utilitarianism," in H. D. Lewis, ed., *Contemporary British Philosophy* (London: Allen and Unwin, 1976), pp. 116–17.

3. I have tried to use this format for an axiomatic contrast of the Rawlsian and utilitarian criteria in "Rawls versus Bentham: An Axiomatic Examination of the Pure Distribution Problem," in *Theory and Decision* 4 (1974); reprinted in N. Daniels, ed., *Reading Rawls* (Oxford: Blackwell, 1975). See also L. Kern, "Comparative Distributive Ethics: An Extension of Sen's Examination of the Pure Distribution Problem," in H. W. Gottinger and W. Leinfellner, eds., *Decision Theory and Social Ethics* (Dordrecht: Reidel, 1978), and J. P. Griffin, "Equality: On Sen's Equity Axiom," Keble College, Oxford, 1978, mimeographed.

4. The equality condition would have to be replaced by a corresponding combination of inequality requirements when the appropriate "continuity" properties do not hold. Deeper difficulties are raised by "nonconvexities" (e.g., increasing marginal utility).

5. J. Harsanyi, "Can the Maximin Principle Serve as a Basis for Morality? A Critique of John Rawls' Theory," *American Political Science Review* 64 (1975).

6. As mentioned in footnote 4, the equality conditions would require modification in the absence of continuity of the appropriate type. Transfers must be carried to the point at which the marginal utility gain of the gainers from any further transfer is *no more than* the marginal utility loss of the losers.

7. Hare (1976), pp. 116–17.

8. John Harsanyi, "Non-linear Social Welfare Functions: A Rejoinder to Professor Sen," in R. E. Butts and J. Hintikka, eds., *Foundational Problems in the Special Sciences* (Dordrecht: Reidel, 1977), pp. 294–95.

9. *Collective Choice and Social Welfare* (San Francisco: Holden-Day, 1970), chapter 6 and section 11.4; "On Weights and Measures: Informational Constraints in Social Welfare Analysis," *Econometrica* 45 (1977). See also T. M. Scanlon's arguments against identifying utility with "urgency" in his "Preference and Urgency," *Journal of Philosophy* 72 (1975).

10. For two highly ingenious examples of such an exercise, see Peter Hammond, "Dual Interpersonal Comparisons of Utility and the Welfare Economics of Income Distribution," *Journal of Public Economics* 6 (1977): 51–57; and Menahem Yaari, "Rawls, Edgeworth, Shapley and Nash: Theories of Distributive Justice Re-examined," Research Memorandum No. 33, Center for

Research in Mathematical Economics and Game Theory, Hebrew University, Jerusalem, 1978.

11. See Harsanyi (1955, 1975, 1977).

12. On this, see Thomas Nagel, "Rawls on Justice," *Philosophical Review* 83 (1973), and "Equality" in his *Mortal Questions* (Cambridge: Cambridge University Press, 1979).

13. The problem is much more complex when the total cake is not fixed, and where the maximization of utility sum need not lead to the equality of total utilities unless some additional assumptions are made, e.g., the absence of incentive arguments for inequality.

14. *On Economic Inequality* (Oxford: Clarendon Press, 1973), pp. 16–20.

15. See John Harsanyi, "Non-linear Social Welfare Functions," *Theory and Decision* 6 (1976): 311–12; Harsanyi (1977); Kern (1978); Griffin (1978); Richard B. Brandt, *A Theory of the Good and the Right* (Oxford: Clarendon Press, 1979), chapter 16.

16. Such an assumption is made in my Weak Equity Axiom, proposed in Sen (1973), but it is unnecessarily demanding for rejecting utilitarianism. See Griffin (1978) for a telling critique of the Weak Equity Axiom, in this exacting form.

17. See Sen (1977), and also my "Welfarism and Utilitarianism," *Journal of Philosophy* 76 (1979).

18. See P. J. Hammond, "Equity, Arrow's Conditions and Rawls' Difference Principle," *Econometrica* 44 (1976); S. Strasnick, "Social Choice Theory and the Derivation of Rawls' Difference Principle," *Journal of Philosophy* 73 (1976); C. d'Aspremont and L. Gevers, "Equity and Informational Basis of Collective Choice," *Review of Economic Studies* 44 (1977); K. J. Arrow, "Extended Sympathy and the Possibility of Social Choice," *American Economic Review* 67 (1977); A. K. Sen, "On Weights and Measures: Informational Constraints in Social Welfare Analysis," *Econometrica* 45 (1977); R. Deschamps and L. Gevers, "Leximin and Utilitarian Rules: A Joint Characterization," *Journal of Economic Theory* 17 (1978); K. W. S. Roberts, "Possibility Theorems with Interpersonally Comparable Welfare Levels," *Review of Economic Studies* 47 (1980); P. J. Hammond, "Two Person Equity," *Econometrica* 47 (1979).

19. P. Suppes, "Some Formal Models of Grading Principles," *Synthese* 6 (1966).

20. Leximin—and maximin—are concerned with conflicts between positional priorities, i.e., between ranks (such as the "worst-off position," "second worst-off position," etc.), and not with interpersonal priorities. When positions coincide with persons (e.g., the *same* person being the worst off in each state), then positional conflicts translate directly into personal conflicts.

21. Theorem 8, Sen (1977). See also Hammond (1979) for extensions of this result.

22. Rawls (1971), pp. 30–31.

23. John Stuart Mill, *On Liberty* (1859), p. 140.

24. Sen (1970), especially chapter 6. Also Sen (1979).

25. T. M. Scanlon (1975), pp. 658–59.

26. Rawls (1971), pp. 60–65.

27. H. L. A. Hart, "Rawls on Liberty and Its Priority," *University of Chicago Law Review* 40 (1973); reprinted in N. Daniels, ed., *Reading Rawls* (Oxford: Blackwell, 1975).

28. John Rawls, "A Kantian Concept of Equality," *Cambridge Review* (February 1975), p. 96.

# 5. HENRY SHUE

Beginning with a characterization of moral rights as providing the rational basis for a justified demand that the actual enjoyment of a substance be socially guaranteed against standard threats, Shue introduces in chapter 1, "Security and Subsistence," the notion of basic rights. "Basic rights," he claims, "are the morality of the depths. They specify the line beneath which no one is to be allowed to sink." They are "social guarantees against actual and threatened deprivations of at least some basic needs." Two of the most important basic rights are a right to physical security and a right to subsistence. Shue argues that if there are any rights at all, then there is a basic right to physical security, because such a right is necessary to the full enjoyment of other rights: No one can fully enjoy these other rights if they can be credibly threatened with murder, rape, beating, or other acts of violence. He then goes on to argue that a right to (at least) subsistence—to "unpolluted air, unpolluted water, adequate food, adequate clothing, adequate shelter, and minimal preventive public health care"—is also basic.

In chapter 2, "Correlative Duties," Shue argues against the position that subsistence rights are less urgent or less basic than rights to physical security. Shue decomposes the position he is attacking into four claims: Subsistence rights are positive rights, rights to physical security are negative rights, the distinction between positive and negative rights is highly significant, and negative rights should take precedence over positive rights. Positive rights put others under a duty to do something, while negative rights require that others refrain from certain conduct. Shue maintains that neither physical security rights nor subsistence rights fit neatly into one of these two categories. Physical security rights, for example, are usually taken to be negative, because it is thought that they require merely that people refrain from unjustified violent acts toward others; against this, Shue asserts that such rights also require a wide range of positive steps to be taken, such as the establishment and maintenance of police forces, criminal courts, penitentiaries and so on.

# Chapters 1–2 of *Basic Rights: Subsistence, Affluence, and U.S. Foreign Policy*

*First published in his* Basic Rights: Subsistence, Affluence, and U.S. Foreign Policy *(Princeton: Princeton University Press, 1980), 13-64, 176-91. SHUE, Henry; BASIC RIGHTS. © 1980 Princeton University Press. Reprinted by permission of Princeton University Press.*

## CHAPTER 1: SECURITY AND SUBSISTENCE

### RIGHTS

A moral right provides (1) the rational basis for a justified demand (2) that the actual enjoyment of a substance be (3) socially guaranteed against standard threats. Since this is a somewhat complicated account of rights, each of its elements deserves a brief introductory explanation.[1] The significance of the general structure of a moral right is, however, best seen in concrete cases of rights, to which we will quickly turn.[2]

A right provides the rational basis for a justified demand. If a person has a particular right, the demand that the enjoyment of the substance of the right be socially guaranteed is justified by good reasons, and the guarantees ought, therefore, to be provided. I do not know how to characterize in general and in the abstract what counts as a rational basis or an adequate justification. I could say that a demand for social guarantees has been justified when good enough reasons have been given for it, but this simply transfers the focus to what count as good enough reasons. This problem pervades philosophy, and I could not say anything very useful about it without saying a lot. But to have a right is to be in a position to make demands of others, and to be in such a position is, among other things, for one's situation to fall under general principles that are good reasons why one's demands ought to be granted. A person who has a right has especially compelling reasons—especially deep principles—on his or her side. People can of course have rights without being able to explain them—without being able to articulate the principles that apply to their cases and serve as the reasons for their demands. This book *[Basic Rights]* as a whole is intended to express a set of reasons that are good enough to justify the demands defended here. If the book is adequate, the principles it articulates are at least one specific example of how some particular demands can be justified. For now, I think, an example would be more useful than an abstract characterization.

The significance of being justified is very clear. Because a right is the basis for a justified demand, people not only may, but ought to, insist. Those who deny rights do so at their own peril. This does not mean that efforts to secure the fulfillment of the demand constituting a right ought not to observe certain constraints. It does mean that those who deny rights can have no complaint when their denial, especially if it is part of a systematic pattern of deprivation, is resisted. Exactly which countermeasures are justified by which sorts of deprivations of rights would require a separate discussion.

A right is the rational basis, then, for a justified demand. Rights do not justify merely requests, pleas, petitions. It is only because rights may lead to demands and not something weaker that having rights is tied as closely as it is to human dignity. Joel Feinberg has put this eloquently for the case of legal rights, or, in his Hohfeldian terminology, claim-rights:

> Legal claim-rights are indispensably valuable possessions. A world without claim-rights, no matter how full of benevolence and devotion to duty, would suffer an immense moral impoverishment. Persons would no longer hope for decent treatment from others on the ground of desert or rightful claim. Indeed, they would come to think of themselves as having no special claim to kindness or consideration from others, so that whenever even minimally decent treatment is forthcoming they would think themselves lucky rather than inherently deserving, and their benefactors extraordinarily virtuous and worthy of great gratitude. The harm to individual self-esteem and character development would be incalculable.

> A claim-right, on the other hand, can be urged, pressed, or rightly demanded against other persons. In appropriate circumstances the right-holder can "urgently, peremptorily, or insistently" call for his rights, or assert them authoritatively, confidently, unabashedly. Rights are not mere gifts or favors, motivated by love or pity, for which gratitude is the sole fitting response. A right is something that can be demanded or insisted upon without embarrassment or shame. When that to which one has a right is not forthcoming, the appropriate reaction is indignation; when it is duly given

there is no reason for gratitude, since it is simply one's own or one's due that one received. A world with claim-rights is one in which all persons, as actual or potential claimants, are dignified objects of respect, both in their own eyes and in the view of others. No amount of love and compassion, or obedience to higher authority, or noblesse oblige, can substitute for those values.[3]

At least as much can be said for basic moral rights, including those that ought to, but do not yet, have legal protection.

That a right provides the rational basis for a justified demand for actual enjoyment is the most neglected element of many rights. A right does not yield a demand that it should be said that people are entitled to enjoy something, or that people should be promised that they will enjoy something. A proclamation of a right is not the fulfillment of a right, any more than an airplane schedule is a flight. A proclamation may or may not be an initial step toward the fulfillment of the rights listed. It is frequently the substitute of the promise in the place of the fulfillment.

The substance of a right is whatever the right is a right to. A right is not a right to enjoy a right—it is a right to enjoy something else, like food or liberty. We do sometimes speak simply of someone's "enjoying a right," but I take this to be an elliptical way of saying that the person is enjoying something or other, which is the substance of a right, and, probably, enjoying it *as* a right. Enjoying a right to, for example, liberty normally means enjoying liberty. It may also mean enjoying liberty in the consciousness that liberty is a right. Being a right is a status that various subjects of enjoyment have. Simply to enjoy the right itself, the status, rather than to enjoy the subject of the right would have to mean something like taking satisfaction that there is such a status and that something has that status. But ordinarily when we say someone is enjoying a right, we mean the person is enjoying the substance of the right.

Being socially guaranteed is probably the single most important aspect of a standard right, because it is the aspect that necessitates correlative duties.[4] A right is ordinarily a justified demand that some other people make some arrangements so that one will still be able to enjoy the substance of the right even if—actually, *especially* if—it is not within one's own power to arrange on one's own to enjoy the substance of the right. Suppose people have a right to physical security. Some of them may nevertheless choose to hire their own private guards, as if they had no right to social guarantees. But they would be justified, and everyone else is justified, in demanding that somebody somewhere make some effective arrangements to establish and maintain security. Whether the arrangements should be governmental or nongovernmental; local, national, or international; participatory or nonparticipatory, are all difficult questions to which I may or may not be able to give definitive or conclusive answers here. But it is essential to a right that it is a demand upon others, however difficult it is to specify exactly which others.

And a right has been guaranteed only when arrangements have been made for people with the right to enjoy it. It is not enough that at the moment it happens that no one is violating the right.[5] Just as a proclamation of a right is not the fulfillment of a right and may in fact be either a step toward or away from actually fulfilling the right, an undertaking to create social guarantees for the enjoyment of various subjects of rights is by no means itself the guaranteeing and may or may not lead to real guarantees. But a right has not been fulfilled until arrangements are in fact in place for people to enjoy whatever it is to which they have the right. Usually, perhaps, the arrangements will take the form of law, making the rights legal as well as moral ones. But in other cases well-entrenched customs, backed by taboos, might serve better than laws—certainly better than unenforced laws.

The vague term "arrangements" is used in order to keep this general introductory explanation neutral on some controversial questions of interpretation. If the "arrangements" for fulfilling, for example, the duty to protect security are to be that every citizen is to be furnished a handgun and local neighborhoods are to elect residents to night patrols, then the right to security has not been socially guaranteed until the handguns have been distributed, the patrols elected, and so on. (The right has still not been guaranteed if this arrangement will usually not work, as I would certainly assume would be the case.) On the other hand, if the "arrangements" are to have well-trained, tax-supported, professional police in adequate numbers, then the right has not been socially guaranteed until the police candidates have in fact been well-trained, enough public funds budgeted to hire an adequate force, and other pieces are in place.

I am not suggesting the absurd standard that a right has been fulfilled only if it is impossible for anyone to be deprived of it or only if no one is ever deprived of it. The standard can only be some reasonable level of guarantee. But if people who walk alone after dark are likely to be assaulted, or if infant mortality is 60 per 1,000 live births, we would hardly say that enjoyment of, respectively, security or subsistence had yet been socially guaranteed. It is for the more precise specification of the reasonable level of social guarantees that we need the final element in the general structure of moral rights: the notion of a standard threat. This notion can be explained satisfactorily only after we look at some cases in detail, and I will take it up in the final section of this chapter.

That a right involves a rationally justified demand for social guarantees against standard threats means, in effect, that the relevant other people have a duty to create, if they do not exist, or, if they do, to preserve effective institutions for the enjoyment of what people have rights to enjoy.[6] From no theory like the present one is it possible to deduce precisely what sort of institutions are needed, and I have no reason to think that the same institutions would be most effective in all places and at all times. On its face, such universality of social institutions is most improbable, although some threats are indeed standard. What is universal, however, is a duty to make and keep effective arrangements, and my later threefold analysis of correlative duties will suggest that these arrangements must serve at least the functions of avoiding depriving people of the substances of their rights, protecting them against deprivation, and aiding them if they are nevertheless deprived of rights.[7] What I am now calling the duty to develop and preserve effective institutions for the fulfillment of rights is a summary of much of what is involved in performing all three of the duties correlative to typical rights, but to discuss duties now would be to jump ahead of the story.

## BASIC RIGHTS

Nietzsche, who holds strong title to being the most misunderstood and most underrated philosopher of the last century, considered much of conventional morality—and not conceptions of rights only—to be an attempt by the powerless to restrain the powerful: an enormous net of fine mesh busily woven around the strong by the masses of the weak.[8] And he was disgusted by it, as if fleas were pestering a magnificent leopard or ordinary ivy were weighing down a soaring oak. In recoiling from Nietzsche's *assessment* of morality, many have dismissed too quickly his insightful *analysis* of morality. Moral systems obviously serve more than one purpose, and different specific systems serve some purposes more fully or better than others, as of course Nietzsche himself also recognized. But one of the chief purposes of morality in general, and certainly of conceptions of rights, and of basic rights above all, is indeed to provide some minimal protection against utter helplessness to those too weak to protect themselves. Basic rights are a shield for the defenseless against at least some of the more devastating and more common of life's threats, which include, as we shall see, loss of security and loss of subsistence. Basic rights are a restraint upon economic and political forces that would otherwise be too strong to be resisted. They are social guarantees against actual and threatened deprivations of at least some basic needs. Basic rights are an attempt to give to the powerless a veto over some of the forces that would otherwise harm them the most.

Basic rights are the morality of the depths. They specify the line beneath which no one is to be allowed to sink. This is part of the reason that basic rights are tied as closely to self-respect as Feinberg indicates legal claim-rights are.[9] And this helps to explain why Nietzsche found moral rights repugnant. His eye was on the heights, and he wanted to talk about how far some might soar, not about how to prevent the rest from sinking lower. It is not clear that we cannot do both.[10]

And it is not surprising that what is in an important respect the essentially negative goal of preventing or alleviating helplessness is a central purpose of something as important as conceptions of basic rights. For everyone healthy adulthood is bordered on each side by helplessness, and it is vulnerable to interruption by helplessness, temporary or permanent, at any time. And many of the people in the world now have very little control over their fates, even over such urgent matters as whether their own children live through infancy.[11] Nor is it surprising that although the goal is negative, the duties correlative to rights will turn out to include positive actions. The infant and the aged do not need to be assaulted in order to be deprived of health, life, or the capacity to enjoy active rights. The classic liberal's main prescription for the good life—do not interfere with thy neighbor—is the only poison they need. To be helpless they need only to be left alone. This is why avoiding the infliction of deprivation will turn out in chapter 2 [of *Basic Rights*, herein 103] not to be the only kind of duty correlative to basic rights.

Basic rights, then, are everyone's minimum reasonable demands upon the rest of humanity.[12] They are the rational basis for justified demands the denial of which no self-respecting person can reasonably be expected to accept. Why should anything be so important? The reason is that rights are basic in the sense used here only if enjoyment of them is essential to the enjoyment of all other rights. This is what is distinctive about a basic right. When a right is genuinely basic, any attempt to enjoy any other right by sacrificing the basic right would be quite literally self-defeating, cutting the ground from beneath itself. Therefore, if a right is basic, other, nonbasic rights may be sacrificed, if necessary, in order to secure the basic right. But the protection of a basic right may not be sacrificed in order to secure the enjoyment of a nonbasic right. It may not be sacrificed because it cannot be sacrificed successfully. If the right sacrificed is indeed basic, then no right for which it might be sacrificed can actually be enjoyed in the absence of the basic right. The sacrifice would have proven self-defeating.[13]

In practice, what this priority for basic rights usually means is that basic rights need to be established securely before other rights can be secured. The point is that people should be able to *enjoy*, or *exercise*, their other rights. The point is simple but vital. It is not merely that people should "have" their other rights in some merely legalistic or otherwise abstract sense compatible with being unable to make any use of the substance of the right. For example, if people have rights to free association, they ought not merely to "have" the rights to free association but also to enjoy their free association itself. Their freedom of association ought to be provided for by the relevant social institutions. This distinction between merely having a right and actually enjoying a right may seem a fine point, but it turns out later to be critical.

What is not meant by saying that a right is basic is that the right is more valuable or intrinsically more satisfying to enjoy than some other rights. For example, I shall soon suggest that rights to physical security, such as the right not to be assaulted, are basic, and I shall not include the right to publicly supported education as basic. But I do not mean by this to deny that enjoyment of the right to education is much greater and richer—more distinctively human, perhaps—than merely going through life without ever being assaulted. I mean only that, if a choice must be made, the prevention of assault ought to supersede the provision of education. Whether a right is basic is independent of whether its enjoyment is also valuable in itself. Intrinsically valuable rights may or may not also be basic rights, but intrinsically valuable rights can be enjoyed only when basic rights are enjoyed. Clearly few rights could be basic in this precise sense.

## SECURITY RIGHTS

Our first project will be to see why people have a basic right to physical security—a right that is basic not to be subjected to murder, torture, mayhem, rape, or assault. The purpose in raising the questions why there are rights to physical security and why they are basic is not that very many people would seriously doubt either that there are rights to physical security or that they are basic. Although it is not unusual in practice for members of at least one ethnic group in a society to be physically insecure—to be, for example, much more likely than other people to be beaten by the police if arrested—few, if any, people would be prepared to defend in principle the contention that anyone lacks a basic right to physical security. Nevertheless, it can be valuable to formulate explicitly the presuppositions of even one's most firmly held beliefs, especially because these presuppositions may turn out to be general principles that will provide guidance in other areas where convictions are less firm. Precisely because we have no real doubt that rights to physical security are basic, it can be useful to see why we may properly think so.[14]

If we had to justify our belief that people have a basic right to physical security to someone who challenged this fundamental conviction, we could in fact give a strong argument that shows that if there are any rights (basic or not basic) at all, there are basic rights to physical security:

> No one can fully enjoy any right that is supposedly protected by society if someone can credibly threaten him or her with murder, rape, beating, etc., when he or she tries to enjoy the alleged right. Such threats to physical security are among the most serious and—in much of the world—the most widespread hindrances to the enjoyment of any right. If any right is to be exercised except at great risk, physical security must be protected. In the absence of physical security people are unable to use any other rights that society may be said to be protecting without being liable to encounter many of the worst dangers they would encounter if society were not protecting the rights.

> A right to full physical security belongs, then, among the basic rights—not because the enjoyment of it would be more satisfying to someone who was also enjoying a full range of other rights,

but because its absence would leave available extremely effective means for others, including the government, to interfere with or prevent the actual exercise of any other rights that were supposedly protected. Regardless of whether the enjoyment of physical security is also desirable for its own sake, it is desirable as part of the enjoyment of every other right. No rights other than a right to physical security can in fact be enjoyed if a right to physical security is not protected. Being physically secure is a necessary condition for the exercise of any other right, and guaranteeing physical security must be part of guaranteeing anything else as a right.

A person could, of course, always try to enjoy some other right even if no social provision were made to protect his or her physical safety during attempts to exercise the right. Suppose there is a right to peaceful assembly but it is not unusual for peaceful assemblies to be broken up and some of the participants beaten. Whether any given assembly is actually broken up depends largely on whether anyone else (in or out of government) is sufficiently opposed to it to bother to arrange an attack. People could still try to assemble, and they might sometimes assemble safely. But it would obviously be misleading to say that they are protected in their right to assemble if they are as vulnerable as ever to one of the most serious and general threats to enjoyment of the right, namely physical violence by other people. If they are as helpless against physical threats with the right "protected" as they would have been without the supposed protection, society is not actually protecting their exercise of the right to assembly.

So anyone who is entitled to anything as a right must be entitled to physical security as a basic right so that threats to his or her physical security cannot be used to thwart the enjoyment of the other right. This argument has two critical premises. The first is that everyone is entitled to enjoy something as a right.[15] The second, which further explains the first, is that everyone is entitled to the removal of the most serious and general conditions that would prevent or severely interfere with the exercise of whatever rights the person has. I take this second premise to be part of what is meant in saying that everyone is entitled to enjoy something as a right, as explained in the opening section of this chapter. Since this argument applies to everyone, it establishes a right that is universal.

## SUBSISTENCE RIGHTS

The main reason for discussing security rights, which are not very controversial, was to make explicit the basic assumptions that support the usual judgment that security rights are basic rights. Now that we have available an argument that supports them, we are in a position to consider whether matters other than physical security should, according to the same argument, also be basic rights. It will emerge that subsistence, or minimal economic security, which is more controversial than physical security, can also be shown to be as well justified for treatment as a basic right as physical security is—and for the same reasons.

By minimal economic security, or subsistence, I mean unpolluted air, unpolluted water, adequate food, adequate clothing, adequate shelter, and minimal preventive public health care. Many complications about exactly how to specify the boundaries of what is necessary for subsistence would be interesting to explore. But the basic idea is to have available for consumption what is needed for a decent chance at a reasonably healthy and active life of more or less normal length, barring tragic interventions. This central idea is clear enough to work with, even though disputes can occur over exactly where to draw its outer boundaries. A right to subsistence would not mean, at one extreme, that every baby born with a need for open-heart surgery has a right to have it, but it also would not count as adequate food a diet that produces a life expectancy of thirty-five years of fever-laden, parasite-ridden listlessness.

By a "right to subsistence" I shall always mean a right to at least subsistence. People may or may not have economic rights that go beyond subsistence rights, and I do not want to prejudge that question here. But people may have rights to subsistence even if they do not have any strict rights to economic well-being extending beyond subsistence. Subsistence rights and broader economic rights are separate questions, and I want to focus here on subsistence.

I also do not want to prejudge the issue of whether healthy adults are entitled to be provided with subsistence *only* if they cannot provide subsistence for themselves. Most of the world's malnourished, for example, are probably also diseased, since malnutrition lowers resistance to disease, and hunger and infestation normally form a tight vicious circle. Hundreds of millions of the malnourished are very young children. A large percentage of the adults, besides being ill and hungry, are also chronically unemployed, so the issue of policy toward healthy adults who refuse to work is largely irrelevant. By a "right to subsistence," then, I shall mean a right to subsistence that includes the provision of subsistence at least to those who cannot provide for themselves. I do not assume that no one else is also entitled to receive subsistence—I simply do not discuss cases of healthy adults who could support themselves but refuse to do so. If there is a right to subsistence in the sense discussed here, at least the people who cannot provide for themselves, including the children, are entitled to receive at least subsistence. Nothing follows one way or the other about anyone else.

It makes no difference whether the legally enforced system of property where a given person lives is private, state, communal, or one of the many more typical mixtures and variants. Under all systems of property people are prohibited from simply taking even what they need for survival. Whatever the property institutions and the economic system are, the question about rights to subsistence remains: If persons are forbidden by law from taking what they need to survive and they are unable within existing economic institutions and policies to provide for their own survival (and the survival of dependents for whose welfare they are responsible), are they entitled, as a last resort, to receive the essentials for survival from the remainder of humanity whose lives are not threatened?

The same considerations that support the conclusion that physical security is a basic right support the conclusion that subsistence is a basic right. Since the argument is now familiar, it can be given fairly briefly.

It is quite obvious why, if we still assume that there are some rights that society ought to protect and still mean by this the removal of the most serious and general hindrances to the actual enjoyment of the rights, subsistence ought to be protected as a basic right:

> No one can fully, if at all, enjoy any right that is supposedly pro-
> tected by society if he or she lacks the essentials for a reasonably
> healthy and active life. Deficiencies in the means of subsistence can
> be just as fatal, incapacitating, or painful as violations of physical
> security. The resulting damage or death can at least as decisively
> prevent the enjoyment of any right as can the effects of security
> violations. Any form of malnutrition, or fever due to exposure,
> that causes severe and irreversible brain damage, for example, can
> effectively prevent the exercise of any right requiring clear thought
> and may, like brain injuries caused by assault, profoundly disturb
> personality. And, obviously, any fatal deficiencies end all possibility
> of the enjoyment of rights as firmly as an arbitrary execution.

Indeed, prevention of deficiencies in the essentials for survival is, if anything, more basic than prevention of violations of physical security. People who lack protection against violations of their physical security can, if they are free, fight back against their attackers or flee, but people who lack essentials, such as food, because of forces beyond their control, often can do nothing and are on their own utterly helpless.[16]

The scope of subsistence rights must not be taken to be broader than it is. In particular, this step of the argument does not make the following absurd claim: Since death and serious illness prevent or interfere with the enjoyment of rights, everyone has a basic right not to be allowed to die or to be seriously ill. Many causes of death and illness are outside the control of society, and many deaths and illnesses are the result of very particular conjunctions of circumstances that general social policies cannot control. But it is not impractical to expect some level of social organization to protect the minimal cleanliness of air and water and to oversee the adequate production, or import, and the proper distribution of minimal food, clothing, shelter, and elementary health care. It is not impractical, in short, to expect effective management, when necessary, of the supplies of the essentials of life. So the argument is: When death and serious illness could be prevented by different social policies regarding the essentials of life, the protection of any human right involves avoidance of fatal or debilitating deficiencies in these essential commodities. And this means fulfilling subsistence rights as basic rights. This is society's business because the problems are serious and general. This is a basic right because failure to deal with it would hinder the enjoyment of all other rights.

Thus, the same considerations that establish that security rights are basic for everyone also support the conclusion that subsistence rights are basic for everyone. It is not being claimed or assumed that security and subsistence are parallel in all, or even very many, respects. The only parallel being relied upon is that guarantees of security and guarantees of subsistence are equally essential to providing for the actual exercise of any other rights. As long as security and subsistence are parallel in this respect, the argument applies equally to both cases, and other respects in which security and subsistence are not parallel are irrelevant.

It is not enough that people merely happen to be secure or happen to be subsisting. They must have a right to security and a right to subsistence—the continued enjoyment of the security and the subsistence must be socially guaranteed. Otherwise a person is readily open to coercion and intimidation through threats of the deprivation of one or the other, and credible threats can paralyze a person and prevent the exercise of any other right as surely as actual beatings and actual protein/calorie deficiencies can.[17] Credible threats can be reduced only by the actual establishment of social arrangements that will bring assistance to those confronted by forces that they themselves cannot handle.

Consequently, the guaranteed security and guaranteed subsistence are what we might initially be tempted to call "simultaneous necessities" for the exercise of any other right. They must be present at any time that any other right is to be exercised, or people can be prevented from enjoying the other right by deprivations or threatened deprivations of security or of subsistence. But to think in terms of simultaneity would be largely to miss the point. A better label, if any is needed, would be "inherent necessities." For it is not that security from beatings, for instance, is separate from freedom of peaceful assembly but that it always needs to accompany it. Being secure from beatings if one chooses to hold a meeting is part of being free to assemble. If one cannot safely assemble, one is not free to assemble. One is, on the contrary, being coerced not to assemble by the threat of the beatings.

The same is true if taking part in the meeting would lead to dismissal by the only available employer when employment is the only source of income for the purchase of food. Guarantees of security and subsistence are not added advantages over and above enjoyment of the right to assemble. They are essential parts of it. For this reason it would be misleading to construe security or subsistence—or the substance of any other basic right—merely as "means" to the enjoyment of all other rights. The enjoyment of security and subsistence is an essential part of the enjoyment of all other rights. Part of what it means to enjoy any other right is to be able to exercise that right without, as a consequence, suffering the actual or threatened loss of one's physical security or one's subsistence. And part of what it means to be able to enjoy any other right is not to be prevented from exercising it by lack of security or of subsistence. To claim to guarantee people a right that they are in fact unable to exercise is fraudulent, like furnishing people with meal tickets but providing no food.

What is being described as an "inherent necessity" needs to be distinguished carefully from a mere means to an end. If A is a means to end B and it is impossible to reach the end B without using the means A, it is perfectly correct to say that A is necessary for B. But when I describe the enjoyment of physical security, for example, as necessary for the enjoyment of a right to assemble, I do not intend to say merely that enjoying security is a means to enjoying assembly. I intend to say that part of the meaning of the enjoyment of a right of assembly is that one can assemble in physical security. Being secure is an essential component of enjoying a right of assembly, so that there is no such thing as a situation in which people do have social guarantees for assembly and do not have social guarantees for security. If they do not have guarantees that they can assemble in security, they have not been provided with assembly as a right. They must assemble and merely hope for the best, because a standard threat to assembling securely has not been dealt with. The fundamental argument is that when one fully grasps what an ordinary right is, and especially which duties are correlative to a right, one can see that the guarantee of certain things (as basic rights) is part of—is a constituent of—is an essential component of—the establishment of the conditions in which the right can actually be enjoyed. These conditions include the prevention of the thwarting of the enjoyment of the right by any "standard threat," at the explanation of which we must soon look.

A final observation about the idea of subsistence rights is, however, worth making here: Subsistence rights are in no way an original, new, or advanced idea. If subsistence rights seem strange, this is more than likely because Western liberalism has had a blind spot for severe economic need.[18] Far from being new or advanced, subsistence rights are found in traditional societies that are often treated by modern societies as generally backward or primitive.

James C. Scott has shown that some of the traditional economic arrangements in Southeast Asia that were in other respects highly exploitative nevertheless were understood by both patrons and clients—to use Scott's terminology—to include rights to subsistence on the part of clients and duties on the part of patrons not only to forbear from depriving clients of subsistence but to provide assistance to any clients who were for any reason deprived:

> If the need for a guaranteed minimum is a powerful motive in peasant life, one would expect to find institutionalized patterns in peasant communities which provide for this need. And, in fact, it is above all within the village—in the patterns of social control and reciprocity that structure daily conduct—where the subsistence

ethic finds social expression. The principle which appears to unify a wide array of behavior is this: "All village families will be guaranteed a minimal subsistence niche insofar as the resources controlled by villagers make this possible." Village egalitarianism in this sense is conservative not radical; it claims that all should have a place, a living, not that all should be equal. . . . Few village studies of Southeast Asia fail to remark on the informal social controls which act to provide for the minimal needs of the village poor. The position of the better-off appears to be legitimized only to the extent that their resources are employed in ways which meet the broadly defined welfare needs of villagers.[19]

As Benedict J. Kerkvliet, also writing about an Asian society, put it: "A strong patron-client relationship was a kind of all-encompassing insurance policy whose coverage, although not total and infinitely reliable, was as comprehensive as a poor family could get."[20]

Many reasons weigh in favor of the elimination of the kind of patron-client relationships that Scott and Kerkvliet have described—no one is suggesting that they should be, or could be, preserved. The point here is only that the institutionalization of subsistence rights is in no way tied to some utopian future "advanced" society. On the contrary, the real question is whether modern nations can be as humane as, in *this* regard, many traditional villages are. If we manage, we may to a considerable extent merely have restored something of value that has for some time been lost in our theory and our practice.

## STANDARD THREATS

Before we turn over the coin of basic rights and consider the side with the duties, we need to establish two interrelated points about the rights side. One point concerns the final element in the account of the general structure of all rights, basic and nonbasic, which is the notion of standard threats as the targets of the social guarantees for the enjoyment of the substance of a right. The other point specifically concerns basic rights and the question whether the reasoning in favor of treating security and subsistence as the substances of basic rights does not generate an impractically and implausibly long list of things to which people will be said to have basic rights. The two points are interrelated because the clearest manner by which to establish that the list of basic rights must, on the contrary, be quite short is to invoke the fact that the social guarantees required by the structure of a right are guarantees, not against all possible threats, but only against what I will call standard threats. In the end we will find a supportive coherence between the account of basic rights and the account of the general structure of most moral rights. We may begin by reviewing the reasons for taking security and subsistence to be basic rights and considering whether the same reasons would support treating many other things as basic rights. Answering that question will lead us to see the role and importance of a conception of standard threats.

Why, then, according to the argument so far, are security and subsistence basic rights? Each is essential to a normal healthy life. Because the actual deprivation of either can be so very serious—potentially incapacitating, crippling, or fatal—even the threatened deprivation of either can be a powerful weapon against anyone whose security or subsistence is not in fact socially guaranteed. People who cannot provide for their own security and subsistence and who lack social guarantees for both are very weak, and possibly helpless, against any individual or institution in a position to deprive them of anything else they value by means of threatening their security or subsistence. A fundamental purpose of acknowledging any basic rights at all is to prevent, or to eliminate, insofar as possible the degree of vulnerability that leaves people at the mercy of others. Social guarantees of security and subsistence would go a long way toward accomplishing this purpose.

Security and subsistence are basic rights, then, because of the roles they play in both the enjoyment and the protection of all other rights. Other rights could not be enjoyed in the absence of security or subsistence, even if the other rights were somehow miraculously protected in such a situation. And other rights could in any case not be protected if security or subsistence could credibly be threatened. The enjoyment of the other rights requires a certain degree of physical integrity, which is temporarily undermined, or eliminated, by deprivations of security or of subsistence. Someone who has suffered exposure or a beating is incapable of enjoying the substances of other rights, although only temporarily, provided he or she receives good enough care to recover the use of all essential faculties.

But as our earlier discussion of helplessness made clear, either the actual or the credibly threatened loss of security or subsistence leaves a person vulnerable to any other deprivations the source of the threat has in mind. Without security or subsistence one is helpless, and consequently one may also be helpless to protect whatever can be protected only at the risk of security or subsistence. Therefore, security and subsistence must be socially guaranteed, if any rights are to be enjoyed. This makes them basic rights.

In the construction of any philosophical argument, a principal challenge is to establish what needs to be established without slipping into the assertion of too much. By "too much" I mean a conclusion so inflated that, even if it is not a reduction to absurdity in the strict sense, it nevertheless strains credulity. The argument for security rights and subsistence rights may seem to suffer this malady, which might be called the weakness of too much strength. Specifically, the argument may be feared to have implicit implications that people have rights to an unlimited number of things, in addition to security and subsistence, that it is difficult to believe that people actually could justifiably demand of others.

Now it is true that we have no reason to believe that security and subsistence are the only basic rights, and chapter 3 [of *Basic Rights*] is devoted to the question of whether some kinds of liberties are also basic rights. But as we shall see in that chapter, it is quite difficult to extend the list of basic rights, and we face little danger that the catalog of basic rights will turn out to be excessively long. Before it becomes perhaps painfully obvious from the case of liberty, it may be helpful to see why in the abstract the list of basic rights is sharply limited even if it may have some members not considered here.

The structure of the argument that a specific right is basic may be outlined as follows, provided we are careful about what is meant by "necessary":

1. Everyone has a right to something.

2. Some other things are necessary for enjoying the first thing as a right, whatever the first thing is.

3. Therefore, everyone also has rights to the other things that are necessary for enjoying the first as a right.

Since this argument abstracts from the substance of the right assumed in the first premise, it is based upon what it normally means for any-thing to be a right or, in other words, upon the concept of a right. So, if the argument to establish the substances of basic rights is summarized by saying that these substances are the "other things . . . necessary" for enjoying any other right, it is essential to interpret "necessary" in the restricted sense of "made essential by the very concept of a right." The "other things" include not whatever would be convenient or useful, but only what is indispensable to anything else's being enjoyed as a right. Nothing will turn out to be necessary, in this sense, for the enjoyment of any right unless it is also necessary for the enjoyment of every right and is, for precisely this reason, qualified to be the substance of a basic right.

Since the concept of a right is a profoundly Janus-faced concept, this conceptual necessity can be explained both from the side of the bearer of the right and, as we will see more fully in chapter 2 [of *Basic Rights*, herein 103] from the side of the bearers of the correlative duties. The content of the basic rights is such that for the bearer of any right (basic or nonbasic) to pursue its fulfillment by means of the trade-off of the fulfillment of a basic right is self-defeating, and such that for the bearer of duties to claim to be fulfilling the duties correlative to any right in spite of not fulfilling the duties correlative to a basic right is fraudulent. But both perspectives can be captured more concretely by the notion of common, or ordinary, and serious but remediable threats or "standard threats," which was introduced earlier as the final element in the explanation of the structure of a right.[21] Certainly from the viewpoint of the bearer of a right it would be false or misleading to assert that a right had been fulfilled unless in the enjoyment of the substance of that right, a person also enjoyed protection against the threats that could ordinarily be expected to prevent, or hinder to a major degree, the enjoyment of the initial right assumed. And certainly from the viewpoint of the bearers of the correlative duties it would be false or misleading to assert that a right had been honored unless social guarantees had been established that would prevent the most common and serious threats from preventing or acutely hindering the enjoyment of the substance of the right. On the side of duties this places especially heavy emphasis upon preventing standard threats, which, as we will see in chapter 2 [of *Basic Rights*, herein 103], is the joint function of the fulfillment of duties to avoid depriving and duties to protect against deprivation.

But the measure of successful prevention of thwarting by ordinary and serious but remediable threats is not utopian. People are neither entitled to social guarantees against every conceivable threat, nor entitled to guarantees against ineradicable threats like eventual serious illness, accident, or death. Another way to indicate the restricted scope of the argument, then, is as follows. The argument rests upon what might be called a transitivity principle for rights: If everyone has a right to $y$, and the enjoyment of $x$ is necessary for the enjoyment of $y$, then everyone also has a right to $x$. But the necessity in question is analytic. People also have rights—according to this argument—only to the additional substances made necessary by the paired concepts of a right and its correlative duties. It is analytically necessary that if people are to be provided with a right, their enjoyment of the substance of the right must be protected against the typical major threats. If people are as helpless against ordinary threats as they would be on their own, duties correlative to a right are not being performed. Precisely what those threats are, and which it is feasible to counter, are of course largely empirical questions, and the answers to both questions will change as the situation changes.[22] In the argument for acknowledging security and subsistence as basic rights I have taken it to be fairly evident that the erosion of the enjoyment of any assumed right by deficiencies in subsistence is as common, as serious, and as remediable at present as the destruction of the enjoyment of any assumed right by assaults upon security.

What is, for example, eradicable changes, of course, over time. Today, we have very little excuse for allowing so many poor people to die of malaria and more excuse probably for allowing people to die of cancer. Later perhaps we will have equally little excuse to allow deaths by many kinds of cancer, or perhaps not. In any case, the measure is a realistic, not a utopian, one, and what is realistic can change. Chapter 4 [of *Basic Rights*] returns to the question of what is realistic now in the realm of subsistence, and consideration of this concrete case will probably also provide the clearest understanding of what constitutes an ordinary and serious but remediable threat.

We noticed in an earlier section that one fundamental purpose served by acknowledging basic rights at all is, in Camus' phrase, that we "take the victim's side," and the side of the potential victims. The honoring of basic rights is an active alliance with those who would otherwise be helpless against natural and social forces too strong for them. A basic right has, accordingly, not been honored until people have been provided rather firm protection—what I am calling "social guarantees"—for enjoying the substance of their basic rights. What I am now stressing is that this protection need neither be ironclad nor include the prevention of every imaginable threat.

But the opposite extreme is to offer such weak social guarantees that people are virtually as vulnerable with their basic rights "fulfilled" as they are without them. The social guarantees that are part of any typical right need not provide impregnable protection against every imaginable threat, but they must provide effective defenses against predictable remediable threats. To try to count a situation of unrelieved vulnerability to standard threats as the enjoyment of basic rights by their bearers or the fulfillment of these rights by the bearers of the correlative duties is to engage in doublespeak, or to try to behave as if concepts have no boundaries at all. To allow such practices to continue is to acquiesce in not only the violation of rights but also the destruction of the concept of rights.

Insofar as it is true that moral rights generally, and not basic rights only, include justified demands for social guarantees against standard threats, we have an interesting theoretical result. The fulfillment of both basic and nonbasic moral rights consists of effective, but not infallible, social arrangements to guard against standard threats like threats to physical security and threats to economic security or subsistence. One way to characterize the substances of basic rights, which ties the account of basic rights tightly to the account of the structure of moral rights generally, is this: The substance of a basic right is something the deprivation of which is one standard threat to rights generally. The fulfillment of a basic right is a successful defense against a standard threat to rights generally. This is precisely why basic rights are basic. That to which they are rights is needed for the fulfillment of all other rights. If the substance of a basic right is not socially guaranteed, attempts actually to enjoy the substance of other rights remain open to a standard threat like the deprivation of security or subsistence. The social guarantees against standard threats that are part of moral rights generally *are the same as* the fulfillment of basic rights.[23] This is why giving less priority to any basic right than to normal nonbasic rights is literally impossible.

## CHAPTER 2: CORRELATIVE DUTIES

### "Negative" Rights and "Positive" Rights

Many Americans would probably be initially inclined to think that rights to subsistence are at least slightly less important than rights to physical security, even though subsistence is at least as essential to survival as security is and even though questions of security do not even arise when subsistence fails. Much official US government rhetoric routinely treats all "economic rights," among which basic subsistence rights are buried amidst many nonbasic rights, as secondary and deferrable, although the fundamental enunciation of policy concerning human rights by the then Secretary of State did appear to represent an attempt to correct the habitual imbalance.[1] Now that the same argument in favor of basic rights to both aspects of personal survival, subsistence and security, is before us, we can examine critically some of the reasons why it sometimes appears that although people have basic security rights, the right, if any, to even the physical necessities of existence like minimal health care, food, clothing, shelter, unpolluted water, and unpolluted air is somehow less urgent or less basic.

Frequently it is asserted or assumed that a highly significant difference between rights to physical security and rights to subsistence is that they are respectively "negative" rights and "positive" rights.[2] This position, which I will now try to refute, is considerably more complex than it at first appears. I will sometimes refer to it as the position that subsistence rights are *positive* and *therefore secondary*. Obviously taking the position involves holding that subsistence rights are positive in some respect in which security rights are negative and further claiming that this difference concerning positive/negative is a good enough reason to assign priority to negative rights over positive rights. I will turn shortly to the explanation of this assumed positive/negative distinction. But first I want to lay out all the premises actually needed by the position that subsistence rights are positive and therefore secondary, although I need to undercut only some—strictly speaking, only one—of them in order to cast serious doubt upon the position's conclusions.

The alleged lack of priority for subsistence rights compared to security rights assumes:

1. The distinction between subsistence rights and security rights is (a) sharp and (b) significant.[3]

2. The distinction between positive rights and negative rights is (a) sharp and (b) significant.

3. Subsistence rights are positive.

4. Security rights are negative.

I am not suggesting that anyone has ever laid out this argument in all the steps it actually needs. On the contrary, a full statement of the argument is the beginning of its refutation—this is an example of the philosophical analogue of the principle that sunlight is the best antiseptic.[4]

In this chapter I will concentrate on establishing that premises 3 and 4 are both misleading. Then I will suggest a set of distinctions among duties that accurately transmits the insight distorted by 3 and 4. Insofar as 3 and 4 are inaccurate, considerable doubt is cast upon 2, although it remains possible that someone can specify some sharply contrasting pair of rights that actually are examples of 2.[5] I will not directly attack premise 1.[6]

Now the basic idea behind the general suggestion that there are positive rights and negative rights seems to have been that one kind of rights (the positive ones) require other people to act positively—to "do something"—whereas another kind of rights (the negative ones) require other people merely to refrain from acting in certain ways—to do nothing that violates the rights. For example, according to this picture, a right to subsistence would be positive because it would require other people, in the last resort, to supply food or clean air to those unable to find, produce, or buy their own; a right to security would be negative because it would require other people merely to refrain from murdering or otherwise assaulting those with the right. The underlying distinction, then, is between acting and refraining from acting; and positive rights are those with correlative duties to act in certain ways and negative rights are those with correlative duties to refrain from acting in certain ways. Therefore, the moral significance, if any, of the distinction between positive rights and negative rights depends upon the moral significance, if any, of the distinction between action and omission of action.[7]

The ordinarily implicit argument for considering rights to subsistence to be secondary would, then, appear to be basically this. Since subsistence rights are positive and require other people to do more than negative rights require—perhaps more than people can actually do—negative rights, such as those to security, should be fully guaranteed first. Then, any remaining resources could be devoted, as long as they lasted, to the positive—and perhaps impossible—task of providing for subsistence. Unfortunately for this argument, neither rights to physical security nor rights to subsistence fit neatly into their assigned sides of the simplistic positive/negative dichotomy. We must consider whether security rights are purely negative and then whether subsistence rights are purely positive. I will try to show (1) that security rights are more "positive" than they are often said to be, (2) that subsistence rights are more "negative" than they are often said to be, and, given (1) and (2), (3) that the distinctions between security rights and subsistence rights, though not entirely illusory, are too fine to support any weighty conclusions, especially the very weighty conclusion that security rights are basic and subsistence rights are not.

In the case of rights to physical security, it may be possible *to avoid violating* someone's rights to physical security yourself by merely refraining from acting in any of the ways that would constitute violations. But it is impossible *to protect* anyone's rights to physical security without taking, or making payments toward the taking of, a wide range of positive actions. For example, at the very least the protection of rights to physical security necessitates police forces; criminal courts; penitentiaries; schools for training police, lawyers, and guards; and taxes to support an enormous system for the prevention, detection, and punishment of violations of personal security.[8] All these activities and institutions are attempts at providing social guarantees for individuals' security so that they are not left to face alone forces that they cannot handle on their own. How much more than these expenditures one thinks would be necessary in order for people actually to be reasonably secure (as distinguished from merely having the cold comfort of knowing that the occasional criminal is punished after someone's security has already been violated) depends on one's theory of violent crime, but it is not unreasonable to believe that it would involve extremely expensive, "positive" programs. Probably no one knows how much positive action would have to be taken in a contemporary society like the United States to significantly reduce the levels of muggings, rapes, murders, and other assaults that violate personal security, and in fact to make people reasonably secure.

Someone might suggest that this blurs rights to physical security with some other type of rights, which might be called rights-to-be-protected-against-assaults-upon-physical-security. According to this distinction, rights to physical security are negative, requiring others only to refrain from assaults, while rights-to-be-protected-against-assaults-upon-physical-security are positive, requiring others to take positive steps to prevent assaults.

Perhaps if one were dealing with some wilderness situation in which individuals' encounters with each other were infrequent and irregular, there might be some point in noting to someone: I am not asking you to cooperate with a system of guarantees to protect me from third parties, but only to refrain from attacking me yourself. But in an organized society, insofar as there were any such things as rights to physical security that were distinguishable from some other rights-to-be-protected-from-assaults-upon-physical-security, no one would have much interest in the bare rights to physical security. What people want and need, as even Mill partly recognized, is the protection of their rights.[9] Insofar as this frail distinction holds up, it is the rights-to-be-protected-against-assaults that any reasonable person would demand from society. A demand for physical security is not normally a demand simply to be left alone, but a demand to be protected against harm.[10] It is a demand for positive action, or, in the words of our initial account of a right, a demand for social guarantees against at least the standard threats.

So it would be very misleading to say simply that physical security is a negative matter of other people's refraining from violations. Ordinarily it is instead a matter of some people refraining from violations and of third parties being prevented from violations by the positive steps taken by first and second parties. The "negative" refraining may in a given case be less significant than the "positive" preventing—it is almost never the whole story. The end-result of the positive preventive steps taken is of course an enforced refraining from violations, not the performance of any positive action. The central core of the right is a right that others not act in certain ways. But the mere core of the right indicates little about the social institutions needed to secure it, and the core of the right does not contain its whole structure. The protection of "negative rights" requires positive measures, and therefore their actual enjoyment requires positive measures. In any imperfect society enjoyment of a right will depend to some extent upon protection against those who do not choose not to violate it.

Rights to subsistence too are in their own way considerably more complex than simply labeling them "positive" begins to indicate. In fact, their fulfillment involves at least two significantly different types of action. On the one hand, rights to subsistence sometimes do involve correlative duties on the part of others to provide the needed commodities when those in need are helpless to secure a supply for themselves, as, for example, the affluent may have a duty to finance food supplies and transportation and distribution facilities in the case of famine. Even the satisfaction of subsistence rights by such positive action, however, need not be any more expensive or involve any more complex governmental programs than the effective protection of security rights would. A food stamp program, for example, could be cheaper or more expensive than, say, an antidrug program aimed at reducing muggings and murders by addicts. Which program was more costly or more complicated would depend upon the relative dimensions of the respective problems and would be unaffected by any respect in which security is "negative" and subsistence is "positive." Insofar as any argument for giving priority to the fulfillment of "negative rights" rests on the assumption that actually securing "negative rights" is usually cheaper or simpler than securing "positive rights," the argument rests on an empirical speculation of dubious generality.

The other type of action needed to fulfill subsistence rights is even more difficult to distinguish sharply from the action needed to fulfill security rights. Rights to physical subsistence often can be completely satisfied without the provision by others of any commodities to those whose rights are in question. All that is sometimes necessary is to protect the persons whose subsistence is threatened from the individuals and institutions that will otherwise intentionally or unintentionally harm them. A demand for the fulfillment of rights to subsistence may involve not a demand to be provided with grants of commodities but merely a demand to be provided some opportunity for supporting oneself.[11] The request is not to be supported but to be allowed to be self-supporting on the basis of one's own hard work.

What is striking is the similarity between protection against the destruction of the basis for supporting oneself and protection against assaults upon one's physical security. We can turn now to some examples that clearly illustrate that the honoring of subsistence rights sometimes involves action no more positive than the honoring of security rights does. Some cases in which all that is asked is protection from harm that would destroy the capacity to be self-supporting involve threats to subsistence of a complexity that is not usually noticed with regard to security, although the adequate protection of security would involve analyses and measures more complex than a preoccupation with police and prisons. The complexity of the circumstances of subsistence should not, however, be allowed to obscure the basic fact that essentially all that is being asked in the name of subsistence rights in these examples is protection from destructive acts by other people.

## SUBSISTENCE RIGHTS AND SCARCITY

The choice of examples for use in an essentially theoretical discussion that does nevertheless have implications for public policy presents an intractable dilemma. Hypothetical cases and actual cases each have advantages and disadvantages that are mirror images of each other's. A description of an actual case has the obvious advantage that it is less susceptible to being tailored to suit the theoretical point it is adduced to support, especially if the description is taken from the work of someone other than the proponent of the theoretical point. Its disadvantage is that if the description is in fact an inaccurate account of the case in question, the mistake about what is happening in that case may appear to undercut the theoretical point that is actually independent of what is happening in any single case. Thus the argument about the theoretical point may become entangled in arguments about an individual instance that was at most only one supposed illustration of the more general point.

Hypothetical cases are immune to disputes about whether they accurately depict an independent event, since, being explicitly hypothetical, they are not asserted to correspond to any one real case. But precisely because they are not constrained by the need to remain close to an independent event, they may be open to the suspicion of having been streamlined precisely in order to fit the theoretical point they illustrate and having thereby become atypical of actual cases.

The only solution I can see is to offer, when a point is crucial, an example of each kind. It is vital to the argument of this book *[Basic Rights]* to establish that many people's lack of the substance of their subsistence rights—of, that is, the means of subsistence like food—is a deprivation caused by standard kinds of threats that could be controlled by some combination of the mere restraint of second parties and the maintenance of protective institutions by first and third parties, just as the standard threats that deprive people of their physical security could be controlled by restraint and protection against nonrestraint. So I will start with a hypothetical case in order to clarify the theoretical point before introducing the partly extraneous complexity of actual events, and then I will quote a description of some actual current economic policies that deprive people of subsistence. The hypothetical case is at the level of a single peasant village, and the actual case concerns long-term national economic strategies. Anyone familiar with the causes of malnutrition in underdeveloped countries today will recognize that the following hypothetical case is in no way unusual.[12]

Suppose the largest tract of land in the village was the property of the descendant of a family that had held title to the land for as many generations back as anyone could remember. By absolute standards this peasant was by no means rich, but his land was the richest in the small area that constituted the universe for the inhabitants of this village. He grew, as his father and grandfather had, mainly the black beans that are the staple (and chief—and adequate—source of protein) in the regional diet. His crop usually constituted about a quarter of the black beans marketed in the village. Practically every family grew part of what they needed, and the six men he hired during the seasons requiring extra labor held the only paid jobs in the village—everyone else just worked his own little plot.

One day a man from the capital offered this peasant a contract that not only guaranteed him annual payments for a ten-year lease on his land but also guaranteed him a salary (regardless of how the weather, and therefore the crops, turned out—a great increase in his financial security) to be the foreman for a new kind of production on his land. The contract required him to grow flowers for export and also offered him the opportunity, which was highly recommended, to purchase through the company, with payments in installments, equipment that would enable him to need to hire only two men. The same contract was offered to, and accepted by, most of the other larger landowners in the general region to which the village belonged.

Soon, with the sharp reduction in supply, the price of black beans soared. Some people could grow all they needed (in years of good weather) on their own land, but the families that needed to supplement their own crop with purchases had to cut back their consumption. In particular, the children in the four families headed by the laborers who lost their seasonal employment suffered severe malnutrition, especially since the parents had originally worked as laborers only because their own land was too poor or too small to feed their families.

Now, the story contains no implication that the man from the capital or the peasants-turned-foremen were malicious or intended to do anything worse than single-mindedly pursue their own respective interests. But the outsider's offer of the contract was one causal factor, and the peasant's acceptance of the contract was another causal factor, in producing the malnutrition that would probably persist, barring protective intervention, for at least the decade the contract was to be honored. If the families in the village had rights to subsistence, their rights were being violated. Society, acting presumably by way of the government, ought to protect them from a severe type of active harm that eliminates their ability even to feed themselves.

But was anyone actually harming the villagers, or were they simply suffering a regrettable decline in their fortunes? If someone was violating their rights, who exactly was the violator? Against whom specifically should the government be protecting them? For, we normally make a distinction between violating someone's rights and allowing someone's rights to be violated while simply minding our own business. It makes a considerable difference—to take an example from another set of basic rights—whether I myself assault someone or I merely carry on with my own affairs while allowing a third person to assault someone when I could protect the victim and end the assault. Now, I may have a duty not to allow assaults that I can without great danger to myself prevent or stop, as well as a duty not to assault people myself, but there are clearly two separable issues here. And it is perfectly conceivable that I might have the one duty (to avoid harming) and not the other (to protect from harm by third parties), because they involve two different types of action.[13]

The switch in land-use within the story might then be described as follows. Even if one were willing to grant tentatively that the villagers all seemed to have rights to subsistence, some of which were violated by the malnutrition that some suffered after the switch in crops, no individual or organization can be identified as the violator: not the peasant-turned-foreman, for example, because—let us assume—he did not foresee the "systemic" effects of his individual choice; not the business representative from the capital because—let us assume—although he was knowledgeable enough to know what would probably happen, it would be unrealistically moralistic to expect him to forgo honest gains for himself and the company he represented because the gains had undesired, even perhaps regretted, "side effects"; not any particular member of the governmental bureaucracy because—let us assume—no one had been assigned responsibility for maintaining adequate nutrition in this particular village. The local peasant and the business representative were both minding their own business in the village, and no one in the government had any business with this village. The peasant and the representative may have attended to their own affairs while harm befell less fortunate villagers, but allowing harm to occur without preventing it is not the same as directly inflicting it yourself. The malnutrition was just, literally, unfortunate: bad luck, for which no one could fairly be blamed. The malnutrition was, in effect, a natural disaster—was, in the obnoxious language of insurance law, an act of God. Perhaps the village was, after all, becoming overpopulated.[14]

But, of course, the malnutrition resulting from the new choice of crop was not a natural disaster. The comforting analogy does not hold. The malnutrition was a social disaster. The malnutrition was the product of specific human decisions permitted by the presence of specific social institutions and the absence of others, in the context of the natural circumstances, especially the scarcity of land upon which to grow food, that were already given before the decisions were made. The harm in question, the malnutrition, was not merely allowed to happen by the parties to the flower-growing contract. The harm was partly caused by the requirement in the contract for a switch away from food, by the legality of the contract, and by the performance of the required switch in crops. If there had been no contract or if the contract had not required a switch away from food for local consumption, there would have been no malnutrition as things were going.[15] In general, when persons take an action that is sufficient in some given natural and social circumstances to bring about an undesirable effect, especially one that there is no particular reason to think would otherwise have occurred, it is perfectly normal to consider their action to be one active cause of the harm. The parties to the contract partly caused the malnutrition.

But the society could have protected the villagers by countering the initiative of the contracting parties in any one of a number of ways that altered the circumstances, and the absence of the appropriate social guarantees is another cause of the malnutrition. Such contracts could, for example, have already been made illegal. Or they could have been allowed but managed or taxed in order to compensate those who would otherwise predictably be damaged by them. Exactly what was done would be, *for the most part*, an economic and political question.[16] But it is possible to have social guarantees against the malnutrition that is repeatedly caused in such standard, predictable ways.

Is a right to subsistence in such a case, then, a positive right in any important ways that a right to security is not? Do we actually find a contrast of major significance? No. As in the cases of the threats to physical security that we normally consider, the threat to subsistence is human activity with largely predictable effects.[17] Even if, as we tend to assume, the motives for deprivations of security tend to be vicious while the motives for deprivations of subsistence tend to be callous, the people affected usually need protection all the same. The design, building, and maintenance of institutions and practices that protect people's subsistence against the callous—and even the merely overenergetic—is no more and no less positive than the conception and execution of programs to control violent crimes against the person. It is not obvious which, if either, it is more realistic to hope for or more economical to pursue. It is conceivable, although I doubt if anyone really knows, that the two are more effectively and efficiently pursued together. Neither looks simple, cheap, or "negative."

This example of the flower contract is important in part because, at a very simple level, it is in fact typical of much of what is happening today among the majority of the people in the world, who are poor and rural, and are threatened by forms of "economic development" that lower their own standard of living.[18] But it is also important because, once again in a very simple way, it illustrates the single most critical fact about rights to subsistence; where subsistence depends upon tight supplies of essential commodities (like food), a change in supply can have, often by way of intermediate price effects, an indirect but predictable and devastating effect on people's ability to survive. A change in supply can transport self-supporting people into helplessness and, if no protection against the change is provided, into malnutrition or death. Severe harm to some people's ability to maintain themselves can be caused by changes in the use to which other people put vital resources (like land) they control. In such cases even someone who denied that individuals or organizations have duties to supply commodities to people who are helpless to obtain them for themselves, might grant that the government ought to execute the society's duty of protecting people from having their ability to maintain their own survival destroyed by the actions of others. If this protection is provided, there will be much less need later to provide commodities themselves to compensate for deprivations.

What transmits the effect in such cases is the local scarcity of the vital commodity. Someone might switch thousands of acres from food to flowers without having any effect on the diet of anyone else where the supply of food was adequate to prevent a significant price rise in response to the cut in supply. And it goes without saying that the price rises are vitally important only if the income and wealth of at least some people is severely limited, as of course it is in every society, often for the rural majority. It is as if an abundant supply sometimes functions as a sponge to absorb the otherwise significant effect on other people, but a tight supply (against a background of limited income and wealth) sometimes functions as a conductor to transmit effects to others, who feel them sharply.

It is extremely difficult merely to mind one's own business amidst a scarcity of vital commodities. It is illusory to think that this first commandment of liberalism can always be obeyed. The very scarcity draws people into contact with each other, destroys almost all area for individual maneuver, and forces people to elbow each other in order to move forward. The tragedy of scarcity, beyond the deprivations necessitated by the scarcity itself, is that scarcity tends to make each one's gain someone else's loss. One can act for oneself only by acting against others, since there is not enough for all. Amidst abundance of food a decision to grow flowers can be at worst a harmless act and quite likely a socially beneficial one. But amidst a scarcity of food, due partly to a scarcity of fertile land, an unmalicious decision to grow flowers can cause death—unless there are social guarantees for adequate nutrition. A call for social guarantees for subsistence in situations of scarcity is not a call for intervention in what were formerly private affairs.

## Two Theses about Economic Deprivation

Our actual case is an economic strategy now being followed in a considerable number of Latin American nations. As already mentioned, it also differs from the hypothetical, but very typical, example of the flower contract by being a matter of macroeconomic strategy. And the actual case differs as well in a respect that is crucial to some of the policy recommendations in chapter 7 [of *Basic Rights*]: the precise relation between the economic decisions and the resulting deprivations of subsistence. In order to be able to characterize this relation accurately we need to draw an important distinction before we look at the description of the case.

"Systemic" deprivation—deprivation resulting from the confluence of many contributing factors—of the kind already seen in the case of the flower contract may or may not be systematic. That is, deprivations that are the result of the interaction of many factors may be (a) accidental—even unpredictable—and relatively easily remediable coincidences in an economic system for which there is no plan or for which the plan does not include the deprivations; or the deprivations may be (b) inherent—perhaps predictable—and acceptable, whether or not positively desirable, elements in a consciously adopted or endorsed economic plan or policy. In the former case they are not systematic but, as I will call them, *accidental*, and in the latter case they are systematic or, I will say, *essential*: essential elements in the strategy that produces them. Essential deprivations can be eliminated only by eliminating the strategy that requires them. Accidental deprivations can be eliminated by making less fundamental changes while retaining the basic strategy, since they are not inherent in the strategy.

The thesis that particular deprivations are accidental often seems to be the explanation recommended by common sense, although we may not ordinarily think explicitly in terms of this distinction. Well-informed people are aware, for example, that the "Brazilian miracle" has left large numbers of the poorest Brazilians worse off than ever, that the Shah's "White Revolution" made relatively small inroads upon malnutrition and infant mortality, that President and Prime Minister Marcos's "New Society" is a similar failure, and so on.[19] But, especially if one assumes that those who dictate economic strategy are reasonable and well-intentioned people, one may infer that these repeated failures to deal with the basic needs of the most powerless are, in spite of the regularity with which they recur, unfortunate but unpredictable by-products of fundamentally benevolent, or anyhow enlightened, economic plans.

Alternatively, one might infer that the continuing deprivations are inherent in the economic strategies being used, and that would lead to the second kind of thesis: that the continuance of the deprivations is essential to the economic strategies. Since this thesis may be less familiar, I would like to quote an example of it at some length. Because this particular formulation is intended by the analyst Richard Fagen to apply only to Latin America (with the exception of Cuba and, of course, to varying degrees in various different countries), a thesis concerning essential deprivation would naturally have to be formulated differently for Africa, Asia, and elsewhere. The following is intended, then, only as one good example, formulated in specifics to cover only a single region, of the second type of thesis:

> —Aggregate economic growth in Latin America over the past decade has been above world averages. The per capita income in the region now exceeds $1,000. . . .

—The actual situation with respect to income distribution and social equity is, in general, appalling. Fifty percent of the region's citizens have incomes of less than $200 per year; one-third receive less than $100. The top five percent of the population controls one-third of the total income. The emphasis on industrialization and export-led growth almost everywhere reinforces and accelerates the neglect of agriculture—at least agriculture in basic foodstuffs for domestic consumption. . . .

—Related to the income distribution and social equity issues is the problem of unemployment. In some countries as many as one out of three persons in the working-age population is unable to find a job of any sort. . . .

—The kind of development that has taken place is reflected in the structure of external indebtedness. Current estimates are that the countries of the region now owe approximately $80 billion in public and publicly guaranteed debt alone. . . .

—The Latin American state is everywhere involved in economic development and management. It is usually the prime borrower abroad, often an important investor at home, frequently a chief partner of foreign capital, and always a source of regulations on everything from wages to import quotas. State capitalism has come to Latin America with a vengeance, and even the governments that claim to give the freest play to market forces are in fact constantly intervening to establish the rules under which "free markets" will be allowed to operate.

The above sketch of Latin American development aids in understanding the nature of contemporary authoritarianism. . . . The linkages are complex, but very largely determine the public policies that will be followed. Creditors want to be paid in dollars or in other international currencies. The international financial institutions are critically concerned with the debtor country's balance of payments. A sharp increase in exports—acknowledged to be the best way to achieve a more favorable balance and repay the debt—is very difficult to achieve in the short run. Also difficult to accomplish is a dramatic increase in capital inflows—except by borrowing even more.

This leaves imports as a natural target for those who would save hard currency. But in order to cut imports—or at least that sector of imports that is least important to ruling elites, economic managers, and most national and international business—mass consumption must be restricted. Since quotas and tariffs are seen as inappropriate policy instruments, to a large extent consumer demand must be managed through restrictions on the real purchasing power of wage-earners—and increases in unemployment.

When coupled with cutbacks in government expenditures (typically in public works and welfare-enhancing subsidies), a huge proportion of the adjustment burden is thus transferred to the working class. In an inflationary economy, the proportional burden is even greater. Needless to say, where minimal possibilities of political expression exist, this kind of adjustment medicine does not go down easily. Repression of trade unions as effective organizations and workers as individuals is in this sense "necessary" for those in charge of managing the economy and for their friends and allies abroad.

Many of these same persons may decry the extreme and brutal measures used in countries such as Brazil, Uruguay, Argentina, Bolivia and Chile to establish and maintain control over the labor movement and hold wages well below the inflationary spiral. Some may even take comfort in the fact that, once the most extreme measures have been used, a partial relaxation of control seems possible at a later date. But minimal honesty requires that the repression in both its physical and financial dimensions be seen as an organic aspect of what is now the prevailing mode of economic development in Latin America. Social and economic human rights do not fare well in such an environment. . . .

What has evolved in Latin America (and by implication in some other areas of the Third World) is a political-economic model that has *no* historical precedent in the now more developed capitalist world. For lack of a more concise phrase, this model can be called illiberal state capitalism, a situation in which state intervention in the economy is substantial, but governmental policies tend to reinforce rather than soften or ameliorate income inequalities, class distinctions, and regional disequilibria.[20]

I take it to be evident that in various countries throughout the world deprivation is sometimes accidental and sometimes essential, and that one has no reason at all to expect that either thesis is applicable to all cases. Each continent, or rather each country, and often each regime, must be analyzed on its own. But it is fairly clear that current regimes include a number of instances of what Fagen calls "illiberal state capitalism" and that in these cases people are deprived of subsistence (and liberty) by their own government's choice of economic strategy.

In this brief theoretical work I obviously cannot attempt to establish under which governments deprivations of subsistence are essential and under which they are accidental, although I have already mentioned some cases I take to be strikingly evident. Illiberal state capitalism is only one prominent source of strategies of essential deprivation, and for us here the main point is the distinction between essential and accidental deprivation, whatever the detailed explanation for which one occurs. Especially when we come in chapter 7 [of *Basic Rights*] to look at specific recommendations for US foreign policy, it will be crucial to keep this underlying distinction between these two explanations of deprivation in mind. In most cases the formulation of policy must take the source of deprivations into account. A government that engages in essential deprivation—that follows an economic strategy in which deprivations of subsistence are inherent in the strategy—fails to fulfill even any duty merely to avoid depriving. Such systematic violation of subsistence rights is surely intolerable. Such a government is a direct and immediate threat to its own people, and they are entitled to resist it in order to defend themselves. But I am getting ahead of the theoretical story.

We turned to the actual case of illiberal state capitalism in Latin America with its macroeconomic strategies of essential deprivation, as well as to the hypothetical case of the village flower contract, which is a kind of contract encouraged by—but not dependent upon—strategies of essential deprivation, in order to see some illustrations of the inaccuracy of the philosophical doctrine that subsistence rights, like all economic rights, are positive, because their fulfillment consists largely of actively providing people with commodities like food. From these cases it is now, I hope, quite clear that the honoring of subsistence rights may often in no way involve transferring commodities to people, but may instead involve preventing people's being deprived of the commodities or the means to grow, make, or buy the commodities. Preventing such deprivations will indeed require what can be called positive actions, especially protective and self-protective actions. But such protection against the deprivation of subsistence is in all major respects like protection against deprivations of physical security or of other rights that are placed on the negative side of the conventional negative/positive dichotomy. I believe the whole notion that there is a morally significant dichotomy between negative rights and positive rights is intellectually bankrupt—that premise 2, as stated in the first section of this chapter, is mistaken. The cases we have considered establish at the very least that the dichotomy distorts when it is applied to security rights and subsistence rights—that premises 3 and 4 were mistaken. The latter is all that needed to be shown.

## AVOIDANCE, PROTECTION, AND AID

Still, it is true that sometimes fulfilling a right does involve transferring commodities to the person with the right and sometimes it merely involves not taking commodities away. Is there not some grain of truth obscured by the dichotomy between negative and positive rights? Are there not distinctions here that are useful to make?

The answer, I believe, is: Yes, there are distinctions, but they are not distinctions between rights. The useful distinctions are among duties, and there are no one-to-one pairings between kinds of duties and kinds of rights. The complete fulfillment of each kind of right involves the performance of multiple kinds of duties. This conceptual change has, I believe, important practical implications, although it will be only in chapter 7 [of *Basic Rights*] that the implications can begin to be illustrated. In the remainder of this chapter I would like to tender a very simple tripartite typology of duties. For all its own simplicity, it goes considerably beyond the usual assumption that for every right there is a single correlative duty, and suggests instead that for every basic right—and many other rights as well—there are three types of duties, all of which must be performed if the basic right is to be fully honored but not all of which must necessarily be performed by the same individuals or institutions. This latter point opens the possibility of distributing each of the three kinds of duty somewhat differently and perhaps confining any difficulties about the correlativity of subsistence rights and their accompanying duties to fewer than all three kinds of duties.

So I want to suggest that with every basic right, three types of duties correlate:

I.     Duties to *avoid* depriving.

II.    Duties to *protect* from deprivation.

III.   Duties to *aid* the deprived.

This may be easier to see in the case of the more familiar basic right, the right to physical security (the right not to be tortured, executed, raped, assaulted, etc.). For every person's right to physical security, there are three correlative duties:

I.     Duties not to eliminate a person's security—duties to *avoid* depriving.

II.    Duties to protect people against deprivation of security by other people—duties to *protect* from deprivation.

III.   Duties to provide for the security of those unable to provide for their own—duties to *aid* the deprived.

Similarly, for every right to subsistence there are:

I.     Duties not to eliminate a person's only available means of subsistence—duties to *avoid* depriving.

II.    Duties to protect people against deprivation of the only available means of subsistence by other people—duties to *protect* from deprivation.

III.   Duties to provide for the subsistence of those unable to provide for their own—duties to *aid* the deprived.

If this suggestion is correct, the common notion that *rights* can be divided into rights to forbearance (so-called negative rights), as if some rights have correlative duties only to avoid depriving, and rights to aid (so-called positive rights), as if some rights have correlative duties only to aid, is thoroughly misguided. This misdirected simplification is virtually ubiquitous among contemporary North Atlantic theorists and is, I think, all the more pernicious for the degree of unquestioning acceptance it has now attained. It is duties, not rights, that can be divided among avoidance and aid, and protection. And—this is what matters—every basic right entails duties of all three types. Consequently the attempted division of rights, rather than duties, into forbearance and aid (and protection, which is often understandably but unhelpfully blurred into avoidance, since protection is partly, but only partly, the enforcement of avoidance) can only breed confusion.

It is impossible for any basic right—however "negative" it has come to seem—to be fully guaranteed unless all three types of duties are fulfilled. The very most "negative"-seeming right to liberty, for example, requires positive action by society to protect it and positive action by society to restore it when avoidance and protection both fail. This by no means implies, as I have already mentioned, that all three types of duties fall upon everyone else or even fall equally upon everyone upon whom they do fall. Although this tripartite analysis of duties is, I believe, perfectly general, I will focus here upon the duties correlative to subsistence rights: subsistence duties.

## The Generality of the Tripartite Analysis

However, perhaps a brief word on the general issue is useful before turning to a fairly detailed analysis of the threefold duties correlative to the rights that most concern us: subsistence rights. Obviously theses of three ascending degrees of generality might be advanced:

All subsistence rights involve threefold correlative duties.

All basic rights involve threefold correlative duties.

Most moral rights involve threefold correlative duties.

I subscribe to all three theses, and I believe that the remainder of this book [*Basic Rights*] offers significant support for all three. But naturally the support will be most thorough for the first thesis and least thorough for the last. For the most part I am content to leave matters at that, because the only point that I am concerned fully to establish is the priority of subsistence rights, that is, their equal priority with all other basic rights. Consequently, the arguments need, strictly speaking, to be thorough only for subsistence rights. But a contrasting pair of observations are also in order.

On the one hand, the argument here is from the particular to the general, not the converse. It is not because I assumed that normal rights involve some, or threefold, duties that I concluded that subsistence rights involve some, and threefold, duties. I explored subsistence rights, as we are about to do, and found that they can be fully accounted for only by means of admitting three kinds of correlated duties. I looked at the same time at security rights and, as we will do in chapter 3 [of *Basic Rights*], at rights to liberty and found again that an adequate explanation involves all three kinds of multiply interrelated duties, thus coming to suspect that all basic rights, at the very least, require the same tripartite analysis of the duty side of the coin.

On the other hand, on the basis of these detailed examinations of these three rights I am indeed tempted to recommend that the most general thesis be made analytically true, that is, that any right not involving the threefold duties be acknowledged to be an exceptional case. If the account of a right given at the beginning of chapter 1 [of *Basic Rights*, herein 84] were made a strict definition, then it would do just this. If a right provides the rational basis for a justified demand that the actual enjoyment of the substance of the right be socially guaranteed against standard threats, then a right provides the rational basis for insisting upon the performance, as needed, of duties to avoid, duties to protect, and duties to aid, as they will shortly be explained. This picture does seem to me to fit all the standard cases of moral rights.[21] If, however, someone can give clear counterexamples to the final step of generalization (the move from duties for basic rights to duties for moral rights generally), I can see little cause for concern, provided the admission of rights that lack some kinds of correlative duties, to the realm of nonbasic rights, is not allowed to devalue the coinage of rights generally.

## SUBSISTENCE DUTIES

The first type of subsistence duty is neither a duty to provide help nor a duty to protect against harm by third parties but is the most nearly "negative" or passive kind of duty that is possible: a duty simply not to take actions that deprive others of a means that, but for one's own harmful actions, would have satisfied their subsistence rights or enabled them to satisfy their own subsistence rights, where the actions are not necessary to the satisfaction of one's own basic rights and where the threatened means is the only realistic one.[22] Duties to avoid depriving require merely that one refrain from making an unnecessary gain for oneself by a means that is destructive for others.

Part of the relation between these subsistence duties to avoid depriving (type I) and subsistence duties to protect from deprivation (type II) is quite straightforward. If everyone could be counted upon voluntarily to fulfill duties to avoid, duties to protect would be unnecessary. But since it would be naive to expect everyone to fulfill his or her duties to avoid and since other people's very survival is at stake, it is clearly necessary that some individuals or institutions have the duty of enforcing the duty to avoid. The duty to protect is, then, in part a secondary duty of enforcing the primary duty of avoiding the destruction of people's means of subsistence. In this respect it is analogous to, for example, the duty of the police to enforce the duty of parents not to starve their children.

The natural institution in many societies to have the task of enforcing those primary duties that need enforcement is the executive branch of some level of government, acting on behalf of the members of society other than the offending individuals or institutions. Which level of government takes operating responsibility is largely a practical matter and might vary among societies. Where the source of harm is, for example, a transnational corporation, protection may need to be provided by the home government or even by multilateral government action.[23] But clearly if duties to avoid depriving people of their last means of subsistence are to be taken seriously, some provision must be made for enforcing this duty on behalf of the rest of humanity upon those who would not otherwise fulfill it. Perhaps it would be worth considering nongovernmental enforcement institutions as the bearers in some cases of the secondary duty to protect, but the primary institution would normally appear to be the government of the threatened person's own nation. It is normally taken to be a central function of government to prevent irreparable harm from being inflicted upon some members of society by other individual members, by institutions, or by interactions of the two. It is difficult to imagine why anyone should pay much attention to the demands of any government that failed to perform this function, if it were safe to ignore its demands.

Duties to aid (type III) are in themselves fairly complicated, and only one kind will be discussed here. At least three subcategories of duties to aid need to be recognized. What they have in common is the requirement that resources be transferred to those who cannot provide for their own survival. First are duties to aid (III-1) that are attached to certain roles or relationships and rest therefore upon only those who are in a particular role or relationship and are borne toward only those other persons directly involved. Some central cases are the duties of parents toward their own young children and the duties of grown children toward their own aged parents. Naturally, important issues can arise even with regard to such relatively clear duties as the duty to provide food to the helplessly young and to the helplessly old, but I have nothing to add here regarding these duties, which are not universal. By their not being universal I mean that although all parents may normally have certain duties toward their own children, no child can justifiably hold that all people, or even all parents, have *this* sort of duty toward it. All people may of course have other duties toward the child, including universal ones, and possibly including one of the other two subcategories of duties to aid that are to be mentioned next.

The only difference between the second and third subcategories of duties to aid is the source of the deprivation because of which aid is needed. In the second case (III-2) the deprivation is the result of failures to fulfill duties to avoid depriving and duties to protect from deprivation—some people have acted in such a way as to eliminate the last available means of subsistence for other people and the responsible government has failed to protect the victims. Thus, the need for assistance is the result of a prior twofold failure to perform duties, and the victims have been harmed by both actions and omissions of actions by other people.

In the third case (III-3) the deprivation is not the result of failures in duty and, in just this sense, the deprivation is "natural," that is, the deprivation suffered is not a case of harm primarily caused by other people. The clearest case of a natural deprivation calling for aid is a natural disaster like a hurricane or an earthquake. As always, questions arise at the borderline between cases—for example, was the death toll increased because the weather bureau or civil defense organization failed to protect with timely warnings? But uncontroversial central cases in which no human beings are much to blame are perfectly familiar, even if not so frequent as we might like to believe.

Where supplies of the necessities of life, or of the resources needed to grow or make the necessities, are scarce, duties of types I and II take on increased importance. The results of the fulfillment only of I and II would already be dramatic in the poorer areas of the world, in which most of the earth's inhabitants eke out their existences. It is easy to underestimate the importance of these two kinds of subsistence duties, which together are intended to prevent deprivation. But to eliminate the only realistic means a person has for obtaining food or other physical necessities is to cause that person, for example, the physical harm of malnutrition or of death by starvation. When physical harm but not death is caused, the effect of eliminating the only means of support can be every degree as serious as the effect of a violation of physical security by means of a bodily assault. The physical effects of malnutrition can be irreversible and far more profound than the physical effects of many an assault in fact are. And when starvation is caused, the ultimate effect of eliminating the only means of support is precisely the same as the effect of murder. Those who are helpless in the face of insuperable obstacles to their continued existence are at least one level worse off than those who are defenseless in the face of assaults upon their physical security. The defenseless will at least be able to maintain themselves if they are provided with protection against threatening assaults. If protected but otherwise left alone, they will manage. But the helpless, if simply left alone—even if they should be protected against all assaults upon their security—will die for lack of the means of subsistence. They will merely, in Coleridge's phrase, "die so slowly that none call it murder."[24]

Now of course differences between deprivations of security and deprivations of subsistence can also be noted, as already mentioned. Normally in a violation of physical security by means of assault or murder, the human agent's central intention is indeed to bring about, or at least includes bringing about, the physical harm or death that is caused for the victim, although obviously one also can injure or kill inadvertently. In the case of the elimination of the means of physical subsistence, the human agent's central intention may at least sometimes be focused on other consequences of his or her action, such as the increased security of income that would result from a multiyear salaried contract to grow flowers rather than a precarious annual attempt to grow food. The harm to the victims may be entirely unintended. Such difference in intention between the two cases is undoubtedly relevant to any assessment of the moral stature respectively of the two persons who partly cause the harm in the two cases. But for the two victims the difference between intended physical harm and unintended physical harm may matter little, since the harmfulness of the action taken may be the same in both cases and may be even greater where unintended.

Nevertheless, it may be arbitrary to assign a role of *the* perpetrator to any one person or group in a case of the deprivation of subsistence. The deprivations in question may in fact be "systemic": the product of the joint workings of individual actions and social institutions no one of which by itself caused the harm. But what follows from this is not that no one is responsible (since everyone is). What follows is that the distinction between duties to avoid (I) and duties to protect (II), which is relatively clear in the abstract, blurs considerably in concrete reality.[25] The division of labor between individual restraint and institutional protection can be worked out in any of several acceptable ways, the full details of which would go considerably beyond the scope of this book *[Basic Rights]*, but between the two kinds of duties, individuals ought not to be deprived by the actions (intentional or unintentional) of others of all hope of sustaining themselves.

This means, however, that duties to protect (II) are not simply secondary duties to enforce the primary duty to avoid (I). We can mark as II-1 the duties to protect that are merely secondary duties to enforce the duty to avoid. But duties to protect also encompass the design of social institutions that do not leave individuals with duties to avoid, the fulfillment of which would necessitate superhuman qualities. This task of constructing institutions can be marked as II-2. In the original example of the flower contract, some would judge that the peasant receiving the offer to switch out of food production, in the circumstances stipulated, could reasonably have been expected to foresee the consequences of the switch and to refrain from making it. But it is probably more realistic neither to expect him to have the information and comprehension necessary to foresee the consequences nor to expect him to choose not to reduce his own insecurity—and certainly an example could readily be constructed in which an individual could not reasonably be expected to know in advance the probable bad consequences for others of his or her action or to give them more weight than improvements in his or her own precarious situation.[26]

For such cases, in which individual restraint would be too much to ask, the duty to protect (II-2) includes the design of laws and institutions that avoid reliance upon unreasonable levels of individual self-control. Many actions that are immoral ought nevertheless not to be made illegal. But one of the best possible reasons for making an act illegal is its contributing to harm as fundamental as the deprivation of someone's last available means of subsistence. And a number of intermediate steps between total prohibition and complete tolerance of an action are possible, such as tax laws that create disincentives of various strengths against the kind of action that would contribute to the deprivation of subsistence from others and create alternative sources of increased economic security for oneself. Social institutions must, at the very least, be designed to enable ordinary human beings, who are neither saints nor geniuses, to do each other a minimum of serious harm.

In sum, then, we find that the fulfillment of a basic right to subsistence involves at least the following kinds of duties:

I. To avoid depriving.

II. To protect from deprivation
   1. By enforcing duty (I) and
   2. By designing institutions that avoid the creation of strong incentives to violate duty (I).

III. To aid the deprived
   1. Who are one's special responsibility,
   2. Who are victims of social failures in the performance of duties (I), (II-1), (II-2) and
   3. Who are victims of natural disasters.

## THE SYSTEMATIC INTERDEPENDENCE OF DUTIES

Fulfillment of a basic right (and, I think, of most other moral rights as well) requires, then, performance by some individuals or institutions of each of these three general kinds of correlative duties. Duties to avoid depriving possibly come closest to failing to be essential, because duties to protect provide for the enforcement of duties to avoid. Even if individuals, organizations, and governments were otherwise inclined to violate rights to security, for example, by failing to fulfill their respective duties to avoid, forceful fulfillment of duties to protect by whomever they fell upon—presumably a national government—could probably produce behavior in compliance with duties to avoid. But reliance on duties to protect rather than duties to avoid would constitute heavy reliance on something like national police power rather than self-restraint by individuals, corporations, and lower-level governments, and would involve obvious disadvantages even if—probably, especially if—the police power were adequate actually to enforce duties to avoid upon a generally reluctant society. Unfortunately this much power to protect would also be enormous power to deprive, which is a lesson about police that even dictators sometimes have to learn the hard way.

Since duties to avoid and duties to protect taken together have only one purpose, to prevent deprivations, the reverse of what was just described is obviously also possible: If everyone who ought to fulfill duties to avoid did so, performance of duties to protect might not be necessary. Law enforcement agencies could perhaps be disbanded in a society of restrained organizational and individual behavior. But although reliance entirely upon duties to protect is undesirable even if possible, a safe complete reliance upon duties to avoid is most improbable in the absence of at least minimal performance of duties to protect. Organizations and individuals who will voluntarily avoid deprivation that would otherwise be advantageous to them because they know that their potential victims are protected cannot be expected to behave in the same way when they know their potential victims are without protection.

The general conclusions about duties to avoid and duties to protect, then, are, first, that strictly speaking it is essential for the guarantee of any right only that either the one or the other be completely fulfilled, but, second, that for all practical purposes it is essential to insist upon the fulfillment of both, because complete reliance on either one alone is probably not feasible and, in the case of duties to protect, almost certainly not desirable.

What division of labor is established by one's account of duties between self-restraint and restraint by others, such as police forces, will obviously have an enormous effect upon the quality of life of those living in the social system in question. I do not want to pursue the questions involved in deciding upon the division, except to note that if either duties to avoid or duties to protect are construed too narrowly, the other duty then becomes unrealistically broad. For example, if a government, in the exercise of its duty to protect, fails to impose constraints upon agribusinesses designed to prevent them from creating malnutrition, the prevention of malnutrition will then depend upon the self-restraint of the agribusinesses. But much evidence suggests that individual agribusinesses are unwilling or unable to take into account the nutritional effect of their decisions about the use of land, local credit and capital, water, and other resources. This is especially true if the agribusiness is producing export crops and most especially if it is investing in a foreign country, the nutritional level of whose people is easily considered irrelevant.[27] If indeed a particular type of corporation has demonstrated an inability to forgo projects that produce malnutrition, given their setting, it is foolish to rely on corporate restraint, and whichever governments have responsibility to protect those who are helpless to resist the corporation's activity—host governments, home government or both—will have to fulfill their duties to protect. If, on the other hand, the corporations would restrain themselves, the governments could restrain them less. How to work this out is difficult and important. The present point is simply that between the bearers of the two duties, the job of preventing deprivation ought to get done, if there is a right not to be deprived of whatever is threatened. And the side that construes its own role too narrowly, if it actually has the power to act, may be as much at fault for contributing to the violation of rights as the side that fails to take up all the resulting slack.

However, as I have already indicated, the duty to protect ought not to be understood only in terms of the maintenance of law enforcement, regulatory, and other closely related agencies. A major and more constructive part of the duty to protect is the duty to design social institutions that do not exceed the capacity of individuals and organizations, including private and public corporations, to restrain themselves. Not only the kinds of acute threats of deprivation that police can prevent, but the kinds of chronic threats that require imaginative legislation and, sometimes, long-term planning fall under the duty to protect.[28]

Nevertheless, it is duties to aid that often have the highest urgency, because they are often owed to persons who are suffering the consequences of failures to fulfill both duties to avoid and duties to protect, that is, they are duties of type III-2. These people will have been totally deprived of their rights to subsistence if they are then not aided either. This greater urgency does not, of course, mean that duties to aid are more compelling overall than the first two types of duty, and indeed it is specifically against duties to aid that complaints that the correlative duties accompanying subsistence rights are too burdensome may seem most plausible. It is important to notice that to the extent that duties to avoid and to protect are fulfilled, duties to assist will be less burdensome. If the fulfillment of duties to protect is sufficiently inadequate, duties to assist may be overwhelming and may seem unrealistically great, as they do today to many people. For example, because the Dutch colonial empire failed to protect the people of Java against the effects of the

Dutch schemes for agricultural exports, the nutritional problems of the majority of Indonesians today strike some people as almost beyond all solution.[29] The colossal failure of the Dutch colonial government in its duties to protect (or, even, to avoid deprivation) has created virtually Sisyphean duties to aid. These presumably fall to some degree upon the Dutch people who are today still profiting from their centuries of spoils. But whoever precisely has these duties to aid—there are plenty to go around—their magnitude has clearly been multiplied by past dereliction in the performance of the other two kinds of duties by the Dutch, among others. We will return in chapter 5 [of *Basic Rights*] to some aspects of the difficult question of how to allocate duties to aid, especially when (chapter 6 [of *Basic Rights*]) they cross national boundaries.

This much, however, is already clear. The account of correlative duties is for the most part a more detailed specification of what the account of rights calls social guarantees against standard threats. Provisions for avoidance, protection, and aid are what are needed for a reasonable level of social guarantees. Making the necessary provisions for the fulfillment of subsistence rights may sometimes be burdensome, especially when the task is to recover from past neglect of basic duties. But we have no reason to believe, as proponents of the negative/positive distinction typically assert, that the performance of the duties correlative to subsistence rights would always or usually be more difficult, more expensive, less practicable, or harder to "deliver" than would the actual performance of the duties correlative to the rights that are conventionally labeled negative and that are more often announced than in fact fulfilled. And the burdens connected with subsistence rights do not fall primarily upon isolated individuals who would be expected quietly to forgo advantages to themselves for the sake of not threatening others, but primarily upon human communities that can work cooperatively to design institutions that avoid situations in which people are confronted by subsistence-threatening forces they cannot themselves handle. In spite of the sometimes useful terminology of third parties helping first parties against second parties, etc., it is worth noting, while assessing the burden of subsistence duties, that the third-party bearers of duties can also become the first-party bearers of rights when situations change. No one is assured of living permanently on one side of the rights/duties coin.

# NOTES

## 1. Security and Subsistence

1. Obviously this is not the usual North Atlantic account of what a right is, although it incorporates, I think, what is correct in the usual accounts. Perhaps the most frequently cited philosophical discussion is the useful one in Joel Feinberg, *Social Philosophy* (Englewood Cliffs: Prentice-Hall, 1973), pp. 55–97. A more recent and extended account is A. I. Melden, *Rights and Persons* (Oxford: Basil Blackwell, 1977). The best collection of recent English and American philosophical essays is probably *Rights*, edited by David Lyons (Belmont, CA: Wadsworth Publishing, 1979). For a broader range of views, in less rigorous form, see *Human Rights: Cultural and Ideological Perspectives*, edited by Adamantia Pollis and Peter Schwab (New York: Praeger Publishers, 1979). For additional references, mostly to work in English, see Rex Martin and James W. Nickel, "A Bibliography on the Nature and Foundations of Rights, 1947-1977," *Political Theory*, 6:3 (August 1978), pp. 395–413. Some older but more wide-ranging bibliographies are *International Human Rights: A Bibliography, 1965-1969*, and *International Human Rights: A Bibliography, 1970-1976*, both edited by William Miller (Notre Dame: University of Notre Dame Law School, Center for Civil Rights, 1976).

2. In saying that these three features constitute "the general structure of a moral right" I do not mean that every moral right always has every one of the three. Wittgenstein, for one, has argued persuasively that we have no particular reason to expect all authentic instances of any concept to have all features—indeed, to have any one feature—in common and that what instance A shares with instance B need not be the same as what instance B shares with instance C. See Ludwig Wittgenstein, *Philosophical Investigations*, 3rd ed. (Oxford: Basil Blackwell, 1967), part I, paragraphs 66–67. What we are left with is the more realistic but more elusive notion of standard, central, or typical cases. The danger then rests in the temptation to dismiss as deviant or degenerate cases what ought to be treated as counterexamples to our general claims. We have no mechanical method for deciding what is standard and what is deviant and so must consider individual cases fairly and thoroughly, as we shall soon be trying to do.

Two important characteristics of this list of features should be emphasized. First, the list of features is, not the premises for, but the conclusion from, the detailed description of individual rights considered in the body of the book *[Basic Rights]*. Thus, the order of presentation is not the order of derivation. These general features were distilled from the cases of security rights, subsistence rights, and liberty rights discussed in the first three chapters [of *Basic Rights*]. These general conclusions are presented here as a means of quickly sketching the bold outlines of what is still to be justified.

Second, most of the argument of the book [*Basic Rights*] depends only upon its being correct to say that all *basic* rights have these three features. Since the features are derived from the detailed consideration only of basic rights, it would be conceivable that basic rights were peculiar in having all three. Yet, many other rights obviously do have this same structure. So I advance the less fully justified broader claim, not merely the safer, narrower claim.

3. Feinberg, pp. 58–59. The terminology of "claim-rights" is of course from Wesley Hohfeld, *Fundamental Legal Conceptions* (New Haven: Yale University Press, 1923).

4. Standard moral rights are, in the categories devised by Hohfeld for legal rights, claim-rights, not mere liberties. Certainly all basic rights turn out to be moral claim-rights rather than moral liberties. See chapter 2 [of *Basic Rights*, herein 103–30].

5. This becomes clearest in the discussion of rights to liberty in chapter 3 [of *Basic Rights*].

6. Who exactly are the relevant people is an extremely difficult question, to which chapter 6 [of *Basic Rights*] is devoted.

7. See chapter 2 [of *Basic Rights*, herein 103–30].

8. For his clearest single presentation of this analysis, see Friedrich Nietzsche, *On the Genealogy of Morals*, edited by Walter Kaufmann and translated by Walter Kaufmann and R. J. Hollingdale (New York: Vintage Books, 1967). Much, but not all, of what is interesting in Nietzsche's account was put into the mouth of Callicles in Plato's *Gorgias*.

9. Many legal claim-rights make little or no contribution to self-respect, but moral claim-rights (and the legal claim-rights based upon them) surely do.

10. Nietzsche was also conflating a number of different kinds of power/weakness. Many of today's politically powerful, against whom people need protection, totally lack the kind of dignified power Nietzsche most admired and would certainly have incurred his cordial disgust.

11. Anyone not familiar with the real meaning of what gets called "infant mortality rates" might consider the significance of the fact that in nearby Mexico seven out of every 100 babies fail to survive infancy—see United States, Department of State, *Background Notes: Mexico*, Revised February 1979 (Washington: Government Printing Office, 1979), p. 1. For far worse current children's death rates still, see chapter 4, note 13 [of *Basic Rights*].

12. It is controversial whether rights are claims only upon members of one's own society or upon other persons generally. For some support for the conclusion assumed here, see chapter 6 [of *Basic Rights*].

13. Since the enjoyment of a basic right is necessary for the enjoyment of all other rights, it is basic not only to nonbasic rights but to other basic rights as well. Thus the enjoyment of the basic rights is an all-or-nothing matter. Each is necessary to the other basic ones as well as to all nonbasic ones. Every

right, including every basic right, can be enjoyed only if all basic rights are enjoyed. An extended discussion of a case of this mutual dependence is found in chapter 3 [of *Basic Rights*].

At the cost of being somewhat premature it may be useful to comment here on an objection that often strikes readers at this point as being a clear counter-example to the thesis that subsistence rights are basic rights in the sense just explained. Mark Wicclair has put the objection especially forcefully for me. The arguments for the thesis have of course not yet been given and occupy much of the remainder of the chapter and, indeed, of the book *[Basic Rights]*.

Suppose that in a certain society people are said to enjoy a certain security right—let us say the right not to be tortured. But they do not in fact enjoy subsistence rights: food, for example, is not socially guaranteed even to people who find it impossible to nourish themselves. The thesis that subsistence rights are basic means that people cannot enjoy any other right if subsistence rights are not socially guaranteed. It follows that the people in the society in ques-tion could not actually be enjoying the right not to be tortured, because their right to adequate food is not guaranteed. But—this is the objection—it would appear that they could enjoy the right not to be tortured even though they were starving to death for lack of food they could do nothing to obtain. The objection grants that starvation is terrible. The theoretical point is, however, said to remain: Starvation without torture is preferable to starvation with torture, and the right not to be tortured is still worth something even in isolation and, in particular, even in the absence of subsistence rights. Subsistence rights are, therefore, not necessary for the enjoyment of all other rights and thus not basic in the relevant sense.

But could there actually be a case of the kind brought forward as a counter-example? Could there actually be a right not to be tortured in the absence of a right to subsistence? The difficulty is that a person who had no social guarantee of, say, food and was in fact deprived of food might, without other recourse, be willing to submit to limited torture in exchange for food. In other words, what is being called a right not to be tortured is open to being undermined by the threat of doing nothing about a shortage of food. If this perverse trade of submission to torture for receipt of food were possible, it would be accurate to say that although the person may *have* a right not to be tortured, he cannot actually *enjoy* the right because he must choose between undergoing torture and undergoing starvation, or malnutrition (to make the alternative involving subsistence much more like torture: painful and damaging but not fatal). Insofar as the person has anything approximating a right not to be tortured, the "right" is a merely conditional one—conditional upon the person's not in fact being without some necessity for subsistence for which the substance of the "right" not to be tortured could, in effect, be sold.

Three ways of trying to save the original objection come to mind. First, it might be suggested that trading the immunity to torture for the means to eat is not an instance of failing to enjoy a right, but an instance of renouncing a right. Only because one has the right not to be tortured does one have something to trade for food.

This response is fairly obviously mistaken. If one's only hope of eating adequately is to submit to torture, one is being coerced into submitting to torture, not renouncing one's right not to be tortured. This is a case of coercion analogous in the relevant respects to the demand, your money or your life. One is not renouncing one's right to the money—one is being forced to surrender one's money in order to stay alive. In prisons, where people are already deprived of the freedom of physical movement ordinarily needed for obtaining their own food, the threat to withhold food as well is in fact a common means of coercion.

Second, it could be noted that the torture-for-food exchange might simply not be available. Certainly in light of the perversity of the bargain, there might be no one in the business of supplying people with food in exchange for the privilege of torturing them. Only some sort of wealthy sadist would engage in this transaction.

Now, of course the exchange described is in fact very unlikely, as is the original situation that constitutes the counterexample. The response to the objection is as fantastical as the objection, but the objector cannot expect otherwise. (In what country are people both provided guarantees against torture and denied guarantees of food for subsistence?) But this second response misses the point. That people were not in fact undergoing torture in order to obtain food (or for any other reason) would not constitute their enjoying a right not to be tortured. Enjoying any right includes, among other things, some social guarantees. It is not merely that one does not undergo objectionable events or that one does undergo desirable events—it includes provisions having been made to see to it that the objectionable does not occur and the desirable does.

Hence, the third way to save the counterexample would be to add to it a prohibition against trading the right not to be tortured for anything else, including what was needed to meet an even more serious threat. The counterexample would have to say: One may not be tortured and one must not surrender, trade, renounce, and so on. this right for anything else. This would be a weak version of something roughly like what was traditionally called inalienability, except that as traditionally understood inalienability was essential to or inherent in a right: It was thought to be somehow absolutely impossible to alienate or trade the right. In the objector's counterexample anyone obviously *could* trade the right not to be tortured for something else. The best that could be done would be an exceptionless and enforceable prohibition against trading away this right. The trade would, perhaps, be illegal. We can call this an alienation-prohibition, in order to distinguish it from the traditional notion of intrinsic inalienability.

With the inclusion of the alienation-prohibition the case may be an actual counterexample, but it is difficult to tell. Possibly one is enjoying a right not to be tortured when one is not only protected against torture but also prevented from exchanging that protection for protection against other threats. As the argument of the book *[Basic Rights]* unfolds, two of the main contentions will be (a) that in order to enjoy any right one must be protected against the standard threats to the right and (b) that the best way to be protected against a standard threat is to have social guarantees for the absence of the threat. Thus, the way to enjoy a right to subsistence is to be guaranteed that no torture, among other things, will be used to implement an economic strategy that produces malnutrition, and the way to enjoy a right not to be tortured is to be guaranteed that no deprivations of subsistence needs like food, among other things, will be used to implement a political strategy that includes torture (not that the latter is a realistic case).

Now instead of protecting the enjoyment of one right against standard threats by also protecting the other rights the enjoyment of which includes social guarantees against the standard threats, one could conceivably "protect" one right in isolation by prohibiting the use of that right to fend off threats against which one has no guarantees because one lacks other rights. This is what is done by the right not to be tortured that includes the alienation-prohibition. But the attempted counterexample has now become quite contorted and exotic. One is being prohibited from saving one's own life (from lack of subsistence) at a cost of pain and damage that one is willing to accept if one must. Is this an example of enjoying one right (not to be tortured) in the absence of the enjoyment of another right (subsistence)? This case is now so different from an ordinary case of enjoying a right (in which, I will contend, part of the right is social guarantees against standard threats) that it is uncertain what to say. Obviously I could not without circularity invoke what I take to be the normal and adequate conception of enjoying a right in order to judge the proffered case not to be a case of enjoying a right and therefore not a counterexample to the thesis that subsistence rights are basic. However, treating this eccentric example as a clear case would be question-begging against my view, I think. So, I leave it to the reader—and to the argument in the text.

14. It is odd that the list of "primary goods" in Rawlsian theory does not mention physical security as such. See John Rawls, *A Theory of Justice* (Cambridge, MA: The Belknap Press of Harvard University Press, 1971), p. 62 and p. 303. The explanation seems to be that security is lumped in with political participation and a number of civil liberties, including freedom of thought, of speech, of press, et al. To do this is to use "liberty" in a confusingly broad sense. One can speak intelligibly of "freedom from" almost anything bad: The child was free from fear, the cabin was free from snakes, the picnic was free from rain. Similarly, it is natural to speak of being free from assault, free from the threat of rape, and so on, but this does not turn all these absences of evils into liberties. Freedom from assault, for example, is a kind of security or safety, not a kind of liberty. It may of course be a necessary condition for the exercise of any liberties, which is exactly what I shall now be arguing, but a necessary condition for the exercise of a liberty may be many things other than another kind of

liberty. The most complete indication of why I believe physical security and liberty—even freedom of physical movement—need to be treated separately is chapter 3 [of *Basic Rights*].

15. At considerable risk of encouraging unflattering comparisons I might as well note myself that in its general structure the argument here has the same form as the argument in H. L. A. Hart's classic, "Are There Any Natural Rights?" *Philosophical Review*, 64:2 (April 1955), pp. 175–91. That is, Hart can be summarized as maintaining: If there are any rights, there are rights to liberty. I am saying: If there are any rights, there are rights to security—and to subsistence. The finer structures of the arguments are of course quite different. I find Hart's inference considerably less obvious than he did. So, evidently, do many thoughtful people in the Third and Fourth Worlds, which counts against its obviousness but not necessarily against its validity. My struggle with the place of some kinds of liberty, construed more narrowly than Hart's, constitutes chapter 3 [of *Basic Rights*].

16. In originally formulating this argument for treating both security and subsistence as basic rights I was not consciously following any philosopher but attempting instead to distill contemporary common sense. As many people have noted, today's common sense tends to be yesterday's philosophy. I was amused to notice recently the following passage from Mill, who not only gives a similar argument for security but notices and then backs away from the parallel with subsistence: "The interest involved is that of security, to everyone's feelings the most vital of all interests. All other earthly benefits are needed by one person, not needed by another; and many of them can, if necessary, be cheerfully forgone or replaced by something else; but security no human being can possibly do without; on it we depend for all our immunity from evil and for the whole value of all and every good, beyond the passing moment, since nothing but the gratification of the instant could be of any worth to us if we could be deprived of everything the next instant by whoever was momentarily stronger than ourselves. Now this most indispensable of all necessaries, after physical nutriment, cannot be had unless. . . . " John Stuart Mill, *Utilitarianism* (Indianapolis: Bobbs-Merrill, 1957), p. 67 (chapter V, 14th paragraph from the end).

17. "Many people, therefore, economically dependent as they are upon their employer, hesitate to speak out not because they are afraid of getting arrested, but because they are afraid of being fired. And they are right." Ira Glasser, "Director's Report: You Can Be Fired for Your Politics," *Civil Liberties*, No. 327 (April 1979), p. 8.

18. Exactly how and why Western liberalism has tended to overlook subsistence is another story, but consider, simply as one symptom, the fact that a standard assumption in liberal theory is that there is only moderate scarcity. This has the effect of assuming that everyone's subsistence is taken care of. You must have your subsistence guaranteed in order to be admitted into the

domain of the theory. Today this excludes from the scope of liberal theory no fewer than 1,000,000,000 people.

The figure of over 1 billion is generally accepted as the minimum number of desperately poor people. The US government's World Hunger Working Group, for example, gave "1.2 billion" as the number of "persons without access to safe drinking water"—see United States, White House, *World Hunger and Malnutrition: Improving the U.S. Response* (Washington: Government Printing Office, 1978), p. 9. This is roughly 25 percent of all the people there are—and a much higher percentage of the children, since in many very poor countries most people are young.

I am not criticizing only people who call themselves "liberals" but also, for example, "neoconservatives." For, as Michael Walzer has perceptively observed, "neoconservatives are nervous liberals, and what they are nervous about is liberalism"—see Michael Walzer, "Nervous Liberals," *New York Review of Books*, 26:15 (October 11, 1979), p. 6.

19. James C. Scott, *The Moral Economy of the Peasant: Rebellion and Subsistence in Southeast Asia* (New Haven: Yale University Press, 1976), pp. 40–41. Scott analyzes the "normative roots of peasant politics" (4) with subtlety and clarity, displaying a coherent and rational conceptual framework implicit in the moral consensus across several peasant societies. I do not mean to suggest, nor does Scott, that all is well in Southeast Asia. For one thing, many traditional village institutions are being eliminated by "modernizing" regimes. With Scott's theory, compare Joel S. Migdal, *Peasants, Politics, and Revolution: Pressures toward Political and Social Change in the Third World* (Princeton: Princeton University Press, 1974); and Samuel L. Popkin, *The Rational Peasant: The Political Economy of Rural Society in Vietnam* (Berkeley: University of California Press, 1979).

For defenses of the suspension of the fulfillment of subsistence rights during an indefinite development period, see Lt. Gen. Ali Moertopo, "Political and Economic Development in Indonesia in the Context of Regionalism in Southeast Asia," *Indonesian Quarterly*, 6:2 (April 1978), pp. 30–47, esp. pp. 32–38; and O. D. Corpuz, "Liberty and Government in the New Society" (Quezon City: University of the Philippines, Office of the President, 1975), photocopy. For cautions from a nutritional anthropologist about the effects of US aid programs on traditional societies, see Norge W. Jerome, "Nutritional Dilemmas of Transforming Economies," in *Food Policy: The Responsibility of the United States in the Life and Death Choices*, ed. by Peter G. Brown and Henry Shue (New York: Free Press, 1977), pp. 275–304.

20. Benedict J. Kerkvliet, *The Huk Rebellion: A Study of Peasant Revolt in the Philippines* (Berkeley: University of California Press, 1977), p. 252. On the importance for Philippine peasants of their deep belief in a right to subsistence, see pp. 252–55. The most comprehensive legal and normative analysis of economic rights in developing countries is "The International

Dimensions of the Right to Development as a Human Right in Relation with Other Human Rights,"United Nations, Economic and Social Council, Commission on Human Rights, E/CN.4/1334 (35th Sess., Agenda item 8, 2 January 1979), (Geneva: Division of Human Rights, 1978).

21. I am grateful to Douglas MacLean for emphasizing the similarity between the notion toward which I am groping here and the one in Thomas M. Scanlon, "Human Rights as a Neutral Concern," in *Human Rights and U.S. Foreign Policy: Principles and Applications,* edited by Peter G. Brown and Douglas MacLean (Lexington, MA: Lexington Books, 1979), pp. 83–92. The Brown and MacLean volume and this volume *[Basic Rights]* are products of the same research effort and are designed to complement each other. On nearly every major issue discussed here, alternative views appear in Brown and MacLean, and I am to some degree indebted to the author of almost every chapter of that companion volume, including those with which I am in sharp disagreement philosophically or politically.

22. Although this admission opens a theoretical door to a certain amount of "relativism," I suspect the actual differences across societies in the standard preventable threats are much less than they conceivably might be. Compare Barrington Moore's thesis that although differences in conceptions of happiness are great and important, virtually everyone agrees upon the "miseries"—Barrington Moore Jr., *Reflections on the Causes of Human Misery and Upon Certain Proposals to Eliminate Them* (Boston: Beacon Press, 1972), especially chapter 1, and *Injustice: The Social Bases of Obedience and Revolt* (White Plains: M. E. Sharpe, 1978). Here, as in many other places, philosophical analysis and political analysis need each other.

The unavoidable mixture of the analytic and the empirical in an element like standard threats is obviously difficult to characterize with any precision. On the one hand, it is clearly part of the meaning of a right that the right-holder may insist that other people take measures to protect the enjoyment of the substance of the right against ordinary, non-inevitable threats—this much is analytic. But which threats are pervasive, which are serious, and which can feasibly be resisted must be discovered from particular situations. Naturally, what is, for example, feasible is a function of how much of the available resources are devoted to the task, as chapter 4 [of *Basic Rights*] will emphasize, and that is a heavily value-laden question, not a mere question of efficiency to be left to the economists. So we can draw no neat line between aspects that require philosophical argument and aspects that require economic and political investigation.

23. The coherence of the account of the general structure of a moral right and the account of a basic right with each other is one consideration in favor of both, although coherence is, needless to say, not enough. I am grateful to Charles R. Beitz for perceptively pressing me to make these underlying connections clearer.

Since fulfilling any one basic right involves creating safeguards for the enjoyment of the substance of that basic right against the other standard threats that are the respective concerns of the other basic rights, no basic right can be completely fulfilled until all basic rights are fulfilled. See note 13 above and, for an extended example, chapter 3 [of *Basic Rights*], and especially note 14. It would appear that just as (and, because?) deprivations of rights tend to be systematically interrelated, the fulfillment of at least the basic rights also comes in a single package.

## 2. Correlative Duties

1. See the Introduction [of *Basic Rights*].

2. For a forceful reaffirmation of this view in the current political context (and further references), see Hugo Adam Bedau, "Human Rights and Foreign Assistance Programs," in *Human Rights and U.S. Foreign Policy*, ed. Peter G. Brown and Douglas MacLean (Lexington, MA: Lexington Books, 1979), pp. 29–44. Also see Charles Frankel, *Human Rights and Foreign Policy*, Headline Series No. 241 (New York: Foreign Policy Association, 1978), especially pp. 36–49, where Frankel advanced a "modest list of fundamental rights" that explicitly excluded economic rights as "dangerously Utopian." A version of the general distinction has recently been reaffirmed by Thomas Nagel—see "Equality," in *Mortal Questions* (New York: Cambridge University Press, 1979), pp. 114–15. An utterly unrealistic but frequently invoked version of the distinction is in Maurice Cranston, *What Are Human Rights?* (London: The Bodley Head, 1973), chapter 8. An interesting attempt to show that the positive/negative distinction is compatible with economic rights is John Langan, "Defining Human Rights: A Revision of the Liberal Tradition," Working Paper (Washington: Woodstock Theological Center, 1979). For a provocative and relevant discussion of "negative responsibility" (responsibility for what one fails to prevent), see Bernard Williams, "A Critique of Utilitarianism," in *Utilitarianism: For & Against* (New York: Cambridge University Press, 1973), pp. 93 ff.

3. Naturally my use of the same argument for the basic status of both security and subsistence is at least an indirect challenge to (1) (b). No question is raised here, however, about (1) (a): the thesis that subsistence and security are sharply distinguishable. People who should be generally sympathetic to my fundamental thesis that subsistence rights are basic rights, do sometimes try to reach the same conclusion by the much shorter seeming route of denying that security and subsistence are importantly different from each other. For example, it is correctly observed that both security and subsistence are needed for survival and then maintained that both are included in a right to survival, or right to life. Though I am by no means hostile to this approach, it does have three difficulties that I believe can be avoided by my admittedly somewhat more circuitous path of argument. First, it is simply not correct that one cannot maintain a clear and

useful distinction between security and subsistence, as, in fact, I hope to have done up to this point. Second, arguments for a general right to life that includes subsistence rights appear to need some premise to the effect that the right to life entails rights to at least some of the means of life. Thus, they face the same "weakness of too much strength"—straining credulity by implying more than most people are likely to be able to believe—that we tried to avoid at the end of chapter 1 [of *Basic Rights*, herein 98ff]. A right-to-the-means-of-life argument might be able to skirt the problem equally well by using a notion of a standard threat to life, analogous to our notion of a standard threat to the enjoyment of rights, but this alternative tack seems, at best, no better off. Third, the concept of a right to life is now deeply infected with ambiguities concerning whether it is a purely negative right, a purely positive right, or, as I shall soon be maintaining with regard to both security and subsistence, an inseparable mixture of positive and negative elements. The appeal for many people of a right to life seems to depend, however, upon its being taken to be essentially negative, while it can fully include subsistence rights only if it has major positive elements.

4. I think one can often show the implausibility of an argument by an exhaustive statement of all the assumptions it needs. I have previously attempted this in the case of one of John Rawls's arguments for the priority of liberty—see "Liberty and Self-Respect," *Ethics*, 85:3 (April 1975), pp. 195–203.

5. I have given a summary of the argument against 3 and arguments against thinking that either the right to a fair trial or the right not to be tortured are negative rights in "Rights in the Light of Duties," in Brown and MacLean, pp. 65–81. I have also argued directly against what is here called 2b and briefly introduced the account of duties presented in the final sections of this chapter. My goal, which I have no illusions about having attained, has been to do as definitive a job on positive and negative rights as Gerald C. MacCallum Jr. did on positive and negative liberty in his splendid article "Negative and Positive Freedom," *Philosophical Review*, 76:3 (July 1967), pp. 312–34.

6. See note 3 above.

7. Elsewhere I have briefly queried the moral significance of the action/omission distinction—see the essay cited in note 5 above. For a fuller discussion, see Judith Lichtenberg, "On Being Obligated to Give Aid: Moral and Political Arguments," Diss., City University of New York, 1978.

8. In fiscal year (FY) 1975 in the United States the cost of the "criminal justice system" was $17 billion, or $71 per capita, *New York Times*, July 21, 1977, p. A3. In several countries that year the total annual income was less than $71 per capita. Obviously such isolated statistics prove nothing, but they are suggestive. One thing they suggest is that adequate provisions for this supposedly negative right would not necessarily be less costly than adequate provisions for some rights supposed to be positive. Nor is it evident that physical security does any better on what Frankel called the test of being "realistically deliverable" (45) and Cranston called "the test of practicability" (66). On Cranston's use of the latter, see chapter 4 [of *Basic Rights*].

9. "To have a right, then, is, I conceive, to have something which society ought to defend me in the possession of"—John Stuart Mill, *Utilitarianism* (Indianapolis: Bobbs-Merrill, 1957), p. 66 (chapter V, 14th paragraph from the end).

10. This is not a point about ordinary language, in which there is obviously a significant difference between "leave me alone" and "protect me against people who will not leave me alone." My thesis is that people who are not already grinding axes for minimal government will naturally and reasonably think in terms of enjoying a considerable degree of security, will want to have done whatever within reason is necessary, and will recognize that more is necessary than refraining campaigns—campaigns urging self-restraint upon would-be murderers, muggers, rapists, et al. I am of course not assuming that existing police and penal institutions are the best forms of social guarantees for security; I am assuming only that more effective institutions would probably be at least equally complex and expensive.

11. Therefore, as we shall see below, the complete fulfillment of a subsistence right may involve not the actual provision of any aid at all but only the performance of duties to avoid depriving and to protect against deprivation.

12. The literature on underdeveloped countries in fact abounds in actual cases that have the essential features of the so-called hypothetical case, and I have simply presented a stylized sketch of a common pattern. Most anecdotes are in the form of "horror stories" about transnational corporations switching land out of the production of the food consumed by the local poor. See, for example, Robert J. Ledogar, *Hungry for Profits: U.S. Food and Drug Multinationals in Latin America* (New York: IDOC, 1976), pp. 92–98 (Ralston Purina in Colombia), and Richard J. Barnet and Ronald E. Müller, *Global Reach: The Power of the Multinational Corporations* (New York: Simon & Schuster, 1974), p. 182 (carnations in Colombia). For a gargantuan case on a regional scale involving cattle ranching, see Shelton H. Davis, *Victims of the Miracle: Development and the Indians of Brazil* (New York: Cambridge University Press, 1977). To a considerable extent the long-term development policy of Mexico for at least thirty of the last forty years has followed this basic pattern of depriving the rural poor of food for subsistence for the sake of greater agricultural production of other crops—see the extremely careful and balanced study by Cynthia Hewitt de Alcantara, *Modernizing Mexican Agriculture: Socioeconomic Implications of Technological Change, 1940–1970*, Report No. 76.5 (Geneva: United Nations Research Institute for Social Development, 1976); and Judith Adler Hellman, *Mexico in Crisis* (New York: Holmes & Meier, 1978), chapter 3. For a sophisticated theoretical analysis of some of the underlying dynamics, see Jeffery M. Paige, *Agrarian Revolution: Social Movements and Export Agriculture in the Underdeveloped World* (New York: Free Press, 1975), which has case studies of Angola, Peru, and Vietnam.

13. That is, they are conceptually distinct; whether this distinction makes any moral difference is another matter. See above, note 7, and the distinctions at the beginning of this chapter.

14. The increasingly frequent and facile appeal to "overpopulation" as a reason not to prevent preventable starvation is considered in chapter 4 [of *Basic Rights*].

15. This much of the analysis is derived from the following important article: Onora O'Neill, "Lifeboat Earth," in *World Hunger and Moral Obligation*, edited by William Aiken and Hugh La Follette (Englewood Cliffs: Prentice-Hall, 1977), pp. 140–64 [first published in *Philosophy and Public Affairs* 4: 3 (spring 1975): 273–92, reprinted herein 1-20]. I return to discussion of the causal complexity of such cases below, pp. 58-60 [herein 125-27].

16. For example, land-use laws might prohibit removing prime agricultural land from food production. Alternatively, land might be allowed to be used in the manner most beneficial to the national balance of payments with tax laws designed to guarantee compensating transfers to increase the purchasing power of the villagers (e.g., food stamps). I return in chapter 5 [of *Basic Rights*] to the question of how to apportion the duties to prevent such social disasters.

17. There are of course nonhuman threats to both security and subsistence, like floods, as well. And we expect a minimally adequate society also to make arrangements to prevent, to control, or to minimize the ill effects of floods and other destructive natural forces. However, for an appreciation of the extent to which supposedly natural famines are the result of inadequate social arrangements, see Richard G. Robbins, *Famine in Russia, 1891-92* (New York: Columbia University Press, 1975); and Michael F. Lofchie, "Political and Economic Origins of African Hunger," *Journal of Modern African Studies* 13:4 (December 1975): 551–67. As Lofchie says: "The point of departure for a political understanding of African hunger is so obvious it is almost always overlooked: the distinction between drought and famine. . . . To the extent that there is a connection between drought and famine, it is mediated by the political and economic arrangements of a society. These can either minimize the human consequences of drought or accentuate its effects" (553). For a demonstration that the weather and other natural factors actually played fairly minor roles in the Great Bengal Famine, see the analysis by Amartya Sen cited in note 17 to chapter 4 ["Starvation and Exchange Entitlements: A General Approach and Its Application to the Great Bengal Famine," *Cambridge Journal of Economics* 1:1 (1977): 33–59], and chapter 4 [of *Basic Rights*] generally. To treat the *absence* of adequate social arrangements as a cause of a famine precipitated by a natural event like a drought or a flood, as these writers and I do, is to assume that it is reasonable to have expected the absent arrangements to have been present.

18. See note 12 above.

19. See chapter 7 [of *Basic Rights*], notes 26-28.

20. Richard R. Fagen, "The Carter Administration and Latin America: Business as Usual?" *Foreign Affairs* 57:3 (America and the World 1978): 663–67. These policies are very similar to those imposed as conditions for loans by the International Monetary Fund. See William Goodfellow, "The IMF and Basic Human Needs Strategies," paper prepared for seminar on "Basic Human Needs: Moral and Political Implications of Policy Alternatives," Woodstock Theological Center, Georgetown University, February 26, 1979; mimeo., p. 4.

With Fagen's analysis, compare Guillermo A. O'Donnell, *Modernization and Bureaucratic-Authoritarianism,* Politics of Modernization Series, No. 9 (Berkeley: University of California, Institute of International Studies, 1973); Fernando Henrique Cardoso and Enzo Faletto, *Dependency and Development in Latin America,* expanded and emended version (Berkeley: University of California Press, 1979), pp. 177–216; and Albert O. Hirschman, "The Turn to Authoritarianism in Latin America and the Search for Its Economic Determinants," in David Collier, ed., *The New Authoritarianism in Latin America* (Princeton: Princeton University Press, 1979), pp. 61–98. Also see Steven Jackson, Bruce Russett, et al., "An Assessment of Empirical Research on *Dependencia*," *Latin American Research Review,* 14:3 (1979): 7–28.

21. On whether an adequate definition can be literally exceptionless, see note 2 to chapter 1 [of *Basic Rights*, herein pp. 131-32].

22. I take the need for the qualification "not necessary to the satisfaction of one's own basic rights" to be fairly obvious. However admirable self-sacrifice may be, it is surely not a basic duty owed to people generally, and the surrender of one's right to subsistence—or security—would in many circumstances constitute a literal sacrifice of oneself, that is, one's life. Unfortunately, the content of a duty does not dictate the identity of its bearers. Chapter 5 [of *Basic Rights*] discusses how to assign in a reasonable way the responsibility for fulfilling various duties.

23. How to bring transnational corporations under some constraints in order to prevent great social harms, like violations of basic rights, is one of our great political challenges. See the discussion in *[Basic Rights]* chapter 7 of recommendation (4) and the relevant notes.

24. I am, of course, not proposing that we start calling it murder, but I am proposing that we acknowledge the parallels and act in appropriately parallel ways.

25. Without becoming anti-intellectual, or even atheoretical, we theorists might remember that a crystal-clear abstract distinction may not only have no positive practical value but may sometimes contribute to vice. Writing about an entirely different matter, Barrie A. Paskins has put the general point eloquently: "We can imagine and describe cases in which we would think torture justified and unjustified. We can state the grounds on which we are

making the discrimination. But what we cannot do is this: *we cannot provide for ourselves, or for those who must act for us in real situations, any way of making our notional distinctions in reality.* What might be claimed about the imaginary example is not that something significantly analogous could not occur but that in reality we cannot enable those who must act to recognize the case for what it is and other cases, by contrast, for what they are. In a real situation we can never be certain that the case in hand is of this kind rather than another. A too vivid imagination blinds us to the dust of war that drifts into the interrogation centre." Barrie A. Paskins, "What's Wrong with Torture?" *British Journal of International Studies* 2 (1976), p. 144. I think this is a profound methodological point with strong implications concerning the now virtually incorrigible habit among moral and political philosophers of relying upon imaginary cases and concerning the "strict compliance" situations and "ideal theory" discussed by John Rawls and Kantians generally. I am trying to develop the methodological point in an essay with the working title "Extreme Cases."

26. On the rationality of peasants, see James C. Scott, *The Moral Economy of the Peasant: Rebellion and Subsistence in Southeast Asia* (New Haven: Yale University Press, 1976), chapters 1 and 2.

27. See note 12 above.

28. I am indebted to John Langan for having emphasized this point. For a different argument, see his paper cited in note 2 above, p. 25.

29. For the classic account, see Clifford Geertz, *Agricultural Involution: The Processes of Ecological Change in Indonesia* (Berkeley: University of California Press for the Association of Asian Studies, 1963), chapters 4 and 5. Although various aspects of Geertz's analysis are naturally no longer accepted, the main points relevant here still stand.

# 6. MICHAEL WALZER

Walzer contends that cultural distinctiveness is a value, and one that can only be preserved within states by controlling immigration. The right of individuals to form distinct and stable groups requires that states have wide latitude in setting their immigration policies. Nonetheless, states are bound by an indeterminate principle of mutual aid or Good Samaritanism to help persons who are destitute, persecuted, or stateless. But this obligation will vary depending upon factors such as whether the state is partially responsible for their status, the ideological convictions of would-be immigrants, their ethnicity, and their immigration alternatives. Finally, no state may establish an immigration policy that results in residents—guest workers—who have no possibility of citizenship.

## The Distribution of Membership

*First published in* Boundaries: National Autonomy and Its Limits, *ed. Peter G. Brown and Henry Shue (Totowa: Rowman & Littlefield, 1981), 1–35.*

### MEMBERS AND STRANGERS

The idea of distributive justice presupposes a bounded world, a community within which distributions take place, a group of people committed to dividing, exchanging, and sharing, first of all among themselves. It is possible to imagine such a group extended to include the entire human race, but no such extension has yet been achieved. For the present, we live in smaller distributive communities. Were the extension ever attempted, its success would depend upon decisions made within these smaller communities and by their members—who distribute decision-making power to one another and avoid, if they possibly can, sharing it with anyone else. When we think today about distributive justice, we think about independent states and commonwealths capable of arranging their own distributions, justly or unjustly. We assume an established group and a fixed population, and so we miss the first and most important distributive question: How is that group constituted?

I don't mean: How *was* it constituted? I am not concerned here with the historical origins of the different groups, but with the decisions they make in the present about their present and future populations. The primary good that we distribute to one another is membership in some human community. And what we do with regard to membership structures all our other distributive choices. It determines with whom we make those choices, from whom we require obedience and collect taxes, to whom we allocate goods and services.

Men and women without membership anywhere are stateless persons. That condition doesn't preclude every sort of distributive relation. Markets, for example, are often open to all comers. But nonmembers are vulnerable and unprotected in the marketplace. Although they participate freely in the exchange of goods, they have no part in those goods that are shared. They are cut off from the communal provision of welfare and security. Even those aspects of welfare and security that are, like public health, collectively distributed are not guaranteed to them, for they have no guaranteed place in the collectivity and are always liable to expulsion. As recent history has amply demonstrated, statelessness is a condition of infinite danger.

But membership and nonmembership are not the only or, for our purposes, the most important set of possibilities. It is also possible to be a member of a poor or a rich country, to live in a densely crowded or a largely empty country, to be the subject of a tyrant or the citizen of a liberal and democratic state. Since human beings are highly mobile, large numbers of men and women regularly attempt to change their residence and their membership, moving from unfavored to favored environments. Affluent and free countries are like elite universities; they are besieged by applicants. They have to decide on their own size and character. Whom should they admit? Ought they to have open admissions? Can they choose among applicants? What are the appropriate criteria for distributing membership?

These are hard questions, and perhaps they are not questions of justice at all. Perhaps, indeed, the positive obligations presupposed by theories of distributive justice exist only within established groups, among men and women already members of a single political community (however they came to be members), while toward outsiders we have only negative obligations—not to kill them, rob them, defraud them, and so on. The moral laws of commerce and war determine what we owe to outsiders, and no other laws apply. This is an attractive view because it matches a moral distinction to a political distinction and so, perhaps, it makes both more plausible than they might otherwise be. But I am inclined to think that the match is wrong. It would appear that at least one positive moral principle—mutual aid or Good Samaritanism—extends across political frontiers, specifying duties owed, as Rawls argues, "not only to definite individuals, say to those cooperating together in some particular social arrangement, but to persons generally."[1] I am not sure how to ground the principle of mutual aid. It can't be the case, as Rawls goes on to say, that "it is only necessary to imagine what a society would be like if it were publicly known that this duty were rejected"—for the difficulty does not arise within any particular society, but only within international society, where many people do in fact believe that the principle of mutual aid has no force, without believing that the consequences of this are intolerable. (If they stood behind the veil of ignorance, would they still find the consequences tolerable? That would probably depend—would certainly depend, if immigration were the issue—upon the view they took of the character of political communities.)

The principle of mutual aid is most commonly recognized when there is no question of community at all, when two strangers meet at sea or in the desert or, as in the Good Samaritan story, by the side of the road. What precisely they owe one another is by no means clear, but it is commonly said of such cases that positive assistance is required if (1) it is needed or urgently needed by one of the parties, and (2) if the risks and costs of giving it are relatively low for the other party. Given these conditions, I ought to stop to help the injured stranger, wherever I meet him, whatever his membership or my own. This is, moreover, an obligation that can be read out in roughly the same form at the collective level. Groups of people ought to help necessitous strangers whom they somehow "discover" in their midst or in their path. But the limit on risks and costs is sharply drawn: I need not take the injured stranger into my home, except briefly, and I certainly need not care for him, or even associate with him, for the rest of my life.[2] My life cannot be shaped and determined by such chance encounters. Whether this right of refusal can also be read out at the collective level is a question that I shall come to only gradually. One of my purposes in this chapter is to explore the requirements of mutual aid upon political communities. Before that, however, I need to say something about the character of the communities and the meaning of membership within them.

If all human beings were strangers to one another, if we had no particular communities and all our meetings were like meetings at sea or in the desert or by the side of the road, then there would be no membership to distribute. Admissions policy would not be an issue. Where and how we lived, and with whom we lived, would depend upon our particular desires, moral understandings, and charitable impulses, and upon the relationships we individually formed. Justice would be nothing more than noncoercion, good faith, and Good Samaritanism. If, by contrast, all human beings were members of a global society, then membership would already have been distributed (equally) and the distribution of other goods would be just so long as it reflected the universal application of whatever standards we had previously thought appropriate in particular communities. The first of these arrangements suggests a kind of global libertarianism, the second a kind of global socialism. These are the two conditions under which the distribution of membership would never arise. Either there would be no such status to distribute or it would simply come (to everyone) with birth. But neither of these arrangements is likely to be realized in the foreseeable future—and there are impressive arguments, which I will come to later on, against both of them. In any case, so long as members and strangers are, as they are at present, two distinct groups, admissions decisions have to be made, men and women taken in or refused. Given the indeterminate requirements of mutual aid, these decisions are not fixed or constrained by any widely accepted standards. That's why the admissions policies of countries are rarely criticized except in terms suggesting that the only relevant criteria are those of charity, not justice. It is certainly possible that a deeper criticism would lead one to deny the member/stranger distinction. But I shall try, nevertheless, to defend that distinction and then to argue that there are (sometimes) moral reasons for constraining the distribution of membership.

The argument will require a careful review of the principles that govern immigration and naturalization policy. But it is worth noting first, briefly, that there are certain similarities between strangers in political space (immigrants) and descendants in time (children). People enter a country by being born to parents already there as well as, and more often, by crossing the frontier. Both these processes can be controlled.

In the first case, however, unless we practice infanticide or sell babies to foreign countries, we are dealing with unborn and hence unknown individuals, effectively with the size of the population only, not with the characteristics of its inhabitants. We might, of course, award the right to give birth differentially to different groups of parents, establishing ethnic quotas (like country-of-origin quotas in immigration policy) or class or intelligence quotas, or allowing right-to-give-birth certificates to be traded on the market. These are ways of regulating who has children and therefore, indirectly, the character of the future population. The method is, however, indirect and inefficient, even with regard to ethnicity, unless the state also regulates intermarriage and assimilation. Short of that, it would still require very high, and probably unacceptable, levels of coercion. So the major issue in politically sponsored birth-control programs is the size of the population only, its growth, stability, or decline: To how many people do we distribute membership? The larger and philosophically more interesting questions—To what sorts of people? and To what particular people?—are most clearly confronted when we turn to the problems involved in admitting or excluding strangers.

## ANALOGUES: NEIGHBORHOODS, CLUBS, FAMILIES

Admissions policies are shaped partly by arguments about economic and political conditions in the host country, partly by arguments about the character and "destiny" of the host country, and partly by arguments about the character of countries (political communities) in general. The last of these is the most important (in theory, at least), for our understanding of countries in general will determine whether particular countries have the right they commonly claim: to distribute membership for (their own) particular reasons. But few of us have ever had any direct experience of what a country is or of what it means to be a member. We often have strong feelings about our country, but we have only dim perceptions of it. As a political community (rather than a place) it is, after all, invisible; we can actually see only its symbols, its offices, and its representatives. I suspect that we understand it best when we compare it to other, smaller associations whose compass we can more easily grasp, whose entire membership, it may be, we can take in at a glance. For we are all members of formal and informal groups of many different sorts; we know their workings intimately. And all these groups have, and necessarily have, admissions policies. Even if we have never served as state officials, even if we have never emigrated from one country to another, we have all had the experience of accepting or rejecting strangers, and we have all had the experience of being strangers, accepted or rejected. I want to draw upon this experience. My argument will be worked through a series of rough comparisons, in the course of which the special character of the political community will, I hope, become increasingly apparent.

Consider, then, three possible analogues for the political community: We can think of countries as neighborhoods, clubs, or families. The list is obviously not exhaustive, but it will serve to illuminate certain key features of admission and exclusion. Universities and companies, though they have some of the characteristics of clubs, distribute social and economic status as well as membership; I will take them up separately. Many domestic associations are parasitic for their memberships, relying on the procedures of other associations. Unions depend upon the hiring policies of companies; parent-teacher organizations depend upon the openness of neighborhoods or the selectiveness of private schools. Political groups are generally like clubs; religious groups are often designed to resemble families. What should countries be like?

The neighborhood is an enormously complex human association, but it has an ideal form that is at least partially reflected (though also increasingly challenged) in contemporary American law. It is an association without an organized or legally enforceable admissions policy. Strangers can be welcomed or not welcomed; they cannot be admitted or excluded. Of course, being welcomed or not welcomed is sometimes effectively the same thing as being admitted or excluded, but the distinction is theoretically important. In principle, individuals and families move into a neighborhood for reasons of their own; they choose but are not chosen. Or rather, in the absence of legal controls, the market controls their movements. Whether they move is determined not only by their own choices but also by their ability to find someone to hire them and someone to rent or sell them a place to live. (The case would be the same in a socialist society, unless people were administratively assigned to jobs and residences. The hiring and renting might involve collective rather than individual decisions, but these would still be market decisions, "private" to the enterprise or the communal apartment building; they would not be neighborhood decisions.) Ideally, the market works independently of the existing composition of the neighborhood. The state upholds this independence by refusing to enforce restrictive covenants and by acting to prevent or minimize discrimination in employment. There are no institutional arrangements capable of maintaining "ethnic purity" (though zoning laws sometimes do maintain class segregation).[3] With reference to any formal criteria, the neighborhood is a random association, "not a selection, but rather a specimen of life as a whole. . . . By the very indifference of space," as Bernard Bosanquet has written, "we are liable to the direct impact of all possible factors."[4]

It was a common argument in classical political economy that national territory should be as "indifferent" as local space. The same writers who defended free trade in the nineteenth century also defended unrestricted immigration. They argued for perfect freedom of contract, without any sort of political restraint. International society, they thought, should take shape as a world of neighborhoods, with individuals moving freely about, seeking private advancement. In their view, as Henry Sidgwick reports it, the only business of state officials is "to maintain order over [a] particular territory . . . but not in any way to determine who is to inhabit this territory, or to restrict the enjoyment of its natural advantages to any particular portion of the human race."[5] Natural advantages (like markets) are open to all comers, within the limits of private-property rights, and if they are used up or devalued by overcrowding, people presumably will move on, into the jurisdiction of new sets of officials.

Sidgwick thinks that this is possibly the "ideal of the future," but he offers three arguments against a world of neighborhoods in the present. First of all, such a world would not allow for patriotic sentiment, and so the "casual aggregates" that would probably result from the free movement of individuals would "lack internal cohesion." Neighbors would be strangers to one another. Second, free movement might interfere with efforts "to raise the standard of living among the poorer classes" of a particular country, since such efforts could not be undertaken with equal energy and equal success everywhere in the world. And third, the promotion of moral and intellectual culture and the efficient working of political institutions might be "defeated" by the continual creation of heterogeneous populations.[6] Sidgwick presents these three arguments as a series of consequentialist considerations that weigh against the benefits of labor mobility and contractual freedom. But they seem to me to have a rather different character. The last two arguments draw their force from the first, but only if the first is conceived in nonutilitarian terms. It is only if patriotic sentiment has some moral basis, only if communal cohesion makes for obligations, only if there are members as well as strangers, that state officials would have any reason to worry especially about the welfare of their own people (and of *all* their own people) and the success of their own culture and politics. For it is at least dubious that the average standard of living of the poorer classes throughout the world would decline under conditions of perfect labor mobility. Nor is there firm evidence that culture cannot thrive in cosmopolitan environments, nor that it is impossible to govern casual aggregations of people. As for the last of these, political theorists long ago discovered that certain sorts of regimes—namely, tyrannical regimes—thrive in the absence of communal cohesion. That perfect mobility leads to tyranny might make for a utilitarian argument against mobility, but such an argument would work only if individual men and women, free to come and go, expressed a desire for some other form of government. And that they might not do.

Perfect labor mobility, however, is probably a mirage, for it is almost certain to be resisted at the local level. Human beings, as I have said, move about a great deal, but this is not because they love to move. They are, most of them, emotionally prone to stay where they are unless their life is very difficult where they are. They experience a tension between love of place and the discomforts of particular places. While some of them leave their homes and become foreigners in new lands, others stay where they are and resent the foreigners in their own land. Hence, if states ever become large neighborhoods, it is likely that neighborhoods will become little states. Their members will organize to defend the local politics and culture against strangers. Historically, neighborhoods have turned into closed communities (leaving aside cases of legal coercion) whenever the state was open: in the cosmopolitan cities of multinational empires, for example, where state officials don't foster any particular identity but permit different groups to build their own institutional structures (as in ancient Alexandria), or in the receiving centers of mass immigration movements (early-twentieth-century New York) where the country is an open but also an alien world—or, alternatively, a world full of aliens. The case is similar where the state doesn't exist at all or in areas where it doesn't function. Where welfare monies are raised and spent locally, for example, as in a seventeenth-century English parish, the local people will seek to exclude newcomers who are likely welfare recipients. It is only the nationalization of welfare (or the nationalization of culture and politics) that opens the neighborhood communities to whoever chooses to come in.

Neighborhoods can be open only if countries are closed, or rather, only if countries are potentially closed. Only if the state makes a selection among would-be members and guarantees the loyalty, security, and welfare of the individuals it selects, can local communities take shape as "indifferent" associations, determined only by personal preference and market capacity. Since we live most immediately at the local level, since individual choice is most dependent upon local mobility, this would seem to be the preferred arrangement. Moreover, politics and culture probably develop best if we do not have to defend them in our neighborhoods; they require the kind of largeness, and also the kind of boundedness, that states provide. I don't mean to deny the value of sectional cultures and ethnic communities, only to describe the rigid parochialism that would be forced upon them in the absence of inclusive and protective states. To tear down the walls of the state is not, as Sidgwick worriedly suggested, to create a world without walls, but rather to create a thousand petty fortresses.

The fortresses too could be torn down, of course. All that is necessary is a global state sufficiently committed to labor mobility and sufficiently powerful to overwhelm the local communities. Then the result would be the world of the political economists, as Sidgwick describes it, a world of radically deracinated men and women. Neighborhoods might maintain some cohesive culture for a generation or two on a voluntary basis, but people would move in, people would move out; soon the cohesion would be gone. The distinctiveness of cultures and groups depends upon closure and cannot be conceived as a stable feature of human life without it. If this distinctiveness is a value, as most people (though some of them are global pluralists and others only local loyalists) seem to believe—more strongly, if individuals have a right to form distinct and stable communities—then closure must be permitted somewhere. At some level of political organization, something like the sovereign state must take shape and claim the authority to make its own admissions policy, to control and sometimes to restrain the flow of immigrants.[7]

But this right to control immigration does not include or entail the right to control emigration. The political community can shape its own population in the one way, but not in the other. This is a distinction that gets reiterated in different forms throughout the account of membership.

The restraint of entry serves to defend the liberty and welfare, the politics and culture of a group of people committed to one another and to their common life. But the restraint of exit replaces commitment with coercion. So far as the coerced members are concerned, there is no longer a community worth defending. States can, perhaps, banish individual citizens or expel aliens living within their borders (if there is some place ready to receive them; I will consider this issue later on). Except in times of national emergency, when everyone is bound to work for the survival of the community, states cannot prevent such people from getting up and leaving. Once again, however, the right to leave one country does not entail the right to enter another (any other). Immigration and emigration are morally asymmetrical.[8] Here the appropriate analogy is with the club, for it is a feature of clubs in domestic society, as I have just suggested it is of states in international society, that they can regulate admissions but cannot bar withdrawals.

Like clubs, countries have admissions committees. In the United States, Congress functions as such a committee, though it rarely makes individual selections. Instead, it establishes general qualifications, categories for admission and exclusion, and numerical quotas (limits). Then admissible individuals are taken in, with varying degrees of administrative discretion, mostly on a first-come, first-served basis. This sort of thing seems eminently defensible, though that does not mean that any particular set of qualifications and categories ought to be defended. To say that states have a right to act in certain areas is not to say that anything they do in those areas is right. One can argue about particular admissions standards by appealing, for example, to the condition and character of the host country. Such arguments have to be judged morally and politically as well as factually. When defenders of restricted immigration into the United States claimed (in 1920, say) that they were defending a homogeneous white and Protestant country, they were involved in a pretense that can plausibly be called immoral as well as inaccurate—as if nonwhite and non-Protestant citizens were invisible men and women who didn't have to be counted in the national census! Earlier Americans, seeing the benefits of economic and geographic expansion, had created a pluralist society, and the moral realities of that society ought to have guided the legislators of the 1920s. If we follow the logic of the club analogy, however, we have to say that the earlier decision might have been different, and the United States might have taken shape as a homogeneous community, an Anglo-Saxon nation-state (assuming what happened in any case—the virtual extermination of the Indians, who, understanding correctly the dangers of invasion, struggled as best they could to keep foreigners from their native lands). Decisions of this sort are subject to constraint, but what the constraints are I am not yet ready to say. It is important now to insist that the distribution of membership in American society, and in any ongoing society, is a matter of political decision. The labor market may be given free rein, as it was for many decades in the United States, but that does not happen by an act of nature or of God; it depends upon choices that are ultimately political. What kind of community do the citizens want to create? With what other men and women do they want to share and exchange social goods?

These are exactly the questions that club members answer when they make membership decisions, though usually with reference to a less extensive community and a more limited range of social goods. In clubs, only the founders choose themselves (or one another); all other members have been chosen by those who were members before them. Individuals may be able to give good reasons why they should be selected, but no one on the outside has a right to be inside. The members decide freely on their future associates, and the decisions they make are authoritative and final. Only when clubs split into factions and fight over property can the state intervene and make its own decision as to who the members are. When states split, however, no legal appeal is possible; there is no superior body. Hence, we might imagine states as perfect clubs, with sovereign power over their own selection processes.[9]

But if this description is accurate as to the law, it is not an accurate account of the moral life of political communities. Clearly, citizens often believe themselves morally bound to open the doors of their country—not to anyone who wants to come in, perhaps, but to a particular group of outsiders, recognized as national or ethnic "relatives." In this sense, states are like families rather than clubs, for it is a feature of families that their members are morally connected to people they have not chosen, who live outside the household. In time of trouble, the household is also a refuge. Sometimes, under the auspices of the state, we take in fellow citizens to whom we are not related, as English country families took in London children during the Blitz, but our more spontaneous beneficence is directed at our own kith and kin. The state recognizes what we can call the family principle when it gives priority in immigration to the relatives of citizens. That is current policy in the

United States, and it seems especially appropriate in a political community largely formed by the admission of immigrants. It is a way of acknowledging that labor mobility has a social price. Since laborers are men and women with families, one cannot admit them for the sake of their labor without accepting some commitment to their aged parents, say, or their sickly brothers and sisters.

In communities differently formed, where the state represents a nation largely in place, another sort of commitment commonly develops, along lines determined by the principle of nationality. In time of trouble, the state is a refuge for members of the nation, whether or not they are residents and citizens. Perhaps the lines of the political community were drawn years ago so as to exclude their villages and towns; perhaps they are the children or grandchildren of emigrants. They have no legal membership rights, but if they are persecuted in the land where they live, they look to their homeland not only with hope but also with expectation. I am inclined to say that such expectations are legitimate. Greeks driven from Turkey, Turks from Greece after the wars and revolutions of the early twentieth century, had to be taken in by the states that bore their collective names. What else are such states for? They don't merely preside over a piece of territory and a random collection of inhabitants; they are also the political expression of a common life and (most often) of a national "family" that is never entirely enclosed within their legal boundaries. After World War II, millions of Germans expelled by Poland and Czechoslovakia were received and cared for by the two Germanys. Even if these states had been free of all responsibility in the expulsions, they would still have had a special obligation to the refugees. Most states recognize obligations of this sort in practice; some do so in law.

## TERRITORY

We might, then, think of countries as national clubs or families. But countries are also territorial states. Although clubs and families own property, they neither require nor (except in feudal systems) possess jurisdiction over territory. Leaving children aside, they do not control the physical location of their members. The state does control physical location—if only for the sake of clubs and families and the individual men and women who make them up—and with this control there come certain obligations. We can best examine these if we consider once again the asymmetry of immigration and emigration.

The nationality principle has one significant limit, commonly accepted in theory, if not always in practice. Though the recognition of national affinity is a reason for permitting immigration, nonrecognition is not a reason for expulsion. This is a major issue in the modern world, for many newly independent states find themselves in control of territory into which alien groups have been admitted under the auspices of the old imperial or colonial regimes. Sometimes these people are forced to leave, the victims of a popular hostility that the new government cannot restrain or can only inadequately restrain. More often, the government itself fosters such hostility and takes positive action to drive out "alien elements," invoking when it does so some version of the club or family analogies. Here, however, the analogies don't apply, for though no "alien" has a right to be a member of a club or family, it is possible, I think, to describe a kind of territorial or locational right.

Hobbes makes the argument in classical form when he lists those rights that are given up and those that are retained when the social contract is signed. The retained rights include self-defense and then "the use of fire, water, free air, *and place to live in*, and . . . all things necessary for life."[10] The right is not, indeed, to a particular place, but it is enforceable against the state, which exists to protect it; the state's claim to territorial jurisdiction derives ultimately from this individual form, and these two can come into conflict. But it can't be said that the first always or necessarily supersedes the second, for the first came into existence for the sake of the second. The state owes something to its inhabitants simply, without reference to their nationality. And the first place to which inhabitants are entitled is surely the place where they and their families have lived and made a life—if not this particular piece of land (or house or apartment), then some other within the same general "place." This claim is particularly powerful when, as in the cases I am considering, people have come where they have come illegally, if they have no other place to go. Then they can claim, as we shall see, the right of asylum. New states and governments, then, must make their peace with the old inhabitants of the land they rule. And countries are likely to take shape as closed territories dominated, perhaps, by particular nations (clubs or families), but always including aliens of one sort or another, whose expulsion would be unjust.

This common arrangement raises one important possibility—that many of the inhabitants of a particular country won't be allowed full membership (citizenship) because of their nationality. I will consider that possibility, and argue for its rejection, when I turn to the specific problems of naturalization. But one might avoid such problems entirely, at least at the level of the state, by opting for a radically different arrangement. Consider once again the neighborhood analogy. Perhaps we should deny to national states, as we deny to ward and precinct organizations and to political parties generally, the collective right of territorial jurisdiction. Perhaps we should insist upon open countries and permit closure only in nonterritorial groups. Open neighborhoods *together with* closed clubs and families—that is the structure of domestic society. Why can't it, why shouldn't it be extended to the global society?

An extension of this sort was actually proposed by the Austrian socialist Otto Bauer, with reference to the old multinational empires of Central and Eastern Europe. Bauer would have organized nations into autonomous corporations, permitting them to tax their members for educational and cultural purposes, but denying them any territorial dominion. Individuals would have been free to move about in political space, within the empire, carrying their national memberships with them, much as individuals move about today in liberal and secular states, carrying their religious memberships and their partisan affiliations. Like churches and parties, the corporations could admit or reject new members in accordance with whatever standards their old members thought appropriate.[11]

The major difficulty here is that all the national communities that Bauer wanted to preserve came into existence and were sustained over the centuries on the basis of geographical coexistence. It isn't any misunderstanding of their histories that leads nations newly freed from imperial rule to seek a firm territorial status. Nations look for countries because in some deep sense they already have countries: The link between people and land is a crucial feature of national identity. Their leaders understand, moreover, that because so many critical issues (including issues of distributive justice, welfare, education, etc.) can be resolved only within geographical units, the focus of political life can never be established elsewhere. "Autonomous" corporations will always be adjuncts, and probably parasitic adjuncts, of territorial states, and to give up the state is to give up any effective self-determination. That's why borders, and the movements of individuals and groups across borders, are bitterly disputed as soon as imperial rule recedes and nations begin the process of "liberation." And, once again, to reverse this process or to repress its effects would require massive coercion on a global scale. There is no easy way to avoid the country (and the proliferation of countries) as we currently know it. Hence the theory of justice must allow for the territorial state, specifying the rights of its inhabitants, and recognizing the collective right of admission and refusal.

## THE CLAIM OF NECESSITY

The argument cannot stop here, however, for the control of territory opens the state to the claim of necessity. Territory is a social good in a double sense. It is living space, earth and water, mineral resources and potential wealth, a resource for the destitute and the hungry. And it is protected living space, with borders and police, a resource for the persecuted and the stateless. These two resources are different, and we might conclude differently with regard to the kinds of claims that can be made on each. But the issue at stake should first be put in general terms. Can a political community exclude destitute and hungry, persecuted and stateless—in a word, necessitous—men and women simply because they are foreigners? Are citizens bound to take in strangers? Let us assume that they have no formal obligations; they are bound by nothing more stringent than the principle of mutual aid or Good Samaritanism. The principle must be applied, however, not to individuals directly but to the citizens as a group, for immigration is a matter of political decision. Individuals participate in the decision making, if the state is democratic, but they decide not for themselves, but for the community generally. And this fact has moral implications. It replaces immediacy with distance, and the personal expense of time and energy with impersonal bureaucratic costs. Mutual aid is more coercive for political communities than it is for individuals because a wide range of benevolent actions are open to the community that will only marginally affect its members considered as a body or even, with possible exceptions, one by one (or family by family, or club by club). These actions include, or may include, the admission of strangers, for admission to a country does not entail the kinds of intimacy that could hardly be avoided in the case of clubs and families. And if this is true, might not admission be morally imperative, at least for *these* strangers, who have no other place to go?

Some such argument, turning mutual aid into a more stringent charge on communities than it can ever be on individuals, probably underlies the common claim that exclusion rights depend upon the territorial extent and population density of particular countries. Thus Sidgwick writes that he "cannot concede to a state possessing large tracts of unoccupied land an absolute right of excluding alien elements."[12] Perhaps, on his view, the citizens can make some selection among necessitous strangers, but they cannot refuse entirely to take them in, so long as they have (a great deal of) available space. A much stronger argument might be made from the other side, so to speak, if we consider the necessitous strangers not as objects of beneficent action, but as desperate men and women, capable of acting on their own behalf. In the *Leviathan*, Hobbes argues that such people, if they cannot earn a living in their own countries, have a right to move into "countries not sufficiently inhabited: where nevertheless they are not to exterminate those they find there, but constrain them to inhabit closer together and not range a great deal of ground to snatch what they find. . . ."[13] Here the "Samaritans" are not themselves active but acted upon and (as we shall see in a moment) charged only with nonresistance.

The Hobbist argument is clearly a defense of European colonization—and also of the subsequent "constraint" of native hunters and gatherers. But it has a wider application. Sidgwick, writing in 1891, probably had in mind the states the colonists had created: the United States, where agitation for the exclusion of immigrants had been at least a sporadic feature of political life all through the nineteenth century, and Australia, then just beginning the great debate over immigration that culminated in the "white Australia" policy. Years later an Australian Minister of Immigration defended that policy in terms that should by now be familiar: "We seek to create a homogeneous nation. Can anyone reasonably object to that? Is not this the elementary right of every government, to decide the composition of the nation? It is just the same prerogative as the head of a family exercises as to who is to live in his own house."[14] But the Australian "family" held a vast territory of which it occupied (and, I shall assume without any further factual reference, still occupies) only a small part. The right of white Australians to the great empty spaces of the subcontinent rested on nothing more than the claim they had staked, and enforced against the aboriginal population, before anyone else. That does not seem a right that one would readily defend in the face of necessitous men and women clamoring for entry. If, driven by famine in the densely populated lands of Southeast Asia, thousands of people were to fight their way into an Australia otherwise closed to them, I doubt that we would want to charge the invaders with aggression. Hobbes's charge might make more sense: "Seeing every man, not only by Right, but also by necessity of Nature, is supposed to endeavor all he can, to obtain that which is necessary for his conservation; he that shall oppose himself against it, for things superfluous, is guilty of the war that thereupon is to follow...."[15]

But Hobbes's conception of "things superfluous" is extraordinarily wide. He means superfluous to life itself, to the bare requirements of physical survival. The argument is more plausible, I think, if we adopt a more narrow conception, shaped to the needs of particular historical communities. We must consider "ways of life" just as, in the case of individuals, we must consider "life plans." Now, let us suppose that the great majority of Australians could maintain their present way of life, subject only to marginal shifts, given a successful invasion of the sort I have imagined. Some individuals would be more drastically affected, of course, for they have come to "need" hundreds or even thousands of empty miles for the life they have chosen. But such needs cannot be given moral priority over the claims of necessitous strangers. Space on that scale is a luxury, as time on that scale is a luxury in more conventional Good Samaritan arguments, and it is subject to a kind of moral encroachment. Assuming, then, that there actually is superfluous land, the claim of necessity would force a political community like that of white Australia to confront a radical choice. Its members could yield land for the sake of homogeneity, or they could give up homogeneity (agree to the creation of a pluralist society) for the sake of the land. And those would be their only choices. White Australia could survive only as little Australia.

I have put the argument in these forceful terms in order to suggest that the collective version of the mutual-aid principle might generate a kind of distributive justice. This is the only kind available to us in a world of members and strangers. Farther than this we cannot go. We cannot describe the littleness of little Australia without attending to the meaning of "things superfluous." To argue, for example, that living space should be distributed in equal amounts to every inhabitant of the globe would be to allow the individual version of the right to a place in the world to override the collective version. Indeed, it would deny that national clubs and families can ever acquire a firm title to a particular piece of territory. A high birth rate in a neighboring land would immediately annul the title and require territorial redistribution. The same difficulty arises with regard to wealth and resources. These too can be superfluous, far beyond what the inhabitants of a particular state require for a decent life (even as they themselves define the meaning of a decent life). Are those inhabitants morally bound to admit immigrants from poorer countries for as long as superfluous resources exist? Or are they bound even longer than that, beyond the limits of mutual aid, until a policy of open admissions ceases to attract and benefit the poorest people in the world? Sidgwick seems to opt for the first of these possibilities; he proposes a primitive and parochial version of Rawls's difference principle: Immigration can be restricted as soon as failure to do so would "interfere materially . . . with the efforts of the government to maintain an adequately high standard of life among the members of the community generally—especially the poorer classes."[16] But the community might well decide to cut off immigration even before that, if it were willing to export (some of) its superfluous wealth. Its members would face a choice similar to that of the Australians. They could share their wealth with necessitous strangers outside their country or with necessitous strangers inside their country. But just how much of their wealth do they have to share? Once again, there must be some limit, short (and probably considerably short) of equality, else communal wealth would be subject to indefinite drainage. The very phrase "communal wealth" would lose its meaning if all resources and all products were globally common. Or rather, there would be only one community, a world state, whose redistributive processes would tend over time to annul the historical particularity of the national clubs and families.

If we stop short of equality, there will continue to be many communities, with different histories, ways of life, climates, political structures, and economics. Some places in the world will still be more desirable than others, either to individual men and women with particular tastes and aspirations, or more generally. Some places will still be uncomfortable for at least some of their inhabitants. Hence immigration will remain an issue even after the claims of distributive justice have been met on a global scale—assuming, still, that global society is and ought to be pluralist in form and that the claims are fixed by some version of collective mutual aid. The different communities will still have to make admissions decisions and will still have a right to make them. If we cannot guarantee the territorial or material base on which a group of people build a common life, we can still say that the common life, at least, is their own and that their comrades and associates are theirs to recognize or choose.

There is, however, one group of needy outsiders whose claims cannot be met by yielding territory or exporting wealth, but only by taking people in. This is the group of refugees whose need is for membership itself, a nonexportable good. The liberty that makes certain countries possible homes for men and women whose politics or religion isn't tolerated where they live is also nonexportable; at least we have found no way of exporting it. These goods can be shared only within the protected space of a particular state. At the same time, admitting refugees doesn't, or doesn't necessarily, decrease the amount of liberty the members enjoy within that space. The victims of political or religious persecution, then, make the most forceful claim for admission. "If you don't take me in," they say, "I shall be killed, persecuted, brutally oppressed by the rulers of my own country." What can we reply?

Toward some refugees, we may well have obligations of the same sort that we have toward fellow nationals. This is obviously the case with regard to any group of people whom we have helped turn into refugees. The injury we have done them makes for an affinity between us; thus Vietnamese refugees had, in a moral sense, been effectively Americanized even before they arrived on these shores. But we can also be found to help men and women persecuted or oppressed by someone else—if they are persecuted or oppressed because they are *like us*. Ideological as well as ethnic affinity can generate bonds across political lines, especially, for example, when we claim to embody certain principles in our communal life and encourage men and women elsewhere to defend those principles. In a liberal state, affinities of this latter sort may be highly attenuated and yet still be morally coercive. Nineteenth-century political refugees in England, for example, were generally not English liberals. They were heretics and oppositionists of all sorts, at war with the autocracies of Central and Eastern Europe. It was chiefly because of their enemies that the English recognized in them a kind of kin. Or consider the thousands of men and women who fled Hungary after the failed revolution of 1956. It is hard to deny them a similar recognition, given the structure of the Cold War, the character of Western propaganda, the sympathy already expressed with East European "freedom fighters." They probably had to be taken in by countries like Britain and the United States. The repression of political comrades, like the persecution of coreligionists, seems to generate an obligation to help, at least to provide a refuge for the most exposed and endangered people. Perhaps every victim of authoritarianism and bigotry is the moral comrade of a liberal citizen; that is an argument I would like to make. But that would press affinity too hard, and it is in any case probably unnecessary. So long as the number of victims is small, the mutual-aid principle will generate similar practical results, and when the number increases, and we are forced to choose among the victims, we shall look, rightfully, for some more direct connection with our own way of life. If, on the other hand, there is no connection at all, antipathy rather than affinity, there can't be a requirement of any sort to take people in. Britain and the United States could hardly have been required, for example, to offer refuge to Stalinists fleeing Hungary in 1956, had the revolution triumphed. Once again, communities must have boundaries, and however these are determined with regard to territory and resources, they depend with regard to population on a sense of relatedness and mutuality. Refugees must appeal to that sense. One wishes them success, but in particular cases, with reference to a particular state, they may well have no right to be successful.

Since ideological (far more than ethnic) affinity is a matter of mutual recognition, there is a lot of room here for political choice—and that means, for exclusion as well as for admission. Hence it might be said that my argument doesn't reach to the desperation of the refugee. Nor does it suggest any way of dealing with the vast numbers of refugees generated by twentieth-century politics. On the one hand, everyone must have a place to live, and a place where a reasonably secure life is possible. On the other hand, this is not a right that can be enforced against particular host states. (The right can't be enforced in practice until there is an international authority capable of enforcing it, and were there such an authority, it would certainly do better to intervene against the state whose brutal policies were driving men and women into exile, and so enable them all to go home.) The cruelty of this dilemma is mitigated to some degree by the principle of asylum. Any refugee who has actually made his escape, who is not seeking but has found (at least a temporary) refuge can claim asylum, a right recognized today, for example, in British law, and then he cannot be deported so long as the only available country to which he might be sent "is one to which he is unwilling to go owing to well-founded fear of being persecuted for reasons of race, religion, nationality . . . or political opinion."[17] Though he is a stranger, and newly come, the rule against expulsion applies to him as if he had already made a life where he is; for there is no other place where he can make a life.

But this principle was designed for the sake of individuals, considered one by one, where their numbers are so small that they cannot have any significant or transforming effect upon the character of the political community. What happens when the numbers are not small? Consider the case of the millions of Russians captured or enslaved by the Nazis in World War II, and overrun by Allied armies in the final offensives of the war. All these people were returned, many of them forcibly returned, to the Soviet Union, where they were immediately shot or sent on to die in labor camps.[18] Those of them who foresaw their fate pleaded for asylum in the West, but for expediential reasons (having to do with war and diplomacy, not with nationality and the problems of assimilation), asylum was denied them. Surely, they should not have been forcibly returned—not once it was known that they would be murdered—and that means that the Western Allies should have been ready to take them in, negotiating among themselves, I suppose, about appropriate numbers. There was no other choice; at the extreme, the claim of asylum is virtually undeniable. I assume that there are in fact limits on our collective liability, but I don't know how to specify the limits.

This last example suggests that the moral conduct of liberal and humane states can be determined by the immoral conduct of authoritarian and brutal states. But if that is true, why stop with the right of asylum? Why be concerned only with men and women actually on our territory who ask to remain, and not with men and women oppressed in their own countries who ask to come in? We seem bound to grant asylum for two reasons: because its denial would require us to use force against helpless and desperate people, and because the numbers likely to be involved, except in unusual cases, are small and the people easily absorbed (so we would be using force for "things superfluous"). But if we offered a refuge to everyone in the world who could plausibly say that he needed it, we might be overwhelmed. The call, "Give me . . . your huddled masses yearning to breathe free . . ." is generous and noble; actually to take in large numbers of refugees is often morally necessary; but the right to restrain the flow remains a feature of communal self-determination.

## ALIENAGE AND NATURALIZATION

The members of a political community have a collective right to shape the resident population, subject always to the limiting factors I have described: national or ideological affinity, the right to place, the claim of necessity. Given these factors, particular countries at particular times are likely to include among their residents men and women who are in different ways alien. These people may be members in their turn of minority or pariah groups, or they may be refugees, immigrants newly arrived. Let us assume that they are rightfully where they are. Can they claim citizenship and political rights within the community where they now live? Does citizenship go with residence? In fact, there is a second admissions process, called naturalization, and the criteria appropriate to this second process remain to be determined. I should stress that what is at stake here is citizenship and not (except in the legal sense of the term) nationality. The national club or family is a community different from the state, for reasons I have already sketched. Hence it is possible, say, for an Algerian immigrant to France to become a French citizen (a French "national") without becoming a Frenchman. But if he isn't a Frenchman, only a resident in France, has he any right to French citizenship?

One might insist, as I shall ultimately do, that the same standards apply to naturalization as to immigration, that every immigrant and every resident is a citizen too or at least a potential citizen. That is why territorial admission is so serious a matter. The members must be prepared to accept the men and women they admit as their own equals in a world of shared obligations; the immigrants must be prepared to share the obligations. But things can be differently arranged. Often, the state controls naturalization strictly, immigration only loosely. Immigrants become resident aliens and, except by special dispensation, nothing more. Why are they admitted? To assist the citizens, to free them from unpleasant work. Then the state is like a family with live-in servants.

That is not an attractive image, for a family with live-in servants is—inevitably, I think—a little tyranny. The principles that rule in the household are the principles of family life. They establish the underlying pattern of mutuality and obligation, of authority and obedience. The servants have no proper place in that pattern, but they have to be assimilated to it. Thus, in the premodern literature on family life, servants are commonly described as children of a special sort: children, because they are subject to command; of a special sort, because they are not allowed to grow up. Parental authority is asserted outside its sphere, over adult men and women who are not and can never be full members of the family. When this assertion is no longer possible, when servants come to be seen as hired workers, the great household begins its slow decline. The pattern of living in is gradually reversed; erstwhile servants seek households of their own.

It is not possible to trace a similar history at the level of the political community. Live-in servants have not disappeared from the modern world. As "guest workers" they play an increasingly important role in its most advanced economies. But before considering the status of guest workers, I want to turn to an older example and consider the status of resident aliens *(metics)* in ancient Athens. The Athenian polis was almost literally a family with live-in servants. Citizenship was an inheritance passed on from parents to children, and a great deal of the city's work was done by residents who could not hope to become citizens. Some of these people were slaves, but I shall not focus on them since the injustice of slavery is not disputed these days, at least not openly. The case of the metics is harder and more interesting.

"We throw open our city to the world," said Pericles in his Funeral Oration, "and never exclude foreigners from any opportunity. . . ." So the metics came willingly to Athens, drawn by economic opportunity, perhaps also by the city's "air of freedom." Most of them never rose above the rank of laborer or "mechanic," but some prospered; in fourth-century Athens, metics were represented among the wealthiest merchants. Athenian freedom, however, they shared only in its negative forms. Though they were required to join in the defense of the city, they had no political rights at all; nor did their descendants. Nor did they share in the most basic of welfare rights: "Foreigners were excluded from the distribution of corn."[19] As the comic poets make clear, these exclusions were politically controversial. How were they defended?

Aristotle (though himself a metic) provides the classic defense, apparently arguing against critics of exclusion who suggested that coresidence and shared labor were sufficient bases for political membership. Aristotle responds: "A citizen does not become such merely by inhabiting a place." Labor, even necessary labor, is no better as a criterion: "You must not posit as citizens all those [human beings] without whom you could not have a city."[20] Citizenship required a certain "excellence" that was not available to everyone. I doubt that Aristotle believed that excellence was transmitted by birth. For him, the existence of members and nonmembers as hereditary castes was probably a matter of convenience. Someone had to do the work of the city, and it was best if the workers were clearly marked out and taught their place from infancy.

Labor itself, the everyday necessity of economic life, put the excellence of citizenship beyond their reach. Ideally, the band of citizens was an aristocracy of the leisured, and its members were aristocrats because they were leisured, not because of any inner gift. Politics took most of their time, though Aristotle would not have said that they ruled over slaves and aliens. Rather, they took turns ruling one another. The others were simply their passive subjects, the "material condition" of their excellence, with whom they had no political relations at all. To admit mechanics to the world of citizens would be to allow economic principles to dominate where politics alone should be supreme.

On Aristotle's view, slaves and aliens lived in the realm of necessity; their existence was determined by the very conditions of economic life. Citizens, by contrast, lived (at least some of the time) in the realm of choice; their lives were determined in the political arena, by their own collective decision making. But the distinction is a false one. In fact, citizens made all sorts of decisions that directly affected, and were authoritative for, the slaves and aliens in their midst—decisions having to do with war, public expenditure, the improvement of trade, the distribution of corn, and so on. Economic conditions were subject to political control, though the extent of that control was always frighteningly limited. Hence slaves and aliens were indeed ruled; their lives were shaped politically as well as economically. They, too, stood within the arena, simply by virtue of being inhabitants of the protected space of the city-state, but they had no voice there. They did not attend the assemblies and juries; they were not consulted about impending decisions; they were never asked to agree or disagree. If we take them to be, despite Aristotle, men and women capable of rational deliberation, then we have to say that they were the subjects of a band of citizen-tyrants, governed without consent.

But hadn't the aliens, at least, consented to these arrangements when they chose to immigrate, knowing the rules by which Athens distributed citizenship? If they had, their children certainly had not; no argument from consent could justify the creation of a hereditary caste of resident aliens. The argument is more plausible if it is applied to contemporary guest workers, who are only temporary residents and who often leave their families behind. It is to these people that I want to turn now, in order to focus on what has become a major issue of public policy throughout the Western world: Can states run their economics with live-in servants, excluded from the company of citizens? The question requires us to consider, more deeply than I have yet done, the meaning of political community.

## GUEST WORKERS

I will not attempt a full description of the experience of contemporary guest workers. Laws and practices differ from one country to another and are constantly changing; the situation is complex and unstable. All that is necessary here is a schematic sketch (drawn chiefly from the practices of West European countries in the early 1970s) designed to highlight those features of the experience that are morally and politically controversial.[21] Imagine, then, a country called Fredonia, a capitalist democracy and welfare state, with strong trade unions and a fairly affluent population. The owners and managers of Fredonia find it increasingly difficult to attract workers to a set of jobs that are or have come to be regarded as exhausting, dangerous, degrading, and dirty. But these jobs are also socially necessary; someone must be found to do them. Domestically, there are only two alternatives, neither of them palatable. The constraints imposed on the labor market by the unions and the welfare state might be broken, and then the most vulnerable segment of the local working class driven to accept the jobs hitherto thought undesirable. But this would require a difficult and dangerous political campaign. Or the wages and working conditions of the undesirable jobs might be dramatically improved so as to attract workers even within the constraints of the local market. But this would raise costs throughout the economy and, what is probably more important, challenge the existing social hierarchy. Rather than adopt either of these drastic measures, the owners and managers, with the help of the Fredonian government, shift the jobs from the domestic to the international labor market, making them available to workers in poorer countries for whom they are less undesirable. The government opens recruiting offices in a number of economically backward countries and draws up regulations to govern the admission of guest workers.

It is crucial that the workers who are admitted should be "guests," not immigrants seeking a new home and a new citizenship. For if they come as future citizens, they would join Fredonia's labor force, temporarily occupying its lower ranks, but benefiting from its unions and welfare programs, and in time reproducing the original dilemma. Moreover, as they advanced, they would come into direct competition with local workers, some of whom they would outdo. Hence the regulations that govern their admission are designed to bar them from the protection of citizenship. They are brought in for a fixed time period, on contract to a particular employer; if they lose their job, they have to leave; they have to leave in any case when their visas expire. They are either prevented or discouraged from bringing dependents along with them, and they are housed in barracks, segregated by sex, on the outskirts of the cities where they work. Mostly they are young men or women in their twenties or thirties; finished with education, not yet infirm, they are a minor drain on Fredonia's welfare services (unemployment insurance is not available to them since they are not permitted to be unemployed in Fredonia). Neither citizens nor potential citizens, they have no political rights. The civil liberties of speech, assembly, association—otherwise strongly defended in Fredonia—are commonly denied to them, sometimes explicitly by state officials, sometimes implicitly by the threat of dismissal and deportation.

Generally, as it becomes clear that foreign workers are a permanent requirement of Fredonia's economy, these conditions are somewhat mitigated. For certain jobs, workers are given longer visas and permitted to bring their families with them, and so they are admitted to some of the benefits of the welfare state. But their position remains precarious. Residence is tied to employment, and the authorities make it a rule that any guest worker who cannot support himself and his family without repeated recourse to state welfare programs can be deported. Hence, in time of recession, many of the guests are forced to leave. In good times, however, the number who choose to come and who find ways to remain is high; soon some 15 percent of the industrial labor force is made up of foreigners. Frightened by this influx, various cities and towns within Fredonia establish residence quotas for guest workers (defending their neighborhoods against an open state). Bound to their jobs, the guests are in any case closely confined in choosing a place to live.

Their existence is harsh and their wages low by the standards prevailing in Fredonia, less so by their own standards. What is most difficult is their homelessness: They work long and hard in a foreign country where they are not encouraged to settle down, where they are always strangers. For those workers who come alone, life in Fredonia is like a self-imposed prison term. They are deprived of normal social, sexual, and cultural activities (of political activity, too, if that is possible in their home country) for a fixed period of time. During that time they live narrowly, saving money and sending it home. Money is the only return Fredonia makes to its guests, and though they export most of it, they are still very cheaply had. The costs of raising and educating workers in Fredonia and paying them what the local labor market requires would be vastly higher than the amount remitted to the guest workers' home countries. So the relation of guests and hosts seems to be a bargain all around; for the harshness of the working days and years is temporary, and the money sent home counts there in a way it could never count in Fredonia.

But what are we to make of Fredonia as a political community? Defenders of the guest worker system might claim that the country is now a neighborhood economically, but politically still a club or family. As a place to live, it is open to anyone who can find work; as a forum or assembly, as a nation or a people, it is closed except to those who meet the requirements set by the present members. The system is a perfect synthesis of labor mobility and patriotic solidarity. But this account somehow misses what is actually going on in Fredonia. The state-as-neighborhood, an "indifferent" association governed only by the laws of the market, and the state-as-club-or-family, with political laws, authority relations, and police, don't simply coexist, like two distinct moments in historical or abstract time. The market for guest workers, while free from the particular political constraints of the domestic labor market, is not free from all political constraints. Indeed, state power plays a crucial role in its creation and then in the enforcement of its rules. Without the denial of political rights and civil liberties and the ever-present threat of deportation, the system would not work. Hence guest workers can't be described merely in terms of their mobility, as men and women free to come and go. While they are guests, they are also subjects. They are ruled, like the Athenian metics, by a band of citizen-tyrants.

But don't they agree to be ruled? Certainly they choose to come knowing roughly what to expect, and they often return knowing exactly what to expect. But this kind of consent, given at a single moment in time, while it is clearly sufficient to legitimize many market transactions, is not sufficient in the political realm. Political authority is precisely the right to make decisions over periods of time, to change the rules, to cope with emergencies; hence it requires the ongoing consent of its subjects. And its subjects are all those men and women resident within the territory over which its rule-making power extends. On the other hand, guest workers really are free to come and go; they can always give up their residence if they find subjection painful. Though they are treated like indentured servants, they are not in fact indented. They can quit their jobs, buy train or airline tickets, and go home; they are citizens elsewhere. If they come voluntarily, to work and not to settle, and if they can leave whenever they want, why should they be granted political or civil rights while they stay? Ongoing consent, it might be argued, is required only from long-term residents. Aside from the explicit provisions of their contracts, the guest workers have no more rights than tourists have.

But guest workers are not, in the usual sense of the word, guests; and they are certainly not tourists. They are workers, above all, and they come (and generally stay for as long as they are allowed) because they need to work, not because they expect to enjoy the visit. They are not on vacation; they do not spend their days as they please. State officials are not polite and helpful to them, giving directions to the museums, enforcing the traffic and currency laws. These guests experience the state as a pervasive and frightening power that shapes their lives and regulates their every move—to which they have no access. Departure is only a formal option, deportation a continuous practical threat. As a group, they constitute a disenfranchised class. They are typically an exploited or oppressed class as well—and they are exploited or oppressed at least in part because they are disenfranchised, incapable of organizing effectively for mutual aid and advancement. Their material condition is unlikely to be improved except by altering their political status. Meanwhile, tyranny is the right name for their subjection. And surely political community requires something else.

The relevant principle here is not mutual aid but political justice. The guests don't need citizenship—not in the same sense in which they might be said to need their jobs. Nor are they injured, helpless, destitute; they are able-bodied and earning money. Nor are they standing, even figuratively, "by the side of the road"; they are living among the citizens. They do socially necessary work and they are deeply enmeshed in the legal system of the country to which they have come. Participants in economy and law, they ought to be able to regard themselves as potential or future participants in politics as well. And they must be possessed of those basic civil liberties the exercise of which is so much preparation for voting and office-holding. They must be set on the road to citizenship. They may choose not to become citizens, to return to their homes, or to stay on as resident aliens. Many, perhaps most, will choose to return because of their emotional ties to their national family and their native land. This will be especially true insofar as the system is genuinely beneficial to them as well as to the people of Fredonia—if they are able to save or remit enough money to make a difference at home. But unless they have that choice, their other choices cannot be taken as so many signs of their acquiescence to the economy and law of Fredonia. And if they do have that choice, the economy and law of Fredonia are likely to look different than they currently do. A firmer recognition of the guests' civil liberties and some enhancement of their opportunities for collective bargaining would be difficult to avoid once they were seen as potential citizens.

I should add that something of the same sort might be obtained in another way. Fredonia might undertake to negotiate formal treaties with the countries from which the guest workers come, setting out in authoritative form a list of "guest rights"—the same rights, roughly, that the workers might win for themselves as union members and political activists in Fredonia.[22] The treaty could include a proviso stipulating its periodic renegotiation, so that the list of rights could be adapted to changing social and economic conditions. Then, even when they were not at home, the original citizenship of the guests would work for them, and they would in some sense be represented in Fredonian decision making. In one way or another, they ought to be able to enjoy the protection of citizenship (or potential citizenship).[23]

Leaving aside international arrangements of the sort just described, the principle of political justice is this: The processes of self-determination through which a territorial state shapes its internal life must be open, and equally open, to all those men and women who live in the territory, work in the local economy, and are subject to local law. Hence, second admissions (naturalization) depend on first admissions (immigration), and are subject only to certain constraints of time and qualification, never to the ultimate constraint of closure. When second admissions are closed, the political community collapses into something very different: a world of members and strangers, with no political boundaries between the two groups, where the strangers are the subjects of the members. Among themselves, perhaps, the members are equal, but it is not their equality but their tyranny that determines the character of the state. Political justice is a bar to permanent alienage—either for particular individuals or for a class of changing individuals. There cannot be a fixed status between citizen and foreigner (though there can be stages in the transition from one of these political identities to the other). Men and women are either subject to the full force of the state's authority or they are not, and if they are subject they must be given a say, and ultimately an equal say, in what that authority does. The citizens of Fredonia, then, have a choice. If they want to bring in new workers, they must be prepared to enlarge their own membership; if they are unwilling to accept new members, they must find ways within the limits of the domestic labor market to get socially necessary work done. And those are their only choices. Their right to choose derives from the existence in this particular territory of a community of citizens, and it is not compatible with the destruction of the community or its transformation into yet another local tyranny.

## MEMBERSHIP AND JUSTICE

The distribution of membership is not pervasively subject to the constraints of justice. Across a considerable range of the decisions that are made, states are simply free to take in strangers (or not)—much as they are free, leaving aside the claims of the needy, to share their wealth with foreign friends, to honor the achievements of foreign artists, scholars, and scientists, and to enter into collective security arrangements with foreign states. But the right to choose an admissions policy is more basic than any of these, for it is not merely a matter of acting in the world, exercising sovereignty, and pursuing national interests. What is at stake here is the shape of the community that acts in the world, exercises sovereignty, and so on. Admission and exclusion are at the core of communal independence. They suggest the deepest meaning of self-determination. Without them, there could not be *communities of character*, historically stable, ongoing associations of men and women with some special commitment to one another and some special sense of their common life.[24]

But self-determination in the area of membership is not absolute. It is a right exercised, most often, by national clubs or families, but it is held in principle by territorial states. Hence it is subject both to the claims of affinity and of place and, when territory is considered as a resource, to the claims of necessity, too. These are the constraints imposed on immigration. The constraints on naturalization are more severe. Every new immigrant, every refugee taken in, every resident and worker must be offered the opportunities of citizenship. If the community is so radically divided that a single citizenship is impossible, then its territory must be divided, too, before the rights of admission and exclusion can be exercised; for these rights are to be exercised only by the political community as a whole (even if in practice some national majority dominates the decision making) and only with regard to foreigners, not by some members of the community with regard to other members. No community can be half slave, half free, and claim that its admissions policies represent acts of self-determination.

The determination of ethnic minorities by all-powerful majorities, or of slaves by masters, or of aliens and guests by an exclusive band of citizens is not communal freedom but oppression. The men and women of the majority group, the masters, the band of citizens: These people are free, of course, to set up a club, make membership as exclusive as they like, write a constitution, and govern one another. But they can't claim territorial jurisdiction and rule over the people with whom they share the territory. To do that is to act outside their sphere, beyond their rights. It is a form of tyranny. Indeed, the rule of masters and citizens over slaves, aliens, and pariahs is probably the most common form of tyranny in human history. The theory of distributive justice, then, must begin with an account of membership rights. It must vindicate at one time the (limited) right of closure, without which there could be no communities at all, and the internal inclusiveness of the existing communities. For it is only as members somewhere that men and women can hope to share in all the other social goods—security, wealth, honor, culture, and political power—that communal life makes possible.

## NOTES

1. John Rawls, *A Theory of Justice* (Cambridge, MA: Harvard University Press, 1971), p. 115; the following quotation is from p. 339.

2. In an argument against free immigration to the new Puritan commonwealth of Massachusetts, John Winthrop stresses the limitations on mutual aid or, as he calls it, "mercy": "1st. A man is not a fit object of mercy except he be in misery. 2nd. We are not bound to exercise mercy to others to the ruin of ourselves. 3rd.... As for hospitality, that rule doth not bind further than for some present occasion, not for continual residence." *Puritan Political Ideas: 1558–1794*, ed. Edmund S. Morgan (Indianapolis: Bobbs-Merrill, 1965), p. 146.

3. The use of zoning laws to bar certain sorts of people from neighborhoods (boroughs, towns), namely, people who don't live in conventional families, is

a new feature of our political history, and I shall not try to comment on it here: See the US Supreme Court's decision in *Village of Belle Terre v. Boraas* (October term, 1973).

4. Bernard Bosanquet, *The Philosophical Theory of the State* (London: Macmillan, 1958; first ed., 1899), p. 286; the discussion of what neighborhood might mean as an "ethical idea" is well worth reading.

5. Henry Sidgwick, *Elements of Politics* (London: Macmillan, 1881), pp. 295–96.

6. Ibid., p. 296.

7. Obviously, the unit from within which closure is attempted can vary a great deal, but the most common alternative to the country is the city, which in classical, medieval, and early modern times always regulated immigration and, what was often more important, naturalization. See, for example, Henri Pirenne on communal exclusivism in the Middle Ages: *Medieval Cities* (Garden City, NY: Doubleday Anchor Books, n. d.), esp. p. 150.

8. Maurice Cranston on the traditional understanding of liberty as a right to move: "It is a tradition which recognizes the right to move in the most literal sense; it does not recognize a natural right to stop and permanently stay. In the language of the French Constitution of 1791, the right of movement is *liberté d'aller, de rester, de partir.*" *What Are Human Rights?* (New York: Taplinger, 1973), p. 32.

9. Winthrop makes the point clearly: "If we here be a corporation established by free consent, if the place of our cohabitation be our own, then no man hath right to come into us... without our consent." *Puritan Political Ideas*, p. 145. I will come back to the question of "place" below.

10. Thomas Hobbes, *The Elements of Law*, part I, chapter 17, paragraph 2.

11. *Austro-Marxism*, ed. Tom Bottomore and Patrick Goode (Oxford: Oxford University Press, 1978), pp. 102–25.

12. *Elements of Politics*, p. 295.

13. *Leviathan*, part II, chapter 30.

14. Quoted in H. I. London, *Non-White Immigration and the "White Australia" Policy* (New York: New York University Press, 1970), p. 98.

15. *Leviathan*, part I, chapter 15.

16. *Elements of Politics*, pp. 296–97.

17. E. C. S. Wade and G. Godfrey Phillips, *Constitutional and Administrative Law*, 9th ed., revised by A. W. Bradley (London: Longman, 1977), p. 424.

18. For the whole ugly story, see Nikolai Tolstoy, *The Secret Betrayal: 1944-1947* (New York: Scribner, 1977).

19. Victor Ehrenberg, *The People of Aristophanes* (New York: Schocken, 1962), p. 153; I have drawn on the entire discussion of foreigners in fifth-century Athens, pp. 147–64.

20. *The Politics*, 3.1.3 and 3.5.2; I have used the translation of Eric Havelock, *The Liberal Temper in Greek Politics* (New Haven: Yale University Press, 1957), pp. 367–69.

21. In my account of guest workers, I rely chiefly on John Berger, *A Seventh Man* (Harmondsworth, England: Penguin Books, 1975); Stephen Castles and Godula Kosack, *Migrant Workers and Class Structure in Western Europe* (Oxford: Oxford University Press, 1973); and Cheryl Bernard, "Migrant Workers and European Democracy," *Political Science Quarterly* 92 (summer 1978): 277–99. I shall say nothing here about the condition of illegal immigrants (who often enough come in with the connivance of government officials). The illegality of their status obviously does not free them from subjection, but only makes it more difficult for them to defend themselves.

22. The argument can he made that the home states ought to insist upon such treaties—that is, they owe it to their citizens, who have every right to continued protection. But home states may not always be able to provide such protection in any effective way.

23. It has been suggested to me that this argument does not plausibly apply to privileged guests: technical advisers, visiting professors, and so on. I concede the point, though I am not sure just how to describe the category "guest workers" so as to exclude these others. But the others are not very important, and it is in the nature of their privileged positions that they are commonly able to call upon the protection of their home states if they ever need it.

24. I have taken the term "communities of character" from Otto Bauer, *Austro-Marxism*, p. 107.

# 7. BRIAN BARRY

In the first section of this paper, Barry argues that considerations of humanity require that rich countries give aid to poor ones. In the second, he argues that considerations of justice also require transfers from rich countries to poor ones. In the third, he takes up the distinction between aid and transfers and argues that, when we get down to the details, the obligations imposed by humanity and justice are different, although not incompatible.

## Humanity and Justice in Global Perspective

*First published in* Nomos XXIV: Ethics, Economics, and the Law, *ed. J. Roland Pennock and John W. Chapman (New York: New York University Press, 1982), 219–52.*

This chapter has three sections. The first argues that considerations of humanity require that rich countries give aid to poor ones. The second argues that considerations of justice also require transfers from rich countries to poor ones. The third picks up the distinction between aid and transfer and argues that, when we get into detail, the obligations imposed by humanity and justice are different, although not incompatible.

## I. HUMANITY

### 1. INTRODUCTION

What is it to act in a way called for by humanity? A humane act is a beneficent act, but not every beneficent act is a humane one. To do something that helps make someone who is already very happy even happier is certainly beneficent, but it would not naturally be described as an act called for by considerations of humanity.

The *Oxford English Dictionary* defines humanity as "Disposition to treat human beings and animals with consideration and compassion, and to relieve their distresses; kindness, benevolence."[1] In this essay I shall understand by "humanity" the relief of distress. As a matter of usage, it seems to me that the *OED* is right to put this before the more extended sense of kindness or benevolence in general. In any case, it is this notion that I want to discuss, and the word "humanity" is the closest representation of it in common use.

There are three questions to be dealt with. First, is it morally obligatory to behave humanely, or is it simply laudable but not morally delinquent to fail so to act? Second, if it is morally obligatory, what implications does it have, if any, for the obligations of rich countries to aid poor ones? Third, if (as I shall suggest) rich countries have a humanitarian obligation to aid poor ones, on what criterion can we determine how much sacrifice the rich countries should be prepared to make?

## 2. The Obligation of Humanity

I shall begin my discussion by taking up and considering the argument put forward by Peter Singer in his article "Famine, Affluence and Morality."[2] Singer puts forward a simple, clear, and forceful case for a humanitarian obligation for those in rich countries to give economic aid to those in poor countries. The premises of his argument are as follows. The first is "that suffering and death from lack of food, shelter, and medical care are bad."[3] The second is given in two alternative forms. One is that "if it is in our power to prevent something bad from happening, without thereby sacrificing anything of comparable moral importance, we ought, morally, to do it."[4] The other, and weaker, form is that "if it is in our power to prevent something very bad from happening, without sacrificing anything morally significant, we ought, morally, to do it."[5] He goes on to say that "an application of this principle [i.e., the second version] would be as follows: If I am walking past a shallow pond and see a child drowning in it, I ought to wade in and pull the child out. This will mean getting my clothes muddy, but this is insignificant, while the death of the child would presumably be a very bad thing."[6] All that has to be added is that the application of the second premise is unaffected by proximity or distance and "makes no distinction between cases in which I am the only person who could possibly do anything and cases in which I am just one among millions in the same position."[7] If we accept these premises, we are committed, Singer claims, to the conclusion that people in the rich countries have a moral obligation to help those in the poor countries.

For the purpose of this chapter, I am going to take it as common ground that one would indeed be doing wrong to walk past Peter Singer's drowning child and do nothing to save it. This of course entails that, at least in the most favorable cases, duties of humanity must exist. In the space available, it hardly makes sense to try to argue for a complete theory of morality from which this can be deduced, and in any case I myself am more sure of the conclusion than of any of the alternative premises from which it would follow. Anyone who disagrees with the claim that there is an obligation to rescue the child in the case as stated will not find what follows persuasive, since I certainly do not think that the case for international aid on humanitarian grounds is *stronger* than the case for rescuing the drowning child.

## 3. Does the Drowning Child Case Extend to International Aid?

The extension of the drowning child case may be challenged along several lines. Here I can only state them and say briefly why I do not think they undercut the basic idea that the case for an obligation to save the drowning child applies also to giving international aid. The appearance of dogmatism is purely a result of compression.

The first argument is that the child may be supposed not to be responsible for his plight (or at any rate it may be on that supposition that the example gets to us) but that countries are responsible for their economic problems. My comments here are two. First, even if it were true that the death by disease and or starvation of somebody in a poor country were to some degree the result of past acts or omissions by the entire population, that scarcely makes it morally decent to hold the individual responsible for his plight; nor, similarly, if his predicament could have been avoided had the policies of his government been different.

Let us move on to consider another way in which a challenge may be mounted to Singer's extension of the argument for a duty to aid from the case of the drowning child to that of famine relief. It may be recalled that Singer explicitly made the shift from one case to the other via the statement that neither proximity nor the one-to-one relation between the victim and the potential rescuer makes any moral difference. Clearly, if this claim is denied, we can again agree on the duty to rescue the drowning child but deny that this is an appropriate analogue to the putative duty of people in rich countries to aid those in poor ones. A number of philosophers have tried to drive a wedge between the cases in this way, but I have to say that I am not very impressed by their efforts. The argument for proximity as a relevant factor is that, if we posit a duty to rescue those near at hand, we keep the duty within narrow bounds and thus do not let it interfere with people's life plans; but, if we allow the duty to range over the whole of mankind, it becomes too demanding. Although some people see merit in this, it appears to me that it is invoked simply because it provides a way of arbitrarily truncating the application of the principle so as to arrive at a convenient answer. I shall go on later to agree that there are limits to what people can be required to sacrifice. But I see no ethically defensible reason for saying that, if we can't (or can't be required to) do anything we might, we should simply contract the sphere of operation of the principle that we are obliged to relieve suffering. Perhaps we should channel our limited humanitarian efforts to where they are most needed, which, if we live in a relatively rich country, is likely to be outside its boundaries.

Singer also made it explicit that, if the case of the drowning child were to be extended to international aid, one would have to rule out the one-to-one relation between the rescuer and the potential rescuee as a morally relevant factor. Attempts have been made to do so, but they likewise seem to me to lack merit. If there are several people who could save the drowning child, it is sometimes said that none of them is particularly responsible for saving it. But if the child drowns because none of them saves it, they are all, I would suggest, morally responsible for its death. Conversely, suppose that several people are drowning at some distance from one another and there is only one person around to save them. It has been argued that since that person cannot do his duty, if that is defined as saving all those whom he might save (assuming that he could save any one of them but cannot save more than one), no such duty exists. The obvious reply to this is that the duty has been incorrectly defined: The duty in this case is to save one, and his duty is not affected by the fact that there are others who cannot be saved.

Finally, it might be accepted that the case of the drowning child would extend to international aid if the aid would do any good, but then denied that it will. The main lines of this argument are two. The first is the one from waste and inefficiency: Aid does not get to the right people; development projects are a disaster; and so on. But I would claim that even if waste is endemic in aid to poor (and probably ill-organized) countries, the difference it makes to health and nutrition is sufficient to make it worth giving if only part of it gets to the people it is supposed to get to. And if, as is all too true, aid in the past has often been inappropriate, the answer is not to withhold aid but to make it more appropriate: no more massive dams, electricity-generating stations, or steel mills, but cheaper, less complex, and more decentralized technology.

The second line of argument is the neo-Malthusian: that the only effect of aid in the long run is to lead to population increase and thus to even more suffering. I agree that if this is the only effect of aid, the humanitarian case for it falls to the ground. But it is clear that economic development combined with appropriate social policies and the widespread availability of contraception can actually reduce the rate of population growth. The implication is thus that aid should be given in large amounts where the social and political conditions are right, so as to get countries through the demographic transition from high birth rate and high death rate to low birth rate and low death rate as rapidly as possible.

Where ideological or religious dogmas result in pronatalist government policies or rejection of contraception by the population, one might conclude that aid would be better withheld, since the only foreseeable effect of economic improvement will be to increase numbers. But can we really be so sure that attitudes will not change? The election of a relatively young and doctrinally reactionary pope does not encourage hopes of any early change in official doctrine. But even without any change at that level, it is striking how, in the developed countries, the practices of Roman Catholics have altered dramatically in just a couple of decades. For example, the Province of Quebec, which had for more than two centuries a birth rate close to the physical maximum, with families of more than ten children quite common, has now one of the lowest birth rates in North America.

## 4. How Far Does the Obligation Extend?

If we accept the conclusion that the rich have some obligation on humanitarian grounds to provide economic aid to the poor, the next question is, How much sacrifice is required? In my view, no simple and determinate criterion is available. This is a problem of the obligation of humanity in general, not a peculiarity of the international context. In the standard case of rescuing someone in danger of drowning, the usual guidance one gets from moral philosophers is that the obligation does not extend to risking one's life, though it does require that one suffer a fair amount of inconvenience. However, the decision in such cases, like that of Singer's drowning child, characteristically has clear and finite limits to its implications. But, given the failure of most people or governments in rich countries to give much aid, it would clearly be possible for individuals to give up a high proportion of their incomes without risking their lives and still leave millions of savable lives in poor countries unsaved. Thus, the question of limits is pressing.

There is an answer that is, in principle, straightforward. It is the one embodied in Singer's claim that one is obliged to help up to the point at which one is sacrificing something of "comparable moral importance." This is, of course, a maximizing form of consequentialism. If you say that pains and pleasures are what is of moral importance, you get Benthamite utilitarianism (in the traditional interpretation, anyway); if you say it is the enjoyment of beauty and personal relationships, you get G. E. Moore's ideal consequentialism; and so on. The trouble with this is, needless to say, that most of us do not see any reason for accepting an obligation to maximize the total amount of good in the universe.

Singer's weaker principle that we should give aid up to the point at which we are sacrificing anything of moral importance seems to me useless: For a Benthamite utilitarian, for example, even getting one's trousers muddy would be in itself an evil—not one comparable to the death of a child, but an evil nonetheless. Even Singer's chosen case would therefore be eliminated on this criterion, let alone any more strenuous sacrifices.

## 5. Conclusion

I conclude, provisionally and in the absence of any plausible alternative, that there is no firm criterion for the amount of sacrifice required to relieve distress. This does not mean that nothing can be said. I think it is fairly clear that there is a greater obligation the more severe the distress, the better off the potential helper would still be after helping, and the higher the ratio of benefit to cost. What is indefinite is where the line is to be drawn. In the words of C. D. Broad, in what may be the best single article in philosophical ethics ever written, "It is no objection to say that it is totally impossible to determine exactly where this point comes in any particular case. This is quite true, but it is too common a difficulty in ethics to worry us, and we know that we are lucky in ethical questions if we can state upper and lower limits that are not too ridiculously far apart."[8]

What, in any case, are we talking about here as the range? We could perhaps wonder whether the level of aid from a country like the United States should be 3 percent of GNP (the level of Marshall aid) or 10 or 25 percent. But, unless we reject the idea of an obligation to aid those in distress altogether, we can hardly doubt that one-quarter of 1 percent is grotesquely too little.

## II. JUSTICE

### 1. THE CONCEPT OF JUSTICE

"Are we not trying to pack too much into the concept of justice and the correlative concept of rights? The question whether it is *wrong* to act in certain ways is not the same question as whether it is *unjust* so to act."[9] I think the answer to Passmore's rhetorical question is in the affirmative. We should not expect to get out of "justice" a blueprint for the good society—nor should we wish to, since that degree of specificity would inevitably limit potential applicability. Surely it ought to be possible for a just society to be rich or poor, cultivated or philistine, religious or secular and (within some limits that are inherent in justice itself) to have more or less of liberty, equality, and fraternity.

Up to this point, I have studiously avoided any reference to justice. I have been talking about the obligation to relieve suffering as a matter of humanity. The fact that the obligation is not derived from justice does not make it a matter of generosity, nor does it entail that it should be left to voluntary action to adhere to it. It is an obligation that it would be wrong not to carry out and that could quite properly be enforced upon rich countries if the world political system made this feasible. And the core of the discussion has been the claim that the obligation to help (and a fortiori the obligation not to harm) is not limited in its application to those who form a single political community.

It is of course open to anyone who wishes to do so to argue that, if the rich have a properly enforceable obligation to give, this is all we need in order to be able to say that the rich must give to the poor as a matter of justice. I have no way of proving that it is a mistake to use the term "just" to mark out the line between, on the one hand, what is morally required and, on the other, what is praiseworthy to do but not wrong to omit doing. All I can say is that such a way of talking seems to me to result in the blunting of our moral vocabulary and therefore to a loss of precision in our moral thinking. Justice, I wish to maintain, is not merely one end of a monochromatic scale that has at the other end sacrifice of self-interest for the good of others to a heroic or saintly degree. Rather, it points to a particular set of reasons why people (or societies) may have duties to one another and to particular features of institutions that make them morally condemnable.[10]

I shall return to the distinction between humanity and justice in Section III, where I shall be able to refer to the results of my discussions of each of them. My plan is to analyze justice under two heads. The first is justice as reciprocity; the second, justice as equal rights. These are both familiar ideas, though I shall give the second a slightly unfamiliar twist. Justice as reciprocity I will discuss in three aspects: justice as fidelity, justice as requital, and justice as fair play.

## 2. JUSTICE AS FIDELITY

The notion of justice as fidelity is that of keeping faith. In addition to covering contract and promises, it extends, in a rather indefinite way, to meeting legitimate expectations not derived from explicit voluntary agreement. Clearly it is an essentially conservative principle and tends if anything to operate contrary to the interests of poor countries, insofar as they often find themselves in the position of seeking to renegotiate disadvantageous deals with transnational corporations within their territories.

## 3. JUSTICE AS REQUITAL

Justice as requital is also a basically conservative principle but can, on occasion, have revisionist implications vis-à-vis justice as fidelity. No simple rule governs what happens when they conflict. Henry Sidgwick, with characteristic caution, said that we have two standards of justice, as the customary distribution and as the ideal distribution, and added that "it is the reconciliation between these two views which is the problem of political justice."[11] I shall not take up that challenge here, but explore the possible implications of justice as requital for international distribution.

The idea of justice as requital is that of a fair return: a fair exchange, a fair share of benefits from some common endeavor, and so on. The most obvious application in the relations between rich and poor countries is whether poor countries are getting fair prices for their exports and paying fair prices for their imports. This, of course, raises the obvious question of what the criterion of a "fair price" is. Suppose, however, that we say, minimally, that it is the prevailing world price. Then it seems clear that, even on this criterion, many poor countries have legitimate complaints about the transfer pricing of transnational corporations. For example, when in the late 1960 the Andean Pact countries (Bolivia, Colombia, Ecuador, and Peru) started taking a serious interest in the pricing policies of transnational corporations operating within their territories, they found overpricing of imports to be the norm, sometimes by factors of hundreds of percent, and, less spectacularly, underpricing of the value of exports.[12] This enabled the companies to attain rates of return on capital of often more than 100 percent while at the same time evading government limits on repatriation of profits. Since the Andean Pact countries have been politically independent for a century and a half and have relatively sophisticated bureaucracies compared with most countries in the Third World, it is inconceivable that similar practices do not obtain in other, more vulnerable countries.

When we turn to the structure of world prices itself, the criterion of justice as requital becomes less helpful. The countries of the Third World, as part of their demands for a "New International Economic Order" have demanded an "Integrated Program" of commodity management that would be designed to push up the prices of raw materials in relation to manufactured products.

The success of the Organization of Petroleum Exporting Countries (OPEC) is, of course, significant here in providing a dazzling example of the effectiveness of a producer cartel. Oil, however, seems to be unique in that it is so cheap to extract and worth so much to consumers. This means that it has always, since the days of the Pennsylvania oilfields, yielded enormous economic rents. The only question has been who captured them. And clearly, until 1973, the Middle Eastern oil producers were getting only a small proportion of the economic rent.

Other commodities are not like oil. It may indeed be possible to push up the prices by restricting supply, but substitution or recycling is likely to set in. From the long-run point of view of the world, this pressure toward conservation would be desirable, no doubt, but the point is that it does not spell a bonanza for the raw material producers.

Clearly, this is only scratching the surface, but I think that it is, at any rate, important to keep in mind that, even if commodity prices could be raised substantially across the board, this would not make most poor countries *appreciably* better off; and it would make some, including the important cases of India and Bangladesh, worse off. Whatever conclusion one wishes to draw, therefore, about the applicability to world prices of justice as requital, the implications are not going to be such as to solve the problem of poor countries that are also resource poor.

## 4. JUSTICE AS FAIR PLAY

We still have to see if any redistributive implications flow from the third branch of justice as reciprocity: justice as fair play. The idea here is that if one benefits (or stands to benefit) from some cooperative practice, one should not be a "free rider" by taking the benefits (or being ready to take them if the occasion arises) while failing to do one's part in sustaining the practice when it is one's turn to do so. Thus, if others burn smokeless fuel in their fireplaces, pack their litter out of the backcountry, or clean up after their dogs, it is unfair for you to refuse to do the same.

The principle of fair play has a potentiality for underwriting a certain amount of redistribution from rich to poor insofar as one practice that might be regarded as prospectively beneficial to all concerned would be the practice of helping those in need. If such a practice existed, it would operate analogously to insurance, which is a contractual way of transferring money from those who have not suffered from certain specified calamities to those who have. The principle of fair play would then hold that it would be unfair to be a free rider on a scheme of helping those in need by refusing to do your part when called upon.

The invocation of this notion of what the sociobiologists call "reciprocal altruism" may appear to provide a new way of distinguishing the drowning child case from that of international aid. Perhaps what motivates us in agreeing that there is an obligation to rescue the child is an unarticulated contextual assumption that the child belongs to our community (however widely we may conceive that "community") and that there are norms within that community calling for low-cost rescue from which we stand to gain if ever we find ourselves in need of rescue. Such feelings of obligation as we have in this case can therefore be adequately explained by supposing that they arise from the application of the principle of fair play. It was, thus, an error to have taken it for granted that an acknowledgment of an obligation to help in the drowning child case must show that we accepted a general principle of an obligation to aid those in distress.

I believe that the objection is formally valid. That is to say, it is possible by invoking the principle of fair play to underwrite the obligation to rescue the drowning child without committing oneself to a universal obligation to rescue. One could respond to this by arguing that the conclusions in Section I of this essay can be reinstated by deriving universal obligations from the existence of world community. I shall consider this argument below. But before doing so, I should like to follow an alternative and more aggressive line.

The point to observe is that, although we may indeed be motivated to agree that we ought to rescue the drowning child by considerations of justice as reciprocity, it does not follow that we are motivated solely by those considerations. Suppose that you are briefly visiting a foreign country, with an entirely alien culture, and have no idea about the local norms of rescue. Would you, if you came across Singer's drowning child, have an obligation to wade in and rescue it? I think that most people would say yes in answer to that question. And, clearly, those who do are acknowledging obligations of humanity as distinct from obligations of justice.

None of this, of course, is intended to suggest that the difficulties in moving from a general obligation of humanity to an obligation on the part of rich countries to give economic aid to poor ones is any less problematic than it appeared earlier. But it does fend off a possible challenge to the move from the drowning child case to the universal obligation to aid. The view I want to maintain is that the answer in the drowning child case is overdetermined where the duty of fair play also underwrites rescue. The strength of the obligation depends upon the circumstances, but it never disappears. Both psychologically and morally, the obligation to aid would be strongest if there were an explicit and generally observed agreement among a group of parents to keep an eye on one another's children: humanity, fidelity, and fair play would then coincide and reinforce each other. The obligation would be perhaps a little less strong but still very strong in a small, stable, and close-knit community with a well-developed tradition of "neighborliness," since the obligation of fair play would here have maximum force. It would be less strong if the norm of rescue were more widely diffused over a whole society, and would of course vary according to the society. (New Zealand would rate much higher than the United States on the strength of the norm of helping strangers within the society, for example.) And, finally, in the absence of any established practice of aiding strangers that would give rise to obligations of fair play, there is still, I am suggesting, an obligation of humanity that does not in any way depend upon considerations of reciprocity.[13]

I have been taking for granted that the existence of a practice of rescue does give rise to an obligation to play one's part. This can be questioned. Somebody might say: "Why should I cooperate with the scheme if I'm willing to renounce any benefits that might be due to me under it?"[14] But the cogency of the objection depends upon the existence of stringent conditions of publicity: It must be possible to make this known to all those in the scheme, and it must be remembered perhaps for decades. (This is essential, since many transfers to those in need are going to be predominantly from the young and middle-aged to the old, so it would undermine the integrity of any such cooperative scheme if people could change their minds about its value as they got older.) Neither condition is generally met. Consider a practice of rescuing the victims of accidents—drowning swimmers are the usually cited case. If this practice exists in a whole society, it is not feasible for those who wish to opt out to notify everybody else in advance. And how many could be counted on to be strong-minded enough to wave away a would-be rescuer when they were in need of help themselves? Even if they could, in many cases the rescuer has to incur the trouble and risk in order to get there (as with rescuing a swimmer) or the victim may be unconscious and thus incapable of spurning help.

It is crucially important to notice, however, that the principle of fair play is conditional; that is to say, it stipulates that it is unfair to be a free rider on an actually existing cooperative practice, and that it *would* be unfair to free ride on other mutually beneficial practices if they did exist. But it does not say that it is unfair for a practice that would, if it existed, be mutually beneficial, not to exist.

As anyone familiar with Rawls's theory of justice will have been aware for some time, we are here on the edge of deep waters. For one strand of Rawls's theory is precisely the notion of justice as reciprocity that is embodied in the principle of fair play. According to Rawls, a society is a scheme of social cooperation, and from this fact we can generate, via the notion of fair play, principles of justice. But, clearly, any actual society simply generates whatever is generated by its actual cooperative practices. If it provides retirement pensions out of social security taxes, it is unfair to be a free rider on the scheme by dodging your share of the cost. And so on. But if I am right about the applicability of the principle of fair play, the most Rawls can say about a society that does not have such a scheme is that it suffers from collective irrationality in that it is passing up a chance to do itself some good. He cannot, I suggest, employ the principle as a step in an argument that such a society is unjust.

I make this point because Charles Beitz, in the last part of his admirable book *Political Philosophy and International Relations*,[15] has argued, within a Rawlsian framework, for a global difference principle. That is to say, income should be redistributed internationally so that the worst-off representative individual in the world is as well off as possible. Beitz acknowledges that he is taking for granted the general validity of Rawls's theory and is simply arguing from within its basic premises for the dropping of Rawls's restriction on the application of the two principles of justice to societies. I have been suggesting that, even within a society, one cannot use the fact that it is a cooperative scheme to argue that it is unfair not to have more extensive cooperation, though not to do so may be collectively irrational. But the international scene presents two further difficulties. First, I think that Rawls is broadly right in (implicitly) denying that the whole world constitutes a single cooperative partnership in the required sense. Second, I do not think that international redistribution can plausibly be said to be advantageous to rich as well as poor countries. Rawls is therefore probably correct in deducing from his system only nonaggression, diplomatic immunity, and the like as mutually advantageous to countries and thus, on his side of the principle of fair play, just. If I am right, however, they are simply collectively rational and give rise to duties of fair play only to the extent that they are instantiated in actual practice.

Beitz's argument for extending the Rawlsian difference principle is in essence that the network of international trade is sufficiently extensive to draw all countries together in a single cooperative scheme. But it seems to be that trade, however multilateral, does not constitute a cooperative scheme of the relevant kind. Trade, if freely undertaken, is (presumably) beneficial to the exchanging parties, but it is not, it seems to me, the kind of relationship that gives rise to duties of fair play. To the extent that justice is involved it is, I would say, justice as requital, that is, giving a fair return. Justice as fair play arises not from simple exchange but from either the provision of public goods that are collectively enjoyed (parks; defense; a litter-free, or unpolluted, environment; and so on) or from quasi-insurance schemes for mutual aid of the kind just discussed. Trade in pottery, ornamentation, and weapons can be traced back to prehistoric times, but we would hardly feel inclined to think of, say, the Beaker Folk as forming a single cooperative enterprise with their trading partners. No more did the spice trade unite East and West.

To the extent that we are inclined to think of the world as more of a cooperative enterprise now, this is, in my judgment, not because trade is more extensive or multilateral, but because there really are rudimentary organs of international cooperation in the form of United Nations agencies and such entities as the International Monetary Fund (IMF) and the World Bank. But the resulting relationships clearly fall short of those of mutual dependence found within societies. And my second point comes in here to draw attention to the fact that the extent of increased cooperation that would really be mutually beneficial is probably quite limited. In particular, redistribution on the insurance principle seems to have little appeal to rich countries. In the foreseeable future, aid to the needy is going to flow from, say, the United States to Bangladesh rather than vice versa. The conditions for reciprocity—that all the parties stand prospectively to benefit from the scheme—simply do not exist. One could, of course, again retreat behind the "veil of ignorance" and argue that, if people did not know to which society they belonged, they would surely choose something like a global difference principle—or at any rate a floor below which nobody should be allowed to fall. And this seems plausible enough. (I have argued it myself in an earlier work.[16]) But this move clearly points up even more sharply than in the case of a single society the degree to which inserting the "veil of ignorance" takes us away from the sphere of the principle of fair play.

## 5. JUSTICE AS EQUAL RIGHTS

In his well-known article "Are There Any Natural Rights?"[17] H. L. A. Hart argues that special rights must presuppose general rights. Before people can act in ways that modify their, and others', rights (paradigmatically by promising), they must, as a matter of elementary logic, have rights that do not stem from such modifications. Putting this in terms of the present discussion, we can say that justice as reciprocity needs a prior assignment of rights before it can get off the ground.

Now we might try to solve the problem of sanctifying the status quo. We could, in other words, simply declare that we are going to push the principle of justice as the fulfillment of reasonable expectations to the limit and say that whatever rights somebody now has are to be taken as the baseline in relation to which all future developments must satisfy the requirements of fidelity, requital, and fair play. If we note that the conservation of value is akin to the Pareto principle, we may observe that this would give us the Virginia school of political economy, especially associated with James Buchanan.

I have criticized his approach elsewhere,[18] and I shall not repeat my criticisms here. But it is surely enough for the present purpose to draw attention to the fact that on the principle of the unquestioned justice of the status quo, the most grotesque features of the existing allocation of rights would be frozen in place forever unless those who suffered from them could find some quid pro quo that would make it worth the while of, say, a shah of Iran or a General Somoza to accept change. But that would be, if it could be found, an improvement in efficiency arising from the reallocation of the existing rights. It would not face the real problem, which was, of course, the injustice of the initial allocation of rights.

Hart's answer to his own question is that the general right that is presupposed by any special rights is an equal right to liberty. He does not give any explicit argument, as far as I can see, for its being equal. But I take it the point is that since a general right is something that is necessarily anterior to any act giving rise to a special right, there is simply no basis for discriminating among people in respect of general rights. In order to discriminate, one would either have to do so on the basis of some quality that is obviously irrelevant to the assignment of rights (e.g., skin color) or on the basis of something the person has done (e.g., made a promise) that provides a reason for attributing different rights to him. But then we get back to the original point, namely that such a differentiation in rights entails that we have an idea of the proper distribution of rights without the special factor adduced. And that must, it seems, be an equal distribution.

In this essay I want to take this idea and apply it to the case of natural resources. I shall suggest that they fit all the requirements for being the subjects of a general right and that therefore everyone has an equal right to enjoy their benefits.

As Hillel Steiner has remarked, "Nozick rightly insists that our commonsense view of what is just—of what is owed to individuals by right—is inextricably bound up with what they *have done* ... [but] unlike other objects, the objects of appropriative rights ... are *not* the results of individuals' past actions.... Appropriative claims, and the rules governing them, can have nothing to do with desert."[19] Consider, for example, Bruce Ackerman's fable of the spaceship and the manna. One of the claimants, "Rusher," says: "I say that the first person who grabs a piece of manna should be recognized as its true owner" and, when asked for a reason, says, "Because people who grab first are better than people who grab second."[20] That, I think, illustrates my point. What exactly is supposed to be the virtue of getting there first, or even worse, in merely having some ancestor who got there first?

The position with regard to countries is parallel to that of individuals. Today the basis of state sovereignty over natural resources is convention reinforced by international declarations such as votes of the United Nations General Assembly in 1970, 1972, and 1974 to the effect that each country has "permanent sovereignty over natural resources" within its territory.[21] It is easy enough to see the basis of the convention. It has a transcendent simplicity and definiteness that must recommend it in international relations. For, in the absence of a "common power," stability depends heavily on conventions that leave the minimum amount of room for interpretation. Within a municipal legal system, by contrast, it is possible to introduce and enforce complex rules limiting the rights of individual appropriation (e.g., restricting the amount of water than can be drawn off from a river) and transferring a portion of the economic rent from the property owner to the state. Moreover, in the absence of a "common power" it is a convention that is relatively easy to enforce—at any rate easier than any alternative. For a state may be presumed, other things being equal, to be in a better position to control the appropriation of the natural resources of its own territory than to control those of some other country.

In practice, of course, things are not always equal, and many Third World countries have found that controlling foreign companies that own their natural resources is no easy matter: An unholy alliance of multinational corporations and their patron governments (for most, this is the United States) stand ready to organize international boycotts, to manipulate institutions such as the World Bank and the IMF against them; and, if all else fails, go in for "destabilization" on the Chilean model. The problem is exacerbated when a country seeks to gain control of the exploitation of its own natural resources by expropriating the foreign-based companies that have been there, often long before the country became independent. For the issue of compensation then arises, and this is likely to be contentious, not only because of the possibility of dispute about the current value of the investment, but also because the country may claim compensation for inadequate (or no) royalties paid on extraction in the past, a claim that (as we noted above) falls under the head of justice as requital.

However, as far as I am aware, no body of opinion in either the North or the South is adverse to the principle that each country is entitled to benefit exclusively from its own natural resources, and to decide whether they should be exploited and, if so, at what rate and in what order. And even the practice has come a long way in the last twenty years. OPEC is of course the outstanding illustration, but the same pattern of improved royalties and more control over the amount extracted and the way in which it is done obtains also in other countries and other commodities.

It would hardly be surprising if, when the principle of national sovereignty over natural resources has been so recently and precariously established, Third World countries should be highly suspicious of any suggestion that natural resources should in future be treated as collective international property. They may well wonder whether this is anything more than a cover for the reintroduction of colonialism. I do not see how such doubts can be allayed by mere assertion. Clearly, everything would depend on the principle's being applied across the board rather than in a one-sided way that lets the industrialized countries act on the maxim "What's yours is mine and what's mine is my own." So far, that is precisely how it has been used, as in the proposals of American chauvinists such as Robert Tucker that the United States should be prepared to occupy the Saudi Arabian oilfields by military force in order to maintain the flow of oil at a "reasonable" price, so that Americans can continue to use up a grossly disproportionate share of the world's oil. Since the United States, if it used only domestically produced oil, would still have one of the world's highest per capita levels of consumption, the effrontery of this proposal for the international control of other countries' oil would be hard to beat.

If the Third World countries were too weak to do anything more than hang on to the present position of national sovereignty over natural resources, we would, it seems to me, have to regard that as the best outcome that can be obtained. It is clearly preferable to the earlier setup, in which countries with the power to do so controlled the natural resources of others. For, although the distribution of natural resources is entirely arbitrary from a moral point of view, it has at any rate the kind of fairness displayed by a lottery. That is presumably better than a situation in which the weak are despoiled of their prizes by force and fraud.

In spite of these forebodings about the potential misuse of the principle that natural resources are the joint possession of the human race as a whole, I think it is worth pursuing. For it is scarcely possible to be satisfied with the present situation from any angle except that of extreme pessimism about the chances of changing it for the better rather than for the worse. The overwhelming fact about the existing system is, obviously, that it makes the economic prospects of a country depend, to a significant degree, on something for which its inhabitants (present or past) can take absolutely no credit and lay no just claim to its exclusive benefits, namely its natural resources—including in this land, water, minerals, sunlight, and so on. The claims of collectivities to appropriate natural resources rest, as do those of individuals, on convention or on law (in this case, such quasi-law as the United Nations resolutions cited above). No doubt, the point has been impressed on people in the West by examples such as Kuwait, the United Arab Emirates, or Saudi Arabia, and it may be that such small numbers of people have never before become so rich without any effort on their own part, simply as a result of sitting on top of rich deposits. But I see no coherent way of saying why there is anything grotesque about, say, the case of Kuwait, without acknowledging that the fault lies in the whole principle of national sovereignty over natural resources. If it were simply a matter of a few million people hitting the jackpot, things would not be bad, but of course the obverse of that is countries that have poor land, or little land per head, and few mineral resources or other sources of energy such as hydroelectric power.

Obviously, some countries are richer than others for many reasons, and some, like Japan, are among the more affluent in spite of having to import almost all their oil and the greatest part of many other natural resources. What, then, about the other advantages that the people in the rich countries inherit—productive capital, good systems of communications, orderly administration, well-developed systems of education and training, and so on? If the point about special rights is that someone must have done something to acquire a special right, what have the fortunate inheritors of all the advantages done to give them an exclusive claim to the benefits flowing from them?

The answer that the defenders of property rights normally give at this point is that, although the inheritors have done nothing to establish any special rights, those who left it to them did do something (namely, help to create the advantages) and had a right to dispose of it to some rather than to others. The special rights of those in the present generation thus derive from the use made by those in the previous generation of *their* special rights.

I cannot, in this already long chapter, undertake here to ask how far this answer takes us. We would have to get into questions that seem to me very difficult, such as the extent to which the fact that people who are no longer alive wanted something to happen, and perhaps even made sacrifices in order to insure that it could happen, provides any basis in justice for determining what those now alive now should do. I shall simply say here that I regard any claims that those now alive can make to special advantages derived from the efforts of their ancestors as quite limited. First, the inheritance must itself have been justly acquired in the first place, and that cannot be said of any country that violated the equal claims of all on natural resources—which means almost all industrial countries. Second, the claims to inheritance seem to me to attenuate with time, so that, although the present generation might legitimately derive some special advantages from the efforts of the preceding one, and perhaps the one before that, the part of what they passed on that was in turn inherited from their predecessors should, I think, be regarded as by now forming part of the common heritage.

Obviously, making this case out would require elaboration beyond the space available. But I do want to emphasize that what follows constitutes, in my view, a minimalist strategy. That is to say, whatever obligations of justice follow from it represent the absolutely rock-bottom requirements of justice in international affairs. To the extent that other advantages can be brought within the net of the principle of equal rights, the obligations of rich countries go beyond what is argued for here.

## 6. INTERNATIONAL INSTITUTIONS

It would be ridiculous to spend time here on a blueprint for a scheme to put into effect the principle that I have been advancing. Its implementation on a worldwide scale, if it happens at all, is going to occur over a period measured in decades and, indeed, centuries. It will depend on both fundamental changes in outlook and on the development of international organs capable of taking decisions and carrying them out with reasonable efficiency and honesty.

The history of domestic redistribution is, I think, very much to the point here in suggesting that there is a virtuous circle in which the existence of redistributive institutions and beliefs in the legitimacy of redistribution are mutually reinforcing and have a strong tendency to become more extensive together over time. When Hume discussed redistribution in the *Enquiry*, the only form of it that he considered was "perfect equality of possessions."[22] The notion of continuous redistribution of income through a system of progressive taxation does not seem to have occurred to him. The Poor Law did, of course, provide a minimum of relief to the indigent, but it was organized by parishes and it is doubtful that the amateurish and nepotistic central administration of the eighteenth century could have handled a national scheme. The introduction of unemployment and sickness benefits and old age pensions in one Western European country after another in the late nineteenth century and early twentieth century was made possible by the development of competent national administrations.

At the same time, these programs constituted a political response to the extension of the suffrage, or perhaps one might more precisely say a response to conditions that, among other things, made the extension of the suffrage necessary for the continued legitimacy of the state. A certain measure of redistribution was the price the privileged were prepared to pay for mass acceptance of their remaining advantages. Once in place, however, such programs have shown a universal tendency to take on a life of their own and to grow incrementally as gaps in the original coverage are filled in and the whole level of benefits is gradually raised. Indeed, it has been found in cross-national studies that the best predictor of the relative size of a given program (say, aid to the blind) within the whole welfare system is the amount of time the program has been running compared with others. In the long run, the programs seem to generate supporting sentiments, so that even Margaret Thatcher and Ronald

Reagan propose only reductions of a few percentage points in programs that even thirty years ago would have seemed quite ambitious.

I do not want to drive the comparison with the international arena into the ground, but I think that, if nothing else, reflecting on domestic experience ought to lead us to look at international transfers from an appropriate time perspective. The United Nations Organization obviously has a lot wrong with it, for example, but its administration is probably less corrupt, self-serving, and inefficient than that which served Sir Robert Walpole. If one takes a time span of thirty years, it is, I suggest, more remarkable that the network of international cooperation has developed as far as it has than that it has not gone further. And in the realm of ideas the notion that poor countries have claims of one sort or another to aid from rich ones has moved from being quite exotic to one that is widely accepted in principle. At any rate in public, the representatives of the rich countries on international bodies no longer deny such a responsibility. They merely seek to evade any binding commitment based on it. But in the long run what is professed in public makes a difference to what gets done because it sets the terms of the discussion.

## 7. International Taxation

It is not at all difficult to come up with proposals for a system by which revenues would be raised on a regular basis from the rich countries and transferred to the poor ones. Accordingly, no elaborate discussion is needed here. If any such scheme ever gained enough momentum to be a serious international issue, economists and accountants would no doubt have a field day arguing about the details. There is no point in anticipating such arguments, even in outline here. However, the relative brevity of treatment here should not lead to any underestimation of its importance. It is in fact the centerpiece of what is being put forward in this essay.

Now, broadly speaking, two alternative approaches are possible. One would be to take up each of the aspects of international justice that have been discussed—and whatever others might be raised—and to base a system of taxes and receipts upon each. This would be messy and endlessly contentious. The alternative, which is, I predict, the only way in which any systematic redistribution will ever take place, if it ever does, is to have one or two comprehensive taxes and distribute the proceeds according to some relatively simple formula among the poor countries.

The most obvious, and in my view the best, would be a tax on the governments of rich countries, assessed as a proportion of gross national product that increases with per capita income, the proceeds to be distributed to poor countries on a parallel basis of negative income tax. Gross national product reflects, roughly, the use of irreplaceable natural resources, the burden on the ecosphere, and advantages derived from the efforts of past generations, and past exploitation of other countries. Ideally, this tax would be supplemented by a severance tax on the extraction of mineral resources and a shadow tax on the value of land and similar resources. (States could be left to collect the money by any means they chose. But their aggregate liability would be assessed by valuing the taxable base and applying the set rate). This would certainly be required to take care of some glaring inequities that would still otherwise remain. But the simple system of transfer based on gross national product would be such an advance over the status quo that it would be a mistake to miss any chance to implement it by pursuing further refinements.

I believe that any other kinds of general tax, that is to say, taxes not related specifically to some aspect of justice, should be rejected. For example, a tax on foreign trade, or on foreign trade in fossil fuels has been proposed.[23] This is so obviously arbitrary that it is hard to see how anyone can have considered it worth mooting. It has the manifest effect of penalizing small countries and countries that export (or import, if one believes that the tax on exports of fossil fuel would be shifted forward) coal and oil. It conversely has an absurdly favorable effect on very large countries that import and export little in relation to the size of the GNPs and are relatively self-sufficient in energy derived from fossil fuels. No doubt the State Department loves it, but why anyone else should be imposed on is a mystery to me.

I have assumed without discussion that resources transferred to satisfy the requirements of justice should go straight to poor countries rather than being channeled through international agencies and dispensed in the form of aid for specific projects. I shall spell out the rationale for this in the next section. But I will simply remark here that nothing I have said about justice rules out additional humanitarian transfers. And these would appropriately be administered by international organizations. The basis for raising such revenues for humanitarian aid would very reasonably be a progressive international shadow income tax, since this would perfectly reflect ability to pay. We might thus envisage a dual system of international taxation—one part, corresponding to the requirements of justice, going directly to poor countries to be spent at their own discretion; the other going to the World Bank or some successor organization less dominated by the donor countries.

# III. THE RELATIONS BETWEEN HUMANITY AND JUSTICE

## 1. INTRODUCTION

I have been arguing that both humanity and justice require a substantial expansion in the scale of economic transfers from rich countries to poor ones. I should now like to show that, as the two rationales are very different, so are their practical implications. This point is, I think, worth emphasizing because those who pride themselves on the possession of sturdy Anglo-Saxon "common sense" tend to conclude that, if we agree on the humanitarian obligation, we are wasting our breath in arguing about claims of injustice—claims for the rectification of alleged unrequited transfers from poor to rich countries in the past that are hard to assess and impossible to quantify or involving more or less abstruse doctrines about the nature of justice in the contemporary world. If we recognize the case for action on simple and straightforward humanitarian grounds, the idea goes, shouldn't we concentrate on putting into place the appropriate aid policies, rather than allow ourselves to get sidetracked into fruitless wrangles about justice? In this context it is often said that the demands made by the countries of the South are "symbolic" or "ideological" and have the effect only of making more difficult the real, practical task of negotiating actual concessions by the countries of the North. The question that seems to me of more import is the following: If an obligation of humanity is accepted, under whatever name, how much difference does it make whether or not the kinds of claims I have been discussing under the heading of "justice" are also conceded?

## 2. RIGHTS AND GOALS

The answer is, I believe, that it makes a great deal of difference. Putting it in the most abstract terms, the obligations of humanity are goal-based, whereas those of justice are rights-based.[24] I would once have expressed the distinction between humanity and justice as one between an aggregative principle and a distributive principle.[25] I now, however, regard that distinction as less fundamental than the one I wish to mark by talking of goal-based and rights-based obligations. The point is that humanity and justice are not simply alternative prescriptions with respect to the same thing. Rather, they have different subject matters.

Humanity, understood as a principle that directs us not to cause suffering and to relieve it where it occurs, is a leading member of a family of principles concerned with what happens to people (and other sentient creatures)—with what I shall call their well-being, intending to include in this such notions as welfare, happiness, self-fulfillment, freedom from malnutrition and disease, and satisfaction of basic needs. Justice, by contrast, is not directly concerned with such matters at all. As well as principles that tell us what are good and bad states of affairs and what responsibilities we have to foster the one and to avert the other, we also have principles that tell us how control over resources should be allocated. If we understand "resources" in a very wide sense, so that it includes all kinds of rights to act without interference from others, to constrain the actions of others, and to bring about changes in the nonhuman environment, then we can say that the subject matter of justice (at any rate, in modern usage) is the distribution of control over material resources. At this high level of generality, it is complemented by the principle of equal liberty, which is concerned with the control over nonmaterial resources. To put it in a slogan, which has the advantages as well as the disadvantages of any slogan, humanity is a question of doing good; justice is a question of power.

When the contrast is stated in those terms, it might seem that bothering about justice is indeed a waste of time and that the bluff Anglo-Saxon advocates of commonsensical utilitarianism have the best of it after all. Why, it may naturally be asked, should we care about the distribution of *stuff* as against the distribution of *welfare*? Isn't this simply commodity fetishism in a new guise?

The easy but inadequate answer is that the concept of justice is, of course, concerned not only with old stuff but the kind of stuff that has the capacity to provide those who use it with the material means of well-being: food, housing, clothing, medical care, and so on. This is correct as far as it goes and shows that being concerned with justice is not irrational. But it is inadequate because it leaves the supporter of justice open to an obvious flanking movement. His opponent may reply: "You say that the only reason for concern about the distribution of the things whose proper allocation constitutes the subject matter of justice is that they are the means to well-being. Very well. But are you not then in effect conceding that your 'deep theory' is goal-based? For what you are saying is that we really are ultimately concerned with the distribution of well-being. We simply take an interest in the distribution of the means of well-being because they are what we can actually allocate. But this means that justice is a derivative principle."

There are two lines of response open at this point. One is to concede that criteria for the distribution of resources are ultimately to be referred to the goal of well-being, but at the same time to deny that it follows from that concession that we can cut out the middleman (or put in the Michelman) and set out our principles for the allocation of resources with an eye directly on the well-being they are likely to produce. Or, more precisely, we may say that among the constituents of well-being is autonomy, and autonomy includes the power to choose frivolously or imprudently. Thus, on one (admittedly controversial) interpretation, Mill's talk of justice in Book V of *Utilitarianism* and his presentation of the "simple principle" of *On Liberty* in terms of rights is all consistent with an underlying utilitarian commitment if we allow for the importance to people of being able to plan their own lives and make their own decisions.

I think that this is by no means an unreasonable view and has more to be said for it than is, perhaps, fashionable to admit. Anyone who wishes at all costs to hold up a monistic ethical position is, I suspect, almost bound to finish up by trying to make some such argument as this. But I think that it is, nevertheless, in the last analysis a heroic attempt to fudge the issue by using the concept of autonomy to smuggle a basically foreign idea into the goal-based notion of advancing well-being.

The alternative is to deny that, in conceding that control over resources is important only because of the connection between resources and well-being, one is thereby committed to the view that principles for the distribution of resources are derivative. According to this view, there simply are two separate kinds of question. One concerns the deployment of resources to promote happiness and reduce misery. The other concerns the ethically defensible basis for allocating control over resources. Neither is reducible, even circuitously, to the other. When they conflict, we get hard questions, such as those involved in the whole issue of paternalism. But there is no overarching criterion within which such conflicts can be solved, as is offered (at least in principle) by the idea that autonomy is an important, but not the only, ingredient in well-being.

As may be gathered, this is the position that I hold. In what follows, I want to show what difference it makes to employ an independent principle of justice in considering issues of international distribution. To make the discussion as clear as possible, I shall draw my contrast with a principle of humanity understood in the kind of pretty straightforward way exemplified in Section I of this chapter. The contrast would be softened the more weight we were to give to autonomy as a component in well-being. Note, however, that even those who might wish to emphasize the importance of individual autonomy are likely to doubt the value to individual well-being of autonomy for states; yet it is precisely the question of autonomy for states that is going to turn out to be the main dividing line between humanity and justice at the international level.

## 3. INTERNATIONAL APPLICATIONS

The point is one of control. The rich countries already mostly concede, at least in verbal declarations, that they have a humanitarian obligation to assist the poor countries economically. The importance to the future of the world of their beginning to live up to those declarations can scarcely be overestimated. I trust that nothing in this chapter will be taken as disparaging humanitarian aid. To the extent that it does in fact relieve problems of poverty, disease, malnutrition, and population growth it is, obviously, of enormous value.

But to see its limitations, let us be really utopian about humanitarian aid. Let us imagine that it is collected on a regular and automatic basis from rich countries according to some formula that more or less reflects ability to pay; for example, a shadow tax on GNP graduated by the level of GNP per capita. And suppose that the proceeds were pooled and dispersed through agencies of the United Nations, according to general criteria for entitlement to assistance.

Now, undoubtedly such a world would be an immense improvement over the present one, just as the modern welfare state has transformed, say, Henry Mayhew's London. But it would still have the division between the donor countries, free to spend "their" incomes as they pleased and the recipient countries, which would have to spend their incomes "responsibly." No doubt, this would be less objectionable if the criteria were drawn up in partnership between donor and recipient countries rather than, as now, being laid down by bodies such as the IMF and the World Bank in whose governing councils the rich countries have a preponderant voice. But funds earmarked and conditional upon approved use would still be basically different from income of the usual kind.

In contrast, transfers that were consequential upon considerations of justice would simply reduce the resources of one set of countries and augment those of another set. The distribution of control of resources would actually be shifted. It is therefore easy to see that the question of justice in the relations between rich and poor countries is by no means a purely "symbolic" one. Real issues are at stake, and it is no self-delusion that leads the poor countries to press for a recognition of the claims of justice and the rich countries to resist.

The conclusion we have reached, then, is that the crucial characteristic of justice is that the obligation to make the transfers required by it does not depend upon the use made of them by the recipient. At this point, I find that the following kinds of objection are usually made: What if the recipient country wastes the resources transferred to it? What if it is going to spend the money on armaments? What if it has a very unequal distribution of income and the additional income will be divided in the same unequal way? Such objections illustrate how difficult it is to get across the idea that if some share of resources is justly owed to a country, then it is (even before it has been actually transferred) as much that country's as it is now normally thought that what a country produces belongs to that country.

The answer that I give is that there are extreme circumstances in which the international community or some particular donor country would be justified in withholding resources owed as a matter of justice to some country. But these are exactly the same extreme conditions under which it would also be justifiable to refuse to pay debts to it or to freeze its assets overseas.

One could envisage a world in which there were indeed an international authority that allowed countries to keep only that income that would be justly distributed internally and used in approved, nonwasteful ways. Such a world would not be at all like ours, since it would accept no principle of national autonomy. It would be a world in which a presently nonexisting world society had inscribed on its banner: "From each according to his ability, to each according to his needs."

The alternative is a world in which the general presumption is of national autonomy, with countries being treated as units capable of determining the use of those resources to which they were justly entitled. This is the world that we now have, and the only modification in the status quo I am arguing for is a redefinition of what justly belongs to a country. It inevitably, as the price of autonomy, permits countries to use their resources in wasteful ways ("theirs," on my interpretation, being of course those in their own territories plus or minus transfers required by justice) and does not insist that a country that allows some to live in luxury while others have basic needs unfulfilled should lose income to which it is entitled as a matter of justice.

My point is that both of the models I have sketched are internally consistent. We could have a system in which there are no entitlements based on justice and in which, assuming that states are still the administrative intermediaries, funds are allocated for worthy purposes and cut off if they are misspent, just as in the United States the federal government cuts off funds to state and local governments that do not comply with various guidelines. Or we could have a world in which, once the demands of just distribution between countries are satisfied, we say that we have justice at the world level, and the question of domestic distribution and national priorities then becomes one for each country to decide for itself.

What is not consistent is to have a world in which those countries that are required by international justice to be donors live under the second system while those that are recipients live under the stern dispensation of the first. If the idea is going to be that countries should have their entitlements reduced if they are wasteful and fail in internal equity, then the obvious place to start is not with some poor country in sub-Saharan Africa or South Asia but with, say, a country that burns one ninth of the world's daily oil consumption on its roads alone and that, in spite of having a quarter of the world's GNP, is unable to provide for much of its population decent medical care, while a substantial proportion live in material conditions of abject squalor that (except for being more dirty and dangerous) recall the cities of Germany and Britain in the aftermath of World War II.

None of this, of course, denies the independent significance of humanity as a criterion in international morality. But we cannot sensibly talk about humanity unless we have a baseline set by justice. To talk about what I ought, as a matter of humanity, to do with what is mine makes no sense until we have established what is mine in the first place. If I have stolen what is rightfully somebody else's property, or if I have borrowed from him and refuse to repay the debt when it is due, and as a result he is destitute, it would be unbecoming on my part to dole out some part of the money that should belong to him, with various strings attached as to the way in which he should spend it, and then go around posing as a great humanitarian. That is, in my judgment, an exact description of the position in which the rich countries have currently placed themselves.

The need for humanitarian aid would be reduced in a world that had a basically just international distribution. It would be required still to meet special problems caused by crop failure owing to drought, destruction owing to floods and earthquakes, and similar losses resulting from other natural disasters. It would also, unhappily, continue to be required to cope with the massive refugee problems that periodically arise from political upheavals.

Beyond that, humanitarian aid in the form of food, technical assistance, or plain money is always a good thing, of course. How much the rich countries would be obliged to give depends first on the extent of redistribution we hold to be required by justice and, second, on the stringency that we assign to the obligation of humanity—how much sacrifice can be demanded to deal with what level of need.

As will be clear, this chapter is concerned only with a preliminary investigation of the principles relevant to an ethical appraisal of international distribution and redistribution. I must therefore leave any more precise statement of implications for future discussions—and not necessarily by me. Ultimately, if anything is to be done, it will require a widespread shift in ideas. Greater precision can be expected to develop *pari passu* with such a shift. I very much doubt the value of single-handed attempts to produce a blueprint in advance of that.

## NOTES

1. *Oxford English Dictionary*, sub. Humanity, 3b. In the light of the central example to be discussed below, it is interesting to note that the title of a society founded in England for the rescuing of drowning persons in 1774 was the Humane Society (*OED*, sub. Humane, 1c).

2. *Philosophy & Public Affairs* 1:229–43 (1972) [reprinted in *Global Ethics: Seminal Essays*, 1–14]. See, for a briefer and more recent statement of the same basic case, Peter Singer, *Practical Ethics* (Cambridge: Cambridge University Press, 1979), chapter 8, pp. 158–81.

3. Ibid., p. 231 [*Global Ethics: Seminal Essays,* 3].

4. Ibid.

5. Ibid.

6. Ibid.

7. Ibid. [*GESE,* 4].

8. C. D. Broad, "On the Function of False Hypotheses in Ethics," *International Journal of Ethics* 26:377–97, at 389–90 (1916).

9. John Passmore, "Civil Justice and Its Rivals," in Eugene Kamenka and Alice Erh-Soon Tay, *Justice* (London: Edward Arnold, 1979) pp. 25–49, at 47 [italics in original].

10. For a sustained argument along these lines, see T. D. Campbell, "Humanity before Justice," *British Journal of Political Science* 4:1–16 (1974).

11. Henry Sidgwick, *The Methods of Ethics* (London: Macmillan, 1907), p. 273.

12. Constantine V. Vaitsos, *Intercountry Income Distribution and Transnational Enterprises* (Oxford: Clarendon Press, 1974), esp. chapter 4.

13. See for an elaboration of these remarks "And Who Is My Neighbor?" *Yale L. J.* 88: 629–58 (1979).

14. Adam Smith expressed this view: "As a man doth, so it shall be done to him, and retaliation seems to be the great law which is dictated to us by nature. Beneficence and generosity we think due to the generous and beneficent. Those whose hearts never open to the feelings of humanity should, we think, be shut out in the same manner, from the affections of all their fellow-creatures, and be allowed to live in the midst of society, as in a great desert, where there is nobody to care for them, or to enquire after them." Adam Smith, *The Theory of Moral Sentiments* (Indianapolis: Liberty Classics, n.d.), p. 160.

15. Princeton, NJ: Princeton University Press, 1979. The part of the book in question was first published in substantially the same form as "Justice and International Relations," *Philosophy & Public Affairs* 4: 360-89 (1975) [reprinted herein 21–48].

16. *The Liberal Theory of Justice* (Oxford: Clarendon Press, 1973), chapter 12.

17. H. L. A. Hart, "Are There Any Natural Rights?" *Philosophical Review* 64: 175–91 (1955).

18. See my extended review in *Theory and Decision,* 12: 95–106 (1980).

19. Hillel Steiner, "The Natural Right to the Means of Production," *The Philosophical Quarterly* 27: 41–49, at 44–45 (1977). The reference to Nozick is to *Anarchy, State, and Utopia* (New York: Basic Books, 1974), p. 154.

20. Bruce A. Ackerman, *Social Justice in the Liberal State* (New Haven: Yale University Press, 1980), p. 38.

21. Oscar Schachter, *Sharing the World's Resources* (New York: Columbia University Press, 1977), p. 124, references n, 52, p. 159.

22. David Hume, *An Enquiry Concerning the Principles of Morals,* 3d ed. (Oxford: Clarendon Press, 1975), pp. 193–94.

23. Eleanor B. Steinberg and Joseph Y. Yager, eds., *New Means of Financing International Needs* (Washington, DC: Brookings Institution, 1978), chapter 3.

24. For a distinction stated in these terms see Ronald Dworkin, "The Original Position," *Chi. L. Rev.* 4: 500-33 (1973), reprinted in Norman Daniels, ed., *Reading Rawls* (Oxford: Basil Blackwell, 1975) pp. 16–53. The relevant discussion is on pp. 38–40 of this reprint.

25. *Political Argument* (London: Routledge and Kegan Paul, 1965), pp. 43–44.

# 8. JOSEPH H. CARENS

Carens draws on three contemporary approaches to political theory—the Rawlsian, the Nozickean, and the utilitarian—to construct arguments for open borders. He argues that all three theories converge upon the open borders position. This he maintains strengthens the case for open borders and reveals its roots in our deep commitment to respect all human beings as free and equal moral persons. In the final part of the essay he considers communitarian objections to his conclusion, especially those of Michael Walzer.

## Aliens and Citizens: The Case for Open Borders

*First published in* The Review of Politics *49: 2 (spring 1987): 251–73.*

Borders have guards and the guards have guns. This is an obvious fact of political life but one that is easily hidden from view—at least from the view of those of us who are citizens of affluent Western democracies. To Haitians in small, leaky boats confronted by armed Coast Guard cutters, to Salvadorans dying from heat and lack of air after being smuggled into the Arizona desert, to Guatemalans crawling through rat-infested sewer pipes from Mexico to California—to these people the borders, guards, and guns are all too apparent. What justifies the use of force against such people? Perhaps borders and guards can be justified as a way of keeping out criminals, subversives, or armed invaders. But most of those trying to get in are not like that. They are ordinary, peaceful people seeking only the opportunity to build decent, secure lives for themselves and their families. On what moral grounds can these sorts of people be kept out? What gives anyone the right to point guns at *them*?

To most people the answer to this question will seem obvious. The power to admit or exclude aliens is inherent in sovereignty and essential for any political community. Every state has the legal and moral right to exercise that power in pursuit of its own national interest, even if that means denying entry to peaceful, needy foreigners. States may choose to be generous in admitting immigrants, but they are under no obligation to do so.[1]

I want to challenge that view. In this essay I will argue that borders should generally be open and that people should normally be free to leave their country of origin and settle in another, subject only to the sorts of constraints that bind current citizens in their new country. The argument is strongest, I believe, when applied to the migration of people from Third World countries to those of the First World. Citizenship in Western liberal democracies is the modern equivalent of feudal privilege—an inherited status that greatly enhances one's life chances. Like feudal birthright privileges, restrictive citizenship is hard to justify when one thinks about it closely.

In developing this argument I will draw upon three contemporary approaches to political theory: first that of Robert Nozick; second that of John Rawls; third that of the utilitarians. Of the three, I find Rawls the most illuminating, and I will spend the most time on the arguments that flow from his theory. But I do not want to tie my case too closely to his particular formulations (which I will modify in any event). My strategy is to take advantage of three well-articulated theoretical approaches that many people find persuasive to construct a variety of arguments for (relatively) open borders. I will argue that all three approaches lead to the same basic conclusion: there is little justification for restricting immigration. Each of these theories begins with some kind of assumption about the equal moral worth of individuals. In one way or another, each treats the individual as prior to the community. These foundations provide little basis for drawing fundamental distinctions between citizens and aliens who seek to become citizens. The fact that all three theories converge upon the same basic result with regard to immigration despite their significant differences in other areas strengthens the case for open borders. In the final part of the essay I will consider communitarian objections to my argument, especially those of Michael Walzer, the best contemporary defender of the view I am challenging.

## ALIENS AND PROPERTY RIGHTS

One popular position on immigration goes something like this: "It's our country. We can let in or keep out whomever we want." This could be interpreted as a claim that the right to exclude aliens is based on property rights, perhaps collective or national property rights. Would this sort of claim receive support from theories in which property rights play a central role? I think not, because those theories emphasize *individual* property rights and the concept of collective or national property rights would undermine the individual rights that these theories wish to protect.

Consider Robert Nozick as a contemporary representative of the property rights tradition. Following Locke, Nozick assumes that individuals in the state of nature have rights, including the right to acquire and use property. All individuals have the same natural rights—that is the assumption about moral equality that underlies this tradition—although the exercise of those rights leads to material inequalities. The "inconveniences" of the state of nature justify the creation of a minimal state whose sole task is to protect people within a given territory against violations of their rights.[2]

Would this minimal state be justified in restricting immigration? Nozick never answers this question directly, but his argument at a number of points suggests not. According to Nozick the state has no right to do anything other than enforce the rights which individuals already enjoy in the state of nature. Citizenship gives rise to no distinctive claim. The state is obliged to protect the rights of citizens and noncitizens equally because it enjoys a de facto monopoly over the enforcement of rights within its territory. Individuals have the right to enter into voluntary exchanges with other individuals. They possess this right as individuals, not as citizens. The state may not interfere with such exchanges so long as they do not violate someone else's rights.[3]

Note what this implies for immigration. Suppose a farmer from the United States wanted to hire workers from Mexico. The government would have no right to prohibit him from doing this. To prevent the Mexicans from coming would violate the rights of both the American farmer and the Mexican workers to engage in voluntary transactions. Of course, American workers might be disadvantaged by this competition with foreign workers. But Nozick explicitly denies that anyone has a right to be protected against competitive disadvantage. (To count that sort of thing as a harm would undermine the foundations of *individual* property rights.) Even if the Mexicans did not have job offers from an American, a Nozickean government would have no grounds for preventing them from entering the country. So long as they were peaceful and did not steal, trespass on private property, or otherwise violate the rights of other individuals, their entry and their actions would be none of the state's business.

Does this mean that Nozick's theory provides no basis for the exclusion of aliens? Not exactly. It means rather that it provides no basis for the *state* to exclude aliens and no basis for individuals to exclude aliens that could not be used to exclude citizens as well. Poor aliens could not afford to live in affluent suburbs (except in the servants' quarters), but that would be true of poor citizens, too. Individual property owners could refuse to hire aliens, to rent them houses, to sell them food, and so on, but in a Nozickean world they could do the same things to their fellow citizens. In other words, individuals may do what they like with their own personal property. They may normally exclude whomever they want from land they own. But they have this right to exclude as individuals, not as members of a collective. They cannot prevent other individuals from acting differently (hiring aliens, renting them houses, etc.).[4]

Is there any room for collective action to restrict entry in Nozick's theory? In the final section of his book, Nozick draws a distinction between nations (or states) and small face-to-face communities. People may voluntarily construct small communities on principles quite different from the ones that govern the state so long as individuals are free to leave these communities. For example, people may choose to pool their property and to make collective decisions on the basis of majority rule. Nozick argues that this sort of community has a right to restrict membership to those whom it wishes to admit and to control entry to its land. But such a community may also redistribute its jointly held property as it chooses. This is not an option that Nozick (or any other property rights theorist) intends to grant to the state.[5]

This shows why the claim "It's our country. We can admit or exclude whomever we want" is ultimately incompatible with a property rights theory like Nozick's. Property cannot serve as a protection for individuals *against* the collective if property is collectively owned. If the notion of collective ownership is used to justify keeping aliens out, it opens the possibility of using the same notion to justify redistributing income or whatever else the majority decides. Nozick explicitly says that the land of a nation is not the collective property of its citizens. It follows that the control that the state can legitimately exercise over that land is limited to the enforcement of the rights of individual owners. Prohibiting people from entering a territory because they did not happen to be born there or otherwise gain the credentials of citizenship is no part of any state's legitimate mandate. The state has no right to restrict immigration.

## MIGRATION AND THE ORIGINAL POSITION

In contrast to Nozick, John Rawls provides a justification for an activist state with positive responsibilities for social welfare. Even so, the approach to immigration suggested by *A Theory of Justice* leaves little room for restrictions in principle. I say "suggested" because Rawls himself explicitly assumes a closed system in which questions about immigration could not arise. I will argue, however, that Rawls's approach is applicable to a broader context than the one he considers. In what follows I assume a general familiarity with Rawls's theory, briefly recalling the main points and then focusing on those issues that are relevant to my inquiry.

Rawls asks what principles people would choose to govern society if they had to choose from behind a "veil of ignorance," knowing nothing about their own personal situations (class, race, sex, natural talents, religious beliefs, individual goals and values, and so on). He argues that people in this original position would choose two principles. The first principle would guarantee equal liberty to all. The second would permit social and economic inequalities so long as they were to the advantage of the least well off (the difference principle) and attached to positions open to all under fair conditions of equal opportunity. People in the original position would give priority to the first principle, forbidding a reduction of basic liberties for the sake of economic gains.[6]

Rawls also draws a distinction between ideal and nonideal theory. In ideal theory one assumes that, even after the "veil of ignorance" is lifted, people will accept and generally abide by the principles chosen in the original position and that there are no historical obstacles to the realization of just institutions. In nonideal theory, one takes account of both historical obstacles and the unjust actions of others. Nonideal theory is thus more immediately relevant to practical problems, but ideal theory is more fundamental, establishing the ultimate goal of social reform and a basis for judging the relative importance of departures from the ideal (e.g., the priority of liberty).[7]

Like a number of other commentators, I want to claim that many of the reasons that make the original position useful in thinking about questions of justice within a given society also make it useful for thinking about justice across different societies.[8] Cases like migration and trade, where people interact across governmental boundaries, raise questions about whether the background conditions of the interactions are fair. Moreover, anyone who wants to be moral will feel obliged to justify the use of force against other human beings, whether they are members of the same society or not. In thinking about these matters we don't want to be biased by self-interested or partisan considerations, and we don't want existing injustices (if any) to warp our reflections. Moreover, we can take it as a basic presupposition that we should treat all human beings, not just members of our own society, as free and equal moral persons.[9]

The original position offers a strategy of moral reasoning that helps address these concerns. The purpose of the "veil of ignorance" is "to nullify the effects of specific contingencies which put men at odds" because natural and social contingencies are "arbitrary from a moral point of view" and therefore are factors which ought not to influence the choice of principles of justice.[10] Whether one is a citizen of a rich nation or a poor one, whether one is already a citizen of a particular state or an alien who wishes to become a citizen—this is the sort of specific contingency that could set people at odds. A fair procedure for choosing principles of justice must therefore exclude knowledge of these circumstances, just as it excludes knowledge of one's race or sex or social class. We should therefore take a global, not a national, view of the original position.

One objection to this global approach is that it ignores the extent to which Rawls's use of the original position and the "veil of ignorance" depends upon a particular understanding of moral personality that is characteristic of modern democratic societies but may not be shared by other societies.[11] Let us grant the objection and ask whether it really matters.

The understanding of moral personality in question is essentially the view that all people are free and equal moral persons. Even if this view of moral personality is not shared by people in other societies, it is not a view that applies only to people who share it. Many members of our own society do not share it, as illustrated by the recent demonstrations by white racists in Forsythe County, Georgia. We criticize the racists and reject their views but do not deprive them of their status as free and equal citizens because of their beliefs. Nor is our belief in moral equality limited to members of our own society. Indeed our commitment to civic equality is derived from our convictions about moral equality, not vice versa. So, whatever we think about the justice of borders and the limitations of the claims of aliens, our views must be compatible with a respect for all other human beings as moral persons.

A related objection emphasizes the "constructivist" nature of Rawls's theory, particularly in its later formulations.[12] The theory only makes sense, it is said, in a situation where people already share liberal-democratic values. But if we presuppose a context of shared values, what need have we for a "veil of ignorance"? Why not move directly from the shared values to an agreement on principles of justice and corresponding institutions? The "veil of ignorance" offers a way of thinking about principles of justice in a context where people have deep, unresolvable disagreements about matters of fundamental importance and yet still want to find a way to live together in peaceful cooperation on terms that are fair to all. That seems to be just as appropriate a context for considering the problem of worldwide justice as it is considering the problem of domestic justice.

To read Rawls's theory only as a constructive interpretation of existing social values is to undermine its potential as a constructive critique of those values. For example, racism has deep roots in American public culture, and in the not-too-distant past people like those in Forsythe County constituted a majority in the United States. If we think the racists are wrong and Rawls is right about our obligation to treat all members of our society as free and equal moral persons, it is surely not just because the public culture has changed and the racists are now in the minority. I gladly concede that I am using the original position in a way that Rawls himself does not intend, but I think that this extension is warranted by the nature of the questions I am addressing and the virtues of Rawls's approach as a general method of moral reasoning.

Let us therefore assume a global view of the original position. Those in the original position would be prevented by the "veil of ignorance" from knowing their place of birth or whether they were members of one particular society rather than another. They would presumably choose the same two principles of justice. (I will simply assume that Rawls's argument for the two principles is correct, though the point is disputed.) These principles would apply globally, and the next task would be to design institutions to implement the principles—still from the perspective of the original position. Would these institutions include sovereign states as they currently exist? In ideal theory, where we can assume away historical obstacles and the dangers of injustice, some of the reasons for defending the integrity of existing states disappear. But ideal theory does not require the elimination of all linguistic, cultural, and historical differences. Let us assume that a general case for decentralization of power to respect these sorts of factors would justify the existence of autonomous political communities comparable to modern states.[13] That does not mean that all the existing features of state sovereignty would be justified. State sovereignty would be (morally) constrained by the principles of justice. For example, no state could restrict religious freedom and inequalities among states would be restricted by an international difference principle.

What about freedom of movement among states? Would it be regarded as a basic liberty in a global system of equal liberties, or would states have the right to limit entry and exit? Even in an ideal world people might have powerful reasons to want to migrate from one state to another. Economic opportunities for particular individuals might vary greatly from one state to another even if economic inequalities among states were reduced by an international difference principle. One might fall in love with a citizen from another land, one might belong to a religion that has few followers in one's native land and many in another, one might seek cultural opportunities that are available only in another society. More generally, one has only to ask whether the right to migrate freely *within* a given society is an important liberty. The same sorts of considerations make migration across state boundaries important.[14]

Behind the "veil of ignorance," in considering possible restrictions on freedom, one adopts the perspective of the one who would be most disadvantaged by the restrictions, in this case the perspective of the alien who wants to immigrate. In the original position, then, one would insist that the right to migrate be included in the system of basic liberties for the same reasons that one would insist that the right to religious freedom be included: It might prove essential to one's plan of life. Once the "veil of ignorance" is lifted, of course, one might not make use of the right, but that is true of other rights and liberties as well. So, the basic agreement among those in the original position would be to permit no restrictions on migration (whether emigration or immigration).

There is one important qualification to this. According to Rawls, liberty may be restricted for the sake of liberty even in ideal theory and all liberties depend on the existence of public order and security.[15] (Let us call this the public order restriction.) Suppose that unrestricted immigration would lead to chaos and the breakdown of order. Then all would be worse off in terms of their basic liberties. Even adopting the perspective of the worst-off and recognizing the priority of liberty, those in the original position would endorse restrictions on immigration in such circumstances. This would be a case of restricting liberty for the sake of liberty and every individual would agree to such restrictions even though, once the "veil of ignorance" was lifted, one might find that it was one's own freedom to immigrate which had been curtailed.

Rawls warns against any attempt to use this sort of public order argument in an expansive fashion or as an excuse for restrictions on liberty undertaken for other reasons. The hypothetical possibility of a threat to public order is not enough. Restrictions would be justified only if there were a "reasonable expectation" that unlimited immigration would damage the public order and this expectation would have to be based on "evidence and ways of reasoning acceptable to all."[16] Moreover, restrictions would be justified only to the extent necessary to preserve public order. A need for some restrictions would not justify any level of restrictions whatsoever. Finally, the threat to public order posed by unlimited immigration could not be the product of antagonistic reactions (e.g., riots) from current citizens. This discussion takes place in the context of ideal theory and in this context it is assumed that people try to act justly. Rioting to prevent others from exercising legitimate freedoms would not be just. So, the threat to public order would have to be one that emerged as the unintended cumulative effect of individually just actions.

In ideal theory we face a world of just states with an international difference principle. Under such conditions, the likelihood of mass migrations threatening to the public order of any particular state seems small. So, there is little room for restrictions on immigration in ideal theory. But what about nonideal theory, where one takes into account both historical contingencies and the unjust actions of others?

In the nonideal, real world there are vast economic inequalities among nations (presumably much larger than would exist under an international difference principle). Moreover, people disagree about the nature of justice and often fail to live up to whatever principles they profess. Most states consider it necessary to protect themselves against the possibility of armed invasion or covert subversion. And many states deprive their own citizens of basic rights and liberties. How does all this affect what justice requires with regard to migration?

First, the conditions of the real world greatly strengthen the case for state sovereignty, especially in those states that have relatively just domestic institutions. National security is a crucial form of public order. So, states are clearly entitled to prevent the entry of people (whether armed invaders or subversives) whose goal is the overthrow of just institutions. On the other hand, the strictures against an expansive use of the public order argument also apply to claims about national security.

A related concern is the claim that immigrants from societies where liberal democratic values are weak or absent would pose a threat to the maintenance of a just public order. Again the distinction between reasonable expectations and hypothetical speculations is crucial. These sorts of arguments were used during the nineteenth century against Catholics and Jews from Europe and against all Asians and Africans. If we judge those arguments to have been proven wrong (not to say ignorant and bigoted) by history, we should be wary of resurrecting them in another guise.

A more realistic concern is the sheer size of the potential demand. If a rich country like the United States were simply to open its doors, the number of people from poor countries seeking to immigrate might truly be overwhelming, even if their goals and beliefs posed no threat to national security or liberal democratic values.[17] Under these conditions, it seems likely that some restrictions on immigration would be justified under the public order principle. But it is important to recall all the qualifications that apply to this. In particular, the need for some restriction would not justify any level of restriction whatsoever or restrictions for other reasons, but only that level of restriction essential to maintain public order. This would surely imply a much less restrictive policy than the one currently in force, which is shaped by so many other considerations besides the need to maintain public order.

Rawls asserts that the priority accorded to liberty normally holds under nonideal conditions as well. This suggests that, if there are restrictions on immigration for public order reasons, priority should be given to those seeking to immigrate because they have been denied basic liberties over those seeking to immigrate simply for economic opportunities. There is a further complication, however. The priority of liberty holds absolutely only in the long run. Under nonideal conditions it can sometimes be justifiable to restrict liberty for the sake of economic gains, if that will improve the position of the worst-off and speed the creation of conditions in which all will enjoy equal and full liberties. Would it be justifiable to restrict immigration for the sake of the worst-off?

We have to be wary of hypocritical uses of this sort of argument. If rich states are really concerned with the worst-off in poor states, they can presumably help more by transferring resources and reforming international economic institutions than by restricting immigration. Indeed, there is reason to suppose more open immigration would help some of the worst-off, not hurt them. At the least, those who immigrate presumably gain themselves and often send money back home as well.

Perhaps the ones who come are not the worst-off, however. It is plausible to suppose that the worst-off don't have the resources to leave. That is still no reason to keep others from coming unless their departure hurts those left behind. But let's suppose it does, as the brain-drain hypothesis suggests. If we assume some restrictions on immigration would be justified for public order reasons, this would suggest that we should give priority to the least skilled among potential immigrants because their departure would presumably have little or no harmful effect on those left behind. It might also suggest that compensation was due to poor countries when skilled people emigrate. But to say that we should actually try to keep people from emigrating (by denying them a place to go) because they represent a valuable resource to their country of origin would be a dramatic departure from the liberal tradition in general and from the specific priority that Rawls attaches to liberty even under nonideal conditions.[18]

Consider the implications of this analysis for some of the conventional arguments for restrictions on immigration. First, one could not justify restrictions on the grounds that those born in a given territory or born of parents who were citizens were more entitled to the benefits of citizenship than those born elsewhere or born of alien parents. Birthplace and parentage are natural contingencies that are "arbitrary from a moral point of view." One of the primary goals of the original position is to minimize the effects of such contingencies upon the distribution of social benefits. To assign citizenship on the basis of birth might be an acceptable procedure, but only if it did not preclude individuals from making different choices later when they reached maturity.

Second, one could not justify restrictions on the grounds that immigration would reduce the economic well-being of current citizens. That line of argument is drastically limited by two considerations: the perspective of the worst-off and the priority of liberty. In order to establish the current citizens' perspective as the relevant worst-off position, it would be necessary to show that immigration would reduce the economic well-being of current citizens below the level the potential immigrants would enjoy if they were not permitted to immigrate. But even if this could be established, it would not justify restrictions on immigration because of the priority of liberty. So, the economic concerns of current citizens are essentially rendered irrelevant.

Third, the effect of immigration on the particular culture and history of the society would not be a relevant moral consideration, so long as there was no threat to basic liberal democratic values. This conclusion is less apparent from what I have said so far, but it follows from what Rawls says in his discussion of perfectionism.[19] The principle of perfectionism would require social institutions to be arranged so as to maximize the achievement of human excellence in art, science, or culture regardless of the effect of such arrangements on equality and freedom. (For example, slavery in ancient Athens has sometimes been defended on the grounds that it was essential to Athenian cultural achievements.) One variant of this position might be the claim that restrictions on immigration would be necessary to preserve the unity and coherence of a culture (assuming that the culture was worth preserving). Rawls argues that in the original position no one would accept any perfectionist standard because no one would be willing to risk the possibility of being required to forgo some important right or freedom for the sake of an ideal that might prove irrelevant to one's own concerns. So, restrictions on immigration for the sake of preserving a distinctive culture would be ruled out.

In sum, nonideal theory provides more grounds for restricting immigration than ideal theory, but these grounds are severely limited. And ideal theory holds up the principle of free migration as an essential part of the just social order toward which we should strive.

## ALIENS IN THE CALCULUS

A utilitarian approach to the problem of immigration can take into account some of the concerns that the original position excludes but even utilitarianism does not provide much support for the sorts of restrictions on immigration that are common today. The fundamental principle of utilitarianism is "maximize utility," and the utilitarian commitment to moral equality is reflected in the assumption that everyone is to count for one and no one for more than one when utility is calculated. Of course, these broad formulations cover over deep disagreements among utilitarians. For example, how is "utility" to be defined? Is it subjective or objective? Is it a question of happiness or welfare as in classical utilitarianism or preferences or interests as in some more recent versions?[20]

However these questions are answered, any utilitarian approach would give more weight to some reasons for restricting immigration than Rawls's approach would. For example, if more immigration would hurt some citizens economically, that would count against a more open immigration policy in any utilitarian theory I am familiar with. But that would not settle the question of whether restrictions were justified, for other citizens might gain economically from more immigration and that would count in favor of a more open policy. More important, the economic effects of more immigration on noncitizens would also have to be considered. If we focus only on economic consequences, the best immigration policy from a utilitarian perspective would be the one that maximized overall economic gains. In this calculation, current citizens would enjoy no privileged position. The gains and losses of aliens would count just as much. Now the dominant view among both classical and neoclassical economists is that the free mobility of capital and labor is essential to the maximization of overall economic gains. But the free mobility of labor requires open borders. So, despite the fact that the economic costs to current citizens are morally relevant in the utilitarian framework, they would probably not be sufficient to justify restrictions.

Economic consequences are not the only ones that utilitarians consider. For example, if immigration would affect the existing culture or way of life in a society in ways that current citizens found undesirable, that would count against open immigration in many versions of utilitarianism. But not in all. Utilitarians disagree about whether all pleasures (or desires or interests) are to count or only some. For example, should a sadist's pleasure be given moral weight and balanced against his victim's pain or should that sort of pleasure be disregarded? What about racial prejudice? That is clearly relevant to the question of immigration. Should a white racist's unhappiness at the prospect of associating with people of color be counted in the calculus of utility as an argument in favor of racial exclusion as reflected, say, in the White Australia policy? What about the desire to preserve a distinctive local culture as a reason for restricting immigration? That is sometimes linked to racial prejudice but by no means always.

Different utilitarians will answer these sorts of questions in different ways. Some argue that only long-term, rational, or otherwise refined pleasures (or desires or interests) should count. Others insist that we should not look behind the raw data in making our calculations. Everyone's preferences should count, not merely the preferences someone else finds acceptable. I favor the former approach, a reconstructive or filtering approach to utility, but I won't try to defend that here. Even if one takes the raw data approach, which seems to leave more room for reasons to restrict immigration, the final outcome is still likely to favor much more open immigration than is common today. Whatever the method of calculation, the concerns of aliens must be counted, too. Under current conditions, when so many millions of poor and oppressed people feel they have so much to gain from migration to the advanced industrial states, it seems hard to believe that a utilitarian calculus that took the interests of aliens seriously would justify significantly greater limits on immigration than the ones entailed by the public order restriction implied by the Rawlsian approach.

## THE COMMUNITARIAN CHALLENGE

The three theories I have discussed conflict with one another on many important issues but not (deeply) on the question of immigration. Each leads on its own terms to a position far more favorable to open immigration than the conventional moral view. It is true that, in terms of numbers, even a public order restriction might exclude millions of potential immigrants given the size of the potential demand. Nevertheless, if the arguments I have developed here were accepted, they would require a radical transformation both of current immigration policies and of conventional moral thinking about the question of immigration.

Some may feel that I have wrenched these theories out of context. Each is rooted in the liberal tradition. Liberalism, it might be said, emerged with the modern state and presupposes it. Liberal theories were not designed to deal with questions about aliens. They assumed the context of the sovereign state. As a historical observation this has some truth, but it is not clear why it should have normative force. The same wrenching out of context complaint could as reasonably have been leveled at those who first constructed liberal arguments for the extension of full citizenship to women and members of the working class. Liberal theories also assumed the right to exclude them. Liberal theories focus attention on the need to justify the use of force by the state. Questions about the exclusion of aliens arise naturally from that context. Liberal principles (like most principles) have implications that the original advocates of the principles did not entirely foresee. That is part of what makes social criticism possible.

Others may think that my analysis merely illustrates the inadequacy of liberal theory, especially its inability to give sufficient weight to the value of community.[21] That indictment of liberal theory may or may not be correct, but my findings about immigration rest primarily on assumptions that I think no defensible moral theory can reject: that our social institutions and public policies must respect all human beings as moral persons and that this respect entails recognition, in some form, of the freedom and equality of every human being. Perhaps some other approach can accept these assumptions while still making room for greater restrictions on immigration. To test that possibility, I will consider the views of the theorist who has done the most to translate the communitarian critique into a positive alternative vision: Michael Walzer.

Unlike Rawls and the others, Walzer treats the question of membership as central to his theory of justice, and he comes to the opposite conclusion about immigration from the one that I have defended:

> Across a considerable range of the decisions that are made, states are simply free to take strangers in (or not).[22]

Walzer differs from the other theorists I have considered not only in his conclusions but also in his basic approach. He eschews the search for universal principles and is concerned instead with "the particularism of history, culture, and membership."[23] He thinks that questions of distributive justice should be addressed not from behind a "veil of ignorance" but from the perspective of membership in a political community in which people share a common culture and a common understanding about justice.

I cannot do full justice here to Walzer's rich and subtle discussion of the problem of membership, but I can draw attention to the main points of his argument and to some of the areas of our disagreement. Walzer's central claim is that exclusion is justified by the right of communities to self-determination. The right to exclude is constrained in three important ways, however. First, we have an obligation to provide aid to others who are in dire need, even if we have no established bonds with them, provided that we can do so without excessive cost to ourselves. So, we may be obliged to admit some needy strangers or at least to provide them with some of our resources and perhaps even territory. Second, once people are admitted as residents and participants in the economy, they must be entitled to acquire citizenship, if they wish. Here the constraint flows from principles of justice, not mutual aid. The notion of permanent "guest workers" conflicts with the underlying rationale of communal self-determination that justified the right to exclude in the first place. Third, new states or governments may not expel existing inhabitants even if they are regarded as alien by most of the rest of the population.[24]

In developing his argument, Walzer compares the idea of open states with our experience of neighborhoods as a form of open association.[25] But in thinking about what open states would be like, we have a better comparison at hand. We can draw upon our experience of cities, provinces, or states in the American sense. These are familiar political communities whose borders are open. Unlike neighborhoods and like countries, they are formally organized communities with boundaries, distinctions between citizens and noncitizens, and elected officials who are expected to pursue policies that benefit the members of the community that elected them. They often have distinctive cultures and ways of life. Think of the differences between New York City and Waycross, Georgia, or between California and Kansas. These sorts of differences are often much greater than the differences across nation-states. Seattle has more in common with Vancouver than it does with many American communities. But cities and provinces and American states cannot restrict immigration (from other parts of the country). So, these cases call into question Walzer's claim that distinctiveness depends on the possibility of formal closure. What makes for distinctiveness and what erodes it is much more complex than political control of admissions.

This does not mean that control over admissions is unimportant. Often local communities would like to restrict immigration. The people of California wanted to keep out poor Oklahomans during the Depression. Now the people of Oregon would like to keep out the Californians. Internal migrations can be substantial. They can transform the character of communities. (Think of the migrations from the rural South to the urban North.) They can place strains on the local economy and make it difficult to maintain locally funded social programs. Despite all this, we do not think these political communities should be able to control their borders. The right to free migration takes priority.

Why should this be so? Is it just a choice that we make as a larger community (i.e., the nation-state) to restrict the self-determination of local communities in this way? Could we legitimately permit them to exclude? Not easily. No liberal state restricts internal mobility. Those states that do restrict internal mobility are criticized for denying basic human freedoms. If freedom of movement within the state is so important that it overrides the claims of local political communities, on what grounds can we restrict freedom of movement across states? This requires a stronger case for the *moral* distinctiveness of the nation-state as a form of community than Walzer's discussion of neighborhoods provides.

Walzer also draws an analogy between states and clubs.[26] Clubs may generally admit or exclude whomever they want, although any particular decision may be criticized through an appeal to the character of the club and the shared understandings of its members. So, too, with states. This analogy ignores the familiar distinction between public and private, a distinction that Walzer makes use of elsewhere.[27] There is a deep tension between the right of freedom of association and the right to equal treatment. One way to address this tension is to say that in the private sphere freedom of association prevails and in the public sphere equal treatment does. You can pick your friends on the basis of whatever criteria you wish, but in selecting people for offices you must treat all candidates fairly. Drawing a line between public and private is often problematic, but it is clear that clubs are normally at one end of the scale and states at the other. So, the fact that private clubs may admit or exclude whomever they choose says nothing about the appropriate admission standards for states. When the state acts it must treat individuals equally.

Against this, one may object that the requirement of equal treatment applies fully only to those who are already *members* of the community. That is accurate as a description of practice, but the question is why it should be so. At one time, the requirement of equal treatment did not extend fully to various groups (workers, blacks, women). On the whole, the history of liberalism reflects a tendency to expand both the definition of the public sphere and the requirements of equal treatment. In the United States today, for example, in contrast to earlier times, both public agencies and private corporations may not legally exclude women simply because they are women (although private clubs still may). A white shopkeeper may no longer exclude blacks from his store (although he may exclude them from his home). I think these recent developments, like the earlier extension of the franchise, reflect something fundamental about the inner logic of liberalism.[28] The extension of the right to immigrate reflects the same logic: equal treatment of individuals in the public sphere.

As I noted at the beginning of this section, Walzer asserts that the political community is constrained by principles of justice from admitting permanent guest workers without giving them the opportunity to become citizens. There is some ambiguity about whether this claim is intended to apply to all political communities or only to ones like ours. If states have a right to self-determination, broadly conceived, they must have a right to choose political forms and political practices different from those of liberal democracies. That presumably includes the right to establish categories of second-class citizens (or, at least, temporary guest workers) and also the right to determine other aspects of admissions policy in accordance with their own principles.[29] But if the question is what *our* society (or one with the same basic values) ought to do, then the matter is different both for guest workers and for other aliens. It is right to assert that *our* society ought to admit guest workers to full citizenship. Anything else is incompatible with our liberal democratic principles. But so is a restrictive policy on immigration.

Any approach like Walzer's that seeks its ground in the tradition and culture of *our* community must confront, as a methodological paradox, the fact that liberalism is a central part of our culture. The enormous intellectual popularity of Rawls and Nozick and the enduring influence of utilitarianism attest to their ability to communicate contemporary understandings and shared meanings in a language that has legitimacy and power in our culture. These theories would not make such sense to a Buddhist monk in medieval Japan. But their individualistic assumptions and their language of universal, ahistorical reason makes sense to us because of *our* tradition, *our* culture, *our* community. For people in a different moral tradition, one that assumed fundamental moral differences between those inside the society and those outside, restrictions on immigration might be easy to justify. Those who are *other* simply might not count, or at least not count as much. But we cannot dismiss aliens on the ground that they are other, because *we* are the products of a liberal culture.

The point goes still deeper. To take *our* community as a starting point is to take a community that expresses its moral views in terms of universal principles. Walzer's own arguments reflect this. When he asserts that states may not expel existing inhabitants whom the majority or the new government regards as alien, he is making a claim about what is right and wrong for *any* state, not just our own or one that shares our basic values. He develops the argument by drawing on Hobbes. That is an argument from a particular tradition, one that may not be shared by new states that want to expel some of their inhabitants. Nonetheless, Walzer makes a universal claim (and one I consider correct). He makes the same sort of argument when he insists that states may not legitimately restrict emigration.[30] This applies to all political communities, not just those that share our understanding of the relation of individual and collective.

Recognition of the particularity of our own culture should not prevent us from making these sorts of claims. We should not try to force others to accept our views, and we should be ready to listen to others and learn from them. But respect for the diversity of communities does not require us to abandon all claims about what other states ought to do. If my arguments are correct, the general case for open borders is deeply rooted in the fundamental values of our tradition. No moral argument will seem acceptable to *us* if it directly challenges the assumption of the equal moral worth of all individuals. If restrictions on immigration are to be justified, they have to be based on arguments that respect that principle. Walzer's theory has many virtues that I have not explored here, but it does not supply an adequate argument for the state's right to exclude.

## CONCLUSION

Free migration may not be immediately achievable, but it is a goal toward which we should strive. And we have an obligation to open our borders much more fully than we do now. The current restrictions on immigration in Western democracies—even in the most open ones like Canada and the United States—are not justifiable. Like feudal barriers to mobility, they protect unjust privilege.

Does it follow that there is *no* room for distinctions between aliens and citizens, no theory of citizenship, no boundaries for the community? Not at all. To say that membership is open to all who wish to join is not to say that there is no distinction between members and nonmembers. Those who choose to cooperate together in the state have special rights and obligations not shared by noncitizens. Respecting the particular choices and commitments that individuals make flows naturally from a commitment to the idea of equal moral worth. (Indeed, consent as a justification for political obligation is least problematic in the case of immigrants.) What is *not* readily compatible with the idea of equal moral worth is the exclusion of those who want to join. If people want to sign the social contract, they should be permitted to do so.

Open borders would threaten the distinctive character of different political communities only because we assume that so many people would move if they could. If the migrants were few, it would not matter. A few immigrants could always be absorbed without changing the character of the community. And, as Walzer observes, most human beings do not love to move.[31] They normally feel attached to their native land and to the particular language, culture, and community in which they grew up and in which they feel at home. They seek to move only when life is very difficult where they are. Their concerns are rarely frivolous. So, it is right to weigh the claims of those who want to move against the claims of those who want to preserve the community as it is. And if we don't unfairly tip the scales, the case for exclusion will rarely triumph.

People live in communities with bonds and bounds, but these may be of different kinds. In a liberal society, the bonds and bounds should be compatible with liberal principles. Open immigration would change the character of the community but it would not leave the community without any character. It might destroy old ways of life, highly valued by some, but it would make possible new ways of life, highly valued by others. The whites in Forsythe County who want to keep out blacks are trying to preserve a way of life that is valuable to them. To deny such communities the right to exclude does limit their ability to shape their future character and destiny, but it does not utterly destroy their capacity for self-determination. Many aspects of communal life remain potentially subject to collective control. Moreover, constraining the kinds of choices that people and communities may make is what principles of justice are for. They set limits on what people seeking to abide by these principles may do. To commit ourselves to open borders would not be to abandon the idea of communal character but to reaffirm it. It would be an affirmation of the liberal character of the community and of its commitment to principles of justice.

# NOTES

This paper was first written for an APSA seminar on citizenship directed by Nan Keohane. Subsequent versions were presented to seminars at the University of Chicago, the Institute for Advanced Study, and Columbia University. I would like to thank the members of these groups for their comments. In addition I would like to thank the following individuals for helpful comments on one of the many drafts: Sot Barber, Charles Beitz, Michael Doyle, Amy Gutmann, Christine Korsgaard, Charles Miller, Donald Moon, Jennifer Nedelsky, Thomas Pogge, Peter Schuck, Rogers Smith, Dennis Thompson, and Michael Walzer.

1. The conventional assumption is captured by the Select Commission on Immigration and Refugee Policy: "Our policy—while providing opportunity to a portion of the world's population—must be guided by the basic national interests of the people of the United States." From *U.S. Immigration Policy and the National Interest: The Final Report and Recommendations of the Select Commission on Immigration and Refugee Policy to the Congress and the President of the United States* (1 March 1981). The best theoretical defense of the conventional assumption (with some modifications) is Michael Walzer, *Spheres of Justice* (New York: Basic Books, 1983), pp. 31–63 [based on his essay "The Distribution of Membership," first published in *Boundaries: National Autonomy and Its Limits*, ed. Peter G. Brown and Henry Shue (Totowa: Rowman & Littlefield, 1981), 1–35, reprinted herein145–77]. A few theorists have challenged the conventional assumption. See Bruce Ackerman, *Social Justice in the Liberal State* (New Haven: Yale University Press, 1980), pp. 89–95; Judith Lichtenberg, "National Boundaries and Moral Boundaries: A Cosmopolitan View" in *Boundaries: National Autonomy and Its Limits*, ed. Peter G. Brown and Henry Shue (Totowa, NJ: Rowman & Littlefield, 1981), pp. 79–100; and Roger Nett, "The Civil Right We Are Not Ready For: The Right of Free Movement of People on the Face of the Earth," *Ethics* 81 (April 1971): 212–27. Frederick Whelan has also explored these issues in two interesting unpublished papers.

2. Robert Nozick, *Anarchy, State, and Utopia* (New York: Basic Books, 1974), pp. 10–25, 88–119.

3. Ibid., pp. 108–113. Citizens, in Nozick's view, are simply consumers purchasing impartial, efficient protection of preexisting natural rights. Nozick uses the terms "citizen," "client," and "customer" interchangeably.

4. Nozick interprets the Lockean proviso as implying that property rights in land may not so restrict an individual's freedom of movement as to deny him effective liberty. This further limits the possibility of excluding aliens. See p. 55.

5. Ibid., pp. 320–23.

6. John Rawls, *A Theory of Justice* (Cambridge, MA: Harvard University Press, 1971), pp. 60–65, 136–42, 243–48.

7. Ibid., pp. 8–9, 244–48.

8. The argument for a global view of the original position has been developed most fully in Charles Beitz, *Political Theory and International Relations* (Princeton, NJ: Princeton University Press, 1979), pp. 125–76, especially 129–36 and 143–53. [Part 3 of Beitz's book, in which the referenced pages are, is based on his essay "Justice and International Relations," first published in *Philosophy and Public Affairs* 4: 4 (summer 1975): 360–389, reprinted herein 21–48, cf. esp. 23-26 and 32-40.] For earlier criticisms of Rawls along the same lines, see Brian Barry, *The Liberal Theory of Justice* (Oxford: Clarendon Press, 1973), pp. 128–33 and Thomas M. Scanlon, "Rawls's Theory of Justice," *University of Pennsylvania Law Review* 121, no. 5 (May 1973): 1066–67. For more recent discussions, see David A. J. Richards, "International Distributive Justice," in *Ethics, Economics, and the Law*, eds. J. Roland Pennock and John Chapman (New York: New York University Press, 1982), pp. 275–99 and Charles Beitz, "Cosmopolitan Ideals and National Sentiments," *Journal of Philosophy* 80, no. 10 (October 1983): 591–600 [reprinted in *Global Ethics: Seminal Essays* 107–17]. None of these discussions fully explores the implications of a global view of the original position for the issue of immigration, although the recent essay by Beitz touches on the topic.

9. Respecting others as free and equal moral persons does not imply that one cannot distinguish friends from strangers or citizens from aliens. See the conclusion for an elaboration.

10. Rawls, *Justice*, pp. 136, 72.

11. John Rawls, "Kantian Constructivism in Moral Theory," *The Journal of Philosophy* 77, no. 9 (September 1980): 515-72.

12. Ibid. See also John Rawls, "Justice as Fairness: Political not Metaphysical," *Philosophy and Public Affairs* 14 (summer 1985): 223–51.

13. Compare Beitz, *Political Theory*, p. 183.

14. For more on the comparison of mobility within a country and mobility across countries, see Joseph H. Carens, "Migration and the Welfare State," in *Democracy and the Welfare State*, ed. Amy Gutmann (Princeton: Princeton University Press, 1987).

15. Rawls, *Justice*, pp. 212–13.

16. Ibid., p. 213.

17. For statistics on current and projected levels of immigration to the U.S., see Michael S. Teitelbaum, "Right Versus Right: Immigration and Refugee Policy in the United States," *Foreign Affairs* 59 (1980): 21–59.

18. For the deep roots of the right to emigrate in the liberal tradition, see Frederick Whelan, "Citizenship and the Right to Leave," *American Political Science Review* 75, no. 3 (September 1981): 636–53.

19. Rawls, *Justice*, pp. 325–32.

20. For recent discussions of utilitarianism, see Richard Brandt, *A Theory of the Good and the Right* (Oxford: Oxford University Press, 1979); Peter Singer, *Practical Ethics* (Cambridge: Cambridge University Press, 1979); R. M. Hare,

*Moral Thinking* (Oxford: Oxford University Press, 1981); and Amartya Sen and Bernard Williams, eds., *Utilitarianism and Beyond* (Cambridge: Cambridge University Press, 1982).

21. For recent communitarian critiques of liberalism, see Alasdair MacIntyre, *After Virtue* (Notre Dame: Notre Dame University Press, 1981), and Michael Sandel, *Liberalism and the Limits of Justice* (New York: Cambridge University Press, 1982). For a critique of the critics, see Amy Gutmann, "Communitarian Critics of Liberalism," *Philosophy and Public Affairs* 14 (Summer 1985): 308–22.

22. Walzer, *Spheres*, p. 61 [cf. herein p. 174].

23. Ibid., p. 5.

24. Ibid., pp. 33, 45–48, 55–61, 42–44 [cf. herein pp. 147, 159-62, 168-74, 156-58].

25. Ibid., pp. 36–39 [cf. herein 149-53].

26. Ibid., pp. 39–41 [cf. herein 153-56].

27. Ibid., pp. 129–64.

28. I am not arguing that the changes in treatment of women, blacks, and workers were *brought about* by the inner logic of liberalism. These changes resulted from changes in social conditions and from political struggles, including ideological struggles in which arguments about the implications of liberal principles played some role, though not necessarily a decisive one. But from a philosophical perspective, it is important to understand where principles lead, even if one does not assume that people's actions in the world will always be governed by the principles they espouse.

29. Compare Walzer's claim that the caste system would be just if accepted by the villages affected (ibid., pp. 313–15).

30. Ibid., pp. 39–40 [cf. herein pp. 153-55].

31. Ibid., p. 38 [cf. herein p. 152].

# 9. DAVID MILLER

Miller's paper begins with the contrast between universalism and particularism in ethics. The special obligations that we normally acknowledge to our fellow countrymen cannot be accounted for in universalist terms. Miller defends national loyalties against the charge that they necessarily depend on beliefs that cannot withstand rational reflection. He contends that national loyalties are in no worse shape than other attachments, and that it counts in their favor that they can support effective practices of distributive justice. This latter point, he maintains, should commend national loyalties even to universalists.

## The Ethical Significance of Nationality

*First published in* Ethics *98: 4 (July 1988): 647–62. Reprinted with permission from The University of Chicago Press. © 1988 by The University of Chicago. All rights reserved.*

### I

My object in this paper is to defend the view that national boundaries may be ethically significant. The duties we owe to our compatriots may be more extensive than the duties we owe to strangers, simply because they are compatriots. On the face of it, such a view is hardly outlandish. On the contrary almost all of us, including our leaders, behave as though it were self-evidently true. We do not, for instance, hesitate to introduce welfare measures on the grounds that their benefits will be enjoyed only by Americans, or Britons, or whomever. Why, then, is it worth defending this view at length? Precisely because there is a powerful thrust in the ethical theories that are most prominent in our culture toward what I shall call universalism: namely, the view that the subject matter of ethics is persons considered merely as such, independent of all local connections and relations; and that the fundamental questions of ethics can be posed in some such form as: What duties do I owe to my fellow human beings? What rights do they have against me?[1] Here the basic principles are worked out without reference to social boundaries. Boundaries may come into the picture at some later point—for instance, as a convenient way of parceling out basic duties—but they themselves never have fundamental ethical significance. The fact that we do normally attribute deeper significance to boundaries is to be explained as some sort of moral error—for instance, as the intrusion of irrational emotional attachments into an arena that ought to be governed by impartial reason.

Although my aim is to show that conationals can rightly make special claims on us, I do not want to suggest that these claims exhaust the ethical universe. There may indeed be duties that we owe to our fellow human beings in the abstract. The point is rather that, once we see why national boundaries make a difference, we shall be in a position to see what space they leave for duties that transcend these limits. Thus the argument is not intended to be a defense of narrow-minded and exclusive nationalism; nor for that matter is it intended to underwrite all national identities regardless of their content. It is directed rather against a naive form of internationalism that is grounded on an inadequate view of ethics and that appears to offer a simple solution to the problem of international obligations but does so at the cost of losing touch with the way we actually think about such issues.

Before embarking on a critique of universalism, I need to explain briefly the idea of nationality that I am counterposing to it. National boundaries, it hardly needs saying, are not the same as borders between states. A state may include more than one national grouping; conversely, people sharing a common national identity may be found living under the auspices of two or more states. How, then, are nations to be individuated? It is fairly clear that no objective criterion, such as language, race, or religion, will be adequate to mark all national distinctions, even though these criteria may enter into particular national identities.[2] Thus nationality is essentially a subjective phenomenon, constituted by the shared beliefs of a set of people: a belief that each belongs together with the rest; that this association is neither transitory nor merely instrumental but stems from a long history of living together that (it is hoped and expected) will continue into the future; that the community is marked off from other communities by its members' distinctive characteristics; and that each member recognizes a loyalty to the community, expressed in a willingness to sacrifice personal gain to advance its interests. We should add, as a final element, that the nation should enjoy some degree of political autonomy. The classic nationalist belief, of course, was that every nation should have its own sovereign state, but I can see no reason for making it part of the definition of a nation that its members should be nationalists in this strong sense. On the other hand, a social group that had no political aspirations at all would surely be counted as an ethnic group rather than as a nation. (I shall say more about the relation between ethnicity and nationality below.)

One feature of this definition deserves underlining. Whether a nation exists depends on whether its members have the appropriate beliefs; it is no part of the definition that the beliefs should in fact be true. This makes the question about the ethical significance of nationality a particularly pointed one. If national allegiances can be based on false beliefs, how is it possible for a purportedly rational institution such as morality to accommodate them?

## II

The view I have called ethical universalism may at first sight seem simply to *be* the ethical point of view. Surely it is definitive of ethics that all of its particular injunctions should be derived from universal, rationally grounded principles?[3] Against this, I want to suggest that such a way of looking at ethics embodies a specific and potentially controversial view of moral agency. The moral subject is seen as an abstract individual, possessed of the general powers and capacities of human beings—especially the power of reason—but not fundamentally committed to any particular persons, groups, practices, institutions, and so forth. In arriving at his most basic principles, the subject can disengage himself from commitments of this latter sort and see himself simply as one member of a moral universe made up of symmetrically placed persons, each of whom likewise possesses only general human capacities. A view of this kind is presented, for example, in Rawls's notion of the original position, in which subjects are asked to choose principles under conditions in which they are deprived of all particular knowledge of their identities, existing commitments, personal values, and so on.[4] Having adopted such an abstract point of view, the subject asks: What duties is it rational for each of us to acknowledge toward all the rest (or, conversely, what rights can each of us claim against all the rest)? Once the basic duties have been established, it is then possible to work out derivative duties for people placed in particular circumstances. Broadly speaking, there are two ways in which this can be done. First, the basic duties can be distributed in such a way that particular persons become responsible for carrying out specific aspects of those duties. To illustrate, suppose that we endorse the basic principle that the needs of children who are not able to look after themselves should be provided for. Feeding in some familiar facts, we can easily derive the subsidiary principle that the primary responsibility for discharging this duty should fall on the parents of each child. Second, the basic rights and duties can empower individuals to create particular duties by voluntary acts—promises, contracts, and so forth. These powers are justified by general considerations about human beings advanced at the basic level.

Most theories of a universalist type do therefore make room for individuals' particular duties, responsibilities, and rights—the duties of parents, colleagues, and so on—but these are never regarded as fundamental commitments. The moral self is defined by its rational capacities, so only general principles can have this basic status; other commitments are contingent and subject to revision if, for example, new facts come to light which demand this. In contrast, consider a second view of ethical agency in which the subject is seen as already deeply embedded in social relationships. Here the subject is partly defined by its relationships and the various rights, obligations, and so forth that go along with these, so these commitments themselves form a basic element of personality. To divest oneself of such commitments would be, in one important sense, to change one's identity. On this view, the agent can still aspire to rationality, but the rationality in question cannot be that of abstract principle. Rather it consists in the capacity to reflect on existing commitments, jettisoning some and reaffirming others, depending on how they stand up to scrutiny. How might such rational appraisal proceed?

First, each commitment can be examined singly to see whether it stands up to the facts of the case, so far as these can be ascertained. For instance, I may have pledged my loyalty to a group of people, but it turns out on closer inspection that the group does not really exist as a group, in the sense that no one, except myself, takes his or her commitment seriously. My commitment is based on false assumptions and, once these are brought to light, it must simply evaporate. (In a similar way, it is possible to *discover* commitments by reflecting on what is already the case.)

Second, one can investigate the coherence of one's existing set of commitments—that is, the extent to which the understanding of personal identity provided by each is consistent with that provided by the others. For instance someone committed both to being a caring father and to being a ruthless tycoon might come to believe that this involved an incoherence—not in the relatively superficial sense that the two commitments might require incompatible actions on certain occasions,[5] but in the deeper sense that he simply could not be both kinds of person at the same time; that the qualities needed to be a good father just could not be reconciled with those needed to be a tycoon. Having reached this point, he must then decide which of his two commitments really is the more fundamental.

These remarks are made to deflect the charge that ethical particularism is simply an irrationalist outlook which elevates our existing prejudices to the status of objective truths. Plainly it does embody a less sweeping notion of rationality than universalism, that tends to identify rationality with the adoption of the impersonal point of view. But it is not so clear that this is finally a drawback.[6] An ethical theory must presumably have practical ambitions in the sense that it aspires to be the theory which people will use to guide their activities. If the theory embodies a view of the subject that is far removed from people's actual experience of agency, what claims can it make on them? Why should they accept its interpretation of rationality? Put slightly differently, the issue is one of ethical motivation. Impartial reason dictates that I should perform such-and-such an action: But why should that give *me* a reason to perform it? These issues have been pursued in far greater depth than is possible here, for instance by Michael Sandel in his critique of the Rawlsian theory of the self[7] and by Bernard Williams in his displacement of "morality"—a term he reserves for universalist theories of obligation—from the central position in ethics.[8] My aim has been not so much to defend particularism as to indicate why it is at least a plausible view, and to show how it differs from universalism.

# III

I now want to show—what may already be intuitively clear—that if nationality is going to have an ethical significance, it must be from a particularist perspective. I do not at this stage attempt to demonstrate that nationality *does* have such a significance. My concern is only to investigate what we need to assume for this even to be a possibility. Universalism can generate surrogates for national attachments but not the genuine article. The main options for the universalist are outlined in Robert Goodin's contribution to this symposium [herein 255–84], so I will simply draw on that discussion to make the point.

If we seek to demonstrate, from universalist premises, that people owe special duties to their compatriots, there are broadly two ways in which we can attempt to do so. First, we can interpret the significance of social boundaries, in contractual or quasi-contractual terms (this approach is likely to recommend itself to Kantians). As Goodin puts it, we are to think of nations as "mutual benefit societies" in which our special obligations to fellow countrymen are derived from our common participation in a practice from which all may expect to benefit—perhaps along the lines of the principle of fair play defended by Hart and Rawls.[9] But this approach is fraught with difficulties. We have first to show that the scope of the mutual benefit practice coincides with existing social boundaries, rather than running within them or across them.[10] Then we have to show that mutual benefit logic accurately models the obligations we do in fact acknowledge to fellow countrymen.[11] Beyond these, there is a further difficulty that is particularly salient for my purposes. Obligations of this kind are clearly tied to established practices. If there currently exists a practice toward which all participants contribute in some way, and in return receive certain benefits, then as a beneficiary I have an obligation to contribute. But in the absence of the practice I clearly have no obligation of this kind, even if the practice would be beneficial to me and others if it did exist (and therefore *ought* to exist). This suggests that, if the contractual argument works at all (leaving aside the two earlier difficulties), it will be targeted on states rather than nations. States, with their codified systems of rules, *might* qualify as mutual benefit societies. Nationality, however, is not so much a cooperative practice as the *grounding* for such a practice. It is because we already share an attachment to our compatriots that we support the setting up of mutual benefit practices and the like. The ethical significance of nationality is not obliterated if, for some reason, the practices in question do not exist.[12] So if we assume that nationality *does* have an ethical significance, it will not be captured in these terms.

An alternative approach is contained in Goodin's suggestion that we see social boundaries as a convenient way of allocating responsibilities that themselves derive from general duties.[13] This in general is how utilitarians may be expected to approach the boundaries issue—essentially as a solution to a coordination problem. This approach, too, has difficulties that occur at different levels. At ground level we face the fact that boundaries enclose sets of people whose mean standards of living vary very greatly, so if the general duty from which the special responsibilities derive is something like a duty to promote welfare (to meet needs, to relieve suffering, etc.), it would seem odd to put the well-off in charge of the well-off and the badly-off in charge of the badly-off. To put this another way, simple coordination rules like "Help the person standing next to you" make sense when, as far as we know, each person is equally in need of help and each is equally able to provide it. But this is hardly an accurate representation of the international scene. De facto, of course, British officials have been "given responsibility" for the welfare of Britons, and so forth, but the question must be whether this is the mode of assigning responsibilities that the general principle demands.

This leads naturally to the second level of difficulty, which is similar to that facing the contractual account. It may be possible to find considerable room for conventions in a consequentialist ethical theory on the grounds that it often matters much more that *someone* should discharge a duty than that some particular person should. But this line of thought leads us toward states as the institutions that currently assign most of the relevant responsibilities. Nationality as such has no place in this picture. If we move away from existing conventions toward those conventions that we can show to be optimal from the point of view of our underlying goal (e.g., the promotion of welfare), along the lines suggested in the last paragraph, it is again difficult to see where nationality can get a foothold. The consideration which, for instance, would justify us in assigning primary responsibility for children to their parents (essentially that parents are very likely to be in the best position to know what the child's interests are) can hardly be extended to nations, composed as they are of people who are mainly strangers to one another, with widely varying patterns of life.

I conclude that the most plausible accounts of special duties from a universalist perspective will give no weight to nationality. The universalist may of course reply, "So much the worse for nationality." I want instead to take the claims of nationality seriously, which therefore means examining them according to particularist criteria. At the end I shall throw some crumbs to comfort the universalist.

## IV

It is perhaps not a surprise that when particularists offer examples to rebut the claims of universalism, they usually choose very specific attachments to make their point, in the expectation that these will carry most weight with their readers. Forster's remark, "If I had to choose between betraying my country and betraying my friend, I hope I should have the guts to betray my country," seems now to represent the conventional wisdom. But does this merely signify a failure of nerve on the part of the particularist? If his aim is to replace the abstract individual as ethical subject with the embedded individual, then it might seem that he should give pride of place, among constitutive attachments, to those that are *not* voluntarily acquired and therefore not a matter of choice. This would leave family, ethnic group, and nation as prime candidates, and of these the family seems, as our century advances, to be taking on more and more the characteristics of a voluntary institution. Why, then, is there so much coyness about holding up national allegiances as precisely the kind of attachments that make up the substance of ethical life, properly understood? Part of the reason, obviously, is the twentieth-century experience of rampant nationalism, an experience distasteful to liberals and the Left alike. But behind this lies a feeling that "the nation" is itself a suspect category and therefore not a fitting object of loyalty. One way of expressing this doubt is to say that nations are, in Benedict Anderson's phrase, "imagined communities."[14] Those who acknowledge national attachments believe themselves to be bound to their compatriots by ties of community, but these ties are in an important sense fictitious. Thus, it is claimed, national allegiances cannot withstand rational reflection, even of the more limited kind recognized by particularists. Such reflection would reveal the imaginary quality of the community in question and, in so doing, destroy it as a possible object of allegiance.

In one sense it is clear that nations cannot be genuine communities. If a community is a face-to-face group based on personal acquaintance and direct practices of mutual aid, then it is obvious enough that nations cannot qualify. But this understanding of community is a very narrow one. Normally we would speak of community in cases where a group is held together by common recognition, a shared culture, and mutually acknowledged obligations, even where the group is spatially dispersed and its members are not all linked by personal acquaintance. It is in this sense that we speak of ethnic groups as constituting communities ("the Jewish community," for instance), and this seems a justifiable extension of the concept.

However, this only serves to sharpen the problem. For it is characteristic of nations that their identities are formed not through spontaneous processes of ethnic self-definition but primarily according to the exigencies of power—the demands of states seeking to assure themselves of the loyalty of their subjects. Nationality is to a greater or lesser degree a manufactured item. This is brought out in Anthony Smith's recent study of the formation of nations out of older ethnic communities.[15] Smith distinguishes broadly between two cases. In the first, the nation is based on a single dominant ethnic group, and the culture of that group is imposed more or less successfully on ethnic minorities falling within the territorial boundaries of the emergent nation. In the second, a dominant culture is lacking and has to be forged in order to create a nation out of a series of disparate ethnic groups. In both cases, but especially the second, nation-building is a work of invention, in particular the invention of a common national past. As Smith puts it, "If the nation is to become a 'political community' on the Western territorial and civic model, it must, paradoxically, seek to create those myths of descent, those historical memories and that common culture which form the missing elements of their ethnic make-up, along with a mutual solidarity. It must differentiate itself from its closest neighbors, distinguish its culture from theirs, and emphasize the historic kinship of its constituent *ethnie* and their common ties of ideological affinity. This is done by creating or elaborating an 'ideological' myth of origins and descent."[16]

Let us take it, then, that nations require histories that are to a greater or lesser degree "mythical" (as judged by the standards of impartial scholarship) and that those stories are not only needed at the time during which a national identity is first being created, but they also pass into that identity itself—so that in order to understand what it means to be French or Greek, one has to accept (some version of)[17] the common story. Do these facts imply that national loyalties cannot withstand rational reflection?

To answer this question we need to make a distinction between beliefs that are constitutive of social relationships and background beliefs that support those constitutive beliefs. To illustrate the former, consider the example of friendship. For A and B to be friends, it must minimally be true that each is willing to put himself out for the other. Suppose that A believes that B would put himself out, but in fact the belief is false. B is merely a fair-weather friend: Should an occasion arise on which he is called on to sacrifice something for A's sake, he will certainly renege. A's loyalties to B are then drained of their value, since the reciprocal attitudes that constitute friendship are not in place. An indicator of this is that A, if he is rational, must want to be informed if indeed it is the case that his "friendship" is not being reciprocated.[18]

But now consider a different case. Suppose there is a family, call them the Smiths, who exemplify all the best features of that institution: There is love, mutual support, and a wide range of activities performed in common. If asked what it is that makes these attitudes to one another appropriate, the Smiths would point, among other things, to the fact that members of the family are biologically related. Suppose now that owing to some dreadful mixup at the hospital, one of the Smith children is in fact not a Smith. We can then say that the family relationship is backed up by a false belief: The love and concern they feel for one another is supported by a supposed genetic connection which in one case fails to obtain. But a falsity of this kind does not mean that the attachment of each member to the family is itself valueless. The *constitutive* beliefs are all in order; each does genuinely identify with the family unit, and his beliefs about the others' attitudes are correct. In contrast to the first case, it would not be rational in these circumstances to want to have the false belief brought to light.[19]

If we apply this distinction to the case of nations, the imagined national past, which as we have seen appears to be an essential element in the process of nation-building, must count as a background (rather than constitutive) belief. It does of course matter (given my definition in Section I above) that nations should see their identities as extending over time, but the constitutive belief is only that there should be some national past. The particular story a nation tells itself about its past is a background belief. It is important that the story should be generally believed—or to put the point more precisely, that there should be substantial convergence in the versions of the story that are believed[20]—but not that it should be historically accurate.[21] Indeed, since the story is told for the purpose of self-definition, and since the nation's self-definition bears on the goals that its members will try to pursue in the future, we should expect a dynamic nation, actively engaged in critical debate on its common purposes, regularly to reinterpret the past as well.

But there may be doubts whether the distinction I have invoked can do all the work that it is needed to do. For even if we can successfully interpret the national past as a background belief, we may not be able to do the same with the national present. Nations need a common view about what they now are; a view about what distinguishes membership of this nation from membership of others. To use an old-fashioned phrase, they need some conception of "national character." But, it might be urged, these beliefs are also to a large extent mythical, in the sense that they attribute a spurious homogeneity to a set of people who, if looked at objectively, vary enormously in values, lifestyles, cultural attributes, and so on. And this observation destroys a *constitutive* belief, because it is constitutive of national identity that members of a nation should have characteristics in common that make it appropriate for them to be lumped together politically rather than parceled out in some other way. Take away national character and all we are left with is de facto boundaries between states.

To rehearse the most persuasive version of this objection, the real bases of social identity are ethnic groups defined by their shared inheritance of strong cultural traits. Nationalities are heterogeneous populations, *masquerading* as ethnic groups, which often in practice means that the dominant ethnic group has its cultural norms paraded as the national culture, with other groups being ignored and by implication disparaged.

As a description of existing national practice, this criticism obviously has much force. But we need to ask to what extent it is essential to the very idea of nationality that it should trespass in this way on ethnicity. The question could be posed in this form: Can we separate nationality from ethnicity without collapsing the former into mere adherence to a set of political institutions? Nationality must be something more than de facto citizenship. It must amount to a common identity that *grounds* citizenship. Can it be this while still being less substantial than ethnic affiliation?

To ask this question is to ask whether there can be a public culture that is shared among groups of people with differing private cultures. How tenable is such a public/private distinction? Some elements of culture seem to fall naturally on one or other side of this dividing line. Political beliefs—beliefs, say, in social equality or in toleration—fall into the public realm. Styles of dress, tastes in food, and forms of music fall into the private realm. Among the more difficult cases are likely to be language and religion. Language is obviously frequently used to designate ethnicity; at the same time it can hardly be considered irrelevant to nationality, since national identity needs linguistic expression (in speeches, histories, and so forth) and the form of the expression, on most theories of language, modifies what is expressed. One need not accept the strong Herder line on the centrality of language to nationality to see that a nation made up of ethnic groups none of which is willing to have its language relegated to the private realm is in difficulties.[22] The problems posed by religion are less sweeping, but in practice many nations surround important occasions (investitures, state funerals, memorials to war dead) with religious ceremony, and the ceremony must draw on some tradition or other. Limited ecumenical gestures are possible: Catholics can be invited to participate in Protestant rites (and vice versa) without much difficulty, but it would be hard to envisage this offer being extended to, say, Buddhists.

It is therefore almost inevitable that there will be areas in which nationality *does* trespass on ethnicity and the fostering of national identity will require the curtailment of certain aspects of ethnic identity in the interests of creating and maintaining a common public culture.[23] The extent of the trespass will depend on the particular national identity in question. To the extent, for instance, to which national rituals can be given secular trappings, there need be no intrusion on the religious element in ethnic self-definition. Equally, some ethnic identities are less vulnerable to intrusion than others. If a group can define itself entirely by, say, descent and private social practices (a group like Italian-Americans, e.g.) there is no reason why ethnic identity and national identity cannot peacefully coexist, one nesting inside the other. So the size of the problem depends on empirical facts. But we cannot in general hope that it will disappear entirely. Either national identity is to a degree fraudulent because it supposes a cultural homogeneity that is denied by the existence of ethnic divisions, or it is genuine, but at the expense of overriding lesser identities, which, so it is argued, are more authentic because they arise in a less artificial way.

# V

How might we respond to this critique of nationality? There are broadly two strategies. One remains within a particularist framework and tries to defend national identities from within—tries, that is, to defend the nation as an object of attachment in cases where this loyalty would conflict with other (especially ethnic) loyalties. The other looks at the issue in universalist terms and tries to show why, on impartialist criteria, it is a good thing for people to have such attachments. These strategies are not incompatible, though particularists will of course view the second as an irrelevance. I shall offer brief sketches of both.

From a particularist perspective, the first move is to show that the nation as an object of allegiance is not necessarily in much worse shape than other possible objects. Taking it for granted, in other words, that it is valuable for individuals to form attachments to various groups and institutions, we go on to challenge the view that there is something especially inappropriate in regarding nationality in this way. In particular, we may challenge the assumption that ethnicity is a more genuine form of allegiance than nationality. What makes this assumption plausible is that it is often fairly easy to see how national identities are being created and manipulated in the interests of those who hold (or aspire to hold) power in particular states. But ethnic identities, too, are far more plastic than they usually appear to be to those who define themselves by these identities. If we look historically at the ways in which specific ethnic groups have adapted their self-definitions and criteria of inclusion to advance their economic interests or social status,[24] we will see that ethnic identity is often as "fictitious" as national identity, in the sense that the self-understanding of an ethnic group relies on an interpretation of the past that is not borne out by the facts. Since, moreover, ethnicity is *defined* by descent, this revelation is liable to be more corrosive than the equivalent revelations about the national past. The point, then, is that ethnic identities tend to adapt spontaneously, in response to the economic or social needs of group members at any moment, whereas national identities tend to be manipulated consciously: This makes the artificiality of national identities more visible, but it is not at all clear that it makes national identities any less eligible as objects of loyalty.

Moving on to the offensive, it can be said in favor of nationality that the nation is potentially a self-sufficient object of allegiance and therefore one that is subject to rational control. If national aspirations are fulfilled, and the nation gains political autonomy, then it has the chance to determine its own destiny—subject, of course, to the activities of other members of the system of states. Some nations are just not viable, either for internal or for external reasons; but where nationality works, so to speak, members of the nation can exercise at the collective level the equivalent of autonomy at the individual level; that is, they can shape their future (including their own future character) by conscious decision, on the basis of a self-understanding informed by a common past.[25] Ethnic groups, having no aspirations to political autonomy, can hold out no such promise. They are at the mercy of nations, and whether a particular ethnic identity remains viable—whether one can maintain it without sacrificing other commitments to an intolerable degree—depends on the contingencies of national politics. That is not an argument for abandoning ethnicity in favor of nationality, but for harmonizing the two: It is an argument for having national allegiances that promise to protect your ethnic ties.[26]

Let me stress that this is not intended as an argument *for* national loyalties, in the sense of an argument that might appeal to someone starting out ethically with a clean slate. In particularist terms there can be no such argument: Crudely speaking, either one has loyalties or one does not (this is too crude, because as I suggested earlier, one may be involved in social relationships that demand loyalty, but initially one may not grasp this fact; so there is room for persuasion). The argument is directed toward someone who feels the pull of nationality but thinks he has good reason to reject that pull; specifically, someone who is willing to entertain particularist commitments but believes that there is something fishy about nationality. To this person I have tried to present the nation as potentially a worthy object of allegiance, though without giving an a priori guarantee that an acceptable national identity will always be available.

## VI

What can be said for nationality from a universalist perspective? Since I have already argued that universalist arguments for limited obligation will not converge on nationality, the answer might seem to be "nothing." However there are forms of universalism that may claim to avoid this conclusion. One is the generalized analogue of what Bernard Williams has nicely labeled "Government House utilitarianism."[27] This is the view that only a select minority are capable of guiding their ethical behavior by universalist criteria; the remainder—the natives, as it were—need a localized set of rules that they do not attempt to derive from universal principles. Williams introduces this view in order to deride it, and we should follow him. A more appealing view looks for reasons *holding for every agent* for not applying universalist criteria directly to one's choice of action. A position of this kind requires that whatever has basic ethical value can in general only be created as a by-product of activities aimed overtly in a different direction. Philip Pettit, for example, has presented such a consequentialist case for acknowledging various specific loyalties.[28] The argument, essentially, is that the security of expectation that these loyalties bring—a consequentialist value—depends on the agents involved *not* taking up a calculating stance when deciding how to act. To make this stick, we would have to show how it is possible for agents to maintain a universalist conception of basic value while regulating their actual behavior by particularist standards (such as loyalties to friends and to groups). Does the universalist standard have practical force, and if so how are agents to avoid consulting it when deciding how to act? Or, to put the point the other way round, can loyalties be genuinely maintained if their ultimate justification (for the agent, not merely for an impartial spectator) is couched in universalist terms? What sort of moral psychology would make this possible? Suppose, though, that these doubts could be resolved and a Pettit-type position maintained. What could be said specifically in favor of nationality as a focus of loyalty?

The answer will depend on which universalist criteria we have in mind. I want to focus here on a particular principle of distributive justice, the principle of distribution according to need. There are two important respects in which this principle depends for its implementation on identifying a relevant community. First, since the principle is comparative in form—it specifies how people are to be treated relative to one another[29]—it requires that its field of application be identified. We have to know *which* people are to have their needs considered. Second, we must also know what is to count as a need. As soon as we move beyond indisputable biological needs, a social element enters the definition. A person's needs will be whatever they must have in order to enjoy a minimally decent existence in *this* society with its particular pattern of life. This is the truth in Michael Walzer's remark that "the idea of distributive justice presupposes a bounded world within which distribution takes place: a group of people committed to dividing, exchanging, and sharing social goods, first of all among themselves."[30] However, we have still to determine what the scope of this "bounded world" should be. There is nothing strictly incoherent in seeking to extend its range to cover the whole globe. Nonetheless, such an extension would be wildly implausible. We do not yet have a global community in the sense that is relevant to justice as distribution according to need. There is no consensus that the needs of other human beings considered merely as such make demands of justice on me, nor is there sufficient agreement about what is to count as a need. It is therefore unrealistic to suppose that the choice lies between distributive justice worldwide and distributive justice within national societies; the realistic choice is between distributive justice of the latter sort, and distributive justice within much smaller units—families, religious communities, and so forth.

The universalist case for nationality, therefore, is that it creates communities with the widest feasible membership, and therefore with the greatest scope for redistribution in favor of the needy. Smaller units would be hampered by their limited resource base; wider units, although advantageous for the reverse reason, would be unable to generate a distributive consensus. Backhanded testimony to the truth of this proposition can be obtained from those classical liberals who have been opposed to distributive justice, and by extension to nationality, as the basis for the state. This was Acton's argument for a multinational state,[31] and the same thought fuels Hayek's anxiety that liberal ideals are currently being threatened by "the inseparable forces of socialism and nationalism," which themselves represent a recrudescence of "tribal sentiments" wholly inappropriate to the "Great Society."[32] The liberal objection to nationality, then, is that it may create a consensus for redistribution at a level that allows redistributive ideals to be implemented politically rather than merely by voluntary transfers.

We may still be tempted to reply: If distributive justice can function only within communities with predefined memberships, so much the worse for distributive justice. Our concern should be with the sick and the starving regardless of membership and regardless of how we conceptualize our obligations to them. The question this raises is whether we should think of ethical concern as a commodity in limited supply, such that if we intensify our concern for our fellow countrymen, we diminish our concern for those outside our borders. I have no space here to tackle this question properly, but it is worth saying that the picture of ethics implied in it is far from self-evident. Indeed a very different picture is intuitively more plausible: So long as different constituencies do not impose conflicting demands on our ethical capacities, a strengthening of commitment to a smaller group is likely to increase our commitment to wider constituencies. Empirically it does not seem that those most committed to distributive justice at home are in consequence less inclined to support foreign aid.

Let me stress in conclusion that I have not attempted here to derive national allegiances from universalist standards. The argument in Section III still stands: If we begin from universalist criteria, we shall not end up with nationality as the optimal basis for special obligations. The point rather is that if we start out with selves already heavily laden with particularist commitments, including national loyalties, we may be able to rationalize those commitments from a universalist perspective. Whether we should *seek* to do so is another matter, and it depends on how successfully we can resist the pull of a universalism which, as I remarked at the outset, is so prominent a feature of contemporary ethical culture.

## NOTES

My thanks are due to the members of the Workshop on Duties Beyond Borders, ECPR Joint Sessions and Workshops, Amsterdam, 10–15 April 1987, for their helpful comments on an earlier draft of this paper.

1. Since the paper hinges on the contrast between univeralism and particularism in ethics, and since, as many now think, the terms "moral" and "morality" tend to bias our thinking in a universalist direction, I try wherever possible to use "ethics" and "ethical" as comprehensive and neutral terms for the phenomena under discussion.

2. See B. Barry, "Self-Government Revisited," in *The Nature of Political Theory*, eds. D. Miller and L. Siedentop (Oxford: Clarendon Press, 1983).

3. A view advanced, e.g., in R. M. Hare, *Moral Thinking* (Oxford: Clarendon Press, 1981).

4. J. Rawls, *A Theory of Justice* (Cambridge, MA: Harvard University Press, 1971), chapter 3.

5. Anyone whose ethical outlook embraces a number of distinct commitments must be prepared to make judgments of priority when the demands of these commitments clash (e.g., whether to put friends or family first in a particular case). But such conflicts do not show that the commitments themselves are mutually incoherent. What I am envisaging in the text are commitments that draw upon incompatible qualities of character, so that someone trying to embrace both would experience a crisis of identity, not merely a problem of practical choice.

6. See the fuller discussion in A. MacIntyre, *Is Patriotism a Virtue?* (Lawrence: University of Kansas, Department of Philosophy, 1984) [reprinted in *Global Ethics: Seminal Essays*, 119–38], sections 3-4 [*GESE* 125–36].

7. M. Sandel, *Liberalism and the Limits of Justice* (Cambridge: Cambridge University Press, 1982).

8. B. Williams, *Ethics and the Limits of Philosophy* (London: Fontana, 1985).

9. R. Goodin, "What Is So Special about Our Fellow Countrymen?" in *Ethics*, 98 (1988): 663–86 [reprinted herein 255–84, at 266–69], section 4; H. L. A. Hart, "Are There any Natural Rights?" in *Political Philosophy*, ed. A. Quinton (Oxford: Oxford University Press, 1967); Rawls, sections 18, 52.

10. For an attempt to derive international obligations in this way, see C. Beitz, *Political Theory and International Relations* (Princeton, NJ: Princeton University Press, 1979) part 3, chapter 3. [Part 3 of Beitz's book is based on his essay "Justice and International Relations," first published in *Philosophy and Public Affairs* 4: 4 (summer 1975): 360–89, reprinted herein 21–48.] For criticism, see B. Barry, "Humanity and Justice in Global Perspective," in *NOMOS XXIV: Ethics, Economics, and the Law*, ed. J. R. Pennock and J. W. Chapman (New York: New York University Press, 1982) [reprinted herein 179–209].

11. See Goodin, section 4 [herein 266–69].

12. I leave aside here the difficult question whether attachments that have no practical expression can survive indefinitely. Certainly there seems to be a feedback mechanism whereby attachments motivate practices of mutual aid that in turn strengthen feelings of attachment.

13. Goodin, section 5 [herein 269–75].

14. B. Anderson, *Imagined Communities: Reflections on the Origin and Spread of Nationalism* (London: Verso, 1983). Anderson draws particular attention to the importance of the printed word in allowing dispersed bodies of people to think of themselves as belonging to a single community.

15. A. D. Smith, *The Ethnic Origins of Nations* (Oxford: Blackwell, 1986).

16. Ibid., p. 147.

17. Very often political disputes within a nation will surface as disputes about the precise character of the national past—see for instance the intense competition between Whig and Tory accounts of English history in eighteenth-century Britain. But the competing accounts will recognizably be different versions of the same general story with many basic facts not in dispute.

18. If A resists the passing on of this information, then the emotion he feels for B is not friendship but love, which (proverbially) is blind.

19. Some may think that it is always rational to divest yourself of irrational beliefs, but this is a superficial view. Here we are on Jon Elster territory. See, e.g., his discussion of "decisions to believe" in J. Elster, *Ulysses and the Sirens* (Cambridge: Cambridge University Press, 1979), section 2.3. The essential point is that there may be beliefs that it is valuable for a person to have in the light of his underlying goals, in which case it is rational for him to set up

mechanisms that ensure that he has them (and, if necessary, protect the beliefs from later rational scrutiny).

20. See n. 17 above.

21. Historical accuracy is not important from the point of view of constituting the nation. In a wider perspective, it may make a good deal of difference how far removed the national myths are from historical truth. If the distance is great, this may have serious repercussions for scholarly research and intellectual toleration generally.

22. Herder's view was that nationality required the perpetuation of a distinct language in every nation. See *Herder on Social and Political Culture*, ed. F. M. Barnard (Cambridge: Cambridge University Press, 1969).

23. I have explored this further in "Socialism and Toleration," in *Justifying Toleration: Conceptual and Historical Perspectives*, ed. S. Mendus (Cambridge: Cambridge University Press 1988).

24. See D. L. Horowitz, "Ethnic Identity" in *Ethnicity: Theory and Experience*, eds. N. Glazer and D. P. Moynihan (Cambridge, MA: Harvard University Press, 1975).

25. I hope it is clear that appealing to national identity in political debate is very different from endorsing the policies pursued at any time by the ruling authority. A patriot can be a radical critic of existing policy (and even, at some level, of existing institutions). This point is well made in MacIntyre, section 4 [*GESE* 129-36].

26. There are of course cases in which harmonization is impossible, since the available national identity contains elements that are directly hostile to the ethnic group in question—the situation of Jews in Nazi Germany, for instance. Here the only option is to formulate an alternative nationality.

27. Williams, pp. 108–10.

28. P. Pettit, "Social Holism and Moral Theory," *Proceedings of the Aristotelian Society* 86 (1985–86): 173–97; P. Pettit and G. Brennan, "Restrictive Consequentialism," *Australasian Journal of Philosophy* 64 (1986): 438–55.

29. For amplification of this point, see my "Social Justice and the Principle of Need," in *The Frontiers of Political Theory*, ed. M. Freeman and D. Robertson (Brighton: Harvester, 1980).

30. M. Walzer, *Spheres of Justice* (Oxford: Martin Robertson, 1983), p. 31 [Chapter 2 of Walzer's book is based on his essay "The Distribution of Membership," first published in *Boundaries: National Autonomy and Its Limits*, ed. Peter G. Brown and Henry Shue (Totowa: Rowman & Littlefield, 1981), 1-35, reprinted herein 145–77, at 145.]

31. See Barry, "Self-Government Revisited," p. 131.

32. F. A. Hayek, *The Mirage of Social Justice*, vol. 2 of *Law, Legislation and Liberty* (London: Routledge and Kegan Paul, 1976), pp. 133–34.

# 10. ROBERT E. GOODIN

Goodin argues that we all have general duties to all persons, but that these duties may be effectively fulfilled through a system of special responsibilities toward compatriots. When such a system works well, everyone's general duties to the members of a country are fulfilled by this country's citizens and government. They take full responsibility in their own country in exchange for others being assigned full responsibility in their respective countries. When such a system fails, however, when a country's citizens and government are unable or unwilling to discharge the special domestic responsibility assigned to them, then, Goodin argues, the general duty devolves back upon everyone.

## What Is So Special about Our Fellow Countrymen?

*First published in* Ethics *98: 4 (July 1988): 663–86. Reprinted with permission from The University of Chicago Press. © 1988 by The University of Chicago. All rights reserved.*

There are some "general duties" that we have toward other people, merely because they are people. Over and above those, there are also some "special duties" that we have toward particular individuals because they stand in some special relation to us. Among those are standardly supposed to be special duties toward our families, our friends, our pupils, our patients. Also among them are standardly supposed to be special duties toward our fellow countrymen.

Where those special duties come from and how they fit with the rest of morality is a moot point. I shall say little about such foundational issues, at least at the outset. In my view, the best way of exploring foundations is by examining carefully the edifice built upon them.

The bit of the edifice that I find particularly revealing is this: When reflecting upon what "special treatment" is due to those who stand in any of these special relations to us, ordinarily we imagine that to be especially *good* treatment. Close inspection of the case of compatriots reveals that that is not completely true, however. At least in some respects, we are obliged to be more scrupulous—not less—in our treatment of nonnationals than we are in our treatment of our own compatriots.[1]

This in itself is a politically important result. It shows that at least some of our general duties to those beyond our borders are at least sometimes more compelling, morally speaking, than at least some of our special duties to our fellow citizens.

This finding has the further effect of forcing us to reconsider the bases of our special duties to compatriots, with yet further political consequences. Morally, what ultimately matters is not nationality per se. It is instead some further feature that is only contingently and imperfectly associated with shared nationality. This further feature may sometimes be found among foreigners as well. When it is, we would have duties toward those foreigners that are similar in their form, their basis, and perhaps even their strength to the duties that we ordinarily acknowledge toward our fellow countrymen.

## I. THE PARTICULARIST'S CHALLENGE

### A

Modern moral philosophy has long been insistently universalistic. That is not to say that it enjoins identical performances, regardless of divergent circumstances. Of course universal laws play themselves out in different ways in different venues and demand different things from differently placed agents. But while their particular applications might vary, the ultimate moral principles, their form and content, has long been regarded as essentially invariant across people. The same basic precepts apply to everyone, everywhere, the same.

A corollary of this universality is impartiality.[2] It has long been supposed that moral principles—and therefore moral agents—must, at root, treat everyone the same. Of course, here again, basic principles that are perfectly impartial can (indeed, usually will) play themselves out in particular applications in such a way as to allow (or even to require) us to treat different people differently. But the ultimate principles of morality must not themselves play favorites.

On this much, at least utilitarians and Kantians—the great contending tribes of modern moral philosophy—can agree. Everyone counts for one, no one for more than one, in the Benthamite calculus. While as an upshot of those calculations some people might gain and others lose, the calculations themselves are perfectly impartial. So too with Kant's Categorical Imperative. Treating people as ends in themselves, and respecting the rationality embodied in others, may require us to do different things to, for, or with different people. But that is not a manifestation of any partiality between different people or their various projects. It is, instead, a manifestation of our impartial respect for each and every one of them.

Furthermore, this respect for universality and impartiality is no mere quirk of currently fashionable moral doctrines. Arguably, at least, those are defining features of morality itself. That is to say, they arguably must be embodied in any moral code in order for it to count as a moral code at all.

## B

Despite this strong attachment to canons of universality and impartiality, we all nonetheless ordinarily acknowledge various special duties. These are different in content and form from the general duties that universalistic, impartial moralities would most obviously generate for us. Whereas our general duties tell us how we should treat anyone, and are hence the same toward everyone, special duties vary from person to person. In contrast to the universality of the general moral law, some people have special duties that other people do not. In contrast to the impartiality of the general moral law, we all have special duties to some people that we do not have to others.[3]

Special duties, in short, bind particular people to particular other people. How this particularism of special duties fits with the universality and impartiality of the general moral law is problematical. Some say that it points to a whole other branch of the moral law, not captured by any of the standard canons. Others, Kantians and utilitarians among them, say that it is derivative in some way or another from more general moral laws. Yet others say that this particularism marks the limits of our psychological capacities for living up to the harsh standards that the general moral law sets for us.[4]

Be all these foundational questions as they may, it is not hard to find intuitively compelling examples of special duties that we would all acknowledge. At the level of preposterous examples so favored among philosophers, consider this case. Suppose your house is on fire. Suppose two people are trapped in the fire, and you will clearly have time to rescue only one before the roof collapses, killing the other. One of those trapped is a great public benefactor who was visiting you. The other is your own mother. Which should you rescue?

This is a story told originally by an impartialist, William Godwin. Being a particularly blunt proto-utilitarian, he had no trouble plunking for the impartialist position: "What magic is there in the pronoun 'my' that should justify us in overturning the decisions of impartial truth?"[5] Nowadays, however, it is a story told more often against impartialists. Few, then or now, have found themselves able to accept the impartialist conclusion with quite such equanimity as Godwin. Many regard the example as a reductio ad absurdum of the impartialist position. And even those who want to stick up for the impartialist side are obliged to concede that impartialists have a case to answer here.[6]

But the debate is not confined to crazy cases like that one. In real life, just as surely as in moral fantasies, we find ourselves involved in special relations of all sorts with other people. And just as we intuitively feel that we should save our own mothers rather than Archbishop Fenelon in Godwin's example, so too do we intuitively feel we should show favoritism of some sort to all those other people likewise. The "mere enumeration" of people linked to us in this way is relatively uncontentious and has changed little from Sidgwick's day to Parfit's. Included in both their lists are family, friends, benefactors, clients, and coworkers, and—especially important, in the present context—compatriots.[7]

Intuitively, we suppose that, on account of those special relations between us, we owe all of those people special treatment of some sort or another: special "kindnesses," "services," or "sacrifices"; "we believe that we ought to try to give them certain kinds of benefit."[8] According to Parfit, "Common-Sense Morality largely consists in such obligations"; and, within commonsense morality, those obligations are particularly strong ones, capable of overriding (at least at the margins) our general duties to aid strangers.[9]

## C

Here, I do not propose to focus (initially, at least) upon the precise strength of those duties. Rather, I want to direct attention to their general tendency. Notice that there is a presumption, running through all those standard discussions of special duties, that the special treatment due to those who are linked to us by some special relation is especially *good* treatment. We are said to be obliged to do more for those people than for unrelated others in an effort to spare them harm or to bring them benefits. To those who stand in some special relation to us, we are said to owe special "kindnesses," "services," or "sacrifices."

That assumption seems to me unwarranted. Agreed, special relations do sometimes permit (and sometimes even require) us to treat those specially related to us better than we need to, absent such a link. Other times, however, special relations permit (and perhaps even sometimes require) us to treat those thus linked to us worse than we would be obliged to treat them, absent such a link.[10] Exploring how that is so, and why, sheds light upon the true nature and strength of special duties. It also, not incidentally, limits the claims for exclusive special treatment that can be entertained under that heading.

## II. THE CASE OF COMPATRIOTS

When discussing what special claims compatriots, in particular, have against us, it is ordinarily assumed that we owe more to our fellow countrymen and less to foreigners. The standard presumption is that "compatriots take priority" over foreigners, "at least in the case of duties to aid"; "the state in determining what use shall be made of its own moneys, may legitimately consult the welfare of its own citizens rather than that of aliens."[11] Thus it makes a salutary start to my analysis to recall that, at least with respect to certain sorts of duties, we must be more scrupulous—not less—in our treatment of foreigners.

In the discussion that follows, "we" will be understood to mean "our community, through its sovereign representatives." In discussing what "we" may and may not do to people, I shall require some rough-and-ready guide to what our settled moral principles actually are. For these purposes, I shall have recourse to established principles of our legal codes: Though the correspondence is obviously less than perfect, presumably the latter at least constitute a rough approximation to the former. Public international law will be taken as indicative of what we may do to foreigners, domestic public law as indicative of what we may do to our compatriots. In both cases, the emphasis will be upon customary higher law rather than upon merely stipulative codes (treaties, statutes, etc.).[12]

Consider, then, all these ways in which we must treat foreigners in general better than we need to treat our compatriots:[13]

*Example a.*—We, through our public officials, may quite properly take the property of our fellow citizens for public purposes, provided they are duly compensated for their losses; this is especially true if the property is within our national boundaries but is even true if it is outside them. We cannot, however, thus commandeer an identical piece of property from a foreigner for an identical purpose in return for identical compensation. This is especially true if the property is beyond our borders;[14] but it is even true if the property is actually in our country, in transit.[15]

*Example b.*—We can conscript fellow citizens for service in our armed forces, even if they are resident abroad.[16] We cannot so conscript foreign nationals, even if they are resident within our own country.[17]

*Example c.*—We can tax fellow citizens, even if they are resident abroad.[18] We cannot so tax foreigners residing abroad on income earned abroad.[19]

*Example d.*—We can dam or divert the flow of a river lying wholly within our national territory to the disadvantage of fellow citizens living downstream. We may not so dam or divert rivers flowing across international boundaries to the disadvantage of foreigners downstream.[20]

*Example e.*—We can allow the emission of noxious factory fumes that damage the persons or property of fellow citizens. We may not do so if those fumes cross international frontiers, causing similar damage to the persons or property of foreigners there.[21]

*Example f.*—We may set arbitrarily low limits on the legal liability of manufacturers for damages done by their production processes or products domestically to our fellow citizens. We may not so limit the damage recoverable from them for harm done across international boundaries to foreigners.[22]

*Example g.*—According to international law, we may treat our fellow citizens "arbitrarily according to [our own] discretion." To aliens within our national territory, however, we must afford their persons and property protection "in accordance with certain rules and principles of international law," that is, "in accordance with ordinary standards of civilization."[23] Commentators on international law pointedly add, "It is no excuse that [a] State does not provide any protection whatever for its own subjects" in those respects.[24]

These are all examples of ways in which we must treat foreigners better than compatriots. In a great many other respects, of course, the conventional wisdom is perfectly right that we owe better treatment to our compatriots than we do to foreigners. For example, we have a duty to protect the persons and property of compatriots against attack, even when they are abroad.[25] Absent treaty obligations, we have no such duty to protect noncitizens beyond our borders. We have a duty—morally, and perhaps even legally—to provide a minimum level of basic necessities for compatriots. Absent treaty obligations, we have no such duty—legally, anyway—to assist needy noncitizens beyond our borders.

Even within our borders, we may treat citizens better in all sorts of ways than we treat noncitizens, just so long as some "reasonable" grounds for those discriminations can be produced and just so long as the protection we provide aliens' persons and property comes up to minimal internationally acceptable standards.[26] Not only are aliens standardly denied political rights, like voting and office-holding, but they are also standardly excluded from "public service." This has, in the past, been interpreted very broadly indeed: In the United States, an alien could have been debarred from being an "optometrist, dentist, doctor, nurse, architect, teacher, lawyer, policeman, engineer, corporate officer, real estate broker, public accountant, mortician, physiotherapist, pharmacist, peddler, pool or gambling-hall operator";[27] in the United Kingdom the range of prohibited occupations has included harbor pilots, masters of merchant ships, and skippers of fishing vessels.[28] Besides all those quasi-public functions from which aliens are excluded, they also suffer other disadvantages of a purely material sort. Perhaps the most significant among them are the rules found in some states denying aliens the right to own land.[29] All of this can be perfectly permissible, both under international law and under higher domestic law.

Thus, the situation is very much a mixed one. Sometimes we are indeed permitted (sometimes even required) to treat our fellow citizens better than we treat those who do not share that status with us. Other times, however, we are required to treat noncitizens better than we need to treat our own fellow citizens.

I pass no judgment on which pattern, on balance, predominates. The point I want to make here is merely that the situation is much more mixed than ordinary philosophical thinking on special duties leads us to expect. That in itself is significant, as I shall now proceed to show.

## III. SPECIAL DUTIES AS MAGNIFIERS AND MULTIPLIERS

In attempting to construe the effect that special relationships have on our moral duties, commonsense morality tends to employ either of two basic models (or both of them: they are nowise incompatible). On the face of things, these two models can only offer reinforcing interpretations for the same one-half of the phenomenon observed in Section II above. Digging deeper to see how such models might account for that other half of the phenomenon drives us toward a model that is even more deeply and familiarly flawed.

### *A*

One standard way of construing the effect of special relationships on our moral duties is to say that special relationships "merely magnify" preexisting moral duties. That is to say, they merely make more stringent duties which we have, in weaker form, vis-à-vis everyone at large; or, "imperfect duties" are transformed by special relationships into "perfect" ones. Thus, perhaps it is wrong to let anyone starve, but it is especially wrong to let kin or compatriots starve. And so on.

That kind of account fits only half the facts, as sketched in Section II above, though. If special relationships were merely magnifiers of preexisting duties, then the magnification should be symmetrical in both positive and negative directions. Positive duties (i.e., duties to provide positive assistance to others) should become more strongly positive vis-à-vis those linked to us by some special relationship. Negative duties (i.e., duties not to harm others) should become more strongly negative vis-à-vis those linked to us by some special relationship. When it comes to our duties in relation to compatriots, however, the former is broadly speaking true, while the latter is not.

It is perfectly true that there is a variety of goods that we may or must provide to compatriots that we may at the same time legitimately deny to nonnationals (especially nonresident nonnationals). Rights to vote, to hold property, and to the protection of their persons and property abroad are among them. In the positive dimension, then, the "magnifier" model is broadly appropriate.[30]

In the negative dimension, it is not. All the examples *a* through *f* in Section II above point to ways in which we may legitimately impose burdens upon compatriots that may not properly be imposed upon nonnationals (especially nonresident nonnationals). We may poison our compatriots' air, stop their flow of water, deprive them of liberty by conscription, deny them legal remedies for damage to their persons and their property—all in a way that we cannot do to nonresident nonnationals. If anything, it is our negative duties toward nonnationals, not our negative duties toward compatriots, that are here magnified.

## B

A second way of construing the effect of special relationships on our moral duties is to say that special relationships "multiply" as well as magnify preexisting duties. That is to say, special relationships do not just make our ordinary general duties particularly stringent in relation to those bound to us by some special relationship; they also create new special duties, over and above the more general ones that we ordinarily owe to anyone and everyone in the world at large. Thus, contracts, for example, create duties de novo. I am under no general duty, strong or weak, to let Dick Merelman inhabit a room in my house; that duty arises only when, and only because, we sign a lease. The special (here, contractual) relationship has created a new duty from scratch.

The "multiplier" model bolsters the "mere magnifier" model's already broadly adequate account of why we have especially strong positive duties toward those linked to us by some special relationship. Sometimes those special relationships strengthen positive duties we owe, less strongly, to everyone at large. Other times, special relationships create new positive duties that we owe peculiarly to those thus linked to us. Either way, we have more and stronger positive duties toward those who stand in special relationships to us than we do the world at large. And that broadly fits the pattern of our special duties vis-à-vis compatriots, as revealed in Section II above.

On the face of it, though, it is hard to see how this multiplier model can account for the weakening of negative duties toward compatriots observed there. If special relationships multiply duties, then we would ordinarily expect that that multiplication would produce more new duties in each direction. Consider the paradigm case of contracts. Sometimes contracts create new special duties enjoining us to help others in ways that we would not otherwise be bound to do. Other times, contracts create new special duties enjoining us not to harm others (e.g., by withdrawing trade, labor, or raw materials) in ways that we would otherwise be at liberty to do. It is hard, on the face of it, at least, to see what the attraction of special duties would be—either for agents who are anxious to incur them or for philosophers who are anxious to impose them—if they make people worse off, opening them up to new harms from which they would otherwise be protected.

Yet, judging from examples *a* through *f* in Section II above, that is precisely what happens in the special relationship between compatriots. Far from simply creating new negative duties among compatriots, that special relationship seems sometimes to have the effect of canceling (or at least weakening or mitigating) some of the negative duties that people owe to others in general. That hardly looks like the result of an act of multiplication. Ordinarily, we would expect that multiplication should produce more—not fewer—duties.

## C

Digging deeper, we find that there may be a way to explain why special relationships have this curious tendency to strengthen positive duties while weakening negative ones. This model quickly collapses into another, more familiar one—and ultimately falls prey to the same objections standardly lodged against it, as Section IV will show. Still, it is worth noting how quickly all the standard theories about special duties, when confronted with certain elementary facts about the case of compatriots, collapse into that familiar and flawed model that ordinarily we might have regarded as only one among many possible ways of filling out those theories.

The crucial move in reconciling standard theories about special duties with the elementary facts about compatriots laid out in Section II is just this: Whether special relationships multiply duties or merely magnify them, the point remains that a relationship is inherently a two-way affair. The same special relation that binds me to you also binds you to me. Special duties for each of us will usually follow from that fact.[31]

Each of us will ordinarily benefit from others' being bound by those extra (or extra strong) duties to do for us things that they are not obliged (or not so powerfully obliged) to do for the world at large. Hence the apparent "strengthening" of positive duties in consequence of special relationships.

Each of us will also ordinarily suffer from those extra (or extra-strong) duties imposing an extra burden on us. Hence the apparent "weakening" of negative duties in consequence of the special relationship. We may legitimately impose burdens upon those standing in special relationships to us that we may not impose upon those in no special relation to us, merely because we have special rights against them, and they have special duties toward us. Those extra burdens upon them are no more, and no less, than the fair price of our being under special duties to provide them with valued assistance.

Many of the findings of Section II above lend themselves quite naturally to some such interpretation. When we say that compatriots may have their incomes taxed, their trucks commandeered, or other liberties curtailed by conscription, that is surely to say little more than that people may be required to do what is required in order to meet their special duties toward their fellow citizens—duties born of their fellow citizens' similar sacrifices to benefit them.[32] When we say that nonnationals (especially nonresident nonnationals) may not be treated in such ways, that is merely to say that we have no such special claims against them nor they any such special duties toward us.

Others of the examples in Section II above (especially examples *d* through *g*) do not lend themselves quite so obviously to this sort of analysis. But perhaps, with a sufficiently long story that is sufficiently rich in lurid details, we might be persuaded that polluting the air, damming rivers, limiting liability for damages, and denying people due process of law really is to the good of all; and suffering occasional misfortunes of those sorts really is just the fair price that compatriots should be required to pay for the benefits that they derive from those broader practices.

Notice that, given this account, the motivational quandary in Section III*B* disappears. People welcome special relationships—along with the attendant special rights and special duties (i.e., along with the strengthening of positive duties and the weakening of negative ones)—because the two come as part of an inseparable package, and people are on net better off as a result of it. That is just to say, their gains from having others' positive duties toward them strengthened exceeds their costs from having others' negative duties toward them weakened, and it is impossible for them to realize the gains without incurring the costs.

Notice, however, how quickly these standard theories of how special relationships work on our moral duties—the magnifier and the multiplier models—have been reduced to a very particular theory about "mutual-benefit societies." Initially, the magnifier and multiplier theories seemed to be much broader than that, open to a much wider variety of interpretations and not committing us to any particular theory about why or how the "magnification" or "multiplication" of duties occurred. Yet if those models are to fit the elementary facts about duties toward compatriots in Section II at all, they must fall back on a sort of mutual-benefit logic that provides a very particular answer to the question of how and why the magnification or multiplication of duties occurred. As Section IV will show, that is not an altogether happy result.

## IV. THE MUTUAL-BENEFIT-SOCIETY MODEL

According to the conventional wisdom about international relations, we have a peculiarly strong obligation to leave foreigners as we found them. "Nonintervention" has long bid fair to constitute the master norm of international law.[33] That is not to say that it is actually wrong to help foreigners, of course. It is, however, to say that it is much, much more important not to harm them than it is to help them. Where compatriots are concerned, almost the opposite is true. According to the flip side of that conventional wisdom, it is deeply wrong to be utterly indifferent toward your fellow countrymen; yet it is perfectly permissible for fellow countrymen to impose hardships on themselves and on one another to promote the well-being of their shared community.

Perhaps the best way to make sense of all this is to say that, within the conventional wisdom about international relations, nation-states are conceptualized as ongoing mutual-benefit societies. Within mutual-benefit-society logic, it would be perfectly permissible to impose sacrifices on some people now so that they themselves might benefit in the future; it may even be permissible to impose sacrifices on some now so that others will benefit, either now or in the future.

Precisely what sorts of contractarian or utilitarian theories are required to underpin this logic can be safely left to one side here. It is the broad outline rather than the finer detail that matters for present purposes. The bottom line is always that, in a mutual-benefit society, imposing harms is always permissible—but only on condition that some positive good comes of it, and only on condition that those suffering the harm are in some sense party to the society in question.

Suppose, now, that national boundaries are thought to circumscribe mutual-benefit societies of this sort.[34] Then the broad pattern of duties toward compatriots and foreigners, respectively, as described in Section II above, becomes perfectly comprehensible. In dealing with other people in general (i.e., those who are not party to the society), the prime directive is "avoid harm": those outside our mutual-benefit society ought not be made to bear any of our burdens; but neither, of course, have they any claim on any of the benefits which we have produced for ourselves, through our own sacrifices. In dealing with others in the club (i.e., compatriots), positive duties wax while negative ones wane: it is perfectly permissible to impose hardships, so long as some positive good somehow comes of doing so; but the point of a mutual-benefit society, in the final analysis, must always be to produce positive benefits for those who are party to it.

There are many familiar problems involved in modeling political communities as mutual-benefit societies.[35] The one to which I wish to draw particular attention here is the problem of determining who is inside the club and who is outside it. Analysis of this problem, in turn, forces us back to the foundational questions skirted at the outset of the article. These will be readdressed in Section V below, where I construct an alternative model of special duties as not very special, after all.

From the legalist perspective that dominates discussion of such duties, formal status is what matters. Who is a citizen? Who is not? That, almost exclusively, determines what we may or must do to people, qua members of the club.

Yet formal status is only imperfectly and contingently related to who is actually generating and receiving the benefits of the mutual-benefit society. The mismatch is most glaring as regards resident aliens: They are often net contributors to the society, yet they are equally often denied its full benefits.[36] The mismatch also appears only slightly less glaringly, as regards natural-born citizens who retain that status although they are and will inevitably (because, e.g., severely handicapped) continue to be net drains on the mutual-benefit society.[37]

In its starkest form, mutual-benefit-society logic should require that people's benefits from the society be strictly proportional to the contributions they have made toward the production of those benefits. Or, minimally, it should require that no one draw out more than he has paid in: The allocation of any surplus created by people's joint efforts may be left open. On that logic, we have special duties toward those whose cooperation benefits us, and to them alone. That they share the same color passport—or, indeed, the same parentage—is related only contingently, at best, to that crucial consideration.

It may well be that mutual-benefit logic, in so stark a form, is utterly inoperable. Constantly changing circumstances mean that everything from social insurance to speculative business ventures might benefit us all in the long run, even if at any given moment some of them constitute net drains on the system. And lines on the map, though inherently arbitrary at the margins, may be as good a way as any of identifying cheaply the members of a beneficially interacting community. So we may end up embracing the formalistic devices for identifying members of the mutual-benefit society, knowing that they are imperfect second-bests but also knowing that doing better is impossible or prohibitively expensive.

The point remains, however, that there are some clear, straightforward adjustments that ought to be made to such "first stab" definitions of membership, if mutual-benefit logic underlay membership. That they are not made—and that we think at least one of them ought not be made—clearly indicates that it is not mutual-benefit logic that underlies membership after all.

Reflect, again, upon the case of resident aliens who are performing socially useful functions over a long period of time. Many societies egregiously exploit "guest workers," denying them many of the rights and privileges accorded to citizens despite the fact that they make major and continuing contributions to the society. Politically and economically, it is no mystery why they are deprived of the full fruits of their labors in this way.[38] But if the moral justification of society is to be traced to mutual-benefit logic, that is transparently wrong. The entry ticket to a mutual-benefit society should, logically, just be conferring net benefits on the society.[39] That membership is nonetheless denied to those who confer benefits on the society demonstrates that the society is not acting consistently on that moral premise. Either it is acting on some other moral premise or else it is acting on none at all (or none consistently, which morally amounts to the same).

Or consider, again, the case of the congenitally handicapped. Though born of native parents in the homeland, and by formalistic criteria therefore clearly qualified for citizenship, such persons will never be net contributors to the mutual-benefit society. If it were merely the logic of mutual benefit that determined membership such persons would clearly be excluded from the benefits of society.[40] (If their parents cared about them, they could give them some of *their* well-earned benefits.) Yet that does not happen, no matter how sure we are that handicapped persons will be net drains on the society for the duration of their lives. And most of us intuitively imagine that it is a good thing, morally, that it does not happen. Thus, society here again seems to be operating on something other than mutual-benefit logic; and here, at least, we are glad that it is.

## V. THE ASSIGNED RESPONSIBILITY MODEL

The magnifier, multiplier, and mutual-benefit-society models all take the specialness of special duties particularly seriously. They treat such duties as if they were, at least in (large) part, possessed of an independent existence or of an independent moral force. I want to deny both of those propositions.

My preferred approach to special duties is to regard them as being merely "distributed general duties." That is to say, special duties are in my view merely devices whereby the moral community's general duties get assigned to particular agents. For this reason, I call mine an "assigned responsibility" model.[41]

This approach treats special duties as much more nearly derivative from general duties than any of the other approaches so far considered. Certainly it is true that, on this account, special duties derive the whole of their moral force from the moral force of those general duties. It may not quite be the case that, existentially, they are wholly derivative from general duties: we cannot always deduce from considerations of general duties alone who in particular should take it upon themselves to discharge them; where the general principle leaves that question open, some further (independent, often largely arbitrary) "responsibility principle" is required to specify it. Still, on this account, special duties are *largely* if not wholly derivative from considerations of general duty.

The practical consequences of this finding are substantial. If special duties can be shown to derive the whole of their moral force from their connections to general duties, then they are susceptible to being overridden (at least at the margins, or in exceptional circumstances) by those more general considerations. In this way, it turns out that "our fellow countrymen" are not so very special after all. The same thing that makes us worry mainly about them should also make us worry, at least a little, about the rest of the world, too.

These arguments draw upon larger themes developed elsewhere.[42] Here I shall concentrate narrowly upon their specific application to the problem of our special duties toward compatriots. The strategy I shall pursue here is to start from the presumption that there are, at root, no distinct special duties but only general ones. I then proceed to show how implementing those general duties gives rise to special duties much like those we observe in the practice of international relations. And finally I shall show how those special duties arising from general duties are much more tightly circumscribed in their extended implications than are the special duties deriving from any of the other models.[43]

## A

Let us start then from the assumption that we all have certain general duties, of both a positive and negative sort, toward one another. Those general injunctions get applied to specific people in a variety of ways. Some are quasi-naturalistic. Others are frankly social in character.

For an example of the former, suppose we operate under some general injunction to save someone who is drowning, if you and you alone can do so. Suppose, further, that you happen to find yourself in such a position one day. Then that general injunction becomes a compelling commandment addressed specifically to you.

The same example is easily adapted to provide an instance of the second mode as well. Suppose, now, that there are hundreds of people on the beach watching the drowning swimmer flounder. None is conspicuously closer or conspicuously the stronger swimmer; none is related to the swimmer. In short, none is in any way "naturalistically" picked out as the appropriate person to help. If all of them tried to help simultaneously, however they would merely get in each other's way; the probable result of such a melee would be multiple drownings rather than the single one now in prospect. Let us suppose, finally, that there is one person who is not naturalistically but, rather, "socially" picked out as the person who should effect the rescue: the duly-appointed lifeguard.[44] In such a case, it is clearly that person upon whom the general duty of rescue devolves as a special duty.

Notice that it is not a matter of indifference whom we choose to vest with special responsibility for discharging our general moral duties. Obviously, some people would, for purely naturalistic reasons, make better lifeguards than others. It is for these naturalistic reasons that we appoint them to the position rather than appointing someone else. But their special responsibility in the matter derives wholly from the fact that they *were* appointed, and not at all from any facts about why they were appointed.

Should the appointed individuals prove incompetent, then of course it is perfectly proper for us to retract their commissions and appoint others in their places. If responsibility is allocated merely upon the bases here suggested, then its reallocation is always a live issue. But it is an issue to be taken up at another level, and in another forum.[45] Absent such a thoroughgoing reconsideration of the allocation of responsibilities, it will almost always be better to let those who have been assigned responsibility get on with the job. In all but the most exceptional cases of clear and gross incompetence on the part of the appointed individual, it will clearly be better to get out of the way and let the duly appointed lifeguard have an unimpeded chance at pulling the drowning swimmer out of the water.

That seems to provide a good model for many of our so-called special duties. A great many general duties point to tasks that, for one reason or another, are pursued more effectively if they are subdivided and particular people are assigned special responsibility for particular portions of the task. Sometimes the reason this is so has to do with the advantage of specialization and division of labor. Other times, it has to do with lumpiness in the information required to do a good job, and the limits on people's capacity for processing requisite quantities of information about a great many cases at once. And still other times it is because there is some process at work (the adversarial system in law, or the psychological processes at work in child development, e.g.) that presuppose that each person will have some particular advocate and champion.[46] Whatever the reason, however, it is simply the case that our general duties toward people are sometimes more effectively discharged by assigning special responsibility for that matter to some particular agents. When that is the case, then that clearly is what should be done.[47]

Thus, hospital patients are better cared for by being assigned to particular doctors rather than having all the hospital's doctors devote one $n$th of their time to each of the hospital's $n$ patients. Someone accused of a crime is better served, legally, by being assigned some particular advocate, rather than having a different attorney appear from the common pool of attorneys to represent him at each different court date.[48] Of course, some doctors are better than others, and some lawyers are better than others; so it is not a matter of indifference which one is handling your case. But any one is better than all at once.

### B

National boundaries, I suggest, perform much the same function. The duties that states (or, more precisely, their officials) have vis-à-vis their own citizens are not in any deep sense special. At root, they are merely the general duties that everyone has toward everyone else worldwide. National boundaries simply visit upon those particular state agents special responsibility for discharging those general obligations vis-à-vis those individuals who happen to be their own citizens.[49]

Nothing in this argument claims that one's nationality is a matter of indifference. There are all sorts of reasons for wishing national boundaries to be drawn in such a way that you are lumped together with others "of your own kind"; these range from mundane considerations of the ease and efficiency of administration to deep psychological attachments and a sense of self that may thereby be promoted.[50] My only point is that those are all considerations that bear on the drawing and redrawing of boundaries; they are not, in and of themselves, the source of special responsibilities toward people with those shared characteristics.[51]

The elementary facts about international responsibilities set out in Section II above can all be regarded as fair "first approximations" to the implications of this assigned responsibility model. States are assigned special responsibility for protecting and promoting the interests of those who are their citizens. Other states do them a prima facie wrong when they inflict injuries on their citizens; it is the prima facie duty of a state, acting on behalf of injured citizens, to demand redress. But ordinarily no state has any claim against other states for positive assistance in promoting its own citizens' interests: That is its own responsibility. Among its own citizens, however, it is perfectly proper that in discharging that responsibility the state should compel its citizens to comply with various schemes that require occasional sacrifices so that all may prosper.[52]

### C

So far, the story is strictly analogous in its practical implications to that told about mutual-benefit societies in Section IV above. Here, as there, we have special duties for promoting the well-being of compatriots. Here, as there, we are basically obliged to leave foreigners as we found them. The rationale is different: Here, it is that we have been assigned responsibility for compatriots, in a way that we have not been assigned any responsibility for foreigners. But the end result is much the same—so far, at least.

There are, however, two important points of distinction between these stories. The first concerns the proper treatment of the useless and the helpless. So far as a mutual-benefit society is concerned, useless members would be superfluous members. Not only may they be cast out, they ought to be cast out. If the raison d'être of the society is mutual benefit, and those people are not benefiting anyone, then it is actually wrong, on mutual-benefit logic, for them to be included. (That is true, at least insofar as their inclusion is in any way costly to the rest of the society—ergo, it is clearly wrong, in those terms, for the severely handicapped to draw any benefits from a mutual-benefit society.) The same is true with the helpless, that is, refugees and stateless persons. If they are going to benefit society, then a mutual-benefit society ought to take them in. But if they are only going to be a net drain on society (as most of the "boat people" presumably appeared to be, e.g.), then a mutual-benefit society not only may but *must* on its own principles, deny them entry. The fact that they are without any other protector in the international system is, for mutual-benefit logic, neither here nor there.

My model, wherein states' special responsibilities are derived from general ones of everyone to everyone, cancels both those implications. States are stuck with the charges assigned to them, whether those people are a net benefit to the rest of society or not. Casting off useless members of society would simply amount to shirking their assigned responsibility.

The "helpless" constitute the converse case. They have been (or, anyway, they are now) assigned to no one particular state for protection. That does not mean that all states may therefore ignore or abuse them, however. Quite the contrary. What justifies states in pressing the particular claims of their own citizens is, on my account, the presumption that everyone has been assigned an advocate/protector.[53] Then and only then will a system of universal special pleading lead to maximal fulfillment of everyone's general duties toward everyone else worldwide.

Suppose, however, that someone has been left without a protector. Either he has never been assigned one, or else the one he was assigned has proven unwilling or unable to provide the sort of protection it was his job to provide. Then, far from being at the mercy of everyone, the person becomes the "residual responsibility" of all.[54] The situation here is akin to that of a hospital patient who, through some clerical error, was admitted with some acute illness without being assigned to any particular physician's list: He then becomes the residual responsibility of all staff physicians of that hospital.

To be sure, that responsibility is an "imperfect" one as against any particular state. It is the responsibility of the set of states, taken as a whole, to give the refugee a home; but it is not the duty of any one of them in particular.[55] At the very least, though, we can say this much: It would be wrong for any state to press the claims of its own citizens strongly, to the disadvantage of those who have no advocate in the system;[56] and it would not be wrong (as, perversely, it would be on the mutual-benefit-society model) for any state to agree to give refugees a home. Both these things follow from the fact that the state's special responsibility to its own citizens is, at root, derived from the same considerations that underlie its general duty to the refugee.

The second important difference between my model and mutual-benefit logic concerns the critique of international boundaries and the obligation to share resources between nations. On mutual-benefit logic, boundaries should circumscribe groups of people who produce benefits for one another. Expanding those boundaries is permissible only if by so doing we can incorporate yet more mutually beneficial collaborators into our society; contracting those boundaries is proper if by so doing we can expel some people who are nothing but liabilities to our cooperative unit. On mutual-benefit logic, furthermore, transfers across international boundaries are permissible only if they constitute mutually beneficial exchanges. The practical consequence of all this is, characteristically, that the rich get richer and the poor get poorer.[57]

On the model I have proposed, none of this would follow. Special responsibilities are, on my account, assigned merely as an administrative device for discharging our general duties more efficiently. If that is the aim, then they should be assigned to agents capable of discharging them effectively; and that, in turn, means that sufficient resources ought to have been given to every such state agent to allow for the effective discharge of those responsibilities. If there has been a misallocation of some sort, so that some states have been assigned care of many more people than they have been assigned resources to care for them, then a reallocation is called for.[58] This follows not from any special theory of justice but, rather, merely from the basis of special duties in general ones.[59]

If some states prove incapable of discharging their responsibilities effectively, then they should either be reconstituted or assisted.[60] Whereas on mutual-benefit logic it would actually be wrong for nations to take on burdens that would in no way benefit their citizens, on my model it would certainly not be wrong for them to do so; and it would in some diffuse way be right for them to do so, in discharge of the general duties that all of them share and that underwrite their own grant of special responsibility for their own citizens in the first place.[61]

## VI. CONCLUSION

Boundaries matter, I conclude. But it is the boundaries around people, not the boundaries around territories, that really matter morally. Territorial boundaries are merely useful devices for "matching" one person to one protector. Citizenship is merely a device for fixing special responsibility in some agent for discharging our general duties vis-à-vis each particular person. At root, however, it is the person and the general duty that we all have toward him that matters morally.

If all has gone well with the assignment of responsibilities, then respecting special responsibilities and the priority of compatriots to which they give rise would be the best way of discharging those general duties. But the assignment of responsibility will never work perfectly, and there is much to make us suppose that the assignment embodied in the present world system is very imperfect indeed. In such cases, the derivative special responsibilities cannot bar the way to our discharging the more general duties from which they are derived. In the present world system, it is often—perhaps ordinarily—wrong to give priority to the claims of our compatriots.

## NOTES

Earlier versions of this article were presented to the European Consortium for Political Research (ECPR) Workshop on "Duties beyond Borders" in Amsterdam and to seminars at the universities of Essex and Stockholm. I am grateful to those audiences, and to Hillel Steiner, for comments.

1. Unlike David Miller, "The Ethical Significance of Nationality," in this issue [*Ethics* 98: 4 (July 1988): 647–62, reprinted herein 235–53], I shall here make no distinction between "state" and "nation," or between "citizenship" and "nationality." In this article, they will be used interchangeably.

2. Or so it is standardly supposed. Actually, there could be a "rule of universal partiality" (e.g., "everyone ought to pursue his own interests," or "everyone ought to take care of his own children"). A variant of this figures largely in my argument in Section V below.

3. The terms "special" and "general" duties—and to a large extent the analysis of them as well—are borrowed from H. L. A. Hart, "Are There Any Natural Rights?" *Philosophical Review* 64 (1955): 175–91.

4. See Robert E. Goodin, *Protecting the Vulnerable* (Chicago: University of Chicago Press, 1985), chapter 1 and the references therein. The strongest arguments for such partiality have to do with the need to center one's sense of self, through personal attachments to particular people and projects; see, e.g., Bernard Williams, *Moral Luck* (Cambridge: Cambridge University Press, 1981), chapter 1. But surely those arguments apply most strongly to more personal links, and only very weakly, if at all, to impersonal links through shared race or nationality. John Cottingham pursues such points in "Partiality, Favouritism and Morality," *Philosophical Quarterly* 36 (1986): 357–73, pp. 370–71.

5. William Godwin, *Enquiry Concerning Political Justice* (1793; reprint, Oxford: Clarendon, 1971), book 2, chapter 2.

6. See, e.g., Williams, *Moral Luck*, pp. 17–18, for the former position; and R. M. Hare, *Moral Thinking* (Oxford: Clarendon, 1981), p. 138, for the latter.

7. Henry Sidgwick, *The Methods of Ethics*, 7th ed. (London: Macmillan, 1907), book 3, chapter 4, section 3; Derek Parfit, *Reasons and Persons* (Oxford: Clarendon, 1984), pp. 95, 485.

8. Sidgwick, *The Methods of Ethics*, book 3, chapter 4, section 3; Parfit, pp. 95, 485.

9. Parfit, p. 95.

10. Sometimes special duties specifically require the opposite. Parents, teachers, and prison wardens are all, from time to time, required by special duties to inflict punishment upon those under their care. But at least some—and arguably all—of these are pains inflicted for the recipient's own greater, long-term good. See Herbert Morris, "A Paternalistic Theory of Punishment," *American Philosophical Quarterly* 18 (1981): 263–71; cf. John Deigh, "On the Right to Be Punished: Some Doubts," *Ethics* 94 (1984): 191–211.

11. Henry Shue, *Basic Rights* (Princeton, NJ: Princeton University Press, 1980), p. 132; Benjamin Cardozo, *People v. Crane*, 214 N.Y. 154, 164, 108 N.E. 427, 437. This report of what constitutes the conventional wisdom is echoed by Thomas Nagel, "Ruthlessness in Public Life," in *Public and Private Morality*, ed. Stuart Hampshire (Cambridge: Cambridge University Press, 1978), pp. 75–93, p. 81; Charles R. Beitz, *Political Theory and International Relations* (Princeton, NJ: Princeton University Press, 1979), p. 163 [herein 37]; and Goodin, *Protecting the Vulnerable*, chapters 1 and 2. Among them, only Cardozo could be said to accept that conventional wisdom uncritically.

12. Unlike stipulative law, which might be made by a small body of people on the spur of the moment, customary law represents the settled judgments of a great many people over some long period. Thus, it is better qualified for use in a quasi-Rawlsian "reflective equilibrium." For other uses of legal principles in such a role, see Robert E. Goodin, *The Politics of Rational Man* (London: Wiley, 1976), chapter 7, and *Protecting the Vulnerable*, chapter 5.

13. These all refer to ways that we must treat foreigners in general, absent specific contractual or treaty commitments. The latter may require better treatment, or permit worst, or both in different respects. The principles set out in the text, however, constitute the normative background against which such contracts or treaties are negotiated.

14. This is true even if it is a piece of movable property, so there is no question of expropriating a piece of another nation's territory. Suppose, e.g., that the British government needs to requisition a privately owned ship to provision troops in the South Atlantic: It may so requisition a ship of British registry, even if it is lying in Dutch waters; it may not so requisition a ship of Dutch registry, even if lying in British waters (except in a case of extreme emergency).

15. Adrian S. Fisher, chief reporter, *Restatement (Second) of the Foreign Relations Law of the United States* (St. Paul, MN: American Law Institute, 1965), section 185c. The "right of safe passage" for people and goods in transit, for purposes of commerce or study, was firmly established even in early modern international law; see Hugo Grotius, *On the Law of War and Peace*, trans. F. W. Kelsey (1625; reprint, Oxford: Clarendon Press, 1925), book 2, chapter 2, sections 13-15; Christian Wolff, *The Law of Nations Treated according to a Scientific Method*, trans. Joseph H. Drake (1749; reprint, Oxford: Clarendon, 1934), section 346; and Emerich de Vattel, *The Law of Nations, or the Principles of Natural Law*, trans. Joseph Chitty (1758; reprint, Philadelphia: T. and J. W. Johnson, 1863), book 2, chapter 10, section 132. This rule, too, is subject to an "extreme emergency" exception.

16. L. Oppenheim, *International Law: A Treatise*, ed. H. Lauterpacht (London: Longman, 1955), 1:288. This, and the similar result in example *c* below, follows from the fact that a state enjoys continuing "personal" sovereignty over its own citizens but possesses merely those powers derived from its "territorial" sovereignty over aliens within its borders. This distinction, emphasized in modern international law (e.g., throughout the first volume of Oppenheim's

treatise, *International Law*), appears in a particularly clear early formulation in Francisco Suárez's 1612 *Treatise on Laws and God the Lawgiver*, in *Selections from Three Works*, trans. and ed. Gwladys L. Williams, Ammi Brown, John Waldron, and Henry Davis (Oxford: Clarendon, 1944), chapter 30, section 12.

17. Oppenheim, 1:288. The practice in the United States, of course, is to conscript alien nationals who are permanently resident in the country into its armed forces; see Alexander M. Bickel, *The Morality of Consent* (New Haven, CT: Yale University Press, 1975), p. 49. But the long-standing rule in international law is that, while we may require resident aliens to help with police, fire, and flood protection, foreigners are exempt from serving in the militia; see Vattel, book 2, chapter 8, sections 105–6 for one early statement of the rule.

18. Oppenheim, 1:288. Bickel, p. 48. Again, this is a long-standing rule of international law; see Wolff, section 324; and Vattel, book 2, chapter 8, section 106. Of course, having the right to tax nationals abroad, states may waive that right (as, e.g., through double-taxation agreements).

19. A partial exception to this rule might be that an alien with permanent residency in one state but temporarily resident in another might be taxable in the first country for earnings in the second; the United States, at least, would try to collect. Some authors maintain that even resident aliens should be exempt from certain sorts of taxes. One example Wolff offers (section 324) is a poll tax: Since aliens are precluded by reason of noncitizenship from voting, they ought for that reason to be exempt from a poll tax, too. Another example, offered by Vattel (book 2, chapter 8, section 106), is that foreigners should be "exempt from taxes...destined for the support of the rights of the nation"; since resident aliens are under no obligation to fight in defense of the nation, they should be under no obligation to pay taxes earmarked for the defense of the nation, either.

20. Oppenheim, 1:290–91, 348, 475.

21. Ibid., 1:291.

22. Thus, e.g., the Price-Anderson Act sets the limit for liability of operators of civilian nuclear reactors within the United States at $560 million. But had the Fermi reactor in Detroit experienced a partial meltdown similar to that at Chernobyl, spreading pollution to Canada, international law would not have recognized the legitimacy of that limit in fixing damages due to Canadians. "It is," according to Oppenheim's *International Law*, 1:350, "a well-established principle that a State cannot invoke its municipal legislation as a reason for avoiding its international obligations."

23. Oppenheim, 1:686–87. Indeed, "black letter" international law—as codified in the American Law Institute's *Restatement (Second) of the Foreign Relations Law of the United States*, section 165(1)(a)—holds that "conduct attributable to a state and causing injury to an alien is wrongful under international law... if it departs from the international standard of justice." For elaboration, see Oppenheim, 1:290, 350, 641; and J. L. Brierly, *The Law of Nations*, 2nd ed. (Oxford: Clarendon, 1936), pp. 172 ff.

24. Oppenheim, 1:687–88. Elsewhere Oppenheim explicitly draws attention to the "paradoxical result" that "individuals, when residing as aliens in a foreign state, enjoy a measure of protection... denied to nationals of a State within its own territory" (1:641, n. 1). In the past, this has been the subject of some controversy. Premodern international lawyers tended to hold that there was some external (God-given) standard of "just suitable" laws that must be adhered to in prescribing differential treatment for aliens; see Suárez, chapter 33, section 7. But early modern writers like Wolff (section 302); and Vattel (book 2, chapter 8, section 100)—right down to Henry Sidgwick, *The Elements of Politics* (London: Macmillan, 1891), pp. 235–36—seemed to suppose that, since the state could refuse admission to aliens altogether, it could impose any conditions it liked upon their remaining in the country, however discriminatory and however short that treatment may fall from any international standards of civilized conduct. At the very least, aliens are not wronged if they are treated no worse than nationals—or so it was thought by many (predominantly European and Latin American) international lawyers prior to 1940 (Ian Brownlie, *Principles of Public International Law* [Oxford: Clarendon, 1966], p. 425). By now, it is decidedly the "prevailing rule" of international law that "there is an international standard of justice that a state must observe in the treatment of aliens, even if the state does not observe it in the treatment of its own nationals, and even if the standard is inconsistent with its own law" (*Restatement [Second] of the Foreign Relations of the United States*, section 165, comment *a*; and Louis B. Sohn and R. R. Baxter, "Responsibility of States for Injuries to the Economic Interests of Aliens (Harvard Law School Draft Convention)," *American Journal of International Law* 55 [1961]: 545–84, pp. 547–48. There is no longer any doubt that "national treatment" is not enough; the only persisting question is whether the international standard demanded should vary with, e.g., the wealth or educational attainments of the people to whom it is being applied—as, e.g., standards of "due diligence" and "reasonable care" perhaps should (Brownlie, p. 427).

25. States are under obligations arising from customary and higher domestic law to do so, even if those obligations are unenforceable under international law, as they seem to be (see Oppenheim, 1:686–87).

26. Suárez, chapter 33, section 7; Wolff, section 303; Sidgwick, *Elements of Politics*, p. 235; Brierly, pp. 172–73; Oppenheim, 1:689–91; Brownlie, pp. 424–48; Gerald M. Rosberg, "The Protection of Aliens from Discriminatory Treatment by the National Government," *Supreme Court Review* (1977), pp. 275–339; Edward S. Corwin, *The Constitution, and What It Means Today*, ed. H. W. Chase and C. R. Ducat (Princeton, NJ: Princeton University Press, 1978), pp. 90–92, and *1980 Supplement*, pp. 159–61; "Developments in the Law: Immigration Policy and the Rights of Aliens," *Harvard Law Review* 96 (1983): 1286–1465.

27. Bickel, pp. 45–46. Also, see Corwin, pp. 90–92, and *1980 Supplement*, pp. 159–61; and "Developments in the Law."

28. Brierly, p. 173; Oppenheim, 1:690.

29. Brierly, p. 173; Bickel, p. 46; "Developments in the Law," pp. 1300–1301.

30. "Broadly," because example *g* above arguably does not fit this pattern. all depends upon whether we construe this as a positive duty to provide iens with something good ("due process of law") or as a negative duty not do something bad to them ("deny them due process of law"). This, in turn, epends upon where we set the baseline of how well off they would have been sent our intervention in the first place.

31. I say "usually" because there are some unilateral power relations (like at of doctor and patient or parent and child) that might imply special duties r one but not the other party to the relationship; see Goodin, *Protecting the ulnerable.*

32. The sacrifices might be actual or merely hypothetical (i.e., should the ccasion arise, they would make the sacrifice).

33. Standard prescriptions along these lines of medieval churchmen were rengthened by each of the early modern international lawyers in turn—Gro- us, Wolff, and Vattel—so that by the time of Sidgwick's *Elements of Politics,* ie "principle of mutual non-interference" (p. 231) could be said to be "the indamental principle" of international morality with no equivocation. It emains so to this day, in the view of most lawyers and of many philosophers; ee, e.g., Michael Walzer, *Just and Unjust Wars* (New York; Basic, 1977), and The Moral Standing of States," *Philosophy and Public Affairs* 9 (1980): 209–29 eprinted in *Global Ethics: Seminal Essays,* 51–71].

34. This thought finds its fullest contemporary expression in the notion of ie "circumstances of justice" that John Rawls, *A Theory of Justice* (Cambridge, IA: Harvard University Press, 1971), pp. 126–30, borrows from David Hume, *Treatise of Human Nature* (London: John Noon, 1739), book 3, part 2, sec- on 2, and *An Enquiry Concerning the Principles of Morals* (London: Cadell, 777), section 3, part 1. Some international relations theorists defend this nalysis at length; see, e.g., Wolff's *Law of Nations,* and Beitz's *Political Theory nd International Relations,* pp. 143–53 [Part 3 of Beitz's book, in which the eferenced pages are, is based on his essay "Justice and International Relations," irst published in *Philosophy and Public Affairs* 4: 4 (summer 1975): 360–89 and eprinted herein 21–48] (cf. his "Cosmopolitan Ideals and National Sentiment," *ournal of Philosophy* 80 [1983]: 591–600, p. 595 [reprinted in *Global Ethics: eminal Essays,* 107–17, at 110–111]). Other commentators seem almost to fall nto this way of talking without thinking (see Nagel, p. 81; and Tony Honoré, The Human Community and the Principle of Majority Rule," in *Community s a Social Ideal,* ed. Eugene Kamenka [London: Edward Arnold, 1982], pp. 47–60, p. 154).

35. These are addressed, in their particular applications to the mutual- enefit model of international obligations, in Brian Barry, "Humanity and ustice in Global Perspective," in *NOMOS XXIV: Ethics, Economics and the Law,* ds. J. R. Pennock and J. W. Chapman (New York: New York University Press,

1982), pp. 219–52, pp. 225–43 [reprinted herein pp. 179–209, pp. 185-201]; and in Goodin, *Protecting the Vulnerable*, pp. 154–60.

36. Both domestic and international law go some way toward recognizing that in many respects resident aliens are much more like citizens than they are like nonresident aliens. But by and large those acknowledgments come *not* in the form of awarding them the same benefits as are enjoyed by citizens but, rather, in the form of imposing many of the same burdens on resident aliens as on citizens. A state may, e.g., compel resident aliens to pay taxes and rates and to serve in local police forces and fire brigades "for the purpose of maintaining public order and safety" in a way it may not require of nonresident aliens; Oppenheim, 1: 680–81.

37. Brian Barry, "Justice as Reciprocity," in *Justice*, ed. Eugene Kamenka and Alice E.-S. Tay (London: Edward Arnold, 1979), pp. 50–78, pp. 68–69; Robert E. Goodin, *Political Theory and Public Policy* (Chicago: University of Chicago Press, 1982), pp. 77–79.

38. The argument here would perfectly parallel that for supposing that, if a workers' cooperative needed more labor, it would hire workers rather than sell more people shares in the cooperative. Demonstrations of this have been developed independently by J. E. Meade, "The Theory of Labour-Managed Firms and of Profit Sharing," *Economic Journal* 82 (1972): 402–28; and David Miller, "Market Neutrality and the Failure of Cooperatives," *British Journal of Political Science* 11 (1981): 309–21.

39. The "participation" model of citizenship is a close cousin to this mutual-benefit-society model. Participating in a society is usually (if not quite always) a precondition for producing benefits for others in that society; and usually (if not quite always) the reason we think participants in society deserve to enjoy the fruits of formal membership is that that is seen as fair return for the benefits they have produced for the society. See "Developments in the Law," pp. 1303–11; and Peter H. Schuck, "The Transformation of Immigration Law," *Columbia Law Review* 84 (1984): 1–90.

40. Since they are, ex hypothesi, congenital handicaps, there is no motive for those who have safely been born without suffering the handicap to set up a mutual insurance scheme to protect themselves against those risks.

41. "Nationality" and the duties to compatriots to which such notions give rise are just the sorts of "institutions" that Henry Shue ("Mediating Duties," this issue [*Ethics* 98:4 (July 1988): 687–704]) shows to be so crucial in implementing any duties of a positive sort. How, precisely, the "assignment" of responsibility is accomplished can safely be left open: sometimes, people and peoples get assigned to some national community by some specific agency (the UN Trusteeship Council, e.g.); more often, assignments are the products of historical accidents and conventions. However they are accomplished, these "assignments" must specify both who is responsible for you and what they are responsible for doing for you. Even so-called perfect duties, which specify the former precisely, are characteristically vague on the latter matter (specifying,

e.g., a duty to provide a "healthful diet" for your children), and require further inputs of a vaguely "institutional" sort to flesh out their content.

42. Goodin, *Protecting the Vulnerable*; Philip Pettit and Robert E. Goodin, "The Possibility of Special Duties," *Canadian Journal of Philosophy* 16 (1986): 651–76.

43. Broadly the same strategy is pursued by Shue in "Mediating Duties," this issue [*Ethics* 98:4 (July 1988): 687–704].

44. This, incidentally, provides an alternative explanation for why we should appoint lifeguards for crowded but not uncrowded beaches. The standard logic—true, too, in its way—is that it is a more efficient allocation of scarce resources since it is more likely that more people will need rescuing on crowded beaches. Over and above all that, however, it is also true that an "obvious" lifesaver will be needed more on crowded than uncrowded beaches to keep uncoordinated helpers from doing each other harm.

45. That is to say that the ascription of "role responsibilities" takes on the same two-tier structure familiar to us from discussions of "indirect consequentialism"; see Hare, pp. 135–40, 201–5; and Bernard Williams, "Professional Morality and Its Dispositions," in *The Good Lawyer*, ed. David Luban (Totowa, N.J.: Rowman & Allanheld, 1983), pp. 259-69.

46. Nagel, p. 81; Williams, *Moral Luck*, chapter 1.

47. Assigning responsibility to some might have the effect of letting others off the hook too easily. It is the job of the police to stop murders, so none of the onlookers watching Kitty Genovese's murder thought it their place to get involved; it is the lifeguard's job to rescue drowning swimmers, so onlookers might stand idly by watching her botch the job rather than stepping in to help themselves; and so on. This emphasizes the importance of back-up responsibilities, to be discussed below, specifying whose responsibility it is when the first person assigned the responsibility fails to discharge it.

48. This is the "division of labor model" of the adversary system discussed by Richard Wasserstrom, "Lawyers as Professionals: Some Moral Issues," *Human Rights* 5 (1975): 1–24, p. 9, and "Roles and Morality," in Luban, ed., pp. 25–37, p. 30.

49. This is, I believe, broadly in line with Christian Wolff's early analysis. Certainly he believes that we have special duties toward our own nations: "Every nation ought to care for its own self, and every person in a nation ought to care for his nation" (section 135). But it is clear from Wolff's preface (sections 9–15) that those special rights and duties are set in the context of, and derived from, a scheme to promote the greater common good of all nations as a whole. Among contemporary writers, this argument is canvassed, not altogether approvingly, by Shue, *Basic Rights*, pp. 139–44; and William K. Frankena, "Moral Philosophy and World Hunger," in *World Hunger and Moral Obligation*, ed. William Aiken and Hugh La Follette (Englewood Cliffs, NJ: Prentice-Hall, 1977), pp. 66–84, p. 81. Hare, pp. 201–2, is more bullish on the proposal.

50. Sidgwick, *Elements of Politics*, chap, 14; Brian Barry, "Self-government Revisited," in *The Nature of Political Theory*, ed. David Miller and Larry

Siedentop (Oxford: Clarendon, 1983), pp. 121–54; Alasdair MacIntyre, "Is Patriotism a Virtue?" (Lawrence: University of Kansas, Lindley Lecture, March 26, 1984 [reprinted in *Global Ethics: Seminal Essays*, 119–38]. Compare Cottingham, pp. 370–74. Notice that the principle urged by David Miller in arguing for "The Ethical Significance of Nationality," (this issue [*Ethics* 98: 4 (July 1988): 647–62, reprinted herein 235–53]) is very much in line with my own in its practical implications: *if* people have national sentiments, then social institutions should be arranged so as to respect them; but Miller gives no reason for believing that people should or must have such sentiments, nor does he pose any objection to people's extending such sentiments to embrace the world at large if they so choose.

51. That is to say, if general duties would be better discharged by assigning special responsibilities to a group of people who enjoy helping one another, then we should so assign responsibilities—not because there is anything intrinsically good about enjoying helping one another, but merely because that is the best means to the intrinsically good discharging of general duties.

52. If example *g* in Section II is construed as a special positive duty toward aliens, as n. 30 above suggests it might be, then it poses something of a problem for all three other models of special responsibilities. All three, for diverse reasons, would expect *positive* duties to be stronger vis-à-vis compatriots, not toward aliens. The assigned responsibility model alone is capable of explaining the phenomenon, as a manifestation of our general duty toward everyone at large that persists even after special responsibilities have been allocated. More will be said of that residual general duty below.

53. Thus, in international law aliens typically have no right themselves to protest directly to host states if they have been mistreated by it; instead, they are expected to petition their home governments, who make representations to the host state in turn (Oppenheim, volume I, chapter 3). Similarly, the reason aliens may be denied political rights in their host states is presumably that they have access to the political process in their home states. It is an implication of my argument here that, if states want to press the special claims of their own citizens to the exclusion of all others, then they have a duty to make sure that everyone has a competent protector—just as if everyone at the seashore wants to bathe undisturbed by any duty to rescue drowning swimmers, then they have a duty to appoint a lifeguard.

54. See Goodin, *Protecting the Vulnerable*, chapter 5; and Pettit and Goodin, "The Possibility of Special Duties," pp. 673–76.

55. Vattel, book 1, chapter 19, section 230; see, similarly, Wolff, sections 147–49; and Grotius, book 2, chapter 2, section 16. Vattel and Wolff specifically assert the right of the exile to dwell anywhere in the world, subject to the permission of the host state—permission that the host may properly refuse only for "good" and "special reasons" (having to do, in Vattel's formulation at least, with the strict scarcity of resources in the nation for satisfying the needs of its preexisting members). The duty of the international community (i.e., the "set

of states as a whole") to care for refugees derives from the fact that refugees "have no remaining recourse other than to seek international restitution of their need," as the point has been put by Andrew E. Shacknove, "Who Is a Refugee?" *Ethics* 95 (1985): 274–84.

56. Similarly, in the "advocacy model" in the law, it is morally proper for attorneys to press their clients' cases as hard as they can if and only if everyone has legal representation; if institutions fail to guarantee that, it is wrong for attorneys to do so. See Wasserstrom, "Lawyers as Professionals," pp. 12–13, and "Roles and Morality," pp. 36–37.

57. Ideally, of course, this model would have both the rich getting richer and the poor getting richer. Even in this ideal world, however, it is almost inevitable that the rich would get richer at a faster rate than the poor. Assuming that the needs of the poor grow more quickly than those of the rich, then in some real sense it may well be inevitable, even in this ideal world, that the poor will actually get (relatively) poorer.

58. Or, as Miller puts it, it is wrong to put the poorly-off in charge of the poorly-off and the well-off in charge of the well-off ("The Ethical Significance of Nationality," this issue [*Ethics* 98: 4 (July 1988): 647–62, reprinted herein 235–53]). That is not a critique of my model but, instead, a critique of existing international boundaries from within my model.

59. Compare Barry, "Self-government Revisited," pp. 234–39.

60. Some have offered, as a reductio of my argument, the observation that one way of "reconstituting" state boundaries as I suggest might be for a particularly poor state to volunteer to become a colony of another richer country. But that would be a true implication of my argument only if (a) citizens of the would-be colony have no very strong interests in their national autonomy and (b) the colonial power truly discharges its duties to protect and promote the interests of the colony, rather than exploiting it. The sense that this example constitutes a reductio of my argument derives, I submit, from a sense that one or the other of those propositions is false. But in that case, it would not be an implication of my argument, either.

61. This duty to render assistance across poorly constituted boundaries might be regarded as a "secondary, backup responsibility" that comes into play when those assigned primary responsibility prove unwilling or unable to discharge it. In *Protecting the Vulnerable*, chapter 5, I argue that such responsibilities come into play whatever the reason for the default on the part of the agent with primary responsibility. There, I also argue that one of our more important duties is to organize political action to press for our community as a whole to discharge these duties, rather than necessarily trying to do it all by ourselves. That saves my model from the counterintuitive consequence that well-off Swedes, knowing that the welfare state will feed their own children if they do not, should send all their own food to starving Africans who would not otherwise be fed rather than giving any of it to their own children.

# 11. JÜRGEN HABERMAS

Habermas argues for three claims. The first is that a commitment to constitutional democracy need not entail that citizens must share a common language, ethnicity, or national culture, but that it does require a shared political culture—a commitment to constitutional patriotism. The second is that the emergence of an identity oriented toward European citizenship will depend not only on economic integration, but also on political mobilization via new social movements and the expansion of communication networks. In this process of identity formation, a common commitment to a set of universalistic values and constitutional principles will be helpful. The third claim is that European states should adopt liberal immigration policies that place limits on immigration to preserve only a common *political*—not national—culture.

## Citizenship and National Identity: Some Reflections on the Future of Europe

First published in German as Staatsbürgerschaft und nationale Identität: Überlegungen zur europäischen Zukunft, *Erker-Galerie AG, Galerie Verlag Presse, 1991. First published in English in* Praxis International *12: 1 (April 1992): 1–19; reprinted as Appendix II in* Between Facts and Norms, *Cambridge MA: MIT Press, 1996.*

Until the mid-eighties, history seemed to be entering that crystalline state known as *posthistoire*. This was Arnold Gehlen's term for the strange feeling that the more things change, the more they remain the same. *Rien ne va plus*—nothing really surprising can happen anymore. Locked in by systemic constraints, all the possibilities seemed to have been exhausted, all the alternatives frozen, and any remaining options drained of meaning. Since then this mood has completely changed.

History is once again on the move, accelerating, even overheating. New problems are shifting the old perspectives. What is more important, new perspectives are opening up for the future, points of view that restore our ability to perceive alternative courses of action.

Three historical movements of our contemporary period, once again in flux, affect the relation between citizenship and national identity: (1) In the wake of German unification, the liberation of the East Central European states from Soviet tutelage, and the nationality conflicts breaking out across Eastern Europe, the question concerning the future of the nation-state has taken on an unexpected topicality. (2) The fact that the states of the European Community are gradually growing together, especially with the caesura that will be created when a common market is introduced in 1993, sheds light on the relation between the nation-state and democracy: The democratic processes constituted at the level of the nation-state lag hopelessly behind the economic integration taking place at a supranational level. (3) The tremendous tide of immigration from the poor regions of the East and South, with which Europe will be increasingly confronted in the coming years, lends the problem of asylum a new significance and urgency. This process exacerbates the conflict between the universalistic principles of constitutional democracy, on the one hand, and the particularistic claims to preserve the integrity of established forms of life, on the other.

These three topics offer an occasion for the conceptual clarification of some normative perspectives from which we can gain a better understanding of the complex relation between citizenship and national identity.

## I. THE PAST AND FUTURE OF THE NATION-STATE

The events in Germany and the Eastern European states have given a new twist to a long-standing discussion in the Federal Republic about the path to a "postnational society."[1] Many German intellectuals have complained, for example, about the democratic deficits of a unification process that is implemented at the administrative and economic levels without the participation of citizens; they now find themselves accused of "postnational arrogance." This controversy over the form and tempo of political unification is fueled not only by the contrary feelings of the disputing parties but also by conceptual unclarities. One side sees the accession of the five new *Länder* to the Federal Republic as restoring the unity of a nation-state torn apart four decades ago. From this viewpoint, the nation represents the prepolitical unity of a community with a shared historical destiny (*Schicksalsgemeinschaft*). The other side sees political unification as restoring democracy and the rule of law in a territory where civil rights have been suspended in one form or another since 1933. From this viewpoint, what used to be West Germany was no less a nation of enfranchised citizens than is the new Federal Republic. This republican usage strips the term "nation-state" of precisely those prepolitical and ethnic-cultural connotations that have accompanied the expression in modern Europe. Dissolving the semantic connections between state citizenship and national identity honors the fact that today the classic form of the nation-state is, with the transition of the European Community to a political union, disintegrating. This is confirmed by a glance back at its genesis in early modernity.

In modern Europe, the premodern form of *empire* that used to unite numerous peoples remained rather unstable, as shown in the cases of the Holy Roman Empire or the Russian and Ottoman empires.[2] A second, federal form of state emerged from the belt of Central European cities. It was above all in Switzerland that a *federation* developed that was strong enough to balance the ethnic tensions within a multicultural association of citizens. But it was only the third form, the centrally administered *territorial state*, that came to have a lasting formative effect on the structure of the European system of states. It first emerged—as in Portugal, Spain, France, England, and Sweden—from kingdoms. Later, as democratization proceeded along the lines of the French example, it developed into the *nation-state*. This state formation secured the boundary conditions under which the capitalist economic system could develop worldwide. That it, the nation-state provided the infrastructure for an administration disciplined by the rule of law, and it guaranteed a realm of individual and collective action free of state interference. Moreover—and this is what primarily interests us here—it laid the foundation for the ethnic and cultural homogeneity that made it possible, beginning in the late eighteenth century, to forge ahead with the democratization of government, albeit at the cost of excluding and oppressing minorities. Nation-state and democracy are twins born of the French Revolution. From a cultural point of view, they both stand under the shadow of nationalism.

This national consciousness is a specifically modern manifestation of cultural integration. The political consciousness of national membership arises from a dynamic that first took hold of the population after processes of economic and social modernization had torn people from their places in the social hierarchy, simultaneously mobilizing and isolating them as individuals. Nationalism is a form of conscious- ness that presupposes an appropriation, filtered by historiography and reflection, of cultural traditions. Originating in an educated bourgeois public, it spreads through the channels of modern mass communication. Both elements, its literary mediation and its dissemination through public media, lend to nationalism its artificial features; its somewhat constructed character makes it naturally susceptible to manipulative misuse by political elites.

The history of the term "nation" reflects the historical genesis of the nation-state.[3] For the Romans, *Natio* was the goddess of birth and origin. *Natio* refers, like *gens* and *populus* but unlike *civitas*, to peoples and tribes who were not yet organized in political associations; indeed, the Romans often used it to refer to "savage," "barbaric," or "pagan" peoples. In this classic usage, then, nations are communities of people of the same descent, who are integrated geographically, in the form of settlements or neighborhoods, and culturally by their common language, customs, and traditions, but who are not yet politically inte- grated through the organizational form of the state. This meaning of "nation" persisted through the Middle Ages and worked its way into the vernacular languages in the fifteenth century. Even Kant still wrote that "those inhabitants ... which recognize themselves as being united into a civil whole through common descent, are called a nation (*gens*)."[4] However, in the early-modern period a competing usage arose: The nation is the bearer of sovereignty. The estates represented the "nation" over against the "king." Since the middle of the eighteenth century, these two meanings of "nation"—community of descent and "people of a state"—have intertwined. With the French Revolution, the "nation" became the source of state sovereignty, for example, in the thought of Emmanuel Sieyès. Each nation is now supposed to be granted the right to political self-determination. The intentional democratic community (*Willensgemeinschaft*) takes the place of the ethnic complex.

With the French Revolution, then, the meaning of "nation" was transformed from a prepolitical quantity into a constitutive feature of the political identity of the citizens of a democratic polity. At the end of the nineteenth century, the conditional relation between ascribed national identity and acquired democratic citizenship could even be reversed. Thus the gist of Ernest Renan's famous saying, "the existence of a nation is... a daily plebiscite," was already directed *against* nationalism. After 1871, Renan could rebut Germany's claims to the Alsace by referring to the inhabitants' French nationality only because he thought of the "nation" as a nation of citizens, and not as a community of descent. The nation of citizens finds its identity not in ethnic and cultural commonalities but in the practice of citizens who actively exercise their rights to participation and communication. At this juncture, the republican strand of citizenship completely parts company with the idea of belonging to a prepolitical community integrated on the basis of descent, shared tradition, and common language. Viewed from this end, the initial fusion of national consciousness with republican conviction only functioned as a catalyst.

The nationalism mediated by the works of historians and romantic writers, hence by scholarship and literature, grounded a collective identity that played a *functional* role for the notion of citizenship that originated in the French Revolution. In the melting pot of national consciousness, the ascriptive features of one's origin were transformed into just so many results of a conscious appropriation of tradition. Ascribed nationality gave way to an achieved nationalism, that is, to a conscious product of one's own efforts. This nationalism was able to foster people's identification with a role that demanded a high degree of personal commitment, even to the point of self-sacrifice; in this respect, general conscription was simply the flip side of civil rights. National consciousness and republican conviction in a sense proved themselves in the willingness to fight and die for one's country. This explains the complementary relation that originally obtained between nationalism and republicanism: One became the vehicle for the emergence of the other.

However, this social-psychological connection does not mean that the two are linked at the conceptual level. National independence and collective self-assertion against foreign nations can be understood as a collective form of freedom. This national freedom does not coincide with the genuinely political freedom that citizens enjoy within a country. For this reason, the modern understanding of this republican freedom can, at a later point, cut its umbilical links to the womb of the national consciousness of freedom that originally gave it birth. The nation-state sustained a close connection between "demos" and "ethos" only briefly.[5] Citizenship was never conceptually tied to national identity.

The concept of citizenship developed out of Rousseau's concept of self-determination. "Popular sovereignty" was initially understood as a delimitation or reversal of royal sovereignty and was judged to rest on a contract between a people and its government. Rousseau and Kant, by contrast, did not conceive of popular sovereignty as the transfer of ruling authority from above to below or as its distribution between two contracting parties. For them, popular sovereignty signified rather the transformation of authority into *self-legislation*. A historical pact, the civil contract, is replaced here by the social contract, which functions as an abstract model for the way in which an authority legitimated only through the implementation of democratic self-legislation is *constituted*. Political authority thereby loses its character of quasi-natural violence: The *auctoritas* of the state should be purged of the remaining elements of *violentia*. According to this idea, "only the united and consenting Will of all—... by which each decides the same for all and all decide the same for each—can legislate."[6]

This idea does not refer to the substantive generality of a popular will that would owe its unity to a prior homogeneity of descent or form of life. The consensus fought for and achieved in an association of free and equal persons ultimately rests only on the unity of a *procedure* to which all consent. This procedure of democratic opinion- and will-formation assumes a differentiated form in constitutions based on the rule of law. In a pluralistic society, the constitution expresses a formal consensus. The citizens want to regulate their living together according to principles that are in the equal interest of each and thus can meet with the justified assent of all. Such an association is structured by relations of mutual recognition in which each person can expect to be respected by all as free and equal. Each and every person should receive a three-fold recognition: They should receive equal protection and equal respect in their integrity as irreplaceable individuals, as members of ethnic or cultural groups, and as citizens, that is, as members of the political community. This idea of a self-determining political community has assumed a variety of concrete legal forms in the different constitutions and political systems of Western Europe and the United States.

In the language of law, though, *"Staatsbürgerschaft," "citoyenneté,"* or "citizenship" referred for a long time only to nationality or member-ship in a state; only recently has the concept been enlarged to cover the status of citizens defined in terms of civil rights.[7] *Membership in a state* assigns a particular person to a particular nation whose existence is recognized in terms of international law. Regardless of the internal organization of state authority, this definition of membership, together with the territorial demarcation of the country's borders, serves to delimit the state in social terms. In the democratic constitutional state, which understands itself as an association of free and equal persons, state membership depends on the principle of voluntariness. Here, the conventional ascriptive characteristics of domicile and birth (*jus soli* and *jus sanguinis*) by no means justify a person's being irrevocably subjected to that government's sovereign authority. These characteristics function merely as administrative criteria for attributing to citizens an assumed, implicit consent, to which the right to emigrate or to renounce one's citizenship corresponds.[8]

Today, though, the expressions *"Staatsbürgerschaft"* or "citizenship" are used not only to denote organizational membership in a state, but also for the status materially defined by civil rights and duties. The Basic Law of the Federal Republic has no explicit parallel to the Swiss notion of active citizenship.[9] However, taking Article 33, section 1, of the Basic Law as its starting point, German legal thought has expanded the package of civil rights and duties, especially the basic rights, to generate an overall status of a similar kind.[10] In the republican view, citizenship has its point of reference in the problem of the legal community's self-organization, whereas its core consists in the rights of political participation and communication. Rolf Grawert, for example, conceives citizenship as "the legal institution through which the individual member of a state is given a collaborative role in the concrete matrix of state actions."[11] The status of citizen fixes in particular the democratic rights to which the individual can reflexively lay claim in order to *change* his material legal status.

In the philosophy of law, two contrary interpretations of this active citizenship vie with each other for pride of place. The role of the citizen is given an individualist and instrumentalist reading in the liberal tradition of natural law starting with John Locke, whereas a communitarian and ethical understanding of this role has emerged in the republican tradition of political philosophy going back to Aristotle. In the first case, citizenship is conceived along the lines of an organizational membership that grounds a legal status. In the second case, it is modeled after a self-determining ethnic-cultural community. In the first interpretation, individuals remain outside the state. In exchange for organizational services and benefits, they make specific contributions, such as voting inputs and tax payments, to the reproduction of the state. In the second interpretation, citizens are integrated into the political community like the parts of a whole, in such a way that they can develop their personal and social identity only within the horizon of shared traditions and recognized political institutions. On the liberal reading, citizens do not differ essentially from private persons who bring their prepolitical interests to bear vis-à-vis the state apparatus. On the republican reading, citizenship is actualized solely in the collective practice of self-determination. Charles Taylor describes these two competing concepts of citizen as follows:

> One [model] focuses mainly on individual rights and equal treatment, as well as a government performance which takes account of the citizen's preferences. This is what has to be secured. Citizen capacity consists mainly in the power to retrieve these rights and ensure equal treatment, as well as to influence the effective decision makers.... [T]hese institutions have an entirely instrumental significance.... [N]o value is put on participation in rule for its own sake....

> The other model, by contrast, defines participation in self-rule as of the essence of freedom, as part of what must be secured. This is ... an essential component of citizen capacity....Full participation in self-rule is seen as being able, at least part of the time, to have some part in the forming of a ruling consensus, with which one can identify along with others. To rule and be ruled in turn means that at least some of the time the governors can be "us," and not always "them."[12]

The holistic model of a community that incorporates its citizens in every aspect of their lives is in many respects inadequate for modern politics. Nevertheless, it has an advantage over the organization model, in which isolated individuals confront a state apparatus to which they are only functionally connected by membership: The holistic model makes it clear that political autonomy is an end in itself that can be realized not by the single individual privately pursuing his own interests but only by all together in an intersubjectively shared practice. The citizen's legal status is constituted by a network of egalitarian relations of mutual recognition. It assumes that each person can adopt the participant perspective of the first-person plural—and not just the perspective of an observer or actor oriented to his own success.

Legally guaranteed relations of recognition do not, however, reproduce themselves of their own accord. Rather, they require the cooperative efforts of a civic practice that no one can be compelled to enter into by legal norms. It is for good reason that modern coercive law does not extend to the motives and basic attitudes of its addressees. A legal duty, say, to make active use of democratic rights has something totalitarian about it. Thus the legally constituted status of citizen depends on the *supportive spirit* of a consonant background of legally noncoercible motives and attitudes of a citizenry oriented toward the common good. The republican model of citizenship reminds us that constitutionally protected institutions of freedom are worth only what a population *accustomed* to political freedom and settled in the "we" perspective of active self-determination makes of them. The legally institutionalized role of citizen must be embedded in the context of a liberal political culture. This is why the communitarians insist that citizens must "patriotically" identify with their form of life. Taylor, too, postulates a shared consciousness that arises from the identification with the consciously accepted traditions of one's own political and cultural community: "The issue is, can our patriotism survive the marginalization of participatory self-rule? As we have seen, a patriotism is a common identification with an historical community founded on certain values....But it must be one whose core values incorporate freedom."[13]

With this, Taylor seems to contradict my thesis that there is only a historically contingent and not a conceptual connection between republicanism and nationalism. Studied more closely, however, Taylor's remarks boil down to the statement that the universalist principles of constitutional democracy need to be somehow anchored in the political culture of each country. Constitutional principles can neither take shape in social practices nor become the driving force for the dynamic project of creating an association of free and equal persons until they are situated in the historical context of a nation of citizens in such a way that they link up with those citizens' motives and attitudes.

As the examples of multicultural societies like Switzerland and the United States demonstrate, a political culture in which constitutional principles can take root need by no means depend on all citizens sharing the same language or the same ethnic and cultural origins. A liberal political culture is only the common denominator for a *constitutional* patriotism (*Verfassungspatriotismus*) that heightens an awareness of both the diversity and the integrity of the different forms of life coexisting in a multicultural society. In a future Federal Republic of European States, the *same* legal principles would also have to be interpreted from the perspectives of *different* national traditions and histories. One's own tradition must in each case be appropriated from a vantage point relativized by the perspectives of other traditions, and appropriated in such a manner that it can be brought into a transnational, Western European constitutional culture. A particularist anchoring of *this kind* would not do away with one iota of the universalist meaning of popular sovereignty and human rights. The original thesis stands: Democratic citizenship need not be rooted in the national identity of a people. However, regardless of the diversity of different cultural forms of life, it does require that every citizen be socialized into a common political culture.

## II. NATION-STATE AND DEMOCRACY IN A UNIFIED EUROPE

The political future of the European Community sheds light on the relation between citizenship and national identity in yet another respect. The concept of citizenship developed by Aristotle was, after all, originally tailored for the size of cities or city-states. The transformation of populations into nations that formed states occurred, as we have seen, under the banner of a nationalism that seemed to reconcile republican ideas with the larger dimensions of modern territorial states. It was in the political forms created by the nation-state that modern trade and commerce arose. And, like the bureaucratic state, the capitalist economy, too, developed a systemic logic of its own. The markets for goods, capital, and labor obey their own logic, independent of the intentions of human subjects. Alongside the administrative power incorporated in government bureaucracies, money has become an anonymous medium of societal integration operating above the participants' heads. This *system integration* competes with the form of integration mediated by the actors' consciousnesses, that is, the *social integration* taking place through values, norms, and mutual understanding. The *political integration* that occurs through democratic citizenship represents one aspect of this general social integration. For this reason, the relation between capitalism and democracy is fraught with tension, something liberal theories often deny.

Examples from the developing countries show that the relation between the development of the democratic constitutional state and capitalist modernization is by no means linear. Nor did the social-welfare compromise, operative in Western democracies since the end of the Second World War, come about automatically. The development of the European Community manifests this same tension between democracy and capitalism in another way. Here it is expressed in the vertical divide between the systemic integration of economy and administration that emerges at the supranational level and the political integration effected only at the level of the nation-state. Hence, the technocratic shape of the European Community reinforces doubts that were already associated with the normative expectations linked with the role of the democratic citizen. Were not these expectations always largely illusory, even within the borders of the nation-state? Did not the temporary symbiosis of republicanism and nationalism merely mask the fact that the concept of the citizen is, at best, suited for the less complex relations of an ethnically homogenous and surveyable polity still integrated by tradition and custom?

Today the "European Economic Community" has become a "European Community" that proclaims the political will to form a "European Political Union." Aside from India, the United States provides the only example for a governmental structure of this sort (which at present would encompass 320 million inhabitants). The United States, though, is a multicultural society united by the same political culture and (at least for now) a single language, whereas the European Union would represent a multilingual state of different nationalities. Even if such an association were to resemble more of a Federal Republic than a federation of semisovereign individual states—a question that is still a matter of controversy—it would have to retain certain features of de Gaulle's "Europe of Fatherlands." The nation-states as we know them would, even in such a Europe, *continue to have* a strong structuring effect.

However, nation-states present a problem along the thorny path to European Union not so much on account of their insuperable claims to sovereignty but because democratic processes have hitherto functioned, imperfectly to be sure, only inside national boundaries. To put it briefly, up to the present the political public sphere has been fragmented into national units. Hence we cannot avoid the question whether a European citizenship can even exist at all. By this I do not mean the possibility of collective political action across national boundaries but the consciousness "of an obligation toward the European common good."[14] As late as 1974, Raymond Aron answered this question with a decisive "No." At the supranational steering level, an extensive European market will soon be set up with legal-administrative instruments. This contrasts with the very limited powers of the European Parliament, a body that will probably be scarcely visible in the political public spheres of the member states. To date, rights of political participation do not effectively extend beyond national boundaries.

The administration of justice by the European Court takes the "Five Freedoms of the Common Market" as its point of orientation and interprets as basic rights the free movement of goods, the free movement of labor, the freedom of entrepreneurial establishment, the freedom to provide services, and the free movement of capital and payments. This corresponds to the powers the Treaty of Rome conferred on the Council of Ministers and the High Commission in Article 3. These in turn are explained in terms of the goal set out in Article 9: "The Community shall be based upon a customs union which shall cover all trade in goods." The internal market and the planned establishment of an autonomous central bank serve the same end. The new level of economic interdependence should give rise to a growing need for coordination in other policy fields as well, such as environmental policy, fiscal and social policy, educational policy. This need for regulation will again be assessed primarily from the standpoint of economic rationality, according to standards of fair competition. Thus far these tasks are accomplished by European organizations that have intermeshed to form a dense administrative network. The new functional elites are, formally speaking, still accountable to the governments and institutions in their respective countries of origin; in reality, however, they have already outgrown their national contexts. Professional civil servants form a bureaucracy that is aloof from democratic processes.

For the citizen, this translates into an ever greater gap between being passively affected and actively participating. An increasing number of measures decided at a supranational level affect the lives of more and more citizens to an ever greater extent. Given that the role of citizen has hitherto been effectively institutionalized only at the level of the nation-state, however, citizens have no promising opportunities to bring up issues and influence European decisions. M. R. Lepsius tersely states, "There is no European public opinion."[15] Does this disparity represent merely a passing imbalance that can be set right by the parliamentarization of the Brussels expertocracy? Or do these bureaucracies, oriented as they are by economic criteria of rationality, merely highlight developments already long under way and inexorably advancing even within nation-states? I allude here to the fact that economic imperatives have become independent of everything else and that politics has been absorbed into the state (*Verstaatlichung*). These developments undermine the status of citizen and contradict the republican claim associated with this status.

Taking England as his example, T. H. Marshall has studied the expansion of citizen rights and duties in connection with capitalist modernization.[16] Marshall's division of such rights into "civil," "political," and "social rights" follows a well-known legal classification. Here, liberal negative rights protect the private legal subject against illegal government infringements of freedom and property; rights of political participation enable the active citizen to take part in democratic processes of opinion- and will-formation; social rights grant clients of the welfare state a minimum income and social security. Marshall advances the thesis that the status of the citizen in modern societies has been expanded and consolidated in a succession of steps. On his analysis, negative liberty rights were first supplemented by democratic rights, and then these two classical types of rights were followed by social rights. Through this process, ever greater sections of the population have acquired their full rights of membership step by step.

Even leaving the historical details aside, this suggestion of a more or less linear development only holds for what sociologists designate by the general term "inclusion." In a society increasingly differentiated along functional lines, an ever greater number of persons acquire an ever larger number of rights of access to, and participation in, an ever greater number of subsystems. Such subsystems include markets, factories, and places of work; government offices, courts, and the military; schools, hospitals, theaters, and museums; political associations and public communications media; political parties, self-governing institutions, and parliaments. For the individual, the number of memberships therewith multiplies, and the range of options expands. However, this image of linear progress emerges from a description that remains neutral toward increases or losses in autonomy. This description is blind to the actual use made of an active citizenship status that allows individuals to play a role in democratically changing their own status. Indeed, only rights of political participation ground the citizen's reflexive, self-referential legal standing. Negative liberties and social rights can, by contrast, be conferred by a paternalistic authority. In principle, the constitutional state and the welfare state are possible without democracy. Even in countries in which all three categories of rights are institutionalized, as in the "democratic and social federal state" defined by the Basic Law, article 20, these negative and social rights are still Janus-faced.

Historically speaking, liberal rights crystallized around the social position of the private-property owner. From a *functionalist* viewpoint, one can conceive them as institutionalizing a market economy, whereas, from a *normative* viewpoint, they guarantee individual freedoms. Social rights signify, from a *functionalist* viewpoint, the installation of welfare bureaucracies, whereas, from a *normative* viewpoint, they grant compensatory claims to a just share of social wealth. It is true that both individual freedom and welfare guarantees can also be viewed as the legal basis for the social independence that first makes it possible to put political rights into effect. But these are empirical, and not conceptually necessary, relationships. Negative liberties and social rights can just as well facilitate the privatistic retreat from a citizen's role. In that case, citizenship is reduced to a client's relationships to administrations that provide services and benefits.

The syndrome of civil privatism and the exercise of citizenship from the standpoint of client interests become all the more probable the more the economy and state—which have been institutionalized through the same rights—develop their own internal systemic logics and push the citizen into the peripheral role of mere organization member. As self-regulating systems, economy and administration tend to close themselves off from their environments and obey only their internal imperatives of money and power. They explode the model of a polity that determines itself through the shared practice of the citizens themselves. The fundamental republican idea of the self-conscious political integration of a "community" of free and equal persons is obviously too concrete and simple for modern conditions. This is true, at least, if one is still thinking of a nation; the republican idea is still more problematic if one's model is an ethnically homogeneous "community of shared destiny" held together by common traditions.

Fortunately, law is a medium that allows for a much more abstract notion of civic, or public, autonomy. Today the public sovereignty of the people has withdrawn into legally institutionalized procedures and the informal, more or less discursive opinion- and will-formation made possible by basic rights. I am assuming here a network of different communicative forms, which, however, must be organized in such a way that one can presume they bind public administration to rational premises. In so doing, they also impose social and ecological limits on the economic system, yet without impinging on its inner logic. This provides a *model of deliberative politics*. This model no longer starts with the macrosubject of a communal whole but with anonymously intermeshing discourses. It shifts the brunt of normative expectations over to democratic procedures and the infrastructure of a political public sphere fueled by spontaneous sources. Today the mass of the population can exercise rights of political participation only in the sense of being integrated into, and having an influence on, an informal circuit of public communication that cannot be organized as a whole but is rather carried by a liberal and egalitarian political culture. At the same time, deliberations in decision-making bodies must remain porous to the influx of issues, value orientations, contributions, and programs originating from a political public sphere unsubverted by power. Only if such an interplay were to materialize between institutionalized opinion- and will-formation and informal public communications could citizenship mean more today than the aggregation of prepolitical individual interests and the passive enjoyment of rights bestowed by a paternalistic authority.

I cannot go into this model in any further detail here.[17] Yet, when we assess the chances for a future European citizenship, we can glean some empirical clues, at least, from the history of the institutionalization of civil rights (in the broad sense) in the nation-state. Clearly, the schema that presents civil rights essentially as the product of class struggle is too narrow.[18] Other types of social movements, above all migrations and wars, have also driven the development of a full-fledged citizenship status. In addition, factors that prompted the juridification of new forms of inclusion also had an impact on the political mobilization of the population, thus contributing to the activation of already existing rights of citizenship.[19] These and similar findings permit a cautiously optimistic extrapolation of the course that European development could take, so that we are not condemned to resignation from the outset.

The European market will set in motion a greater horizontal mobility and multiply the contacts among members of different nationalities. In addition to this, immigration from Eastern Europe and the poverty-stricken regions of the Third World will heighten the multicultural diversity of society. This will no doubt give rise to social tensions. But if those tensions are dealt with productively, they can foster a political mobilization that will give additional impetus to the new endogenous social movements already emergent within nation-states—I am thinking of the peace, environmental, and women's movements. These tendencies would strengthen the relevance that public issues have for the lifeworld. At the same time, there is a growing pressure of problems that can be solved only at a coordinated European level. Under these conditions, communication complexes could develop in Europe-wide public spheres. These publics would provide a favorable context both for new parliamentary bodies of regions that are now in the process of merging and for a European Parliament furnished with greater authority.

To date, in the member states the policy of the European Community is not yet an object of a legitimating public debate. By and large, national public spheres are still culturally isolated from one another. That is, they are rooted in contexts in which political questions become significant only against the background of each nation's own history. In the future, however, a common *political* culture could differentiate itself from the various *national* cultures. A differentiation could appear between a Europe-wide *political* culture and the various *national* traditions in art and literature, historiography, philosophy, and so on, which have been branching out since early modernity. Cultural elites and the mass media would have an important role to play in this process. Unlike the American variant, a European constitutional patriotism would have to grow together from various nationally specific interpretations of the same universalist principles of law. Switzerland provides an example for how a common politicocultural self-understanding can emerge by differentiation from the cultural orientations of different nationalities.

In this context, our task is less to reassure ourselves of our common origins in the European Middle Ages than to develop a new political self-consciousness commensurate with the role of Europe in the world of the twenty-first century. Hitherto, history has granted the empires that have come and gone but *one* appearance on the world stage. This is just as true of the modern states—Portugal, Spain, England, France, and Russia—as it was for the empires of antiquity. By way of exception, Europe as a whole is now being given a *second* chance. But it will be able to make use of this opportunity not on the terms of its old-style power politics but only under the changed premises of a nonimperialist process of reaching understanding with, and learning from, other cultures.

# III. IMMIGRATION AND THE CHAUVINISM OF AFFLUENCE: A DEBATE

Hannah Arendt's diagnosis—that stateless persons, refugees, and those deprived of rights would come to symbolize this century—has proved frighteningly accurate. The "displaced persons" that the Second World War left in a devastated Europe have long since been replaced by asylum seekers and immigrants flooding into a peaceful and prosperous Europe from the South and the East. The old refugee camps can no longer accommodate the flood of new immigrants. Statisticians anticipate that in coming years 20 to 30 million immigrants will come from Eastern Europe alone. This problem can be solved only by the joint action of the European states involved. In the process, a dialectic that has already taken place on a smaller scale during the process of German unification would repeat itself. The transnational movements of immigrants function as sanctions that compel Western Europe to fulfill a responsibility that has fallen on it with the bankruptcy of state socialism. Either Europe must make the utmost effort to quickly improve conditions in the poorer regions of Central and Eastern Europe or it will be flooded by asylum seekers and immigrants.

Experts are debating the capacity of the economic system to absorb these groups of people. But the readiness to politically integrate immigrants seeking economic betterment also depends on how the indigenous populations *perceive* the social and economic problems posed by immigration. This should be the sole matter for discussion. Throughout Europe, right-wing xenophobic reactions against the "corrupting influence of foreigners" has increased. The relatively deprived classes, whether they feel endangered by social decline or have already slipped into segmented marginal groups, identify quite openly with the ideologized supremacy of their own collectivity and reject everything foreign. This is the underside of a chauvinism of affluence that is on the rise everywhere. Thus the "asylum problem" also brings to light the latent tension between citizenship and national identity.

One example is the nationalistic and anti-Polish sentiments in the new German *Länder*. There the newly acquired status of citizenship in the Federal Republic was coupled with the hope that the Republic's frontier of affluence would move straightaway toward the Oder and Neisse Rivers. Their newly gained citizenship also gives many of them the ethnocentric satisfaction that they will no longer be treated as second-class Germans. They forget that the rights of the citizen guarantee liberty because they contain universal human rights. Article 4 of the Revolutionary Constitution of 1793, which defined "The Status of Citizen," was already quite consistent in granting *every* adult foreigner who lived for one year in France not just the right to remain within the country but also active citizenship rights.

In the Federal Republic, as in most Western legal systems, the legal status of aliens, homeless foreigners, and stateless persons has at least become more like the status of citizens. Because the architectonic of the Basic Law is defined by the idea of human rights, *every* inhabitant enjoys the protection of the Constitution. Foreigners have the same duties, entitlements, and legal protections as do native citizens; with few exceptions, they also receive equal treatment with regard to economic status. The large number of statutes that are indifferent to membership status relativizes the real significance of its absence. The human-rights component of citizenship will be strengthened through supranational rights, and especially through European Civil Rights, which might even affect the core opportunities for exercising political influence. The Federal Constitutional Court's decision of October 31, 1990, is notable in this context. Though it declared unconstitutional the right of foreigners to vote in municipal and district elections (i.e., the local voting right of foreigners), its justification at least acknowledged the principles raised by the petitioners: "Behind this view obviously stands the notion that the idea of democracy, and especially the idea of liberty contained in it, implies that a congruence should be established between the possessors of democratic political rights and those who are permanently subject to a specific government. This is the proper starting point."[20]

These trends simply mean that the normative content of a citizenship largely dissociated from national identity does not provide arguments for restrictive or obstructionist asylum and immigration policies. However, it remains an open question whether the European Community of today, in expectation of large streams of immigrants, can and ought to pursue foreigner and immigration policies as liberal as those of the Jacobins in their day. The pertinent *discussion in moral-theoretical*, to which I restrict myself here, turns on the concept of "special duties," those special obligations that exist only within the social boundaries of a community. The state, too, forms a concrete legal community that imposes special obligations on its members. Economic immigrants, more than asylum seekers, confront members of the European states with the problem of whether one can justify the priority of special membership-based duties over universal obligations that transcend state boundaries. I will recapitulate this recent topic of philosophical discussion in five steps.

(a) *Special obligations* are owed by specific persons to other specific persons who "are close" to them as "members," such as members of one's own family, friends and neighbors, and fellow citizens of one's political community or nation. Parents have special obligations toward their children, and vice versa; consulates in foreign countries have special obligations toward their own citizens in need of protection, and these in turn have obligations toward the institutions and laws of their own land. In this context, we think primarily of positive duties, which are indeterminate insofar as they demand acts of solidarity, care, and commitment in ways that cannot be fixed in exact terms. One cannot reasonably expect that everyone should provide help on every occasion. Special obligations, which arise from the fact that one belongs to particular communities, can be understood as socially ascribing, and substantively specifying, such naturally indeterminate duties.

Utilitarians have attempted to ground special duties in the mutual benefit that members of a polity gain from one another through their reciprocal services. Even nations and states are conceived as such "mutual-benefit societies."[21] According to this model, each member can expect that the long-term profit gained through exchange relationships with the other members is proportional to the services he himself contributes in his interactions with others. On this basis, one can justify a reciprocity of special duties and rights, which prohibits, for example, the underprivileging of guest workers. Of course, this model cannot ground any duties toward members who cannot contribute as much (e.g., the handicapped, the ill, and the elderly) or toward those in need of help (e.g., foreigners seeking asylum). The instrumental ethnocentrism of reciprocal benefit expectations would suggest an immigration policy that granted entry to foreigners only if there were reasonable prospects that they would not burden the existing balance of contributions and claims (e.g., in a social-security or national-insurance system).

(b) This counterintuitive result is a reason to abandon the utilitarian approach in favor of a model that explains special duties not in terms of the reciprocal benefits of an exchange of services among those belonging to a collectivity but in terms of the coordinating capacities of a centrally established, moral division of labor.[22] For special obligations do not vary in direct proportion to the social distance between individuals, as though the claims of those who are near to us should always have priority over those who are far. This intuition applies only within the close confines of family and neighborhood. But it is misleading insofar as all those persons beyond these intimate circles are equally close and distant. Normally, we perceive these "strangers" under the category of the "other," whether they are fellow citizens of our own nation or not. Special obligations toward "others" do not result primarily from belonging to a concrete community. They issue rather from the abstract action coordination effected by *legal* institutions. By assigning particular obligations to particular categories of persons or agents, these institutions socially and substantively specify and make binding those positive duties that otherwise remain indeterminate. On this view, special duties issue from the institutionally mediated assignment of specific responsibilities to particular addressees active in a moral division of labor. In the framework of such a legally regulated moral division of labor, the social boundaries of a legal community have only the function of regulating the distribution of responsibilities. This does not mean that our obligations in general end at these boundaries. Rather, national governments also have to see to it that citizens fulfill their positive duties toward nonmembers, such as asylum seekers. Naturally, this does not yet tell us what these duties consist in.

(c) The moral point of view obligates us to assess this problem impartially, and thus not just from the one-sided perspective of an inhabitant of an affluent region but also from the perspective of immigrants who are seeking their well-being there. In other words, they seek a free and dignified existence and not just political asylum. In John Rawls's well-known thought experiment of the original position, individuals behind a "veil of ignorance" do not know the society into which they were born or their position in that society. If one applies this moral test to our problem, then the outcome for a world society is obvious:

> Behind the "veil of ignorance," in considering possible restrictions on freedom, one adopts the perspective of the one who would be most disadvantaged by the restrictions, in this case the perspective of the alien who wants to immigrate. In the original position, then, one would insist that the right to migrate be included in the system of basic liberties for the same reasons that one would insist that the right to religious freedom be included: it might prove essential to one's plan of life.[23]

Legitimate restrictions of immigration rights could at most be justified in the light of competing considerations, for example, the need to avoid social conflicts and burdens on a scale that would seriously endanger the public order or economic reproduction of society. Criteria of ethnic descent, language, and education—or even an "attestation of belonging to the cultural community" of the land of immigration, as in the case of *Statusdeutschen* ("German by status")—could not justify privileges in the process of immigration and naturalization.

(d) The communitarians, by contrast, point to a fact that the above-mentioned individualistic approaches overlook. Contrary to what the model of the legally regulated moral division of labor suggests, the social boundaries of a political community do not have just a *functional* meaning. Rather, they regulate one's belonging to a historical community of shared destiny and a political form of life that is constitutive for the citizens' very identity: "Citizenship is an answer to the question, 'Who am I?' and 'What should I do?' when posed in the public sphere."[24] Membership in a political community grounds special duties, behind which stands a patriotic identification. This kind of loyalty reaches beyond the validity of institutionally prescribed legal duties: "Each member recognizes a loyalty to the community, expressed in a willingness to sacrifice personal gain to advance its interests."[25] The misgivings about an exclusively moral and legal view of the problem draw support from the communitarian concept of citizenship, which we have already encountered. Such conceptions are no longer appropriate for the conditions of complex societies, but they do highlight an *ethical* component that should not be ignored.

The modern state, too, represents a political form of life that cannot be translated without remainder into the abstract form of institutions designed according to general legal principles. This form of life comprises the *politicocultural* context in which universalistic constitutional principles must be implemented, for only a population *accustomed* to freedom can keep the institutions of freedom alive. For that reason, Michael Walzer is of the opinion that the right of immigration is limited by the right of a political community to preserve the integrity of its form of life. In his view, the right of citizens to self-determination includes the right of self-assertion for each particular form of life.[26]

(e) This argument, of course, can be read in two opposed ways. On the communitarian reading, additional normative restrictions should be imposed on liberal immigration rights. In addition to the

functional restrictions that result from the conditions for the reproduction of the socioeconomic system, there are restrictions that secure
the ethnic-cultural substance of the particular form of life. With this
the argument takes on a *particularistic* meaning, wherein citizenship is
intertwined, not with a national identity, but with historically specific
cultural identities. Thus Herman R. van Gunsteren, fully in the spirit of
Arendt, formulates the following condition for admission to citizenship
in a democratic polity:

> The prospective citizen must be capable and willing to be a mem-
> ber of this particular historical community, its past and future, its
> forms of life and institutions within which its members think and
> act. In a community that values autonomy and judgment of its
> members, this is obviously not a requirement of pure conformity.
> But it is a requirement of knowledge of the language and the
> culture and of acknowledgment of those institutions that foster
> the reproduction of citizens who are capable of autonomous and
> responsible judgment.[27]

Nonetheless, the requisite "competence to act as a member of *this*
particular polity"[28] must be understood in another sense completely,
namely, a *universalistic* one, as soon as the political community itself
implements universalistic constitutional principles. The identity of the
political community, which also must not be violated by immigration,
depends primarily on the legal principles anchored in the *political culture*
and not on an *ethical-cultural* form of life as a whole. It follows that one
must expect only that immigrants willingly engage in the political culture of their new home, without necessarily abandoning the cultural life
specific to their country of origin. The *political acculturation* demanded
of them does not extend to the whole of their socialization. Rather,
by importing new forms of life, immigrants can expand or multiply
the perspectives from which the shared political constitution must
be interpreted: "People live in communities with bonds and bounds,
but these may be of different kinds. In a liberal society, the bonds and
bounds should be compatible with liberal principles. Open immigration
would change the character of the community, but it would not leave
the community without any character."[29]

The discussion we have traced through steps (a) through (e) finally
yields the following normative conclusion: The European states should

agree on a liberal immigration policy. They must not circle their wagons and use a chauvinism of affluence as cover against the onrush of immigrants and asylum seekers. Certainly the democratic right to self-determination includes the right to preserve one's own *political* culture, which forms a concrete context for rights of citizenship, but it does not include the right to self-assertion of a privileged *cultural* form of life. Within the constitutional framework of the democratic rule of law, diverse forms of life can coexist equally. These must, however, overlap in a common political culture that in turn is open to impulses from new forms of life.

Only a democratic citizenship that does not close itself off in a particularistic fashion can pave the way for a *world citizenship*, which is already taking shape today in worldwide political communications. The Vietnam War, the revolutionary changes in Eastern and Central Europe, as well as the Gulf War, are the first *world-political* events in the strict sense. Through the electronic mass media, these events were brought instantaneously before a ubiquitous public sphere. In the context of the French Revolution, Kant made reference to the reactions of a participating public. At that time, he identified the phenomenon of a world public sphere, which today is becoming political reality for the first time in a cosmopolitan matrix of communication. Even the superpowers cannot ignore the reality of worldwide protests. The ongoing state of nature between bellicose states that have already forfeited their sovereignty has at least begun to appear obsolescent. Even if we still have a long way to go before fully achieving it, the cosmopolitan condition is no longer merely a mirage. State citizenship and world citizenship form a continuum whose contours, at least, are already becoming visible.

## NOTES

First published as a monograph by Erker-Verlag, St. Gallen, 1991. I am grateful to Ingeborg Maus and Klaus Günther for critical advice and suggestions.

1. P. Glotz, *Der Irrweg des Nationalstaats* (Stuttgart, 1990); J. Habermas, *Vergangenheit als Zukunft* (Zürich, 1991), trans. and ed. M. Pensky *The Past as Future* (Lincoln, NE, 1994).

2. On the following, see M. R. Lepsius, "Der europäische Nationalstaat," in Lepsius, *Interessen, Ideen und Institutionen* (Opladen 1990), pp. 256ff.

3. See the article entitled "Nation" in *Historisches Wörterbuch der Philosophie*, vol. 6, pp. 406–14.

4. Immanual Kant, *Anthropology from a Pragmatic Point of View*, trans. V. L. Dowdell, rev. and ed. H. H. Rudnich (Carbondale, Ill., 1978), p. 225.

5. M. R. Lepsius "Ethos und Demos," in Lepsius, *Interessen*, pp. 247–55.

6. Immanuel Kant, *Metaphysical Elements of Justice*, trans. J. Ladd (New York, 1965), section 46, p. 78.

7. On the following, see R. Grawert, "Staatsangehörigkeit und Staatsbürgerschaft," *Der Staat* 23 (1984): 179–204.

8. P. H. Shuck and R. M. Smith, *Citizenship without Consent* (New Haven, CT, 1985), chapter 1. Admittedly, not everywhere is the normative meaning of national citizenship consistently uncoupled from ascriptive characteristics of descent. Article 116 of the Basic Law of the Federal Republic, for example, introduces a notion of so-called *Statusdeutschen* ("German by status"), someone who belongs to the German people according to an objectively confirmed "attestation of membership in the cultural community," without being a German citizen. Such a person enjoys the privilege of being able to become a German citizen, although this is now disputed at a constitutional level.

9. R. Winzeler, *Die politischen Rechte des Aktivbürgers nach schweizerischem Bundersrecht* (Bern, 1983).

10. K. Hesse, *Grundzüge des Verfassungsrechts* (Heidelberg, 1990), p. 113, states, "In their function as subjective rights, [the basic rights] determine and secure the foundations of the individual's legal status. In their function as [objective] basic elements of the democratic constitutional order, they insert the individual into this order, which can in turn become a reality only if these rights are actualized. The status of the individual in terms of constitutional law, as grounded in and guaranteed by the basic rights laid out in the Basic Law, is a material legal status, i.e., a status with concretely specified contents over which neither the individual nor government authorities have unlimited control. This constitutional status forms the core of the general status of citizenship that, along with the basic rights,... is laid down in law."

11. R. Grawert, "Staatsvolk und Staatsangehörigkeit," in J. Isensee and P. Kirchof, eds., *Handbuch des Staatsrechts* (Heidelberg, 1987), p. 685; see also pp. 684ff.

12. C. Taylor, "Cross-Purposes: The Liberal-Communitarian Debate," in N. Rosenblum, ed., *Liberalism and the Moral Life* (Cambridge, MA, 1989), pp. 178–79.

13. Taylor, "Cross-Purposes," p. 178.

14. P. Kielmannsegg, "Ohne historisches Vorbild," *Frankfurter Allgemeine Zeitung*, December 7, 1990.

15. M. R. Lepsius, *Die Europäische Gemeinschaft* (Frankfurt am Main, 1990).

16. T. H. Marshall, *Citizenship and Social Class* (Cambridge, MA, 1950).

17. See chapter 7, section 7.2, "Democratic Procedure and the Problem of Its Neutrality" in *Between Facts and Norms: Contributions to a Discourse Theory of Law and Democracy*, Jürgen Habermas, translated by William Rehg (Cambridge, MA: MIT Press, 1996), 302–14.

18. B. S. Turner, *Citizenship and Capitalism* (London, 1986).

19. J. M. Barbalet, *Citizenship* (Stratford, England, 1988).

20. *Europäische Grundrechtszeitschrift* (1990): 443.

21. R. Goodin, "What Is So Special about Our Fellow Countrymen?" *Ethics* 98 (1988): 663–86 [reprinted herein 255–84].

22. H. Shue, "Mediating Duties," *Ethics* 98 (1988): 687–704.

23. J. H. Carens, "Aliens and Citizens: The Case for Open Borders," *Review of Politics* 49 (1987): 258 [reprinted herein 211–33, at 218].

24. H. R. van Gunsteren, "Admission to Citizenship," *Ethics* 98 (1988): 732.

25. D. Miller, "The Ethical Significance of Nationality," *Ethics* 98 (1988): 648 [reprinted herein 235–53, at 237].

26. Michael Walzer, *Spheres of Justice* (New York, 1983), pp. 31–63 [based on his essay "The Distribution of Membership," first published in *Boundaries: National Autonomy and Its Limits*, ed. Peter G. Brown and Henry Shue (Totowa: Rowman & Littlefield, 1981), 1–35, reprinted herein 145–77].

27. Gunsteren, "Admission to Citizenship," p. 736.

28. Ibid.

29. Carens, "Aliens and Citizens," p. 271 [herein 230].

# 12. DAVID HELD

Held surveys the history of democratic theory and considers the conditions in which democratic institutions have come to exist. He then examines the significance and proper role of democratic institutions in the contemporary global context. He argues for the extension of democratic institutions across state borders toward a democratic cosmopolitan global order.

## Democracy: From City-States to a Cosmopolitan Order?

*First published in* Political Studies *(special issue) 40: s1 (August 1992): 10–39.*

Democracy seems to have scored a historic victory over alternative forms of governance.[1] Nearly everyone today professes to be a democrat. Political regimes of all kinds throughout the world claim to be democracies. Yet what these regimes say and do is often substantially different from one to another. Democracy bestows an aura of legitimacy on modern political life: Laws, rules and policies appear justified when they are "democratic." But it was not always so. The great majority of political thinkers from ancient Greece to the present day have been highly critical of the theory and practice of democracy. A uniform commitment to democracy is a very recent phenomenon. Moreover, democracy is a remarkably difficult form of government to create and sustain. The history of twentieth-century Europe alone makes this clear: fascism, Nazism, and Stalinism came very close to obliterating democracy altogether.

Against this background, it is unsettling that some recent political commentators have proclaimed (by means of a phrase borrowed most notably from Hegel) the "end of history"—the triumph of the West over all political and economic alternatives. The revolutions that swept across Central and Eastern Europe at the end of 1989 and the beginning of

1990 stimulated an atmosphere of celebration. Liberal democracy was championed as the agent of progress, and capitalism as the only viable economic system: Ideological conflict, it was said, is being steadily displaced by universal democratic reason and market-oriented thinking.[2] But such a view is quite inadequate in a number of respects.

In the first instance, the "liberal" component of liberal democracy cannot be treated simply as a unity. There are distinctive liberal traditions that embody quite different conceptions from each other of the individual agent, of autonomy, of the rights and duties of subjects, and of the proper nature and form of community. In addition, the "celebratory" view of liberal democracy neglects to explore whether there are any tensions, or even perhaps contradictions, between the "liberal" and "democratic" components of liberal democracy; for example, between the liberal preoccupation with individual rights or "frontiers of freedom" which "nobody should be permitted to cross," and the democratic concern for the regulation of individual and collective action; that is, for public accountability.[3] Those who have written at length on this question have frequently resolved it in quite different directions. Furthermore, there is not simply one institutional form of liberal democracy. Contemporary democracies have crystallized into a number of different types, which makes any appeal to a liberal position vague at best.[4] An uncritical affirmation of liberal democracy essentially leaves unanalyzed the whole meaning of democracy and its possible variants.

This chapter seeks to address this lacuna, first, by examining the development of different models of democracy; second, by considering the conditions of application of these models; third, by exploring the meaning of democracy in the context of the progressive enmeshment today of states and societies in regional and global networks; and finally, by assessing the proper form and scope of democracy in relation to systems of international governance. The first two sets of issues will be examined in the next section, and the second two sets in the subsequent one. It will be argued, ultimately, that democracy can result from, and only from, a nucleus, or federation, of democratic states and societies. Or, to put the point differently, national democracies require international democracy if they are to be sustained and developed in the contemporary era. Paradoxically, perhaps, democracy has to be extended and deepened within and between countries for it to retain its relevance in the twenty-first century.

If the case for rethinking democracy in relation to the interconnectedness of states and societies is established successfully, a new agenda will have been created for democratic theory and practice. It is important to be clear about the meaning of "new" in this context. The agenda will not be new in the sense of being without precedent; others before have sought to understand the impact of the international order on the form and operation of domestic politics within democratic states. Others before have also sought to set out the normative implications of changes in the international order for the role and nature of democratic government. Nor will the agenda be new in the sense that traditional questions of democratic theory will be wholly displaced. On the contrary, questions will remain about the proper form of citizenship, the nature of individual rights and duties and the extent of participation and representation, for instance. But the agenda will be new to the extent that the case is made that a theory of democracy (whether focusing on philosophical or empirical-analytic concerns) requires a theory of the interlocking processes and structures of the global system. For a theory of democracy must offer, it will be maintained, an account both of the changing meaning of democracy within the global order and of the impact of the global order on the development of democratic associations. Democratic institutions and practices have to be articulated with the complex arena of national and international politics, and the mutual interpenetration of the national and international must be mapped. Political understanding, and the successful pursuit of democratic political theory, are dependent on the outcome of these tasks.[5] Before pursuing them, however, the concept of democracy itself requires some clarification.

## MODELS OF DEMOCRACY

Within the history of democratic theory lies a deeply rooted conflict about whether democracy should mean some kind of popular power (a form of politics in which citizens are engaged in self-government and self-regulation) or an aid to decision making (a means of conferring authority on those periodically voted into office). This conflict has given rise to three basic variants or models of democracy, which it is as well to bear in mind. First, there is direct or participatory democracy, a system of decision making about public affairs in which citizens are directly involved. This was the "original" type of democracy found in ancient Athens, among other places. Second, there is liberal or representative democracy, a system of rule embracing elected "officers" who undertake to "represent" the interests or views of citizens within the framework of the "rule of law." Third, there is a variant of democracy based on a one-party model (although some may doubt whether this is a form of democracy at all). Until recently the Soviet Union, East European societies, and many Third World countries have been dominated by this conception. The following discussion deals briefly with each of these models in turn, developing concepts and issues that will be drawn upon in later argument.

## THE ACTIVE CITIZEN AND REPUBLICAN GOVERNMENT

Athenian democracy has long been taken as a fundamental source of inspiration for modern Western political thought. This is not to say that the West has been right to trace many elements of its democratic heritage exclusively to Athens; for, as recent historical and archaeological research has shown, some of the key political innovations, both conceptual and institutional, of the nominally Western political tradition can be traced to older civilizations in the East. The city-state or *polis* society, for example, existed in Mesopotamia long before it emerged in the West.[6] Nonetheless, the political ideals of Athens—equality among citizens, liberty, respect for the law and justice—have been taken as integral to Western political thinking, and it is for this reason that Athens constitutes a useful starting point.

The Athenian city-state, ruled as it was by citizen-governors, did not differentiate between state and society. In ancient Athens, citizens were at one and the same time subjects of political authority and the creators of public rules and regulations. The people *(demos)* engaged in legislative and judicial functions, for the Athenian concept of citizenship entailed their taking a share in these functions, participating *directly* in the affairs of "the state."[7] Athenian democracy required a general commitment to the principle of civic virtue: dedication to the republican city-state and the subordination of private life to public affairs and the common good. "The public" and "the private" were intertwined. Citizens could properly fulfill themselves and live honorably only in and through the *polis*. Of course, who was to count as a citizen was a tightly restricted matter; among the excluded were women and a substantial slave population.

The Athenian city-state—eclipsed ultimately by the rise of empires, stronger states, and military regimes—shared features with republican Rome. Both were predominantly face-to-face societies and oral cultures; both had elements of popular participation in governmental affairs, and both had little, if any, centralized bureaucratic control. Furthermore, both sought to foster a deep sense of public duty, a tradition of civic virtue or responsibility to "the republic"—to the distinctive matters of the public realm. And in both polities, the claims of the state were given a unique priority over those of the individual citizen. But if Athens was a democratic republic, contemporary scholarship generally affirms that Rome was, by comparison, an essentially oligarchical system.[8] Nevertheless, from antiquity, it was Rome that was to prove the most durable influence on the dissemination of republican ideas.

Classical republicanism received its most robust restatement in the early Renaissance, especially in the city-states of Italy. The meaning of the concept of "active citizenship in a republic" became a leading concern. Political thinkers of this period were critical of the Athenian formulation of this notion; shaped as their views were by Aristotle, one of the most notable critics of Greek democracy, and by the centuries-long impact of republican Rome, they recast the republican tradition. While the concept of the *polis* remained central to the political theory of Italian cities, most notably in Florence, it was no longer regarded as a means to self-fulfillment.[9] Emphasis continued to be placed on the importance of civic virtue but the latter was understood as highly fragile, subject particularly to corruption if dependent solely upon the political involvement of any one major grouping: the people, the aristocracy or the monarchy. A constitution that could reflect and balance the interests of all leading political factions became an aspiration. Niccolò Machiavelli thus argued that all singular constitutional forms (monarchy, aristocracy, and democracy) were unstable, and only a governmental system combining elements of each could promote the kind of political culture on which civic virtue depends.[10] The best example of such a government was, he proclaimed, Rome: Rome's mixed government (with its system of consuls, Senate, and tribunes of the people) was directly linked to its sustained achievements.

The core of the Renaissance republican case was that the freedom of a political community rested upon its accountability to no authority other than that of the community itself. Self-government is the basis of liberty, together with the right of citizens to participate—within a constitutional framework that creates distinct roles for leading social forces—in the government of their own common business.[11] As one commentator put it, "the community as a whole must retain the ultimate sovereign authority," assigning its various rulers or chief magistrates "a status no higher than that of elected officials."[12] Such "rulers" must ensure the effective enforcement of the laws created by the community for the promotion of its own good; for they are not rulers in a traditional sense, but "agents or *ministri* of justice."

In Renaissance republicanism, as well as in Greek democratic thought, a citizen was someone who participated in "giving judgment and holding office."[13] Citizenship meant participation in public affairs. This definition is noteworthy because it suggests that theorists within these traditions would have found it hard to locate citizens in modern democracies, except perhaps as representatives or officeholders. The limited scope in contemporary politics for the active involvement of citizens would have been regarded as most undemocratic.[14] Yet the idea that human beings should be active citizens of a political order—citizens of their states—and not merely dutiful subjects of a ruler has had few advocates from the earliest human associations to the early Renaissance.[15]

The demise in the West of the idea of the active citizen, one whose very being is affirmed in and through political action, is hard to explain fully. But it is clear enough that the antithesis of *homo politicus* is the *homo credens* of the Christian faith: the citizen whose active judgment is essential is displaced by the true believer.[16] Although it would be quite misleading to suggest that the rise of Christianity effectively banished secular considerations from the lives of rulers and ruled, it unquestionably shifted the source of authority and wisdom from this-worldly to otherworldly representatives. During the Middle Ages, the integration of Christian Europe came to depend above all on two theocratic authorities: the Roman Catholic Church and the Holy Roman Empire. There was no theoretical alternative to their account of the nature of power and rule.[17] Not until the end of the sixteenth century, when it became apparent that religion had become a highly divisive force and that the powers of the state would have to be separated from the duty of rulers to uphold any particular faith, did the nature and limits of political authority, law, rights, and obedience become a preoccupation of European political thought from Italy to England.[18]

## Liberal Representative Democracy

Modern liberal and liberal democratic theories have constantly sought to justify the sovereign power of the state while at the same time justifying limits on that power.[19] The history of this attempt since Thomas Hobbes is the history of arguments to balance might and right, power and law, duties and rights. On the one hand, states must have a monopoly of coercive power in order to provide a secure basis on which trade, commerce, religion, and family life can prosper. On the other hand, by granting the state a regulatory and coercive capability, political theorists were aware that they had accepted a force that could, and frequently did, deprive citizens of political and social freedoms.

Liberal democrats provided the key institutional innovation to try to overcome this dilemma: representative democracy. The liberal concern with reason, law and freedom of choice could only be upheld properly by recognizing the political equality of all mature individuals. Such equality would ensure not only a secure social environment in which people would be free to pursue their private activities and interests, but also a state which, under the watchful eye of the electorate, would do what was best in the general or public interest. Thus, liberal democrats argued, the democratic constitutional state, linked to other key institutional mechanisms, particularly the free market, would resolve the problems of ensuring both authority and liberty.

Two classic statements of the new position can be found in the philosophy of James Madison and in the work of one of the key figures of nineteenth-century English liberalism: Jeremy Bentham. In Madison's account, "pure democracies" (by which he means societies "consisting of a small number of citizens, who assemble and administer the government in person") have always been intolerant, unjust, and unstable.[20] By contrast, representative government overcomes the excesses of "pure democracy" because regular elections force a clarification of public issues, and the elected few, able to withstand the political process, are likely to be competent and capable of "discerning the true interest of their country."

The central concern of Madison's argument is not the rightful place of the active citizen in the life of the political community but, instead, the legitimate pursuit by individuals of their interests, and government as a means for the enhancement of these interests. Although Madison himself sought clear ways of reconciling particular interests with what he called modern "extended republics," his position signals a clear shift from the classical ideals of civic virtue and the public realm to liberal preoccupations.[21] He conceived of the representative state as the chief mechanism to aggregate individuals' interests and to protect their rights. In such a state, he believed, security of person and property would be sustained and politics could be made compatible with the demands of large nation-states, with their complex patterns of trade, commerce and international relations.[22]

In parallel with this view, Bentham held that representative democracy "has for its characteristic object and effect... securing its members against oppression and depredation at the hands of those functionaries which it employs for its defence."[23] Democratic government is required to protect citizens, from the despotic use of political power, whether it be by a monarch, the aristocracy, or other groups. The representative state thus becomes an umpire or referee while individuals pursue in civil society, according to the rules of economic competition and free exchange, their own interests. The free vote and the free market are both essential, for a key presupposition is that the collective good can be properly realized in most domains of life only if individuals interact in competitive exchanges, pursuing their utility with minimal state interference. Significantly, however, this argument has another side. Tied to the advocacy of a "minimal state," whose scope and power need to be strictly limited, there is a strong commitment to certain types of state intervention: for instance, to regulate the behavior of the disobedient, and to reshape social relations and institutions if, in the event of the failure of laissez-faire, the greatest happiness of the greatest number is not achieved—the only scientifically defensible criterion, Bentham held, of the public good.

From classical antiquity to the seventeenth century, democracy was largely associated with the gathering of citizens in assemblies and public meeting places. By the early nineteenth century it was beginning to be thought of as the right of citizens to participate in the determination of the collective will through the medium of elected representatives.[24] The theory of representative democracy fundamentally shifted the terms of reference of democratic thought: The practical limits that a sizable citizenry imposes on democracy, which had been the focus of so much critical (antidemocratic) attention, were practically eliminated. Representative democracy could now be celebrated as both accountable and feasible government, potentially stable over great territories and time spans.[25] It could even be heralded, as James Mill put it, as "the grand discovery of modern times" in which "the solution of all difficulties, both speculative and practical, will be found."[26] Accordingly, the theory and practice of popular government shook off its traditional association with small states and cities, opening itself to become the legitimating creed of the emerging world of nation-states. But who exactly was to count as a legitimate participant, or a "citizen" or "individual," and what his or her exact role was to be in this new order, remained either unclear or unsettled. Even in the work of the enlightened John Stuart Mill, ambiguities remained: The idea that all citizens should have equal political weight in the polity remained outside his actual doctrine, along with that of most of his contemporaries.[27]

It was left by and large to the extensive and often violently suppressed struggles of working-class and feminist activists in the nineteenth and twentieth centuries to accomplish a genuinely universal suffrage in some countries. Their achievement was to remain fragile in places such as Germany, Italy, and Spain, and was in practice denied to some groups, for instance, many African-Americans in the US before the civil rights movement in the 1950s and 1960s. However, through these struggles the idea that the rights of citizenship should apply equally to all adults became slowly established; many of the arguments of the liberal democrats could be turned against existing institutions to reveal the extent to which the principles and aspirations of equal political participation and equal human development remained unfulfilled. It was only with the actual achievement of citizenship for all adult men and women that liberal democracy took on its distinctively contemporary form: a cluster of rules and institutions permitting the broadest participation of the majority of citizens in the selection of representatives who alone can make political decisions (that is, decisions affecting the whole community).

This cluster includes elected government; free and fair elections in which every citizen's vote has an equal weight; a suffrage that embraces all citizens irrespective of distinctions of race, religion, class, sex, and so on; freedom of conscience, information, and expression on all public matters broadly defined; the right of all adults to oppose their government and stand for office; and associational autonomy—the right to form independent associations including social movements, interest groups, and political parties.[28] The consolidation of representative democracy, thus understood, has been a twentieth-century phenomenon; perhaps one should even say a late-twentieth-century phenomenon. For it is only in the closing decades of this century that democracy has been securely established in the West and widely adopted in principle as a suitable model of government beyond the West.

## MARXISM AND ONE-PARTY DEMOCRACY

The struggle of liberalism against tyranny, and the struggle by liberal democrats for political equality, represented a major step forward in the history of human emancipation, as Karl Marx and Friedrich Engels readily acknowledged. But for them, and for the Marxist tradition more broadly, the great universal ideals of "liberty, equality, and justice" cannot be realized simply by the "free" struggle for votes in the political system together with the "free" struggle for profit in the marketplace. Advocates of the democratic state and the market economy present these institutions as the only ones under which liberty can be sustained and inequalities minimized. However, according to the Marxist critique, the capitalist economy, by virtue of its internal dynamics, inevitably produces systematic inequality and massive restrictions on real freedom. The formal existence of certain liberties is of little value if they cannot be exercised in practice. Therefore, although each step toward formal political equality is an advance, its liberating potential is severely curtailed by inequalities of class.

In class societies the state cannot become the vehicle for the pursuit of the common good or public interest. Far from playing the role of emancipator, protective knight, umpire, or judge in the face of disorder, the agencies of the liberal representative state are enmeshed in the struggles of civil society. Marxists conceive of the state as an extension of civil society, reinforcing the social order for the enhancement of particular interests. Their argument is that political emancipation is only a step toward human emancipation: that is, the complete democratization of both society and the state. In their view, liberal democratic society fails when judged by its own promises.

Among these promises are, first, political participation, or general involvement mediated by representatives in decisions affecting the whole community; second, accountable government; and third, freedom to protest and reform.[29] But "really existing liberal democracy," as one Marxist recently put it, fails to deliver on any of these promises. For it is distinguished by the existence of a largely passive citizenry (significant numbers of eligible citizens do not vote in elections, for example); by the erosion and displacement of parliamentary institutions by unelected centers of power (typified by the expansion of bureaucratic authority and of the role of functional representatives); and by substantial structural constraints on state action and, in particular, on the possibility of the piecemeal reform of capitalism (the flight of capital, for example, is a constant threat to elected governments with strong programs of social reform).[30]

Marx himself envisaged the replacement of the liberal democratic state by a "commune structure": the smallest communities, which were to administer their own affairs, would elect delegates to larger administrative units (districts, towns); these in turn would elect candidates to still larger areas of administration (the national delegation).[31] This arrangement is known as the "pyramid" structure of "delegative democracy": All delegates are revocable, bound by the instructions of their constituency, and organized into a "pyramid" of directly elected committees. The postcapitalist state would not therefore bear any resemblance to a liberal, parliamentary regime. All state agencies would be brought within the sphere of a single set of directly accountable institutions. Only when this happens will "that self-reliance, that freedom, which disappeared from earth with the Greeks, and vanished into the blue haze of heaven with Christianity," as the young Marx put it, gradually be restored.[32]

In the Marxist-Leninist account, the system of delegative democracy is to be complemented, in principle, by a separate but somewhat similar system at the level of the Communist Party. The transition to socialism and communism necessitates the "professional" leadership of a disciplined cadre of revolutionaries.[33] Only such a leadership has the capacity to organize the defense of the revolution against counterrevolutionary forces, plan the expansion of the forces of production, and supervise the reconstruction of society. Since all fundamental differences of interest are class interests, since the working-class interest (or standpoint) is the progressive interest in society, and since during and after the revolution it has to be articulated clearly and decisively, a revolutionary party is essential. The party is the instrument that can create the framework for socialism and communism. In practice, the party has to rule; and it was only in the "Gorbachev era" in the Soviet Union (from 1984 to August 1991) that a pyramid of councils, or "Soviets," from the central authority to those at local village and neighborhood level, was given anything more than a symbolic or ritualistic role in the postrevolutionary period.

## DEMOCRACY, THE STATE, AND CIVIL SOCIETY

What should be made of these various models of democracy in contemporary circumstances? The classical participatory model cannot easily be adapted to stretch across space and time. Its emergence in the context of city-states, and under conditions of "social exclusivity," was an integral part of its successful development. In complex industrial societies, marked by a high degree of social, economic, and political differentiation, it is very hard to envisage how a democracy of this kind could succeed on a large scale.

The significance of these reflections is reinforced by examining the fate of the conception of democracy advocated by Marx and Engels and their followers. In the first instance, the "deep structure" of Marxist categories—with its emphasis on the centrality of class, the universal standpoint of the proletariat, and a conception of politics that is rooted squarely in production—ignores or severely underestimates the contributions to politics of other forms of social structure, collectivity, agency, identity, interest, and knowledge. Second, as an institutional arrangement that allows for mediation, negotiation, and compromise among struggling factions, groups, or movements, the Marxist model does not stand up well under scrutiny, especially in its Marxist-Leninist form. A system of institutions to promote discussion, debate, and competition among divergent views—a system encompassing the formation of movements, pressure groups, and/or political parties with independent leaderships to help press their cases—appears both necessary and desirable. Further, the changes in Central and Eastern Europe after 1989 seem to provide remarkable confirmatory evidence of this, with their emphasis on the importance of political and civil rights, a competitive party system, and the "rolling back of the state"—that is, the freeing of civil society from state domination.

One cannot escape the necessity, therefore, of recognizing the importance of a number of fundamental liberal tenets concerning the centrality, in principle, of an "impersonal" structure of public power, of a constitution to help guarantee and protect rights, of a diversity of power centers within and outside the state, and of mechanisms to promote competition and debate among alternative political platforms. What this amounts to, among other things, is confirmation of the fundamental liberal notion that the "separation" of state from civil society must be an essential element of any democratic political order. Conceptions of democracy that depend on the assumption that the state could ever replace civil society, or vice versa, must be treated with caution.

To make these points is not, however, to affirm any one liberal democratic model as it stands, although many advocates of democracy appear to take this view. It is one thing to accept the arguments concerning the necessary protective, conflict-mediating, and redistributive functions of the democratic state, quite another to accept these as prescribed in existing accounts of liberal democracy. Advocates of liberal democracy have tended to be concerned, above all else, with the proper principles and procedures of democratic government. But by focusing on "government," they have drawn attention away from a thorough examination of the relation between formal rights and actual rights; between commitments to treat citizens as free and equal and practices that do neither sufficiently; between concepts of the state as, in principle, an independent authority, and state involvement in the reproduction of the inequalities of everyday life; between notions of political parties as appropriate structures for bridging the gap between state and society and the array of power centers that such parties and their leaders cannot reach. To ignore these questions is to risk the establishment of "democracy" in the context of a sea of political, economic, and social inequality. And it is to risk the creation of, at best, a very partial form of democratic politics—a form of politics in which the involvement of some bears a direct relation to the limited participation or nonparticipation of others.

The implications of these points are, I believe, of considerable significance. For democracy to flourish it has to be reconceived as a double-sided phenomenon: concerned, on the one hand, with the reform of state power and, on the other hand, with the restructuring of civil society. This entails recognizing the indispensability of a process of what I have elsewhere called "double democratization": the interdependent transformation of both state and civil society.[34] Such a process must be premised on the principles that the division between state and civil society must be a central aspect of democratic life, and that the power to make decisions must be free of the inequalities and constraints that can be imposed by an unregulated system of private capital, as Marx foresaw. But, of course, to recognize the importance of both these points is to recognize the necessity of recasting substantially their traditional connotations.[35]

In short, if democratic life involves no more than casting a periodic vote, citizens' activities will be largely confined to the "private" realm of civil society, and the scope of their actions will depend largely on the resources they can command. Few opportunities will exist for citizens to act as citizens; that is, as participants in public life. But if democracy is understood as a double-sided process, this state of affairs might be redressed by creating opportunities for people to establish themselves "in their capacity of being citizens."[36] The "active citizen" could once again return to the center of public life, involving him- or herself in the realms of both state and civil society. Of course, the nature of this involvement would differ in each of these realms, according to its organizational and institutional features. But opportunities will at least have been created for all those affected by the decision-making structures of their communities to participate in the latters' regulation—or so the story of democracy has so far suggested. However, democracy has another side.

## DEMOCRACY, GLOBALIZATION, AND INTERNATIONAL GOVERNANCE

Throughout the nineteenth and twentieth centuries democratic theory has tended to assume a "symmetrical" and "congruent" relationship between political decision makers and the recipients of political decisions.[37] In fact, symmetry and congruence have often been taken for granted at two crucial points: first, between citizen-voters and the decision makers whom they are, in principle, able to hold to account; and second, between the "output" (decisions, policies, and so on) of decision makers and their constituents—ultimately, "the people" in a delimited territory.

Even the critics of modern democracies have tended to share this assumption; following the narrative of democracy as conventionally told, they have thought of the problem of political accountability as, above all, a national problem. Contemporary representative structures are, they hold, insufficiently responsive to their citizens; and, in discussing various forms of participatory democracy, or contemporary interpretations of the relevance of republicanism, they place emphasis on making the political process more transparent and intelligible, more open to, and reflective of, the heterogeneous wants and needs of "the people."[38]

But the problem, for defenders and critics alike of modern democratic systems, is that regional and global interconnectedness contests the traditional national resolutions of the key questions of democratic theory and practice. The very process of governance can escape the reach of the nation-state. National communities by no means exclusively make and determine decisions and policies for themselves, and governments by no means determine what is right or appropriate exclusively for their own citizens.[39] To take some recent examples: a decision to increase interest rates in an attempt to stem inflation or exchange-rate instability is most often taken as a "national" decision, although it may well stimulate economic changes in other countries. Similarly, a decision to permit the "harvesting" of the rain forests may contribute to ecological damage far beyond the borders that formally limit the responsibility of a given set of political decision makers. These decisions, along with policies on issues as diverse as investment, arms procurement, and AIDS, are typically regarded as falling within the legitimate domain of authority of a sovereign nation-state. Yet, in a world of regional and global interconnectedness, there are major questions to be put about the coherence, viability, and accountability of national decision-making entities themselves.

Further, decisions made by quasi-regional or quasi-supranational organizations such as the European Community, the North Atlantic Treaty Organization, or the International Monetary Fund diminish the range of decisions open to given national "majorities." The idea of a community that rightly governs itself and determines its own future—an idea at the very heart of the democratic polity itself—is, accordingly, today deeply problematic. Any simple assumption in democratic theory that political relations are, or could be, "symmetrical" or "congruent" appears unjustified.

If the inadequacy of this assumption can be fully shown, issues are raised that go to the heart of democratic thought. The idea that *consent* legitimates government and the state system more generally has been central to nineteenth- and twentieth-century liberal democrats.[40] The latter have focused on the ballot box as the mechanism whereby the individual citizen expresses political preferences and citizens as a whole periodically confer authority on government to enact laws and regulate economic and social life. The principle of "majority rule," or the principle that decisions that accrue the largest number of votes should prevail, is at the root of the claim of political decisions to be regarded as worthy or legitimate.[41] But the very idea of consent through elections, and the particular notion that the relevant constituencies of voluntary agreement are the communities of a bounded territory or a state, become problematic as soon as the issue of national, regional, and global interconnectedness is considered and the nature of a so-called "relevant community" is contested. Whose consent is necessary and whose participation is justified in decisions concerning, for instance, AIDS, or acid rain, or the use of nonrenewable resources? What is the relevant constituency: national, regional, or international? To whom do decision makers have to justify their decisions? To whom should they be accountable? Further, what are the implications for the idea of legitimate rule of decisions taken in polities, with potentially life-and-death consequences for large numbers of people, many of whom might have no democratic stake in the decision-making process?

Territorial boundaries demarcate the basis on which individuals are included in and excluded from participation in decisions affecting their lives (however limited the participation might be), but the outcomes of these decisions must often "stretch" beyond national frontiers. The implications of this are considerable, not only for the categories of consent and legitimacy, but for all the key ideas of democracy: the nature of a constituency, the meaning of representation, the proper form and scope of political participation, and the relevance of the democratic nation-state, faced with unsettling patterns of relations and constraints in the international order, as the guarantor of the rights, duties, and welfare of subjects. Of course, these considerations would probably come as little surprise to those nations and countries whose independence and identity have been deeply affected by the hegemonic reach of empires, old and new, but they do come as a surprise to many in the West.

In order to explore the significance of these matters further, it is necessary to examine why for most of the nineteenth and twentieth centuries democracy *in* nation-states has not been accompanied by democratic relations *among* states; why the interstate system is now coming under pressure in a way that makes the relation between democracy within borders and democracy across borders a more urgent concern; why contemporary circumstances are creating the possibility of rethinking democracy at regional and global levels; and why democracy at such levels is an important condition for the development of democracy within local and national communities. I shall endeavor to show that democracy within a nation-state or region requires democracy within a network of interwoven international forces and relations; and that such a requirement is thwarted by the "deep structure" of the sovereign state order and the grafting on to this structure of the United Nations system in the immediate aftermath of the Second World War. Nonetheless, one can glimpse the possibility, I shall also seek to show, of an alternative to this state of affairs.

## SOVEREIGNTY AND THE WESTPHALIAN ORDER

The history of the modern interstate system, and of international relations more generally, has borne little relation to any democratic principle of organization. In the arena of world politics, Hobbes's way of thinking about power and power relations has often been regarded as the most insightful account of the meaning of the state at the global level.[42] Hobbes drew a comparison between international relations and the state of nature, describing the international system of states as being in a continuous "posture of war."[43] A war of "all against all" is a constant threat, since each state is at liberty to act to secure its own interests unimpeded by any higher religious or moral strictures.

In the study of international affairs, Hobbes's account has become associated with the "realist" theory of international politics.[44] Realism posits, in the spirit of Hobbes's work, that the system of sovereign states is inescapably anarchic in character; and that this anarchy forces all states, in the inevitable absence of any supreme arbiter to enforce moral behavior and agreed international codes, to pursue power politics in order to attain their vital interests. This realpolitik view of states has had a significant influence on both the analysis and practice of international relations in recent times, as it offers a convincing prima facie explanation of the chaos and disorder of world affairs. In this account, the modern system of nation-states is a "limiting factor" that will always thwart any attempt to conduct international relations in a manner that transcends the politics of the sovereign state.

A concomitant of each and every modern state's claim to supreme authority is a recognition that such a claim gives other states an equal entitlement to autonomy and respect within their own borders. In the context of the rapid erosion of "Christian society" from the late sixteenth century, the development of sovereignty can be interpreted as part of a process of mutual recognition whereby states granted each other rights of jurisdiction in their respective territories and communities. Accordingly, sovereignty involved the assertion by the modern state of independence; that is, of its possession of sole rights to jurisdiction over a particular people and territory. And in the world of relations among states, the principle of the sovereign equality of all states gradually became adopted as the paramount principle governing the formal conduct of states toward one another, however representative or unrepresentative were their particular regimes.

The conception of international order that emerged to clarify and formalize the interstate system has been referred to as the "Westphalian" model (after the Peace of Westphalia of 1648, which brought to an end the German phase of the Thirty Years' War).[45] The model covers a period from 1648 to 1945 (although some would argue it still holds today).[46] It depicts the emergence of a world community consisting of sovereign states that settle their differences privately and often by force;

that engage in diplomatic relations but otherwise minimal cooperation; that seek to place their own national interest above all others; and that accept the logic of the principle of effectiveness, that is, the principle that might eventually makes right in the international world—that appropriation becomes legitimation.[47] The model of Westphalia is summarized in Table 1. 1.[48]

This framework of international affairs had a lasting and paradoxical quality rich in implications: an increasingly developed and interlinked states system endorsed the right of each state to autonomous and independent action. As one commentator has aptly noted, the upshot of this was that states were "not subject to international moral requirements because they represent separate and discrete political orders with no common authority among them."[49] In this situation, the world consists of separate political powers, pursuing their own interests, backed ultimately by their organization of coercive power.[50]

The consolidation of the modern states system resulted from the expansion of Europe across the globe. If the Iberian monarchies led the early wave of "European globalization," their position was eroded in the seventeenth century by the Dutch, and subsequently by the English. Key features of the modern states system—the centralization of political power, the expansion of administrative rule, the legitimation of power through claims to representation, the emergence of massed armies—which existed in Europe in embryo in the sixteenth century, were to become prevalent features of the entire global system.[51]

While the diffusion of European power mainly occurred through the medium of seagoing military and commercial endeavors, Europe became connected to a global system of trade and production relationships. At the center of the latter were new and expanding capitalistic economic mechanisms that had their origins in the sixteenth century, or in what is sometimes called the "long sixteenth century," running from about 1450 to 1640.[52] Capitalism was from the beginning an international affair:[53] capital never allowed its aspirations to be determined by national boundaries alone. Consequently, the emergence of capitalism ushered in a fundamental change in the world order: It made possible, for the first time, genuinely global interconnections among states and societies; it penetrated the distant corners of the world and brought far-reaching changes to the dynamics and nature of political rule.

The development of the world capitalist economy initially took the form of the expansion of market relations, driven by a growing need for

---

TABLE 1.1
The Model of Westphalia

---

1. The world consists of, and is divided by, sovereign states that recognize no superior authority.
2. The processes of lawmaking, the settlement of disputes and law enforcement are largely in the hands of individual states subject to the logic of "the competitive struggle for power."
3. Differences among states are often settled by force: The principle of effective power holds sway. Virtually no legal fetters exist to curb the resort to force; international legal standards afford minimal protection.
4. Responsibility for cross-border wrongful acts are a "private matter" concerning only those affected; no collective interest in compliance with international law is recognized.
5. All states are regarded as equal before the law: Legal rules do not take account of asymmetries of power.
6. International law is oriented to the establishment of minimal rules of coexistence; the creation of enduring relationships among states and peoples is an aim, but only to the extent that it allows national political objectives to be met.
7. The minimization of impediments on state freedom is the "collective" priority.

---

raw materials and other factors of production. Capitalism stimulated this drive and was, in turn, stimulated by it. It is useful to make a distinction between the expansion of capitalist market relations based on the desire to buy, sell, and accumulate mobile resources (capital), and the formation of industrial capitalism involving highly distinctive class relations—based initially on those who own and control the means of production and those who have only their laboring capacity to sell. It is only with the development of capitalism in Europe after 1500, and in particular with the formation of the capitalist organization of production from the middle of the eighteenth century, that the activities of capitalists and the capitalist system began to converge.[54] From this period, the objectives of war became linked to economic objectives: military endeavor and conquest became more directly connected with the pursuit of economic advantage than they had been in earlier periods.[55]

The globalization of economic life—broadly, the growth of complex economic interconnections among states and societies—has not by any means been, of course, a uniform process, affecting each region and country in a similar way. From the outset this process has involved great costs for the autonomy and independence of many: for example, the progressive collapse of non-European civilizations, among them the Muslim, Indian, and Chinese; the disorganizing effects of Western rule on a large number of small societies; and the interlinked degradation of the non-European and European worlds caused by the slave trade. In fact, globalization has been characterized both by "hierarchy" and "unevenness."[56] Hierarchy denotes the structure of economic globalization: its domination by those constellations of economic power concentrated in the West and North. With the decline of Europe's empires in the twentieth century and the end of the Cold War, economic globalization has arguably become more significant than ever as the determinant of hierarchy and the front line of geopolitics. It is likely that the economic summits of the leading industrial countries will supplant superpower summits as the primary arena within which to discern new contours of hierarchy and power. While there may be uncertainty about the precise distribution of influence at the center of the advanced industrial countries, the hierarchical structure of the economic processes of globalization firmly places the leading economic powers of the West or North in central positions.

The other side of hierarchy is unevenness. This refers to the asymmetrical effects of economic globalization upon the life-chances and well-being of peoples, classes, ethnic groupings, movements, and the sexes. The contours of these processes of "unevenness" are not difficult to discern, although they will not be documented here. They are broadly correlated with geography, race, and gender and, accordingly, with the clusters of poverty and deprivation found among the countries of the South, among nonwhites and among women. However, the existence of significant poverty in the North (in Europe and the US), the persistence of unemployment in the most advanced industrial countries (even during periods of marked growth), and the fate of many indigenous peoples indicate the approximate nature of conceiving of unevenness in these terms alone. Unevenness is a phenomenon of both international and national development. The categories of social and political stratification must, therefore, be thought of as denoting systematic divisions within and across territories.[57]

The effective power that sovereignty bestows is, to a significant degree, connected to the economic resources at the disposal of a state or people.

Clearly the resources a polity can mobilize will vary according to its position in the global structure of economic relations, its place in the international division of labor, and the support it can muster from regional economic networks.[58] The growing awareness in many Western countries that their sovereignty is under pressure from a variety of sources and forces places before them (often for the first time) issues that have been apparent to many countries for a long time. The struggle for sovereignty and autonomy in many Third World countries was closely related to the struggle for freedom from colonial domination. De jure sovereignty has been of the utmost importance to those countries that had previously been denied it; but de jure sovereignty is not of course the same thing as de facto or practical sovereignty. The often weak and debt-ridden economies of many Third World countries leave them vulnerable and dependent on economic forces and relations over which they have little, if any, control. Although the internationalization of production and finance places many instruments of economic control beyond even the most powerful countries, the position of those at the lower end of the globalization hierarchy, experiencing the worst effects of unevenness, is substantially worse.

Political independence often provides at best only a brief respite from the processes of marginalization in the world economy. In countries such as those of the sub-Sahara, where the boundaries of the state (with two small exceptions) do not correspond to the boundaries of any states that existed before colonization, where there has been no "established habit" of exercising central authority and accepting its role, and where some of the most elementary human securities have often been absent, independence has been fraught with many types of difficulty.[59] Against this background, the achievement of any form of democracy is significant. Nevertheless, the achievement is handicapped by vulnerability to the international economy, by a fragile resource base that is threatening to the autonomy of political organizations, and by social groups often deeply divided by extreme poverty, hardship, and ill-health as well as by ethnic, cultural, and other considerations. In addition, it is handicapped by the very *structure* of the international political system that leaves individual states, locked into the competitive pursuit of their own security and interests, without systematic means to pursue the accountability and regulation of some of the most powerful forces ordering national and international affairs. It is political and economic might that ultimately determines the effective deployment of rules and resources within and across borders in the Westphalian world.

## THE INTERNATIONAL ORDER AND THE UNITED NATIONS CHARTER

The titanic struggles of the First and Second World Wars led to a growing acknowledgment that the nature and process of international governance would have to change if the most extreme forms of violence against humanity were to be outlawed, and the growing interconnectedness and interdependence of nations recognized. Slowly, the subject, scope, and very sources of the Westphalian conception of international regulation, particularly its conception of international law, were all called into question.[60]

First and foremost, opinion moved against the doctrine that international law, as Oppenheim put it, is a "law between states only and exclusively."[61] Single persons and groups became recognized as subjects of international law. It is generally accepted, for example, that persons as individuals are subjects of international law on the basis of such documents as the Charters of the Nuremberg and Tokyo War Crimes Tribunals, the Universal Declaration of Human Rights of 1948, the Covenants on Civil and Political Rights of 1966, and the European Convention on Human Rights of 1950.

Opinion has also moved against the doctrine that international law is primarily about political and strategic (state) affairs. According to this position, international law is concerned progressively with orchestrating and regulating economic, social, and environmental matters. Linked to substantial increases in the number of "actors" in world politics—for example, the UN, the UN Economic and Social Council, the UN Conference on Trade and Development (UNCTAD), the World Bank, the International Monetary Fund, the Food and Agricultural Organization, and the World Health Organization—there have been many pressures to increase the scope of international law. Faced with this development, there are those who characterize the changing reach of international law as being ever less concerned with the freedom or liberty of states, and ever more with the general welfare of all those in the global system who are able to make their voices count.[62]

Finally, the influential legal doctrine that the only true source of international law is the consent of states—either their expressed consent, or their implied consent—has been fundamentally challenged. Today, a number of sources of international law jostle for recognition. These include the traditional sources such as international conventions or treaties (general or particular) that are recognized by states; international custom or practice that provides evidence of an accepted rule or set of rules; and the underlying principles of law recognized by "civilized nations." They also include the "will of the international community," which can assume the "status of law" or be the "basis of international legal obligation" under certain circumstances.[63] The latter represents a break in principle with the requirement of individual state consent in the making of international rules and responsibilities.[64]

Although the Westphalian model of international law had its critics throughout the modern era, particularly during the ill-fated efforts of the League of Nations, it was not until after the Second World War that a new model of international law and accountability was widely advocated and accepted, culminating in the adoption of the UN Charter. The image of international regulation projected by the Charter (and related documents) was one of "states still jealously, 'sovereign'," but linked together in a "myriad of relations"; under pressure to resolve disagreements by peaceful means and according to legal criteria; subject in principle to tight restrictions on the resort to force; and constrained to observe "certain standards" with regard to the treatment of all persons on their territory, including their own citizens.[65] Of course, how restrictive the provisions of the Charter have been to states, and to what extent they have been actually operationalized, are important questions. Before addressing them, however, leading elements of the Charter model should be sketched (see Table 1.2).[66]

The shift in the structure of international regulation from the Westphalian to the UN Charter model raised fundamental questions about the nature and form of international law, questions that point to the possibility of a significant disjuncture between the law of nation-states—of the states system—and of the wider international community. At the heart of this shift lies a conflict between claims made on behalf of individual states and those made on behalf of an alternative organizing principle of world affairs: ultimately, a democratic community of states, with equal voting rights in the General Assembly of nation-states, openly and collectively regulating international life while constrained to observe the UN Charter and a battery of human rights conventions. However, this conflict has not been settled, and it would be quite misleading to conclude that the era of the UN Charter model simply displaced the Westphalian logic of international governance. The essential reason for this is that the Charter framework represents, in many respects, an extension of the interstate system.

---

**Table 1.2**
**The UN Charter Model**

---

1.   The world community consists of sovereign states, connected through a dense network of relations, both ad hoc and institutionalized. Single persons and groups are regarded as legitimate actors in international relations (albeit with limited roles).

2.   Certain peoples oppressed by colonial powers, racist regimes, or foreign occupants are assigned rights of recognition and a determinate role in articulating their future and interests.

3.   There is a gradual acceptance of standards and values that call into question the principle of effective power; accordingly, major violations of given international rules are not in theory to be regarded as legitimate. Restrictions are placed on the resort to force, including the unwarranted use of economic force.

4.   New rules, procedures, and institutions designed to aid lawmaking and law enforcement in international affairs are created.

5.   Legal principles delimiting the form and scope of the conduct of all members of the international community, and providing a set of guidelines for the structuring of international rules, are adopted.

6.   Fundamental concern is expressed for the rights of individuals, and a corpus of international rules is created seeking to constrain states to observe certain standards in the treatment of all, including their own citizens.

7.   The preservation of peace, the advancement of human rights, and the establishment of greater social justice are the stated collective priorities; "public affairs" include the whole of the international community. With respect to certain values—peace, the prohibition of genocide—international rules now provide in principle for the personal responsibility of state officials and the attribution of criminal acts to states.

8.   Systematic inequalities among peoples and states are recognized and new rules—including the concept of "the common heritage of mankind"[67]—are established to create ways of governing the distribution, appropriation, and exploitation of territory, property, and natural resources.

---

The organizations and procedures of the UN were designed partly to overcome weaknesses in the League of Nations. Its "architecture," therefore, was drawn up to accommodate the international power structure as it was understood in 1945. The division of the globe into powerful nation-states, with distinctive sets of geopolitical interests, was built into the Charter conception. As a result, the UN was virtually immobilized as an autonomous actor on many pressing issues.[68] One of the most obvious manifestations of this was the special veto power accorded to the five Permanent Members of the UN Security Council. This privileged political status added authority and legitimacy to the position of each of the major powers; for although they were barred in principle from the use of force on terms contrary to the Charter, they were protected against censure and sanctions in the event of unilateral action in the form of their veto. Moreover, the Charter gave renewed credence (through Article 51) to unilateral strategic state initiatives if they were necessary in "self-defense," since there was no clear delimitation of the meaning of this phrase. In addition, while the Charter placed new obligations on states to settle disputes peacefully and laid down certain procedures for passing judgment on alleged acts of self-defense, these procedures have rarely been used and there has been no insistence on compliance with them. The possibility of mobilizing the collective coercive measures envisaged in the Charter itself against illegitimate state action has, furthermore, never materialized, and even the UN's peacekeeping missions have been restricted generally to areas in which the consent of the territorial state in question has first been given.

The UN's susceptibility to the agendas of the most powerful states has been reinforced by its dependence on finance provided by its members. This position of vulnerability to state politics is underscored by the absence of any mechanism to confer some kind of direct UN status on regional and transnational functional or cultural forces (agencies, groups, or movements) that often might have a significant perspective on international questions. In sum, the UN Charter model, despite its good intentions, failed effectively to generate a new principle of organization in the international order—a principle that might break fundamentally with the logic of Westphalia and generate new democratic mechanisms of political coordination and change.

Nonetheless, it would be wrong simply to leave the argument here. The UN Charter system has been distinctively innovative and influential in a number of respects. It has provided an international forum in which all states are in certain respects equal, a forum of particular value to Third World countries and to those seeking a basis for "consensus" solutions to international problems. It has provided a framework for decolonization, and for the pursuit of the reform of international economic institutions.

Moreover, it has provided a vision, valuable in spite of all its limitations, of a new world order based upon a meeting of governments and, under appropriate circumstances, of a supranational presence in world affairs championing human rights.[69] Further, some of the deficiencies attributed to the UN can be better placed at the door of the states system itself, with its deep structural embeddedness in the global capitalist economy.

It might, accordingly, be a considerable step forward in the cross-border regulation of world affairs if the UN system were to live up to its Charter. Among other things, this would involve pursuing measures to implement key elements of the rights Conventions, enforcing the prohibition on the discretionary right to use force, activating the collective security system envisaged in the Charter itself and, more generally, ensuring compliance with the Charter's main articles.[70] In addition, if the Charter model were extended—for example, by adding the requirement of compulsory jurisdiction in the case of disputes falling under the UN rubric, or by providing means of redress through a new international human rights court in the case of human rights violations, or by making a (near) consensus vote in the General Assembly a legitimate source of international law, or by modifying the veto arrangement in the Security Council and rethinking representation on it to allow for an adequate regional presence—a basis might be established for the Charter model to generate political resources of its own, and to act as an autonomous decision-making center.

While each move in this direction would be significant, particularly in enhancing the prospects of world peace, it would still represent, at best, a movement toward a very partial or "thin" form of democracy in international affairs. Certainly, each state would enjoy formal equality in the UN system, and regional interests would be better represented. But it would still be possible for a plethora of different kinds of political regimes to participate on an equal footing in the Charter framework; the dynamics and logic of the interstate system would still represent an immensely powerful principle of organization in global affairs, especially with its military machinery largely intact; the massive disparities of power and asymmetries of resources in the hierarchical and uneven global political economy would be left virtually unaddressed; the changing structure of the global order reflected in discussion about the proper subject, scope, and sources of international law would remain marginal to the model; and transnational actors, civil associations, non-governmental organizations and social movements might still have a minimal role in this governance system. It would remain, then, a state-centered or sovereignty-centered model of international politics, and would lie at some considerable distance from what might be called a "thicker" democratic ordering of international affairs. Furthermore, it would lie at some distance from an adequate recognition of the transformations being wrought in the wake of globalization—transformations that are placing increasing strain on both the Westphalian and Charter conceptions of international governance.

## COSMOPOLITAN DEMOCRACY AND THE
## NEW INTERNATIONAL ORDER

There is a striking paradox to note about the contemporary era: From Africa to Eastern Europe, Asia to Latin America, more and more nations and groups are championing the idea of "the rule of the people"; but they are doing so at just that moment when the very efficacy of democracy as a national form of political organization appears open to question. As substantial areas of human activity are progressively organized on a global level, the fate of democracy, and of the independent democratic nation-state in particular, is fraught with difficulty.

It could be objected that there is nothing particularly new about global interconnections, and that the significance of global interconnections for politics has, in principle, been plain for people to see for a long time. Such an objection could be elaborated by emphasizing, as I have done, that a dense pattern of global interconnections began to emerge with the initial expansion of the world economy and the rise of the modern state from the late sixteenth century. Further, it could be suggested that domestic and international politics have been interwoven throughout the modern era: Domestic politics has always to be understood against the background of international politics, and the former is often the source of the latter.[71] However, it is one thing to claim that there are elements of continuity in the formation and structure of modern states, economies, and societies, quite another to claim that there is nothing new about aspects of their form and dynamics. For there is a fundamental difference between, on the one hand, the development of particular trade routes, or select military and naval operations that have an impact on certain towns, rural centers, and territories, and, on the other hand, an international order involving the emergence of a global economic system that stretches beyond the control of any single state (even of dominant states); the expansion of networks of transnational relations and communications over which particular states have limited influence; the enormous growth in international organizations and regimes that can limit the scope for action of the most powerful states; and the development of a global military order, and the buildup of the means of "total" warfare as an enduring feature of the contemporary world, which can reduce the range of policies available to governments and their citizens. While trade routes and military expeditions can link distant populations together in long loops of cause and effect, contemporary developments in the international order link peoples through multiple networks of transaction and coordination, reordering the very notion of distance itself.[72]

It needs to be emphasized that processes of globalization do not necessarily lead to growing global integration; that is, to a world order marked by the progressive development of a homogeneous or unified society and politics. For globalization can generate forces of both fragmentation and unification. Fragmentation or disintegrative trends are possible for several reasons. The growth of dense patterns of interconnectedness among states and societies can increase the range of developments affecting people in particular locations. By creating new patterns of transformation and change, globalization can weaken old political and economic structures without necessarily leading to the establishment of new systems of regulation. Further, the impact of global and regional processes is likely to vary under different international and national conditions—for instance, a nation's location in the international economy, its place in particular power blocs, its position with respect to the international legal system. In addition, globalization can engender an awareness of political difference as much as an awareness of common identity; enhanced international communications can highlight conflicts of interest and ideology, and not merely remove obstacles to mutual understanding.

In positive terms, globalization implies at least two distinct phenomena. First, it suggests that political, economic, and social activity is becoming worldwide in scope. And, second, it suggests that there has been an intensification of levels of interaction and interconnectedness within and among states and societies.[73] What is new about the modern global system is the spread of globalization through new dimensions of activity—technological, organizational, administrative, and legal, among others—each with its own logic and dynamic of change; and the chronic intensification of patterns of interconnectedness mediated by such phenomena as the modern communications industry and new information technology. Politics unfolds today, with all its customary uncertainty and indeterminateness, against the background of a world shaped and permeated by the movement of goods and capital, the flow of communication, the interchange of cultures, and the passage of people.[74]

In this context, the meaning and place of democratic politics, and of the contending models of democracy, have to be rethought in relation to a series of overlapping local, regional, and global processes and structures.[75] It is essential to recognize at least three elements of globalization: first, the way processes of economic, political, legal, and military interconnectedness are changing the nature, scope, and capacity of the sovereign state from above, as its "regulatory" ability is challenged and reduced in some spheres; second, the way local groups, movements and nationalisms are questioning the nation-state from below as a representative and accountable power system; and, third, the way global interconnectedness creates chains of interlocking political decisions and outcomes among states and their citizens, altering the nature and dynamics of national political systems themselves. Democracy has to come to terms with all three of these developments and their implications for national and international power centers. If it fails to do so, it is likely to become ever less effective in determining the shape and limits of political activity. The international form and structure of politics and civil society have, accordingly, to be built into the foundations of democratic thought and practice.

Three distinct requirements arise: first, that the territorial boundaries of systems of accountability be recast so that those issues that escape the control of a nation-state—aspects of monetary management, environmental questions, elements of security, new forms of communication—can be brought under better democratic control; second, that the role and place of regional and global regulatory and functional agencies be rethought so that they might provide a more coherent and useful focal point in public affairs; and third, that the articulation of political institutions with the key groups, agencies, associations, and organizations of international civil society be reconsidered to allow the latter to become part of a democratic process—adopting, within their very modus operandi, a structure of rules and principles compatible with those of democracy.

How might this approach to democracy be developed? What are its essential characteristics? Addressing these questions requires recalling earlier arguments about the need to conceive democracy as a double-sided process, while reappraising the proper domain for the application of this process.[76] For if the above arguments are correct, democracy has to become a transnational affair if it is to be possible both within a restricted geographic domain and within the wider international community. The possibility of democracy today must, in short, be linked to an expanding framework of democratic institutions and agencies. I refer to such a framework as "the cosmopolitan model of democracy."[77] The framework can be elaborated by focusing initially on some of its institutional requirements.

In the first instance, the "cosmopolitan model of democracy" presupposes the creation of regional parliaments (for example, in Latin America and Africa) and the enhancement of the role of such bodies where they already exist (the European Parliament) in order that their decisions become recognized, in principle, as legitimate independent sources of regional and international law. Alongside such developments, the model anticipates the possibility of general referenda, cutting across nations and nation-states, with constituencies defined according to the nature and scope of controversial transnational issues. In addition, the opening of international governmental organizations to public scrutiny and the democratization of international "functional" bodies (on the basis perhaps of the creation of elected supervisory boards that are in part statistically representative of their constituencies) would be significant.

Hand in hand with these changes, the cosmopolitan model of democracy assumes the entrenchment of a cluster of rights, including civil, political, economic, and social rights, in order to provide shape and limits to democratic decision making.[78] This requires that they be enshrined within the constitutions of parliaments and assemblies (at the national and international level); and that the influence of international courts is extended so that groups and individuals have an effective means of suing political authorities for the enactment and enforcement of key rights, both within and beyond political associations.

In the final analysis, the formation of an authoritative assembly of all democratic states and societies—a re-formed UN, or a complement to it—would be an objective. The UN, as previously noted, combines two contradictory principles of representation: the equality of all countries (one country, one vote in the General Assembly) and deference to geopolitical strength (special veto power in the Security Council to those with current or former superpower status). An authoritative assembly of all democratic states and societies would seek unreservedly to place principles of democratic representation above those of superpower politics. Moreover, unlike the General Assembly of the UN, it would not, to begin with at least, be an assembly of all nations; for it would be an assembly of democratic nations which would draw in others over time, perhaps by the sheer necessity of being a member if their systems of governance are to enjoy legitimacy in the eyes of their own populations. As such, the new assembly in its early stages can best be thought of as a complement to the UN, which it would either replace over time or accept in a modified form as a "second chamber"—a necessary meeting place for all states irrespective of the nature of their regimes.

Of course, the idea of a new democratic international assembly is open to a battery of objections commonly put to similar schemes. Would it have any teeth to implement decisions? How would democratic international law be enforced? Would there be a centralized police and military force?[79] And so forth. These concerns are significant. But many of them can be met and countered. For instance, it needs to be stressed that any global legislative institution should be conceived above all as a "standard-setting" institution. Although a distinction ought to be made between legal instruments that would have the status of law independently of any further negotiation or action on the part of a region or state or local government, and instruments that would require further discussion with them, implementation of the detail of a broad range of recommendations would be a matter for nonglobal levels of governance.[80] In addition, the question of law enforcement at a regional and global level is not beyond resolution in principle: a proportion of a nation-state's police and military (perhaps a growing proportion over time) could be "seconded" to the new international authorities and placed at their disposal on a routine basis. To this end, avenues could be established to meet the concern that "covenants, without the sword, are but words."[81]

Equally, only to the extent that the new forms of "policing" are locked into an international democratic framework would there be good grounds for thinking that a new settlement could be created between coercive power and accountability. If such a settlement seems like a fantasy, it should be emphasized that it is a fantasy to imagine that one can advocate democracy today without confronting the range of issues elaborated here. If the emerging international order is to be democratic, these issues have to be considered, even though their details are, of course, open to further specification.

The implications of all this for international civil society are in part clear. A democratic network of states and civil societies is incompatible with the existence of powerful sets of social relations and organizations that can, by virtue of the very bases of their operations, systematically distort democratic conditions and processes. At stake are, among other things, the curtailment of the power of corporations to constrain and influence the *political* agenda (through such diverse measures as the public funding of elections, the use of "golden shares," and citizen directors), and the restriction of the activities of powerful transnational interest groups to pursue their interests unchecked (through, for example, the regulation of bargaining procedures to minimize the use of "coercive tactics" within and between public and private associations, and the enactment of rules limiting the sponsorship of political representatives by sectional interests, whether these be particular industries or trade unions).

If individuals and peoples are to be free and equal in determining the conditions of their own existence, there must be an array of social spheres—for instance, privately and cooperatively owned enterprises, independent communications media, and autonomously run cultural centers—that allow their members control of the resources at their disposal without direct interference from political agencies or other third parties.[82] At issue here is a civil society that is neither simply planned nor merely market oriented but, rather, open to organizations, associations, and agencies pursuing their own projects, subject to the constraints of democratic processes and a common structure of action.[83]

The key features of this model are set out in Table 1.3. The cosmopolitan model of democracy presents a program of possible transformations with short- and long-term political implications. It does not present an all-or-nothing choice, but rather lays down a direction of possible change with clear points of orientation (see appendix).

Would a cosmopolitan framework of democracy, assuming its details could be adequately fleshed out, have the organizational resources—procedural, legal, institutional, and military—to alter the dynamics of resource production and distribution, and of rule creation and enforcement, in the contemporary era? It would be deeply misleading to suggest that it would initially have these capabilities. Nevertheless, its commitment to the extension and deepening of mechanisms of democratic accountability across major regions and

---

TABLE 1.3
The Cosmopolitan Model of Democracy

---

1. The global order consists of multiple and overlapping networks of power including the political, social, and economic.
2. All groups and associations are attributed rights of self-determination specified by a commitment to individual autonomy and a specific cluster of rights. The cluster is composed of rights within and across each network of power. Together, these rights constitute the basis of an empowering legal order—a "democratic international law."
3. Lawmaking and law enforcement can be developed within this framework at a variety of locations and levels, along with an expansion of the influence of regional and international courts to monitor and check political and social authority.
4. Legal principles are adopted that delimit the form and scope of individual and collective action within the organizations and associations of state *and* civil society. Certain standards are specified for the treatment of all, which no political regime or civil association can legitimately violate.
5. As a consequence, the principle of noncoercive relations governs the settlement of disputes, though the use of force remains a collective option in the last resort in the face of tyrannical attacks to eradicate democratic international law.
6. The defense of self-determination, the creation of a common structure of action, and the preservation of the democratic good are the overall collective priorities.
7. Determinate principles of social justice follow: The *modus operandi* of the production, distribution, and exploitation of resources must be compatible with the democratic process and a common framework of action.

---

international structures would help regulate resources and forces that are already beyond the reach of national democratic mechanisms and movements. Moreover, its commitment to the protection and strengthening of human rights, and to the further development of a regional and international court system, would aid the process whereby individuals and groups could sue their governments for the enactment of key human rights.

In addition, the establishment of regional authorities as major independent voices in world politics might contribute further to the erosion of the old division of the world by the US and the former USSR.

Likewise, the new institutional focus at the global level on major transnational issues would go some way toward eradicating sectarian approaches to these questions, and to countering "hierarchy" and some of the major asymmetries in life-chances. Finally, new sets of regional and global rules and procedures might help prevent public affairs from becoming a quagmire of infighting among nations wholly unable to settle pressing collective issues.

Of course, there would be new possible dangers—no political scheme is free from such risks. But what would be at issue would be the beginning of the creation of a new international democratic culture and spirit—one set off from the partisan claims of the nation-state. Such developments might take years, if not decades, to become entrenched. But 1989-91 has shown that political change can take place at an extraordinary speed, itself no doubt partially a result of the process of globalization.

## CONCLUSION

In order to avoid possible misunderstandings about the arguments offered above, it might be useful, by way of a conclusion, to emphasize the terrain they occupy and the ground they reject. This can be done by assessing critically a number of conceptual polarities frequently found in political discourse: globalism versus cultural diversity; constitutionalism versus politics; political ambition versus political feasibility; participatory or direct democracy versus liberal representative democracy, and global governance from above versus the extension of grassroots associations from below. Although these polarities provide much of the tension that charges the debate about the possibility of democracy beyond borders, there are good reasons for doubting their coherence.

To begin with, globalism and cultural diversity are not simply opposites. For global interconnectedness is already forming a dense web of relations linking cultures one to another. The issue is how and in what way cultures are linked and interrelated, not how a sealed cultural diversity can persist in the face of globalization.

Second, the juxtaposition of constitutionalism—or the elaboration of theoretical models of principles of political organization—with politics as a practical activity, sets up another false polarity. Politics typically operates within a framework—albeit a shifting framework—of rules. Politics is rarely without some pattern, and is most often about the nature of the rules that will shape and delimit political activity. For politics is at root about the ways in which rules and resources are distributed, produced and legitimated. The question is whether politics will be shaped by an explicit, formal constitution or model that might, in principle, be open and contestable, or whether politics will be subject to an unwritten constitution, which is altogether more difficult to invoke as a defense in the face of unaccountable systems of power.

Third, the question of feasibility cannot simply be set up in opposition to the question of political ambition. For what is ambitious today might be feasible tomorrow. Who anticipated the remarkable changes of 1989–90 in Eastern Europe? Who foresaw the fall of communism in the Soviet Union? The growing interconnectedness between states and societies is generating consequences, intended and unintended, for the stability of regimes, governments, and states. While the question of political feasibility is of the utmost significance, it would be naive to juxtapose it simply with programs of political ambition.

Fourth, versions of participatory democracy cannot simply be opposed to liberal representative democracy. Programs of participatory or direct democracy are fraught with complexities and questions. Likewise, liberal representative democracy does not simply mean one set of possible institutions or forms. The nature of liberal democracy is itself an intensely contested issue. So while there seem to be good grounds for accepting the liberal distinction between state and civil society, there are not equally good grounds for uncritically accepting either of these in their liberal form. The juxtaposition of participation with liberal representative democracy leaves most of political analysis to one side.

Fifth, the problems of global governance from above cannot be solved through the extension of grassroots democracy alone. For the questions have to be posed: Which grassroots, and which democracy? There are many social movements—for instance, right-wing nationalist movements or the Eugenics movement—that highlight how the very nature of a grassroots movement can be contested and fought over. Grassroots movements are by no means merely noble or wise. Like most social, economic, or political forms, they can appear in a variety of shapes, with a variety of patterns of internal organization. An appeal to the nature or inherent goodness of grassroots associations and movements bypasses the necessary work of theoretical analysis.

Today, any attempt to set out a position of what could be called "embedded utopianism" must begin both from where we are—the existing pattern of political relations and processes—and from an analysis of what might be: desirable political forms and principles.[84] If utopia is to be embedded, it must be linked into patterns and movements as they are. But if this context of embeddedness is not simply to be affirmed in the shapes and patterns generated by past groups and movements, it has to be assessed according to standards, criteria, and principles. These, in my view, follow from a theory of democracy.

Finally, if the history and practice of democracy has until now been centered on the idea of locality (the city-state, the community, the nation), it is likely that in the future it will be centered on the international or global domain. It would be immensely naive to claim that there are any straightforward solutions to the problems posed by global interconnectedness, with its complex and often profoundly uneven effects; but there is, without doubt, an inescapably important set of questions to be addressed. Certainly, one can find many good reasons for being optimistic about finding a path forward, and many good reasons for thinking that at this juncture democracy will face another critical test.

# APPENDIX

## OBJECTIVES OF THE COSMOPOLITAN MODEL OF DEMOCRACY: ILLUSTRATIVE ISSUES

|   | Short-term | Long-term |
|---|---|---|
| **POLITY/GOVERNANCE** | | |
| 1. | Reform of UN Security Council (to give the Third World a significant voice) | Global parliament (with limited revenue-raising capacity) connected to regions, nations, and localities |
| 2. | Creation of a UN second chamber (on the model of the EC?) | New Charter of Rights and Duties locked into different domains of power |
| 3. | Enhanced political regionalization (EC and beyond) | Separation of political and economic interests; public funding of electoral processes |
| 4. | Compulsory jurisdiction before the International Court. New International Criminal Court and new Human Rights Court for the pursuit of rights | Interconnected global legal system |
| 5. | Establishment of a small but effective, accountable, international military force | Permanent "secondment" of a growing proportion of a nation-state's coercive capability to regional and global institutions. Aim: demilitarization and transcendence of war system |
| **CIVIL SOCIETY** | | |
| 1. | Enhancement of nonstate, nonmarket solutions in the organization of civil society | Creation of a diversity of self-regulating associations and groups in civil society |
| 2. | Introduction of limits to private ownership of key "public-shaping" institutions: media, information, and so on | Systematic experimentation with different democratic organizational forms in civil society |
| 3. | Provision of resources to those in the most vulnerable social positions to defend and articulate their interests | Multisectoral economy and pluralization of patterns of ownership and possession |

# NOTES

1. I should like to thank Richard Falk, Anthony Giddens, Jack Hayward, Quentin Skinner, David Scott-Macnab, Saul Mendlovitz, and John Thompson for many constructive comments on this chapter. It seeks to draw together and expand upon a number of themes discussed in my recent writings, particularly in *Models of Democracy* (Cambridge: Polity Press, 1987), ch. 9; "Democracy, the Nation-State and the Global System," in D. Held (ed.), *Political Theory Today* (Cambridge: Polity Press, 1991); and "Democracy and Globalization," *Alternatives* 16:2 (1991).

2. See F. Fukuyama, "The End of History," *The National Interest* 16 (1989) and "A Reply to My Critics," *The National Interest* 18 (1989/90). For a more detailed commentary on these texts, see D. Held, "Liberalism, Marxism and Democracy," *Theory and Society* 22:2 (April 1993): 249–81.

3. I. Berlin, *Four Essays on Liberty* (Oxford: Oxford University Press, 1969), pp. 164ff.

4. See, for example, A. Lizphart, *Democracies* (New Haven, CT: Yale University Press, 1984), and R. Dahl, *Democracy and Its Critics* (New Haven, CT: Yale University Press, 1989).

5. A fuller account of the nature and scope of political theory as outlined here can be found in the "Introduction" to Held, *Political Theory Today*, pp. 1–21.

6. See M. Bernal, *Black Athena*, vol. 1 (London: Free Association Books, 1987), and P. Springborg, *Western Republicanism and the Oriental Prince* (Cambridge: Polity Press, 1992).

7. When referring to the Greek *polis*, some scholars prefer to use the term "city-republic" on the grounds that the concept of the state was an early modern formulation. For some of the issues underpinning this preference see Held, *Models of Democracy*, ch. 2.

8. M. Finley, *Politics in the Ancient World* (Cambridge: Cambridge University Press, 1983), pp. 84ff.

9. See J. G. A. Pocock, *The Machiavellian Moment: Florentine Political Thought and the Atlantic Republican Tradition* (Princeton, NJ: Princeton University Press, 1975), pp. 64–80.

10. See N. Machiavelli, *The Discourses* (Harmondsworth: Penguin, 1983), pp. 104–11.

11. The republican view emphasizes, in short, that the freedom of citizens consists above all in their unhindered pursuit of their self-chosen ends. The highest political ideal is the civic freedom of an independent, self-governing republic.

12. Q. Skinner, "The State," in T. Ball, J. Farr, and R. Hanson, eds., *Political Innovation and Conceptual Change* (Cambridge: Cambridge University Press, 1989), p. 105.

13. Aristotle, *The Politics* (Harmondsworth: Penguin, 1981), p. 169.

14. See M. Finley, *Democracy Ancient and Modern* (London: Chatto and Windus, 1973).

15. The concern with aspects of "self-government" in Renaissance Italy had a significant influence in seventeenth- and eighteenth-century England, France, and America. The problem of how civic life was to be constructed, and public life sustained, was faced by diverse thinkers. While the meaning of the ideal of active citizenship was progressively altered—and denuded of many of its most challenging implications—threads of this ideal remained and continued to have an impact. It is possible to trace "radical" and "conservative" strains of republicanism throughout the early modern period. Cf. Pocock, *The Machiavellian Moment,* and G. S. Wood, *The Creation of the American Republic: 1776–1787* (Chapel Hill: University of North Carolina Press, 1969).

16. Pocock, *The Machiavellian Moment,* p. 550.

17. H. Bull, *The Anarchical Society* (London: Macmillan, 1977), p. 27.

18. Q. Skinner, *The Foundations of Political Thought,* vol. 1 (Cambridge: Cambridge University Press, 1978), p. 352.

19. See D. Held, "The Development of the Modern State," in S. Hall and B. Gieben, eds., *Formations of Modernity* (Cambridge: Polity Press, 1992).

20. J. Madison, *The Federalist Papers,* ed. R. Fairfield (New York: Doubleday, 1966), No. 10, p. 20.

21. Madison, *The Federalist Papers,* No. 10, pp. 21–22.

22. See R. W. Krouse, "Classical Images of Democracy in America: Madison and Tocqueville," in D, Duncan, ed., *Democratic Theory and Practice* (Cambridge: Cambridge University Press, 1983), pp. 58–78.

23. J. Bentham, *Constitutional Code, Book 1,* in *The Works of Jeremy Bentham,* vol. IX (Edinburgh: W. Tait, 1843), p. 47.

24. N. Bobbio, *Democracy and Dictatorship* (Cambridge: Polity Press, 1989), p. 144.

25. See Dahl, *Democracy and Its Critics,* pp. 28–30.

26. Quoted in G. H. Sabine, *A History of Political Theory* (London: George G. Harrap, 3rd ed., 1963), p. 695.

27. See Held, *Models of Democracy,* chapter 3.

28. See N. Bobbio, *Which Socialism?* (Cambridge: Polity Press, 1987), p. 66, and Dahl, *Democracy and Its Critics,* pp. 221 and 233.

29. Bobbio, *Which Socialism?,* pp. 42–44.

30. A. Callinicos, *The Revenge of History: Marxism and the East European Revolutions* (Cambridge: Polity Press, 1991), pp. 108–9.

31. K. Marx, *The Civil War in France* (Peking: Foreign Languages Press, 1970), pp. 67–70.

32. Marx, Letter 2, from the *Deutsch-Französische Jahrbücher* (Paris, 1844).

33. See, for example, V. I. Lenin, *What Is To Be Done?* (Moscow: Progress Publishers, 1947).

34. Held, *Models of Democracy,* chapter 9.

35. For texts that seek to do this, see Held, *Models of Democracy*, chapters 8 and 9; Held, "Democracy, the Nation-State and the Global System," pp. 227–35; and J. Keane, *Democracy and Civil Society* (London: Verso, 1988). See also Keane's "Democracy and the Media: Without Foundations," in *Prospects for Democracy: North, South, East, West*, ed. David Held (Stanford: Stanford University Press, 1993), pp. 235–53.

36. H. Arendt, *On Revolution* (New York: Viking Press, 1963), p. 256.

37. Held, "Democracy, the Nation-State and the Global System," p. 198. Some of the material in the following paragraphs is adapted from pp. 201–5 of that essay.

38. Cf., for example, C. B. Macpherson, *The Life and Times of Liberal Democracy* (Oxford: Oxford University Press, 1977); C. Pateman, *The Problem of Political Obligation* (Cambridge: Polity Press, 2nd ed., 1985); and B. Barber, *Strong Democracy* (Berkeley and Los Angeles: University of California Press, 1984).

39. C. Offe, *Disorganized Capitalism* (Cambridge: Polity Press, 1985), pp. 286ff.

40. R. Hanson, "Democracy," in T. Ball, J. Farr, and R. Hanson, eds., *Political Innovation and Conceptual Change* (Cambridge: Cambridge University Press, 1989), pp. 68–69.

41. Cf. Dahl, *Democracy and Its Critics*, chapters 10 and 11.

42. See, for example, R. Aron, *Peace and War: A Theory of International Relations* (New York: Doubleday, 1966).

43. T. Hobbes, *Leviathan* (Harmondsworth: Penguin, 1968), pp. 187–8.

44. Cf. H. J. Morgenthau, *Politics among Nations* (New York: Knopf, 1948); M. Wight, *Power Politics* (Harmondsworth: Penguin, 1986); and S. Smith, "Reasons of State," in D. Held and C. Pollitt, eds., *New Forms of Democracy* (London: Sage, 1987).

45. See R. Falk, "The Interplay of Westphalia and Charter Conceptions of the International Legal Order," in R. Falk and C. Black, eds., *The Future of the International Legal Order*, vol. 1 (Princeton, NJ: Princeton University Press, 1969); R. Falk, *A Study of Future Worlds* (New York: Free Press, 1975), chapter 2; and A. Cassese, *International Law in a Divided World* (Oxford: Clarendon Press, 1986), especially pp. 393ff. While the emergence of this model can be linked directly to the Peace of Westphalia, important qualifications ought also to be noted. First, the basic conception of territorial sovereignty was outlined well before this settlement (although not generally assented to). Second, there were few, if any, references in the classic texts of early modern political theory to an intrinsically territorial state; as T. Baldwin put it, "political theory had still to catch up with practice." On both these points, see T. Baldwin, "The Territorial State," in H. Gross and T. R. Harrison, eds., *Cambridge Essays in Jurisprudence* (Oxford: Clarendon Press, 1993).

46. By a "model," I mean a theoretical construction designed to reveal and explain the main elements of a political form or order and its underlying structure of relations. Models in this context are "networks" of concepts and

generalizations about aspects of the political, economic, and social spheres.

47. A. Cassese, "Violence, War and the Rule of Law in the International Community," in D. Held, ed., *Political Theory Today* (Cambridge: Polity Press, 1991), p. 256.

48. These points are adapted from Falk, "The Interplay of Westphalia and Charter Conceptions of the International Legal Order," and Cassese, *International Law in a Divided World*, pp. 396–99.

49. C. Beitz, *Political Theory and International Relations* (Princeton, NJ: Princeton University Press, 1979), p. 25.

50. The resort to coercion or armed force by nonstate actors is also, arguably, an almost inevitable outcome in such a world. For communities contesting established territorial boundaries have, as Baldwin succinctly wrote, "little alternative but to resort to arms in order to establish 'effective control' over the area they seek as their territory, and in that way make their case for international recognition (cf. Eritrea, East Timor, Kurdistan ...)." See Baldwin, "The Territorial State."

51. See G. Modelski, *Principles of World Politics* (New York: Free Press, 1972).

52. See F. Braudel, *Capitalism and Material Life* (London: Weidenfeld & Nicolson, 1973).

53. I. Wallerstein, *The Capitalist Economy* (Cambridge: Cambridge University Press, 1979), p. 19.

54. C. Tilly, *Coercion, Capital and European States, AD 990–1990* (Oxford: Blackwell, 1990), pp. 17 and 189.

55. See M. Mann, *The Sources of Social Power,* vol. 1 (Cambridge: Cambridge University Press, 1986), pp. 510–16.

56. The following analysis is indebted to R. Falk, "Economic Dimensions of Global Civilization: A Preliminary Perspective" (working paper prepared for the Cairo meeting of the Global Civilization Project, October 1990), pp. 2–12.

57. See R. W. Cox, *Production, Power, and World Order: Social Forces in the Making of History* (New York: Columbia University Press, 1987), chapter 9.

58. I do not mean this to be an "economistic" point. There are obviously other important factors involved in determining a state's effective power. See D. Held, *Political Theory and the Modern State* (Cambridge: Polity Press, 1989), chapter 8.

59. See G. Hawthorn's "Sub-Saharan Africa," in *Prospects for Democracy: North, South, East, West*, ed. David Held (Stanford: Stanford University Press, 1993), pp. 330–54. Cf. R. H. Jackson and C. G. Rosberg, "Why Africa's Weak States Persist: The Empirical and the Juridical in Statehood," *World Politics*, 35: 1 (1982): 1-24.

60. For an overview see Bull, *The Anarchical Society*, chapter 6.

61. See L. Oppenheim, *International Law*, vol. 1 (London: Longman, 1905), chapter 1.

62. Cf., for example, B. Röling, *International Law in an Expanded World* (Amsterdam: Djambatan, 1960); W. Friedmann, *The Changing Structure of International Law* (London: Stevens & Son, 1964); and Cassese, *International Law in a Divided World,* especially chapters 7–9.

63. Cf. Bull, *The Anarchical Society,* pp. 147–58; C. Jenks, *Law, Freedom and Welfare* (London: Stevens & Son, 1963), chapter 5; and R. Falk, *The Status of Law in International Society* (Princeton, NJ: Princeton University Press, 1970), chapter 5.

64. It is interesting to note that the tradition of natural law thinking, which informed early modern international law in particular, recognized a certain tension between the requirement of governmental consent and the existence of international rights and duties.

65. Cassese, "Violence, War and the Rule of Law," p. 256.

66. I have drawn these points from Cassese, *International Law in a Divided World,* pp. 398–400.

67. First propounded in the late 1960s, the concept of "the common heritage of mankind" has been enshrined in two notable treaties: the Convention on the Moon and Other Celestial Bodies (1979) and the Convention on the Law of the Sea (1982). The concept has been proposed as a device to exclude a state or private right of appropriation over certain resources and to permit the development of these resources, where appropriate, for the benefit of all, with due regard paid to environmental protection.

68. See Falk, *A Study of Future Worlds,* pp. 69-72; R. Falk, *A Global Approach to National Policy* (Cambridge, MA: Harvard University Press, 1975), pp. 169–96; Cassese, *International Law in a Divided World,* pp. 142–3, 200–201, 213–14 and 246–50.

69. Cf. R. Falk, "Reflections on Democracy and the Gulf War," *Alternatives* 16:2 (1991), p. 272.

70. In making these proposals I do not wish to imply that the UN Charter itself is a fully coherent document. It includes some contradictory stipulations and procedures; some of its clauses are vague at best; and some of its recommendations can generate conflicting priorities. It is, in short, open to conflicts of interpretation which would have to be addressed thoroughly if it were to take on a more robust role.

71. P. Gourevitch, "The Second Image Reversed: The International Sources of Domestic Politics," *International Organization* 32 (1978).

72. Or, as Anthony Giddens usefully put it, globalization can be defined as "the intensification of worldwide social relations which link distant localities in such away that local happenings are shaped by events occurring many miles away and vice versa," in *Consequences of Modernity* (Cambridge: Polity Press, 1990), p. 64.

73. See A. McGrew, "Conceptualizing Global Politics," in A. McGrew, P. Lewis, et al., *Global Politics* (Cambridge: Polity Press, 1992), pp. 1–28.

74. C. W. Kegley and E. R. Wittkopf, *World Politics* (Basingstoke: Macmillan, 1989), p. 511.

75. I have discussed these processes and structures in "Democracy, the Nation-State and the Global System," pp. 207–27, and at greater length in *Democracy and the Global Order: From the Modern State to Cosmopolitan Governance,* (Cambridge and Stanford: Polity Press and Stanford University Press, 1995).

76. See Section "Democracy, the State, and Civil Society" above, pp. 321–24.

77. In previous publications I have referred to this as "the federal model," but given the current controversy about "federalism" in Europe, the term has become unhelpful in conveying my intentions. I would like to thank Daniele Archibugi for pressing this point. A central theme of my work *Democracy and the Global Order* is what I now prefer to call "the cosmopolitan model of democracy," or, better still, of "democratic autonomy." Of course, anyone who seeks to use the term "cosmopolitan" needs to clarify its meaning, especially in relation to Kant's thought. I seek to do this in *Democracy and the Global Order.*

78. It is beyond the scope of this chapter to set out my particular conception of rights, which I link to the notion of a "common structure of action": the necessary conditions for people in principle to enjoy free and equal political participation. See Held, "Democracy, the Nation-State and Global System," pp. 227–35, and, particularly, Held, *Democracy and the Global Order.*

79. Among other difficulties to be faced would be the rules determining the assembly's representative base. One country, one vote? Representatives allocated according to population size? Would major international functional organizations be represented? Cf. I. McLean, "Forms of Representation and Systems of Voting," in D. Held, ed., *Political Theory Today* (Cambridge: Polity Press, 1991), pp. 190–96, and J. Burnheim, *Is Democracy Possible?* (Cambridge: Polity Press, 1985), pp. 82–124.

80. European Community law embodies a range of relevant distinctions among legal instruments and types of implementation that are helpful to reflect on in this context. However, I leave open these complex issues in this chapter.

81. Hobbes, *Leviathan,* p. 223.

82. The models for the organization of such spheres are, it must be readily acknowledged, far from settled. See D. Held and C. Pollitt, eds., *New Forms of Democracy* (London: Sage, 1986).

83. The proposed European Social Charter embodies principles and rules that are compatible with the idea of generating elements of a common structure of action. If operationalized it would, in principle, alter the structure and functioning of market processes in a number of ways. While the Charter falls considerably short of what I have in mind as a common structure of action, and its details require extensive consideration that I shall not offer here, it is a useful illustration of the possibility of legislation to alter the background conditions and operations of the economic organizations of civil society.

84. Cf. R. Falk, "Positive Prescriptions for the Near Future" (Princeton, NJ: Princeton University, Center for International Studies, World Order Studies Program Occasional Paper, No. 20, 1991), pp. 8–10.

# 13. THOMAS POGGE

Pogge proposes to understand human rights as being primarily moral claims on social institutions rather than on the conduct of governments and other actors. On this variant of institutional moral cosmopolitanism, individual and collective agents have a human-rights-based negative duty not to participate in imposing on others an unjust institutional scheme. Pogge is especially concerned to bring such a human-rights standard to bear on the prevailing global institutional order which, in our highly interdependent world, has the most profound impact on human rights fulfillment worldwide. He argues that, so focused, his standard would support global institutional reforms toward a vertical dispersal of sovereignty, with governmental authority and patriotic sentiment widely dispersed over a plurality of nested territorial units. Such reforms would tend to increase prospects for peace, reduce severe poverty and oppression, enhance democratic participation, and stem ecological degradation.

## Cosmopolitanism and Sovereignty

*First published in* Ethics *103: 1 (October 1992): 48–75. Reprinted with permission from The University of Chicago Press. © 1992 by The University of Chicago. All rights reserved.*

The human future suddenly seems open. This is an inspiration; we can step back and think more freely. Instead of containment or détente, political scientists are discussing grand pictures: the end of history, or the inevitable proliferation and mutual pacifism of capitalist democracies. And politicians are speaking of a new world order. My inspiration is a little more concrete. After developing a rough, cosmopolitan specification of our task to promote moral progress, I offer an idea for gradual global institutional reform. Dispersing political authority over nested territorial units would decrease the intensity of the struggle for power and wealth within and among states, thereby reducing the incidence of war, poverty, and oppression. In such a multilayered institutional order, borders could be redrawn more easily to accord with the aspirations of peoples and communities.

## INSTITUTIONAL COSMOPOLITANISM BASED ON HUMAN RIGHTS

Three elements are shared by all cosmopolitan positions. First *individualism*: The ultimate units of concern are *human beings*, or *persons*[1]—rather than, say, family lines, tribes, or ethnic, cultural, or religious communities, nations, or states. The latter may be units of concern only indirectly, in virtue of their individual members or citizens. Second *universality*: The status of ultimate unit of concern attaches to *every* living human being *equally*[2]—not merely to some subset, such as men, aristocrats, Aryans, whites, or Muslims. Third *generality*: This special status has global force. Persons are ultimate units of concern *for everyone*—not only for their compatriots, fellow religionists, or such like.

Let me separate three cosmopolitan approaches by introducing two distinctions. The first is that between legal and moral cosmopolitanism. *Legal* cosmopolitanism is committed to a concrete political ideal of a global order under which all persons have equivalent legal rights and duties—are fellow citizens of a universal republic.[3] *Moral* cosmopolitanism holds that all persons stand in certain moral relations to one another: We are required to respect one another's status as ultimate units of moral concern—a requirement that imposes limits on our conduct and, in particular, on our efforts to construct institutional schemes. This view is more abstract, and in this sense weaker than, legal cosmopolitanism: It may support the latter for certain empirical circumstances, but it may, for different circumstances, support less uniform arrangements such as a system of autonomous states or even a multitude of self-contained communities. Here I present a variant of moral cosmopolitanism before examining below whether this position supports reforms that would bring our global order closer to the ideal of legal cosmopolitanism.

The central idea of moral cosmopolitanism is that every human being has a global stature as an ultimate unit of moral concern. Such moral concern can be fleshed out in countless ways. One may focus on subjective goods and ills (human happiness, desire fulfillment, preference satisfaction, or pain avoidance) or on more objective ones (such as human need fulfillment, capabilities, opportunities, or resources). Also, one might relativize these measures, for instance, by defining the key ill as *being worse off than anyone need be*, as *being dominated by others*, or as *falling below the mean*—which is equivalent to replacing straightforward aggregation (sum-ranking or averaging) by a maximin or egalitarian standard. In order to get to my topic quickly, I do not discuss these matters, but simply opt for a variant of moral cosmopolitanism that is formulated in terms of *human rights* (with straightforward interpersonal aggregation).[4] In doing so, I capture what most other variants likewise consider essential. And my further reflections can, in any case, easily be generalized to other variants of moral cosmopolitanism.

My second distinction lies *within* the domain of the moral. It concerns the nature of the moral constraints to be imposed. An *institutional* conception postulates certain fundamental principles of social *justice*. These apply to institutional schemes and are thus second-order principles: standards for assessing the ground rules and practices that regulate human interactions. An *interactional* conception, by contrast, postulates certain fundamental principles of *ethics*. These principles, like institutional ground rules, are first-order in that they apply directly to the conduct of persons and groups.

Interactional cosmopolitanism assigns direct responsibility for the fulfillment of human rights to other individual and collective agents, whereas institutional cosmopolitanism assigns such responsibility to institutional schemes. On the latter view, the responsibility of persons is then indirect—a shared responsibility for the justice of any practices one helps to impose: One ought not to cooperate in the imposition of a coercive institutional order that avoidably leaves human rights unfulfilled without making reasonable efforts to protect its victims and to promote institutional reform.[5]

Institutional and interactional conceptions are compatible and thus may be combined in a mutually complementary way.[6] Here I focus, however, on a variant of institutional cosmopolitanism while leaving open the question of its supplementation by a variant of interactional cosmopolitanism. I hope to show that making the institutional view primary leads to a more plausible and more pertinent overall morality. To do this, let me begin by exploring how the two approaches yield different understandings of human rights and their fulfillment.

On the interactional view, human rights impose constraints on conduct, while on the institutional view they impose constraints, in the first instance, on shared practices. The latter approach has two straightforward limitations. First, its applicability is contingent, in that human rights are activated only through the emergence of social institutions.

Where such institutions are lacking, human rights are merely latent, incapable of being either fulfilled or unfulfilled. Thus, if we accept a purely institutional conception of human rights, then we need some additional moral conception to formulate moral constraints on conduct in a disorganized state of nature.

Second, the cosmopolitanism of the institutional approach is contingent as well, in that the *global* moral force of human rights is activated only through the emergence of a *global* institutional order, which triggers obligations to promote any feasible reforms of this order that would enhance the fulfillment of human rights. So long as there is a plurality of self-contained cultures, the responsibility for unfulfilled human rights does not extend beyond their boundaries. (On the interactional approach suggested by Luban, by contrast, human rights would impose duties on persons anywhere to give possible aid and protection in specified cases of need.) It is only because all human beings are now fellow participants in a single, global institutional order—involving such institutions as the territorial state, a system of international law and diplomacy as well as a global economic system of property rights and markets for capital, goods, and services—that all unfulfilled human rights have come to be, at least potentially, everyone's responsibility.[7]

These two limitations do not violate generality. Each person has a duty toward *every* other person not to cooperate in imposing an unjust institutional order upon her, even while this duty triggers human-rights-based obligations only to fellow participants in the same institutional scheme. This is analogous to how the duty to keep one's promises is general even while it triggers obligations only toward persons to whom one has actually made a promise.

We see here how the institutional approach makes available an appealing intermediate position between two interactional extremes: It goes beyond simple libertarianism, according to which we may ignore harms that we do not directly bring about, without falling into a utilitarianism of rights, which commands us to take account of all relevant harms whatsoever, regardless of our causal relation to these harms.[8]

Consider a human right not to be enslaved. On an interactional view, this right would constrain persons, who must not enslave one another. On an institutional view, the right would constrain legal and economic institutions: ownership rights in persons must not be recognized or enforced. This leads to an important difference regarding the moral role of those who are neither slaves nor slaveholders. On the interactional view, such third parties have no responsibility toward existing slaves, unless the human right in question involved, besides the negative duty not to enslave, also a positive duty to protect or rescue others from enslavement. Such positive duties have been notoriously controversial. On the institutional view, by contrast, some third parties may be implicated far more directly in the unfulfilled human right. If they are not making reasonable efforts toward institutional reform, the more privileged participants in an institutional scheme in which slavery is permitted or even enforced—even those who own no slaves themselves—are here seen as cooperating in the enslavement, in violation of a *negative* duty. The institutional view thus broadens the circle of those who share responsibility for certain deprivations and abuses beyond what a simple libertarianism would justify, and it does so without having to affirm positive duties.

To be sure: Working for institutional reform is doing something (positive). But, in the context of practices, this—as even libertarians recognize—does not entail that the duty in question is therefore a positive one: The negative duty not to abuse just practices may also generate positive obligations, as when one must act to keep a promise or contract one has made. Once one is a participant in social practices, it may no longer be true that one's negative duties require merely forbearance.

The move from an interactional to an institutional approach thus blocks one way in which today's rich and mighty in the world's affluent regions like to see themselves as morally disconnected from the fate of the poor in the developing countries. It overcomes the claim that one need only refrain from violating human rights directly, that one cannot plausibly be required to become a soldier in the global struggle against human rights violators and a comforter of their victims worldwide. This claim is not refuted but shown to be irrelevant. We are asked to be concerned about unfulfilled human rights not simply insofar as they exist at all, but only insofar as they are produced by social institutions in whose coercive imposition we participate. Our negative duty not to cooperate in the imposition of unjust social institutions triggers obligations to promote feasible reforms that would enhance the fulfillment of human rights. This understanding of human rights as moral claims on national and global institutional schemes accords well with how human rights are understood in the Universal Declaration of Human Rights. Its Article 28 reads: "Everyone is entitled to a social *and international* order in which the rights and freedoms set forth in this Declaration can be fully realized" (my emphasis).

One may think that a shared responsibility for the justice of any social institutions one helps impose cannot plausibly extend beyond our national institutional scheme, in which we participate as citizens, and which we can most immediately affect. But such a limitation is untenable. The existing global institutional order is neither natural nor God-given, but rather shaped and upheld by the more powerful governments and by other actors they control (such as the UN, EU, IMF, World Bank, NATO, and OECD). At least the more privileged and influential citizens of the more powerful and approximately democratic countries bear then a collective responsibility for their governments' role in upholding this global order and for their government's failure to reform it toward greater human-rights fulfillment.

There are two primary strategies for attempting to limit the practical importance of this shared responsibility. A more philosophical strategy seeks to show that any institutional scheme should be held responsible only for deprivations it *establishes*, that is, mandates or at least authorizes. A human-rights standard should then classify such a scheme as acceptable so long as no severe deprivations are established by it, irrespective of any severe deprivations this scheme merely—however predictably and however avoidably—*engenders*. And we should therefore not count against the current global order the fact that it tends to engender a high incidence of war, torture, and starvation, because nothing in the existing (written or unwritten) international ground rules calls for such deprivations—they actually forbid both torture and the waging of aggressive war. Their prevalence therefore indicates no flaw in our global order and, a fortiori, no negative duties on our part (though we do of course have some more local negative duties to see to it that *our* government does not bring about torture, starvation, or an unjust war).

This position is implausible. It would be blatantly irrational to assess social institutions without regard to the effects they predictably engender—blatantly irrational, for example, to design a penal code or a tax code without regard to the effects it will actually produce through, for example, the compliance and reward incentives it provides. Longer jail terms may lower crime rates, thus reducing aggregate jail time, and lower tax rates may expand the tax base, thus increasing tax revenues—or they may have the opposite effect. A legislature would not be doing its job if it made such decisions without regard to their engendered consequences. It would be similarly irresponsible to think about the design and reform of global institutions without regard to *their* engendered consequences.

It does not follow that a plausible standard for assessing social institutions must treat established and engendered consequences on a par. A human right to physical security, for instance, though it should be sensitive to the risks an institutional scheme may impose on (some of) its participants through the high crime rate it engenders, should certainly be *more* sensitive to the risks it produces through officially authorized or even mandated assaults. (We should not, to give a simple illustration, authorize a "reform" of police procedures that would cause an extra 90 assaults by police against suspects, even if its contribution to deterrence would also reduce by 100 the number of similarly severe assaults by criminals against citizens.) These differentiations can and should be incorporated into any plausible conception of human rights, which should avoid, then, the kind of purely recipient-oriented view of deprivations that is embodied in consequentialist and contractualist (Rawlsian original-position) theorizing. With these differentiations in place, we can count engendered deprivations (such as poverty in a market system or insecurity due to crimes) as relevant to the fulfillment of human rights without committing to a purely recipient-oriented assessment of social institutions that would assign to engendered deprivations the same weight as it assigns to (equally severe) established deprivations.[9]

The sensitivity of the institutional approach to engendered deprivations suggests a further contrast to the interactional approach, concerning the way each understands what it means for a human right to be unfulfilled. It cannot plausibly be required of an institutional scheme, for example, that it reduce the incidence of criminal assaults to zero. This would be impossible; and approximating such an ideal as closely as possible would require a police state. The institutional approach thus should count a person's human right to physical security as adequately fulfilled if the integrity of her body is *reasonably* secure.[10] This entails that, even in the presence of a shared institutional scheme, some of what count as human rights violations on the interactional view (e.g., certain assaults) do not count as unfulfilled human rights on the institutional view (because the victims enjoy a high level of physical security which made the assault they actually suffer highly unlikely). Conversely, some of what count as unfulfilled human rights on the institutional view (e.g., inadequate protection associated with a considerable risk of assault) may not register on the interactional view (because some insufficiently protected persons are not actually assaulted).

A second, more empirical strategy for attempting to limit the practical importance of our shared responsibility for global institutions seeks to downplay the extent to which our global institutional scheme is causally responsible for current deprivations: "Unfulfilled human rights and their distribution have local explanations. In some countries torture is rampant, while it is virtually non-existent in others. Some regions are embroiled in frequent wars, while others are not. In some countries democratic institutions thrive, while others bring forth a succession of autocrats. And again, some poor countries have developed rapidly, while others are getting poorer year by year. Therefore our global institutional scheme has very little to do with the deplorable state of human rights fulfillment on earth."[11]

This challenge appeals to true premises but draws an invalid inference. Our global institutional scheme can obviously not figure in the explanation of *local* variations in the underfulfillment of human rights, but only in the *macro*explanation of its *global* incidence. This parallels how Japanese culture may figure in the explanation of the Japanese suicide rate or how the laxity of US handgun legislation may figure in the explanation of the North American homicide rate, without thereby explaining particular suicides/homicides or even intercity differentials in rates. In these parallel cases the need for a macroexplanation is obvious from the fact that there are other societies whose suicide/homicide rates are significantly lower. In the case of *global* institutions, the need for a macroexplanation of the overall incidence of unfulfilled human rights is less obvious because—apart from some rather inconclusive historical comparisons—the contrast to observable alternative global institutional schemes is lacking. Still, it is highly likely that there are feasible (i.e., practicable and accessible) alternative global regimes that would tend to engender lower rates of deprivation. This is clear, for example, in regard to economic institutions, where our experience with various national and regional schemes suggests that free markets must be regulated or complemented in certain ways if extreme poverty, entailing effective exclusion from political participation as well as from educational and medical opportunities, is to be avoided. This supports a generalization to the global plane, to the conjecture that the current global economic order must figure prominently in the explanation of the fact that our world is one of vast and increasing international inequalities in income and wealth (with consequent huge differentials in national rates of infant mortality, life expectancy, disease, and malnutrition). Such a macroexplanation does not preempt microexplanations of why one poor country is developing rapidly and why another is not. It would explain why so few are while so many are not.

Let me close the more abstract part of the discussion with a sketch of how this institutional view might understand social and economic human rights and how it might thus relate to the notion of distributive justice. A man sympathetic to the moral claims of the poor, Michael Walzer, has written: "The idea of distributive justice presupposes a bounded world, a community, within which distributions take place, a group of people committed to dividing, exchanging, and sharing, first of all among themselves."[12] This is precisely the picture of distributive justice that Robert Nozick (among others) has so vigorously attacked. To the notion of dividing, he objects that "there is no *central* distribution, no person or group entitled to control all the resources, jointly deciding how they are to be doled out."[13] And as for the rest, he would allow persons to do all the exchanging and sharing they like, but would strongly reject any enforced sharing implemented by some redistribution bureaucracy.

The institutional approach involves a conception of distributive justice that differs sharply from the one Walzer supports and Nozick attacks. Here the issue of distributive justice is not how to distribute a given pool of resources or how to improve upon a given distribution but, rather, how to choose or design the economic ground rules, which regulate property, cooperation, and exchange and thereby condition production and distribution. (On the particular view I have defended, for example, we should aim for a set of economic ground rules under which each participant would be able to meet her basic social and economic needs.) A conception of distributive justice understood in this way, as providing a standard for the moral assessment of alternative feasible schemes of economic institutions, is prior to both production and distribution occurring under such schemes and therefore involves neither the idea of an already existing pool of stuff to be doled out nor the idea of already owned resources to be *re*-distributed.

The institutional conception of distributive justice also does not presuppose the existence of a community of persons committed first of all to share with one another. Rather, it has a far more minimal rationale: We face a choice of economic ground rules that is partly open—not determined by causal necessity, nor preempted by some God-given or natural or neutral scheme that we must choose irrespective of its effects. This choice has a tremendous impact on human lives, an impact from which persons cannot be insulated and cannot insulate themselves. Our present global economic regime produces a stable pattern of widespread malnutrition and starvation among the poor (with some 20 million persons dying every year from hunger and trivial diseases), and there are likely to be feasible alternative regimes that would not produce similarly severe deprivations. If this is so, the victims of such avoidable deprivations are not merely poor and starving, but impoverished and starved through an institutional scheme coercively imposed upon them. There is an injustice in this economic scheme, which it would be wrong for its more affluent participants to perpetuate. And that is so quite independently of whether we and the starving are united by a communal bond or committed to sharing resources with one another—just as murdering a person is wrong irrespective of such considerations. This is what the assertion of social and economic human rights amounts to within the proposed institutional cosmopolitanism.[14]

This institutional cosmopolitanism does not, as such, entail crisp practical conclusions. One reason for this is that I have not—apart from allusions to the Universal Declaration—given a full list of well-defined human rights together with relative weights or priority rules. Another reason is that this institutional cosmopolitanism bears on the burning issues of the day only in an indirect way, mediated by empirical regularities and correlations about how existing institutional schemes, compared to feasible modifications thereof, tend to affect the incidence of unfulfilled human rights (as roughly indicated by rates of infant mortality, child abuse, crime, war, malnutrition, poverty, personal dependence, and exclusion from education or health care).

The intervention of such empirical matters, and the openness of the notion of human rights, do not mean that no conclusions can be drawn about the burning issues—only that what we can conclude is less precise and less definite than one might have hoped.

## THE IDEA OF STATE SOVEREIGNTY

Before discussing how we should think about sovereignty in light of the proposed institutional cosmopolitanism, let me define this term, in a somewhat unusual way, as a two-place relation:

A is *sovereign* over B if and only if

1.  A is a governmental body or officer ("agency"), and

2.  B are persons, and

3.  A has unsupervised and irrevocable authority over B
    (a) to lay down rules constraining B's conduct, or
    (b) to judge B's compliance with rules, or
    (c) to enforce rules against B through preemption, prevention, or punishments, or
    (d) to act in B's behalf toward other agencies (ones that do or do not have authority over B) or persons (ones whom A is sovereign over, or not).

A has *absolute sovereignty* over B if and only if

1.  A is sovereign over B, and

2.  no other agency has any authority over A or over B which is not both supervised and revocable by A.

Any A having (absolute) sovereignty over some B can then be said to be an (absolute) sovereign (the one-place predicate).[15]

Central to contemporary political thought and reality is the idea of the autonomous territorial state as the preeminent mode of political organization. In the vertical dimension, sovereignty is very heavily concentrated at a single level—it is states and only states that merit separate colors on a political map of our world. For nearly every human being, and for almost every piece of territory, there is exactly one government with preeminent authority over, and primary responsibility for, this person or territory. And each person is thought to owe primary political allegiance and loyalty to this government with preeminent authority over him or her. Such governments check and dominate the decision making of smaller political units as well as supranational decisions, which tend to be made through intergovernmental bargaining.[16]

From the standpoint of a cosmopolitan morality—which centers around the fundamental needs and interests of individual human beings, and of *all* human beings—this concentration of sovereignty at one level is no longer defensible. What I am proposing instead is not the idea of a centralized world state, which is really a variant of the preeminent-state idea. Rather, the proposal is that governmental authority—or sovereignty—be widely dispersed in the vertical dimension. What we need is *both* centralization *and* decentralization—a kind of second-order decentralization away from the now dominant level of the state. Thus, persons should be citizens of, and govern themselves through, a number of political units of various sizes, without any one political unit being dominant and thus occupying the traditional role of state. And their political allegiance and loyalties[17] should be widely dispersed over these units: neighborhood, town, county, province, state, region, and world at large. People should be politically at home in all of them, without converging on any one of them as the lodestar of their political identity.[18]

Before defending and developing this proposal by reference to the institutional cosmopolitanism set forth above, let me address two types of objection to any vertical division of sovereignty.

Objections of type 1 dispute that sovereignty can be divided at all. The traditional form of this objection rests on the belief that a *juridical condition* (as distinct from a lawless state of nature) presupposes an absolute sovereign. This dogma of absolute sovereignty arises (e.g., in Hobbes and Kant) roughly as follows. A juridical condition, by definition, involves a recognized decision mechanism that uniquely resolves any dispute. This mechanism requires some agency because a mere written or unwritten code (constitution, holy scripture) cannot settle disputes about its own interpretation. But so long as this agency is limited or divided—whether horizontally (i.e., by territory or by governmental function) or vertically (as in my proposal)—a juridical condition has not been achieved because there is no recognized way in which conflicts over the precise location of the limit or division can be authoritatively resolved. A genuine state of peace requires then an agency of last resort—ultimate, supreme, and unconstrained. Such an agency may still be limited by (codified or uncodified) obligations. But these can obligate merely *in foro interno* (in conscience) because to authorize subjects, or some second agency, to determine whether the first agency is overstepping its bounds would enable conflicts about this question for which there would be no reliable legal path of authoritative resolution.[19]

This argument, which—strictly construed—would require an absolute world sovereign, has been overtaken by the historical facts of the last two hundred years or so, which show conclusively that what cannot work in theory works quite well in practice. Law-governed coexistence is possible without a supreme and unconstrained agency. There is, it is true, the possibility of *ultimate* conflicts: of disputes in regard to which even the legally correct method of resolution is contested. To see this, one need only imagine how a constitutional democracy's three branches of government might engage in an all-out power struggle, each going to the very brink of what, on its understanding, it is constitutionally authorized to do. From a theoretical point of view, this possibility shows that we are not insured against, and thus live in permanent danger of, constitutional crises. But this no longer undermines our confidence in a genuine division of powers: We have learned that such crises need not be frequent or irresolvable. From a practical point of view, we know that constitutional democracies can endure and can ensure a robust juridical condition.

This same point applies in the vertical dimension as well: Just as it is nonsense to suppose that, in a juridical condition, sovereignty *must* rest with one of the branches of government, it is similarly nonsensical to think that in a multilayered scheme sovereignty *must* be concentrated on one level exclusively. As the history of federalist regimes clearly shows, a vertical division of sovereignty can work quite well in practice, even while it leaves some conflicts over the constitutional allocation of powers without a reliable legal path of authoritative resolution.

Objections of type 2 oppose, more specifically, a *vertical* dispersal of sovereignty: There are certain vertically indivisible governmental functions that form the core of sovereignty. Any political unit exercising these core functions must be dominant—free to determine the extent to which smaller units within it may engage in their own local political decision making, even while its own political process is immune to regulation and review by larger political units of which it forms a part. If there is to be any vertical distribution of sovereignty at all, it must therefore be lopsided in favor of those governments in the vertical order, which have authority over the core functions. The political units coordinate to these dominant governments, and only they, deserve the title of "country" (or "state," if one leaves aside the use of this word within the US).

To be assessable, such a claim stands in need of two clarifications, which are rarely supplied. First, when one thinks about it more carefully, it turns out to be surprisingly difficult to come up with examples of indivisible governmental functions. Eminent domain, economic policy, foreign policy, judicial review; the control of natural resources, security forces, education, health care, and income support; the regulation and taxation of resource extraction and pollution, of work and consumption, can all be handled at various levels and indeed *are* so handled in existing federal regimes and confederations. So what are the governmental functions that supposedly are vertically indivisible? And, second, is their indivisibility supposed to be derived from a conceptual insight, from empirical exigencies, or from moral desiderata? And which ones?

Since I cannot here discuss all possible type 2 objections, let me concentrate on one paradigm case: Walzer's claim that the authority to fix membership, to admit and exclude, is at least part of an indivisible core of sovereignty: "At some level of political organization something like the sovereign state must take shape and claim the authority to make its own admissions policy, to control and sometimes to restrain the flow of immigrants."[20] Walzer's "must" does not reflect a conceptual or empirical necessity, for in those senses the authority in question quite obviously *can* be divided—for example, by allowing political units on all levels to veto immigration. It is on moral grounds that Walzer rejects such an authority for provinces, towns, and neighborhoods: It would "create a thousand petty fortresses."[21] But if smaller units are to be precluded from controlling the influx of new members, then immigration must be controlled at the state level: "Only if the state makes a selection among would-be members and guarantees the loyalty, security, and welfare of the individuals it selects, can local communities take shape as 'indifferent' associations, determined only by personal preference and market capacity."[22] The asserted connection is again a moral one: It is certainly factually possible for local communities to exist as indifferent associations even while no control is exercised over migration at all; as Walzer says, "the fortresses too could be torn down, of course."[23] Walzer's point is, then, that the insistence on openness (to avoid a thousand petty fortresses) is asking too much of neighborhoods, unless the state has control over immigration: "The distinctiveness of cultures and groups depends upon closure ....If this distinctiveness is a value, ... then closure must be permitted somewhere."[24]

But is the conventional model really supported by the rationale Walzer provides? To be sure, Walzer is right to claim that the value of protecting cohesive neighborhood cultures is better served by national immigration control than by no control at all.[25] But it would be much better served still if the state could admit only immigrants who are planning to move into a neighborhood that is willing to accept them.

Moreover, since a neighborhood culture can be as effectively destroyed by the influx of compatriots as by that of immigrants, neighborhoods would do even better, if they had some authority to select from among prospective domestic newcomers or to limit their number. Finally, neighborhoods may often want to bring in new members from abroad—persons to whom they have special ethnic, religious, or cultural ties—and they would therefore benefit from a role in the national immigration control process that would allow them to facilitate the admission of such persons. Thus there are at least three reasons for believing that Walzer's rationale—cohesive neighborhood cultures ought to be protected without becoming petty fortresses—is actually *better* served by a division of the authority to admit and exclude than by the conventional concentration of this authority at the level of the state.

## SOME MAIN REASONS FOR A VERTICAL DISPERSAL OF SOVEREIGNTY

Having dealt with some preliminary obstacles, let me now sketch four main reasons that favor, over the status quo, a world in which sovereignty is widely distributed vertically.

1. *Peace/Security.* Under the current regime, interstate rivalries are settled ultimately through military competition, including the threat and use of military force. Moreover, within their own territories, national governments are free to do virtually anything they like. Such governments therefore have very powerful incentives and very broad opportunities to develop their military might. This is bound to lead to the further proliferation of nuclear, biological, chemical, and conventional weapons of mass destruction. And in a world in which dozens of competing governments control such weapons, the outbreak of devastating wars is only a matter of time. It is not feasible to reduce and eliminate national control over weapons of mass destruction through a program that depends on the voluntary cooperation of each and every national government. What is needed, therefore, is a centrally enforced end to the proliferation of such weapons and their gradual abolition—in violation of the prevalent idea of state sovereignty. Such a program, if implemented soon, is much less dangerous than continuing the status quo and could therefore—provided it increases the security of all on fair terms that are effectively adjudicated and enforced—win broad support from peoples and governments.

2. *Reducing Oppression.* Under the current global regime, national governments are effectively free to control "their" populations in whatever way they see fit. Many make extensive use of this freedom by torturing and murdering their domestic opponents, censoring information, suppressing and subverting democratic procedures, prohibiting emigration, and so forth. These massive deprivations could be reduced through a vertical dispersal of sovereignty over various layers of political units that would check and balance one another as well as publicize one another's abuses.

3. *Global Economic Justice.* The magnitude and extent of current economic deprivations calls for some modification in the prevailing global scheme of economic cooperation.[26] One plausible reform would involve a global levy on the use of natural resources to support the economic development in the poorest areas. Such a levy would tend to equalize per capita endowments and would also encourage conservation. Reforms for the sake of economic justice would again involve some centralization—though without requiring anything like a global welfare bureaucracy.[27]

Global economic justice is an end in its own right, which requires, and therefore supports, a reallocation of political authority. But it is also important as a means toward the first two objectives. War and oppression result from the contest for power within and among political units, which tends to be the more intense the higher the stakes. In fights to govern states, or to redraw their borders, far too much is now at stake by way of control over people and resources. We can best lower the stakes by dispersing political authority among several levels *and* institutionally securing economic justice at the global level.

This important point suggests why my first three considerations—though each supports some centralization—do not on balance support a centralized world state. While such a world state could lead to significant progress in terms of peace and economic justice, it also poses significant risks of oppression. Here the kind of multilayered scheme I propose has the great advantages of affording plenty of checks and balances and of assuring that, even when some political units turn tyrannical and oppressive, there will always be other, *already fully organized* political units (above, below, or on the same level) that can render aid and protection to the oppressed, publicize the abuses, and, if necessary, fight the oppressors. The prospect of such organized resistance would have a deterrent effect as governments would understand that repression is more likely to reduce than enhance their power.

There are two further important reasons against a centralized world state. Cultural and social diversity are likely to be far better protected when the interests of cultural communities at all levels are represented (externally) and supported (internally) by coordinate political units. And the scheme I propose could be gradually reached from where we are now (through what I have called second-order decentralization), while a centralized world state—involving, as it does, the annihilation of existing states—would seem reachable only through revolution or in the wake of some global catastrophe.

4. *Ecology*. Modern processes of production and consumption are liable to generate significant negative externalities that, to a large and increasing extent, transcend national borders. In a world of competing autonomous states, the internalization of such externalities is generally quite imperfect because of familiar isolation, assurance, and coordination problems. Treaties among a large number of very differently situated actors require difficult and time-consuming bargaining and negotiations, which often lead to only very slight progress, if any. And even when treaties are achieved, doubts about the full compliance of other parties tend to erode each party's own commitment to make good-faith efforts toward compliance.

Now one might think that this fourth reason goes beyond my institutional cosmopolitanism, because there is no recognized human right to a clean and healthy environment. Why should people not be free to live in a degraded natural environment if they so choose? In response: Perhaps they should be, but for now they will not have had a choice. The degradation of our natural environment inescapably affects us all. And yet, most people are effectively excluded from any say about this issue which, in the current state-centric model, is regulated by national governments unilaterally or through intergovernmental bargaining heavily influenced by huge differentials in economic and military might.

This response suggests replacing *Ecology* with a deeper and more general fourth reason labeled *Democracy*: Persons have a right to an institutional order under which those significantly and legitimately[28] affected by a political decision have a roughly equal opportunity to influence the making of this decision—directly or through elected delegates or representatives.[29] Such a human right to equal opportunity for political participation also supports greater local autonomy in matters of purely local concern than exists in most current states or would exist in a world state, however democratic. In fact, it supports just the kind of multilayered institutional scheme I have proposed.

Before developing this idea further, let me consider an objection. One might say, against a human right to equal opportunity for political participation, that what matters about political decisions is that they be correct, not that they be made democratically by those concerned. But this objection applies, first of all, only to political choices that are morally closed and thus *can* be decided correctly or incorrectly. I believe that we should reject a view on which almost all political choices are viewed as morally closed (with the correct decision determined, perhaps, through utility differentials), but I have no space here to defend this belief. Second, even when political choices *are* morally closed, the primary and ultimate responsibility for their being made correctly should lie with the persons concerned. Of course, some other decision procedure—such as a group of experts—may be more reliable for this or that kind of decision, and such procedures (judges, parliaments, cabinets, central banks, etc.) should then be put in place. This should be done, however, by *the people* delegating, or abstaining from, such decisions. It is ultimately up to them, and not to self-appointed experts, to recognize the greater reliability of, and to institutionalize, alternative decision-making procedures.

Given a human right to equal opportunity for political participation so conceived, the proper vertical distribution of sovereignty is determined by considerations of three kinds. The first favors decentralization, the second centralization, while the third may correct the resulting balance in either direction.

First, decision making should be decentralized as far as possible. This is desirable in part, of course, in order to minimize the decision-making burdens on individuals. But there are more important reasons as well. Insofar as decisions are morally closed, outsiders are more likely to lack the knowledge and sensitivities to make responsible judgments—and the only practicable and morally acceptable way of delimiting those who are capable of such judgments is by rough geographical criteria. Insofar as decisions are morally open, the goal must be to maximize each person's opportunity to influence the social conditions that shape her life—which should not be diluted for the sake of enhancing persons' opportunities to influence decisions of merely local significance elsewhere. At least persons should be left free to decide for themselves to what extent to engage in such exchanges. The first consideration does not then rule out voluntary creation of common decision-making mechanisms (whose structure would, however, tend to reflect the bargaining power of the political units involved, whose willing participation it must elicit). Such discretionary centralization may be rational, for example, in cases of conflict between local and global rationality (tragedy-of-the-commons cases: fishing, grazing, pollution) and also in regard to desired projects that require many contributors because they involve coordination problems or economies of scale, for example, or because they are simply too expensive (construction and maintenance of transportation and communication systems, research and technology, space programs, and so forth).

The second consideration favors centralization insofar as this is necessary to avoid excluding persons from the making of decisions that significantly and legitimately affect them. Such decisions are of two—possibly three—kinds. First, inhabiting the same natural environment and being significantly affected by what others do to it, our human right to an equal opportunity for political participation extends to regulating the use of this environment. Second, since the lives each of us can lead are very significantly shaped by prevailing social institutions—those defining property rights and markets, for example, and those structuring child rearing and the exercise of political authority—our human right to an equal opportunity for political participation extends to the choice and design of such institutions. These two kinds of decision arise directly from Kant's point that human beings cannot avoid affecting one another: through direct contact and through their impact on the natural world in which they coexist. A right to participate in decisions of the third kind is more controversial. There are contexts, one might say, in which we act as a species and thus should decide together how to act. Examples might be our conduct toward other biological species (extinction, genetic engineering, cruelty), ventures into outer space, and the preservation of our human heritage (ancient skeletons and artifacts, great works of art and architecture, places of exceptional natural beauty). In all these cases it would seem wrong for one person, group, or state to take irreversible steps unilaterally.

The significance of the second consideration depends heavily on empirical matters, though it does so in a rather straightforward and accessible way. It is evident that this consideration in favor of centralization has become far more significant over the past few centuries.

This is so partly because of rising population density, but much more importantly because of heightened global interdependence. Such interdependence is to some extent merely a function of vastly more powerful technologies, which bring it about that what a population does within its own national territory—stockpiling weapons of mass destruction, cutting down vegetation essential for the reproduction of oxygen, emitting pollutants that are destroying the ozone layer and cause global warming—now often imposes very significant harms and risks on outsiders. These externalities bring into play the political human rights of these outsiders, thereby morally undermining the conventional insistence on absolute state autonomy. Such technologies have also facilitated today's truly global capital and commodity markets, which communicate crashes and crises from any region to any other and enable even minor shocks—the devaluation of the Thai currency, a change in British interest rates, or a commodity futures trading frenzy in Chicago—literally to make the difference between life and death for large numbers of people half a world away, in Africa, for instance, where many countries are heavily dependent on foreign loans and on the exportation of minerals and cash crops. Such interdependence is not bad as such (it can hardly be scaled back in any case), but it does require democratic centralization of decision making: As persons become ever more strongly affected by the structure of global economic institutions, they become entitled to a political role in shaping them. The possibility of free bargaining over the design of such social institutions does not satisfy the equal-opportunity principle, as is illustrated in the case of commodity markets by the fact that African populations simply lack the bargaining power that would allow them significantly to affect how such markets are organized. (This argument withstands the communitarian claim that we must reject supranational democratic processes for the sake of the value of national autonomy. Such rejection does indeed enhance the national autonomy of the advantaged populations of the developed countries. But their gain comes at the expense of poorer populations who, despite fictional or de jure state sovereignty, have virtually no control over the most basic parameters that shape their lives—a problem heightened by the fact that even their own, rather weak governments face strong incentives to cater to foreign interests in preference to those of their constituents.)

The first two considerations by themselves yield the result that the authority to make decisions of some particular kind should rest with the democratic political process of a unit that (i) is as small as possible but still (ii) includes as equals all persons significantly and legitimately affected by decisions of this kind. In practice, some trading-off is required between these two considerations because there cannot always be an established political process that includes as equals all and only those significantly affected. A matter affecting the populations of two provinces, for example, might be referred to the national parliament or be left to bargaining between the two provincial governments. The former solution serves (ii) at the expense of (i): involving many persons who are not legitimately affected. The latter solution serves (i) at the expense of (ii): giving the persons legitimately affected not an equal opportunity to influence the matter, but one that depends on the relative bargaining power of the two provincial governments.

The first two considerations would suffice on the ideal-theory assumption that any decisions made satisfy all moral constraints with regard to both procedure (the equal-opportunity requirement) and output (this and other human rights). This assumption, however, could hardly be strictly true in practice. And so a third consideration must come into play: What would emerge as the proper vertical distribution of sovereignty from a balancing of the first two considerations alone should be modified—in either direction—if such modification significantly increases the democratic nature of decision making or its reliability (as measured in terms of human rights fulfillment). Let me briefly discuss how this third consideration might make a difference.

On the one hand, one must ask whether it would be a gain for human rights fulfillment on balance to transfer decision-making author-ity "upward" to larger units—or (perhaps more plausibly) to make the political process of smaller units subject to regulation and/or review by the political process of the next larger one. Such authority would allow the larger political unit, solely on human rights grounds, to require revi-sions in the structure of the political process of the smaller one and/or to invalidate its political decisions, and perhaps also to enforce such revisions and invalidations.[30]

Even when such a regulation and review authority really does protect human rights, it has some costs in terms of the political human rights of the members of the smaller unit. But then, of course, the larger unit's regulation and review process may itself be unreliable and thus may produce unfulfilled human rights either by overturning unobjectionable structures or decisions (at even greater cost to the political human rights of members of the smaller unit) or by forcing the smaller unit to adopt structures and decisions that directly lead to unfulfilled human rights.

On the other hand, there is also the less familiar inverse question: whether the third consideration might support a move in the direction of *de*centralization. Thus one must ask to what extent the political process of a larger unit is undemocratic or unreliable, and whether it might be a gain for human rights fulfillment on balance to transfer decision-making authority "downward" to smaller units—or to invest the political process of such subunits with review authority. Such an authority might, for instance, allow provincial governments, on human rights grounds, to block the application of national laws in their province. This authority is justified if and only if its benefits (laws that were passed in an undemocratic manner or would have led to unfulfilled human rights are not applied) outweigh its costs (unobjectionable laws are blocked in violation of the political rights of members of the larger unit).

How such matters should be weighed is a highly complex question that I cannot here address with any precision. Let me make two points nevertheless. First, a good deal of weight should be given to the actual views of those whose human rights are unfulfilled and for whose benefit a regulation and/or review authority might thus be called for. If most blacks in some state of the US would rather suffer discrimination than see their state government constrained by the federal government, then the presumption against such an authority should be much weightier than if the opposition came only from whites. This is not to deny that victims of injustice may be brainwashed or may suffer from false consciousness of various sorts. It may still be possible to make the case for a regulation and/or review authority. But it should be significantly more difficult to do so.

Second, commonalities of language, religion, ethnicity, or history are strictly irrelevant. Such commonalities do not give people a claim to be part of one another's political lives, nor does the lack of such commonalities argue against restraints. The presence or absence of such commonalities may still be empirically significant, however. Thus suppose that the members of some smaller unit share religious or ethnic characteristics that in the larger unit are in the minority (e.g., a Muslim province within a predominantly Hindu country). Our historical experience with such cases may well support the view that a regulation and review authority by the larger unit would probably be frequently abused or that a review authority by the smaller unit would tend to enhance human rights fulfillment overall. The relevance of such information brings out that the required balancing does not depend on value judgments alone. It also depends on empirically based expectations about how alternative arrangements would actually work in one or another concrete context.

The third consideration must also play a central role in a special case: the question of where decisions about the proper allocation of decision making should be made. For example: Should a dispute between a provincial parliament and a national legislature over which of them is properly in charge of a particular decision be referred to the provincial or the national supreme court? Here again a particular locus of decision making must be justified by showing that it is likely to be more reliable than its alternative.

Nothing definite can be said about the ideal number of levels or the exact distribution of legislative, executive, and judicial functions over them. These matters might vary in space and time, depending on the prevailing empirical facts to be accommodated by the second and third considerations (externalities, interdependence; unreliability problems) and on persons' preferences as shaped by the historical, linguistic, religious, or other cultural ties among them. The human right to an equal opportunity for political participation also leaves room for a wide variety, hence regional diversity, of decision-making procedures—direct or representative, with or without political parties, and so on. Democracy may take many forms.

## THE SHAPING AND RESHAPING OF POLITICAL UNITS

One great advantage of the proposed multilayered scheme is that it can be reached gradually from where we are now. This requires moderate centralizing and decentralizing moves involving the strengthening of political units above and below the level of the state. In some cases, such units will have to be created, and so we need some idea about how the geographical shape of new political units is to be determined. Or, seeing that there is considerable dissatisfaction about even the geographical shape of existing political units, we should ask more broadly: What principles ought to govern the geographical separation of political units on any level?

Guided again by the cosmopolitan ideal of democracy, I suggest these two procedural principles as a first approximation:

(1) The inhabitants of any contiguous territory of reasonable shape may decide, through some majoritarian or supermajoritarian procedure, to join an existing political unit whose territory is contiguous with theirs and whose population is willing—as assessed through some majoritarian or supermajoritarian procedure—to accept them as members.[31] This liberty is subject to two conditions: The territory of the newly enlarged political unit must have a reasonable shape. And any newly contracted political unit must either remain viable in a contiguous territory of reasonable shape or be willingly incorporated, pursuant to this same liberty, into another political unit or other political units.

(2) The inhabitants of any contiguous territory of reasonable shape, if sufficiently numerous, may decide, through some majoritarian or supermajoritarian procedure, to constitute a new political unit. This liberty is constrained in three ways: There may be subgroups whose members are free, pursuant to (1), to reject membership in the unit to be formed in favor of membership in another political unit. There may be subgroups whose members are free, pursuant to (2), to reject membership in the unit to be formed in favor of forming their own political unit.[32] And any newly contracted political unit must either remain viable in a contiguous territory of reasonable shape or be willingly incorporated, pursuant to the first clause of (1), into another political unit or other political units.

It will be said that acceptance of such principles would trigger an avalanche of applications. It is surely true that many existing groups are unhappy with their current membership status; there is a significant backlog, so to speak, that might pose a serious short-term problem. Once this backlog will have been worked down, however, there may not be much redrawing activity as people will then be content with their political memberships, and most borders will be supported by stable majorities.

Moreover, as the advocated vertical dispersal of sovereignty is implemented, conflicts over borders will lose much of their intensity. In our world, many such conflicts are motivated by morally inappropriate considerations—especially the following two: There is competition over valuable or strategically important territories and groups because control over them importantly affects the distribution of international bargaining power (economic and military potential) for the indefinite future. And there are attempts by the more affluent to interpose borders between themselves and the poor in order to circumvent widely recognized duties of distributive justice among compatriots.[33] Under the proposed multilayered scheme—in which the political authority currently exercised by national governments is both constrained and dispersed over several layers, and in which economic justice is institutionalized at the global level and thus inescapable—territorial disputes on any level would be only slightly more intense than disputes about provincial or county lines are now. It is quite possible that my two principles are not suitable for defining a right to secession in our present world of excessively sovereign states.[34] But their plausibility will increase as the proposed second-order decentralization progresses.[35]

Finally, the incidence of applications can be reduced through two reasonable amendments: First, the burden of proof, in appealing to either of the two principles, should rest with the advocates of change, who must map out an appropriate territory, mobilize the support of its population, and so forth. This burden would tend to discourage frivolous claims. Second, it may be best to prescribe some supermajoritarian procedure (requiring, say, that proponents must outnumber opponents plus nonvoters in two referenda one year apart). Some such provision would especially help prevent areas changing back and forth repeatedly (with outside supporters moving in, perhaps, in order to tip the scales).

Let me briefly illustrate how the two principles would work in the case of nested political units. Suppose the Kashmiris agree that they want to belong together as one province but are divided on whether this should be a province of India or of Pakistan. The majority West Kashmiris favor affiliation with Pakistan, the East Kashmiris favor affiliation with India. There are four plausible outcomes: A united Kashmiri province of Pakistan (P), a united Kashmiri province of India (I), a separate state of Kashmir (S), and a divided Kashmir belonging partly to Pakistan and partly to India (D). Since the East Kashmiris can, by principle (2), unilaterally insist on D over P, they enjoy some protection against the West Kashmiri majority. They can use this protection for bargaining, which may result in outcome S (if this is the second preference on both sides) or even in outcome I (if that is the second preference of the West Kashmiris while the East Kashmiris prefer D over P).[36]

The conventional alternatives to the proposed cosmopolitan way of settling the borders of political units reserve a special role either for historical states and their members (compatriots) or for nations and their

members (fellow nationals). The former version is inherently conservative, the latter potentially revisionist (by including, e.g., the Arab, Kurd-
ish, and Armenian nations and by excluding multinational states like the
Soviet Union or the Sudan). The two key claims of such a position are:
(A) Only (encompassing) groups of compatriots/fellow nationals have
a right to self-government. (B) Such government may be exercised even
over unwilling geographical subgroups of compatriots/fellow nationals,
who at most have a liberty of individual emigration.[37] Those who hold
such a conventional position are liable to reject the cosmopolitan view
as excessively individualist, contractarian, or voluntaristic. Examples of
this sentiment are easy to find: "The more important human groupings
need to be based on shared history, and on criteria of nonvoluntaristic
(or at least not wholly contractarian) membership to have the value
that they have."[38] Insofar as this is an empirical claim—about the preconditions of authentic solidarity and mutual trust, perhaps—I need
not disagree with it.[39] If indeed a political unit is far more valuable
for its members when they share a common descent and upbringing
(language, religion, history, culture), then people will recognize this
fact and will themselves seek to form political units along these lines.
I don't doubt that groups seeking to change their political status under
the two principles would for the most part be groups characterized by
such unchosen commonalities.

But would I not allow any other group to change its political status,
even if this means exchanging a more valuable for a less valuable membership? Margalit and Raz ridicule this idea through their examples of
"the Tottenham Football Club supporters," "the fiction-reading public,"
and "the group of all the people whose surnames begin with a 'g' and
end with an 'e.' "[40] Yet these examples—apart from being extremely
far-fetched—are ruled out by the contiguity requirement, which a "vol-
untarist" can and, I believe, should accept in light of the key function of
government: to support common rules among persons who cannot avoid
influencing one another through direct interaction and through their
impact on a shared environment. A more plausible example would then
be that of the inhabitants of a culturally and linguistically Italian border
village who prefer an (ex hypothesi) less valuable membership in France
over a more valuable membership in Italy. Here I ask: Do they not,
France willing, have a right to err? Or should they be forced to remain
in, or be turned over to, a larger political unit against their will?

This example brings out the underlying philosophical value conflict.
Cosmopolitanism is committed to the freedom of individual persons and

therefore envisions a pluralist global institutional scheme. Such a scheme is compatible with political units whose membership is homogeneous with respect to some partly unchosen criteria (nationality, ethnicity, native language, history, religion, etc.), and it would certainly engender such units. But it would do so only because persons *choose* to share their political life with others who are like themselves in such respects—not because persons are entitled to be part of one another's political lives if and only if they share certain unchosen features.

One way of supporting the conventional alternative involves rejecting the individualist premise that only human beings are ultimate units of moral concern.[41] One could then say that, once the moral claims of states/nations are taken into account alongside those of persons, one may well find that, all things considered, justice requires institutional arrangements that are inferior, in human rights terms, to feasible alternatives—institutional arrangements, for example, under which the interest of Italy in its border village would prevail over the expressed interest of the villagers.

This justificatory strategy faces two main problems. It is unclear how states/nations can have interests or moral claims that are not reducible to interests and moral claims of their members (which can be accommodated within a conception of human rights). This idea smacks of bad metaphysics,[42] and also is dangerously subject to political/ideological manipulation (as exemplified by Charles de Gaulle who was fond of adducing the interests of *la nation* against those of his French compatriots). Moreover, it is unclear why this idea should work here, but not in the case of other kinds of (sub- and supranational) political units, nor in that of religious, cultural, and athletic entities. Why need we not also take into account the moral claims of Catholicism, art, or soccer?

These problems suggest the other justificatory strategy, which accepts the individualist premise but then formulates the political rights of persons with essential reference to the state/nation whose members they are. This strategy has been defended, most prominently, by Michael Walzer, albeit in a treatise that focuses on international ethics (interactions) rather than international justice (social institutions). Walzer approvingly quotes Westlake: "The duties and rights of states are nothing more than the duties and rights of the men who compose them," adding "the rights ... [to] territorial integrity and political sovereignty ... belong to states, but they derive ultimately from the rights of individuals, and from them they take their force. ... States are neither organic wholes nor mystical unions."[43]

The key question is, of course, how such a derivation is supposed to work. There are two possibilities. The direct route would be to postulate either a human right to be jointly governed with one's compatriots/fellow nationals[44] or a human right to an equal opportunity to participate in the exercise of sovereignty over one's compatriots/fellow nationals. The former of these rights is implausibly demanding on others (the Bavarians can insist on being part of Germany, even if all the other Germans wanted nothing to do with them) and would still fail to establish claim (B), unless it were also unwaivable—a duty, really. The latter right is implausibly demanding on those obligated to continue to abide by the common will merely because they have once (however violently) been incorporated into a state or merely because they have once shared solidarity and sacrifices.

The indirect, instrumental route would involve the empirical claim that human rights (on a noneccentric definition) are more likely to be fulfilled, or are fulfilled to a greater extent, if there is, for each person, one political unit that decisively shapes her life and is dominated by her compatriots/fellow nationals. This route remains open on my cosmopolitan conception (via the third consideration), though the relevant empirical claim would not seem to be sustainable on the historical record.

Supposing that this sort of argument fails on empirical grounds, the proposed institutional cosmopolitanism would favor a global order in which sovereignty is widely distributed vertically, while the geographical shape of political units is determined by the autonomous preferences of situated individuals in accordance with principles (1) and (2).

## CONCLUSION

From our angle, the world looks in good shape. We live in clean and safe surroundings, economically and physically secure under an alliance of governments that have "won the Cold War." We have every reason to be content with the global order we have shaped. But resting content with it is doubly myopic. It ignores that we are only 15 percent of humankind: Much larger numbers must live, despite hard work, on incomes of 1/50 the purchasing power of ours and hence in constant confrontation with infant mortality, child labor, hunger, squalor, and disease. Fully one-third of all human beings still die from poverty-related causes. In view of such massive deprivations and unprecedented inequalities, we cannot decently avoid reflection on global institutional reform. Resting content with the status quo also ignores the future: More and more, the transnational imposition of externalities and risks is becoming a two-way street, as no state or group of states, however rich and well-armed, can effectively insulate itself from external influences—from military and terrorist attacks, illegal immigrants, epidemics and the drug trade, pollution and climate change, price fluctuations, and scientific-technological and cultural innovations. Bringing these potentially highly disruptive risks and externalities under effective control requires a global institutional reform involving significant reductions in national sovereignty. To be morally acceptable and politically feasible, such a reform must be capable of functioning without heavy and continuing enforcement and therefore must bring to poorer societies not merely a reduction in their formal sovereignty, but also economic sufficiency and democratic governance. This essay was meant to show how the main elements of such a global institutional reform might be conceived, and justified in terms of a cosmopolitan human-rights standard, in a way that is broadly sharable internationally.


## NOTES

This essay has benefited from many incisive comments and suggestions by Andreas Follesdal, Bonnie Kent, Ling Tong, and my fellow participants at the "Ethicon East/West Dialogue Conference on the Restructuring of Political and Economic Systems" (Berlin, January 1991). While the essay has been updated in various ways, I have made no effort to change its tone, reflecting the spirit of 1990, the year of its composition.

1. The differences between these two concepts are not essential to the present discussion.

2. This emphasis on equality is compatible with the view that the weight agents ought to give to the human rights of others may vary with their relation to them—that agents have stronger moral reasons to secure human rights in their own country, for example, than abroad—so long as this is not seen as being due to a difference in the moral significance of these rights, impersonally considered. (I can believe that the flourishing of all children is equally important and also that I should show greater concern for the flourishing of my own children than for that of others.)

There is some debate about the extent to which we should give weight to the interests of future persons and also to those of past ones (whose deaths are still recent). I leave this issue aside because it is at right angles to the debate between cosmopolitanism and its alternatives.

3. One recent argument for a world state is advanced in Kai Nielsen, "World Government, Security, and Global Justice," in Steven Luper-Foy, ed. *Problems of International Justice* (Boulder: Westview Press 1988).

4. I have in mind here a rather minimal conception of human rights, one that rules out truly severe abuses, deprivations, and inequalities while still being compatible with a wide range of political, moral, and religious cultures. The recent development of, and progress within, both governmental and nongovernmental international organizations supports the hope, I believe, that such a conception might, in our world, become the object of a worldwide overlapping consensus. See also my essay "Human Flourishing and Universal Justice" in *Social Philosophy and Policy* 16 (1999): 333–61.

5. Interactional cosmopolitanism has been defended in numerous works. A paradigmatic statement is offered in David Luban's essay "Just War and Human Rights" in Charles Beitz et al., eds. *International Ethics* (Princeton: Princeton University Press 1985), at 209 [first published in *Philosophy and Public Affairs* 9: 2 (winter 1980): 160-81, at 174, reprinted in *Global Ethics: Seminal Essays*, 29–50 at 41]: "A human right, then, will be a right whose beneficiaries are all humans and whose obligors are all humans in a position to effect the right." Substantially similar moral positions are advanced in Peter Singer: "Famine, Affluence and Morality," in *Philosophy and Public Affairs* 1 (1972): 229–43 [reprinted in *Global Ethics: Seminal Essays*, 1–14]; James Rachels, "Killing and Starving to Death," in *Philosophy* 54 (1979), 159-171; Shelly Kagan, *The Limits of Morality* (Oxford: Oxford University Press 1989); Peter Unger, *Living High and Letting Die: Our Illusion of Innocence* (Oxford: Oxford University Press 1996) [sections 1–3 of chapter 1 and chapter 2 reprinted in *Global Ethics: Seminal Essays*, 325–78]. Robert Nozick's *Anarchy, State, and Utopia* (New York: Basic Books 1974)—however surprising the rights he singles out as fundamental—is also an instance of interactional cosmopolitanism. For institutional cosmopolitanism, see Onora Nell [O'Neill], "Lifeboat Earth," in *Philosophy and Public Affairs* 4 (1975): 273–92 [reprinted herein 1–20]; Thomas Nagel, "Poverty and Food: Why Charity Is Not Enough," in Peter Brown and Henry Shue, eds., *Food Policy: The Responsibility of the United States in the Life and Death Choices* (New York: The Free Press, 1977), 54–62 [reprinted herein 49–59]; Charles Beitz: *Political Theory and International Relations* (Princeton: Princeton University Press, 1979), part 3 [based on his essay "Justice and International Relations," first published in *Philosophy and Public Affairs* 4: 4 (summer 1975): 360–89, reprinted herein 21–48]; Charles Beitz: "Cosmopolitan Ideals and National Sentiment," *Journal of Philosophy* 80 (1983): 591–600 [reprinted in *Global Ethics: Seminal Essays*, 107–17]; and Thomas Pogge: *Realizing Rawls* (Ithaca: Cornell University Press, 1989), part 3. Henry Shue's influential book *Basic Rights* (Princeton: Princeton University Press, 1996 [1980]) [chapters 1 and 2 reprinted herein 83–144] seems to me to waver between both variants of moral cosmopolitanism, leaving unclear whether Shue means the weight of our duties to protect and to aid the deprived to depend on whether we are

or are not involved in (imposing on them the social institutions that produce) their deprivation.

6. This is done, for example, by John Rawls, who asserts both a natural duty to uphold and promote just social institutions as well as various other natural duties that do not presuppose shared social institutions, such as duties to avoid injury and cruelty, duties to render mutual aid, and a duty to bring about just social institutions where none presently exist. See John Rawls, *A Theory of Justice* (Cambridge: Harvard University Press, 1971), 114f and 334.

7. These two limitations are compatible with the belief that we have a duty to *create* a comprehensive institutional scheme. Thus Kant believed that any persons and groups who cannot avoid affecting one another ought to enter into a juridical condition. See "Theory and Practice" in Hans Reiss, ed., *Kant's Political Writings* (Cambridge: Cambridge University Press, 1970), p. 73 (Ak 8:289).

8. The expression "utilitarianism of rights" is due to Nozick (op. cit., 28). Such a view, suggested by the sentence quoted from Luban (note 5 above), relates the goal of maximizing rights fulfillment directly to agents. It takes a consequentialist approach in *ethics* and thus admits of the usual alternative specifications: A utilitarianism of rights might be of the ideal or real as well as of the act, rule, or motive variety. There are also noninteractional versions of consequentialism, such as Bentham's utilitarianism, which is meant to apply to social institutions (such as a society's penal system).

9. The distinction between the established and the engendered effects of social institutions as well as the question of its moral significance are extensively discussed in my *Realizing Rawls*, §§ 2–4. The rejection of purely recipient-oriented modes of assessment (such as that enshrined in Rawls's original position) is of more recent vintage: "Three Problems with Contractarian-Consequentialist Ways of Assessing Social Institutions," in *Social Philosophy and Policy* 12 (1995): 241–66.

10. This notion is defined in probabilistic terms, perhaps by taking account of various personal characteristics. Thus it is quite possible that the human right to physical security is today fulfilled in the US for middle-aged whites or suburbanites but not for black youths or inner-city residents.

11. The explanatory move urged in this fictitious interjection is extremely common among social theorists and philosophers. Let me give two representative examples: "It is not the sign of some collective derangement or radical incapacity for a political community to produce an authoritarian regime. Indeed, the history, culture, and religion of the community may be such that authoritarian regimes come, as it were, naturally, reflecting a widely shared world view or way of life"—Michael Walzer: "The Moral Standing of States" in *Philosophy and Public Affairs* 9 (1980): 209–29 at 224f [reprinted in *Global Ethics: Seminal Essays*, 51–71 at 65f]. "The great social evils in poorer societies are likely to be oppressive government and corrupt elites"—John Rawls, "The Law of Peoples," in Stephen Shute and Susan Hurley, eds., *On Human Rights*

(New York: Basic Books 1993), 77 [reprinted herein 421–60, at 448]. It is more fully criticized in part 3 of my "The Bounds of Nationalism" in *Rechtsphiloso-phische Hefte* 7 (1997): 55–90.

12. Michael Walzer: "The Distribution of Membership" in Peter Brown and Henry Shue, eds.: *Boundaries* (Totowa: Rowman Littlefield 1981), 1 [reprinted herein 145–77, at 145]. Cf. the largely identical chapter 2 of Michael Walzer, *Spheres of Justice* (New York: Basic Books, 1983), p. 31.

13. Nozick, *Anarchy*, 149.

14. This understanding of human rights is further elaborated in my "How Should Human Rights be Conceived?" in *Jahrbuch für Recht und Ethik* 3 (1995): 103–20, and "Menschenrechte als moralische Ansprüche an globale Institutionen," in Stefan Gosepath and Georg Lohmann, eds., *Die Philosophie der Menschenrechte* (Frankfurt: Suhrkamp, 1998), pp. 378–400.

15. It is quite possible, and not without historical justification, to define sovereignty the way I have defined absolute sovereignty. In that case sovereignty would not survive division, and the expression "distribution of sovereignty" would be an oxymoron.

16. The central organs of the European Union constitute a promising exception to this generalization. For further discussion, see my "How to Create Supra-National Institutions Democratically: Some Reflections on the European Union's 'Democratic Deficit,'" in Andreas Follesdal and Peter Koslowski, ed., *Democracy and the European Union* (Berlin: Springer Verlag, 1998), pp. 160–85.

17. This includes the sentiments of patriotism, if such there must be. Beitz points out two respects in which patriotic allegiance to political units may be desirable: It supports a sense of shared loyalty ("Cosmopolitan Ideals," p. 599 [*GESE* 114–15]). And it allows one to see oneself as a significant contributor to a common cultural project: "Just as we can see ourselves as striving to realize in our own lives various forms of individual perfection, so we can see our countries as striving for various forms of social and communal perfection" ("Cosmopolitan Ideals," 600 [*GESE* 115]). Neither of these considerations entails that Britain, say, must be the sole object of your patriotic allegiance, rather than some combination of Glasgow, Scotland, Britain, Europe, humankind, and perhaps even such geographically dispersed units as the Anglican Church, the World Trade Union Movement, PEN, or Amnesty International.

18. Many individuals might, of course, identify more with one of their citizenships than with the others. But in a multilayered scheme, such prominent identifications would be less frequent and, most important, would not converge: Even if some residents of Glasgow would see themselves as primarily British, others would identify more with Europe, with Scotland, with Glasgow, or with humankind at large.

19. This dogma—prefigured in Thomas Aquinas, Dante Alighieri, Marsilius of Padua, and Jean Bodin—is most fully stated in chapters 14, 26 and 29

of Thomas Hobbes, *Leviathan* (Harmondsworth: Penguin, 1981 [1651]), who also introduces the idea of obligations *in foro interno*. For Kant's statements of it, see "Theory and Practice" in Reiss, 75 and 81 (Ak 8:291f, 8:299), and *Metaphysical Elements of Justice* in Reiss, 144f (Ak 6:319). The dogma maintained its hold well into the twentieth century, when it declined with the Austinian conception of jurisprudence. See John Austin, *The Province of Jurisprudence Determined* (London: Weidenfeld and Nicolson, 1955 [1832]), Geoffrey Marshall, *Parliamentary Sovereignty and the Commonwealth* (Oxford: Oxford University Press, 1957), part 1; S. I. Benn and R. S. Peters, *Social Principles and the Democratic State* (London: Allen and Unwin, 1959), chapters 3 and 12; and Herbert L. A. Hart, *The Concept of Law* (Oxford: Oxford University Press, 1994 [1961]).

20. Walzer, "The Distribution of Membership," 10 [herein p. 153].

21. Ibid., 9 [herein p. 153].

22. Ibid.

23. Ibid.

24. Ibid., 9-10 [herein p. 153].

25. Ibid., 9 [herein pp. 152-153].

26. 1.3 billion persons, 22 percent of the world's population, live below the international poverty line, which means that their daily income has less purchasing power that one Dollar had in the US in 1985, less purchasing power than $1.55 had in the US in 1999. As a consequence of such severe poverty, 841 million persons (14 percent) are today malnourished, 880 million (15 percent) without access to health services, 1 billion (17 percent) without adequate shelter, 1.3 billion (22 percent) without access to safe drinking water, 2 billion (33 percent) without electricity, and 2.6 billion (43 percent) without access to sanitation—United Nations Development Programme: *Human Development Report, 1998* (New York: Oxford University Press, 1998), p. 49. The effects of such severe poverty on children are especially appalling. The International Labor Organization (www.ilo.org) reports that at least 120 million children between the ages of 5 and 14 work full time; the number is 250 million, or more than twice as many, if we include those for whom work is a secondary activity. Many of these children are forced to work under cruel conditions in mines, quarries, and factories as well as in agriculture, construction, prostitution, textile, and carpet production. See also United Nations Children's Fund, *The State of the World's Children, 1998* (New York: Oxford University Press, 1998), reporting on children deprived of even basic education as well as on child deaths from easily and cheaply preventable or curable diseases such as diarrhea, pneumonia, and measles.

27. For further discussion of such a reform—backed perhaps by the idea that the world's resources should be owned or controlled by all its inhabitants as equals—see Beitz, *Political Theory*, 136–43 [cf. herein pp. 27-32], and my "A Global Resources Dividend" in David A. Crocker and Toby Linden, eds.,

*Ethics of Consumption: The Good Life, Justice, and Global Stewardship* (Lanham, MD: Rowman & Littlefield, 1998), pp. 501–36.

28. The qualification "legitimately" is necessary to rule out claims such as this: "I should be allowed a vote on the permissibility of homosexuality in all parts of the world, because the knowledge that homosexual acts are performed anywhere causes me great distress." I cannot enter a discussion of this proviso here, except to say that the arguments relevant to its specification are by and large analogous to the standard arguments relevant to the specification of Mill's no-harm principle: "the sole end for which mankind are warranted, individually or collectively, in interfering with the liberty of action of any of their number is self-protection"—John Stuart Mill, *On Liberty* (Indianapolis: Hackett, 1978 [1859]), p. 9.

29. I understand *opportunity* as being impaired only by (social) *disadvantages*—not by (natural) *handicaps*. This is plausible only on a narrow construal of "handicap." Although being black and being female are natural features, they reduce a person's chances to influence political decisions only in certain social settings (in a racist/sexist culture). Such reductions should therefore count as due to disadvantage rather than handicap.

By contrast, those whose lesser ability to participate in public debate is due to their low intelligence are not disadvantaged but handicapped. Provided they had access to an adequate education, they do not count as having a less-than-equal opportunity.

The postulated human right is not a group right. Of course, the inhabitants of a town may appeal to this right to show that it was wrong for the national government, say, to impose some political decision that affects only them. In such a case, the townspeople form a group of those having a grievance. But they do not have a grievance *as a group*. Rather, *each* of them has such a grievance of not having been given her due political weight—just the grievance she would have had, had the decision been made by other townspeople with her excluded.

30. The larger political unit may not take such action in defense of its own values or interests. Nor may it act in defense of procedural or substantive constraints to which the smaller unit may have chosen to commit itself; the interpretation of such constraints is left to the courts of the smaller unit (just as federal courts in the US must defer to the courts of each state in regard to the interpretation of that state's laws and constitution).

31. I won't try to be precise about "reasonable shape." The idea is to rule out areas with extremely long borders, or borders that divide towns, integrated networks of economic activity, or the like. Perhaps the inhabitants in question should have to be minimally numerous; but I think the threshold could be quite low. If a tiny border village wants to belong to the neighboring province, why should it not be allowed to switch?

The contiguity condition needs some relaxing to allow territories consisting of a small number of internally contiguous areas whose access to one another is not controlled by other political units. The US would satisfy this relaxed condition through secure access among Puerto Rico, Alaska, Hawaii, and the remaining forty-eight contiguous states.

32. What if minority subgroups are geographically dispersed (like the Serbs in Croatia)? In such cases, there is no attractive way of accommodating those opposed to the formation of the new political unit. The second proposed principle would let the preference of the majority within the relevant territory prevail nevertheless. This is defensible, I think, so long as the fulfillment of human rights is not at stake. In such cases it seems plausible, if legitimate preferences are opposed and some must be frustrated, to let the majority prevail.

33. See Allen Buchanan, *Secession* (Boulder: Westview Press, 1991), pp. 114–25, and my "Loopholes in Moralities," in *Journal of Philosophy* 89 (1992): 79–98, at 88–90.

34. *This* topic is extensively discussed by Buchanan. While he takes the current states system for granted and makes realistic adjustments of his theory of secession to this system, my aim is to give yet one more reason for a somewhat different global order by showing that it would render realistic a morally more appealing theory of secession. See also Buchanan's chapter herein. A more sustained argument for the moral appeal of this theory in terms of democratic self-government is provided in Daniel Philpott: "In Defense of Self-Determination," in *Ethics* 105 (1995): pp. 352–85. See also Christopher Wellman, "A Defense of Secession and Political Self-Determination," in *Philosophy and Public Affairs* 24 (1995): pp. 142–71, and the early, pioneering contribution by Harry Beran, *The Consent Theory of Political Obligation* (London: Croom Helm Publishers, 1987).

35. For example: As European states will increasingly become subject to global and regional constraints—regarding military might, pollution, exploitation of resources, treatment of its citizens, etc.—the importance of whether there is one state (Czechoslovakia) or two states (one Czech, one Slovak) would tend to decline: for the Slovaks, for the Czechs, and for any third parties.

36. Obviously, this story is not meant to reflect the actual situation on the Indian subcontinent.

37. While the precise definition of "nation" and "nationality" is not essential to this discussion, I do assume that nationality is not defined entirely in voluntaristic terms (e.g., "a nation is a group of persons all of whom desire to constitute one political unit of which they are the only members"), in which case the first claim would become trivial and the second empty. The definition may still contain significant voluntaristic elements, as in Renan's proposal: "A nation is a grand solidarity constituted by the sentiment of sacrifices which one has made and those one is disposed to make again. It supposes a past ..."—quoted in Brian Barry, "Self-Government Revisited," in David Miller and Larry Siedentop, eds., *The Nature of Political Theory* (Oxford: Clarendon Press, 1983), p. 136. So long as some nonvoluntaristic element is present, at least one of the two claims can get off the ground: Those who want to belong

together as one political unit may be prevented from doing so when they lack an appropriate history of solidarity and sacrifices.

38. Avishai Margalit and Joseph Raz: "National Self-Determination," *Journal of Philosophy* 87 (1990): pp. 439–61, at 456 [reprinted in *Global Ethics: Seminal Essays*, 181–206, at 199].

39. Though one should ask how this claim squares with the history of the United States, in the nineteenth century, say. Those who enjoyed the rights of citizenship were highly heterogeneous in descent and upbringing, and they came as immigrants, through sheer choice. I do not believe these facts significantly reduced the level of solidarity and mutual trust they enjoyed, compared to the levels enjoyed in the major European states of that period. A careful study of this case might well show that people *can* be bound together by a common decision to follow the call of a certain constitution and ideology as well as the promise of opportunities and adventure. If so, this would suggest that what matters for solidarity and mutual trust is the *will* to make a political life together and that such will is possible without unchosen commonalities. This result would hardly be surprising, seeing how easily the closest friendships we form can do without commonalities in facial features, native language, cultural background, and religious convictions.

40. Margalit and Raz, 443 and 456 [*GESE* 185 and 199].

41. For an example, see Brian Barry, "Do Countries Have Moral Obligations?" in S. M. McMurrin, ed., *The Tanner Lectures on Human Values II* (Salt Lake City: University of Utah Press, 1981), pp. 27–44.

42. Rawls makes this point: "We want to account for the social values, for the intrinsic good of institutional, community, and associative activities, by a conception of justice that in its theoretical basis is individualistic. For reasons of clarity among others, we do not want to ... suppose that society is an organic whole with a life of its own distinct from and superior to that of all its members in their relations with one another"—*A Theory of Justice*, p. 264.

43. Michael Walzer, *Just and Unjust Wars* (New York: Basic Books, 1977), p. 53. See also Michael Walzer, "The Moral Standing of States," p. 219 [*GESE* 60–61].

44. Walzer suggests this tack: "Citizens of a sovereign state have a right, insofar as they are to be ravaged and coerced at all, to suffer only at one another's hands"—*Just and Unjust Wars*, p. 86.

# 14. JEREMY WALDRON

Distinguishing two classes of theories of what individuals owe the state: theories of acquired obligation and theories of natural duty, Waldron claims that the latter have been relatively neglected in the philosophical literature. His first concern here is to examine objections to these theories, and to rebut them. A second, positive, goal is to develop his own natural duty theory, one that can accommodate these objections. A formulation of justice as a fundamental natural duty from Rawls's *A Theory of Justice* sets the scene. According to this account, the duty of justice is twofold: So long as the basic structure of our society is just (or "as just as it is reasonable to expect in the circumstances"), we each have a natural duty to comply and to play our part. Insofar as just social institutions are lacking, we are to strive to bring them about. Waldron examines two objections against this view—the "Special Allegiance" objection and the "Application" objection—and finds that neither is insurmountable.

## Special Ties and Natural Duties

*First published in* Philosophy and Public Affairs *22: 1 (winter 1993): 3–30.*

### I

Philosophical accounts of what we owe the state can be divided into two classes: theories of acquired obligation and theories of natural duty. Theories of acquired obligation are more familiar in political philosophy: Our obligation to the state is said to be based on consent[1] or, using the principle of fair play, on the willing receipt of benefits from others' cooperation.[2] The theory that we have a *natural* duty to support the laws and institutions of a just state—the theory that the requirement of obedience is not contingent on anything we have said or done—is less well known and the literature discussing it much less extensive.

This is surprising because, at first glance, the idea of natural duty promises a better account of our moral relation to the law. The law does not predicate its demand for compliance on any contingency such as consent or receipt of benefits. Though few citizens comply with all the laws all the time, those who think there is a moral requirement of obedience usually think that, because they believe the laws roughly represent the just demands of life in society.[3] Even those who express their *philosophical* view in terms of acquired obligation tend to push it in the direction of natural duty. Either they assimilate an individual's receipt of benefits from a system (for the purposes of the principle of fair play) to his being treated justly by the system,[4] or, if they adopt the consent approach, they turn tacit consent into hypothetical consent, defining a just system as one from which, hypothetically, consent would not be withheld.[5] Philosophers toy with something *like* the theory of natural duty in almost all their thought about what people owe to the state.

It is odd, then, that there has been so little in the way of *direct* discussion of the natural duty idea. A version of it was propounded in John Rawls's book *A Theory of Justice*,[6] but it has not received the discussion that other parts of the book have generated. I suspect this is because the theory is thought to be subject to some rather quick and devastating objections. In this article, I will say what those objections are and show how they can be dealt with. The point is not simply to rebut them. I want to develop an account that responds adequately to philosophical concerns about this way of characterizing what we owe to the state.

## II

To understand the objections, we need a formulation of the theory. John Rawls states it in the following terms:

> From the standpoint of justice as fairness, a fundamental natural duty is the duty of justice. This duty requires us to support and to comply with just institutions that exist and apply to us. It also constrains us to further just arrangements not yet established, at least when this can be done without too much cost to ourselves. Thus if the basic structure of society is just, or as just as it is reasonable to expect in the circumstances, everyone has a natural duty to do his part in the existing scheme. Each is bound to these institutions independent of his voluntary acts, performative or otherwise.[7]

Notice that Rawls uses the phrase "just, or as just as it is reasonable to expect in the circumstances." No state in the world is perfectly just; many are egregiously unjust. However, in this article I will discuss only the duties we owe to *just* political institutions. Though this makes the discussion a bit artificial, it is important for the purposes of exposition.[8] Rawls's critics have denied that the natural duty theory would work to bind people even to institutions that *were* perfectly just. If we can rebut these criticisms and develop a plausible account for the ideal case, then—perhaps in subsequent articles—we can see what follows from this theory about duties that are owed to states that fall short of what justice requires.[9]

Let us take the passage from Rawls quoted above as a fair summary of the theory. What are the difficulties that stand in the way of its acceptance? There are, as I see it, two related objections.

## THE "SPECIAL ALLEGIANCE" OBJECTION

The first objection is that a theory basing the requirement of obedience simply on the quality of legal and political institutions is unable to explain the special character of a person's allegiance to the particular society in which he lives.[10] I may concede that I am bound to the government of my country insofar as it is just. But what makes it *my* country? Most of us think that is an important aspect of political obligation, for we do not think of ourselves as bound simply to *any* government that happens to be just. The objection is that the natural duty theory cannot explain the moral force of "*my* country" in this regard.

Suppose two countries, say, New Zealand and France, have legal systems that are just.[11] The Rawlsian theory certainly requires the citizens of New Zealand to support New Zealand institutions and requires the citizens of France to support French institutions. So far, so good. However, exactly the same reasoning also requires a Frenchman to support New Zealand institutions and a New Zealander to support French institutions. Since what Rawls postulates is a duty to support just institutions *as such*, his approach does not establish anything special about the relation between the New Zealander and New Zealand. It seems incapable of capturing the particularity or intimacy of that political relationship.

Theories of consent, by contrast, are in much better shape on this issue. They have no difficulty explaining what is distinctive about a New

Zealander's obligations to New Zealand and a Frenchman's obligations to France. In each case, the obligation derives from a promise made to the government or to the other citizens of the country in question. The New Zealander has agreed with his fellow citizens, explicitly or tacitly, to abide by their laws, and he has made no such agreement with the French. That is why his moral situation is special with regard to the laws of New Zealand. The same is true of arguments based on the principle of fair play. A person living in New Zealand has received the benefits of life lived by others in accordance with New Zealand law; he therefore has an obligation to do his part in the particular scheme of cooperation from which he has benefited. However, he has received few if any benefits from the law-abidingness of Frenchmen; so he acquires in fairness no obligation to support or obey their laws.

The objection may seem wrongheaded inasmuch as it neglects an important phrase in the Rawlsian formula quoted earlier: The duty is "to support and to comply with just institutions that exist and *apply to us.*" Maybe French law does not "apply" to New Zealanders, so the difficulty does not really arise. On this account, what is special about my relation to my own country is that its laws are the only ones that apply to me. But the insertion of a phrase is not an answer to a philosophical objection. And anyway, all this maneuver achieves is the opening up of the Rawlsian theory to a second challenge.

## THE "APPLICATION" OBJECTION

The second objection is that the theory fails to explain how a particular institution comes to be the one to which individuals owe obedience and support. The theory assumes that in most cases there simply *is* an institutional structure in society that "applies to us," and that if it is just, we have a duty to support it. But the notion of an institution's "applying" to a person needs elucidation.

Is "application" simply a matter of the institution's purporting to address the individual's situation or his claims? If the answer is yes, there may be all sorts of institutions that "apply" to him. An insurgent movement may appoint "officials" and enact "laws" to "apply" to all the members of the society whose government they are trying to overthrow. Do we want to say that the only thing that determines whether people are bound to such an organization is the justice of its demands? Do we really want to abandon all interest in whether they have agreed to submit themselves to its jurisdiction or whether they have brought themselves under its auspices in some other way, for example, by the acceptance of benefits?[12]

The Rawlsian theory offers no account, or a plainly inadequate account, of the existence of political and legal institutions. The problem is that if we try to articulate a satisfactory account of "application," we tend to end up abandoning what is distinctive about the natural duty account. The temptation is to say that an institution "applies" to me only if I have voluntarily brought myself under its auspices, or to impose some other similar condition (such as receipt of benefits) on any inference from the justice of the institution to a duty of obedience.[13] But then we are back with *acquired* political obligation. The theory of natural duty fails to provide a real alternative to the traditional Lockean approach. That is the second objection.

## III

Though the two objections are connected, I shall answer them one at a time, because I think that is the best way to highlight the neglected strengths as well as the notorious weaknesses of the natural duty approach. I will begin with the objection about special allegiance.

It is not in dispute that the citizens of one country may have *some* duty or obligation to the institutions and laws of another (at least when those institutions and laws are just).

A first example is obvious enough. A New Zealander visiting France is morally bound to obey just provisions of French law, even though they may be different from the provisions of New Zealand law. He should drive on the right side of the road, he should not evade occupancy tax in hotel rooms, he should answer questions put to him by members of the *gendarmerie* even though he might have no obligation to answer such questions if they were posed by a constable in New Zealand.

The idea that two *different* sets of laws might both be just should not require much explanation. For some cases, like the rule of the road, justice does not dictate the particular substance of the rule. The right-hand rule and the left-hand rule are equally just; what matters is that one rule is settled upon. Other cases—for example, those concerning taxes and commercial law—may involve fragments of different systems, each of which, taken as a whole, satisfies the same principles of justice. Thus, for example, a consumption tax may be calibrated to achieve the same distributive effect overall as an earned income tax. A negative income tax may have the same effect as a carefully administered welfare system. Still other cases may involve the application of similar background principles to diverse local conditions, or the integration of local customs, traditions, and ways of doing things into the wider fabric of justice.

It is no objection to the natural duty theory that it requires the New Zealander visiting France to obey French law and vice versa. However, it is no advantage either. Theories of acquired obligation can explain this as well (if they can explain anything). By choosing to enter France (when he could have gone elsewhere or stayed at home) the New Zealander makes a clear, though implicit, decision to abide by French laws, if only for a short period of time. The New Zealander must know that this is the condition under which his visa was issued, the condition under which the French officials have admitted him, and the condition under which the French people have authorized tourism and immigration arrangements. Or, if the consent theory is rejected, the principle of fair play can explain the tourist's obligation. Sojourning in France, he enjoys the benefits of its social, legal, and economic arrangements, and so for the time being he ought to cooperate in the production of those benefits. This case, then, does not indicate any difference of explanatory power between theories of natural duty and theories of acquired obligation.

A second case is easier for the natural duty theory to explain than its rivals. There are things a Frenchman could do *in France* that would undermine the laws and institutions of New Zealand. We need not play with hypotheticals: A real-life example comes to mind. In 1985, French officials conspired to arrange a terrorist attack by their agents on a ship, the *Rainbow Warrior*, belonging to the Greenpeace organization. The vessel was used by Greenpeace to harass the French in their conduct of nuclear weapons tests in the South Pacific. It was bombed by agents of the French military, operating covertly in New Zealand, while it lay in Auckland harbor. Owing to their Clouseau-like incompetence, the French operatives immediately responsible were apprehended by the New Zealand police and eventually pleaded guilty to charges of manslaughter (for one Greenpeace activist had died in the attack). But it is not the attack itself that is the focus of my example; it is what happened afterward. During the investigation of the attack, French officials were unhelpful to the New Zealand police, and it is widely believed that they urged their operatives to perjure themselves in the New Zealand courts. Once the saboteurs were convicted, the French persuaded the British and American governments to put economic pressure on New Zealand to secure their release. Thus in various ways officials of the French government living and working in France conspired to undermine the operation of the criminal justice system in New Zealand.[14]

Now we do not need anything like a duty to uphold just institutions to explain the wrongness of the bombing or of the conspiracy to mount the attack. That can be understood quite independently of any duty or obligation to uphold particular laws. It would be wrong whether there were legal institutions in New Zealand or not.[15]

But many would say it was also wrong of the French officials subsequently to obstruct the investigation of the *Rainbow Warrior* affair, to counsel their operatives to perjure themselves, and to interfere with their punishment. That thought *does* seem best captured by the claim that if the criminal justice system of a country is fair, everyone everywhere has a duty not to obstruct it, whether they owe any particular allegiance to that system and live under its laws or not. In this case, obstructing justice in New Zealand was both a possibility and a temptation. The French had a lot to lose if justice were allowed to run its course.

Theories of acquired political obligation cannot explain why it was wrong of them to do this. Not even the most diluted theory of tacit consent is going to yield the conclusion that the officials in Paris had made an implicit promise not to undermine the criminal justice system of a small country on the other side of the world. And no argument from fair play can be made either, for it is unlikely that they ever received benefits from the operation of New Zealand law.[16] The only principle that explains our thought on the matter is one that holds that everyone everywhere has a duty not to undermine just institutions, even when those institutions have nothing directly to do with them.

Let us try a hypothetical example. Suppose a rich playboy with a taste for anarchy contrives to corrupt the judiciary of a foreign country for the sheer fun of it. He bribes the judges to return false verdicts in an array of cases that have nothing to do with him, so that later he can expose yet another legal system as rotten. Surely this action is wrong. But again, the only explanation of its wrongness is that the rich anarchist has violated a duty he has not to undermine the administration of justice—*anywhere*. Neither consent theory nor the principle of fair play can explain what is wrong with his gratuitous interference.

There are two points to be made about the argument so far. First, I assume that proponents of consent and fair play theories share our intuitions about these cases. Since their own theories cannot explain them, they will have to admit that there *is* a duty of the kind Rawls mentions—a duty that applies to everyone with regard to just institutions everywhere. That is not a fatal admission. Their view need not be that consent or fair play is the only principle operating in the area. The first objection is not that there is no such thing as a natural duty to support just institutions, but rather that such a duty cannot by itself account for the special character of political obligation.

Second, if there *is* a natural duty that explains why it is wrong for a French official to obstruct justice in New Zealand and wrong for an anarchist to undermine a legal system for the sheer fun of it, presumably the very same duty also holds between an individual and the laws and institutions of his *own* country. Once again, this is not incompatible with theories of consent or fair play. Maybe there are many layers to the moral issue of what one owes to the state.[17]

## IV

What can the proponent of natural duty say about the difference between a Frenchman's relation to the just institutions of New Zealand and a New Zealander's relation to those institutions?

I want to develop my account of this difference in several stages: (A) I shall first identify two relations in which an individual may stand to a given principle of justice $P_1$. (B) Corresponding to that distinction, I shall define two relations in which an individual might stand to an institution administering $P_1$. Stages (A) and (B) are both abstract: We are to consider the idea of an individual's relation to a principle, and then the idea of an individual's relation to an institution administering that principle. The idea of an institution's administering $P_1$ includes the idea of certain individuals being required by further principles—$P_2$, $P_3$, and so on—to behave in a certain way with regard to the administration of $P_1$. For example, if $P_1$ is "To each according to his need," the other principles may comprise requirements such as "Administer $P_1$ impartially" (addressed to an official) and "Do not demand more than you need" (addressed to a subject of the institution in question).

At a third stage, (C), I want to shift the discussion from the abstract specification of principles and institutions to their concrete realization.[18] It is all very well to outline the variety of rules that *would* be required for the administration of $P_1$ by an institution; but we still have to deal with the question of which organizations are *in fact* entitled to occupy that institutional role, that is, which organizations are *in fact* entitled to demand our participation, compliance, and support in their administration of a principle like $P_1$. As we address this question—as we move from stage (B) to stage (C)—we will also be moving from our attempt to deal with the first objection to our attempt to deal with the second.

(A) Let us begin with a cute example. Hobbes has five children and one cake. He decides that the fair way to divide the cake is to give each child an equal share: "To each an equal amount of cake" is his principle. A neighbor's child, called Calvin, is watching these proceedings from across the fence. Astutely, Calvin points out to Hobbes that the principle "To each an equal amount of cake" entitles him (Calvin) to a slice as well. Hobbes responds that Calvin has misunderstood the principle. The formulation is elliptical, and the principle it abbreviates is not "To each and every one in the world (or even, to each and every one in the neighborhood) an equal amount of cake," but rather "To each *of Hobbes's children* an equal amount of cake." The principle is intended to be limited in its application.

Now Calvin may complain that this is a bad principle to work with inasmuch as it rests on an arbitrary distinction between Hobbes's children and other kids in the neighborhood. Such a complaint may be justified in certain circumstances, but it is not always justified. Hobbes may know for a fact that his neighbor has already served cake to the children on the far side of the fence, so that Calvin does not need any of the cake that Hobbes is now serving to his brood. There may even be a rule in the neighborhood, born out of long experience with incidents like this: "Each parent is to serve his own cake to his own kids."

A principle of distributive justice may thus have a limited application: I shall call such principles "range-limited." In the case we have been discussing, Calvin turns out not to be within the range of Hobbes's principle. He is an *outsider* so far as Hobbes's distribution of cake is concerned. Formally, an individual is within the range of a given principle $P_1$ (and thus an *insider* with regard to that principle) just in case he figures in the set of persons (or any of the sets of persons), referred to in the fullest statement of $P_1$, to whose conduct, claims, and/or interests the requirements of $P_1$ are supposed to apply. Substantively, an individual is within the range of a principle if it is part of the point and justification of the principle to deal with his conduct, claims, and interests along with those of any other persons it deals with.[19]

I hope it is clear where we are heading: I am going to argue that a New Zealander's special relation to the legal institutions of New Zealand is largely captured by the fact that he is an insider with regard to the set of range-limited principles administered by those institutions. However, this account will only work—for Rawls's theory of a natural duty to support *just* institutions—if it is possible for the principles administered by the legal institutions of a country to be both just and limited in their range.

Many recent discussions of social justice presuppose such limitations as a matter of course.[20] John Rawls's theory, for example, is presented as "a reasonable conception of justice for the basic structure of society conceived for the time being as a closed system isolated from other societies."[21] On that approach we could settle what was just for New Zealand and New Zealanders without saying anything about the resources or inhabitants of any other country.

However, the assumption that justice may be confined within the borders of a single society is unsatisfactory. There are vast disparities of wealth between the inhabitants of different countries. The poorest person in New Zealand is considerably better off than most people in Bangladesh, and one feels uneasy about making a passionate case in the name of justice for enhancing the well-being of the former while putting completely to one side all claims that might be made on the Bangladeshis' behalf. Certainly, if we are to use range-limited principles, we must have an argument *justifying* our use of them, and that argument, at least, should not simply treat the Bangladeshis as though they did not exist.

The best candidate in our tradition for such an argument is found in the political theory of Immanuel Kant. Like other contractarians, Kant thought of the state as an arrangement into which people enter for the resolution of conflict and the establishment of a secure system of property. However, Kant believed that morally it was not an open question whether we should enter into such arrangements or not: "If you are so situated as to be unavoidably side by side with others, you ought to abandon the state of nature and enter, with all others, a juridical state of affairs, that is, a state of distributive legal justice."[22] The reason has to do with the avoidance of the "fighting" and "wild violence" that will otherwise ensue among those who find themselves disputing possession of the same resources: "Even if we imagine men to be ever so good natured and righteous before a public lawful state of society is established, individual men, nations, and states can never be certain that they are secure against violence from one another, because each will have his own right to do what *seems just and good to him*, entirely independent of the opinion of the others.[23] The basic principle of morality so far as material resources are concerned is, in Kant's account, that people must act toward one another so that each external object can be used as someone's property.[24] If a stable system of resource use is to be made possible, then a person claiming possession or use of a resource "must also be allowed to compel everyone else with whom he comes into conflict over the question of whether such an object is his to enter, together with him, a society under a civil constitution."[25]

Now, although Kant acknowledges that in principle all humans share the earth,[26] clearly those with whom I come into conflict will in the first instance be my near neighbors. Since no one can afford to wait until all possible conflicts arise so that all can be definitively settled at once, the Kantian approach implies that I should enter quickly into a form of society with those immediately adjacent to me, those with whose interests my resource use is likely to pose the most frequent and dangerous conflicts. These conflicts at any rate must be resolved quickly on the basis of just political and legal institutions, in order to avoid arbitrariness and violence. Throughout the rest of this article, I shall use the notion of "a territory" to refer to any area within which conflicts must be settled if *any* stable system of resource use is to be possible among the inhabitants.

Certainly such resolutions are provisional. As the sphere of human interaction expands, further conflicts may arise, and the scope of the legal framework must be extended and if necessary rethought, according to the same Kantian principle. But in the meantime, it is important to find a just basis for settling those conflicts that are immediately unavoidable, a basis that is just between the parties to those conflicts.

# V

It seems, then, that principles of justice can be limited in their range, at least on a *pro tem* basis. This is sufficient to establish the distinction between insiders and outsiders that I need for the remainder of the argument. I move now to the second stage of the argument, to consider the administration of principles by institutions.

(B) Principles cannot conduct distributions by themselves: They must be administered by working institutions. What would an institution L have to be like in order to administer a range-limited principle of distributive justice $P_1$? What demands would L have to make on the behavior of those who were insiders and on the behavior of those who were outsiders with regard to $P_1$?

The first demand made by L would be, of course, the demand of justice embodied in $P_1$ itself. Suppose $P_1$ is limited in its range to the interests of A and B: It dictates that a certain fund of resources be divided equally between them. Then $P_1$ requires of A that he not take more than an equal share. For A to accept $P_1$ is for A to accept that requirement, and for L to administer $P_1$ is for L to supervise and enforce it.

Secondly, L will have to require that A and B *accept* its supervision in this regard. Suppose A and B disagree about the interpretation of $P_1$ or about what counts as an equal share. A third person, C, may come along and offer an opinion. A or B or both may turn on C and say that it is none of her business; in some contexts that may be an apt reply. Suppose, however, that C is a functionary of L and acting in her official capacity. If A and B accept L's supervision, this changes the picture for them. To accept L's supervision is to say (among other things) that it is for officials of L to arbitrate disputes about the application of $P_1$. Their determination is to be accepted, if any third party's determination is. No doubt there are also other aspects of A's and B's accepting supervision by L. In general, if $P_1$ is to be administered by L, then those who are insiders with regard to $P_1$ are morally required to abide by the following principle, $P_2$: "Accept the supervision of L with regard to the implementation of $P_1$."

Like $P_1$, $P_2$ will be a range-limited principle. Since it is the point of L to administer $P_1$ (perhaps among other principles), A and B mark themselves as insiders in relation to L by accepting $P_2$. In general, a person is an insider in relation to an institution if and only if it is part of the point of that institution to do justice to some claim of his among all the claims with which it deals.[27] So, for example, a New Zealand resident is an insider in relation to the fiscal and welfare institutions of New Zealand, for it is part of the point of those institutions to do justice to his claims to income and assistance along with all the other claims that they address. The aim of the institutions is to determine what burdens it is fair to impose, and what benefits it is fair to confer, on this person and on others in New Zealand in the course of that overall enterprise.[28]

A third demand that will have to be made if $P_1$ is to be administered effectively by L is this: that both insiders and outsiders refrain from attacking or sabotaging L in its attempts to put $P_1$ into operation. Even the most just institution is vulnerable to human interference, whether that is motivated by greed or some other antisocial impulse. In order to operate, an institution administering $P_1$ will have to promulgate or otherwise get accepted a third principle, $P_3$: "Do not undermine the administration of $P_1$ by L."

Unlike $P_1$ and $P_2$, $P_3$ will be a principle of unlimited range. It will address anyone and everyone whose actions might possibly affect the administration of $P_1$. Those whose conduct with regard to L is constrained only by this third principle may be called outsiders in relation to the institution L.[29]

$P_3$ is entirely consequentialist in conception. The claim made in its behalf will be that everyone should recognize that there is value in justice being done, even when they are not those among whom it is being done in this particular instance. For that reason, they should refrain from interfering with it.[30] Suppose, as before, that L has put into effect a just distribution between A and B regarding a certain fund of resources. A mischievous outsider, C, has it in mind to do something that will undermine or upset that distribution. Why should she refrain? Because her intervention may have an effect that is bad from a moral point of view, namely, that A gets more (or less) of the fund than he is entitled to (as against B). Though B's is the only claim that A's is balanced against in this distribution, the justice of A and B each getting his fair share can be recognized from an impersonal point of view, and the badness of that distribution's being upset can therefore be acknowledged even by someone who does not have a direct stake in the matter.[31] If A were to seize more than his fair share, that would be direct injustice; the moral requirement not to do that is precisely what the initial principle of justice, $P_1$, amounts to (so far as A is concerned). When C upsets the distribution between A and B, the *result* is injustice even though C's action is not itself a violation of $P_1$ in the way that a greedy encroachment by A would be. C's act is wrong because of its consequences.

I believe this distinction between insiders and outsiders explains much of the specialness of an individual's relation to the institutions of his own country, at least so far as moral requirement is concerned. It gives a reasonably clear sense to the Rawlsian formulation that a person owes support to just institutions that "apply to him." The laws of New Zealand do not purport to address conflicts involving the ordinary claims and rights of Frenchmen. So, no matter how just those laws are, the relation of most Frenchmen to them is at most an external relation: There are things they can do to undermine the legal system in New Zealand, but they are not bound internally to their determinations of justice.[32] By contrast, a New Zealander *does* have the special insider relation to the laws of his own country. They have been set up precisely to address the question of the rights and duties of someone in his position vis-à-vis his fellow New Zealanders. That is the sense in which they apply to him.

Notice that this answer to the first objection does not make specialness merely contingent. In his original formulation of the "special allegiance" objection, Ronald Dworkin considered the following response: "We can construct a practical contingent argument for the special duty. Britons have more opportunity to aid British institutions than those of other nations whose institutions they also think mainly just."[33] But, he goes on, "This practical argument fails to capture the intimacy of the special duty." Dworkin is right about that. However, the distinction I have developed is a distinction in principle. Though it does not flow from citizenship as such, it depends on the difference between being one of the parties in respect of whose interests a just institution is just, and being a person who is merely capable of interfering with a just institution in some way. It is a difference in the content and structure of the natural duty, not a difference that depends on contingent facts and opportunities.

I concede that there may be other elements of patriotic affect and allegiance that this account does not capture.[34] Though I have lived for years in the United States, I feel a fierce loyalty to New Zealand—and for its institutions as well as its sports teams!—a loyalty that has nothing to do with any special application to my interests of the principles of justice it administers. I suspect that, in the end, these ties must be explained by reference to the idea of *nation* rather than polity, and birth and acculturation rather than any juridical connection. Nation, birth, and allegiance in this sense are matters on which modern political philosophers have had embarrassingly little to say.[35] I am comforted, however, by the thought that theories of acquired obligation—theories based on consent or on the principle of fairness—have even less to say on these matters than theories of natural duty.

# VI

An institution will be able to administer a range-limited principle of justice $P_1$ only if most of the people to whom it applies accept $P_2$ and only if most others also accept $P_3$. But how do we establish that a given organization is to fill this role? If an organization simply announces that it wishes to fill the role of institutional administrator of $P_1$ and shows itself capable of doing so, is this sufficient to establish that insiders and outsiders (with regard to $P_1$) are actually bound to that organization by principles like $P_2$ and $P_3$, respectively? This leads us to stage (C) of the argument and to the nub of our discussion.

(C) The disconcerting thing about the theory of natural duty is that it envisages moral requirements binding us to a political organization (a would-be state) quite apart from our agreement to be so bound, and quite apart from any benefits the organization has conferred on us (not counting those benefits whose conferral follows from its being a just organization). We suddenly find ourselves faced with a body of people purporting to do justice in our territory. In order for them to pursue that aim, they must elicit a certain amount of compliance and support from us. The natural duty theory is that they are entitled to that compliance and support simply by virtue of the quality of organization that they have put together.

Is this acceptable? Are there any other conditions we should stipulate, apart from the requirement that the organization be just—in its own workings and in the principles it proposes to apply?

One obvious additional condition is that the organization be *capable* of doing justice in the territory and over the claims that it purports to address. No one, surely, is morally bound to support a lost cause; or if they are so bound, for example, by personal ties of promise or fealty, they are not bound to an ineffective organization merely by virtue of the just character of what it would do if it were not ineffective. This point applies to collapsing anciens régimes as well as to governments-in-exile, hopeless insurgencies, and so on.

Whether an organization is effective will depend partly on whether people are prepared to accept it. In our notation, that includes whether they accept and follow the principles such as $P_2$ and $P_3$ that are necessary for its operation. But there is no vicious circle here: I am not saying that one is bound to follow these principles only if the organization L is effective and that L is effective only if one follows these principles. The point is rather that a person must be assured that sufficient others are disposed to comply with the principles before he can reasonably think L is effective and thus before he can reasonably think that he is bound to follow the principles. In some situations, this will generate collective action problems of a type familiar to students of Hobbes.[36] But often it will not. Most of us, when we awake to a consideration of these matters, find ourselves faced with an organization to which the people around us are already lending their support. The effectiveness condition, therefore, is usually already fulfilled for most societies under modern conditions.

But not always. Occasionally there is more than one organization purporting to do justice in a certain territory. I have in mind cases such as Northern Ireland, where in certain Catholic enclaves the IRA purports to administer rules of social conduct (knee-capping muggers, collecting funds to support "law enforcement," distributing welfare assistance, and so on) in a way that rivals the parallel, though much more highly organized, apparatus of the British state. Or consider a situation like that of modern Lebanon, where in certain areas there are several rival and apparently parallel state or proto-state apparatuses. In cases like these, if both rival organizations are in fact just,[37] does either of them have a claim of natural duty on us?

It is no good responding that it does not matter because if both are just their demands will coincide. We have already seen that that need not be the case. The organizations may make different and incompatible demands that nevertheless address all the main issues of justice in society adequately or nearly adequately. And of course each will need to raise money to fund the cost of *its* actually doing what justice requires. If we have a duty to support just institutions, does it follow that we have a duty to support *both* institutions in a case like this? That is a question about the duty of justice owed by insiders, that is, the persons in the territory patrolled by these rival institutions. We can also ask a similar question about the duties of outsiders. If there are two rival states or proto-states in a territory, do outsiders have a duty to refrain from interfering with both of them, or only one (which one?), or neither?

Clearly we need another condition to deal with these issues. I want to suggest that the natural duties come into play only where the organization in question passes not only tests of justice and effectiveness, but also a test of legitimacy. What must be established is that there is a good reason to recognize *this* organization, as opposed to any rival organization, as *the one* to do justice in the given territory or with regard to the claims that are at issue. To the extent that such reasons exist, the organization is "legitimate." Legitimacy, then, is an exclusive characteristic: Only one organization may be legitimate with regard to a given set of claims or with regard to the issues of justice arising in a given territory.

The explication of the legitimacy requirement has three parts to it: (i) We must recall why it is important for there to be institutions doing justice. (ii) We must show why it is important for there to be only *one* such institution in a territory. (iii) We must indicate grounds on which it might be appropriate to favor the claims of one particular organization over those of its rivals.

(i) The first step takes us back to the Kantian theory we noted in Section IV. The setting up of political institutions, Kant argued, is the way to avoid or mitigate the disagreements and conflicts that will otherwise inevitably arise even among people attempting in good faith to follow the dictates of justice. Because the stakes are high, these conflicts always threaten to issue in violence. Such violence will involve death and suffering, and, as Thomas Hobbes famously pointed out, the anxiety and unpredictability that accompany it will make it difficult for anyone to pursue a decent life.[38] Political institutions are capable of making things better in this regard: They can mediate and arbitrate disputes, they can develop practices of impartiality, and they can collect together sufficient force to uphold their determinations. There is therefore a clear moral interest in their establishment.

(ii) The reasons for having political institutions are also reasons for ensuring, if possible, that there is just *one* in each territory. In *Anarchy, State and Utopia*, Robert Nozick imagined that some of the inhabitants of a territory might join one enforcement-and-arbitration organization and some might join another. The reasons that led people to join these organizations would, he said, also lead to fighting between them.[39] If anything, such violence will be worse than that of the Hobbesian "war of all against all," because the battles will be better organized. The moral interest in reducing such fighting provides a reason for all of us to join and support the same organization, and that gives each of us a reason to join and support whatever organization others are joining and supporting. Once again, this may involve collective action problems; but it need not, and even if it does, the problems are not necessarily intractable.[40]

There are other reasons, too. Justice is partly a matter of cooperation. Though in most human situations (even those in which institutions are lacking) individuals can distinguish between just and unjust courses of action, they will often feel that things would go better from the point of view of justice, and that their own actions would make more of a difference if they could be sure that others were following the same goals as they were. A single person contributing to charity, for example, may see his own donation as a drop in the ocean—worthwhile in itself, no doubt, but in the long run essentially futile in comparison to the magnitude of the problem. He may think that a problem like world poverty is adequately addressed only if all or almost all well-off people make an organized effort to do something about it. In other words, it may make a difference to what it is just for me to do whether I have the assurance that others are cooperating with me.[41] An institution with authority over a large number of people may help provide this assurance. But usually that assurance can be provided only if the number of institutions addressing the problem that concerns me is limited (perhaps to one). Too great a plurality of institutions may dissolve the advantages of an assured scheme of cooperation and reintroduce the chaos of a number of crosscutting initiatives, each of which seems futile in itself.

For some cases, the importance of singling out one organization to do justice in a given area stems paradoxically from the plurality of possible just schemes. The point is clearest in the case of simple coordination problems. A scheme that required motorists to drive on the left would be just. And so would a scheme that required motorists to drive on the right. But this plurality does not mean we can allow rival schemes to operate in the same territory. The problem of coordination here will not be solved unless one and only one is chosen. Though either would be just and though either would be better than no solution at all, common sense requires that one of them be rejected.

Now we cannot use coordination problems as a model for all issues of justice and political obligation.[42] But many of the issues of choice with regard to just institutions do have this character. Suppose we establish something like a Rawlsian difference principle as a fundamental criterion of economic justice.[43] There may still be choices to be made about the best institutional structures for achieving this: a negative income tax, for example, or some more familiar scheme of welfare support. Some of these choices are made on the basis of which structure is more likely to be just, given the contingent circumstances and history of each society. But some of them may simply be arbitrary: welfare scheme W together with fiscal scheme X may be every bit as just as welfare scheme Y together with fiscal scheme Z. It will matter that we settle on one combination, but it may not particularly matter which.

The example also illustrates another point about the need for a single scheme of justice. As Rawls has stressed, the institutions of a society operate as a single structure and, for the purposes of a theory of justice, have to be assessed as a whole.[44] It may not be possible to say that the taxation scheme of a society is just until we consider how it fits with the property system, the education system, the welfare system, and so on. Because justice is in this sense systematic, and because systematicity may depend on there being a unique set of interrelated institutions, it seems that any claim that justice can make on us presupposes the identification of one set of organized institutions as *the system* that makes a claim on us, if any system does.

(iii) The reasons for having a single scheme of justice in a society give us our best grip on the criteria for political legitimacy. To the extent that the underlying reason has to do with strategic choice in something like a coordination game, anything that establishes the salience of one system over others will be a reason for preferring it. In most cases, the fact that there *is* a state and that it is, for all practical purposes, dominant and unchallenged in a territory will be sufficient. This is the organization that deserves our support in the enterprise of doing justice if any organization does.

What if there is competition between two or more plausible contenders? How should we choose which to support? Since effectiveness is one of the conditions we have imposed, there may be reason to choose the more powerful contender. Alternatively (if this does not amount to the same thing), we may have reason to choose the organization with the greater popular support.

This criterion might seem to reintroduce the idea of government by consent—the very idea that natural duty theories are trying to replace. The idea seems to be that if most people in a territory agree that some organization L is *the* system to keep order and mete out justice in that territory, then their consent confers legitimacy on L and provides *me* with a basis for identifying L as the institution deserving of my support and allegiance.

However, this does not amount to a reintroduction of the consent theory of obligation (though it may help to explain why consent is so often appealed to in this context). For one thing, consent is being suggested here as one possible ground for legitimacy; it is not the only possible ground. The sheer existence of an institution as dominant and unchallenged may suffice to establish its salience, whether it is popularly supported or not. For another thing, the consent that establishes legitimacy in this sense affects the duties not only of those who give their consent but of outsiders, too. Once a Frenchman has identified the institutions that are supported by the people of New Zealand, he is bound (as a matter of natural duty) to regard those institutions as the ones he must not attempt to subvert or undermine even though he himself has never agreed to support them.

In general, the use of consent in relation to legitimacy is quite different in its logic from its use as a direct ground of obligation.[45] In the latter case, consent is represented as a promise; in the former case, it is more like a permission or nomination. Few of us think that hypothetical promises can create real obligations; but we do often believe that hypothetical consent can confer real permissibility on what would otherwise be wrongful intrusions. A surgeon pondering whether to operate on an unconscious accident victim does not have to wait for actual consent; she can proceed on the basis of her best sense of what the accident victim would have agreed to if he had been conscious.

Also, consent in this context is not incompatible with majoritarianism, as it is in classic theories of social contract. One cannot be voted into a social contract, because there the image of consent is being used to explain individualized obligation and it is part of the logic of that image that one's own obligations can be generated only by one's own agreement. But if the consent of a community is being used to establish institutional salience, or to provide the assurance one needs for cooperative action, then the agreement of a majority of the inhabitants of a country may suffice. The advantage of the natural duty approach is that the *obligatoriness* of respecting an institution's demands of justice is secured independently of consent, as a matter of moral background. Consent is used here simply to establish which institutions may appropriately embody those demands.[46]

Indeed, for this latter purpose, propositions about *hypothetical* consent (even hypothetical majority consent) might be sufficient (though again they are not sufficient as direct grounds of obligation).[47] If a pair of rival institutional systems, $L_1$ and $L_2$, in a territory T are such that most of the people of T would clearly agree to be governed by $L_1$ rather than by $L_2$ if they were asked, and if almost everyone in T knows this about the two systems, then it seems that $L_1$ is clearly the salient choice as *the* system to which allegiance is owed on grounds of justice, if such allegiance is owed to any institutional system. That the people of T have not *actually* consented to $L_1$ is neither here nor there. They have a natural duty to support whatever institution can be identified as the appropriate one to do justice in their territory; and these hypothetical propositions about their consent (or the consent of most of them) are sufficient basis for that identification.

Popular consent may, finally, be relevant to institutional choice as an aspect of justice. In our models so far, we have imagined institutions administering substantive principles of social justice; we imagined that $P_1$ was something like "To each according to his need" or "To each equally" and that it applied to the distribution of material resources. But institutions will also have to address the distribution of political power. Most of us think that, in this regard, an institution is just only if it is democratic: that is, only if it proposes to settle disagreements about what justice requires by some form of voting among all the people who are subject to its jurisdiction. The idea of a natural duty to support just institutions may therefore involve the idea of a natural duty to support democratic institutions, institutions that embody regular appeals to popular consent. Even so, the requirement to support such a regime is based on the justice of its political system; it is not based directly on consent.

## VII

The position we have reached is that an organization that is just, effective, and legitimate (in the sense of being singled out as *the* salient organization for this territory) has *eo ipso* a claim on our allegiance. Though popular consent may be implicated in its justice, its effectiveness, or its legitimacy, the moral requirement that we support and obey such an organization is not itself based on any promise that we have made.

Despite the conditions we have imposed, someone might still balk at the general idea behind this position. Can an organization simply *impose* itself on us, morally, in this way?

There comes a point when the theorist of natural duty must stop treating this question as an objection and simply insist that the answer is yes. His affirmative answer is, after all, what distinguishes a theory of natural duty from theories of acquired political obligation.

To defend the answer, he will emphasize two considerations: first, the moral importance of justice; and second, the moral significance of the difficulties that attend the pursuit of justice without political institutions. We have rehearsed the second consideration already. The pursuit of justice often requires coordination, among those who are attempting to do justice and among the various spheres in which they are attempting to do it. Institutions are necessary for that coordination. Without them, there will be more injustice. So to the extent that the avoidance of injustice is a moral imperative, the establishment of coordinating institutions is a moral imperative.[48] In addition, there are the considerations about conflict that were also discussed earlier. The pursuit of justice in an institutional vacuum leads to conflict among persons who have different views about what justice requires, and that in turn issues in violence, suffering, and anxiety. These things are worth avoiding in themselves: They are additional evils (that is, evils over and above injustice itself) attendant on the conflicting efforts of a number of people to avoid the primary evils of injustice.

In all of this, the assumption of the natural duty approach is that the pursuit of justice is a moral imperative. This proposition is one that needs to be understood carefully. At the beginning of *A Theory of Justice*, Rawls writes: "Justice is the first virtue of social institutions, as truth is of systems of thought. A theory however elegant and economical must be rejected or revised if it is untrue; likewise laws and institutions no matter how efficient and well-arranged must be reformed or abolished if they are unjust."[49] But the analogy is misleading. To say that *if* I propound a theory it is important that the theory be true is not the same as saying that it is important that I propound a true theory. From the point of view of truth, there may be no problem with silence or theoretical reticence. Analogously, Rawls seems to be saying in this passage that *if* we have social and political institutions, it is important that they be just. In fact, the importance of justice goes beyond this. It is morally imperative that the demands of justice be pursued *period*. If institutions are necessary for their pursuit, then it is morally imperative that such institutions be established. Our duty of justice is not satisfied by ensuring that whatever institutions we happen to have are just; it is satisfied only by our doing our part to establish just institutions. The point, once again, is the Kantian one. Because we are not to regard remaining in the state of nature as a permissible option, we may not say that whether we are bound to legal institutions is a matter of whether we happen to promise our cooperation. Our cooperation in establishing and sustaining political institutions that promote justice is morally required. That is the backbone of the natural duty position.

Once we see this, we see how to deal with an alleged counterexample put forward by A. John Simmons in articulating the second of our original objections—the "application" objection. Simmons asked us to imagine an organization simply arriving on the scene and announcing that it proposes to do justice.

> Imagine ... that a group a benighted souls off in Montana organizes an "Institute for the Advancement of Philosophers," designed to help philosophers by disseminating papers, creating new job opportunities, offering special unemployment benefits, etc. Moreover, these benefits are distributed strictly according to the demands of justice; and they are made possible by the philosophers who pay "dues" to the Institute. ... One day the Institute ... decides to expand its operations eastward, and I receive in the mail a request that I pay my dues. Does this institution "apply to me"? There is a very weak sense in which we might say that it does; it is an institution for philosophers and I am a philosopher (of sorts). I may even stand to benefit from its operations in the future. But am I *duty-bound* to pay my dues, in accordance with the "rules" of the Institute?[50]

Simmons thinks the answer is no, irrespective of the justice of the Institute: "People cannot simply force institutions on me, no matter how just, and force on me a moral bond to do my part."[51]

The example is ambiguous, so far as the justice of the Institute is concerned. An institution can be just in two ways: (a) it can be just in the way it operates; and (b) it can be just in the sense that it is doing something that justice requires. Simmons stipulates that the Institute is just in sense (a): comparing the charges it levies with the benefits it distributes, it deals fairly with the revenues it raises. But to establish that it is a just institution in a sense that would engage the Rawlsian principle, one has to show more than that. One has to show that it is just in raising the levy in the first place. That involves considering both the benefits it offers and the other purposes on which philosophers might want to spend their money. It involves showing that, as a matter of justice, it is imperative that people do what they can to support philosophers (over and above the general schemes of social support to which they are already contributing). Our readiness to agree with Simmons's verdict on the hypothetical stems, I suspect, from the belief that this cannot be shown. We think that a philosopher may fairly resist the Institute's demands by saying, "I concede that your organization is just so far as its internal workings are concerned. I even concede that helping philosophers is a nice thing to do. But I deny that it is important from the point of view of justice to offer philosophers this assistance, so I don't see that I am doing anything wrong in refusing your request for my support, at least so far as the natural duty theory is concerned."

Suppose the case were different. Suppose the benighted souls off in Montana were to set up an institute to give aid to the homeless. Suppose, moreover, that the founders of this institute were right in thinking that their organization is not only just in sense (a)—that is, with regard to its internal workings—but just also in sense (b). They believe that the homeless are entitled, as a matter of justice not charity, to much more than they are currently receiving under state welfare arrangements. If they were right about that—if it really *were* a demand of *justice* that they were responding to—then, assuming their institute was effective and not competing with any other organization to address this problem, the theory of natural duty *might* yield the conclusion that we are morally bound to support it. As soon as we became aware of the organization, of the true nature of the problem it was addressing, and of its position as the only organization in the country proposing to deal justly with homelessness, maybe we *would* be bound to send off our check for the amount it determined we should contribute. That conclusion might seem counterintuitive and certainly uncomfortable. But I wonder how much of this discomfort is due to our bad faith about justice, rather than to any specific difficulty about the duties that we owe to institutions.

## NOTES

I am grateful to Leslie Green, Kenneth Kress, Michael Moore, and Eric Rakowski for earlier discussion of these ideas. A first draft of this article was prepared under the auspices of the Program in Ethics and Public Life, Cornell University. I am particularly grateful to Henry Shue for his support and his comments. A later draft was presented to a Philosophy Department seminar at Princeton University; comments and criticisms received on that occasion are also much appreciated. I am also indebted to the Editors of *Philosophy & Public Affairs* for their criticisms.

1. Arguments basing political obligation on agreement are of course as old as the *Crito*. The classic exposition of the theory of tacit consent is John Locke, *Two Treatises of Government*, ed. Peter Laslett (Cambridge: Cambridge

University Press, 1988), II, paras. 87–89, 119–22 (pp. 323–25, 347–49). For a modern discussion, see Leslie Green, *The Authority of the State* (Oxford: Clarendon Press, 1988), chapter 6.

2. The principle of fair play is defended in H. L. A. Hart, "Are There Any Natural Rights?" in *Theories of Rights*, ed. Jeremy Waldron (Oxford: Oxford University Press, 1984), p. 85. See also John Rawls, *A Theory of Justice* (Cambridge, MA: Harvard University Press, 1971), pp. 108–14, 342–50; and George Klosko, "The Obligation to Contribute to Discretionary Public Goods," *Political Studies* 37 (1990): 196–214.

3. See Tom Tyler, *Why People Obey the Law* (New Haven: Yale University Press, 1990).

4. See A. John Simmons, *Moral Principles and Political Obligations* (Princeton: Princeton University Press, 1979), pp. 109–14.

5. See Hanna Pitkin, "Obligation and Consent," *American Political Science Review* 59 (1965): 996; and 60 (1966): 39, 44.

6. Rawls, *A Theory of Justice*, pp. 114–17, 333–37.

7. Ibid., p. 115.

8. See ibid., pp. 8–9, for this order of exposition.

9. One important topic that Rawls does address concerns the tension between social justice as a substantive standard and justice in the distribution of political power. If people disagree in good faith about what justice requires, then their operation of a just system of political choice may require some of them to put up with policies whose justice they dispute. See ibid., pp. 195–201, 221–34.

10. See, for example, Ronald Dworkin, *Law's Empire* (Cambridge, MA: Harvard University Press, 1986), p. 193: "That duty . . . does not provide a good explanation of legitimacy, because it does not tie political obligation sufficiently tightly to the particular community to which those who have the obligation belong; it does not show why Britons have a special duty to support the institutions of Britain."

11. I shall use New Zealand and France as examples throughout this article because they satisfy the following conditions: (1) neither society is so egregiously unjust that it would strain credibility to use it as a paradigm for the purposes of this argument; (2) they are distant enough from one another that there is no question of their really being part of one big society (as France and Britain are part of the European Community); (3) there are relatively few cases where New Zealand courts have to make decisions about the rights of people living in France and vice versa; but (4) there are things that the citizens of the one country can do to promote or undermine justice in the institutions of the other. If France and New Zealand are thought bad examples, any other pair of countries satisfying these conditions will do, though condition (4) was dramatically illustrated for this pair in the *Rainbow Warrior* affair, when operatives of the French state blew up and destroyed a vessel lying at anchor in Auckland harbor in July 1985.

12. The objection is put forward by A. John Simmons. See Simmons, *Moral Principles*, pp. 147–52. I will discuss Simmons's version of the objection in more detail in Section VII.

13. See ibid., p. 151, for Simmons's notion of "strong" application.

14. There are excellent accounts in Richard Shears and Isobelle Gidley, *The Rainbow Warrior Affair* (London: Unwin, 1986); and John Dyson, *Sink the Rainbow: An Enquiry into the "Greenpeace Affair"* (London: Victor Gollancz, 1986).

15. To put it another way, the idea of natural law suffices to explain why it is wrong to blow up a ship with the danger of loss of life. See Locke, *Two Treatises*, II, para. 9 (pp. 272–73), for the claim that the magistrates of one country may rely on natural law if they wish to punish aliens.

16. However, the French police would have received normal cooperation from the New Zealand police in the past in homicide and antiterrorist inquiries, so that the withdrawal of cooperation in the *Rainbow Warrior* case might be seen as a failure of reciprocity.

17. Rawls argues that at least some citizens and officials have an obligation to the laws and institutions of their society based on the principle of fairness in addition to the normal bond of natural duty: see Rawls, *A Theory of Justice*, pp. 336–50. For a critique of this "two-tier" approach, see Green, *The Authority of the State*, pp. 244–46.

18. Rawls notes that an institution may be thought of in two ways: "first as an abstract object, that is as a possible form of conduct expressed by a system of rules; and second, as the realization in the thought and conduct of certain persons at a certain time and place of the actions specified by those rules" (Rawls, *A Theory of Justice*, p. 55).

19. I am simplifying a bit here. Of course $P_1$ need not refer to an individual A by name in order for him to be within its range. Usually what it will do is use some phrase like "every citizen" and A will be within the range of the principle just in case he satisfies that description.

20. Some even *define* justice meta-ethically in terms of *local* understandings. This, I take it, is Michael Walzer's approach in *Spheres of Justice: A Defense of Pluralism and Equality* (Oxford: Basil Blackwell, 1983): "Every substantive account of distributive justice is a local account" (p. 314) and "The very phrase 'communal wealth' would lose its meaning if all resources and all products were globally common."

21. Rawls, *A Theory of Justice*, p. 8.

22. Immanuel Kant, *The Metaphysical Elements of Justice*, trans. John Ladd (Indianapolis: Bobbs-Merrill, 1965) section 42, p. 71.

23. Ibid., section 44, p. 76.

24. Ibid., section 6, p. 60.

25. Ibid., section 8, p. 65.

26. Kant writes elsewhere of "that *right to the earth's surface* which the human race shares in common," a cosmopolitan right that establishes the basis

of a "universal community": Immanuel Kant, *Perpetual Peace: A Philosophical Sketch*, in *Kant's Political Writings*, ed. Hans Reiss (Cambridge: Cambridge University Press, 1970), pp. 106–8.

27. See note 19 above.

28. What about the situation where a French company is temporarily doing business in New Zealand, or where a New Zealander has a claim against some property or person in France? We develop rules of private international law to determine (sometimes arbitrarily but not unjustifiably) which forum is competent to determine such issues. If it is a New Zealand court and it makes its determination justly, then the French party *is* bound in justice to accept the determination, and that is a requirement—like $P_2$—on a par with a New Zealander's duty to accept the just determinations of local courts. The only thing that distinguishes the French party from a New Zealander in this respect is that special circumstances have to arise before French claims are adjudicated in New Zealand courts, whereas for New Zealanders such adjudications are (properly) a matter of course.

29. Insiders are of course also subject to $P_3$. Apart from grabbing more than he is entitled to under $P_1$, an insider might try to obstruct or undermine its administration in other ways for purely malicious reasons.

30. The situation is complicated somewhat by the fact that outsiders may sometimes justly demand to be treated as insiders. Suppose an outsider interferes with the local administration of $P_1$ because he wants to promote a principle of wider range—principle $P_1^*$— that deals justly with his claims as well as those previously dealt with under $P_1$. The outsider in question may be a Bangladeshi and $P_1^*$ may be a principle of global redistribution. Perhaps in this case there is no moral basis for condemning his interference. Who, after all, is entitled to object if his interference is calculated to bring about the administration of $P_1^*$? Certainly not those who are insiders with regard to $P_1$, for they have claims of justice only against one another, not against those whose interests are neglected in the administration of that principle. Still, $P_3$ applies to *some* acts of interference by such outsiders, namely, those that do not enhance the prospects for $P_1$'s being replaced by $P_1^*$. And it certainly applies to the actions of outsiders such as Frenchmen who do not have this special interest in the replacement of $P_1$ by a principle of wider range. (I assume here that both Frenchmen and New Zealanders are better off under the range-limited principles that are already being administered in their respective societies than they would be under any just principle of wider range.)

31. This helps explain torts of interference with contractual relations. Though a contract between A and B creates purely *in personam* rights, C can wrong B by inciting A to violate these rights.

32. Except, that is, in the extraordinary case in which some property of his is governed by New Zealand courts for the purposes of some dispute, under private international law. See note 28 above.

33. Dworkin, *Law's Empire*, p. 193.

34. This paragraph is in response to a criticism by Mark Johnson.

35. Recent communitarian discussions of patriotism and loyalty are all predicated on the idea that I owe something to the community that is currently making my life and the exercise of my rights possible. See, for example, Alasdair MacIntyre, *Is Patriotism a Virtue? The Lindley Lecture* (Lawrence: University of Kansas, 1984), [reprinted in *Global Ethics: Seminal Essays*, 119–38], and Charles Taylor, "Atomism," in his *Philosophy and the Human Sciences: Philosophical Papers* 2 (Cambridge: Cambridge University Press, 1985). These accounts do not explore the idea of an allegiance that is more atavistic and that stands quite independently of the communal attachments I currently enjoy. The best recent account is Neil MacCormick, "Nation and Nationalism," in his *Legal Right and Social Democracy: Essays in Legal and Social Philosophy* (Oxford: Clarendon Press, 1982).

36. See the excellent discussion in Jean Hampton, *Hobbes and the Social Contract Tradition* (Cambridge: Cambridge University Press, 1986), chapter 6. Hampton shows that these collective action problems are not Prisoners' Dilemmas.

37. I do not mean to suggest the truth of this hypothesis (about justice) in either the Irish or the Lebanese case, but simply to consider what would follow if it *were* true (and what does follow to the extent that it *is* true).

38. Thomas Hobbes, *Leviathan*, ed. Richard Tuck (Cambridge: Cambridge University Press, 1991), chapter 13, pp. 89–90.

39. Robert Nozick, *Anarchy, State and Utopia* (New York: Basic Books, 1984), pp. 12–17.

40. See Hampton, *Hobbes and the Social Contract Tradition*.

41. See Don Regan, *Utilitarianism and Cooperation* (Oxford: Clarendon Press, 1980) for an excellent detailed argument to this effect.

42. See Leslie Green, "Law, Co-ordination and the Common Good," *Oxford Journal of Legal Studies* 3 (1983): 299–324.

43. The difference principle holds that inequalities of wealth and power are acceptable only if they redound to the benefit of the least favored group in society; see Rawls, *A Theory of Justice*, pp. 75–79.

44. Ibid., pp. 7, 170–71. See also John Rawls, "The Basic Structure as Subject," *American Philosophical Quarterly* 14 (1977): 159–65.

45. There is a more expensive discussion of this in Jeremy Waldron, "Theoretical Foundations of Liberalism," *Philosophical Quarterly* 37 (1987): 135–40.

46. This use of consent is different again from its use within Rawlsian-style contractarianism. There the image of consent is deployed as a model-theoretic device for establishing what justice actually amounts to; it has no political or institutional significance, either with regard to obligation or with regard to legitimacy (in the sense I am discussing).

47. For the argument that hypothetical consent cannot generate actual obligation, see Ronald Dworkin, *Taking Rights Seriously* (London: Duckworth, 1977), pp. 150–59.

48. For a dissenting view, see Nozick, *Anarchy, State and Utopia*, chapters 2–6. It is Nozick's contention in this part of the book that the moral force of constraints of right and justice does not translate automatically into a moral imperative of submission to and cooperation with whatever organization seems best positioned to uphold and enforce such rights. Nozick's position is based partly on his particular conception of rights as agent-relative side-constraints: that A has a right against B that B not attack him does not, on Nozick's account, provide any third party C with either a duty or a moral justification for restraining or helping to restrain B from attacking A. I am grateful to the editors of *Philosophy & Public Affairs* for pressing this point.

49. Rawls, *A Theory of Justice*, p. 3.

50. Simmons, *Moral Principles*, p. 148.

51. Ibid.

# 15. JOHN RAWLS

Rawls develops a set of principles for international justice, which he calls the law of peoples. These principles are justified by appeal to a version of his well-known original position argument. The argument here proceeds in two steps, one including only representatives of liberal democratic peoples in the original position, the other including representatives of decent hierarchical peoples. The outcome is a set of principles that includes a commitment to a limited set of human rights, and the protection of the sovereignty of peoples that honor those rights.

## The Law of Peoples

*First published in* On Human Rights: The Oxford Amnesty Lectures, *ed. Stephen Shute and Susan Hurley (New York: Basic Books, 1993), 41–82, 220–30.*

One aim of this essay is to sketch—in a short space, I can do no more than that—how the law of peoples[1] may be developed out of liberal ideas of justice similar to but more general than the idea I called justice as fairness and presented in my book *A Theory of Justice* (1971). By the law of peoples I mean a political conception of right and justice[2] that applies to the principles and norms of international law and practice. In section 58 of the above work I indicated how from justice as fairness the law of peoples might be developed for the limited purpose of addressing several questions of just war. In this essay my sketch of that law covers more ground and includes an account of the role of human rights. Even though the idea of justice I use to do this is more general than justice as fairness, it is still connected with the idea of the social contract: The procedure of construction, and the various steps gone through, are much the same in both cases.

A further aim is to set out the bearing of political liberalism once a liberal political conception of justice is extended to the law of peoples. In particular, we ask: What form does the toleration of nonliberal societies take in this case? Surely tyrannical and dictatorial regimes cannot be accepted as members in good standing of a reasonable society of peoples. But equally not all regimes can reasonably be required to be liberal, otherwise the law of peoples itself would not express liberalism's own principle of toleration for other reasonable ways of ordering society nor further its attempt to find a shared basis of agreement among reasonable peoples. Just as a citizen in a liberal society must respect other persons' comprehensive religious, philosophical, and moral doctrines provided they are pursued in accordance with a reasonable political conception of justice, so a liberal society must respect other societies organized by comprehensive doctrines, provided their political and social institutions meet certain conditions that lead the society to adhere to a reasonable law of peoples.

More specifically, we ask: Where are the reasonable limits of toleration to be drawn? It turns out that a well-ordered nonliberal society will accept the same law of peoples that well-ordered liberal societies accept. Here I understand a well-ordered society as being peaceful and not expansionist; its legal system satisfies certain requisite conditions of legitimacy in the eyes of its own people; and, as a consequence of this, it honors basic human rights (section 4). One kind of nonliberal society satisfying these conditions is illustrated by what I call, for lack of a better term, a well-ordered hierarchical society. This example makes the point, central for this argument, that although any society must honor basic human rights, it need not be liberal. It also indicates the role of human rights as part of a reasonable law of peoples.

## 1. HOW A SOCIAL CONTRACT DOCTRINE IS UNIVERSAL IN ITS REACH

I begin by explaining the way in which a social contract doctrine with its procedure of construction is universal in its reach.

Every society must have a conception of how it is related to other societies and of how it is to conduct itself toward them. It lives with them in the same world and except for the very special case of isolation of a society from all the rest—long in the past now—it must formulate certain ideals and principles for guiding its policies toward other peoples. Like justice as fairness, the more general liberal conception I have in mind—as specified in section 3—begins with the case of a hypothetically closed and self-sufficient liberal democratic society and covers only political values and not all of life. The question now arises as to how that conception can be extended in a convincing way to cover a society's relations with other societies to yield a reasonable law of peoples. In the absence of this extension to the law of peoples, a liberal conception of political justice would appear to be historicist and to apply only to societies whose political institutions and culture are liberal. In making the case for justice as fairness, and for similar more general liberal conceptions, it is essential to show that this is not so.

The problem of the law of peoples is only one of several problems of extension for these ideas of justice. There is the additional problem of extending these ideas to future generations, under which falls the problem of just savings. Also, since the ideas of justice regard persons as normal and fully cooperating members of society over a complete life, and having the requisite capacities to do this, there arises the problem of what is owed to those who fail to meet this condition, either temporarily or permanently, which gives rise to several problems of justice in health care. Finally, there is the problem of what is owed to animals and the rest of nature.

We would eventually like an answer to all these questions, but I doubt that we can find one within the scope of these ideas of justice understood as political conceptions. At best they may yield reasonable answers to the first three problems of extension: to other societies, to future generations, and to certain cases of health care. With regard to the problems which these liberal ideas of justice fail to address, there are several things we might say. One is that the idea of political justice does not cover everything and we should not expect it to. Or the problem may indeed be one of political justice but none of these ideas is correct for the question at hand, however well they may do for other questions. How deep a fault this shows must wait until the question itself can be examined, but we should not expect these ideas, or I think any account of political justice, to handle all these matters.

Let's return to our problem of extending liberal ideas of justice similar to but more general than justice as fairness to the law of peoples. There is a clear contrast between these and other familiar views in the way they are universal in reach. Take, for example, Leibniz's or Locke's doctrines: These are universal both in their source of authority and in their formulation. By that I mean that their source is God's authority or the divine reason, as the case may be; and they are universal in that their principles are stated so as to apply to all reasonable beings everywhere. Leibniz's doctrine is an ethics of creation. It contains the idea of morals as the *imitatio Dei* and applies straightway to us as God's creatures endowed with reason. In Locke's doctrine, God having legitimate authority over all creation, the natural law—that part of God's law that can be known by our natural powers of reason—everywhere has authority and binds us and all peoples.

Most familiar philosophical views—such as rational intuitionism, (classical) utilitarianism, and perfectionism—are also formulated in a general way to apply to us directly in all cases. Although they are not theologically grounded, let's say their source of authority is (human) reason, or an independent realm of moral values, or some other proposed basis of universal validity. In all these views the universality of the doctrine is the direct consequence of its source of authority and of how it is formulated.

By contrast, a constructivist view such as justice as fairness, and more general liberal ideas, do not begin from universal first principles having authority in all cases.[3] In justice as fairness the principles of justice for the basic structure of society are not suitable as fully general principles: They do not apply to all subjects, not to churches and universities, or to the basic structures of all societies, or to the law of peoples. Rather, they are constructed by way of a reasonable procedure in which rational parties adopt principles of justice for each kind of subject as it arises. Typically, a constructivist doctrine proceeds by taking up a series of subjects, starting, say, with principles of political justice for the basic structure of a closed and self-contained democratic society. That done, it then works forward to principles for the claims of future generations, outward to principles for the law of peoples, and inward to principles for special social questions. Each time the constructivist procedure is modified to fit the subject in question. In due course all the main principles are on hand, including those needed for the various political duties and obligations of individuals and associations.[4] Thus, a constructivist liberal doctrine is universal in its reach once it is extended to give principles for all politically relevant subjects, including a law of peoples for the most comprehensive subject, the political society of peoples. Its authority rests on the principles and conceptions of practical reason, but always on these as suitably adjusted to apply to different subjects as they arise in sequence; and always assuming as well that these principles are endorsed on due reflection by the reasonable agents to whom the corresponding principles apply.

At first sight, a constructivist doctrine of this kind appears hopelessly unsystematic. For how are the principles that apply to different cases tied together? And why do we proceed through the series of cases in one order rather than another? Constructivism assumes, however, that there are other forms of unity than that defined by completely general first principles forming a consistent scheme. Unity may also be given by an appropriate sequence of cases and by supposing that the parties in an original position (as I have called it) are to proceed through the sequence with the understanding that the principles for the subject of each later agreement are to be subordinate to those of subjects of all earlier agreements, or else coordinated with and adjusted to them by certain priority rules. I shall try out a particular sequence and point out its merits as we proceed. There is in advance no guarantee that it is the most appropriate sequence and much trial and error may be needed.

In developing a conception of justice for the basic structure or for the law of peoples, or indeed for any subject, constructivism does not view the variation in numbers of people alone as accounting for the appropriateness of different principles in different cases. That families are smaller than constitutional democracies does not explain why different principles apply to them. Rather, it is the distinct structure of the social framework, and the purpose and role of its various parts and how they fit together, that explain why there are different principles for different kinds of subjects. Thus, it is characteristic of a constructivist idea of justice to regard the distinctive nature and purpose of the elements of society, and of the society of peoples, as requiring persons, within a domain where other principles leave them free, to act from principles designed to fit their peculiar roles. As we shall see as we work out the law of peoples, these principles are identified in each case by rational agents fairly, or reasonably, situated given the case at hand. They are not derived from completely general principles such as the principle of utility or the principle of perfectionism.

## 2. THREE PRELIMINARY QUESTIONS

Before showing how the extension to the law of peoples can be carried out, I go over three preliminary matters. First, let's distinguish between two parts of justice as fairness, or of any other similar liberal and constructivist conception of justice. One part is worked up to apply to the domestic institutions of democratic societies, their regime and basic structure, and to the duties and obligations of citizens. The other part is worked up to apply to the society of political societies and thus to the political relations between peoples.[5] After the principles of justice have been adopted for domestic justice, the idea of the original position is used again at the next higher level.[6] As before, the parties are representatives, but now they are representatives of peoples whose basic institutions satisfy the principles of justice selected at the first level. We start with the family of societies, each well-ordered by some liberal view meeting certain conditions (justice as fairness is an example), and then work out principles to govern their relations with one another. Here I mention only the first stage of working out the law of peoples. As we shall see in section 4, we must also develop principles which govern the relations between liberal and what I shall call hierarchical societies. It turns out that liberal and hierarchical societies can agree on the same law of peoples and thus this law does not depend on aspects peculiar to the Western tradition.

It may be objected that to proceed in this way is to accept the state as traditionally conceived, with all its familiar powers of sovereignty. These powers include first, the right to go to war in pursuit of state policies—Clausewitz's pursuit of politics by other means—with the aims of politics given by a state's rational prudential interests.[7] They include second, the state's right to do as it likes with people within its own borders. The objection is misapplied for this reason. In the first use of the original position domestic society is seen as closed, since we abstract from relations with other societies. There is no need for armed forces and the question of the government's right to be prepared militarily does not arise, and would be denied if it did. The principles of domestic justice allow a police force to keep domestic order, but that is another matter, and although those domestic principles are consistent with a qualified right of war in a society of peoples, they do not of themselves support that right. That is up to the law of peoples itself, still to be constructed. And, as we shall see, this law will also restrict a state's internal sovereignty, its right to do as it likes to people within its own borders.

Thus, it is important to see that in this working out of the law of peoples, a government as the political organization of its people is not, as it were, the author of its own power. The war powers of governments, whatever they should be, are only those acceptable within a reasonable law of peoples. Presuming the existence of a government whereby a people is domestically organized with institutions of background justice does not prejudge these questions. We must reformulate the powers of sovereignty in light of a reasonable law of peoples and get rid of the right to war and the right to internal autonomy, which have been part of the (positive) international law for the two and a half centuries following the Thirty Years' War, as part of the classical states system.[8]

Moreover, these ideas accord with a dramatic shift in how international law is now understood. Since World War II international law has become far more demanding than in the past. It tends to restrict a state's right to wage war to cases of self-defense (this allows collective security), and it also tends to limit a state's right of internal sovereignty.[9] The role of human rights connects most obviously with the latter change as part of the effort to provide a suitable definition of, and limits on, a government's internal sovereignty, though it is not unconnected with the first. At this point I leave aside the many difficulties of interpreting these rights and limits, and take their general meaning and tendency as clear enough. What is essential is that our elaboration of the law of peoples should fit—as it turns out to do—these two basic changes, and give them a suitable rationale.

The second preliminary matter concerns the question: In working out the law of peoples, why do we start (as I said above) with those societies well-ordered by liberal views somewhat more general than justice as fairness? Wouldn't it be better to start with the world as a whole, with a global original position, so to speak, and discuss the question whether, and in what form, there should be states, or peoples, at all? Some writers (I mention them later) have thought that a social contract constructivist view should proceed in this manner, that it gives an appropriate universality from the start.

I think there is no clear initial answer to this question. We should try various alternatives and weigh their pluses and minuses. Since in working out justice as fairness I begin with domestic society, I shall continue from there as if what has been done so far is more or less sound. Thus I build on the steps taken until now, as this seems to provide a suitable starting point for the extension to the law of peoples. A further reason for proceeding thus is that peoples as corporate bodies organized by their governments now exist in some form all over the world. Historically speaking, all principles and standards proposed for the law of peoples must, to be feasible, prove acceptable to the considered and reflective public opinion of peoples and their governments.

Suppose, then, that we are (even though we are not) members of a well-ordered society. Our convictions about justice are roughly the same as those of citizens (if there are any) in the family of societies well-ordered by liberal conceptions of justice and whose social and historical conditions are similar to ours. They have the same kinds of reasons for affirming their mode of government as we do for affirming ours. This common understanding of liberal societies provides an apt starting point for the extension to the law of peoples.

Finally, I note the distinction between the law of peoples and the law of nations, or international law. The latter is an existing, or positive, legal order, however incomplete it may be in some ways, lacking, for example, an effective scheme of sanctions such as normally characterizes domestic law. The law of peoples, by contrast, is a family of political concepts with principles of right, justice, and the common good, that specify the content of a liberal conception of justice worked up to extend to and to apply to international law. It provides the concepts and principles by which that law is to be judged.

This distinction between the law of peoples and the law of nations should be straightforward. It is no more obscure than the distinction between the principles of justice that apply to the basic structure of domestic society and the existing political, social, and legal institutions that actually realize that structure.

## 3. THE EXTENSION TO LIBERAL SOCIETIES

The three preliminary matters settled, I turn to the extension of liberal ideas of justice to the law of peoples. I understand these ideas of justice to contain three main elements: (i) a list of certain basic rights and liberties and opportunities (familiar from constitutional democratic regimes); (ii) a high priority for these fundamental freedoms, especially with respect to claims of the general good and of perfectionist values; and (iii) measures assuring for all citizens adequate all-purpose means to make effective use of their freedoms. Justice as fairness is typical of these conceptions except that its egalitarian features are stronger. To some degree the more general liberal ideas lack the three egalitarian features of the fair value of the political liberties, of fair equality of opportunity, and of the difference principle. These features are not needed for the construction of a reasonable law of peoples and by not assuming them our account has greater generality.

There are two main stages to the extension to the law of peoples and each stage has two steps. The first stage of the extension I call the ideal, or strict compliance, theory, and unless otherwise stated, we work entirely in this theory. This means that the relevant concepts and principles are strictly complied with by all parties to the agreements made and that the requisite favorable conditions for liberal or hierarchical institutions are on hand. Our first aim is to see what a reasonable law of peoples, fully honored, would require and establish in this case.

To make the account manageable, we suppose there are only two kinds of well-ordered domestic societies, liberal societies and hierarchical societies. I discuss at the first step the case of well-ordered liberal democratic societies. This leads to the idea of a well-ordered political society of societies of democratic peoples. After this I turn to societies that are well-ordered and just, often religious in nature and not characterized by the separation of church and state. Their political institutions specify a just consultation hierarchy, as I shall say, while their basic social institutions satisfy a conception of justice expressing an appropriate conception of the common good. Fundamental for our rendering of the law of peoples is that both liberal and hierarchical societies accept it. Together they are members in good standing of a well-ordered society of the just peoples of the world.

The second stage in working out the law of peoples is that of nonideal theory, and it also includes two steps. The first step is that of noncompliance theory. Here we have the predicament of just societies, both democratic and hierarchical, as they confront states that refuse to comply with a reasonable law of peoples. The second step of this second stage is that of unfavorable conditions. It poses the different problem of how the poorer and less technologically advanced societies of the world can attain historical and social conditions that allow them to establish just and workable institutions, either liberal or hierarchical. In actual affairs, nonideal theory is of first practical importance and deals with problems we face every day. Yet, for reasons of space, I shall say very little about it (sections 6–7).

Before beginning the extension we need to be sure that the original position with the veil of ignorance is a device of representation for the case of liberal societies. In the first use of the original position, its function as a device of representation means that it models what we regard—you and I, and here and now[10]—as fair conditions for the parties, as representatives of free and equal citizens, to specify the terms of cooperation regulating the basic structure of their society. Since that position includes the veil of ignorance, it also models what we regard as acceptable restrictions on reasons for adopting a political conception of justice. Therefore, the conception the parties would adopt identifies the conception of justice that we regard—you and I, here and now—as fair and supported by the best reasons.

Three conditions are essential: First, the original position represents the parties (or citizens) fairly, or reasonably; second, it represents them as rational; and third, it represents them as deciding between available principles for appropriate reasons. We check that these three conditions are satisfied by observing that citizens are indeed represented fairly, or reasonably, in virtue of the symmetry and equality of their representatives' situation in the original position. Next, citizens are represented as rational in virtue of the aim of their representatives to do the best they can for their essential interests as persons. Finally, they are represented as deciding for appropriate reasons: The veil of ignorance prevents their representatives from invoking reasons deemed unsuitable, given the aim of representing citizens as free and equal persons.

At the next level, when the original position is used to extend a liberal conception to the law of peoples, it is a device of representation because it models what we would regard—you and I, here and now[11]—as fair conditions under which the parties, this time as representatives of societies well-ordered by liberal conceptions of justice, are to specify the law of peoples and the fair terms of their cooperation.

The original position is a device of representation because, as before, free and equal peoples are represented as both reasonably situated and rational, and as deciding in accordance with appropriate reasons. The parties as representatives of democratic peoples are symmetrically situated, and so the peoples they represent are represented reasonably. Moreover, the parties deliberate among available principles for the law of peoples by reference to the fundamental interests of democratic societies in accordance with, or as presupposed by, the liberal principles of domestic justice. And finally, the parties are subject to a veil of ignorance: They do not know, for example, the size of the territory, or the population, or the relative strength of the people whose fundamental interests they represent. Although they know that reasonably favorable conditions obtain that make democracy possible, they do not know the extent of their natural resources, or level of their economic development, or any such related information. These conditions model what we, as members of societies well-ordered by liberal conceptions of justice, would accept as fair—here and now—in specifying the basic terms of cooperation between peoples who, as peoples, regard themselves as free and equal. We use the original position at the second level as a device of representation as we did at the first.

I assume that working out the law of peoples for liberal democratic societies only will result in the adoption of certain familiar principles of justice, and will also allow for various forms of cooperative association among democratic peoples and not for a world state. Here I follow Kant's lead in *Perpetual Peace* (1795) in thinking that a world government—by which I mean a unified political regime with the legal powers normally exercised by central governments—would be either a global despotism or else a fragile empire torn by frequent civil strife as various regions and peoples try to gain political autonomy.[12] On the other hand, it may turn out, as I sketch below, that there will be many different kinds of organizations subject to the judgment of the law of democratic peoples, charged with regulating cooperation between them, and having certain recognized duties. Some of these organizations (like the United Nations) may have the authority to condemn domestic institutions that violate human rights, and in certain severe cases to punish them by imposing economic sanctions, or even by military intervention. The scope of these powers is all peoples' and covers their domestic affairs.

If all this is sound, I believe the principles of justice between free and democratic peoples will include certain familiar principles long recognized as belonging to the law of peoples, among them the following:

1. Peoples (as organized by their governments) are free and independent and their freedom and independence is to be respected by other peoples.

2. Peoples are equal and parties to their own agreements.

3. Peoples have the right of self-defense but no right to war.

4. Peoples are to observe a duty of nonintervention.

5. Peoples are to observe treaties and undertakings.

6. Peoples are to observe certain specified restrictions on the conduct of war (assumed to be in self-defense).

7. Peoples are to honor human rights.

This statement of principles is of course incomplete; other principles would need to be added. Further, they require much explanation and interpretation, and some of them are superfluous in a society of well-ordered democratic peoples, for instance, the sixth regarding the conduct of war and the seventh regarding human rights. The main point is that given the idea of a society of free and independent democratic peoples, who are ready to recognize certain basic principles of political justice governing their conduct, principles of this kind constitute the charter of their association.[13] Obviously, a principle such as the fourth—that of nonintervention—will have to be qualified in the general case. Although suitable for a society of well-ordered democratic peoples who respect human rights, it fails in the case of disordered societies in which wars and serious violations of human rights are endemic. Also, the right to independence, and equally the right to self-determination, hold only within certain limits, to be specified by the law of peoples for the general case. Thus, no people has the right to self-determination, or a right to secession, at the expense of the subjugation of another people;[14] nor can a people protest their condemnation by the world society when their domestic institutions violate the human rights of certain minorities living among them. Their right to independence is no shield from that condemnation, or even from coercive intervention by other peoples in grave cases.

There will also be principles for forming and regulating federations (associations) of peoples, and standards of fairness for trade and other cooperative arrangements. There should be certain provisions for mutual assistance between peoples in times of famine and drought, and were it feasible, as it should be, provisions for ensuring that in all reasonably developed liberal societies people's basic needs are met.[15] These provisions will specify duties of assistance in certain situations, and they will vary in stringency depending on the severity of the case.

An important role of a people's government, however arbitrary a society's boundaries may appear from a historical point of view,[16] is to be the representative and effective agent of a people as they take responsibility for their territory and the size of their population, as well as for maintaining its environmental integrity and its capacity to sustain them. The idea here appeals to the point of the institution of property: Unless a definite agent is given responsibility for maintaining an asset and bears the loss for not doing so, that asset tends to deteriorate. In this case the asset is the people's territory and its capacity to sustain them in perpetuity; the agent is the people themselves as politically organized. They must recognize that they cannot make up for irresponsibility in caring for their land and conserving their natural resources by conquest in war or by migrating into other people's territory without their consent.[17]

These remarks belong to ideal theory and indicate some of the responsibilities of peoples in a just society of well-ordered liberal societies. Since the boundaries of peoples are often historically the outcome of violence and aggression, and some peoples are wrongly subjected to others, the law of peoples in its nonideal part should, as far as possible, contain principles and standards—or at least some guidelines—for coping with these matters.

To complete this sketch of the law of peoples for well-ordered liberal societies only, let's consider under what conditions we can reasonably accept this part of the law of peoples and regard it as justified.

There are two conditions beyond the three requirements earlier noted in discussing the original position as a device of representation. These requirements were: that the parties (as representatives of free and equal peoples) be represented as reasonably situated, as rational, and as deciding in accordance with appropriate reasons. One of the two further conditions is that the political society of well-ordered democratic peoples should itself be stable in the right way.[18] Given the existence of a political society of such peoples, its members will tend increasingly over time to accept its principles and judgments as they come to understand the ideas of justice expressed in the law among them and appreciate its benefits for all liberal peoples.

To say that the society of democratic peoples is stable in the right way is to say that it is stable with respect to justice, that is, that the institutions and practices among peoples always more or less satisfy the relevant principles of justice, although social conditions are presumably always changing. It is further to say that the law of peoples is honored not simply because of a fortunate balance of power—it being in no people's interest to upset it—but because, despite the possibly shifting fortunes of different peoples, all are moved to adhere to their common law accepting it as just and beneficial for all. This means that the justice of the society of democratic peoples is stable with respect to the distribution of fortune among them. Here fortune refers not to a society's military success or the lack of it, but to other kinds of success: its achievement of political and social freedom, the fullness and expressiveness of its culture, the economic well-being of its citizens.

The historical record suggests that, at least so far as the principle against war is concerned, this condition of stability would be satisfied in a society of just democratic peoples. Although democratic societies have been as often involved in war as nondemocratic states[19] and have often vigorously defended their institutions, since 1800, as Michael Doyle points out, firmly established liberal societies have not gone to war with one another.[20] And in wars in which a number of major powers were engaged, such as the two World Wars, democratic states have fought as allies on the same side. Indeed, the absence of war between democracies is as close as anything we know to an empirical law in relations between societies.[21] This being so, I shall suppose that a society of democratic peoples, all of whose basic institutions are well-ordered by liberal conceptions of justice (though not necessarily by the same conception) will be stable in the right way as above specified. The sketch of the law of such peoples therefore seems to meet the condition of political realism given by that of stability for the right reasons.

Observe that I state what I call Doyle's law as holding between well-established and well-ordered liberal democracies that are significant if not major powers. The reasons for this law's holding (supposing it does) are quite compatible with actual democracies, marked as they are by considerable injustice and oligarchic tendencies, intervening, often covertly, in smaller countries whose democracies are less well established and secure. Witness the United States' overturning the democracies of Allende in Chile, Arbenz in Guatemala, Mossadegh in Iran, and, some would add, the Sandinistas in Nicaragua. Whatever the merits of these regimes, covert operations against them can be carried out by a government bureaucracy at the urging of oligarchic interests without the knowledge or criticism of the public, and presenting it with a fait accompli. All this is made easier by the handy appeal to national security given the situation of superpower rivalry in the Cold War, which allowed those democracies, however implausibly, to be cast as a danger. While democratic peoples are not expansionist, they do defend their security interest, and this an oligarchic government can easily manipulate in a time of superpower rivalry to support covert interventions once they are found out.[22]

The last condition for us to accept this sketch of the law of democratic peoples as sound is that we can, as citizens of liberal societies, endorse the principles and judgments of this law on due reflection. We must be able to say that the doctrine of the law of peoples for such societies, more than any other doctrine, ties together our considered political convictions and moral judgments at all levels of generality, from the most general to the more particular, into one coherent view.

# 4. EXTENSION TO HIERARCHICAL SOCIETIES

Recall from section 3 that the extension of liberal ideas of justice to the law of peoples proceeds in two stages, each stage having two steps. The first stage is that of ideal theory and we have just completed the first step of that: the extension of the law of peoples to well-ordered liberal societies only. The second step of ideal theory is more difficult: It requires us to specify a second kind of society—a hierarchical society, as I shall say—and then to state when such a society is well-ordered. Our aim is to extend the law of peoples to these well-ordered hierarchical societies and to show that they accept the same law of peoples liberal societies do. Thus, this shared law of well-ordered peoples, both liberal and hierarchical, specifies the content of ideal theory. It specifies the kind of society of well-ordered peoples all people should want and it sets the regulative end of their foreign policy. Important for us, it has the obvious corollary that nonliberal societies also honor human rights.

To show all this we proceed thus. First, we state three requirements for any well-ordered hierarchical regime. It will be clear that satisfying these requirements does not entail that a regime be liberal. Next, we confirm that, in an original position with a veil of ignorance, the representatives of well-ordered hierarchical regimes are reasonably situated as well as rational, and are moved by appropriate reasons. In this case also, the original position is a device of representation for the adoption of law among hierarchical peoples. Finally, we show that in the original position the representatives of well-ordered hierarchical societies would adopt the same law of peoples that the representatives of liberal societies do. That law thus serves as a common law of a just political society of well-ordered peoples.

The first of the three requirements for a hierarchical society to be well-ordered is that it must be peaceful and gain its legitimate aims through diplomacy and trade, and other ways of peace. It follows that its religious doctrine, assumed to be comprehensive and influential in government policy, is not expansionist in the sense that it fully respects the civic order and integrity of other societies. If it seeks wider influence, it does so in ways compatible with the independence of, and the liberties within, other societies. This feature of its religion supports the institutional basis of its peaceful conduct and distinguishes it from leading European states during the religious wars of the sixteenth and seventeenth centuries.

A second fundamental requirement uses an idea of Philip Soper. It has several parts. It requires first, that a hierarchical society's system of law be such as to impose moral duties and obligations on all persons within its territory.[23] It requires further that its system of law be guided by a common good conception of justice, meaning by this a conception that takes impartially into account what it sees not unreasonably as the fundamental interests of all members of society. It is not the case that the interests of some are arbitrarily privileged, while the interests of others go for naught. Finally, there must be sincere and not unreasonable belief on the part of judges and other officials who administer the legal order that the law is indeed guided by a common good conception of justice. This belief must be demonstrated by a willingness to defend publicly the state's injunctions as justified by law. Courts are an efficient way of doing this.[24] These aspects of a legal order are necessary to establish a regime's legitimacy in the eyes of its own people. To sum up the second requirement we say: The system of law is sincerely and not unreasonably believed to be guided by a common good conception of justice. It takes into account people's essential interests and imposes moral duties and obligations on all members of society.

This second requirement can be spelled out further by adding that the political institutions of a well-ordered hierarchical society constitute a reasonable consultation hierarchy. They include a family of representative bodies, or other assemblies, whose task is to look after the important interests of all elements of society. Although in hierarchical societies persons are not regarded as free and equal citizens, as they are in liberal societies, they are seen as responsible members of society who can recognize their moral duties and obligations and play their part in social life.

With a consultation hierarchy there is an opportunity for different voices to be heard, not, to be sure, in a way allowed by democratic institutions, but appropriately in view of the religious and philosophical values of the society in question. Thus, individuals do not have the right of free speech as in a liberal society; but as members of associations and corporate bodies they have the right at some point in the process of consultation to express political dissent and the government has an obligation to take their dissent seriously and to give a conscientious reply. That different voices can be heard is necessary because the sincere belief of judges and other officials has two components: honest belief and respect for the possibility of dissent.[25] Judges and officials must be willing to address objections. They cannot refuse to listen to them on the grounds that they think those expressing them are incompetent and cannot understand. Then we would not have a consultation hierarchy but a purely paternalistic regime.

In view of this account of the institutional basis of a hierarchical society, we can say that its conception of the common good of justice secures for all persons at least certain minimum rights to means of subsistence and security (the right to life),[26] to liberty (freedom from slavery, serfdom, and forced occupations) and (personal) property, as well as to formal equality as expressed by the rules of natural justice[27] (for example, that similar cases be treated similarly). This shows that a well-ordered hierarchical society also meets a third requirement: It respects basic human rights.

The argument for this conclusion is that the second requirement rules out the violation of these rights. For to satisfy it, a society's legal order must impose moral duties and obligations on all persons in its territory and it must embody a reasonable consultation hierarchy which will protect human rights. A sincere and reasonable belief on the part of judges and other officials that the system of law is guided by a common good conception of justice has the same result. Such a belief is simply unreasonable, if not irrational, when those rights are infringed.

There is a question about religious toleration that calls for explicit mention. Whereas in hierarchical societies a state religion may be on some questions the ultimate authority within society and control government policy on certain important matters, that authority is not (as I have said) extended politically to other societies. Further, their (comprehensive) religious or philosophical doctrines are not unreasonable: They admit a measure of liberty of conscience and freedom of thought, even if these freedoms are not in general equal for all members of society as they are in liberal regimes.[28] A hierarchical society may have an established religion with certain privileges. Still, it is essential to its being well-ordered that no religions are persecuted, or denied civic and social conditions that permit their practice in peace and without fear.[29] Also essential, and this because of the inequality of religious freedom, if for no other reason, is that a hierarchical society must allow for the right of emigration.[30] The rights noted here are counted as human rights. In section 5 we return to the role and status of these rights.

An institutional basis that realizes the three requirements can take many forms. This deserves emphasis, as I have indicated only the religious case. We are not trying to describe all possible forms of social order consistent with membership in good standing of a reasonable society of peoples. Rather, we have specified three necessary conditions for membership of a reasonable society of peoples and then shown by example that these conditions do not require a society to be liberal.

This completes the account of the requirements imposed on the basic institutions of a well-ordered hierarchical society. My aim has been to outline a conception of justice that, although distant from liberal conceptions, still has features that give to societies regulated accordingly the moral status required to be members in good standing in a reasonable society of well-ordered peoples. It is important to see, as I have noted, that an agreement on a law of peoples ensuring human rights is not an agreement only liberal societies can make. We must now confirm this.

Hierarchical societies are well-ordered in terms of their own conceptions of justice.[31] This being so, their representatives in an appropriate original position would adopt the same principles as those sketched above that would be adopted by the representatives of liberal societies. Each hierarchical society's interests are understood by its representatives in accordance with or as presupposed by its conception of justice. This enables us to say in this case also that the original position is a device of representation.

Two considerations confirm this. The first is that, in view of the common good conception of justice held in a hierarchical society, the parties care about the good of the society they represent, and so about its security as assured by the laws against war and aggression. They also care about the benefits of trade and assistance between peoples in time of need. All these help protect human rights. In view of this, we can say that the representatives of hierarchical societies are rational. The second consideration is that they do not try to extend their religious and philosophical doctrines to other peoples by war or aggression, and they respect the civic order and integrity of other societies. Hence, they accept—as you and I would accept[32]—the original position as fair between peoples and would endorse the law of peoples adopted by their representatives as specifying fair terms of political cooperation between them and other societies. Thus, the representatives are reasonably situated and this suffices for the use of the original position as a device of representation in extending the law of peoples to hierarchical societies.[33]

Note that I have supposed that the parties as representatives of peoples are to be situated equally, even though the conception of justice of the hierarchical society they represent allows basic inequalities between its members. For example, some of its members are not granted equal liberty of conscience. There is, however, no inconsistency in this: A people sincerely affirming a nonliberal conception of justice may still think their society should be treated equally in a just law of peoples, even though its members accept basic inequalities among themselves. Though a society lacks basic equality, it is not unreasonable for that society to insist on equality in making claims against other societies.

About this last point, two observations. One is that although the original position at the first level, that of domestic justice, incorporates a political conception of the person rooted in the public culture of a liberal society, the original position at the second level, that of the law of peoples, does not. I emphasize this fact, since it enables a liberal conception of justice to be extended to yield a more general law of peoples without prejudging the case against nonliberal societies.

This leads to a second observation. As mentioned earlier, the law of peoples might have been worked out by starting with an all-inclusive original position with representatives of all the individual persons of the world.[34] In this case the question of whether there are to be separate societies and of the relations between them will be settled by the parties behind a veil of ignorance. Offhand it is not clear why proceeding this way should lead to different results than, as I have done, proceeding from separate societies outward. All things considered, one might reach the same law of peoples in either case. The difficulty with an all-inclusive, or global, original position is that its use of liberal ideas is much more troublesome, for in this case we are treating all persons, regardless of their society and culture, as individuals who are free and equal, and as reasonable and rational, and so according to liberal conceptions. This makes the basis of the law of peoples too narrow.

Hence I think it best to follow the two-level[35] bottom-up procedure, beginning first with the principles of justice for the basic structure of domestic society and then moving upward and outward to the law of peoples. In so doing our knowledge of how peoples and their governments have acted historically gives us guidance in how to proceed and suggests questions and possibilities we might not otherwise have thought of. But this is simply a point of method and settles no questions of substance. These depend on what can actually be worked out.

One might well be skeptical that a liberal social contract and constructivist[36] idea of justice can be worked out to give a conception of the law of peoples universal in its reach and also applying to nonliberal societies. Our discussion of hierarchical societies should put these doubts to rest. I have noted the conditions under which we could accept the law of liberal peoples we had sketched as sound and justified. In this connection we considered whether that law was stable with respect to justice, and whether, on due reflection, we could accept the judgments that its principles and precepts led us to make. If both these things hold, we said, the law of liberal peoples as laid out could, by the criteria we can now apply, be accepted as justified.

Parallel remarks hold for the wider law of peoples including well-ordered hierarchical societies. Here I simply add, without argument or evidence, but hoping it seems plausible, that these societies will honor a just law of peoples for much the same reasons liberal peoples will do so, and that both we and they will find the judgments to which it leads acceptable to our convictions, all things considered. I believe it is of importance here that well-ordered hierarchical societies are not expansionist and their legal order is guided by a common good conception of justice ensuring that it honors human rights. These societies also affirm a peaceful society of peoples and benefit therefrom as liberal societies do. All have a common interest in changing the way in which politics among peoples—war and threats of war—has hitherto been carried on.

We may therefore view this wider law of peoples as sound and justified. This fundamental point deserves emphasis: There is nothing relevantly different between how, say, justice as fairness is worked out for the domestic case in *A Theory of Justice*, and how the law of peoples is worked out from more general liberal ideas of justice. In both cases we use the same fundamental idea of a reasonable procedure of construction in which rational agents fairly situated (the parties as representatives of citizens in one case and of peoples or societies in the other) select principles of justice for the relevant subject, either their separate domestic institutions or the shared law of peoples. As always, the parties are guided by the appropriate reasons as specified by a veil of ignorance. Thus, obligations and duties are not imposed by one society on another; instead, reasonable societies agree on what the bonds will be. Once we confirm that a domestic society, or a society of peoples, when regulated by the corresponding principles of justice, is stable with respect to justice (as previously defined), and once we have checked that we can endorse those principles on due reflection, then in both domains the ideals, laws, and principles of justice are justified in the same way.[37]

## 5. HUMAN RIGHTS

A few of the features of human rights as we have described them are these. First, these rights do not depend on any particular comprehensive moral doctrine or philosophical conception of human nature, such as, for example, that human beings are moral persons and have equal worth, or that they have certain particular moral and intellectual powers that entitle them to these rights. This would require a quite deep philosophical theory that many if not most hierarchical societies might reject as liberal or democratic, or in some way distinctive of the Western political tradition and prejudicial to other cultures.

We therefore take a different tack and say that basic human rights express a minimum standard of well-ordered political institutions for all peoples who belong, as members in good standing, to a just political society of peoples.[38] Any systematic violation of these rights is a serious matter and troubling to the society of peoples as a whole, both liberal and hierarchical. Since they must express a minimum standard, the requirements that yield these rights should be quite weak.

Recall that we postulated that a society's system of law must be such as to impose moral duties and obligations on all its members and be regulated by what judges and other officials reasonably and sincerely believe is a common good conception of justice. For this condition to hold, the law must at least uphold such basic rights as the right to life and security, to personal property, and the elements of the rule of law, as well as the right to a certain liberty of conscience and freedom of association, and the right to emigration. These rights we refer to as human rights.

Next we consider what the imposition of these duties and obligations implies, including (1) a common good conception of justice and (2) good faith on the part of officials to explain and justify the legal order to those bound by it. For these things to hold does not require the liberal idea that persons are first citizens and as such free and equal members of society who hold those basic rights as the rights of citizens. It requires only that persons be responsible and cooperating members of society who can recognize and act in accordance with their moral duties and obligations. It would be hard to reject these requirements (a common good conception of justice and a good faith official justification of the law) as too strong for a minimally decent regime. Human rights, understood as resulting from these requirements, could not be rejected as peculiarly liberal or special to our Western tradition. In that sense, they are politically neutral.[39]

To confirm this last point, I consider an alleged difficulty. Many societies have political traditions that are different from Western individualism in its many forms. In considering persons from a political point of view, these traditions are said to regard persons not as citizens first with the rights of citizens but rather as first being members of groups: communities, associations, or corporations.[40] On this alternative, let's say associationist, view, whatever rights persons have arise from this prior membership and are normally enabling rights, that is, rights that enable persons to perform their duties in the groups to which they belong. To illustrate with respect to political rights: Hegel rejects the idea of one person one vote on the grounds that it expresses the democratic and individualistic idea that each person, as an atomic unit, has the basic right to participate equally in political deliberation.[41] By contrast, in the well-ordered rational state, as Hegel presents it in *The Philosophy of Right*, persons belong first to estates, corporations, and associations. Since these social forms represent the rational[42] interests of their members in what Hegel views as a just consultation hierarchy, some persons will take part in politically representing these interests in the consultation process, but they do so as members of estates and corporations and not as individuals, and not all individuals are involved.

The essential point here is that the basic human rights as we have described them can be protected in a well-ordered hierarchical state with its consultation hierarchy; what holds in Hegel's scheme of political rights holds for all rights.[43] Its system of law can fulfill the conditions laid down and ensure the right to life and security, to personal property and the elements of the rule of law, as well as the right to a certain freedom of conscience and freedom of association. Admittedly it ensures these rights to persons as members of estates and corporations and not as citizens. But that does not matter. The rights are guaranteed and the requirement that a system of law must be such as to impose moral rights and duties is met. Human rights understood in the light of that condition cannot be rejected as peculiar to our Western tradition.

Human rights are a special class of rights designed to play a special role in a reasonable law of peoples for the present age. Recall that the accepted ideas about international law changed in two basic ways following World War II, and this change in basic moral beliefs is comparable to other profound historical changes.[44] War is no longer an admissible means of state policy. It is only justified in self-defense and a state's internal sovereignty is now limited. One role of human rights is precisely to specify limits to that sovereignty.

Human rights are thus distinct from, say, constitutional rights, or the rights of democratic citizenship,[45] or from other kinds of rights that belong to certain kinds of political institutions, both individualist and associationist. They are a special class of rights of universal application and hardly controversial in their general intention. They are part of a reasonable law of peoples and specify limits on the domestic institutions required of all peoples by that law. In this sense they specify the outer boundary of admissible domestic law of societies in good standing in a just society of peoples.[46]

Human rights have these three roles:

1) They are a necessary condition of a regime's legitimacy and of the decency of its legal order.

2) By being in place, they are also sufficient to exclude justified and forceful intervention by other peoples, say by economic sanctions, or in grave cases, by military force.

3) They set a limit on pluralism among peoples.[47]

## 6. NONIDEAL THEORY: NONCOMPLIANCE

So far we have been concerned solely with ideal theory. By developing a liberal conception of justice we have reviewed the philosophical and moral grounds of an ideal conception of a society of well-ordered peoples and of the principles that apply to its law and practices. That conception is to guide the conduct of peoples toward one another and the design of common institutions for their mutual benefit.

Before our sketch of the law of peoples is complete, however, we must take note of, even though we cannot properly discuss, the questions arising from the highly nonideal conditions of our world with its great injustices and widespread social evils. Nonideal theory asks how the ideal conception of the society of well-ordered peoples might be achieved, or at least worked toward, generally in gradual steps. It looks for policies and courses of action likely to be effective and politically possible as well as morally permissible for that purpose. So conceived, nonideal theory presupposes that ideal theory is already on hand for, until the ideal is identified, at least in outline, nonideal theory lacks an objective by reference to which its questions can be answered. And although the specific conditions of our world at any given time—the status quo—do not determine the ideal conception of the society of well-ordered peoples, those conditions do affect answers to the questions of nonideal theory. They are questions of transition: In any given case, they start from where a society is and seek effective ways permitted by the law of peoples to move the society some distance toward the goal.

We may distinguish two kinds of nonideal theory. One kind deals with conditions of noncompliance, that is, with conditions in which certain regimes refuse to acknowledge a reasonable law of peoples. These we may call outlaw regimes. The other kind of nonideal theory deals with unfavorable conditions, that is, with the conditions of peoples whose historical, social, and economic circumstances make their achieving a well-ordered regime, whether liberal or hierarchical, difficult if not impossible.

I begin with noncompliance theory. As we have said, a reasonable law of peoples guides the well-ordered regimes in facing outlaw regimes by specifying the goal they should always have in mind and indicating the means they may use or must avoid in pursuing the goal.

Outlaw regimes are a varied lot. Some are headed by governments that seem to recognize no conception of right and justice at all; often their legal order is at bottom a system of coercion and terror. The Nazi regime is a demonic example of this. A more common case, philosophically more interesting and historically more respectable, are those societies—they would scoff at being referred to as outlaw regimes—whose rulers affirm comprehensive doctrines that recognize no geographic limits to the legitimate authority of their established religious or philosophical views. Spain, France, and the Hapsburgs all tried at some time to subject much of Europe and the world to their will.[48] They hoped to spread true religion and culture, sought dominion and glory, not to mention wealth and territory. Such societies are checked only by a balance of power, but as this is changing and unstable, the hegemonic theory of war, so-called, fits nicely.[49]

The law-abiding societies—both liberal and hierarchical—can at best establish a modus vivendi with the outlaw expansionist regimes and defend the integrity of their societies as the law of peoples allows. In this situation the law-abiding societies exist in a state of nature with the outlaw regimes, and they have a duty to their own and to one another's societies and well-being, as well as a duty to the well-being of peoples subjected to outlaw regimes, though not to their rulers and elites. These several duties are not all equally strong, but there is always a duty to consider the more extensive long-run aims and to affirm them as overall guides of foreign policy. Thus, the only legitimate grounds of the right to war against outlaw regimes is defense of the society of well-ordered peoples and, in grave cases, of innocent persons subject to outlaw regimes and the protection of their human rights. This accords with Kant's idea that our first political duty is to leave the state of nature and submit ourselves along with others to the rule of a reasonable and just law.[50]

The defense of well-ordered peoples is only the first and most urgent task. Another long-run aim, as specified by the law of peoples, is to bring all societies eventually to honor that law and to be full and self-standing members of the society of well-ordered peoples, and so secure human rights everywhere. How to do this is a question of foreign policy; these things call for political wisdom, and success depends in part on luck. These are not matters to which political philosophy has much to add. I venture several familiar points.

For well-ordered peoples to achieve this long-run aim they should establish among themselves new institutions and practices to serve as a kind of federative center and public forum of their common opinion and policy toward the other regimes. This can either be done separately or within institutions such as the United Nations by forming an alliance of well-ordered peoples on certain issues. This federative center may be used both to formulate and to express the opinion of the well-ordered societies. There they may expose to public view the unjust and cruel institutions of oppressive and expansionist regimes and their violations of human rights.

Even these regimes are not altogether indifferent to this kind of criticism, especially when the basis of it is a reasonable and well-founded law of peoples that cannot be easily dismissed as simply liberal or Western. Gradually over time the well-ordered peoples may pressure the outlaw regimes to change their ways; but by itself this pressure is unlikely to be effective. It must be backed up by the firm denial of all military aid, or economic and other assistance; nor should outlaw regimes be admitted by well-ordered peoples as members in good standing into their mutually beneficial cooperative practices.

## 7. NONIDEAL THEORY: UNFAVORABLE CONDITIONS

A few words about the second kind of nonideal theory, that of unfavorable conditions. By these I mean the conditions of societies that lack the political and cultural traditions, the human capital and know-how, and the resources, material and technological, that make well-ordered societies possible. In noncompliance theory we saw that the goal of well-ordered societies is somehow to bring the outlaw states into the society of well-ordered peoples. The outlaw societies in the historical cases we mentioned above were not societies burdened by unfavorable resources, material and technological, or lacking in human capital and know-how; on the contrary, they were among the most politically and socially advanced and economically developed societies of their day. The fault in those societies lay in their political traditions and the background institutions of law, property, and class structure, with their sustaining beliefs and culture. These things must be changed before a reasonable law of peoples can be accepted and supported.

We must ask the parallel question: What is the goal specified by nonideal theory for the case of unfavorable conditions? The answer is clear. Eventually each society now burdened by unfavorable conditions should be raised to, or assisted toward, conditions that make a well-ordered society possible.

Some writers have proposed that the difference principle, or some other liberal principle of distributive justice, be adopted to deal with this problem and to regulate accordingly the economic inequalities in the society of peoples.[51] Although I think the difference principle is reasonable for domestic justice in a democratic society, it is not feasible as a way to deal with the general problem of unfavorable conditions among societies. For one thing, it belongs to the ideal theory for a democratic society and is not framed for our present case. More serious, there are various kinds of societies in the society of peoples and not all of them can reasonably be expected to accept any particular liberal principle of distributive justice; and even different liberal societies adopt different principles for their domestic institutions. For their part, the hierarchical societies reject all liberal principles of domestic justice. We cannot suppose that they will find such principles acceptable in dealing with other peoples. In our construction of the liberal law of peoples, therefore, liberal principles of domestic distributive justice are not generalized to answer questions about unfavorable conditions.

Confirming this is the fact that in a constructivist conception there is no reason to think that the principles that apply to domestic justice are also appropriate for regulating inequalities in a society of peoples. As we saw at the outset, each kind of subject—whether an institution or an individual, whether a political society or a society of political societies—may be governed by its own characteristic principles. What these principles are must be worked out by a suitable procedure beginning from a correct starting point. We ask how rational representatives suitably motivated, and reasonably situated with respect to one another, would be most strongly moved to select among the feasible ideals and principles to apply to the subject in question. Since the problem and subject are different in each case, the ideals and principles adopted may also be different. As always, the whole procedure and the principles it yields must be acceptable on due reflection.

Although no liberal principle of distributive justice would be adopted for dealing with unfavorable conditions, that certainly does not mean that the well-ordered and wealthier societies have no duties and obligations to societies burdened by such conditions. For the ideal conception of the society of peoples that well-ordered societies affirm directs that in due course all societies must reach, or be assisted to, the conditions that make a well-ordered society possible. This implies that human rights are to be recognized and secured everywhere, and that basic human needs are to be met. Thus, the basis of the duty of assistance is not some liberal principle of distributive justice. Rather, it is the ideal conception of the society of peoples itself as consisting of well-ordered societies, with each people, as I have said, a full and self-standing member of the society of peoples, and capable of taking charge of their political life and maintaining decent political and social institutions as specified by the three requirements earlier surveyed.[52]

I shall not attempt to discuss here how this might be done, as the problem of giving economic and technological aid so that it makes a sustained contribution is highly complicated and varies from country to country. Moreover the problem is often not the lack of natural resources. Many societies with unfavorable conditions don't lack for resources. Well-ordered societies can get on with very little; their wealth lies elsewhere: in their political and cultural traditions, in their human capital and knowledge, and in their capacity for political and economic organization. Rather, the problem is commonly the nature of the public political culture and the religious and philosophical traditions that underlie its institutions. The great social evils in poorer societies are likely to be oppressive government and corrupt elites; the subjection of women abetted by unreasonable religion, with the resulting overpopulation relative to what the economy of the society can decently sustain. Perhaps there is no society anywhere in the world whose people, were they reasonably and rationally governed, and their numbers sensibly adjusted to their economy and resources, could not have a decent and worthwhile life.

These general remarks indicate what is so often the source of the problem: the public political culture and its roots in the background social structure. The obligation of wealthier societies to assist in trying to rectify matters is in no way diminished, only made more difficult. Here, too, in ways I need not describe, an emphasis on human rights may work, when backed by other kinds of assistance, to moderate, albeit slowly, oppressive government, the corruption of elites, and the subjection of women.[53]

## 8. CONCLUDING REFLECTIONS

I have not said much about what might be called the philosophical basis of human rights. This is because, despite their name, human rights are a special class of rights explained by their role in a liberal conception of the law of peoples acceptable to both well-ordered liberal and hierarchical societies. I have therefore sketched how such a law of peoples might be worked out on the basis of a liberal conception of justice.[54] Within this framework I have indicated how respect for human rights is one of the conditions imposed on any political regime to be admissible as a member in good standing into a just political society of peoples. Once we understand this, and once we understand how a reasonable law of peoples is developed out of the liberal conception of justice and how this conception can be universal in its reach, it is perfectly clear why those rights hold across cultural and economic boundaries, as well as the boundaries between nation states, or other political units. With our two other conditions, these rights determine the limits of toleration in a reasonable society of peoples.

About these limits, the following observation: If we start with a well-ordered liberal society that realizes an egalitarian conception of justice such as justice as fairness,[55] the members of that society will nevertheless accept into the society of peoples other liberal societies whose institutions are considerably less egalitarian. This is implicit in our beginning with liberal conceptions more general than justice as fairness as defined in section 3. But citizens in a well-ordered egalitarian society will still view the domestic regimes of those societies as less congenial to them than the regime of their own society.

This illustrates what happens whenever the scope of toleration is extended: The criteria of reasonableness are relaxed.[56] In the case we have considered, we seek to include other than liberal societies as members in good standing of a reasonable society of peoples. Hence when we move to these societies, their domestic regimes are less, often much less, congenial to us. This poses the problem of the limits of toleration. Where are these limits to be drawn? Clearly, tyrannical and dictatorial regimes must be outlawed, and also, for basic liberal reasons, expansionist states like those of the Wars of Religion. The three necessary conditions for a well-ordered regime—that it respect the principles of peace and not be expansionist, that its system of law meet the essentials of legitimacy in the eyes of its own people, and that it honor basic human rights—are proposed as an answer as to where those limits lie. These conditions indicate the bedrock beyond which we cannot go.

We have discussed how far many societies of the world have always been, and are today, from meeting these three conditions for being a member in good standing of a reasonable society of peoples. The law of peoples provides the basis for judging the conduct of any existing regime, liberal as well as nonliberal. And since our account of the law of peoples was developed out of a liberal conception of justice, we must address the question whether the liberal law of peoples is ethnocentric and merely Western.

To address this question, recall that in working out the law of peoples we assumed that liberal societies conduct themselves toward other societies from the point of view of their own liberal political conception. Regarding this conception as sound, and as meeting all the criteria they are now able to apply, how else are they to proceed? To the objection that to proceed thus is ethnocentric or merely Western, the reply is: no, not necessarily. Whether it is so turns on the content of the political conception that liberal societies embrace once it is worked up to provide at least an outline of the law of peoples.

Looking at the outline of that law, we should note the difference between it and the law of peoples as it might be understood by religious and expansionist states that reject the liberal conception. The liberal conception asks of other societies only what they can reasonably grant without submitting to a position of inferiority, much less to domination. It is crucial that a liberal conception of the law of peoples not ask well-ordered hierarchical societies to abandon their religious institutions and adopt liberal ones. True, in our sketch we supposed that traditional societies would affirm the law of peoples that would hold among just liberal societies. That law is therefore universal in its reach: It asks of other societies only what they can accept once they are prepared to stand in a relation of equality with all other societies and once their regimes accept the criterion of legitimacy in the eyes of their own people. In what other relations can a society and its regime reasonably expect to stand?

Moreover, the liberal law of peoples does not justify economic sanctions or military pressure on well-ordered hierarchical societies to change their ways, provided they respect the rules of peace and their political institutions satisfy the essential conditions we have reviewed. If, however, these conditions are violated, external pressure of one kind or another may be justified depending on the severity and the circumstances of the case. A concern for human rights should be a fixed part of the foreign policy of liberal and hierarchical societies.

Looking back at our discussion, let's recall that besides sketching how the law of peoples might be developed from liberal conceptions of right and justice, a further aim was to set out the bearing of political liberalism for a wider world society once a liberal political conception of justice is extended to the law of peoples. In particular, we asked: What form does the toleration of nonliberal societies take in this case? Although tyrannical and dictatorial regimes cannot be accepted as members in good standing of a reasonable society of peoples, not all regimes can reasonably be required to be liberal. If so, the law of peoples would not express liberalism's own principle of toleration for other reasonable ways of ordering society. A liberal society must respect other societies organized by comprehensive doctrines, provided their political and social institutions meet certain conditions that lead the society to adhere to a reasonable law of peoples.

I did not try to present an argument to this conclusion. I took it as clear that if other nonliberal societies honored certain conditions, such as the three requirements discussed in section 4, they would be accepted by liberal societies as members in good standing of a society of peoples. There would be no political case to attack these nonliberal societies militarily, or to bring economic or other sanctions against them to revise their institutions. Critical commentary in liberal societies would be fully consistent with the civic liberties and integrity of those societies.

What conception of toleration of other societies does the law of peoples express? How is it connected with political liberalism? If it should be asked whether liberal societies are, morally speaking, better than hierarchical societies, and therefore whether the world would be a better place if all societies were liberal, those holding a comprehensive liberal view could think it would be. But that opinion would not support a claim to rid the world of nonliberal regimes. It could have no operative force in what, as a matter of right, they could do politically. The situation is parallel to the toleration of other conceptions of the good in the domestic case. Someone holding a comprehensive liberal view can say that their society would be a better place if every one held such a view. They might be wrong in this judgment even by their own lights, as other doctrines may play a moderating and balancing role given the larger background of belief and conviction, and give society's culture a certain depth and richness. The point is that to affirm the superiority of a particular comprehensive view is fully compatible with affirming a political conception of justice that does not impose it, and thus with political liberalism itself.

Political liberalism holds that comprehensive doctrines have but a restricted place in liberal democratic politics in this sense: Fundamental constitutional questions and matters concerning basic rights and liberties are to be settled by a public political conception of justice, exemplified by the liberal political conceptions, and not by those wider doctrines. For given the pluralism of democratic societies—a pluralism best seen as the outcome of the exercise of human reason under free institutions, and which can only be undone by the oppressive use of state power—affirming such a public conception and the basic political institutions that realize it is the most reasonable basis of social unity available to us.

The law of peoples, as I have sketched it, is simply the extension of these same ideas to the political society of well-ordered peoples. That law, which settles fundamental constitutional questions and matters of basic justice as they arise for the society of peoples, must also be based on a public political conception of justice and not on a comprehensive religious, philosophical, or moral doctrine. I have sketched the content of such a political conception and tried to explain how it could be endorsed by well-ordered societies, both liberal and hierarchical. Except as a basis of a modus vivendi, expansionist societies of whatever kind could not endorse it; but in principle there is no peaceful solution in their case except the domination of one side or the peace of exhaustion.

## NOTES

I am indebted to many people for helping me with this essay. I have indicated specific debts in notes to the text. More general debts I should like to acknowledge are to Ronald Dworkin and Thomas Nagel for discussions about my earlier attempts to consider the law of peoples at their seminars at New York University in the fall of 1990 and 1991; to T. M. Scanlon and Joshua Cohen for valuable criticism and comments; to Michael Doyle and Philip Soper for instructive correspondence; and as always to Burton Dreben. I am especially indebted to Erin Kelly, who has read all the drafts of this essay and proposed many improvements, most of which I have adopted. Her criticisms and suggestions have been essential in my getting right, as I hope, the line of reasoning in section 4.

1. The name "law of peoples" derives from the traditional *ius gentium*, and the way I use it is closest to its meaning in the phrase "ius gentium intra se" (laws of peoples among themselves). In this meaning it refers to what the laws of all peoples had in common. See R. J. Vincent, *Human Rights and International Relations* (Cambridge, England: Cambridge University Press, 1986), p. 27. Taking these laws to be a core paired with principles of justice applying to the laws of peoples everywhere gives a meaning related to my use of the law of peoples.

2. A political conception of justice has the following three features: (1) it is framed to apply to basic political, economic, and social institutions; in the case of domestic society, to its basic structure, in the present case to the law and practices of the society of political peoples; (2) it is presented independently

of any particular comprehensive religious, philosophical, or moral doctrine, and though it may be derived from or related to several such doctrines, it is not worked out in that way; (3) its content is expressed in terms of certain fundamental ideas seen as implicit in the public political culture of a liberal society. See my *Political Liberalism* (New York: Columbia University Press, 1993), 11–15.

3. In this and the next two paragraphs I draw on the first section of my "The Basic Structure as Subject" (1978), reprinted in *Political Liberalism*.

4. For a detailed example of how this is done in the case of the four-stage sequence of original position, constitutional convention, the legislature, and the courts, see *A Theory of Justice* (Cambridge, MA: Harvard University Press, 1971), pp. 195–201. A briefer statement is found in my "The Basic Liberties and Their Priority" (1982), reprinted in *Political Liberalism*.

5. By peoples I mean persons and their dependents seen as a corporate body and as organized by their political institutions, which establish the powers of government. In democratic societies persons will be citizens, while in hierarchical and other societies they will be members.

6. See *A Theory of Justice*, 378ff., where this process is very briefly described.

7. It would be unfair to Clausewitz not to add that for him the state's interests can include regulative moral aims of whatever kind, and thus the aims of war may be to defend democratic societies against tyrannical regimes, somewhat as in World War II. For him the aims of politics are not part of the theory of war, although they are ever present and may properly affect the conduct of war. On this, see the instructive remarks of Peter Paret, "Clausewitz," in *The Makers of Modern Strategy: From Machiavelli to the Nuclear Age*, ed. Peter Paret (Princeton, NJ: Princeton University Press, 1986), pp. 209–13. The view in my text characterizes the *raison d'état* as pursued by Frederick the Great. Or so Gerhard Ritter says in *Frederick the Great*, trans. Peter Paret (Berkeley: University of California Press, 1968). See chapter 10, and the statement on p. 197.

8. These powers Charles Beitz characterizes as belonging to what he calls the morality of states in part II of his *Political Theory and International Relations* (Princeton, NJ: Princeton University Press, 1979). They depend, he argues, on a mistaken analogy between individuals and states.

9. Stanley Hoffman, *Janus and Minerva: Essays in the Theory and Practice of International Politics* (Boulder, CO, and London: Westview Press, 1987), p. 374.

10. Note: "You and I" are "here and now" citizens of the same liberal democratic society and we are working out the liberal conception of justice in question.

11. In this case "you and I" are citizens of liberal democratic societies but not of the same one.

12. Kant says at Ak: VIII:367: "The idea of international law presupposes the separate existence of independent neighboring states. Although this con-

dition is itself a state of war (unless federative union prevents the outbreak of hostilities), this is rationally preferable to the amalgamation of states under one superior power, as this would end in one universal monarchy, and laws always lose in vigor what government gains in extent; hence a condition of soulless despotism falls into anarchy after stifling seeds of good." This attitude to universal monarchy was shared by other writers of the eighteenth century. See, for example, Hume's "Of the Balance of Power" (1752) in *Essays: Moral, Political, and Literary*, ed. Eugene F. Miller (Indianapolis: Liberty Fund, 1985), pp. 332–41. F. H. Hinsley, *Power and the Pursuit of Peace: Theory and Practice in the History of Relations between States* (Cambridge, England: Cambridge University Press, 1967), 162ff., also mentions Montesquieu, Voltaire, and Gibbon. Hinsley also has an instructive discussion of Kant's ideas in chapter 4. See also Patrick Riley, *Kant's Political Philosophy* (Totowa, NJ: Rowman & Littlefield, 1983), chapters 5 and 6. Thomas Nagel, in his *Equality and Partiality* (New York: Oxford University Press, 1991), 169ff., 174, gives strong reasons supporting the same conclusion.

13. See Terry Nardin, *Law, Morality, and the Relations of States* (Princeton, NJ: Princeton University Press, 1983), 269ff., who stresses this point.

14. A clear example regarding secession is whether the South had a right to secede from 1860 to 1861. By this test it had no such right, since it seceded to perpetuate its domestic institution of slavery. This is as severe a violation of human rights as any, and it extended to nearly half the population.

15. By basic needs I mean roughly those that must be met if citizens are to be in a position to take advantage of the rights, liberties, and opportunities of their society. They include economic means as well as institutional rights and freedoms.

16. From the fact that boundaries are historically arbitrary it does not follow that their role in the law of peoples cannot be justified. To wit: That the boundaries between the several states of the United States are historically arbitrary does not argue to the elimination of our federal system, one way or the other. To fix on their arbitrariness is to fix on the wrong thing. The right question concerns the political values served by the several states in a federal system as compared with the values served by a central system. The answer is given by states' function and role: by the political values they serve as subunits, and whether their boundaries can be, or need to be, redrawn, and much else.

17. This remark implies that a people has at least a qualified right to limit immigration. I leave aside here what these qualifications might be.

18. See my "The Domain of the Political and Overlapping Consensus," *New York University Law Review* 64 (1989): 245, section VII.

19. See Jack S. Levy, "Domestic Politics and War," an essay in *The Origin and Prevention of Major Wars*, ed. Robert I. Rotberg and Theodore K. Rabb (Cambridge England: Cambridge University Press, 1989), p. 87. Levy refers to

several historical studies that have confirmed the finding of Melvin Small and J. David Singer in "The War-Proneness of Democratic Regimes, 1816–1965," *Jerusalem Journal of International Relations* vol. 1 (1976): 50–69, mentioned in note 21 below.

20. See Michael W. Doyle's two-part article, "Kant, Liberal Legacies, and Foreign Affairs," *Philosophy and Public Affairs* 12 (3 & 4) (summer and autumn 1983): 205–35, 323–53. [Part I is reprinted in *Global Ethics: Seminal Essays*, 73–106.] A survey of the evidence is in the first part, pp. 206–32 [*GESE* 75–96]. Doyle says: "These conventions [those based on the international implications of liberal principles and institutions] of mutual respect have formed a cooperative foundation for relations among liberal democracies of a remarkably effective kind. *Even though liberal states have become involved in numerous wars with nonliberal states, constitutionally secure liberal states have yet to engage in war with one another.* [Italicized in the original.] No one should argue that such wars are impossible; but preliminary evidence does appear to indicate ... a significant predisposition against warfare between liberal states" (p. 213) [*GESE* 80–81].

21. See Levy, "Domestic Politics and War," p. 88. In these studies most definitions of democracy are comparable to that of Small and Singer as listed by Levy in a footnote: (1) regular elections and the participation of opposition parties, (2) at least 10 percent of the adult population being able to vote for (3) a parliament that either controlled or shared parity with the executive branch (ibid., p. 88). Our definition of a liberal democratic regime goes well beyond this definition.

22. On this see Alan Gilbert, "Power-Rivalry Motivated Democracy," *Political Theory* 20 (1992): 681, and esp. 684ff.

23. Here I draw upon Philip Soper's *A Theory of Law* (Cambridge, MA: Harvard University Press, 1984), esp. pp. 125–47. Soper holds that a system of law, as distinct from a system of mere commands coercively enforced, must be such as to give rise, as I have indicated, to moral duties and obligations on all members of society, and judges and other officials must sincerely and reasonably believe that the law is guided by a common good conception of justice. The content of a common good conception of justice is such as to impose morally binding obligations on all members of society. I mention some of the details of Soper's view here, but I do so rather freely and not with the intent of explaining his thought. As the text shows, my aim is to indicate a conception of justice that, while not a liberal conception, still has features that give to societies regulated accordingly the moral standing required to be members of a political society adhering to a reasonable law of peoples. However, we must be careful in understanding this second requirement. For Soper it is part of the definition of a system of law. It is a requirement that a scheme of rules must satisfy to be a system of law properly thus called. See *A Theory of Law*, chapter 4, pp. 91–100. I don't follow Soper in this respect; nor do I reject this

idea either, as Soper makes a strong case for it. Rather, it is put aside and the requirement is adopted as a substantive moral principle explicable as part of the law of peoples worked up from a liberal conception of justice. The reason for doing this is to avoid the long debated jurisprudential problem of the definition of law. Also, I don't want to have to argue that the antebellum South, say, didn't have a system of law. I am indebted to Samuel Freeman for valuable discussion of these points.

24. Soper, *A Theory of Law*, pp. 112, 118.

25. Ibid., p. 141.

26. Henry Shue, *Basic Rights: Subsistence, Affluence, and U.S. Foreign Policy* (Princeton, NJ: Princeton University Press, 1980) [chapters 1 and 2 reprinted herein 83–144]. Shue, p. 23 [herein p. 93], and Vincent, *Human Rights and International Relations*, interpret subsistence as including certain minimum economic security, and both hold that subsistence rights are basic. One must agree with this since the reasonable and rational exercise of all liberties, of whatever kind, as well as the intelligent use of property, always implies having certain general all-purpose economic means.

27. On the rules of natural justice, see H. L. A. Hart, *The Concept of Law* (Oxford: Clarendon Press, 1961), p. 156ff.

28. One might raise the question here as to why religious or philosophical doctrines that deny full and equal liberty of conscience are not unreasonable. I did not say, however, that they are reasonable, but rather that they are not unreasonable. One should allow, I think, a space between the reasonable or the fully reasonable, which requires full and equal liberty of conscience, and the unreasonable, which denies it entirely. Traditional doctrines that allow a measure of liberty of conscience but do not allow it fully are views that lie in that space and are not unreasonable. On this see my *Political Liberalism*, Lecture II, section 3.

29. On the importance of this, see Judith Shklar's *Ordinary Vices* (Cambridge, MA: Harvard University Press, 1984), in which she presents what she calls the "liberalism of fear." See especially the introduction and chapters 1 and 6. She once called this kind of liberalism that of "permanent minorities." See her *Legalism: Law, Morals, and Political Trials* (Cambridge, MA: Harvard University Press, 1963), p. 224.

30. Subject to certain qualifications, liberal societies must also allow for this right.

31. These are not political conceptions of justice in my sense; see note 2 above.

32. Here "you and I" are members of hierarchical societies but again not the same one.

33. Here I am indebted to Lea Brilmayer of New York University for pointing out to me that in my sketch of the law of peoples (October 1990), I failed to state these conditions satisfactorily.

34. Brian Barry, in his splendid *Theories of Justice* (Berkeley: University of California Press, 1989), discusses the merits of doing this. See pp. 183–89ff.

Along the way he raises serious objections to what he takes to be my view of the principles of distributive justice for the law of peoples. I do not discuss these important criticisms here, but I do mention questions related to them hereafter.

35. We can go on to third and later stages once we think of groups of societies joining together into regional associations or federations of some kind, such as the European Community, or a commonwealth of the republics in the former Soviet Union. It is natural to envisage future world society as in good part comprised of such federations together with certain institutions, such as the United Nations, capable of speaking for all the societies of the world.

36. Justice as fairness is such an idea. For our purposes other more general liberal ideas of justice fit the same description. Their lacking the three egalitarian elements of justice as fairness noted in the first paragraph of section 3 does not affect this.

37. There are, however, some differences. The three requirements of legitimacy discussed in this section are to be seen as necessary conditions for a society to be a member in good standing of a reasonable society of peoples; and many religious and philosophical doctrines with their different conceptions of justice may lead to institutions satisfying these conditions. In specifying a reasonable law of peoples, societies with such institutions are viewed as well-ordered. However, those requirements do not specify a political conception of justice in my sense (see note 2 above). For one thing, I suppose that a society's common good conception of justice is understood as part of its comprehensive religious or philosophical doctrine. Nor have I suggested that such a conception of justice is constructivist, and I assume it is not. Whether the three requirements for legitimacy can themselves be constructed within a social contract view is another question. I leave it open here. The point, though, is that none of these differences affect the claim in the text that in both domains the ideals and principles of justice are justified in the same way.

38. Here I draw upon T. M. Scanlon's instructive discussion in "Human Rights as a Neutral Concern," in *Human Rights and U.S. Foreign Policy*, ed. Peter G. Brown and Douglas MacLean (Lexington, MA: Lexington Books, 1979).

39. Scanlon emphasizes this point in "Human Rights," pp. 83, 89–92. It is relevant when we note later in sections 6 and 7 that support for human rights should be part of the foreign policy of well-ordered societies.

40. See R. J. Vincent, "The Idea of Rights in International Ethics," in *Traditions of International Ethics*, ed. Terry Nardin and David Mapel (Cambridge, England: Cambridge University Press, 1992), pp. 262–65.

41. Hegel, *The Philosophy of Right* (1821), section 308.

42. The meaning of *rational* here is closer to *reasonable* than to *rational* as I have used these terms. The German is *vernünftig*, and this has the full force

of reason in the German philosophical tradition. It is far from the economist's meaning of *rational*, given by *zweckmässig* or *rationnell*.

43. There is a complication about Hegel's view in that some rights are indeed rights of individuals. For him the rights to life, security, and (personal) property are grounded in personhood; and liberty of conscience follows from being a moral subject with the freedom of subjectivity. I am indebted to Frederick Neuhouser for discussing these points with me.

44. See Keith Thomas, *Man and the Natural World: A History of the Modern Sensibility* (New York: Pantheon Books, 1983) for an account of the historical change in attitudes toward animals and nature.

45. See Judith Shklar's illuminating discussion of these in her *American Citizenship: The Quest for Inclusion* (Cambridge, MA: Harvard University Press, 1991), with her emphasis on the historical significance of slavery.

46. This fact about human rights can be clarified by distinguishing among the rights that have been listed as human rights in various international declarations. Consider the Universal Declaration of Human Rights of 1948. First, there are human rights proper, illustrated by Article 3: "Everyone has a right to life, liberty and security of person"; and by Article 5: "No one shall be subjected to torture or to cruel, inhuman or degrading treatment or punishment." Articles 3 to 18 may fall under this heading of human rights proper, pending certain questions of interpretation. Then there are human rights that are obvious implications of these rights. These are the extreme cases described by the special conventions on genocide (1948) and on apartheid (1973). These two classes comprise the human rights.

Of the other declarations, some seem more aptly described as stating liberal aspirations, such as Article 1 of the Universal Declaration of Human Rights of 1948: "All human beings are born free and equal in dignity and rights. They are endowed with reason and conscience and should act towards one another in a spirit of brotherhood." Others appear to presuppose specific kinds of institutions, such as the right to social security, in Article 22, and the right to equal pay for equal work, in Article 23.

47. Nardin, *Law, Morality, and the Relations of States*, p. 240, citing David Luban's "The Romance of the Nation-State," *Philosophy and Public Affairs* 9 (4) (summer 1980): 392–97, 396.

48. On this, see Ludwig Dehio, *The Precarious Balance: Four Centuries of the European Power Struggle* (New York: Alfred A. Knopf, 1962).

49. Robert Gilpin, "The Theory of Hegemonic War," in *The Origin and Prevention of Major Wars*, ed. Rotberg and Rabb, pp. 15–38.

50. See Kant, *Rechtslehre*, sections 44 and 61. [*The Theory of Right*, part 1 of *The Metaphysics of Morals*, in *Kant: Political Writings*, trans. H. B. Nisbet, ed. Hans Reiss (Cambridge, 1970, 1991), sections 44 and 61.]

51. Beitz, *Political Theory and International Relations*; part III [based on his essay "Justice and International Relations," first published in *Philosophy*

*and Public Affairs* 4: 4 (summer 1975): 360–89, reprinted herein 21–48] gives a sustained discussion. This principle is defined in my *A Theory of Justice*, section 13. I do not review the principle here because, as my text says, I believe all liberal distributive principles are unsuitable for the case we are considering.

52. With much of Beitz's view the law of peoples agrees. Thus it seems that he thinks of the difference principle between societies as "a resource redistribution principle that would give each society a fair chance to develop just political institutions and an economy capable of satisfying its members' basic needs" (141 [cf. herein 30]). And "it [the resource distribution principle] provides assurance to persons in resource-poor societies that their adverse fate will not prevent them from realizing economic conditions sufficient to support just social institutions and to protect human rights" (142 [cf. herein 31]). (Beitz, *Political Theory and International Relations*). The law of peoples accepts Beitz's goals for just institutions, securing human rights, and meeting basic needs. But, as I suggest in the next paragraph, persons' adverse fate is more often to be born into a distorted and corrupt political culture than into a country lacking resources. The only principle that does away with that misfortune is to make the political traditions and culture of all peoples reasonable and able to sustain just political and social institutions that secure human rights. It is this principle that gives rise to the duties and obligations of assistance. We do not need a liberal principle of distributive justice for this purpose.

53. That the insistence on human rights may help here is suggested by Amartya Sen's work on famines. He has shown in *Poverty and Famines: An Essay on Entitlement and Deprivation* (Oxford: Clarendon Press, 1981), by an empirical study of four well-known historical cases (Bengal, 1943; Ethiopia, 1972–74; Sahel, 1972–73; and Bangladesh, 1974), that food decline need not be the main cause of famine, or even a cause, nor even present. But sometimes it can be an important cause of famine, for example, in Ireland in the 1840s and in China from 1959 to 1961. In the cases Sen studies, while a drop in food production may have been present, it was not great enough to lead to famine given a decent government that cares for the well-being of all of its people and has in place a reasonable scheme of backup entitlements provided through public institutions. For Sen "famines are economic disasters, not just food crises" (162). In the well-known historical cases they revealed faults of the political and social structure and its failure to institute appropriate policies to remedy the effects of shortfalls in food production. After all, there would be massive starvation in any modern Western democracy were there not schemes in place to remedy the losses in income of the unemployed. Since a government's allowing people to starve when this is preventable is a violation of their human rights, and if well-ordered regimes as we have described them will not allow this to happen, then insisting on human rights is exerting pressure in the direction of decent governments and a decent society of peoples. Sen's book with Jean Drèze, *Hunger and Public Action* (Oxford: Clarendon Press, 1989) confirms

these points and stresses the success of democratic regimes in coping with these problems. See their summary statement in chapter 13: 257–79. See also the important work of Partha Dasgupta, *An Inquiry into Well-Being and Destitution* (Oxford: Clarendon Press, 1993), chapters 1–2, 5, and passim.

54. It might be asked why the law of peoples as here constructed is said to be liberal when it is also accepted by well-ordered hierarchical societies. I have called it liberal because the law of peoples is presented as an extension from liberal conceptions of domestic justice. I do not mean to deny, however, that a well-ordered hierarchical society may have conceptions of justice that can be extended to the law of peoples and that its content would be the same as that of liberal conceptions. For the present I leave this question open. I would hope that there are such conceptions in all well-ordered hierarchical societies, as this would widen and strengthen the support for the law of peoples.

55. Three egalitarian elements are the fair value of equal political rights and liberties, fair equality of opportunity, and the difference principle, all to be understood as specified in my *A Theory of Justice*.

56. In the domestic case we are led in parallel fashion to count many comprehensive doctrines reasonable that we would not, in our own case, regard as worthy of serious consideration. See my *Political Liberalism*, Lecture II, section 3.1 and the footnote.

# 16. THOMAS POGGE

This response to John Rawls's 1993 Oxford Amnesty Lecture, which presented the first version of his proposed "law of peoples" (then still without a "duty of assistance"), focuses on Rawls's rejection of any egalitarian distributive principle applicable to global institutional arrangements. Pogge offers both an internal and an external critique of the original-position argument. The internal critique accepts that the parties in the global original position are motivated as Rawls stipulates: by the goal that the people each represents should be a stable well-ordered society. This goal would incline them, Pogge argues, to favor global institutional arrangements that mitigate rather than aggravate international economic inequalities. The reason is that large international inequalities render poor societies vulnerable to corruption from abroad that endangers the stability of their domestic order. The external critique questions why the parties in the global original position should lack any interest in the relative or absolute economic well-being of the members of the peoples they represent. If they had even a slight such interest, they would again favor global institutional arrangements that mitigate international economic inequalities. Pogge goes on to develop a concrete global institutional reform idea—broadly supportable with Rawlsian, ecological, and Lockean considerations—that would help mitigate international economic inequalities. This reform centers around a Global Resources Dividend, or GRD. Humankind at large is to be viewed as owning a minority stake in all planetary resources (including air, water, and soil used for the discharging of pollutants). As with preferred stock, this stake does not entitle everyone to participate in deciding how resources are to be used; this authority is to remain with the society in whose territory resources are located. But the stake does entitle all to a share of the economic benefits of resource utilization. Because the global poor are otherwise excluded from such a share, the funds raised through the GRD are to be spent on their emancipation.

# An Egalitarian Law of Peoples

*First published in* Philosophy and Public Affairs *23: 3 (summer 1994): 195–224.*

In 1993, expanding on a brief sketch composed more than twenty years earlier, John Rawls offered a more detailed extension of his theory of justice to the international domain.[1] Like that first sketch, the "law of peoples" he now proposed had no egalitarian distributive component. In my own extension of Rawls's framework, I had argued that a criterion of global justice must be sensitive to international social and economic inequalities.[2] Here I take another look at this issue in light of Rawls's new and more elaborate deliberations about it.

Rawls's conception of domestic justice has three components that, in his view (LP 51 [herein 428]), qualify it for the predicate "egalitarian":

(1) His first principle of justice requires that institutions maintain the fair value of the political liberties, so that persons similarly motivated and endowed have, irrespective of their economic and social class, roughly equal chances to gain political office and to influence the political decisions that shape their lives (cf. *TJ* 225).

(2) His second principle of justice requires that institutions maintain fair equality of opportunity, so that equally talented and motivated persons have roughly equal chances to obtain a good education and professional position irrespective of their initial social class (cf. *TJ* 73, 301).

(3) His second principle also requires that, insofar as they generate social or economic inequalities, social institutions must be designed to the maximum benefit of those at the bottom of these inequalities (the difference principle—cf. *TJ* 76f).

Each of these egalitarian components furnishes separate grounds on which the current basic structure of the United States can be criticized for producing excessive inequalities.

Analogous points can be made about our current world order:

(1) It fails to give members of different peoples roughly equal chances to influence the transnational political decisions that shape their lives.

(2) It fails to give equally talented and motivated persons roughly equal chances to obtain a good education and professional position irrespective of the society into which they were born.

(3) It also generates international social and economic inequalities that are not to the maximum benefit of the world's worst-off persons.

These observations are certainly true. The question is: Do they show faults in the existing global order?

Rawls's law of peoples contains no egalitarian distributive principle of any sort; and he seems then to be committed to the view that none of the three analogous criticisms is valid, even though he explicitly attacks only the analogue to his third egalitarian concern: the proposal of a global difference principle. My own view still is that all three of the analogous egalitarian concerns are valid in a world characterized by the significant political and economic interdependencies that exist today and will in all likelihood persist into the indefinite future. Here I will, however, defend against Rawls a much weaker claim: A plausible conception of global justice must be sensitive to international social and economic inequalities.

My focus on this one disagreement should not obscure the fact that I agree with much in this Amnesty Lecture—both substantively and methodologically. Substantively, I agree with his view that a just world order can contain societies governed by a conception of justice that differs from his own political liberalism by being nonpolitical, nonliberal, or both (LP 42f, 46 [herein 421f, 424]); and that a main demand to make upon how their institutions work domestically is that they secure human rights (LP 61–63, 68–71 [herein 435–38, 441–43]). And I agree methodologically as well that it is too early to tell how his idea of the original position should best be adapted to the complexities of our interdependent world (LP 50, 65f [herein 427, 439]). This original position—initially devised to deal with a closed, self-contained society (*TJ* 4, 8, 457)—is an imagined deliberative forum in which prospective citizens are represented by "the parties." All these individual representatives are to do the best they can for their clients, whose distinguishing features are, however, concealed by a "veil of ignorance." The parties are to seek agreement on a public criterion of justice without knowing the particular creeds, values, tastes, desires, and endowments of those they represent or even the natural and historical context of their clients' society. This idea might be extended to the world at large in various ways. One main strategy is Rawls's: Apply the two principles to the basic structure of a national society, and then reconvene the parties for a second session to deal with the relations among such societies. Another main strategy is to start with a global original position that deals with the world at large, even asking, as Rawls puts it (somewhat incredulously?), "whether, and in what form, there should be states, or peoples, at all" (LP 50 [herein 427]). Variants of this second strategy have been entertained by David Richards, Thomas Scanlon, Brian Barry, Charles Beitz, and myself. I can leave aside this second strategy here, because international egalitarian concerns can easily be accommodated within the first strategy; as we shall see, Rawls simply decides against doing so.

My focus on one disagreement should also not obscure the fact that there are others. Two of these are relevant here. First, I do not believe that the notion of "a people" is clear enough and significant enough in the human world to play the conceptual role and to have the moral significance that Rawls assigns to it. In many parts of the globe, official borders do not correlate with the main characteristics that are normally held to identify a people or a nation—such as a common ethnicity, language, culture, history, tradition. Moreover, whether some group does or does not constitute a people would seem, in important ways, to be a matter of more-or-less rather than either-or. I have suggested that these complexities might be better accommodated by a multilayered institutional scheme in which the powers of sovereignty are vertically dispersed rather than heavily concentrated on the single level of states [herein 355-90].[3] But I will set aside this topic as well. Let us assume that there really is a clear-cut distinction between peoples and other kinds of groupings, that every person belongs to exactly one people, and that each national territory really does, nearly enough, contain all and only the members of a single people. In this highly idealized case, egalitarian concerns would seem to be least pressing. Hence, if I can make them plausible for this case, they should be plausible for more realistic scenarios as well.

Second, I do not believe that Rawls has an adequate response to the historical arbitrariness of national borders—to the fact that most borders have come about through violence and coercion. He writes:

> From the fact that boundaries are historically arbitrary it does not follow that their role in the law of peoples cannot be justified. To wit: that the boundaries between the several states of the United States are historically arbitrary does not argue to the elimination of our federal system, one way or the other. To fix on their arbitrariness is to fix on the wrong thing. The right question concerns the political values served by the several states in a federal system as compared with the values served by a central system. The answer is given by states' function and role: by the political values they serve as subunits, and whether their boundaries can be, or need to be, redrawn, and much else (LP 223n16 [herein 454n16]).

Let us suppose that the mere fact of historical arbitrariness is indeed no argument against the status quo, that a forward-looking justification suffices. What such a justification should be able to justify is threefold: that there should be boundaries at all, that they should be where they are now, and that they should have the institutional significance they currently have. I am not interested in the first two issues: Let there be national borders and let them be just where they are today. The issue I am raising is the third: How can Rawls justify the enormous distributional significance national borders now have, and in a Rawlsian ideal world would continue to have, for determining the life prospects of persons born into different states? How can he justify that boundaries are, and would continue to be, associated with ownership of, full control over, and exclusive entitlement to all benefits from, land, natural resources, and capital stock? It is revealing that, in the midst of discussing national borders, Rawls switches to considering state borders within the US, which have virtually no distributional significance. It does not really matter whether one is born in Kansas or in Iowa, and so there is not much to justify, as it were. But it matters a great deal whether one is born a Mexican or a US citizen, and so we do need to justify to a Mexican why we should be entitled to life prospects that are so much superior to hers merely because we were born on the other side of some line—a difference that, on the face of it, is no less morally arbitrary than differences in sex, in skin color, or in the affluence of one's parents. Justifying this is more difficult when national borders are historically arbitrary or, to put it more descriptively, when the present distribution of national territories is indelibly tainted with past unjust conquest, genocide, colonialism, and enslavement. But let me set aside this difficulty as well and focus on moral rather than historical arbitrariness. Let us assume that peoples have come to be matched up with territories in the morally most benign way one can conceive.

My defense, against Rawls, of an egalitarian law of peoples labors then under a self-imposed triple handicap: I accept Rawls's stipulation that global justice is addressed in a second session of the original position, featuring representatives of peoples who take the nation-state system as a given; I accept Rawls's fantasy that the world's population neatly divides into peoples cleanly separated by national borders; and I waive any support my egalitarian view could draw from the role that massive past crimes have played in the emergence of current national borders. I make these concessions strictly for the sake of the argument of Sections I-V and otherwise stand by my earlier contrary positions.

## I. A GLOBAL RESOURCES DIVIDEND

Some of the arguments Rawls advances against incorporating an egalitarian component into the law of peoples are pragmatic, mainly having to do with inadequate administrative capabilities and the dangers of a world government. To make it easier for you to assess these worries, I want to put before you a reasonably clear and specific institutional proposal and thereby give our central disagreement a concrete institutional form. I lack the space, however, to develop and defend a complete criterion of global justice and to show what specific institutional arrangements would be favored by this criterion. I will therefore employ a shortcut. I will make an institutional proposal that virtually any plausible egalitarian conception of global justice would judge to be at least a step in the right direction. Rawls's law of peoples, by contrast, would not call for such a step. It would permit the step among consenting peoples, but would not view it as required or suggested by justice.

When sketching how a property-owning democracy might satisfy the difference principle, Rawls entertains a proportional income or consumption tax with a fixed exemption. The tax rate and exempt amount are to be set so as maximally to benefit the lowest economic position in the present and future generations. Focusing on one such (as he says) instrument "frees us from having to consider the difference principle on every question of policy."[4]

I have proposed a similar instrument to control international inequality: a global resources dividend, or GRD.[5] The basic idea is that, while each people owns and fully controls all resources within its national territory,[6] it must pay a dividend on any resources it chooses to extract. The Saudi people, for example, would not be required to extract crude oil or to allow others to do so. But if they chose to do so nonetheless, they would be required to pay a proportional dividend on any crude extracted, whether it be for their own use or for sale abroad. This idea could be extended, along the same lines, to reusable resources: to land used in agriculture and ranching, for example, and, especially, to air and water used for the discharging of pollutants.

The burdens of the GRD would not be borne by the owners of resources alone. The dividend would lead to higher prices for crude oil, minerals, and so forth. Therefore, some of the GRD on oil would ultimately fall upon the Japanese (who have no oil of their own, but import a good bit), even while the dividend would be actually paid by the peoples who own oil reserves and choose to extract them. This point significantly mitigates the concern that the GRD proposal might be arbitrarily biased against some rich peoples, the resource-rich, and in favor of others. This concern is further mitigated by the GRD's pollution component.

The GRD is then a charge on consumption. But it affects different kinds of consumption differentially. The cost of gasoline will contain a much higher GRD portion than the cost of a ticket to an art museum. The GRD falls on goods and services roughly in proportion to their resource content: in proportion to how much value each takes from our planet. It can therefore be motivated not only forward-lookingly, in consequentialist and contractualist terms, but also backward-lookingly: as a proviso on unilateral appropriation, which requires compensation to those excluded thereby. Nations (or persons) may appropriate and use resources, but humankind at large still retains a kind of minority stake, which, somewhat like preferred stock, confers no control but a share of the material benefits. In this picture, my proposal can be presented as a modern Lockean proviso. It differs from Locke's own proviso by giving up the vague and unwieldy[7] condition of "leaving enough and as good for others": One may use unlimited amounts, but one must share some of the economic benefit. It is nevertheless similar enough to the original so that even such notoriously anti-egalitarian thinkers as John Locke and Robert Nozick might find it plausible.[8]

National governments would be responsible for paying the GRD, and, with each society free to raise the requisite funds in any way it likes, no new administrative capabilities would need to be developed. Since extraction and pollution activities are relatively easy to quantify, the assurance problem would be manageable and total collection costs could be negligible.

Proceeds from the GRD are to be used toward the emancipation of the present and future global poor: toward assuring that all have access to education, health care, means of production (land) and/or jobs to a sufficient extent to be able to meet their own basic needs with dignity and to represent their interests effectively against the rest of humankind: compatriots and foreigners. In an ideal world of reasonably just and well-ordered societies, GRD payments could be made directly to the governments of the poorest societies, based on their per capita income (converted through purchasing power parities) and population size. These data are readily available and easy to monitor—reliable and comprehensive data are currently being collected by the United Nations, the World Bank, the IMF, and various other organizations.[9]

GRD payments would enable the governments of the poorer peoples to maintain lower tax rates, higher tax exemptions and/or higher domestic spending for education, health care, microloans, infrastructure, and so on than would otherwise be possible. Insofar as they would actually do this, the whole GRD scheme would require no central bureaucracy and certainly nothing like a world government, as governments would simply transfer the GRD amounts to one another through some facilitating organization, such as the World Bank, perhaps, or the UN. The differences to traditional development aid are: Payments would be a matter of entitlement rather than charity and—there being no matching of "donors" and recipients—they would not be conditional upon rendering political or economic favors to a donor or upon adopting a donor's favored political or economic institutions.[10] Acceptance of GRD payments would be voluntary: A just society may certainly shun greater affluence if it, democratically, chooses to do so.

In a nonideal world like ours, corrupt governments in the poorer states pose a significant problem. Such governments may be inclined, for example, to use GRD funds to underwrite indispensable services while diverting any domestic tax revenue saved to the rulers' personal use. A government that behaves in this way may be cut off from GRD funds.[11] In such cases it may still be possible to administer meaningful development programs through existing UN agencies (World Food Program, WHO, UNICEF, for instance) or through suitable non-governmental organizations (such as Oxfam). If GRD funds cannot be used effectively to improve the position of the poor in a particular country, then there is no reason to spend them there. They should rather be spent where they can make more of a difference in reducing poverty and disadvantage.

There are then three possibilities with regard to any country that is poor enough in aggregate to be eligible for GRD funds: Its poorer citizens may benefit through their government, they may benefit from development programs run by some other agency, or they may not benefit at all. Mixtures are, of course, also possible. (A country might receive 60 percent of the GRD funds it is eligible for, one-third of this through the government and two-thirds through other channels.) How are these matters to be decided? And by whom? The decisions are to be made by the facilitating organization, but pursuant to clear and straightforward general rules. These rules are to be designed, and possibly revised, by an international group of economists and international lawyers. Its task is to devise the rules so that the entire GRD scheme has the maximum possible positive impact on the world's poorest persons—the poorest quintile, say—in the long run. The qualification "in the long run" indicates that incentive effects must be taken into account. Governments and also the wealthier strata of a people stand to gain from GRD spending in various ways ("trickle-up") and therefore have an incentive to ensure that GRD funds are not cut off. The rules should be designed to take advantage of this incentive. They must make it clear to members of the political and economic elite of GRD-eligible countries that, if they want their society to receive GRD funds, they must cooperate in making these funds effective toward enhancing the opportunities and the standard of living of the domestic poor.[12]

Specifying how GRD funds should best be raised poses some complex problems, among them the following four: First, setting GRD rates too high may significantly dampen economic activity—in extreme cases so much that revenues overall would decline. It must be noted, however, that the funds raised through the GRD scheme do not disappear: They are spent by, and for the benefit of, the global poor and thereby generate effective market demand that spurs economic activity. Second, imposing any GRD on land use for cultivation of basic commodities (grains, beans, cotton, etc.) might increase their prices and thereby have a deleterious effect on the position of the globally worst-off. Hence it may make sense to confine any GRD on land to land used in other ways (e.g., to raise cattle or grow tobacco, coffee, cocoa, or flowers). Third, the setting of GRD rates should also take into account the interests of the future globally worst-off. The GRD should target the extraction of nonrenewable resources liable to run out within a few decades in preference to that of resources of which we have an abundant supply; it should target the discharging of pollutants that will persist for centuries in preference to the discharging of pollutants that decay more quickly. Finally, while designing the GRD is inevitably difficult and complicated, the GRD itself should be easy to understand and to apply. It should, for example, be based on resources and pollutants whose extraction or discharge is reasonably easy to monitor or estimate, in order to ensure that every people is paying its fair share and also to assure every people that this is so.

The general point behind these brief remarks is that GRD liabilities should be targeted so as to optimize their collateral effects. What is perhaps surprising is that these effects may on the whole be positive, on account of the GRD's considerable benefits for environmental protection and conservation. These benefits are hard to secure in a less concerted way because of familiar collective-action problems ("tragedy of the commons").

What about the overall magnitude of the GRD? In light of today's vast global social and economic inequalities, one may think that a massive GRD scheme would be necessary to support global background justice. But I do not think this is so. Current inequalities are the cumulative result of decades and centuries in which the more-developed peoples used their advantages in capital and knowledge to expand these advantages ever further. They show the power of long-term compounding rather than overwhelmingly powerful centrifugal tendencies of our global market system. Even a rather small GRD may then be sufficient continuously to balance these ordinary centrifugal tendencies of market systems enough to prevent the development of excessive inequalities and to maintain in equilibrium a rough global distributional profile that preserves global background justice.

I cannot here work through all the complexities involved in determining the appropriate magnitude of the GRD scheme. To achieve some concreteness nevertheless, let us, somewhat arbitrarily, settle for a GRD of up to 1 percent of world product—or less than 1 percent if a smaller amount would better advance the interests of the globally worst-off in the long run. Almost any egalitarian conception of global justice would probably recognize this proposal as an improvement over the status quo. A 1 percent GRD would currently raise revenues of roughly $300 billion per annum. This amount is quite large relative to the total income of the world's poorest 1 billion persons and, if well targeted and effectively spent, would make a phenomenal difference to them even within a few years. On the other hand, the amount is rather small for the rest of us: close to the annual defense budget of the U.S. alone and also a good bit less than the market price of the annual crude oil production, which is in the neighborhood of $500 billion (ca. 69 million barrels per day at about $20 per barrel). Thus the entire revenue goal could be raised by targeting a small number of resource uses—ones whose discouragement seems especially desirable for the sake of future generations. A $2-per-barrel GRD on crude oil extraction, for example, would raise about one-sixth of the overall revenue target while increasing the price of petroleum products by about 5 cents a gallon. It would have some substitution effects, welcome in terms of conservation and environmental protection; and, if it had any dampening effect on overall economic activity at all, this effect would be quite slight.

Having tried to show that introducing a 1 percent GRD would be an instantly feasible and morally attractive institutional reform of the existing global order,[13] let me now focus on its plausibility as a piece of ideal theory. To do this, we append my GRD proposal to Rawls's law of peoples.[14] The resulting alternative to Rawls is not my considered position on global justice. Its point is rather to allow us to focus sharply on the topic of international inequality. Egalitarian concerns will be vindicated, if it can be shown that the amended law of peoples is morally more plausible than Rawls's original—and especially so, if this can be shown on Rawlsian grounds.

## II. RAWLS'S POSITION ON INTERNATIONAL DISTRIBUTIVE JUSTICE

In his initial sketch, Rawls's brief discussion of international justice was characterized by a tension between three views:

1.  He speaks of the second session of the original position as featuring *persons* from the various societies who make a rational choice of principles so as best to protect their interests while "they know nothing about the particular circumstances of their own society, its power and strength in comparison with other nations, *nor do they know their place in their own society*" (*TJ* 378, my emphasis). I called this reading $R_1$ (*RR* 242f).

2.  On the same page, Rawls also speaks of this second session as featuring "representatives of *states* [who are] to make a rational choice to protect their interests" (*TJ* 378, my emphasis). Here, "the national interest of a just state is defined by the principles of justice that have already been acknowledged. Therefore such a nation will aim above all to maintain and to preserve its just institutions and the conditions that make them possible" (*TJ* 379). I called this reading $R_2$ (*RR* 243f).

3.  Rawls also wanted to endorse the traditional (pre–World War II) principles of international law as outlined by James Brierly.

I have tried to show (*RR* §21) that no two of these views are compatible.

Rawls has now fully resolved the tension by clearly and consistently endorsing the second view, $R_2$—without, however, offering any reasons for favoring it over $R_1$. He stipulates that the parties "are representatives of peoples" (LP 48 [herein 426]) and "subject to a veil of ignorance: They do not know, for example, the size of the territory, or the population, or the relative strength of the people whose fundamental interests they represent. Although they know that reasonably favorable conditions obtain that make democracy possible, they do not know the extent of their natural resources, or level of their economic development, or any such related information" (LP 54 [herein 430]).

And what are those fundamental interests of a people? As in his initial account of $R_2$, Rawls takes each people to have only one such fundamental interest: that its domestic institutions satisfy its conception of justice (LP 54, 64 [herein 430, 438]). And while the parties to the first session of the original position do not know the particular conceptions of the good of the persons they represent, Rawls assumes, without justifying the disanalogy, that each party to the second session does know what conception of domestic justice "her" people subscribes to. It would seem that the various delegates would then favor different versions of the law of peoples, each one especially hospitable to a particular conception of domestic justice.[15] Rawls claims, however, that within a certain range of conceptions of domestic justice, the interests of peoples regarding the law of peoples coincide: Delegates of peoples whose conception of domestic justice is either *liberal* or *hierarchical* would all favor exactly the same law of peoples (LP 60 [herein 435]). This is then the law of peoples that we, as members of a society with a liberal conception of justice, should endorse: It is hospitable to liberal regimes and to the more palatable nonliberal regimes as well. The regimes it does not accommodate are "outlaw regimes" of various sorts and those committed to an expansionist foreign policy (LP 72f [herein 444f]). Rawls's law of peoples cannot be justified to them as being (behind the veil of ignorance) in their interest as well. But this fact cannot count against it from our point of view—which, after all, is the one to which we seek to give systematic expression.

Given this structure of his account, Rawls decides to run the second session twice: Once to show that delegates of peoples with any liberal conception of domestic justice would favor his law of peoples and then to show that delegates of peoples with any hierarchical conception of domestic justice would do so as well.[16] He does not actually perform either of these two runs in any detail, and I am quite unclear as to how the second is supposed to go.

In the next two sections, I shall focus exclusively on the liberal run, in which "the parties deliberate among available principles for the law of peoples by reference to the fundamental interests of democratic societies in accordance with, or as presupposed by, the liberal principles of domestic justice" (LP 54 [herein 430]). A *liberal* conception of justice is defined (LP 51 [herein 428]) as one that

— demands that certain rights, liberties, and opportunities be secure for all citizens,
— gives this demand a high priority vis-à-vis other values and interests, and
— demands that all citizens should have adequate means to take advantage of their rights, freedoms, and opportunities.

Liberal conceptions of justice may differ from Rawls's by being comprehensive rather than political, for example, or by lacking some or all of the three egalitarian components he incorporates.

Rawls makes each delegate assume that her people is interested exclusively in being constituted as a just liberal society and he asserts that delegates with this sole interest would adopt his law of peoples, which lacks any egalitarian component. I will now argue against his stipulation that the delegates have only this one interest (Section III) and then against his claim that delegates with this sole interest would adopt his law of peoples (Section IV). If only one of my two arguments succeeds, Rawls's account is in trouble.

## III. AGAINST RAWLS'S STIPULATION

An obvious alternative to the stipulation is this: Each delegate assumes that her people has an ultimate interest not only in the justice of its domestic institutions, but also in the well-being of its members (beyond the minimum necessary for just domestic institutions). Each delegate assumes, that is, that her people would, other things equal, prefer to have a higher rather than a lower average standard of living.[17]

Delegates so described would favor the GRD amendment. This is clearly true if, like the parties to the domestic session, they deliberate according to the maximin rule.[18] But it is also true if they focus on average expectations: The GRD amendment would benefit all peoples by reducing pollution and environmental degradation. It is unclear whether it would have a positive or negative effect on per capita income for the world at large. But it would keep national per capita incomes closer together and thereby, given the decreasing marginal significance of income for well-being, raise the average standard of living as anticipated in the original position. An increase in national per capita income at the bottom matters more than an equal decrease in national per capita income at the top—in terms of a people's ability to structure its social world and national territory in accordance with its collective values and preferences, for example, and also in terms of its members' quality of life.

We need not stipulate that a people's interest in well-being is strong relative to its interest in domestic justice. For suppose we have each delegate assume that her people's interest in well-being is very slight and subordinate to the interest in domestic justice. Then the delegate will care relatively little about what her people would gain through the amendment in case it would otherwise be poorer. But then she will also care little about what it would lose through the amendment in case it would otherwise be more affluent. She would care little both ways, and therefore would still have reason to adopt the amendment if, as I have argued, the gains outweigh the losses.

I conclude that, if a delegate assumes her people to have an interest in well-being, and be it ever so slight, then she will favor my amendment—regardless of whether she seeks to maximize her people's average or worst-case expectations. Rawls must therefore posit the opposite: Each delegate assumes that her people has no interest at all in its standard of living (beyond its interest in the minimum necessary for just domestic institutions). This is, of course, precisely what his stipulation entails. But why should we find this stipulation plausible once we see what it excludes?

There are several reasons to find it *implausible*. There are, for one thing, variants of liberalism that—unlike Rawls's own—are committed to continued economic growth and progress; and a people committed to one of them should be presumed to want to avoid economic stagnation and decline. There are also cosmopolitan variants of liberalism that extend the egalitarian concerns that Rawls confines to the domestic case to all human beings worldwide; and a people committed to one of them should be presumed to want to avoid relative deprivation for itself as well as for others.

The stipulation also has implausible side effects. In explicating the outcome of the liberal run of his second session, Rawls writes: "There should be certain provisions for mutual assistance between peoples in times of famine and drought and, were it feasible, as it should be, provisions for ensuring that in all reasonably developed liberal societies people's basic needs are met" (LP 56 [herein 432]). Does he really mean what this sentence suggests: that provisions are called for to meet basic needs only in reasonably developed societies? His account may well leave him no other choice. In his second session, each delegate cares solely about her people's achieving domestic justice. However, helping a people meet their basic needs may not enable them to achieve domestic justice, if their society is still quite undeveloped. Hence aid to members of such societies is not a requirement of global justice on Rawls's stipulation. His law of peoples requires basic food aid, say, only to peoples who but for their poverty would be able to maintain just domestic institutions.

Now it would be outrageous to suggest that Rawls deems it a matter of moral indifference whether members of undeveloped societies are starving or not. But, given his stipulation, he would have to say that such aid is an ethical duty, which we might discharge individually, or collectively through our government. International *justice* requires institutions designed to meet basic needs in societies where this contributes to domestic justice, but not in societies where it does not. Yet this looks counterintuitive: Why, after all, do liberals want the law of peoples to be supportive of the internal justice of all societies, if not for the sake of the persons living in them? And if our concern for the domestic justice of societies is ultimately a concern for their individual members, why should we focus so narrowly on how well a law of peoples accommodates their interest in living under just domestic institutions and not also, more broadly, on how well it accommodates their underlying and indisputable interest in secure access to food, clothing, shelter, education, and health care, even where a reasonably developed liberal society is still out of the question?

The danger here is not merely moral implausibility, but also philosophical incoherence between Rawls's conceptions of domestic and of global justice. According to the latter, a just domestic regime is an end in itself. According to the former, however, it is not an end in itself, but rather something we ought to realize for the sake of individual human persons, who are the ultimate units of moral concern. Our natural duty to create and uphold just domestic institutions is a duty owed to them (*TJ* 115). Their well-being is the *point* of social institutions and therefore, through the first session of the original position, gives content to Rawls's conception of domestic justice.

The incoherence might be displayed as follows. Suppose the parties to the first, domestic session knew that the persons they represent are the members of one society among a plurality of interdependent societies; and suppose they also knew that a delegate will represent this society in a subsequent international session, in which a law of peoples is to be adopted. How would they describe to this delegate the fundamental interests of their society? Of course they would want her to push for a law of peoples that is supportive of the kind of national institutions favored by the two principles of justice they have, according to Rawls, adopted for the domestic case. But their concern for such domestic institutions is derivative on their concern for the higher-order interests of the individual human persons they themselves represent in the domestic original position. Therefore, they would want the delegate to push for the law of peoples that best accommodates, on the whole, those higher-order interests of individuals.[19] They would want her to consider not only how alternative proposals for a law of peoples would affect their clients' prospects to live under just domestic institutions, but also how these proposals would affect their clients' life prospects in other ways—for example through the affluence of their society. This point, by the way, strongly suggests that those committed to a Rawlsian (or, indeed, any other liberal) conception of domestic justice should want the delegates to any global original position to be conceived as representatives of persons rather than peoples.

I suspect that Rawls wants his second session of the original position to be informed by the interests of peoples, conceived as irreducible to the interests of persons, because the latter would inject an individualistic element that he deems unacceptable to hierarchical societies. The problem he sees is real enough, but his solution accommodates the hierarchicals at the expense of not being able to accommodate the liberals. I will return to this point in Section V.

## IV. AGAINST RAWLS'S REASONING

The foregoing arguments notwithstanding, let us now allow the stipulation. Let us assume that each people really does have only the one interest in the justice of its own domestic institutions, and that its delegate to the second session of the original position is instructed accordingly. Would such delegates prefer Rawls's law of peoples over my more egalitarian alternative? The answer, clearly, is NO: They would at most be indifferent between the two proposals. I don't know why Rawls thinks otherwise. But he may have been misled by an unrecognized presumption that a laissez-faire global economic order is the natural or neutral benchmark that the delegates would endorse unless they have definite reasons to depart from it.

This presumption would explain his discussion of a global difference principle, which is peculiar in two respects. First, Rawls considers such a principle only in regard to one part of nonideal theory: coping with unfavorable conditions (LP 75 [herein 446f]), although it has generally, if not always, been proposed as an analogue to the domestic difference principle, which is used primarily to design the ideal basic structure.[20] Second, the tenor of his remarks throughout is that a global difference principle is too strong for the international case, that it demands too much from hierarchical societies (e.g., LP 75[herein 446f]). This suggests a view of the difference principle as a principle of *re*distribution, which takes from some to give to others: The more it redistributes, the more demanding is the principle. But this view of the difference principle loses an insight that is crucial to understanding Rawls's own, domestic difference principle: There is no prior distribution, no natural baseline or neutral way of arranging the economy, relative to which the difference principle could be seen to make *re*distributive modifications. Rather, there are countless ways of designing economic institutions, none initially privileged, of which one and only one will be implemented. The difference principle selects the scheme that ought to be chosen. The selected economic ground rules, whatever their content, do not *re*distribute, but rather govern how economic benefits and burdens get distributed in the first place.

This point is crucial for Rawls's reply to Nozick's critique. Nozick wants to make it appear that laissez-faire institutions are natural and define the baseline distribution which Rawls then seeks to revise ex post through redistributive transfers. Nozick views the first option as natural and the second as making great demands upon the diligent and the gifted. He allows that, with unanimous consent, people can make the switch to the second scheme; but, if some object, we must stick to the first.[21] Rawls can respond that a libertarian basic structure and his own more egalitarian liberal-democratic alternative are options on the same footing: The second is, in a sense, demanding on the gifted, if they would do better under the first—but then the first is, in the same sense and symmetrically, demanding on the less gifted, who would do much better under the second scheme.

In his discussion of the global difference principle, Rawls's presentation of the issue is the analogue to Nozick's in the domestic case. It is somehow natural or neutral to arrange the world economy so that each society has absolute control over, and unlimited ownership of, all natural resources within its territory. Any departures from this baseline, such as my GRD proposal, are demanding and, it turns out, too demanding on some societies. I want to give the analogue to the Rawlsian domestic response: Yes, egalitarian institutions are demanding upon naturally and historically favored societies, because they would do better in a scheme with unlimited ownership rights. But then, symmetrically, a scheme with unlimited ownership rights is at least equally demanding upon naturally and historically disfavored societies, since they and their members would do much better under a more egalitarian global basic structure.

I have argued that Rawls has given no reason why the delegates— even if each of them cares solely about her people's prospects to live under just domestic institutions—should prefer his inegalitarian law of peoples over more egalitarian alternatives. Might they have a reason for the opposite preference? I believe that they do. In a world with large international inequalities, the domestic institutions of the poorer societies are vulnerable to being corrupted by powerful political and economic interests abroad. This is something we see all around us: politicians and businesspeople from the rich nations self-servingly manipulating and interfering with the internal political, judicial, and economic processes of Third World societies.

Rawls is presumably aware of this phenomenon, but he fails to see its roots in gross international inequality: In poorer societies, he writes, "the problem is commonly the nature of the public political culture and the religious and philosophical traditions that underlie its institutions. The great social evils in poorer societies are likely to be oppressive government and corrupt elites" (LP 77 [herein 448]). Now Rawls is surely right that many poor countries have corrupt institutions and ruling elites, which do not serve the interests of the people and contribute to their poverty. But the inverse is certainly true as well: Relative poverty breeds corruptibility and corruption. Powerful foreign governments support their favorite faction of the local elite and often manage to keep or install it in power—through financial and organizational help for winning elections, if possible, or through support for security forces, coups d'état, or "revolutions" otherwise. Third World politicians are bribed or pressured by firms from the rich societies to cater to their sex tourism business, to accept their hazardous wastes and industrial facilities, and to buy useless products at government expense.

Agribusinesses, promising foreign exchange earnings that can be used for luxury imports, manage to get land use converted from staple foods to export crops: Wealthy foreigners get coffee and flowers year-round, while many locals cannot afford the higher prices for basic foodstuffs. Examples could be multiplied; but I think it is indisputable that the oppression and corruption in the poorer countries, which Rawls rightly deplores, are by no means entirely homegrown. So it is true, but not the whole truth, that governments and institutions of poor countries are often corrupt: They are actively being corrupted, continually and very significantly, by private and official agents from vastly more wealthy societies. It is entirely unrealistic to expect that such foreign-sponsored corruption can be eradicated without reducing the enormous differentials in per capita GNP.

So long as the delegates to Rawls's second session are merely presumed to know that large international inequalities *may* have a negative impact upon the domestic justice of the poorer societies, they have a tie-breaking reason to favor a more egalitarian law of peoples over Rawls's.[22]

## V. ANOTHER WAY OF UNDERSTANDING RAWLS'S LIBERAL DELEGATES

If only one of my two arguments is sound, then delegates of liberal societies would prefer a more egalitarian law of peoples over Rawls's inegalitarian alternative. I suppose Rawls would regret this fact, if it destroys the desired coincidence between the law of peoples adopted by delegates of liberal societies (at step 1 of his second session) and the law of peoples adopted by delegates of hierarchical societies (at step 2). But this coincidence fails, in any case, on account of human rights.

Rawls claims that both sets of delegates would adopt precisely the same law of peoples (LP 60 [herein 435]), which includes a list of human rights (LP 62f, 68, 70 [herein 437, 441, 442]) featuring minimum rights to life (means of subsistence and security), to liberty (freedom from slavery, serfdom, and forced occupations), to personal property, to "a measure" (LP 63 [herein 437]) of liberty of conscience and freedom of thought and "a certain" (LP 68 herein 441]) freedom of association (compatible with an established religion), to emigration, and to the rule of law and formal equality as expressed by the rules of natural justice (for example, that similar cases be treated similarly). He gives no reason, and I can see none, historical or philosophical, for believing that hierarchical societies, as such, would incorporate these human rights into their favored law of peoples. Perhaps many such societies can honor these rights while retaining their hierarchical, nonliberal character, as Rawls suggests (LP 70 [herein 442]); but this hardly shows that they would choose to be bound by them. Human rights are not essential to hierarchical societies, as they are essential to liberal ones.

Not only is it highly doubtful that delegates of hierarchical societies would choose to commit themselves to so much; it is also quite unclear why delegates of liberal societies would not want to incorporate more than Rawls's list, which specifically excludes freedom of speech (LP 62 [herein 436f]), democratic political rights (LP 62, 69f [herein 436f, 441f]), and equal liberty of conscience and freedom of thought (LP 63, 65 [herein 437, 439]).

Rawls's quest for a "politically neutral" (LP 69 [herein 442]) law of peoples—one that liberals and hierarchicals would independently favor on the basis of their respective values and interests—thus holds little promise: Those who are really committed to a liberal conception of justice will envision a law of peoples which demands that persons everywhere enjoy the protection of the full list of human rights as well as adequate opportunities and material means that are not radically unequal. The friends of hierarchical societies will prefer a world order that is much less protective of the basic interests of persons as individuals. The former will want the interests of persons to be represented in the second session of the original position. The latter will care only about the interests of peoples.

Occasionally, Rawls suggests a different picture, which jettisons the claim to political neutrality. On this picture, the law of peoples he proposes is not what liberals would ideally want, but rather is affected by the existence of hierarchical societies. The alleged coincidence of the results of the two runs of the second session is then not luck, but design. It comes about because good liberals seek to accommodate hierarchical societies by adjusting their ideal of global justice so as to "express liberalism's own principle of toleration for other reasonable ways of ordering society" (LP 43 [herein 422]).[23] Just as Rawls himself may be expressing this desire by conceiving the second session of the original position in nonindividualistic terms, he may conceive of his liberal delegates as having a similar desire to adopt a law of peoples acceptable to hierarchical societies. This could explain their—otherwise incredible—decisions against certain human rights (precisely those most offensive to the hierarchicals) and against any egalitarian principle.

This picture is not at all that of a negotiated compromise in which the liberal delegates agree to surrender their egalitarian concerns and some human rights in exchange for the hierarchical delegates accepting the remainder. Such a bargaining model is quite un-Rawlsian and also does not fit with his account, on which the two groups of delegates deliberate in mutual isolation. The toleration model is more noble than this: The liberal delegates, informed that their societies share a world with many hierarchical societies, seek to design a law of peoples that hierarchical societies, on the basis of their values and interests as such, can reasonably accept. Yet, for all its nobility, the toleration model has a drawback that the bargaining model avoids: It is rather one-sided. The hierarchicals, unencumbered by any principle of toleration, get their favorite law of peoples, while the liberals, "to express liberalism's own principle of toleration," surrender their egalitarian concerns and some important human rights.[24] This fits the witty definition of a liberal as someone who will not take her own side in any disagreement.

What goes wrong here is that Rawls, insofar as he is committed to this picture, does not clearly distinguish two views, and hence is prone to accept the second with the first:

(1)  Liberalism involves a commitment to tolerance and diversity that extends beyond the family of liberal conceptions: A liberal world order will therefore leave room for certain kinds of nonliberal national regimes.

(2)  Liberalism involves a commitment to tolerance and diversity that extends beyond the family of liberal conceptions: It would thus be illiberal to impose a liberal global order on a world that contains many peoples who do not share our liberal values.

By acknowledging (1), we are not compromising our liberal convictions. To the contrary: We would be compromising our liberal convictions if we did not envision a liberal world order in this way. A world order would not be genuinely liberal if it did not leave room for certain nonliberal national regimes. Those who acknowledge (2), by contrast, *are* compromising their liberal convictions for the sake of accommodating those who do not share them. Liberals should then accept (1) and reject (2).

This reasoning is the analogue to what Rawls himself would say about the domestic case. Consider:

(1')   A liberal society must leave room for certain nonliberal communities and lifestyles.

(2')   It would be illiberal to impose liberal institutions on a society that contains many persons who do not share our liberal values.

Rawls would clearly accept (1') and reject (2'). He could give the following rationale: While our society can contain many different kinds of communities, associations, and conceptions of the good, some liberal in character and others not, it can be structured or organized in only one way. If my neighbor wants to be a Catholic and I an atheist, we can both have our way, can both lead the life each deems best. But if my neighbor wants the US to be organized like the Catholic Church and I want it to be a liberal state, we can *not* both have our way. There is no room for accommodation here, and, if I really believe in egalitarian liberal principles, I should politically support them and the institutions they favor against their opponents. These institutions will not vary with the shifting political strength of groups advocating various religious, moral, or philosophical doctrines.[25]

My rationale is the analogue to this: While the world can contain societies that are structured in a variety of ways, some liberal and some not, it cannot itself be structured in a variety of ways. If the Algerians want their society to be organized as a religious state consistent with a just global order and we want ours to be a liberal democracy, we can both have our way. But if the Algerians want the world to be organized according to the Koran, and we want it to accord with liberal principles, then we can *not* both have our way. There is no room for accommodation here, and, if we really believe in egalitarian liberal principles—in every person's equal claim to freedom and dignity—then we should politically support these principles, and the global institutions they favor, against their opponents. These institutions will not vary with the shifting political strength of states committed to various conceptions of domestic justice.

I conclude that Rawls has failed to show that the law of peoples liberals would favor and the law of peoples favored by hierarchicals either coincide by sheer luck or can be made to coincide by morally plausible design. We should then work toward a global order that—though tolerant of certain nonliberal regimes, just as a liberal society is tolerant of certain nonliberal sects and movements—is itself decidedly liberal in character, for example by conceiving of individual persons and of them alone as ultimate units of equal moral concern. This quest will put us at odds with many hierarchical societies whose ideal of a fully just world order will be different from ours.

It may seem then that my more assertive liberalism will lead to greater international conflict. And this may well be so in the area of human rights. But it may not be so in the area here at issue: international inequality. Rawls rejects all egalitarian distributive principles of international justice on the ground (among others) that they are inseparable from liberal values and therefore unacceptable to hierarchical societies (LP 75 [herein 446f]).[26] But in the real world, the chief opponents of proposals along the lines of my GRD are the affluent liberal societies. We are, after all, also the wealthy ones and account for a vastly disproportionate share of global resource depletion and pollution. If we submitted the GRD proposal to the rest of the world, most societies would probably accept it with enthusiasm.[27]

Given that institutional progress is politically possible, it would be perverse to oppose it by saying to the rest of the world: "We care deeply about equality, and we would very much like it to be the case that you are not so much worse off than we are. But, unfortunately, we do not believe that you ultimately care about equality the way we do. Therefore we feel entitled to refuse any global institutional reforms that would lead to greater international equality." One reason this would be perverse is that those touting hierarchical values and those suffering most from global inequality are rarely the same. Those whose lot a GRD would do most to improve—poor women and rural laborers in the Third World, for example—rarely give the hierarchical values of their rulers and oppressors their considered and reflective endorsement.[28]

## VI. THE PROBLEM OF STABILITY

Delegates of liberal societies might *prefer* an egalitarian law of peoples and yet *adopt* Rawls's inegalitarian alternative.[29] For they might believe that a scheme like the GRD would simply not work: The moral motives ("sense of justice") that a just world order would engender in peoples and their governments would not be strong enough to ensure compliance. There would always be some wealthy peoples refusing to pay their fair share, and this in turn would undermine others' willingness to participate. In short: The GRD scheme is practicable only if backed by sanctions.[30] And sanctions presuppose a world government, which the delegates have abundant reasons to reject.

In response, I accept the claim that the GRD scheme would have to be backed by sanctions. But sanctions do not require a world government. They could work as follows: Once the agency facilitating the flow of GRD payments reports that a country has not met its obligations under the scheme, all other countries are required to impose duties on imports from, and perhaps also similar levies on exports to, this country to raise funds equivalent to its GRD obligations plus the cost of these enforcement measures. Such decentralized sanctions stand a very good chance of discouraging *small*-scale defections. Our world is now, and is likely to remain, highly interdependent economically; most countries export and import between 10 percent and 50 percent of their gross domestic product. None of them would benefit from shutting down foreign trade for the sake of avoiding a GRD obligation of around 1 percent of GDP. And each would have reasons to meet its GRD obligation voluntarily: to retain full control over how the funds are raised, to avoid paying for enforcement measures in addition, and to avoid the negative publicity associated with noncompliance.

This leaves the problem of *large*-scale defections, and the related problem of getting most of the more affluent societies to agree to something like the GRD scheme in the first place. This scheme could not work in our world without the willing cooperation of most of the wealthier countries. You may be tempted to look at the world as it is and conclude that the hope for such willing cooperation is not realistic. So you would have the delegates to any global original position choose Rawls's law of peoples after all. And you might then give the following speech to the global poor: "We care deeply about equality, and we would very much like it to be the case that you are not so much worse off than we are. But, unfortunately, it is not realistic to expect that we would actually comply with more egalitarian global institutions. Since no one would benefit from a futile attempt to maintain impracticable institutions, we should all just rest content with the global inequalities of the status quo."

This little speech is not quite as nefarious as I have made it sound, because the "we" in the first sentence denotes a significantly smaller group than the "we" in the second, which refers to the entire population of the First World. Still, if it is true that reflection on our (wide sense) liberal values would support a preference for more egalitarian global economic institutions, then we (narrow sense) should at least try to stimulate such reflection in our compatriots before declaring such institutions to be impracticable. We should seek to make it become widely recognized among citizens of the developed West that such institutions are required by justice. I have already suggested one reason for believing that this may be a feasible undertaking—a scheme like the GRD can be justified by appeal to different (and perhaps incompatible) values prominent in Western moral thought:

(a) It can be supported by libertarian arguments as a modern Lockean proviso on unilateral appropriation (cf. 467f, above).[31]

(b) It can be supported as a general way of mitigating the effects of grievous historical wrongs (see pp. 465f, above) that cannot be mitigated in any more specific fashion.[32]

(c) It is also supported by forward-looking considerations as exemplified in the hypothetical-contract (Rawls) and consequentialist traditions.

These rationales are not unassailable. For one thing, they all hinge upon empirical facts of interdependence:

(a) Peoples must share the same planet with its limited resources.

(b) The common history that has produced peoples and national territories as they now exist and will continue to exist in the foreseeable future is replete with massive wrongs and injustices.

(c) Existing peoples interact within a single global framework of political and economic institutions, which tends to produce and reproduce rather stable patterns of inequalities and deprivations.

To undermine those rationales and the moral conclusion they support, First-Worlders often downplay these interdependencies and think of real societies as "self-sufficient" (*TJ* 4), "closed," "isolated" (*TJ* 8), and "self-contained" (*TJ* 457).[33] Like the closely related notion that the causes of Third World poverty are indigenous (cp. 479f above), this fiction is a severe distortion of the truth—most clearly in the especially relevant case of today's most unfortunate societies, which are still reeling from the effects of slavery and colonial oppression and exploitation and are also highly vulnerable to global market forces and destabilization from abroad.

The three rationales are also frequently confronted with notions of national partiality: It is perfectly permissible for us and our government, in a spirit of patriotic fellow-feeling, to concentrate on promoting the interests of our own society and compatriots, even if foreigners are much worse off. I need not deny this claim, only to qualify it: Partiality is legitimate only in the context of a *fair* competition. This idea is familiar and widely accepted in the domestic case: It is perfectly all right for persons to concentrate on promoting the interests of themselves and their relatives, provided they do so on a "level playing field" whose substantive fairness is continually preserved. Partiality toward one's family is decidedly not acceptable when we, as citizens, face political decisions in which that level playing field itself is at stake. It would be morally wrong, for example, even (or perhaps especially) if one's children are white boys, to use one's political influence to oppose equal access to higher education for women or blacks. Most citizens in the developed West understand and accept this point without question. It should not be all that hard to make them understand that for closely analogous reasons national partiality is morally acceptable only on condition that the fairness of international competition is continually preserved, and that it is morally wrong in just the same way for the rich Western states to use their vastly superior bargaining power to impose upon the poor societies a global economic order that tends to perpetuate and perhaps aggravate their inferiority.[34]

If the three rationales can be properly developed and defended against these and other challenges, a moral commitment to something like the GRD scheme could gradually emerge and become widespread in the developed West. Even if this were to occur, however, there would still be the further question of whether our governments could be moved to introduce and comply with such institutions. I think that an affirmative answer to this question can be supported by some historical evidence. Perhaps the most dramatic such evidence is provided by the suppression of the slave trade in the nineteenth century. Great Britain was in the forefront of these efforts, actively enforcing a ban on the entire maritime slave trade irrespective of a vessel's ownership, registration, port of origin, or destination. Britain bore the entire cost of its enforcement efforts and could not hope to gain significant benefits from them—in fact, Britain bore additional opportunity costs in the form of lost trade, especially with Latin America. States do sometimes act for moral reasons.[35]

It should also be said that institutional reforms establishing a GRD need not go against the national interest of the developed states. I have already said that the GRD would slow pollution and resource depletion and thereby benefit all peoples in the long run. Let me now add that the fiction of mutual independence, and the cult of state sovereignty associated with it, have become highly dangerous in the modern world. Technological progress offers rapidly expanding possibilities of major devastations, of which those associated with nuclear, chemical, or biological weapons and accidents are only the most dramatic and the most obvious. If responsibility for guarding against such possibilities remains territorially divided over some two hundred national governments, the chances of avoiding them in the long run are slim. No state or group of states can protect itself against all externally induced gradual or catastrophic deteriorations of its environment. The present geopolitical constellation offers a unique opportunity for bringing the more dangerous technologies under central international control. If the most powerful states were to try to mandate such control unilaterally, they would likely encounter determined resistance and would have to resort to force. It would seem more promising to pursue the same goal in a multilateral fashion, by relaxing the idea of state sovereignty in a more balanced way: We, the First World, give up the notion that all our great affluence is ours alone, fit to be brought to bear in our bargaining with the rest of the world so as to entrench and expand our advantage; they, the rest, give up the notion that each society has a sovereign right to develop and control by itself all the technological capacities we already possess.

This scenario shows another reason for believing that it may be possible for a commitment to the GRD scheme to become and remain widespread among our compatriots in the First World: We, too, like the global poor, have a strong interest in a gradual erosion of the doctrine of absolute state sovereignty through a strengthening concern for the welfare of humankind at large,[36] though our interest is more long-term than theirs. It may seem that a commitment motivated along these lines would be excessively prudential. But then our concern to protect our environment is not merely prudential, but also moral: We do care about the victims of Bhopal and Chernobyl as well as about future generations. And once the new institutions begin to take hold and draw the members of different societies closer together, the commitment would in any case tend gradually to assume a more moral character.

I conclude that there is no convincing reason to believe that a widespread moral commitment on the part of the more affluent peoples and governments to a scheme like the GRD could not be sustained in the world as we know it. Delegates of liberal societies as Rawls conceives them would therefore not merely *prefer*, but would *choose*, my more egalitarian law of peoples over his inegalitarian alternative. In doing so, they would also envision a more democratic world order, a greater role for central organizations, and, in this sense, more world government than we have at present—though nothing like *a* world government on the model of current national governments.

"The politician," Rawls writes, "looks to the next election, the statesman to the next generation, and philosophy to the indefinite future."[37] Our task as philosophers requires that we try to imagine new, better political structures and different, better moral sentiments. We must be realistic, but not to the point of presenting to the parties in the original position the essentials of the status quo as unalterable facts.

## NOTES

Work on this paper was supported by a Laurance S. Rockefeller fellowship at the Princeton University Center for Human Values. Written for a conference on the "Ethics of Nationalism" at the University of Illinois at Urbana-Champaign, it was also presented to audiences at Princeton, Harvard, New York, Stanford, and Oxford Universities. I am grateful for the barrage of forceful criticisms I have received—in particular from Brian Barry, Alyssa Bernstein, Lea Brilmayer, Tony Coady, John Cooper, Roger Crisp, Peter de

Marneffe, Alan Houston, Frances Kamm, Elizabeth Kiss, Christine Korsgaard, Ling Tong, Stuart White, and the editors of *Philosophy and Public Affairs*, in which this article was first published (vol. 23 (3): 195–224, summer 1994); reprinted with permission.

1. John Rawls, "The Law of Peoples," in *On Human Rights*, eds. Stephen Shute and Susan Hurley (New York: Basic Books, 1993), pp. 41–82, 220–30 [reprinted herein 421–60]. Page numbers preceded by LP refer to this lecture. The earlier sketch is on pp. 378f of *A Theory of Justice* (Cambridge, MA: Harvard University Press, 1971); henceforth *TJ*.

2. See chapter 6 of *Realizing Rawls* (Ithaca: Cornell University Press 1989); henceforth *RR*.

3. "Cosmopolitanism and Sovereignty," *Ethics* 103 (1992): 48–75 [reprinted herein 355–90].

4. John Rawls, "Justice as Fairness: Revisited, Revised, Recast," 1992 typescript, p. 136 [*Justice as Fairness: A Restatement*, ed. Erin Kelly (Cambridge, MA: Harvard University Press, 2001), p. 162].

5. *RR* 256n18, 264f. See also "An Institutional Approach to Humanitarian Intervention," *Public Affairs Quarterly* 6 (1992): 89–103, p. 96. More recently: "A Global Resources Dividend" in David Crocker, ed., *The Ethics of Consumption and Stewardship* (Totowa: Rowman and Littlefield, 1997).

6. This accommodates Rawls's remark that "unless a definite agent is given responsibility for maintaining an asset and bears the loss of not doing so, that asset tends to deteriorate" (LP 57 [herein 432]).

7. Consider: Must we leave enough and as good for future generations? For how many? Are air and water pollution ruled out entirely because the air and water left behind is not as good?

8. Cf. John Locke, *Second Treatise*, §§27, 33; Robert Nozick, *Anarchy, State, and Utopia* (New York: Basic Books, 1974), pp. 175–77 and chapter 4.

9. One may think that domestic income distribution should be taken into account as well. Even if two states have the same per capita income, the poor in the one may still be much worse off than the poor in the other. The problem with taking account of this fact is that it may provide a perverse incentive to governments to neglect their domestic poor in order to receive larger GRD payments. This incentive is bad, because governments might act on it, and also because governments might, wrongly, be thought to act or be accused of acting on it (appearance and assurance problems).

10. For a detailed account of how the latter feature renders current aid highly inefficient, if not useless, see the cover story, "Why Aid is an Empty Promise," *The Economist* 331/7862 (May 7, 1994): pp. 13–14, 21–24.

11. For a contrary conception, see Brian Barry, "Humanity and Justice in Global Perspective" in *NOMOS XXIV: Ethics, Economics, and the Law*, ed. J. R. Pennock and J. W. Chapman (New York: New York University Press, 1982), pp. 219–52 [reprinted herein 179–209]. Barry holds that the governments of poor societies should receive funds regardless of their domestic policies.

12. In some GRD-eligible countries there may well be factions of the ruling elite for whom these incentives would be outweighed by their interest in keeping the poor uneducated, impotent, and dependent. Still, the incentives will shift the balance of forces in the direction of reform.

13. This is a bit of an exaggeration: I have not yet given you any reason not to dismiss my GRD proposal as unfeasible in the political sense. This I hope to do in the final section.

14. Rawls characterizes this law of peoples by the following list of principles (LP 55 [herein 431]): "(1) Peoples (as organized by their governments) are free and independent and their freedom and independence is to be respected by other peoples. (2) Peoples are equal and parties to their own agreements. (3) Peoples have the right of self-defense but no right to war. (4) Peoples are to observe a duty of nonintervention. (5) Peoples are to observe treaties and undertakings. (6) Peoples are to observe certain specified restrictions on the conduct of war (assumed to be in self-defense). (7) Peoples are to honor human rights." Though this list is not meant to be complete (ibid. [herein 432]), the complete list would not contain an egalitarian distributive principle (LP 75f [herein 446f]). Throughout, Rawls makes no attempt to show that representatives of peoples would, in his second session of the original position, adopt these principles. The presentation is far less rigorous than the one he had offered in support of his two principles of domestic justice. My response in this essay is then not so much a critique of Rawls as a detailed and, I hope, constructive invitation to defend his conclusions.

15. I say that any global (session of the) original position features *delegates* rather than parties or representatives. This is my expression, not Rawls's. Its sole purpose is to make more perspicuous that the reference is to deliberators about global rather than domestic institutions.

16. See LP 52 and 60 [herein 429 and 435] for Rawls's distinction of these two steps, as he calls them, of his account of international ideal theory.

17. Rawls makes the analogous stipulation for the domestic session of the original position, remarking that it cannot hurt a person to have greater means at her disposal: One can always give them away or forgo their use (*TJ* 142f).

18. This rule prescribes that choices should be evaluated on the basis of their worst possible outcomes. Of the available options, one ought to favor the one with the best worst-case scenario.

19. For Rawls's account of the three higher-order interests of the persons whom the parties to the first, domestic session represent, see his *Political Liberalism* (New York: Columbia University Press, 1993), pp. 74f, 106.

20. In the penultimate draft of "The Law of Peoples," Rawls did argue also against the global difference principle as a proposal for ideal theory, but he has deleted those arguments.

21. See *Anarchy, State, and Utopia* pp. 167–74, 198–204, 280–92.

22. While the delegates to an $R_2$-type second session would view my modification as an improvement, they would presumably like even better

the addition of a more statist egalitarian component, such as Brian Barry's proposal cited in note 11. This does not worry me, because it was only for the sake of the argument that I have here accepted Rawls's $R_2$ setup, which treats peoples, not persons, as ultimate units of moral concern. I am confident that a more plausible construal of a global original position—G, for example, as defended in *RR* §§22–23—would support something very much like the GRD as an essential part of a fully just law of peoples.

23. Another, related reason might be, as Rawls remarks in another context, that "all principles and standards proposed for the law of peoples must, to be feasible, prove acceptable to the considered and reflective public opinion of peoples and their governments" (LP 50 [herein 427]).

24. And probably some additional human rights as well, if I was right to argue that the hierarchical delegates would not adopt even the truncated list that Rawls incorporates into his law of peoples.

25. In supporting his view that our conception of justice should not, in the manner of (2'), be sensitive to what competing views happen to be prevalent among our compatriots, Rawls also stresses that such sensitivity would render this conception "political in the wrong way," thus leading to some of the problems associated with institutions that reflect a modus vivendi. (See *Political Liberalism*, lecture IV, esp. pp. 141–48.) This concern, too, has an analogue on the global plane (see *RR*, chapter 5).

26. I believe, to the contrary, that rather a lot could be said to support the GRD scheme in terms of nonliberal values prevalent in many hierarchical societies today, though I cannot undertake this task here.

27. Witness the debates during the 1970s, in UNCTAD and the General Assembly of the United Nations, about a new international economic order.

28. Should I apologize for my liberal bias here, for being concerned with endorsement by individual persons rather than by whole peoples (as expressed, presumably, by their governments and "elites")?

29. The problem I try to deal with in this final section is not one raised by Rawls, who holds that the delegates would even *prefer* his law of peoples. So nothing I say in response to the problem is meant to be critical of him.

30. One might justify including this claim among the general knowledge available to the delegates by pointing to how lax many states have been about paying their much smaller membership dues to the UN.

31. Cf. the far more radical idea that on a Lockean account "each individual has a right to an equal share of the basic nonhuman means of production" (i.e., means of production other than labor that are not themselves produced: resources in the sense of my GRD), as presented in Hillel Steiner, "The Natural Right to the Means of Production," *Philosophical Quarterly* 27 (1977): 41–49, p. 49, and further developed in G. A. Cohen, "Self-Ownership, World Ownership, and Equality: Part II," *Social Philosophy and Policy* 3 (1986): 77–96, pp. 87–95.

32. Nozick entertains this backward-looking rationale for the difference principle: If we cannot disentangle and surgically neutralize the effects of past wrongs, then implementing Rawls's difference principle may be the best way of satisfying Nozick's principle of rectification at least approximately. See *Anarchy, State, and Utopia*, p. 231.

33. Rawls describes societies in this way only for purposes of a "first approximation." See *Political Liberalism*, p. 272.

34. For a different argument, to the effect that unqualified partiality constitutes a loophole, see my "Loopholes in Moralities," *Journal of Philosophy* 89 (1992): 79–98, pp. 84–98.

35. I owe this example to W. Ben Hunt. Obviously, much more could and should be said about the various similarities and dissimilarities between this nineteenth-century case and our current global situation. I mention the case here mainly as a preliminary, but I think powerful, empirical obstacle to the claim that governments never act contrary to what they take to be in their own, or their society's, best interest. There are, I believe, many other less dramatic, but also more recent, counterexamples to this claim.

36. Note the success of recent programs under which Third World governments are forgiven some of their foreign debts in exchange for their undertaking certain environmental initiatives in their territory.

37. "The Idea of an Overlapping Consensus," *Oxford Journal of Legal Studies* 7 (1987): 1–25, p. 24.

# 17. MARTHA C. NUSSBAUM

Nussbaum defends a version of the capabilities approach to justice. This approach holds that justice is centrally concerned with making possible the realization of certain human functionings or capabilities. She demonstrates how this approach can guide development policy to ensure that women have equal capabilities with men. And she argues that her version of the capabilities approach can adequately answer the most serious charges made by relativists against ethical universalism.

## Human Capabilities, Female Human Beings

*First published in* Women, Culture and Development: A Study of Human Capabilities, *ed. Martha C. Nussbaum and Jonathan Glover (Oxford: Oxford University Press, 1995), 61–104.*

> Human beings are not by nature kings, or nobles, or courtiers, or rich. All are born naked and poor. All are subject to the miseries of life, to frustrations, to ills, to needs, to pains of every kind. Finally, all are condemned to death. That is what is really the human being; that is what no mortal can avoid. Begin, then, by studying what is the most inseparable from human nature, that which most constitutes humanness.
>
> —*Jean-Jacques Rousseau,* Emile, *Book IV*

Women, a majority of the world's population, receive only a small share of developmental opportunities. They are often excluded from education or from the better jobs, from political systems or from adequate health care. ... In the countries for which relevant data are available, the female human development index is only 60 percent that of males.

—Human Development Report, 1993, *United Nations Development Programme*

Were our state a pure democracy there would still be excluded from our deliberations women, who, to prevent depravation of morals and ambiguity of issue, should not mix promiscuously in gatherings of men.

—*Thomas Jefferson*

Being a woman is not yet a way of being a human being.

—*Catharine MacKinnon*

# 1. FEMINISM AND COMMON HUMANITY

Begin with the human being: with the capacities and needs that join all humans, across barriers of gender and class and race and nation.[1] To a person concerned with the equality and dignity of women, this advice should appear in one way promising. For it instructs us to focus on what all human beings share rather than on the privileges and achievements of a dominant group, and on needs and basic functions rather than on power or status. Women have rarely been kings, or nobles, or courtiers, or rich. They have, on the other hand, frequently been poor and sick and dead.

But this starting point will be regarded with skepticism by many contemporary feminists. For it is all too obvious that throughout the history of political thought, both Western and non-Western, such allegedly unbiased general concepts have served in various ways to bolster male privilege and to marginalize women. Human beings are not born kings, or nobles, or courtiers. They are, or so it seems,[2] born male and female. The nakedness on which Rousseau places such emphasis reveals a difference that is taken by Rousseau himself to imply profound differences in capability and social role. His remarks about human nature are the prelude to his account of Emile's education. Sophie, Emile's female companion, will be said to have a different "nature" and a different education. Whether, as here, women are held to be bearers of a different "nature" from unmarked "human nature," or whether they are simply said to be degenerate and substandard exemplars of the same "nature," the result is usually the same: a judgment of female inferiority, which can then be used to justify and stabilize oppression.[3]

I shall argue nonetheless that we should in fact begin with a conception of the human being and human functioning in thinking about women's equality in developing countries. This notion can be abused. It can be developed in a gender-biased way. It can be unjustly and prejudicially applied. It can be developed in ways that neglect relevant differences among women of different nationalities, classes, and races. But I shall argue that, articulated in a certain way (and I shall be emphatically distinguishing my approach from others that use an idea of "human nature") it is our best starting point for reflection. It is our best route to stating correctly what is wrong with the situations that confronted Saleha Begum and Metha Bai,[4] the best basis for claims of justice on their behalf, and on behalf of the huge numbers of women in the world who are currently being deprived of their full "human development."

I note that the concept of the human being has already been central to much of the best feminist and internationalist thinking. Consider, for example, J. S. Mill's remarks on "human improvement" in *The Subjection of Women*; Amartya Sen's use of a notion of "human capability" to confront gender-based inequalities; the Sen-inspired use of a notion of "human development" in the UN Report to describe and criticize gender-based inequalities; Susan Moller Okin's proposal for a "humanist justice" in her recent major work of feminist political theory; Catharine MacKinnon's graphic description of women's current situation, quoted as my epigraph; and, of course, the role that various accounts of "human rights," or even "The Rights of Man," have played in claiming justice for women.[5] Much the same can be said more generally, I think, about internationalist thought.[6] To cite just one example, I take my proposal to be the feminist analogue of the proposal recently made by Ghanaian philosopher Kwame Anthony Appiah when he wrote, "We will only solve our problems if we see them as human problems arising out of a special situation, and we shall not solve them if we see them as African problems, generated by our being somehow unlike others."[7]

My proposal is frankly universalist and "essentialist." That is, it asks us to focus on what is common to all rather than on differences (although, as we shall see, it does not neglect these), and to see some capabilities and functions as more central, more at the core of human life, than others. Its primary opponents on the contemporary scene will be "anti-essentialists" of various types, thinkers who urge us to begin not with sameness but with difference—both between women and men and across groups of women—and to seek norms defined relatively to a local context and locally held beliefs.[8] This opposition takes many forms, and I shall be responding to several distinct objections that opponents may bring against my universalist proposal. But I can begin to motivate my enterprise by telling several true stories of conversations that have taken place at WIDER, in which the relativist position[9] seemed to have alarming implications for women's lives. I have in some cases conflated two separate conversations into one; otherwise things happened as I describe them.[10]

1. At a conference on "Value and Technology," an American economist who has long been a left-wing critic of neoclassical economics delivers a paper urging the preservation of traditional ways of life in a rural area of India, now under threat of contamination from Western development projects. As evidence of the excellence of this rural way of life, he points to the fact that, whereas we Westerners experience a sharp split between the values that prevail in the workplace and the values that prevail in the home, here, by contrast, there exists what the economist calls "the embedded way of life"; the same values obtaining in both places. His example: Just as in the home a menstruating woman is thought to pollute the kitchen and therefore may not enter it, so too in the workplace a menstruating woman is taken to pollute the loom and may not enter the room where looms are kept. Amartya Sen objects that this example is repellent, rather than admirable: Surely such practices both degrade the women in question and inhibit their freedom. The first economist's collaborator, an elegant French anthropologist (who would, I suspect, object violently to a purity check at the seminar room door), replies to Sen. Doesn't he realize that there is, in these matters, no privileged place to stand? This, after all, has been shown by both Derrida and Foucault. Doesn't he know that he is neglecting the otherness of Indian ideas by bringing his Western essentialist values into the picture?[11]

2. The same French anthropologist now delivers her paper. She expresses regret that the introduction of smallpox vaccination to India by the British eradicated the cult of Sittala Devi, the goddess to whom one used to pray in order to avert smallpox. Here, she says, is another example of Western neglect of difference. Someone (it might have been me) objects that it is surely better to be healthy rather than ill, to live rather

than to die. The answer comes back: Western essentialist medicine conceives of things in terms of binary oppositions: life is opposed to death, health to disease.[12] But if we cast away this binary way of thinking, we will begin to comprehend the otherness of Indian traditions.

At this point Eric Hobsbawm, who has been listening to the proceedings in increasingly uneasy silence, rises to deliver a blistering indictment of the traditionalism and relativism that prevail in this group. He lists historical examples of ways in which appeals to tradition have been used to support oppression and violence.[13] His final example is that of National Socialism in Germany. In the confusion that ensues, most of the relativist social scientists—above all those from far away, who do not know who Hobsbawm is—demand that he be asked to leave the room. The radical American economist, disconcerted by this apparent tension between his relativism and his affiliation with the left, convinces them, with difficulty, to let Hobsbawm remain.

3. We shift now to another conference two years later, a philosophical conference organized by Amartya Sen and me.[14] Sen makes it clear that he holds the perhaps unsophisticated view that life is opposed to death in a very binary way, and that such binary oppositions can and should be used in development analysis. His paper[15] contains much universalist talk of human functioning and capability; he begins to speak of freedom of choice as a basic human good. At this point he is interrupted by the radical economist of my first story, who insists that contemporary anthropology has shown that non-Western people are not especially attached to freedom of choice. His example: A new book on Japan has shown that Japanese males, when they get home from work, do not wish to choose what to eat for dinner, what to wear, and so on. They wish all these choices to be taken out of their hands by their wives. A heated exchange follows about what this example really shows. I leave it to your imaginations to reconstruct it. In the end, the confidence of the radical economist is unshaken: Sen and I are both victims of bad universalist thinking, who fail to respect "difference."[16]

Here we see the relativist position whose influence in development studies motivated the work that has led to the present volume [*Women, Culture and Development*]. The phenomenon is an odd one. For we see here highly intelligent people, people deeply committed to the good of women and men in developing countries, people who think of themselves as progressive and feminist and antiracist, people who correctly argue that the concept of development is an evaluative concept requiring normative argument[17]—effectively eschewing normative argument and taking up positions that converge, as Hobsbawm correctly saw, with the positions of reaction, oppression, and sexism. Under the banner of their fashionable opposition to "essentialism" march ancient religious taboos, the luxury of the pampered husband, educational deprivation, unequal health care, and premature death. (And in my own universalist Aristotelian way, I say it at the outset, I do hold that death is opposed to life in the most binary way imaginable, and freedom to slavery, and hunger to adequate nutrition, and ignorance to knowledge. Nor do I believe that it is only, or even primarily, in Western thinking that such oppositions are, and should be, important.)

The relativist challenge to a universal notion of the human being and human functioning is not always accompanied by clear and explicit philosophical arguments. This is especially true in the material from development studies to which I have referred, where the philosophical debate concerning relativism in ethics and in science is not confronted, and universalism is simply denounced as the legacy of Western conceptions of "*episteme*"[18] that are alleged to be in league with imperialism and oppression.[19] The idea behind this volume [*Women, Culture and Development*] as a whole was that to sort out various strands in the philosophical debate on these questions would be of the first importance in making further progress on women's issues; and the papers by Alcoff ["Democracy and Rationality: A Dialogue with Hilary Putnam," pp. 225–34], Benhabib ["Cultural Complexity, Moral Interdependence, and the Global Dialogical Community," pp. 235–58], Glover ["The Research Programme of Development Ethics," pp. 116–39], and Hilary Putnam ["Pragmatism and Moral Objectivity," pp. 199–224] carry out various aspects of this antirelativist project. Here, then, I shall simply set out rather schematically and briefly, for the purposes of my own argument, several objections to the use of a universal notion of human functioning in development analysis to which I shall later respond.

## 2. THE ASSAULT ON UNIVERSALISM

Many critics of universalism in ethics are really critics of metaphysical realism who assume that realism is a necessary basis for universalism. I shall argue that this assumption is false. By metaphysical realism I mean the view (commonly held in both Western and non-Western philosophical traditions) that there is some determinate way the world is, apart from the interpretive workings of the cognitive faculties of living beings. Far from requiring technical metaphysics for its articulation, this is a very natural way to view things, and is in fact a very common daily-life view, in both Western and non-Western traditions. We did not make the stars, the earth, the trees: They are what they are there outside of us, waiting to be known. And our activities of knowing do not change what they are.

On such a view, the way the human being essentially and universally is will be part of the independent furniture of the universe, something that can in principle be seen and studied independently of any experience of human life and human history. Frequently it is held that a god or gods have this sort of knowledge, and perhaps some wise humans also. This knowledge is usually understood to have normative force. The heavenly account of who we are constrains what we may legitimately seek to be.[20] It is this conception of inquiry into the nature of the human that the Marglins are attacking in their critique of what they call Western *episteme*. They clearly believe it to be a necessary prop to any ethical universalism.

The common objection to this sort of realism is that such extra-historical and extra-experiential metaphysical truths are not in fact available. Sometimes this is put skeptically: The independent structure may still be there, but we cannot reliably grasp it. More often, today, doubt is cast on the coherence of the whole realist idea that there is some one determinate structure to the way things are, independent of all human interpretation. This is the objection that nonphilosophers tend to associate with Jacques Derrida's assault on the "metaphysics of presence,"[21] which he takes to have dominated the entirety of the Western philosophical tradition, and with Richard Rorty's closely related assault on the idea that the knowing mind is, at its best, a "mirror of nature."[22] But it actually has a far longer and more complicated history, even within Western philosophy, beginning at least as early as Kant's assault on transcendent metaphysics, and perhaps far earlier, in some of Aristotle's criticisms of Platonism.[23] A similar debate was long familiar in classical Indian philosophy, and no doubt it has figured in other philosophical traditions as well.[24] Contemporary arguments about realism are many and complex, involving, frequently, technical issues in the philosophy of science and the philosophy of language.

The debate about realism appears to be far from over. The central issues continue to be debated with vigor and subtlety, and a wide range of views is currently on the table. On the other hand, the attack on realism has been sufficiently deep and sufficiently sustained that it would appear strategically wise for an ethical and political view that seeks broad support not to rely on the truth of metaphysical realism, if it can defend itself in some other way. If, then, all universalist and humanist conceptions in ethics are required to regard the universal conception of the human being as part of the independent furniture of the world, unmediated by human self-interpretation and human history, such conceptions do appear to be in some difficulty, and there may well be good reasons to try to do without them.

But universalism does not require such support.[25] For universal ideas of the human do arise within history and from human experience, and they can ground themselves in experience. Indeed, if, as the critics of realism allege, we are always dealing with our own interpretations anyhow, they must acknowledge that universal conceptions of the human are prominent and pervasive among such interpretations, hardly to be relegated to the dustbin of metaphysical history along with rare and recondite philosophical entities such as the Platonic forms. As Aristotle so simply puts it, "One may observe in one's travels to distant countries the feelings of recognition and affiliation that link every human being to every other human being."[26] Or, as Kwame Anthony Appiah eloquently tells the story of his bicultural childhood, a child who visits one set of grandparents in Ghana and another in rural England, who has a Lebanese uncle and who later, as an adult, has nieces and nephews from more than seven different nations, comes to notice not unbridgeable alien "otherness," but a great deal of human commonality, and comes to see the world as a "network of points of affinity."[27] Pursuing those affinities, one may accept the conclusions of the critics of realism while still believing that a universal conception of the human being is both available to ethics and a valuable starting point. I shall be proposing a version of such an account, attempting to identify a group of especially central and basic human functions that ground these affinities.

But such an experiential and historical universalism[28] is still vulnerable to some, if not all, of the objections standardly brought against universalism. I therefore need to introduce those objections, and later to test my account against them.

## 2.1. NEGLECT OF HISTORICAL AND CULTURAL DIFFERENCES

The opposition charges that any attempt to pick out some elements of human life as more fundamental than others, even without appeal to a transhistorical reality, is bound to be insufficiently respectful of actual historical and cultural differences. People, it is claimed, understand human life and humanness in widely different ways: and any attempt to produce a list of the most fundamental properties and functions of human beings is bound to enshrine certain understandings of the human and to demote others. Usually, the objector continues, this takes the form of enshrining the understanding of a dominant group at the expense of minority understandings. This type of objection is frequently made by feminists and can claim support from many historical examples, in which the human has indeed been defined by focusing on the characteristics of males, as manifested in the definer's culture.

It is far from clear what this objection shows. In particular it is far from clear that it supports the idea that we ought to base our ethical norms, instead, on the current preferences and the self-conceptions of people who are living what the objector herself claims to be lives of deprivation and oppression.[29] But it does show at least that the project of choosing one picture of the human over another is fraught with difficulty, political as well as philosophical.

## 2.2. NEGLECT OF AUTONOMY

A different objection is presented by liberal opponents of universalism; my relativist opponents, the Marglins, endorse it as well. (Many such objectors, though not, I believe, the Marglins, are themselves willing to give a universal account of the human in at least some ways, holding freedom of choice to be everywhere of central importance.) The objection is that by determining in advance what elements of human life have most importance, the universalist project fails to respect the right of people to choose a plan of life according to their own lights, determining what is central and what is not.[30] This way of proceeding is "imperialistic." Such evaluative choices must be left to each citizen. For this reason, politics must refuse itself a determinate theory of the human being and the human good.

## 2.3. Prejudicial Application

If we operate with a determinate conception of the human being that is meant to have some normative moral and political force, we must also, in applying it, ask which beings we shall take to fall under the concept. And here the objector notes that, all too easily—even if the conception itself is equitably and comprehensively designed—the powerless can be excluded. Aristotle himself, it is pointed out, held that women and slaves were not full-fledged human beings; and since his politics were based on his view of human functioning, the failure of these beings (in his view) to exhibit the desired mode of functioning contributed to their political exclusion and oppression.

It is, once again, hard to know what this objection is supposed to show. In particular, it is hard to know how, if at all, it is supposed to show that we would be better off without such determinate universal concepts. For it could be plausibly argued that it would have been even easier to exclude women and slaves on a whim if one did not have such a concept to contend with. Indeed, this is what I shall be arguing.[31] On the other hand, it does show that we need to think not only about getting the concept right but also about getting the right beings admitted under the concept.

Each of these objections has some merit. Many universal conceptions of the human being have been insular in an arrogant way, and neglectful of differences among cultures and ways of life. Some have been neglectful of choice and autonomy. And many have been prejudicially applied. But none of this shows that all such conceptions must fail in one or more of these ways. But at this point I need to advance a definite example of such a conception, in order both to display its merits and to argue that it can in fact answer these charges.

# 3. A CONCEPTION OF THE HUMAN BEING: THE CENTRAL HUMAN CAPABILITIES

Here, then, is a sketch for an account of the most important functions and capabilities of the human being, in terms of which human life is defined. The basic idea is that we ask ourselves, "What are the characteristic activities[32] of the human being? What does the human being do, characteristically, as such—and not, say, as a member of a particular group, or a particular local community?" To put it another way, what are the forms of activity, of doing and being, that constitute the human form of life and distinguish it from other actual or imaginable forms of life, such as the lives of animals and plants, or, on the other hand, of immortal gods as imagined in myths and legends (which frequently have precisely the function of delimiting the human)?[33]

We can get at this question better if we approach it via two somewhat more concrete questions that we often really ask ourselves. First is a question about personal continuity. We ask ourselves what changes or transitions are compatible with the continued existence of that being as a member of the human kind, and what are not. (Since continued species identity seems to be at least necessary for continued personal identity, this is also a question about the necessary conditions for continuing as one and the same individual.) Some functions can fail to be present without threatening our sense that we still have a human being on our hands; the absence of others seems to signal the end of a human life. This question is asked regularly, when we attempt to make medical definitions of death in a situation in which some of the functions of life persist, or to decide, for others or (thinking ahead) for ourselves, whether a certain level of illness or impairment means the end of the life of the being in question.[34]

The other question is a question about kind inclusion. We recognize other humans as human across many differences of time and place, of custom and appearance. Kwame Anthony Appiah writes about the experience of seeing his heterogeneous nieces and nephews playing together, and the term "the human future" naturally occurs to him.[35] Much though we may love our dogs and cats, we recognize such scenes as crucially different from scenes of a child playing with a dog or cat. On what do we base these recognitions? We often tell ourselves stories, on the other hand, about anthropomorphic creatures who do not get classified as human, on account of some feature of their form of life and functioning. On what do we base these exclusions? In short, what do we believe must be there, if we are going to acknowledge that a given life is human?[36]

This inquiry proceeds by examining a wide variety of self-interpretations of human beings in many times and places. Especially valuable are myths and stories that situate the human being in some way in the universe, between the "beasts" on the one hand and the "gods" on the other; stories that ask what it is to live as a being with certain abilities that set it apart from the rest of the world of nature and with, on the other hand, certain limits that derive from membership in the world of nature. The idea is that people in many different societies share a general outline of such a conception. This is not surprising, since they do recognize one another as members of the same species,[37] marry one another, have children together, and so forth—and indeed do tell one another such stories, without much difficulty of translation. This convergence gives us some reason for optimism, that if we proceed in this way, using our imaginations, we will have in the end a theory that is not the mere projection of local preferences, but is fully international and a basis for cross-cultural attunement.

Several important methodological points must now be emphasized:

1.  The procedure through which this account of the human is derived is neither ahistorical nor a priori. It is an attempt to set down a very general record of broadly shared experiences of human beings within history. A related point can be made about the results of the inquiry: they do not claim to be ahistorical or a priori truth, but, rather, an especially deep and continuous sort of experiential and historical truth.

2.  On the other hand, the guiding questions of the inquiry direct it to cross national and temporal boundaries, looking for features that ground recognitions of humanness across these boundaries. Thus we can expect that its results will embody what is continuous rather than rapidly changing, international rather than local.

3.  The account is neither a biological account nor a metaphysical account. (For these reasons I have avoided using the term "human nature," which is usually associated with attempts to describe the human being either from the point of view of an allegedly value-free science or from the point of view of normative, often theological, metaphysics.) The inquiry pays attention to biology, but as it figures in and shapes human experience. It is an evaluative and, in a broad sense, ethical inquiry. It asks us to evaluate components of lives, asking which ones are so important that we would not call a life human without them. The result of this inquiry is, then, not a list of value-neutral facts, but a normative conception.[38]

4.     The account is meant to be both tentative and open-ended. We allow explicitly for the possibility that we will learn from our encounters with other human societies to recognize things about ourselves that we had not seen before, or even to change in certain ways, according more importance to something we had thought more peripheral. (We may also shift to reach a political consensus.)

5.     The account is not intended to deny that the items it enumerates are to some extent differently constructed by different societies. It claims only that in these areas there is considerable continuity and overlap, sufficient to ground a working political consensus.[39]

6.     Although the account appeals to consensus in this way, it should be understood that the consensus is acceptable only if it is reached by reasonable procedures, where the notion of reasonableness has normative content.[40] In this way it is different from consensus as mere overlap.[41]

7.     The list is heterogeneous: for it contains both limits against which we press and capabilities through which we aspire. This is not surprising, since we began from the intuitive idea of a creature who is both capable and needy.

8.     The concept "human being," as this view understands it, is in one way like the concept "person" as used elsewhere in moral philosophy: that is, it is a normative ethical concept. On the other hand, because of its link with an empirical study of a species-specific form of life, and with what is most central in such a form of life, it may prove more difficult to withhold from certain beings in an arbitrary way (see Section 7 below). This may commend it to feminists: for the label "person" has frequently been withheld from women, without substantial argument.[42]

Here then, as a first approximation, is a story about what seems to be part of any life we will count as a human life:

## 3.1. Level One of the Conception of the Human Being: The Shape of the Human Form of Life

### 3.1.1. Mortality

All human beings face death and, after a certain age, know that they face it. This fact shapes more or less every other element of human life. Moreover, all human beings have an aversion to death. Although in many circumstances death will be preferred to the available alternatives, the death of a loved one, or the prospect of one's own death, is an occasion for grief and/or fear. If we encountered an immortal anthropomorphic being, or a mortal being who showed no aversion to death and no tendency at all to avoid death, we would judge, in both of these cases, that the form of life was so different from our own that the being could not be acknowledged as human.

### 3.1.2. The Human Body

We live all our lives in bodies of a certain sort, whose possibilities and vulnerabilities do not as such belong to one human society rather than another. These bodies, similar far more than dissimilar (given the enormous range of possibilities) are our homes, so to speak, opening certain options and denying others, giving us certain needs and also certain possibilities for excellence. The fact that any given human being might have lived anywhere and belonged to any culture is a great part of what grounds our mutual recognitions; this fact, in turn, has a great deal to do with the general humanness of the body, its great distinctness from other bodies. The experience of the body is culturally shaped, to be sure; the importance we ascribe to its various functions is also culturally shaped. But the body itself, not culturally variant in its nutritional and other related requirements, sets limits on what can be experienced and valued, ensuring a great deal of overlap.

There is much disagreement, of course, about how much of human experience is rooted in the body. Here religion and metaphysics enter the picture in a nontrivial way. Therefore, in keeping with the nonmetaphysical character of the list, I shall include at this point only those features that would be agreed to be bodily even by determined dualists. The more controversial features, such as thinking, perceiving, and emotion, I shall discuss separately, taking no stand on the question of dualism.

*1. Hunger and thirst: the need for food and drink.* All human beings need food and drink in order to live; all have comparable, though varying, nutritional requirements. Being in one culture rather than another does not make one metabolize food differently. Furthermore, all human beings have appetites that are indices of need. Appetitive experience is to some extent culturally shaped; but we are not surprised to discover much similarity and overlap. Moreover, human beings in general do not wish to be hungry or thirsty (though of course they might choose to fast for some reason). If we discovered someone who really did not experience hunger and thirst at all, or, experiencing them, really did not care about eating and drinking, we would judge that this creature was (in Aristotle's words) "far from being a human being."

*2. Need for shelter.* A recurrent theme in myths of humanness is the nakedness of the human being, its relative unprotectedness in the animal world, its susceptibility to heat, cold, and the ravages of the elements. Stories that explore the difference between our needs and those of furry or scaly or otherwise protected creatures remind us how far our life is constituted by the need to find protection through clothing and housing.

*3. Sexual desire.* Though less urgent as a need than the needs for food, drink, and shelter (in the sense that one can live without its satisfaction), sexual need and desire are features of more or less every human life, at least beyond a certain age. It is, and has all along been, a most important basis for the recognition of others different from ourselves as human beings.

*4. Mobility.* Human beings are, as the old definition goes, featherless bipeds—that is, creatures whose form of life is in part constituted by the ability to move from place to place in a certain characteristic way, not only through the aid of tools that they have made, but with their very own bodies. Human beings like moving about and dislike being deprived of mobility. An anthropomorphic being who, without disability, chose never to move from birth to death would be hard to view as human.

### 3.1.3. Capacity for Pleasure and Pain

Experiences of pain and pleasure are common to all human life (though, once again, both their expression and, to some extent, the experience itself may be culturally shaped). Moreover, the aversion to pain as a fundamental evil is a primitive and, it appears, unlearned part of being a human animal. A society whose members altogether lacked that aversion would surely be judged to be beyond the bounds of humanness.

### 3.1.4. Cognitive Capability: Perceiving, Imagining, Thinking

All human beings have sense-perception, the ability to imagine, and the ability to think, making distinctions and "reaching out for understanding."[43] And these abilities are regarded as of central importance. It is an open question what sorts of accidents or impediments to individuals in these areas will be sufficient for us to judge that the life in question is not really human any longer. But it is safe to say that if we imagine a group of beings whose members totally lack sense-perception, or totally lack imagination, or totally lack reasoning and thinking, we are not in any of these cases imagining a group of human beings, no matter what they look like.

### 3.1.5. Early Infant Development

All human beings begin as hungry babies, aware of their own help-lessness, experiencing their alternating closeness to and distance from that, and those, on whom they depend. This common structure to early life[44]—which is clearly shaped in many different ways by different social arrangements—gives rise to a great deal of overlapping experience that is central in the formation of desires, and of complex emotions such as grief, love, and anger. This, in turn, is a major source of our ability to recognize ourselves in the emotional experiences of those whose lives are very different in other respects from our own. If we encountered a group of apparent humans and then discovered that they never had been babies and had never, in consequence, had those experiences of extreme dependency, need, and affection, we would, I think, have to conclude that their form of life was sufficiently different from our own that they could not be considered part of the same kind.

### 3.1.6. Practical Reason

All human beings participate (or try to) in the planning and managing of their own lives, asking and answering questions about what is good and how one should live. Moreover, they wish to enact their thought in their lives—to be able to choose and evaluate, and to function accordingly. This general capability has many concrete forms, and is related in complex ways to the other capabilities, emotional, imaginative, and intellectual. But a being who altogether lacks this would not be likely to be regarded as fully human, in any society.

### 3.1.7. Affiliation with Other Human Beings

All human beings recognize and feel some sense of affiliation and concern for other human beings. Moreover, we value the form of life that is constituted by these recognitions and affiliations. We live with and in relation to others, and regard a life not lived in affiliation with others to be a life not worth the living. (Here I would really wish, with Aristotle, to spell things out further. We define ourselves in terms of at least two types of affiliation: intimate family and/or personal relations, and social or civic relations.)

### 3.1.8. Relatedness to Other Species and to Nature

Human beings recognize that they are not the only living things in their world: that they are animals living alongside other animals, and also alongside plants, in a universe that, as a complex interlocking order, both supports and limits them. We are dependent upon that order in countless ways; and we also sense that we owe that order some respect and concern, however much we may differ about exactly what we owe, to whom, and on what basis. Again, a creature who treated animals exactly like stones and could not be brought to see any difference would probably be regarded as too strange to be human. So too would a creature who did not in any way respond to the natural world.

### 3.1.9. Humor and Play

Human life wherever it is lived, makes room for recreation and laughter. The forms play takes are enormously varied—and yet we recognize other humans, across cultural barriers, as the animals who laugh. Laughter and play are frequently among the deepest and also the first modes of our mutual recognition. Inability to play or laugh is taken, correctly, as a sign of deep disturbance in a child; if it proves permanent we will doubt whether the child is capable of leading a fully human life. An entire society that lacked this ability would seem to us both terribly strange and terribly frightening.

### 3.1.10. Separateness

However much we live with and for others, we are, each of us, "one in number,"[45] proceeding on a separate path through the world from birth to death. Each person feels only his or her own pain and not anyone else's. Each person dies without entailing logically the death of anyone else. When one person walks across the room, no other person follows automatically. When we count the number of human beings in a room, we have no difficulty figuring out where one begins and the other ends. These obvious facts need stating, since they might have been otherwise. We should bear them in mind when we hear talk about the absence of individualism in certain societies. Even the most intense forms of human interaction, for example sexual experience, are experiences of responsiveness, not of fusion. If fusion is made the goal, the result is bound to be disappointment.

### 3.1.11. Strong Separateness

Because of separateness, each human life has, so to speak, its own peculiar context and surroundings—objects, places, a history, particular friendships, locations, sexual ties—that are not exactly the same as those of anyone else, and in terms of which the person to some extent identifies herself. Though societies vary a great deal in the degree and type of strong separateness that they permit and foster, there is no life yet known that really does (as Plato wished) fail to use the words "mine" and "not mine" in some personal and nonshared way. What I use, live in, respond to, I use, live in, respond to from my own separate existence. And on the whole, human beings recognize one another as beings who wish to have at least some separateness of context, a little space to move around in, some special items to use or love.

This is a working list. It is put out to generate debate. It has done so and will continue to do so, and it will be revised accordingly.

As I have said, the list is composed of two different sorts of items; limits and capabilities. As far as capabilities go, to call them parts of humanness is to make a very basic sort of evaluation. It is to say that a life without this item would be too lacking, too impoverished, to be human at all. Obviously, then, it could not be a good human life. So this list of capabilities is a ground-floor or minimal conception of the good. (In the sense that it does not fully determine the choice of a way of life, but simply regulates the parameters of what can be chosen, it plays, however, the role traditionally played in liberal political theory by a conception of the right.)[46]

With the limits, things are more complicated. In selecting the limits for attention, we have, once again, made a basic sort of evaluation, saying that these things are so important that life would not be human without them. But what we have said is that human life, in its general form, consists of the awareness of these limits plus a struggle against them. Humans do not wish to be hungry, to feel pain, to die. (Separateness is highly complex, both a limit and a capability. Much the same is true of many of the limits implied by the shape and the capacities of the body.) On the other hand, we cannot assume that the correct evaluative conclusion to draw is that we should try as hard as possible to get rid of the limit altogether. It is characteristic of human life to prefer recurrent hunger plus eating to a life with neither hunger nor eating; to prefer sexual desire and its satisfaction to a life with neither desire nor satisfaction. Even where death is concerned, the desire for immortality, which many human beings certainly have, is a peculiar desire: For it is not clear that the wish to lose one's finitude completely is a desire that one can coherently entertain for oneself or for someone one loves. It seems to be a wish for a transition to a way of life so wholly different, with such different values and ends, that it seems that the identity of the individual will not be preserved. So the evaluative conclusion, in mapping out a ground-floor conception of the good (saying what functioning is necessary for a life to be human) will have to be expressed with much caution, clearly, in terms of what would be a humanly good way of countering the limitation.

## 4. THE TWO THRESHOLDS

Things now get very complicated. For we want to describe two distinct thresholds: a threshold of capability to function beneath which a life will be so impoverished that it will not be human at all; and a somewhat higher threshold, beneath which those characteristic functions are available in such a reduced way that, though we may judge the form of life a human one, we will not think it a *good* human life. The latter threshold is the one that will eventually concern us when we turn to public policy: for we don't want societies to make their citizens capable of the bare minimum. My view holds, with Aristotle, that a good political arrangement is one "in accordance with which anyone whatsoever might do well and live a flourishing life."[47]

These are clearly, in many areas, two distinct thresholds, requiring distinct levels of resource and opportunity. One may be alive without being well nourished. As Marx observed, one may be able to use one's senses without being able to use them in a fully human way. And yet there is need for caution here. For in many cases the move from human life to good human life is supplied by the citizen's own powers of choice and self-definition, in such a way that once society places them above the first threshold, moving above the second is more or less up to them. This is especially likely to be so, I think, in areas such as affiliation and practical reasoning, where in many cases once social institutions permit a child to cross the first threshold its own choices will be central in raising it above the second. (This is not always so, however: for certain social conditions, for example certain mindless forms of labor or, we may add, traditional hierarchical gender relations, may impede the flourishing of affiliation and practical reason, while not stamping it out entirely.) On the other hand, it is clear that where bodily health and nutrition, for example, are concerned, there is a considerable difference between the two thresholds, and a difference that is standardly made by resources over which individuals do not have full control. It would then be the concern of quality-of-life assessment to ask whether all citizens are capable, not just of the bare minimum, but of *good life* in these areas. Clearly there is a continuum here. Nor will it in practice be at all easy to say where the upper threshold, especially, should be located.

I shall not say much about the first threshold, but shall illustrate it by a few examples. What is an existence that is so impoverished that it cannot properly be called a human life? Here we should count, I believe, many forms of existence that take place at the end of a human life—all those in which the being that survives has irretrievably lost sensation and consciousness (in what is called a "permanent vegetative condition"); and also, I would hold, some that fall short of this, but in which the capacity to recognize loved ones, to think and to reason, has irreversibly decayed beyond a certain point. I would include the extreme absence of ability to engage in practical reasoning that is often the outcome of the notorious frontal lobotomy. I would also include an absence of mobility so severe that it makes speech, as well as movement from place to place, impossible.

It follows from this that certain severely damaged infants are not human ever, even if born from two human parents: again, those with global and total sensory incapacity and/or no consciousness or thought; also, I think, those with no ability at all to recognize or relate to others. (This of course tells us nothing about what we owe them morally, it just separates that question from moral questions about human beings.)[48]

Again, we notice the evaluative character of these threshold judgments. The fact that a person who has lost her arms cannot play a piano does not make us judge that she no longer lives a human life; had she lost the capacity to think and remember, or to form affectionate relationships, it would have been a different matter.

Many such disasters are not to be blamed on social arrangements, and in those cases the first threshold has no political implications. But many are, where bad nutrition and health care enter in. The role of society is even more evident if we think of a more controversial group of first-threshold cases, in which the nonhuman outcome was environmentally caused: the rare cases of children who have grown up outside a human community, or in a severely dysfunctional home, and utterly lack language and reason, or lack social abilities in an extreme and irreversible way. We can focus the political question more productively, however, if we now turn from the question of mere human life to the question of good life, the level we would really like to see a human being attain.

Here, as the next level of the conception of the human being, I shall now specify certain basic functional capabilities at which societies should aim for their citizens, and which quality of life measurements should measure. In other words, this will be an account of the second threshold—although in some areas it may coincide, for the reasons I have given, with the first: Once one is capable of human functioning in this area one is also capable, with some further effort and care, of good functioning. I introduce this list as a list of capabilities to function, rather than of actual functionings, since I shall argue that capability, not actual functioning, should be the goal of public policy.

## 4.1. LEVEL 2 OF THE CONCEPTION OF THE HUMAN BEING: BASIC HUMAN FUNCTIONAL CAPABILITIES

1.   Being able to live to the end of a human life of normal length,[49] not dying prematurely, or before one's life is so reduced as to be not worth living.

2.  Being able to have good health; to be adequately nour-
    ished;[50] to have adequate shelter;[51] having opportuni-
    ties for sexual satisfaction, and for choice in matters
    of reproduction;[52] being able to move from place to
    place.

3.  Being able to avoid unnecessary and nonbenefi-
    cial pain, so far as possible, and to have pleasurable
    experiences.

4.  Being able to use the senses; being able to imagine, to
    think, and to reason—and to do these things in a way
    informed and cultivated by an adequate education,
    including, but by no means limited to, literacy and
    basic mathematical and scientific training.[53] Being
    able to use imagination and thought in connection
    with experiencing and producing spiritually enriching
    materials and events of one's own choice; religious,
    literary, musical, and so forth. I believe that the protec-
    tion of this capability requires not only the provision
    of education, but also legal guarantees of freedom of
    expression with respect to both political and artistic
    speech, and of freedom of religious exercise.

5.  Being able to have attachments to things and persons
    outside ourselves; to love those who love and care for
    us, to grieve at their absence; in general, to love, to
    grieve, to experience longing and gratitude.[54] Support-
    ing this capability means supporting forms of human
    association that can be shown to be crucial in their
    development.[55]

6.  Being able to form a conception of the good and to
    engage in critical reflection about the planning of
    one's own life. This includes, today, being able to seek
    employment outside the home and to participate in
    political life.

7.  Being able to live for and to others, to recognize and
    show concern for other human beings, to engage in

various forms of social interaction; to be able to imagine the situation of another and to have compassion for that situation; to have the capability for both justice and friendship. Protecting this capability means, once again, protecting institutions that constitute such forms of affiliation, and also protecting the freedoms of assembly and political speech.

8. Being able to live with concern for and in relation to animals, plants, and the world of nature.

9. Being able to laugh, to play, to enjoy recreational activities.

10. Being able to live one's own life and nobody else's. This means having certain guarantees of noninterference with certain choices that are especially personal and definitive of selfhood, such as choices regarding marriage, childbearing, sexual expression, speech, and employment.

10a. Being able to live one's own life in one's own surroundings and context. This means guarantees of freedom of association and of freedom from unwarranted search and seizure; it also means a certain sort of guarantee of the integrity of personal property, though this guarantee may be limited in various ways by the demands of social equality, and is always up for negotiation in connection with the interpretation of the other capabilities, since personal property, unlike personal liberty, is a tool of human functioning rather than an end in itself.

My claim is that a life that lacks any one of these capabilities, no matter what else it has, will fall short of being a good human life. So it would be reasonable to take these things as a focus for concern, in assessing the quality of life in a country and asking about the role of public policy in meeting human needs. The list is certainly general—and this is deliberate, in order to leave room for plural specification and also for further negotiation. But I claim that it does, rather like a set of constitutional guarantees, offer real guidance in the ongoing historical process of further refinement and specification, and far more accurate guidance than that offered by the focus on utility, or even on resources.

A few comments are in order about the relationship of this version of the list to other versions I have published previously. First, taking some lessons from the *Human Development Report*, it is considerably more specific about matters such as education and work, so as to give the development theorist something concrete to measure. Second, it is far more explicitly concerned with guarantees of personal liberty of expression, reproductive choice, and religion.[56] This was not only called for in general, but called forth by the attempt to articulate the specific requisites of equal female capability.[57] Third, in accordance with its commitment to the distinction between ends and means, it understands "property rights" as instrumental to other human capabilities,[58] and therefore to a certain extent, as up for negotiation in general social planning.

The list is, emphatically, a list of separate components. We cannot satisfy the need for one of them by giving a larger amount of another. All are of central importance and all are distinct in quality. This limits the trade-offs that it will be reasonable to make, and thus limits the applicability of quantitative cost-benefit analysis. At the same time, the items on the list are related to one another in many complex ways. For example our characteristic mode of nutrition, unlike that of sponges, requires moving from here to there. And we do whatever we do as separate beings, tracing distinct paths through space and time. Notice that reproductive choices involve both sexual capability and issues of separateness, and bind the two together in a deep and complex way.

A further comment is in order, concerning the relationship of this threshold list to an account of human equality. A commitment to bringing all human beings across a certain threshold of capability to choose represents a certain sort of commitment to equality: for the view treats all persons as equal bearers of human claims, no matter where they are starting from in terms of circumstances, special talents, wealth, gender, or race. On the other hand, I have said nothing so far about how one should regard inequalities that persist once the threshold level has been attained for all persons. To some extent I feel this would be premature, since the threshold level has so rarely been attained for the complete capability set. On the other hand, one can imagine a situation—perhaps it could be that of the USA or Japan, given certain large changes in health support here, or educational distribution there, that would meet threshold conditions and still exhibit inequalities of attainment between the genders or the races. We have two choices here: either to argue that this situation actually contains capability failure after all; or to grant that the capability view needs to be supplemented by an independent theory of equality. I am not yet certain what I want to say about this, but I am inclined to the first alternative, since I think that gender inequality of the sort one sees in a prosperous nation does nonetheless push the subordinated racial or gender group beneath an acceptable threshold of autonomy, dignity, and emotional well being. Indeed, subordination is itself a kind of capability failure, a failure to attain complete personhood. So I am inclined to say that, properly fleshed out, the second threshold would be incompatible with systematic subordination of one group to another.

## 5. THE ROLE OF THE CONCEPTION IN DEVELOPMENT POLICY

My claim is that we urgently need a conception of the human being and human functioning in public policy. If we try to do without this sort of guidance when we ask how goods, resources, and opportunities should be distributed, we reject guidance that is, I think, superior to that offered by any of the other guides currently available.

I shall focus here on the area of most concern to our project: the assessment of the quality of life in a developing country, with special attention to the lives of women. For the time being, I shall take the nation-state as my basic unit, and the question I shall ask is, "How is the nation doing, with respect to the quality of life of its citizens?" In other words, I shall be asking the sort of question asked by the UN *Human Development Report*. I shall not propose a general theory about how the needs revealed by such an assessment should be met: whether by centralized government planning, for example, or through a system of incentives, and whether through direct subsidies or through the provision of opportunities for employment. Nor shall I ask what responsibilities richer nations have to poorer nations, in ensuring that the needs of all human beings are met the world over. That is an urgent question, and it must at a later date be confronted. For now, however, I shall focus on the correct understanding of the goal, where each separate nation is concerned.

The basic claim I wish to make—concurring with Amartya Sen—is that the central goal of public planning should be the *capabilities* of citizens to perform various important functions. The questions that should be asked when assessing quality of life in a country are (and of course this is a central part of assessing the quality of its political arrangements) "How well have the people of the country been enabled to perform the central human functions?" and, "Have they been put in a position of mere human subsistence with respect to the functions, or have they been enabled to live well?" In other words, we ask where the people are, with respect to the second list. And we focus on getting as many people as possible above the second threshold, with respect to the interlocking set of capabilities enumerated by that list.[59] Naturally, the determination of whether certain individuals and groups are across the threshold is only as precise a matter as the determination of the threshold; and I have left things deliberately somewhat open-ended at this point, in keeping with the procedures of the *Human Development Report*, believing that the best way to work toward a more precise determination is to allow the community of nations to hammer it out after an extended comparative inquiry, of the sort the report makes possible. Again, we will have to answer various questions about the costs we are willing to pay to get all citizens above the threshold, as opposed to leaving a small number below and allowing the rest a considerably above-threshold life quality. Here my claim is that capability-equality, in the sense of moving all above the threshold, should be taken as the central goal. As with Rawls's difference principle, so here: Inequalities in distribution above the threshold should be tolerated only if they move more people across it;[60] once all are across, societies are to a great extent free to choose the other goals that they wish to pursue.

The basic intuition from which the capability approach starts, in the political arena, is that human capabilities exert a moral claim that they should be developed. Human beings are creatures such that, provided with the right educational and material support, they can become fully capable of the major human functions, can cross the first and second thresholds. That is, they are creatures with certain lower-level capabilities (which I have elsewhere called "basic capabilities")[61] to perform the functions in question. When these capabilities are deprived of the nourishment that would transform them into the high-level capabilities that figure on my list, they are fruitless, cut off, in some way but a shadow of themselves. They are like actors who never get to go on the stage, or a musical score that is never performed. Their very being makes forward reference to functioning. Thus if functioning never arrives on the scene, they are hardly even what they are. This may sound like a metaphysical idea, and in a sense it is (in that it is an idea discussed in Aristotle's *Metaphysics*). But that does not mean that it is not a basic and pervasive empirical idea, an idea that underwrites many of our daily practices and judgments in many times and places. I claim that just as we hold that a child who dies before getting to maturity has died especially tragically—for her activities of growth and preparation for adult activity now have lost their point—so too with capability and functioning more generally: We believe that certain basic and central human endowments have a claim to be assisted in developing, and exert that claim on others, and especially, as Aristotle saw, on government. We shall see the work this consideration can do in arguments for women's equality. I think it is the underlying basis, in the Western philosophical tradition, for many notions of human rights. I suggest, then, that in thinking of political planning we begin from this notion, thinking of the basic capabilities of human beings as needs for functioning, which give rise to correlated political duties.

There is, then, an empirical basis for the determination that a certain being is one of the ones to which our normative conception and its associated duties applies. It is the gap between potential humanness and its full realization that exerts a moral claim. If the worker described by Marx as not capable of a truly human use of his senses[62] had really been a nonhuman animal, the fact that he was given a form of life suited to such an animal would not be a tragedy. If women were really turtles, the fact that being a woman is not yet a way of being a human being would not be, as it is, an outrage. There is, of course, enormous potential for abuse in determining who has these basic capabilities. The history of IQ testing is just one chapter in an inglorious saga of prejudiced capability-testing that goes back at least to the Noble Lie of Plato's *Republic*. Therefore we should, I think, proceed as if every offspring of two human parents has the basic capabilities, unless and until long experience with the individual has convinced us that damage to that individual's condition is so great that it could never in any way arrive at the higher capability level.

The political and economic application of this approach is evident in a variety of areas. Amartya Sen has developed a number of its concrete implications in the areas of welfare and development economics, and has focused particularly on its application to the assessment of women's quality of life.[63] With his advice, the UN *Human Development*

*Reports* have begun to gather information and to rank nations in accordance with the type of plural-valued capability-focused measuring the approach suggests. In a closely related study, Iftekhar Hossein has used the approach to give an account of poverty as capability failure.[64] Independently, a very similar approach has been developed by Finnish and Swedish social scientists, above all Erik Allardt and Robert Erikson.[65] Wishing to develop ways of gathering information about how their people are doing that would be more sensitive and informationally complete than polls based on ideas of utility, they worked out lists of the basic human capabilities for functioning and then examined the performance of various groups in the population—above all women and minorities—in these terms, thus anticipating the procedures of the *Human Development Report*, which devotes a great deal of attention to gender differences, urban-rural differences, and so forth.

The "capabilities approach" has clear advantages over other current approaches to quality-of-life assessment. Assessment that uses GNP per capita as its sole measure fails to concern itself with the distribution of resource and thus can give high marks to countries with enormous inequalities. Nor does this approach examine other human goods that are not reliably correlated with the presence of resources: infant mortality, for example, or access to education, or the quality of racial and gender relations, or the presence or absence of political freedoms. The *Human Development Report* for 1993 informs us, for example, that the United Arab Emirates has real GNP per capita of $16,753—tenth-highest in the world, higher, for example, than Norway or Australia—while overall, in the aggregation of all the indicators of life quality, it ranks only sixty-seventh in the world (out of 173 nations measured). Its adult literacy rate is 55%, far lower than any of the 60 countries generally ahead of it, and also than many generally below it. (Both Norway and Australia have adult literacy of 99%.) The maternal mortality rate of 130 per 100,000 live births is comparatively high. The proportion of women progressing beyond secondary education is very low, and only 6% of the labor force is female (as opposed, for example, to 42% in Seychelles, 35% in Brazil, 43% in China, 47% in Vietnam, 26% in India, and 20% in Nigeria). In fact, in all the world only Algeria (4%) has a lower proportion of females in the labor force, only Iraq (6%) ties it, and only Qatar (7%), Saudi Arabia (7%), Libya (9%), Jordan (10%), Pakistan (11%), Bangladesh (7%), and Afghanistan (8%) come close. Evidence links female wage-earning outside the home strongly to female health care and life-expectancy.[66] And in fact, we find that the ratio of females to males in the United Arab Emirates is the amazing 48:100, lowest in all the world. If this is discounted as employment related, we may pursue the other countries in our low external employment comparison class. The ratio of females to males in nations in which there is no reason to suppose sexual discrimination in nourishment and health care is, Sen has shown, about 106:100 in Europe and North America—or, if we focus only on the developing world, taking sub-Saharan Africa as our "norm," 102:100. In Qatar it is 60:100, in Saudi Arabia 84, in Libya 91, in Jordan 95, in Pakistan 92, in Bangladesh 94, in Afghanistan 94.

These are some of the numbers that we start noticing if we focus on capabilities and functioning rather than simply on GNP. They are essential to the understanding of how women are doing. In fact, they are the numbers from which Sen's graphic statistics regarding "missing women" emerge. (The number of "missing women" is the number of extra women who would be in a given country if that country had the same sex ratio as sub-Saharan Africa.) They strongly support Martha Chen's argument that the right to work is a right basic to the lives of women not only in itself, but for its impact on other basic capabilities and functionings. Saleha Begum's employment led to better nutritional and health status for herself and, indeed, her children and family. Metha Bai may soon become one of the statistics from which the number of missing women is made.

Would other available approaches have done the job as well? The common approach that measures quality of life in terms of utility—polling people concerning the satisfaction of their preferences—would have missed the obvious fact that desires and subjective preferences are not always reliable indicators of what a person really needs. Preferences, as Amartya Sen's work has repeatedly shown, are highly malleable.[67] The rich and pampered easily become accustomed to their luxury, and view with pain and frustration a life in which they are treated just like everyone else. Males are a special case of this: We do not need to go abroad to know that males frequently resent a situation in which they are asked to share child care and domestic responsibilities on an equal basis.[68] The poor and deprived frequently adjust their expectations and aspirations to the low level of life they have known. Thus they may not demand more education, better health care. Like the women described in Sen's account of health surveys in India, they may not even know what it is to feel healthy.[69] Like the rural Bangladeshi women so vividly described in Martha Chen's *A Quiet Revolution*,[70] they may not even know what it means to have the advantages of education. We may imagine that many women in the countries I have mentioned would not fight, as Seleha Begum did, for participation in the workforce; nor would they be aware of the high correlation between work outside the home and other advantages. As Sen argues, they may have fully internalized the ideas behind the traditional system of discrimination, and may view their deprivation as "natural." Thus if we rely on utility as our measure of life quality, we most often will get results that support the status quo and oppose radical change.[71]

If these criticisms apply to approaches that focus on utility in general, they apply all the more pointedly to the sort of local-tradition relativism espoused by the Marglins, in which the measure of quality of life will be the satisfaction of a certain group of preferences, namely the traditional ones of a given culture. Indeed, it is illuminating to consider how close, in its renunciation of critical normative argument, the Marglin approach is to the prevailing economic approaches of which it presents itself as a radical critique. A preference-based approach that gives priority to the preferences of traditional culture is likely to be especially subversive of the quality of life of women who have been on the whole badly treated by prevailing traditional norms. And one can see this clearly in the Marglins' own examples. For menstruation taboos impose severe restrictions on women's power to form a plan of life and to execute the plan they have chosen. They are members of the same family of traditional attitudes about women and the workplace that made it difficult for Saleha Begum to support herself and her family, that make it impossible for Metha Bai to sustain the basic functions of life. And the Japanese husband who allegedly renounces freedom of choice actually enhances it, in the ways that matter, by asking the woman to look after the boring details of life. One can sympathize with many of the Marglins' goals—respect for diversity, desire to preserve aspects of traditional life that appear to be rich in spiritual and artistic value—without agreeing that extreme relativism of the sort they endorse is the best way to pursue these concerns.

As for liberal approaches that aim at equality in the distribution of certain basic resources, these have related problems, since these, too, refuse to take a stand on the ends to which the resources are means.[72] Wealth and income are not good in their own right; they are good only insofar as they promote human functioning. Second, human beings have widely varying needs for resources, and any adequate definition of who is "better off" and "worse off" must reflect that fact.[73] Women who have traditionally not been educated, for example, may well require more of the relevant resources to attain the same capability level: that is why, in the case discussed by Martha Chen, the Bangladesh Rural Advancement Committee created a special female literacy program, rather than a program that distributed equal resources to all. Third, by defining being "well-off" in terms of possessions alone, the liberal fails to go deep enough in imagining the impediments to functioning that are actually present in many lives—in their conditions of labor or exclusion from labor, for example, in their frequently unequal family responsibilities, in the obstacles to self-realization imposed by traditional norms and values.[74] The stories of Saleha Begum and Metha Bai are vivid examples of such unequal obstacles. No right-to-work effort, and no expenditure of resources in that connection, were necessary in order to make men capable of working in the fields in Bangladesh. No male of Metha Bai's caste would have to overcome threats of physical violence in order to go out of the house to work for life-sustaining food.

## 6. ANSWERING THE OBJECTIONS: HUMAN FUNCTIONING AND PLURALISM

I have commended the human-function view by contrast to its rivals on the development scene. But I must now try to show how it can answer the objections I described earlier.

Concerning *neglect of historical and cultural difference*, I can begin by insisting that this normative conception of human capability and functioning is general, and in a sense vague, for precisely this reason. The list claims to have identified in a very general way components that are fundamental to any human life. But it allows in its very design for the possibility of multiple specifications of each of the components. This is so in several different ways. First, the constitutive circumstances of human life, while broadly shared, are themselves realized in different forms in different societies. The fear of death, the love of play, relationships of friendship, and affiliation with others, even the experience of the bodily appetites never turn up in simply the vague and general form in which we have introduced them there, but always in some specific and historically rich cultural realization, which can profoundly shape not only the conceptions used by the citizens in these areas, but also their experiences themselves. Nonetheless, we do have in these areas of our common humanity sufficient overlap to sustain a general conversation, focusing on our common problems and prospects. And sometimes the common conversation will permit us to criticize some conceptions of the grounding experiences themselves, as at odds with other things human beings want to do and to be.

When we are choosing a conception of good functioning with respect to these circumstances, we can expect an even greater degree of plurality to become evident. Here the approach wants to retain plurality in two significantly different ways: what I may call the way of *plural specification*, and what I may call the way of *local specification*.

Plural specification means what its name implies. Public policy, while using a determinate conception of the good at a high level of generality, leaves a great deal of latitude for citizens to specify each of the components more concretely, and with much variety, in accordance with local traditions, or individual tastes. Many concrete forms of life, in many different places and circumstances, display functioning in accordance with all the major capabilities.

As for local specification: Good public reasoning, I believe and have argued, is always done, when well done, with a rich sensitivity to the concrete context, to the characters of the agents and their social situation. This means that in addition to the pluralism I have just described, the Aristotelian needs to consider a different sort of plural specification of the good. For sometimes what is a good way of promoting education in one part of the world will be completely ineffectual in another. Forms of affiliation that flourish in one community may prove impossible to sustain in another. In such cases, the Aristotelian must aim at some concrete specification of the general list that suits, and develops out of, the local conditions. This will always most reasonably be done in a participatory dialogue[75] with those who are most deeply immersed in those conditions. For though Aristotelianism does not hesitate to criticize tradition where tradition perpetrates injustice or oppression, it also does not believe in saying anything at all without rich and full information, gathered not so much from detached study as from the voices of those who live the ways of life in question. Martha Chen's work, both here and in her book, gives an excellent example of how such sensitivity to the local may be combined with a conviction that the central values on the list are worth pursuing even when tradition has not endorsed them.

The liberal charges the capability approach with *neglect of autonomy*, arguing that any such determinate conception removes from the citizens the chance to make their own choices about the good life. This is a complicated issue: Three points can be stressed. First, the list is a list of capabilities, not a list of actual functions, precisely because the conception is designed to leave room for choice. Government is not directed to push citizens into acting in certain valued ways; instead, it is directed to make sure that all human beings have the necessary resources and conditions for acting in those ways. It leaves the choice up to them. A person with plenty of food can always choose to fast. A person who has been given the capability for sexual expression can always choose celibacy. The person who has access to subsidized education can always decide to do something else instead. By making opportunities available, government enhances, and does not remove, choice.[76] It will not always be easy to say at what point someone is really capable of making a choice, especially in areas where there are severe traditional obstacles to functioning. Sometimes our best strategy may well be to look at actual functioning and infer negative capability (tentatively) from its absence.[77] But the conceptual distinction remains very important.

Second, this respect for choice is built deeply into the list itself, in the architectonic role it gives to practical reasoning. One of the most central capabilities promoted by the conception will be the capability of choice itself.[78] We should note that the major liberal view in this area (that of John Rawls) agrees with our approach in just this area. For Rawls insists that satisfactions that are not the outgrowth of one's very own choices have no moral worth; and he conceives of the two moral powers (analogous to our practical reasoning), and of sociability (corresponding to our affiliation) as built into the definition of the parties in the original position, and thus as necessary constraints on any outcome they will select.[79]

Finally, the capability view insists that choice is not pure spontaneity, flourishing independent of material and social conditions. If one cares about autonomy, then one must care about the rest of the form of life that supports it, and the material conditions that enable one to live that form of life. Thus the approach claims that its own comprehensive concern with flourishing across all areas of life is a better way of promoting choice than is the liberal's narrower concern with spontaneity alone, which sometimes tolerates situations in which individuals are in other ways cut off from the fully human use of their faculties.

I turn now to the objection about application; it raises especially delicate questions where women are concerned.

# 7. WHO GETS INCLUDED? WOMEN AS HUMAN BEINGS

In a now well-known remark, which I cite here as an epigraph, the feminist lawyer Catharine MacKinnon claimed that "being a woman is not yet a way of being a human being."[80] This means, I think, that most traditional ways of categorizing and valuing women have not accorded them full membership in the human species, as that species is generally defined. MacKinnon is no doubt thinking in particular of the frequent denials to women of the rational nature that is taken to be a central part of what it is to be human. It is sobering to remind oneself that quite a few leading philosophers, including Aristotle and Rousseau, the "fathers" (certainly not mothers) of my idea, did deny women full membership in human functioning as they understood that notion. If this is so, one might well ask, of what use is it really to identify a set of central human capabilities? For the basic (lower-level) capacity to develop these can always be denied to women, even by those who grant their centrality. Does this problem show that the human function idea is either hopelessly in league with patriarchy or, at best, impotent as a tool for justice?

I believe that it does not. For if we examine the history of these denials we see, I believe, the great power of the conception of the human as a source of moral claims. Acknowledging the other person as a member of the very same kind would have generated a sense of affiliation and a set of moral and educational duties. That is why, to those bent on shoring up their own power, the stratagem of splitting the other off from one's own species seems so urgent and so seductive. But to deny humanness to beings with whom one lives in conversation and interaction is a fragile sort of self-deceptive stratagem, vulnerable to sustained and consistent reflection, and also to experiences that cut through self-deceptive rationalization.[81] Any moral conception can be withheld, out of ambition or hatred or shame. But the conception of the human being, spelled out, as here, in a roughly determinate way, in terms of circumstances of life and functions in these circumstances, seems much harder to withhold than other conceptions that have been made the basis for ethics—"rational being," for example, or (as I have suggested) "person."

To illustrate this point, I now turn to the earliest argument known to me in the Western philosophical tradition that uses a conception of the human being for feminist ends. It is not the first feminist argument in the Western tradition: For Plato's *Republic* precedes (and influences) it.[82] But Plato's argument in favor of equal education for women is heavily qualified by his élitism with respect to all functions for all human beings; thus it is able to generate only élitist conclusions for males and females alike. Platonic justice is not the "humanist justice" of Susan Okin's powerful phrase. The argument I have in mind is, instead, the first argument of the Roman Stoic thinker Musonius Rufus in his brief treatise "That Women Too Should Do Philosophy," written in the first century A.D.[83] This argument is all the more interesting in that it, in effect, uses Aristotelian concepts to correct Aristotle's mistake about women—showing, I think, that an Aristotelian who is both internally consistent and honest about the evidence cannot avoid the egalitarian normative conclusion that women, as much as men, should receive a higher education (for that is in effect what is meant by doing philosophy).[84]

The argument has a tacit premise. It is that—at least with respect to certain central functions of the human being—the presence in a creature of a basic (untrained, lower-level) capability to perform the functions in question, given suitable support and education, exerts a claim on society that those capabilities should be developed to the point at which the person is fully capable of choosing the functions in question. This premise needed no argument in the philosophical culture of Greco-Roman antiquity, since that moral claim is more or less taken to be implicit in the notion of capability itself. I have tried to give it intuitive support in the argument of this paper.

The argument itself now follows with a truly radical simplicity. Its second premise consists of an appeal to the experience of the imaginary recalcitrant male interlocutor. Women, he is asked to concede on the basis of experience, do in fact have the basic capabilities to perform a wide variety of the most important human functions. They have the five senses. They have the same number of bodily parts, implying similar functional possibilities in that sphere. They have the ability to think and reason, just as males do. And, finally, they have responsiveness to ethical distinctions, making (whether well or badly) distinctions between the good and the bad. Some time is then spent establishing a third premise: that "higher education" of the sort offered by the Stoic ideal of liberal education, is necessary for the full development of the perceptual, intellectual, and moral capabilities. Conclusion: Women, like men, should have this education.

The puzzle, for us, is the second premise. Why does the interlocutor accept it? We see from the surrounding material that the interlocutor is a husband who interacts with his wife in a number of areas of life that are explicitly enumerated: planning and managing a household (where she is the one who manages most of the daily business); having and raising children (where he observes, or imagines, her in labor, enduring risk and pain for the sake of the family and, later, caring for and educating the child); having sexual relations with him, and refusing to have sex with others; having a real friendship with him, based on common contemporary ideas of "sharing life together";[85] deciding how to treat the people around her; being fair, for example, to the household staff; and, finally, confronting all the dangers and the moral ambiguities of the politics of first century A.D. Rome—refusing to capitulate, he says, to the unjust demands of a tyrant. In all of these operations of life, the argument seems to be, he tacitly acknowledges, in fact strongly relies upon, his wife's capability to engage in practical reasoning and ethical distinction making. Indeed, he is depicted as someone who would like these things done *well*—for he wants his wife not to reason badly when political life gets tough, or to treat the servants with cruelty, or to botch the education of the children. So in his daily life he acknowledges her humanity, her possession of the basic (lower-level) capabilities for fully human functioning. How, then, Musonius reasonably asks him, can he consistently deny her what would be necessary in order to develop and fulfill that humanity?

This, I believe, is an impressively radical argument. And it led to (or reflected) a social situation that marked a high point for women in the Western tradition for thousands of years since and to come.[86] We do not need to show that the views of Musonius on women were perfect in all respects; in many ways they were not. But his argument shows, I believe, the power of a universal conception of the human being in claims of justice for women. For the interlocutor might have refused to acknowledge that his wife was a "person": It was to some extent up to him to define that rather refined and elusive concept. He could not fail to acknowledge that she was a human being, with the basic capability for the functions in question. For he had acknowledged that already, in his daily life.

## 8. WOMEN AND MEN: TWO NORMS OR ONE?

But should there *be* a single norm of human functioning? It has often been argued, in both non-Western and Western traditions, that there should be two different standards of human functioning and capability, corresponding to the different "natures" of the male and the female. Usually these overlap in the areas of bodily health, mobility, and perception, but differ sharply in the areas of practical reason and affiliation. Most commonly, citizenship, public activity, and full practical autonomy are assigned to males, care for home and family to females. We must now confront the claims of this position.

Those who recognize separate spheres of functioning for males and females have taken up two importantly-different positions, which we need to be careful to distinguish. The first, which I shall call Position A, assigns to both males and females the same general normative list of functions, but suggests that males and females should exercise these functions in different spheres of life. The second, which I shall call Position B, insists that the list of functions, even at a high level of generality, should be different. (It is B rather than A that is usually associated with the claim that males and females have different "natures".)

Position A is compatible with a serious interest in equality and in gender justice. For what it says, after all, is that males and females have the same basic needs for capability development and should get what they need. It is determined to ensure that both get to the higher (developed) level of capability with respect to all the central functions. It simply holds that this can (and perhaps should) be done in separate spheres. It is a kind of gender-based local specification. A is, after all, the position of Musonius, who holds that the major functions of affiliation and practical reason may be exercised by the woman in the management of the home and by the man in the public sphere.[87] It evidently seems to him convenient, given women's childbearing role, that the customary divisions of duties should not be overturned, and he believes that all the major capabilities can flourish in either sphere. Is this any more problematic than to say that human functioning in India can, and even should, take a different concrete form from functioning in England?

The difficulty is, however, that once we have recognized the extent to which gender divisions have been socially constructed in morally arbitrary and injurious ways, and once we insist, instead, on using common humanity as our moral and political basis, it is difficult to see what good arguments there are for Position A, which just happens to maintain in place divisions that have often proven oppressive to women. What could such arguments be?

I have mentioned biological differences. But how much separation of function is really suggested by women's childbearing, especially today?

Even in the fourth century B.C., Plato was able to see that the situation of males and females is not very different from the situation of male and female hunting dogs: The female needs a period of rest for childbearing and nursing, but this in no way requires, or even suggests, a lifelong differentiation of functions. Advances in the control of reproduction are making this less and less plausible. And it should be evident to all that the disability imposed by childbearing for the member of the labor force is to a large extent constructed, above all by the absence of support for child care, both from the public sphere and from employers. Other bodily differences that have standardly been mentioned—for example, differences in bodily strength that have often been held to imply a differentiation of functions—are increasingly being found to be based on bad scientific argument,[88] and are also less and less plausible as bases for functional differentiation. Military functions, for example, depend less and less upon bodily strength and more and more on education. The recognition of this by the US Congress in its recent equalization of military roles simply grants what should long ago have been obvious.

One might also point to contingent social facts. Societies are already divided along gender lines. So if we are going to move to a situation in which women will be capable of exercising all the major functions, it will be prudent to develop the resources of that gender-divided structure, seeking greater independence and fulfillment for women within it, rather than trying to break it up. This, I think, is what is really going on in Musonius. As a Greek-speaking philosopher in Nero's Rome, he hasn't the ghost of a chance of making institutional changes of the sort recommended in Stoic views of the ideal city, in which males and females were to be fully equal citizens with no distinction of spheres and even no distinction of clothing![89] He does have a hope of convincing individual husbands to allow their wives access to education, so he does what he can. Much the same is true in Martha Chen's *A Quiet Revolution*. Neither Chen nor her colleagues proposed to jettison all gender divisions within the village. Instead, they found "female jobs" that were somewhat more dignified and important than the old jobs, jobs that looked continuous with traditional female work but were outside the home and brought in wages.

Frequently this is a prudent strategy in bringing about real social change. As Martha Chen shows, the "revolution" in women's quality of life never would have taken place but for the caution of the women, who at each stage gave the men of the village reason to believe that the transformations were not overwhelmingly threatening and were good for the well-being of the entire group. On the other hand, such pragmatic decisions in the face of recalcitrant realities do not tell us how things ought to be. To hold that a gender-divided two-spheres result is an acceptable specification of the norm is deeply problematic. For very often the traditionally female norm is socially devalued, and the traditionally male functions powerfully connected with important advantages. In Musonius's Rome, a husband can be both a citizen and a household manager; a wife does not have the choice to be a citizen. In Metha Bai's contemporary India, the confinement of women to the domestic sphere cuts them off from the choice to earn a living, a powerful determinant of overall capability status. In short, "separate but equal" assignments usually serve the ends of a dominant group and perpetuate the oppression of the powerless.[90]

This point needs particular attention in thinking about divisions of labor within the family. It seems perfectly reasonable that in any household there should be a division of labor, even a long-standing one, with some members gaining greater skills at one task, some at another. It would already be great progress, vis-à-vis the current state of things in all known countries, if domestic duties were equally divided by time and effort. But even in that utopian situation, assignment of tasks along traditional gender-divided lines may be suspect, on account of its possible association with lack of respect and self-respect. If all and only girls are taught to cook, for example, this does not seem to be a morally neutral case of functional specialization (like teaching one child the piano, another the clarinet); for it reinforces stereotypes that are associated, historically, with the denial to women of citizenship and autonomy.

I conclude that there are no good arguments for position A, and that even the prudent use of A in promoting gradual social change should be viewed with caution, and with a constant awareness of more genuinely equal norms.

I turn now to Position B, which has been influentially defended by many philosophers, including Rousseau and some of his contemporary followers.[91] This position may be criticized in a number of different ways. First, we should insist that, insofar as it rests on the claim that there are two different sets of basic capabilities, this claim has not been borne out by any responsible scientific evidence. As Anne Fausto-Sterling's *Myths of Gender* repeatedly shows, experiments that allegedly show strong gender divisions in basic (untrained) abilities are full of scientific flaws; these flaws removed, the case for such differences is altogether inconclusive.

Second, we should note that even what is claimed without substantiation in this body of scientific material usually does not amount to a difference in what I have been calling the central basic capabilities. What is alleged is usually a differential statistical distribution of some specific capacity for a high level of excellence, not for crossing the threshold, and excellence in some very narrowly defined function (say, geometrical ability), rather than in one of our large-scale capabilities such as the capability to perform practical reasoning (which may, recall, be done in a number of different ways, in accordance with the particular tastes and abilities of the individual). So: Even if the claim were true, it would not be a claim about capabilities in our capacious sense; nor, since it is a statistical claim, would it have any implications for the ways in which individuals should be treated. So the political consequences of such gender differences in our scheme of things, even had they been established, would be nil.

Finally, we must also note that it is in principle next to impossible, right now, to do the sort of research that would be required if such differences were ever to be convincingly established. For it has been shown that right now, from birth on, babies of the two sexes are differently treated by parents and other adults, in accordance with the perception of their external genitalia. They are handled differently, spoken to differently, given different toys. Their emotions are labeled differently—thus a crying infant tends to be labeled "angry" if the observer believes it to be a boy, and "frightened" if the observer believes it to be a girl.[92] This means that in the present gender-divided state of things we cannot get beneath culture reliably enough to get the necessary evidence about basic capabilities. I think this supports the conclusion I defended earlier: The potential for error and abuse in capability testing is so great that we should proceed as if every individual has the basic capabilities.

But we can also criticize Position B in a different way. For I believe that it can also be shown that the differentiated conceptions of male and female functioning characteristically put forward by B are internally inadequate, and fail to give us viable norms of human flourishing.[93]

What do we usually find, in the versions of B that our philosophical tradition bequeaths to us? (Rousseau's view is an instructive example.) We have, on the one hand, males who are "autonomous," capable of practical reasoning, independent and self-sufficient, allegedly good at political deliberation. These males are brought up not to develop strong emotions of love and feelings of deep need that are associated with the awareness of one's own lack of self-sufficiency. For this reason they are not well equipped to care for the needs of their family members, or, perhaps, even to notice those needs. On the other hand, we have females such as Rousseau's Sophie, brought up to lack autonomy and self-respect, ill equipped to rely on her own practical reasoning, dependent on males, focused on pleasing others, good at caring for others. Is either of these viable as a complete life for a human being?

It would seem not. The internal tensions in Rousseau's account are a good place to begin seeing this; they have been well described by Susan Okin and Jane Roland Martin. Rousseau, in *Emile*, places tremendous emphasis on compassion as a basic social motivation. He understands compassion to require fellow feeling, and a keen responsiveness to the sufferings of others. And yet, in preparing Emile for autonomous citizenship, in the end he shortchanges these emotional functions, allocating caring and responsiveness to the female sphere alone. It appears likely that Emile will be not only an incomplete person but also a defective citizen, even by the standards of citizenship recognized by Rousseau himself.

With Sophie, things again go badly. Taught to care for others, but not taught that her life is her own to plan, she lives under the sway of external influences and lacks self-government. As Rousseau himself shows, in his fascinating narrative of the end of her life, she comes to a bad end through her lack of judgment. Moreover—as Musonius already argued to his Roman husband, defending equal functioning—she proves to be a bad partner and deficient in love. For love, as we come to see, requires judgment and constancy if it is to be truly deep and truly perceptive. So each of them fails to live a complete human life; and each fails, too, to exemplify fully and well the very functions for which they were being trained, since those functions require support from other functions for which they were not trained. The text leads its thoughtful reader to the conclusion that the capabilities that have traditionally marked the separate male and female spheres are not separable from one another without a grave functional loss. They support and educate one another. So society cannot strive for completeness by simply adding one sphere to the other. It must strive to develop in each and every person the full range of human capabilities.

This more inclusive notion of human functioning admits tragic conflict. For it insists on the separate value and the irreplaceable importance of a rich plurality of functions. And the world does not always guarantee that individuals will not be faced with painful choices among these functions, in which, in order to pursue one of them well they must neglect others (and thus, in many cases, subvert the one as well). But this shows once again, I believe, the tremendous importance of keeping some such list of the central functions before us as we assess the quality of life in the countries of the world and strive to raise it. For many such tragedies—like many cases of simple capability failure—result from unjust and unreflective social arrangements. One can imagine, and try to construct, a society in which the tragic choices that faced Emile and Sophie would not be necessary, in which both males and females could learn both to love and to reason.

Being a woman is indeed not yet a way of being a human being. Women in much of the world lack support for the most central human functions, and this denial of support is frequently caused by their being women. But women, unlike rocks and plants and even dogs and horses, are human beings, have the potential to become capable of these human functions, given sufficient nutrition, education, and other support. That is why their unequal failure in capability is a problem of justice. It is up to us to solve this problem. I claim that a conception of human functioning gives us valuable assistance as we undertake this task.[94]

## NOTES

[Note added by author in 2007:] This paper represents an early and rather primitive stage of my thinking about human capabilities. More developed versions are found in my books *Women and Human Development: The Capabilities Approach* (Cambridge University Press, 2000), and *Frontiers of Justice: Disability, Nationality, Species Membership* (Harvard University Press, 2006). Among the important developments in the view, the most important are: (1) my endorsement of a form of Rawlsian "political liberalism," in such a way that the capabilities list is introduced not as a comprehensive view of a flourishing life, but only as the source for political principles that can potentially be endorsed as the basis for a decent common life by people who share different comprehensive doctrines of the good; (2) an account of political justification and of the relationship between my view and views in both the Utilitarian and social-contract traditions; (3) an account of the role of a notion of human equality in the capability approach, in which some capabilities are thought to be distributed adequately only if they are distributed equally (e.g., freedom of religion, the right to vote, the right to education), whereas others (e.g., the right to suitable housing) are taken to be distributed adequately once an ample social minimum is attained; (4) a major revision in the notion of "basic capabilities," with the result that being born of two human parents is sufficient for being a bearer of fully equal human dignity, with only a few exceptions, such as the person in a permanent vegetative state and the anencephalic child; in other words, so long as some kind of intentional focusing and striving is present, the person, however severely disabled, has entitlements fully equal to those of the so-called "normal" person; (5) an account of political implementation, which makes it clear that the capabilities list is a basis for international discussion and persuasion only, but that implementation is the job of governments chosen by and accountable to the people, except in extreme cases of genocide and other traditionally recognized occasions for humanitarian intervention.

1. The argument of this paper is closely related to that of several other papers of mine, to which I shall refer frequently in what follows: "Nature, Function, and Capability," *Oxford Studies in Ancient Philosophy*, suppl. vol. 1 (1988): 145–84; "Non-Relative Virtues: An Aristotelian Approach," *Midwest Studies in Philosophy* 13 (1988): 32–53, and, in an expanded version, in M. Nussbaum and A. Sen, eds., *The Quality of Life* (Oxford: Clarendon Press, 1993), pp. 242–76; "Aristotelian Social Democracy," in R. B. Douglass, G. Mara, and H. Richardson, eds., *Liberalism and the Good* (New York: Routledge, 1990), pp. 203–52; "Aristotle on Human Nature and the Foundations of Ethics," in *World, Mind, and Ethics: Essays on the Philosophy of Bernard Williams*, ed. R. Harrison and J. Altham eds. (Cambridge: Cambridge University Press, 1995); "Human Functioning and Social Justice: In Defense of Aristotelian Essentialism," *Political Theory* 20 (1992): 202–46.

2. By this I mean that the difference in external genitalia figures in social life as it is interpreted by human cultures; thus we are never dealing simply with facts given at birth, but always with what has been made of them (see below, section 8 for discussion of the role of culture in biological claims about male/female differences). Thus, even the common distinction between "gender," a cultural concept, and "sex," the allegedly pure biological concept, is inadequate to capture the depth of cultural interpretation in presenting even the biological "facts" to human beings, from the very start of a child's life. See Anne Fausto-Sterling, *Myths of Gender* (2nd ed., New York: Basic Books, 1992). I have discussed these issues further in "Constructing Love, Desire, and Care," in D. Estlund and M. Nussbaum, eds., *Sex, Preference, and Family: Essays on Law and Nature* (New York: Oxford University Press, 1997), pp. 17–43, and in my *Sex and Social Justice* (New York: Oxford University Press, 1999), pp. 253–275.

3. For a historical argument along these lines from the history of Western scientific thought, see Thomas Laqueur, *Making Sex* (Berkeley and Los

Angeles: University of California Press, 1989). The papers in this volume [*Women, Culture and Development*] by Amartya Sen ["Gender Inequality and Theories of Justice," 259–73], Xiaorong Li ["Gender Inequality in China and Cultural Relativism," 407–25], and Roop Rekha Verma ["Femininity, Equality, and Personhood," 433–43] show that the use of ideas of nature to convey a false sense of appropriateness, "justifying" unjust practices, is by no means confined to the Western tradition.

4. See Martha Chen's "A Matter of Survival: Women's Right to Employment in India and Bangladesh," in *Women, Culture and Development: A Study of Human Capabilities*, ed. Martha C. Nussbaum and Jonathan Glover (Oxford: Oxford University Press, 1995), 37-57.

5. J. S. Mill, *The Subjection of Women* (Indianapolis: Bobbs Merrill, 1988); Amartya Sen, "Gender and Cooperative Conflicts," in I. Tinker, ed., *Persistent Inequalities* (New York: Oxford University Press, 1990); "Gender Inequality and Theories of Justice" in *Women, Culture and Development*, pp. 259-73, and "More Than 100 Million Women Are Missing," *New York Review of Books; Human Development Report, 1993,* for the United Nations Development Programme (UNDP) (New York and Oxford: Oxford University Press, 1993); Susan Moller Okin, *Justice, Gender, and the Family* (New York: Basic Books, 1989), see my review of Okin, "Justice for Women," *New York Review of Books* (October 1992); Catharine MacKinnon, remark cited by Richard Rorty in "Feminism and Pragmatism," *Michigan Quarterly Review* 30 (1989): 263. MacKinnon has since acknowledged the remark.

6. For a compelling argument linking feminism and internationalism, see Onora O'Neill, "Justice, Gender, and International Boundaries," in M. Nussbaum and A. Sen, eds., *The Quality of Life*, pp. 303–23.

7. Kwame Anthony Appiah, *In My Father's House: Africa in the Philosophy of Culture* (New York and Oxford: Oxford University Press, 1992), pp. 136.

8. On the other hand, it is closely related to Kantian approaches using the universal notion of personhood. See, for example, Onora O'Neill, "Justice, Gender, and International Boundaries," with my commentary (324–35). In the present volume [*Women, Culture and Development*], see the papers of Onora O'Neill ["Justice, Capabilities, and Vulnerabilities," 140–52], Ruth Anna Putnam ["Why Not a Feminist Theory of Justice?" 298–331], and Roop Rekha Verma ["Femininity, Equality, and Personhood," 433–43]. Below I shall be making some criticisms of the concept of "person" in feminist argument, and related criticisms of liberal Kantian approaches (on which see also ASD and my review of Okin). But these differences are subtle and take place against a background of substantial agreement. See also David Crocker, "Functioning and Capability: The Foundation of Sen's and Nussbaum's Development Ethics," *Political Theory* 20 (1992): 584ff.

9. By relativism, I mean the view that the only available criterion of adjudication is some local group or individual. Thus relativism, as I understand it,

is a genus of which the brand of reliance on individuals' subjective preferences frequently endorsed in neoclassical economics is one species. (Economists, of course, are relativist only about value, not about what they construe as the domain of scientific "fact.") This affinity will later be relevant to my comments on the Marglin project. My opponents also frequently employ the term "post-modernist" to characterize their position: This is a vaguer term, associated in a very general way with the repudiation of both metaphysical realism (to be defined below) and universalism.

10. Much of the material described in these examples is now published in *Dominating Knowledge: Development, Culture, and Resistance*, ed. F. A. Marglin and S. A. Marglin (Oxford: Clarendon Press, 1990). The issue of "embedded-ness" and menstruation taboos is discussed in S. A. Marglin, "Losing Touch: The Cultural Conditions of Worker Accommodation and Resistance," pp. 217–82, and related issues are discussed in S. A. Marglin, "Toward the Decolonization of the Mind," 1–28. On Sittala Devi, see F. A. Marglin, "Smallpox in Two Systems of Knowledge," 102–44; and for related arguments see Ashis Nandy and Shiv Visvanathan, "Modern Medicine and Its Non-Modern Critics," 144–84.

11. For Sen's own account of the plurality and internal diversity of Indian values, one that strongly emphasizes the presence of a rationalist and critical strand in Indian traditions, see M. Nussbaum and A. Sen, "Internal Criticism and Indian Relativist Traditions," in M. Krausz, ed., *Relativism* (Notre Dame, IN: Notre Dame University Press, 1989)—a paper originally presented at the same WIDER conference and refused publication by the Marglins in its proceedings; and "India and the West," *New Republic* (7 June 1993).

12. S. A. Marglin, in "Toward the Decolonization," 22–23, suggests that binary thinking is peculiarly Western. But such oppositions are pervasive in all traditions with which I have any acquaintance: in the *Upanishads*, for example (see the epigraph to "Human Functioning"), in Confucian thought (see, again, the epigraph to "Human Functioning"), in Ibo thought (see, for many examples, Chinua Achebe's *Things Fall Apart* [London: William Heinemann, 1958]). Critics of such oppositions have not explained how one can speak coherently without bouncing off one thing against another. I believe that Aristotle was right to hold that to say anything at all one must rule out something, at the very least the contradictory of what one puts forward. The arguments of Nietzsche, which are frequently put forward as if they undermine all binary oppositions, actually make far more subtle and concrete points about the origins of certain oppositions, and the interests served by them.

13. See E. Hobsbawm and T. Ranger, eds., *The Invention of Tradition* (Cambridge: Cambridge University Press, 1983). In his *New Republic* piece, Sen makes a similar argument about contemporary India: The Western construction of India as mystical and "other" serves the purposes of the fundamentalist BJP, who are busy refashioning history to serve the ends of their own political power. An eloquent critique of the whole notion of the "other," and of the associated

"nativism," where Africa is concerned, can be found in Appiah (above n. 7), especially in the essays "The Postcolonial and the Postmodern," pp. 137–57 and "Topologies of Nativism," pp. 47–72.

14. The proceedings of this conference are now published as Nussbaum and Sen, eds., *The Quality of Life* (n. 1 above).

15. "Capability and Well-Being," in Nussbaum and Sen, pp. 30–53.

16. Marglin has since published this point in "Toward the Decolonization." His reference is to Takeo Doi, *The Anatomy of Dependence* (Tokyo: Kedansho, 1971). On women and men in Japan, see *Human Development Report, 1993*, p. 26: "Japan, despite some of the world's highest levels of human development, still has marked inequalities in achievement between men and women. The 1993 human development index puts Japan first. But when the HDI is adjusted for gender disparity, Japan slips to number 17.... Women's average earnings are only 51 percent those of men, and women are largely excluded from decision-making positions.... Their representation is even lower in the political sphere.... In legal rights in general, Japan's patrilineal society is only gradually changing to offer women greater recognition and independence. Japan now has political and non-governmental organizations pressing for change...." The question of freedom of choice is thus on the agenda in Japan in a large way, precisely on account of the sort of unequal functioning vividly illustrated in Marglin's example, where menial functions are performed by women, in order that men may be free to perform their managerial and political functions.

17. See S. A. Marglin, "Toward the Decolonization."

18. See S. A. Marglin, "Losing Touch." I put the term in quotes to indicate that I am alluding to Marglin's use of the term, not to the concept as I understand it.

19. See S. A. Marglin, "Toward the Decolonization" and "Losing Touch." Similar claims are common in feminist argument. For example, in *The Feminist Theory of the State* (Cambridge, MA: Harvard University Press, 1989), Catharine MacKinnon argues that "objectivity" as traditionally conceived in the Western epistemological tradition is causally linked to the objectification and abuse of women. This line of argument is effectively criticized in Louise M. Antony, "Quine as Feminist: The Radical Import of Naturalized Epistemology," in L. M. Antony and C. Witt, eds., *A Mind of One's Own: Feminist Essays on Reason and Objectivity* (Boulder, CO: Westview Press, 1992), pp. 185–225. See also the detailed examination of MacKinnon's argument in the same volume by Sally Haslanger, in "On Being Objective and Being Objectified," 85–125. MacKinnon's fundamental contributions in the areas of sexual harassment and pornography do not depend on this analysis, and are actually undermined by it. The core of her thought actually reveals a strong commitment to a type of ethical universalism, as my epigraph indicates. See, in the Antony volume, the persuasive analysis by Liz Rappaport, "Generalizing Gender: Reason and Essence in the Legal Thought of Catharine MacKinnon," pp. 127–43.

Alcoff's contribution in the present volume ["Democracy and Rationality: A Dialogue with Hilary Putnam" in *Women, Culture and Development*, pp. 225–34] continues the debate about feminism and reason; and see also L. Alcoff and E. Potter, eds., *Feminist Epistemologies* (New York: Routledge, 1993). For a healthy skepticism about the role of "anti-essentialism" within feminism, see Seyla Benhabib, "Feminism and the Question of Postmodernism," in *Situating the Self: Gender, Community, and Postmodernism in Contemporary Ethics* (New York: Routledge, 1992), pp. 203–42; Sabina Lovibond, "Feminism and Postmodernism," *New Left Review* 178 (November–December 1989): 5–28; Val Moghadam, "Against Eurocentrism and Nativism," *Socialism and Democracy* (fall/winter 1989): 81–104; Moghadam, *Gender, Development, and Policy: Toward Equity and Empowerment*, UNU/WIDER Research for Action series (November 1990).

20. For an account of this sort of normative argument, see Alasdair MacIntyre, *After Virtue* (Notre Dame, IN: Notre Dame University Press, 1989).

21. J. Derrida, *Of Grammatology*, trans. G. Spivak (Baltimore: Johns Hopkins University Press, 1976). The term is meant to suggest the idea that reality is simply "there" and that knowledge consists in being "present" to it, without any interfering barrier or mediation.

22. R. Rorty, *Philosophy and the Mirror of Nature* (Princeton, NJ: Princeton University Press, 1979).

23. See, for example, G. E. L. Owen, *"Tithenai ta Phainomena"*, in *Logic, Science, and Dialectic* (London: Duckworth, 1986), and M. Nussbaum, *The Fragility of Goodness: Luck and Ethics in Greek Tragedy and Philosophy* (Cambridge: Cambridge University Press, 1986). See also Hilary Putnam, *Aristotle after Wittgenstein*, Lindlay Lecture, University of Kansas, 1991.

24. See the illuminating discussion in B. K. Matilal, *Perception* (Oxford: Clarendon Press, 1985). It is worth noting that this fundamental work is not cited anywhere in Marglin and Marglin, although Matilal was present at the conference and delivered a paper critical of the Marglins' characterization of Indian traditions. This paper was dropped from the volume. Matilal also described the implications of the realism debate for Indian ethical thought: see "Ethical Relativism and the Confrontation of Cultures," in Krausz, ed., *Relativism* (Notre Dame, IN: Notre Dame University Press, 1989), pp. 339–62.

25. There is a longer version of my criticism of contemporary attacks on universalism in "Human Functioning." See also "Skepticism about Practical Reason in Literature and the Law," *Harvard Law Review* 107 (1994): 714–44. In both of these papers I study the surprising convergence between "left" and "right" in the critique of normative argument, the "postmodern" positions of many thinkers on the left proving, often, difficult to distinguish from claims about the arbitrariness of evaluation in neoclassical economics. In Barbara Herrnstein Smith's *Contingencies of Value* (Durham, NC: Duke University Press, 1988), we even see a fusion of the two positions, a postmodernism concluding

that, in the absence of transcendent standards, we should understand value judgments as attempts to maximize expected utility.

26. Aristotle, *Nicomachean Ethics* VIII.I, 1155a 21–22. I discuss this passage in "Aristotle on Human Nature" and "Non-Relative Virtues."

27. K. A. Appiah, *In My Father's House*, pp. vii–viii: "If my sisters and I were 'children of two worlds', no one bothered to tell us this; we lived in one world, in two 'extended' families divided by several thousand miles and an allegedly insuperable cultural distance that never, so far as I can recall, puzzled or perplexed us much." Appiah's argument does not in any sense neglect distinctive features of concrete histories; indeed, one of its purposes is to demonstrate how varied, when concretely seen, histories really are. But his argument, like mine, seeks a subtle balance between perception of the particular and recognition of the common. In his essay "The Postcolonial and the Postmodern" (pp. 137–57), Appiah shows that it is all too often the focus on "otherness" that produces a lack of concrete engagement with individual lives. Speaking of the sculpture "Yoruba Man with Bicycle" that appears on the cover of the book, Appiah comments: "The *Man with a Bicycle* is produced by someone who does not care that the bicycle is the white man's invention—it is not there to be Other to the Yoruba Self; it is there because someone cared for its solidity; it is there because it will take us further than our feet will take us...." (157).

28. In this category, as closely related to my own view, I would place the "internal-realist" conception of Hilary Putnam articulated in *Reason, Truth, and History* (Cambridge: Cambridge University Press, 1981), *The Many Faces of Realism* (La Salle: Open Court Publishing, 1987), and *Realism with a Human Face* (Cambridge, MA: Harvard University Press, 1990); and also the views of Charles Taylor, for example, in *Sources of the Self: The Making of Modern Identity* (Cambridge, MA: Harvard University Press, 1989), and "Explanation and Practical Reason," in Nussbaum and Sen, eds., *The Quality of Life*, pp. 208–31.

29. In this sense I am thoroughly in agreement with Susan Okin's reply to the charge of "substitutionalism" that has been made against her book, and in agreement with both Okin and Ruth Anna Putnam that it is a mistake to conceive of the moral point of view as constituted by the actual voices of all disadvantaged parties; see Okin's "Inequalities between the Sexes in Different Cultural Contexts," pp. 274–97 and Putnam's "Why Not a Feminist Theory of Justice?" pp. 298–331 in *Women, Culture and Development*. See my further comments below, Section 5.

30. Can the Marglins consistently make this objection while holding that freedom of choice is just a parochial Western value? It would appear not; on the other hand, F. A. Marglin (here differing, I believe, from S. A. Marglin) also held in oral remarks delivered at the 1986 conference that logical consistency is simply a parochial Western value.

31. The politics of the history of Western philosophy have been interpreted this way, with much plausibility though perhaps insufficient historical

argumentation, by Noam Chomsky, in *Cartesian Linguistics* (New York: Harper & Row, 1966). Chomsky argues that Cartesian rationalism, with its insistence on innate essences, was politically more progressive, more hostile to slavery and imperialism, than empiricism, with its insistence that people were just what experience had made of them. My analysis of Stoic feminist argument (below Section 7) bears this out.

32. The use of this term does not imply that the functions all involve doing something especially "active." (See here Sen, "Capability and Well-Being," in *The Quality of Life*, pp. 30–53.) In Aristotelian terms, and in mine, being healthy, reflecting, being pleased, are all "activities."

33. For further discussion of this point, and examples, see "Aristotle on Human Nature."

34. Ibid. discusses the treatment of this point in contemporary medical ethics. Could one cease to be one's individual self without ceasing to be human? This is ruled out, I think, in Aristotle's conception, but is possible in some other metaphysical conceptions. But the sort of case that would most forcefully raise this possibility is not the sort involving illness or impairment, but instead the sort involving personality or memory change; and I shall not attempt to deal with such cases here.

35. Appiah, *In My Father's House*, p. viii.

36. In "Aristotle on Human Nature," there is a more extended account of this procedure and how it justifies.

37. This of course is not incompatible with calling certain groups non-human or subhuman for political purposes. But such denials are usually either transparent propaganda or forms of self-deception, which can be unmasked by critical argument. See below for a case involving women; and for an extensive analysis of the psychology of such self-deception, and its unmasking, see Raoul Hilberg, *The Destruction of the European Jews*, abridged edition (New York: Holmes & Meier, 1985), pp. 274–93.

38. In order to make this clear, I speak of it as a conception of the good, at a very minimal and general level. The phrase I have elsewhere used is "the thick vague theory of the good." The term "thick" contrasts this account, in its comprehensiveness, with Rawls's "thin" theory of the good, which is designed to avoid even partial comprehensiveness.

39. On this see especially "Non-Relative Virtues."

40. I have discussed my own views about practical rationality elsewhere, particularly in "The Discernment of Perception," in *Love's Knowledge* (New York: Oxford University Press, 1990). A related account, which I admire and to a large extent agree with, is given by Henry Richardson in *Practical Deliberation about Final Ends* (Cambridge University Press, 1994). Richardson's account is closely related, as well, to the pragmatist conception supported by Hilary Putnam in his "Pragmatism and Moral Objectivity" in *Women, Culture and Development*, pp. 199–224.

Should the conception of reasonableness be defined with reference to *democratic* procedures, as Seyla Benhabib has recommended? I see the attractions of this proposal, but I have not followed it. First of all, it seems to me that democratic procedures as they actually are do not always embody reasonableness; so to describe what makes a democratic procedure reasonable we will have to have a notion of the reasonable that is to at least some extent independent of the notion of democracy. Second, to build democracy into the ground level of the conception of the human from the start prevents us from raising later on the question of what political arrangement will best secure to citizens the list of human capabilities, in a wide variety of circumstances. It may turn out that the answer will always be "democracy." But even then, I think it will rarely be *just* democracy (ancient Athenian or New England town-meeting style). No modern democratic state is a pure democracy, and it should at this point remain an open question as to what role should be played by relatively undemocratic institutions such as the US Supreme Court in promoting the capabilities of citizens.

41. For Rawls's use of a notion of consensus, see Rawls, "The Idea of an Overlapping Consensus," *Oxford Journal of Legal Studies* 7 (1987), and now *Political Liberalism* (New York: Columbia University Press, 1993). Rawls's notion of consensus appears ambiguous between the two notions I identify here. See, on this, the exchange between Joshua Cohen and Jean Hampton in *The Idea of Democracy* (New York: Oxford University Press, 1992). Cohen argues that Rawls needs, and can consistently defend, the weaker "overlap" reading; Hampton argues that, whatever Rawls intends, the plausibility of his argument rests on his opting for the normative reading. I concur with Hampton.

42. To cite only a few recent examples with serious practical consequences: in the United States in the 1890s, the Supreme Court, denying a Virginia woman's appeal against a law forbidding women to practice law, judged that it was up to the state Supreme Court "to determine whether the word 'person'" in the statute on which the woman based her appeal "is confined to males." (*In re Lockwood*, 154 US 116, discussed in Okin, *Women*, p. 251 and n. 10, and see Sunstein's "Gender, Caste, and Law" in *Women, Culture and Development*, pp. 332–59.) In Massachusetts in 1932, women were denied eligibility for jury service, although the law stated that "every person qualified to vote" was eligible. The state Supreme Court wrote: "No intention to include women can be deduced from the omission of the word 'male'"(*Commonwealth v. Welosky*, 276 Mass. 398, cert. denied, 284 US 684 [1932]), discussed in Okin, *Women*, p. 251 and n. 11. Such readings no doubt reflect faithfully enough the views that the Founders had about the term "person" when they used it in the Constitution: See my Jefferson epigraph. Although this construal of the term does not prevail today in American law, its legacy is with us in countless more informal ways.

43. Aristotle, *Metaphysics* I.I.

44. I discuss this issue in much more detail in Lecture 3 of my 1993 Gifford Lectures, University of Edinburgh, in chapter 4 of *Upheavals of Thought: The Intelligence of Emotions* (New York: Cambridge University Press, 2001).

45. Aristotle, ubiquitously in the accounts of substance.

46. On these issues, see further in "Aristotelian Social Democracy."

47. Aristotle, *Politics* VII.I: see "Nature, Function, and Capability."

48. It may support what James Rachels calls "moral individualism" (*Created from Animals* [Oxford and New York: Oxford University Press, 1990]), in which our moral obligations flow from the endowments of the individual creature with whom we are dealing, rather than from its species, and our goal should be to promote—or at least not to impede—the form of flourishing of which the being is basically capable. On this view such an infant should get the same treatment that we would give to an animal of similar endowment. But we may also decide to give the fact that it is an offspring of humans some moral weight; nothing I have said here rules that out.

49. Although "normal length" is clearly relative to current human possibilities and may need, for practical purposes, to be to some extent relativized to local conditions, it seems important to think of it—at least at a given time in history—in universal and comparative terms, as the *Human Development Report* does, to give rise to complaint in a country that has done well with some indicators of life quality but badly on life expectancy. And although some degree of relativity may be put down to the differential genetic possibilities of different groups (the "missing women" statistics, for example, allow that on the average women live somewhat longer than men), it is also important not to conclude prematurely that inequalities between groups—for example, the growing inequalities in life expectancy between blacks and whites in the USA—are simply genetic variation, not connected with social injustice.

50. The precise specification of these health rights is not easy, but the work currently being done on them in drafting new constitutions in South Africa and Eastern Europe gives reason for hope that the combination of a general specification of such a right with a tradition of judicial interpretation will yield something practicable. It should be noticed that I speak of health, not just health care: and health itself interacts in complex ways with housing, with education, with dignity. Both health and nutrition are controversial as to whether the relevant level should be specified universally, or relatively to the local community and its traditions: for example, is low height associated with nutritional practices to be thought of as "stunting," or as felicitous adaptation to circumstances of scarcity? For an excellent summary of this debate, see S. R. Osmani, ed., *Nutrition and Poverty*, WIDER series (Oxford: Clarendon Press, 1990), especially the following papers: on the relativist side, T. N. Srinivasan, "Undernutrition: Concepts, Measurements, and Policy Implications," 97–120; on the universalist side, C. Gopalan, "Undernutrition: Measurement and Implications," 17–48; for a compelling adjudication of the debate, coming out on the

universalist side, see Osmani, "On Some Controversies in the Measurement of Undernutrition," 121–61.

51. There is a growing literature on the importance of shelter for health: e.g., that the provision of adequate housing is the single largest determinant of health status for HIV–infected persons. Housing rights are increasingly coming to be constitutionalized, at least in a negative form—giving squatters grounds for appeal, for example, against a landlord who would bulldoze their shanties. On this as a constitutional right, see proposed Articles 11, 12, and 17 of the South African Constitution, in a draft put forward by the ANC committee, adviser Albie Sachs, where this is given as an example of a justiciable housing right.

52. I shall not elaborate here on what I think promoting this capability requires, since there is a WIDER project and conference devoted to this topic.

53. A good example of an education right that I would support is given in the ANC South African Constitution draft, Article 11: "Education shall be free and compulsory up to the age of sixteen, and provision shall be made for facilitating access to secondary, vocational and tertiary education on an equal basis for all. Education shall be directed toward the development of the human personality and a sense of personal dignity, and shall aim at strengthening respect for human rights and fundamental freedoms and promoting understanding, tolerance and friendship amongst South Africans and between nations." The public (or otherwise need-blind) provision of higher education will have to be relative to local possibilities, but it is at least clear that the USA lags far behind most other countries of comparable wealth in this area.

54. On the emotions as basic human capabilities, see, in addition to my "Emotions and Women's Capabilities," in *Women, Culture and Development*, pp. 360–95, my 1993 Gifford Lectures, *Upheavals of Thought: The Intelligence of Emotions* (Cambridge: Cambridge University Press, 2001), and my *Hiding from Humanity: Disgust, Shame, and the Law* (Princeton: Princeton University Press, 2004). My omission of anger from this list of basic emotional capabilities reveals an ambivalence about its role that I discuss at length, both in Gifford Lectures 3 and 10, and in *The Therapy of Desire: Theory and Practice in Hellenistic Ethics* (Princeton, NJ: Princeton University Press, 1994), chs. 7, 11, and 12. See also "Equity and Mercy," *Philosophy and Public Affairs* (spring 1993).

55. In my 1993 Gifford Lectures, I spell out what I think this entails where "the family" is concerned. On the whole, I am in agreement with Susan Okin that some form of intimate family love is of crucial importance in child development, but that this need not be the traditional Western nuclear family. I also agree with Okin that the important educational role of the family makes it all the more crucial that the family should be an institution characterized by justice, as well as love. See Okin, *Justice, Gender, and the Family*.

56. "Aristotelian Social Democracy" said that a list of such liberties needed to be added to the Aristotelian scheme, but it did not include them in the account of capabilities itself. These issues are further developed in a WIDER

project and conference on reproductive rights and women's capabilities.

57. For reproductive choice as an equality issue, see Sunstein's "Gender, Caste, and Law" in *Women, Culture and Development*, pp. 332–59, and also his "Gender, Reproduction, and Law" presented at the conference on reproductive rights and women's capabilities at WIDER in 1993.

58. On this see also "Aristotelian Social Democracy."

59. With Sen, I hold that the capability set should be treated as an interlocking whole: for my comments on his arguments, see "Nature, Function, and Capability." Tensions will frequently arise among members of the list, and I shall comment on some of those below. But it should be clear by now that the architectonic role of practical reasoning imposes strict limits on the sort of curb on personal autonomy that will be tolerated for the sake of increased nutritional well-being, etc.

60. Chris Bobonich "Internal Realism, Human Nature, and Distributive Justice: A Response to Martha Nussbaum," *Modern Philology* (May 1993), supplement, 74–92, worries that this will impose enormous sacrifices. But I think that this is because he has not imagined things in detail, nor thought about my claim that once people have what they basically need, they can get all sorts of other good things through their own efforts. If I have enough food to be well nourished, more food will just rot on the shelf or make me fat. If my basic health needs are met, it seems right that I should not be able to claim expensive unnecessary luxuries (say, cosmetic surgery) at the public expense so long as even one person in my country is without support for basic needs. And so forth. One must take seriously the Aristotelian idea, which is basic to both Sen's and my programs, that resources are just tools for functioning and have a limit given by what is needed for that functioning. Above that limit, they are just a heap of stuff, of no value in themselves.

61. See "Nature, Function, and Capability," with reference to Aristotle.

62. Marx, *Economic and Philosophical Manuscripts of 1844*, discussed in "Nature, Function, Capability" and "Aristotle on Human Nature."

63. See especially Sen's "Gender Inequality and Theories of Justice," in *Women, Culture and Development*, pp. 259–73; also "More Than 100 Million Women Are Missing," *New York Review of Books* 37 (1990): 61–66.

64. Iftekhar Hossein, "Poverty as Capability Failure," Ph.D. dissertation in Economics, Helsinki University, 1990.

65. See Allardt, "Having, Loving, Being: An Alternative to the Swedish Model of Welfare Research," and Erikson, "Descriptions of Inequality: The Swedish Approach to Welfare Research," in Nussbaum and Sen, *The Quality of Life*, pp. 88–94 and 67–84.

66. See Sen, "More Than 100 Million Women."

67. Sec also Jon Elster, *Sour Grapes* (Cambridge: Cambridge University Press, 1983); Cass R. Sunstein, "Preferences and Politics," *Philosophy and Public Affairs* 20 (1991): 3–34.

68. Päivi Setälä, Professor of Women's Studies at the University of Helsinki, informs me that recent studies show that even in Finland, only 40 percent of the housework is done by males. This, in the second nation in the world (after New Zealand, in 1906) to give females the vote, a nation as committed to sex equality as any in the world. We can assume that the situation is causally related to male preferences.

69. On the disparity between externally observed health status and self-reports of satisfaction about health, see Sen, *Commodities and Capabilities* (Amsterdam: North-Holland, 1985).

70. Martha Chen, *A Quiet Revolution: Women in Transition in Rural Bangladesh* (Cambridge, MA: Schenkman, 1983). I describe this account of a rural women's literacy project, and its large-scale impact on women's quality of life, in "Non-Relative Virtues," "Aristotelian Social Democracy," and "Human Functioning and Social Justice."

71. This is a criticism of economic utilitarianism, not of sophisticated philosophical forms of utilitarianism that build in means to filter or correct preferences. Nonetheless, the human-functioning approach would still object to the role played by the commensurability of values in utilitarianism, and to the related suggestion that for any two distinct ends we can, without loss of what is relevant for choice, imagine trade-offs in purely quantitative terms. Furthermore, most forms of utilitarianism are committed to aggregating utilities across lives, and thus to neglecting separateness, which I have defended as fundamental. I have addressed some of these questions elsewhere, for example, in "The Discernment of Perception" in *Love's Knowledge*, and in "The Literary Imagination in Public Life," *New Literary History* (fall 1993). Sen's work has addressed them in greater detail. I therefore leave them to one side for the purposes of the present inquiry.

72. For a detailed consideration of these approaches, see "Aristotelian Social Democracy," "Human Functioning," with references to related arguments of Sen. "Aristotelian Social Democracy" contains a detailed account of the relationship between Rawls's resourcism and my project, which is a particularly subtle one. Rawls is willing to take a stand on certain items: Thus liberty and the social conditions of self-respect figure on his list of "primary goods," as well as wealth and income. On the other hand, he has repeatedly denied that his index of primary goods could, or should, be replaced by an index of functionings as in the *Human Development Report*.

73. This is the central point repeatedly made by Sen against Rawls; for an overview, see "Capability and Well-Being" in *The Quality of Life*, with references.

74. In Rawls's liberalism the problem is even more acute, since the parties who are either well or not well off are "heads of households," usually taken to be male, who are alleged to deliberate on behalf of the interests of their family members. But women cannot in fact rely on the altruism of males to guarantee

their economic security, or even survival. In addition to Sen's work on this issue, see Susan Moller Okin, *Justice, Gender, and the Family*. In my review of Okin, I offer this as a reason for Okin to be more critical of resource-based liberalism than she is.

75. Martha Chen and her fellow development workers, in the project described in *A Quiet Revolution*, were indebted in their practice to Paolo Freire's notion of "participatory dialogue."

76. Sen has stressed this throughout his writing on the topic. For an overview, see "Capability and Well-Being."

77. This is the strategy used by Erikson's Swedish team, when studying inequalities in political participation: see "Descriptions of Inequality." The point was well made by Bernard Williams in his response to Sen's Tanner Lectures [the one delivered May 22, 1979 is reprinted herein 61–81]: see Williams, "The Standard of Living: Interests and Capabilities," in G. Hawthorn, ed., *The Standard of Living* (Cambridge: Cambridge University Press, 1987). To give just one example of the issue, we will need to ask to what extent laws regulating abortion, sodomy laws, the absence of civil rights laws, etc., restrict the capability for sexual expression of women and homosexuals in a given society. The gay American military officer who chooses celibacy for fear of losing his job has not, in the relevant sense, been given a capability of choosing.

78. Sec also Sen, *Commodities and Capabilities*.

79. The relevant textual references are gathered and discussed in "Aristotelian Social Democracy."

80. The remark was cited by Richard Rorty in "Feminist and Pragmatism," *Michigan Quarterly Review* 30 (1989): 231; it has since been confirmed and repeated by MacKinnon herself.

81. See n. 37 above on Raoul Hilberg's account, in *The Destruction of the European Jews*, of the Nazi device of categorizing Jews as animals or inanimate objects, and the vulnerability of that stratagem to "breakthroughs," in which the mechanisms of denial were caught off guard.

82. The most comprehensive and incisive account of Plato's arguments about women is now in Stephen Halliwell, *Plato: Republic*, Book V (Warminster: Aris and Phillips, 1992), Introduction and commentary to the relevant passages. See also Okin, *Women in Western Political Thought*.

83. For Musonius's collected works, see the edition by O. Hense (Leipzig: Teubner Library, 1905). Other works with radical conclusions for women's issues include "Should Boys and Girls Have the Same Education?" (answering yes to that question); "Should One Raise All the Children Who Are Born?" (arguing against infanticide, a particular threat to female offspring); "On the Goal of Marriage" (arguing against the sexual double standard and in favor of equal sexual fidelity for both sexes; arguing as well against the common view that female slaves were available for sexual use).

84. Stoics are of course highly critical of much that passes for higher educa-

tion, holding that the traditional "liberal studies" are not "liberal" in the right way, that is, do not truly "free" the mind to take charge of its own reasoning. See Seneca, *Moral Epistle*, p. 88.

85. See Musonius, "On the Goal of Marriage." Similar conceptions are defended by Seneca and Plutarch. On this shift in thinking about the marital relationship, see the useful discussion in Foucault, *History of Sexuality*, vol. III, trans. R. Hurley (New York: Pantheon, 1985).

86. On the way in which Christianity disrupted the emerging feminist consensus, see G. E. M. de Ste. Croix, *The Class Struggle in the Ancient Greek World* (London: Duckworth, 1987).

87. See the last section of "That Women Too," where he answers the male interlocutor's imaginary objection that educated women will spend too much time sitting around and talking, and neglect their practical duties, by telling him that the very same issue arises for him: He too has practical duties that may seem less interesting than talking about ideas, and he too should make sure that he doesn't neglect them. It is, I think, because Musonius has a pretty low view of the worth of male public life that he can easily view that sphere as equivalent and equal to the female sphere.

88. See Anne Fausto-Sterling, *Myths of Gender*.

89. For the evidence, see Malcolm Schofield, *The Stoic Idea of the City* (Cambridge: Cambridge University Press, 1992).

90. Is the Nigerian situation depicted in Nzegwu's paper an exception? We can agree with her that the traditional system in which women controlled certain vital agricultural functions, and men others, was somewhat better, in capability terms, than the system of confinement to the domestic sphere imposed by British colonialism, without being altogether sure that the traditional system was morally acceptable. This would depend on a closer scrutiny of the whole system of functionings and capabilities, as affected by gender divisions. I am no expert in Ibo culture, clearly; but the traditional Ibo families depicted in Chinua Achebe's novels, for example, do not seem to me to manifest full gender equality in capability. Okonkwo (in *Things Fall Apart*) can decide to beat his wife; she cannot choose to beat him in return, or even to stop him, in all but the most egregious of cases. Okonkwo can choose to take another wife; no wife of his can choose another husband. The reason why Okonkwo keeps wishing that Ezinma had been a boy rather than a girl is that he perceives that, being a girl, she is debarred from many functions for which she seems well suited. His fear of being seen as a "woman" is, by contrast, a fear of capability failure.

91. On Rousseau, see Okin, *Women*, and Jane Roland Martin, *Reclaiming a Conversation* (New Haven: Yale University Press, 1985). On some related contemporary arguments, for example those of Allan Bloom, see Okin, *Justice*, ch. 1.

92. On all this, see Fausto-Sterling.

93. Here I am in agreement with the general line of argument in Okin, *Women*, and Martin, *Reclaiming*, and with the related arguments in Nancy

Chodorow's *The Reproduction of Mothering*, which I discuss in my other chapter ["Emotions and Women's Capabilities," in *Women, Culture and Development*, pp. 360–95].

94. I am grateful to all the members of our meeting for valuable comments, and especially to Amartya Sen for valuable discussions and to David Crocker, Jonathan Glover, Cass Sunstein, and Susan Wolf for helpful written comments. I am also grateful to Chris Bobonich, David Estlund, and Henry Richardson for comments on related earlier work.

# 18. DARREL MOELLENDORF

Moellendorf argues that, due to the particular constructivist procedure he employs in "The Law of Peoples," Rawls is unable to justify his claim that there is a relationship between limiting the internal and external sovereignty of states. An alternative constructivist procedure is plausible, but it extends the ideal theory of global justice to include liberal democratic and egalitarian principles. The alternative procedure and expanded set of principles justify a principle of international resource redistribution and weaken the general prohibitions against intervention.

## Constructing the Law of Peoples

*First published in* Pacific Philosophical Quarterly *77: 2 (June 1996): 132–54.*

In this paper I shall argue that due to the constructivist procedure that John Rawls employs in "The Law of Peoples," he is unable to justify his claim that there is a relationship between limiting the internal and external sovereignty of states. An alternative constructivist procedure is viable, but it extends the ideal theory of international justice to include liberal democratic and egalitarian principles. The procedure and principles have significant implications for nonideal theory as well, insofar as they justify a principle of international resource redistribution and weaken general prohibitions against intervention.

1

In *Political Liberalism*, John Rawls argues that the principles of justice have a different status than in *A Theory of Justice*, where they constitute a comprehensive liberal conception of justice.[1] In *Political Liberalism* they constitute a political liberal conception (*PL* 11).[2] In order for the principles to qualify as political, they must be freestanding, that is not derived exclusively from any one of the many comprehensive moral, philosophical, and theological doctrines that citizens of liberal democracies hold (*PL* 12). Rawls prefers a political conception of justice because it affords the opportunity of wider assent to the principles of justice, resulting in greater stability for the order based upon them. This difference in status is the result of a difference in procedure. Although the original position in each of the two works situates parties in the same manner, the original position in *Political Liberalism* is developed as a procedure of construction. The procedure involves modeling conceptions of persons and society which are derived not from metaphysical claims about human nature or the essence of human society, but from ideas which are said to have common currency in the liberal democratic tradition (*PL* 14). Modeling such conceptions of persons and society is key, if the outcome is to be political and not comprehensive.

Rawls employs this constructivist procedure not only in *Political Liberalism*, but also in a recent paper entitled "The Law of Peoples." Here he develops a set of principles that are supposed to constitute the body of international justice. In addition, Rawls draws certain conclusions about the limits of liberal principles, if they are to be political and not comprehensive. In particular, the set of principles constructed in "The Law of Peoples" is liberal only in the very limited sense that it recognizes human rights. In fact, he suggests that principles that are liberal to any greater degree would have to be comprehensive rather than political principles, and would therefore violate the liberal principle of tolerance.

Bruce Ackerman seems to agree that if Rawls's procedure of construction is based upon ideas of persons and society that are drawn from the liberal democratic tradition, then the resulting principles will be of narrow application. So much the worse for Rawls's theory, he thinks. In a remarkably unfair missive, he even chastises Rawls's theory as an apology for the self-aggrandizement of political elites, xenophobia, and the injustices of the present international distribution of resources.[3]

Rawls on the other hand takes his account in "The Law of Peoples" to be a significant departure from conventional international law.

> We must reformulate the powers of sovereignty in light of a reasonable law of peoples and get rid of the right to war and the right to

internal autonomy, which have been part of the (positive) international law for the two and a half centuries following the Thirty Years' War as part of the classical states system. (42 [herein 427])

As Rawls notices in a footnote to this quotation, arguments in defense of state sovereignty typically have been based upon an analogy between individuals and states.[4] The danger of such an analogy, on liberal grounds at least, is that it might serve to subordinate the interests of the individual to those of sovereign states. In *A Theory of Justice*, Rawls draws an analogy between the equal rights of citizens in a constitutional regime and the equal rights of states under the law of the peoples (*TJ* 378). The attempt to reformulate the powers of sovereignty in "The Law of Peoples" appears to back away from the analogy between individuals and states.

The disanalogy is, however, only partially endorsed. Rawls is willing to pierce the shell of state sovereignty in order to prohibit human rights violations and limit the legitimate use of force between states, but he is not willing to write liberal democratic and egalitarian principles of justice into the law of peoples. I shall argue that this is a mistake. But it is also a mistake to see the conclusion that Rawls draws as necessarily following from the limitations of a procedure of construction that models the conceptions of persons and society drawn from the liberal democratic tradition, as Ackerman does.[5] In fact, this is not at all Rawls's procedure of construction in "The Law of Peoples," although I shall argue that it should have been.

In the second section I shall explain Rawls's construction of the law of peoples and show the inadequacy of his partial disposal of sovereignty. In this section I shall also identify an expanded set of principles of the law of peoples that pays even less homage than Rawls's principles to the idea of sovereignty. In the third section I shall argue that an alternative construction procedure would better establish the relationship between the constraints on internal and external sovereignty that Rawls asserts, and would derive the expanded set of principles identified in the second section. The fourth section will compare Rawls's construction with one that I offer. It will look at the modeling done in *Political Liberalism*, "The Law of Peoples," and in the third section of this paper. This will involve, in part, looking at how rights are derived from each the three procedures. In the fifth and sixth sections I shall defend the expanded set of principles of the law of peoples against two different interpretations of the charge that they would provide an excessively narrow basis of agreement. Finally, I shall look at how my procedure answers certain concerns of nonideal theory. The result, I hope, will be fruitful both for understanding something about Rawls's constructivist procedure and a liberal theory of international justice.

## 2

The first stage of Rawls's construction of the law of peoples is the construction of an ideal theory. This stage assumes that reasonably favorable conditions for democracy exist (45 [herein 430]). The construction proceeds in two steps. The first is a construction that applies, with a significant caveat, to relations among liberal democratic states, the second expands relations to include well-ordered non-liberal, or what Rawls calls hierarchical, states. It is my belief that Rawls tailors the construction, and thus the conclusion, of the first step in order to fit the second step, and that this is unwarranted.

As soon as Rawls begins the construction of the law of peoples, he compares it to the more familiar construction, in *Political Liberalism*, of the principles of justice which should govern liberal societies. In *Political Liberalism* the original position is said to model fair conditions among free and equal citizens because their representatives are situated symmetrically and equally. Citizens are modeled as rational in virtue of their representatives' full pursuit of their interests. Finally, the veil of ignorance models reasonableness by preventing decisions based upon known advantages over others. The original position for the law of peoples is set up in exactly the same manner except that seated behind the veil of ignorance are representatives of peoples and not citizens (45 [herein 430]).[6] The veil of ignorance prevents the representatives of peoples from knowing their territory and population size, level of economic development, wealth of natural resources, and their strength. In a footnote Rawls defines peoples as "persons and their dependents seen as a corporate body and as organized by their political institutions, which establish the powers of government" (41 [herein 453, n. 5]). As the last clause makes clear, peoples are in fact states. This is corroborated by the introduction to *Political Liberalism* where he states that he prefers the term "peoples" over the term "states" (*PL* xxviii).[7] Thus, Rawls reintroduces the analogy between citizens and states through the procedure of construction he employs.

This is confirmed when Rawls explains why he chooses an original position with representatives of peoples (states) rather than of all the people of the world.

> Since in working out justice as fairness I begin with domestic society, I shall continue from there as if what has been done so far is more or less sound. So I simply build on the steps taken until now, as this seems to provide a suitable starting point for the extension to the law of peoples. A further reason for proceeding thus is that peoples as corporate bodies organized by their governments now exists in some form all over the world. Historically speaking, all principles and standards proposed for the law of peoples must, to be feasible, prove acceptable to the considered reflective public opinion of peoples and their governments. (42-43 [herein 427])

The use of a procedure that draws upon an analogy between citizens and states is justified by Rawls in this passage as a minimum standard of realism, which requires that the law of the peoples not call into question the existence of the international state system. Closely related to this standard is another that stipulates that a law of peoples not require a world state, which, Rawls believes, following Kant, would produce global despotism (46 [herein 431]). Rawls meets both standards by having the parties in this new original position be representatives of states.

I mentioned at the outset of this section that the first set of principles of justice that Rawls constructs using the device of this new original position applies to relations between liberal democratic states, with a caveat. Although liberal, the states even at this first stage are not all egalitarian. The principles of justice that govern them need not include the fair value of political liberties, fair equality of opportunity, and the difference principle. Thus, despite Rawls's claim to the contrary in the above quotation, he is not simply continuing from the construction of justice as fairness. He is instead backing away from the most significant accomplishments of that construction. In omitting the principles of egalitarian justice (e.g., the fair value of political liberties, fair equality of opportunity, and the difference principle), Rawls says merely, "These features are not needed for the construction of a reasonable law of peoples, and by not assuming them our account has greater generality" (43-44 [herein 428]).

The seven principles that Rawls suggests representatives of liberal democratic, but not necessarily egalitarian, states would agree upon in the original position are the following (46 [herein 431]):

(1)   Peoples (as organized by their governments) are free and independent, and their freedom and independence is to be respected by other peoples.

(2)   Peoples are equal parties to their own agreements.

(3)   Peoples have the right to self-defense but not war.

(4)   Peoples observe the duty of nonintervention.

(5)   Peoples are to observe treaties and undertakings.

(6)   Peoples are to observe certain specified restrictions on the conduct of war (assumed to be in self-defense).

(7)   Peoples are to honor human rights.

He does not clarify how these principles are derived from the modeling that occurs in this new original position. But we may suppose the following: Principle (1) is derived from the interests that states have in pursuing their rational advantage; (2), (4), (5), and (6) are derived from the capacity of states to propose and abide by fair terms of cooperation; and (3) is derived from both the rational interests of states and their ability to propose and abide by fair terms of cooperation.

The inclusion of (7) is more problematic. It is not obvious why representatives who are pursuing the rational advantage of states would agree on a proposition that protects the interests of individuals. Perhaps it is because the protection of human rights just is a part of the conception of justice that all states at this step are presumed to share since they are liberal and democratic. It would, then, cost them nothing to include it.

Rawls contends that there is an important relationship between principle (7) and principles (3) and (4). Principles (3) and (4) are to be included only if principle (7) is also included. Rawls holds that respecting human rights is a necessary condition for prohibiting wars of intervention. At least, that is what the following passage suggests:

> Obviously, a principle such as the fourth—that of nonintervention—will have to be qualified in the general case. While suitable

> for a society of well-ordered democratic peoples who respect
> human rights, it fails in the case of a society of disordered societies
> in which wars and serious violations of human rights are endemic.
> (47 [herein 432])

In addition, he states unambiguously that principle (7) is a sufficient
condition for the inclusion of principles (3) and (4) (59 [herein 443]).
The importance of this should not escape us. Rawls sees the power of
the state to engage in war as being justifiably constrained if and only if
the sovereignty of the state in its internal relations is also constrained.
Thus, Rawls can legitimately claim that he has reformulated the powers
of sovereignty.

Here, however, two difficulties arise. First, Rawls offers no argument
that wars of intervention are illegitimate if and only if human rights
are observed. Nor has he clearly justified the inclusion of the principle
demanding respect for human rights. Principles (3) and (4) would be
decided upon by representatives of states because of the interest that
states have in pursuing their rational advantage and because of their
willingness to abide by fair terms which permit each to engage in such
a pursuit without infringing on the ability of others to do so. Principle
(7) is there because this new original position at this first step included
only representatives of states honoring human rights. Were the parties
to this new original position only representatives of states which violate
human rights, (7) would not be included among the list, but there is no
reason to think that (3) and (4) would not be.

Second, there appears to be an omission in this set. If principle (7)
follows from the character of the states as liberal and democratic, one
would also expect an eighth principle:

(8)　Peoples are to honor the principles of liberal democracy.

The reason that representatives of liberal democratic states would
include principle (8) is the same as the (presumed) reason that they would
include (7). It is part of the conception of justice of the states represented
by the parties because these states are liberal democratic regimes. Thus, the
states need not modify their behavior in any way by including (7) or (8).
Furthermore, since the shell protecting a range of internal affairs of the
state has already been pierced by principle (7), the need to preserve sovereignty could not be invoked as reason for not including principle (8).

In line with this reasoning, if the participants in this original position were seen to represent egalitarian liberal democratic states, then one could expect a ninth principle:

(9)    Peoples are to honor principles of egalitarian distributive justice.

Including principles (8) and (9) accords well with a liberal democratic egalitarian outlook which recognizes that states institutionalize political coercion. The order which is maintained by a system of units of institutionalized coercion may not, unless guarantees are provided, represent the legitimate interests of the citizens.

To analogize between individuals and states obscures the important difference that within states there may exist relations of illegitimate coercion. Rawls, of course, is aware of this danger, as all liberals are. He contends that, "No people has the right to self-determination, or a right to secession, at the expense of another people" (47 [herein 432]). He cites an example of this the abrogation of a right to secede by the American South because it perpetuated institutions of slavery. There are clear liberal democratic and egalitarian grounds upon which to object to institutions of slavery. But there are also clear grounds to object to the institutional denial of civil and democratic rights and institutionally based illegitimate material inequalities. Liberal democratic egalitarian values, lexically ordered, may find slavery more objectionable than the denial of civil and democratic rights and the existence of great inequalities, but they would nonetheless find these latter objectionable.

Recall that Rawls seems to view the inclusion of principle (7) as necessary and sufficient for the inclusion of principles (3) and (4). But just as the absence of human rights in a state might be reason, although perhaps not sufficient reason, to intervene, so the absence of liberal democracy and egalitarian justice might be reason, although not sufficient, to intervene. Since Rawls's construction does not provide an argument that respecting human rights is a necessary and sufficient condition for prohibiting wars of intervention, he is in a poor position to resist including respect for liberal democracy and egalitarian justice as individually necessary conditions and as collectively sufficient conditions.

The omission of (8) and (9) does not sit well with Rawls's obvious concern about illegitimate state coercion. Why, then, does he not include them? His explanation for including representatives of nonegalitarian states, cited above, is telling. He is concerned that the principles that would follow from an original position which included only representatives of liberal democratic egalitarian states would exclude from possible agreement a wide range of states that are not egalitarian. So, he tailored the first step to omit (9), but he merely neglected to include (8). To include principles (8) and (9) as products of the first step would result in a set of principles that would be unacceptable in the second step.

At the second step of the ideal theory Rawls attempts to extend the law of peoples to include well-ordered nonliberal hierarchical states. These are states that ensure neither egalitarian justice nor liberal and democratic rights. They impose duties on their citizens to pursue a common good and are peaceful and respectful of human rights. Representatives of such states can be modeled by the same original position that modeled liberal democratic states because such states can be seen as reasonable and rational. They do not try to extend their conception of the good life by war, and they have an ordered civil civic life. Thus, they can accept an original position that models fairness among peoples (states) (54 [herein 438]). In addition, they have a conception of the good that can be modeled by the pursuit of rational advantage by their representatives in the original position.

Representatives of well-ordered hierarchical states would agree to principles (1) through (7) for the same reasons that representatives of liberal democratic societies do. Principle (1) is derived from the interests that states have in pursuing their rational advantage; (2), (4), (5), and (6) are derived from the capacity of states to propose and abide by fair terms of cooperation. Principle (3) is derived both from the rational interests of states and their capacity to propose and abide by fair terms of cooperation. Principle (7) is included because it is part of the conception of justice that well-ordered states have. Clearly principles (8) and (9) would be rejected by representatives of well-ordered hierarchical states.

Rawls does not attempt to justify his omission of principle (8) at the first step. And his exclusion of (9) seems motivated by a desire to provide a set of principles with greater generality (43–44 [herein 428]). The motivation for omitting both principles appears to be to make the extension in the second step possible. This is hardly satisfying since one of the main conclusions that Rawls wishes to establish is that liberal and well-ordered hierarchical states will accept the same law of peoples

(37 [herein 422]). Furthermore, Rawls's account appears internally ad hoc insofar as it permits piercing the shell of sovereignty in order to defend human rights, but not in order to defend liberal democracy or egalitarianism. He seems to have neglected Kant's advice not to advance a political morality that is tailored to the concerns of the statesman.

> I can easily conceive of a moral politician, i.e., one who so chooses political principles that they are consistent with those of morality; but I cannot conceive of a political moralist, one who forges a morality in such a way that it conforms to the statesman's advantage.[8]

This advice applies also to worries about whether existing state leaders would accept principles (8) and (9). The goal of political morality is not to establish principles that leaders are likely to accept, but ones that they ought to accept, that is ones to which citizens might hold them accountable.[9]

Liberal democratic egalitarians have special reason to be suspicious. Since states institutionalize political coercion, a representative of a nonliberal democratic or nonegalitarian state may represent the interests of the dominant powers of that state without representing the wishes of all its citizens, particularly those who advocate liberal democratic egalitarianism. Because principles (1) through (7) are congenial to the interests of well-ordered hierarchical states, Rawls claims that they would be accepted by citizens of well-ordered hierarchical regimes without even considering that such citizens might find the order under which they live to be oppressive (54 [herein 438f]).

There remains the specific question of whether the property of greater generality for the set of principles justifies the evacuation of liberal-democratic and egalitarian content. I shall examine this question in sections five and six. But before doing so, in Section 3, I explore an alternative construction of the law of peoples that can establish the relationship between restrictions on internal and external sovereignty that Rawls wishes to assert, and in 4, I compare these two constructions with certain claims from *Political Liberalism*.

## 3

Rawls asserts that the constructivist procedure is alterable according to the subject with which it is dealing (39 [herein 424]). The structure of the procedure is a function of the structure of the social framework about which the procedure is deciding.

> I add that in developing a conception of justice for the basic structure or for the law of peoples, or indeed for any subject, constructivism does not view the variation in numbers of people alone as accounting for the appropriateness of different principles in different cases ... Rather, it is the distinct structure of the social framework, and the purpose and role of its various parts and how they fit together, that explains there being different principles for different kinds of subjects. (40 [herein 425])

Rawls is also willing to admit that the particular procedure of construction that he has adopted in "The Law of Peoples" may not be the best fit for the subject-matter (40 [herein 425]). He gives passing consideration to an entirely different construction of the law of peoples, a construction that would include in the original position not representatives of states, but representatives of all of the individual persons of the world (54–55 [herein 439]). Such a construction would break once and for all the analogy between states and individuals. But Rawls rejects this construction for the familiar reason that it makes the basis of agreement of the law of peoples too narrow (55 [herein 439]). He might also have rejected this construction because it fails to conform to his minimum standard of realism by allowing the international system of states to be called into question.

He does not consider a third construction that places in the original position representatives of persons taken to be the citizens of states. These representatives would be ignorant of the state, and its character, that the represented citizens inhabit.[10] But because this is a construction of an ideal theory, they would know that reasonably favorable conditions for democracy exist. This construction conforms to Rawls's minimal standards of realism since citizens are organized into states, but it breaks the analogy between states and individuals since the interests of persons that get primary representation. States' interests are represented just insofar as these interests serve the interests of their citizens.

It might be objected that such a construction seems to allow too much knowledge behind the veil. In particular that persons are known to be citizens of states might be thought to be unjustified. If this were the case, then our choice might be between Rawls's construction and a construction that represents all the persons of the world. But if the original positions of *A Theory of Justice* and *Political Liberalism*, which employ representatives of citizens of a state, are justified, then so must be this construction, which utilizes the same representatives. Furthermore, this setup adheres to what Rawls regards as the requirements of political realism. This third construction is the one that Rawls needs in order to justify the relationship between limits on internal and external sovereignty that he wishes to assert. However, this procedure goes farther than Rawls wishes, as it establishes principles (8) and (9) as well.

In this third construction, the original position situates free and equal representatives of persons (taken to citizens of states) thought to be reasonable and rational. Such representatives would be far less concerned with the interests of states and far more concerned with the freedom and ability of persons to pursue their own conceptions of the good life within a fair system of cooperation than would be representatives of states. They would desire that both state institutions and the international order reflect this concern.

Representatives of persons taken to be the citizens of states would not be likely to choose Rawls's third and fourth principles, if principles (8) and (9) were not also included. If the only way that rational persons could be prevented from living according to their legitimate conceptions of the good life were through the violation of their human rights, then rationality and reason would dictate forgoing the power of intervention once human rights had been assured. This is because after assuring respect for human rights, a representative of the citizens of states would have no reason to worry that those persons she represented might be stranded in a state that prohibited the pursuit of legitimate conceptions of the good life. But clearly illiberal, undemocratic, and nonegalitarian social orders can also prevent persons from living according to their legitimate conceptions of the good life. Principles prohibiting the right to forcefully intervene into a state's affairs would be an irrational choice in the absence of assurances of the kind that principles (8) and (9) provide.

In the absence of any knowledge of which state's citizens she represents and the state's social and political arrangements, the representative of citizens would want assurances that individuals can freely pursue their legitimate conceptions of the good life or that they may struggle against social circumstances that make that impossible, and that in such a struggle they may with justice request, and reasonably expect, aid. Once full assurance that citizens can freely pursue their legitimate conceptions of the good life is provided, then wars of intervention should be prohibited. Thus, respect for human rights, the principles of liberal democracy, and the principles of egalitarian justice are individually necessary conditions, and collectively sufficient condition, for prohibiting wars of intervention.

One might argue that representatives of the citizens of states, having knowledge of the history of interventions in the twentieth century which were liberating in name only, would choose respect for sovereignty over principles (8) and (9) out of a concern that interventions might well turn into acts of imperialist aggression. But as a matter of ideal theory this procedure produces a set of principles that includes (3) and (4) as well as (7) through (9). Under ideal theory, imperialism is impermissible because interventions are impermissible. I shall discuss the concern about imperialist or illiberal interventions further in Section 7, where I take up certain concerns appropriate for nonideal theory.

**4**

In this section I shall argue that the parallels between "The Law of Peoples" account of the original position and the *Political Liberalism* account involve the former in the infraction of modeling states in an inappropriate manner. In addition, I shall argue that individual rights can only be justified by representing the interests of individuals in the original position, not the interests of states. Finally, I shall argue that a law of peoples specified by principles (1) through (9) is political and not comprehensive because it models the interests and powers of persons taken to be citizens of states and a conception of intrastate society in an appropriate fashion, and does not rest on metaphysical conceptions.

Let's turn first to *Political Liberalism*. The compound question this book seeks to answer is the following: "How is it possible for there to exist over time a just and stable society of free and equal citizens who still remain profoundly divided by reasonable religious, philosophical, and moral doctrines?" (*PL* 47) A requirement for such a just and stable society is a political conception of justice that draws on certain shared political conceptions from the liberal democratic tradition. The central organizing ideas of the account that Rawls gives are those of society as a fair system of cooperation over time, citizens as free and equal, and a well-ordered society as a society effectively regulated by a political conception of justice (*PL* 14).

Utilizing each of the above ideas involves modeling them in appropriate ways in the structure of the original position or the psychology of its parties. It is far too much, and more than the argument of this paper requires, to show how every aspect of each of these three ideas gets modeled. Instead I shall focus on two related aspects of persons—persons as free and rational citizens.

In the liberal democratic tradition, understanding citizens as free involves two assumptions about their moral powers. First, they are capable of forming and rationally revising their conception of the good (*PL* 30). Second, they view themselves as self-authenticating sources of valid claims on others and the state (*PL* 31). These two powers constitute a citizen's rational autonomy (*PL* 72). The original position models these powers—and therefore a citizen's rational autonomy—in two ways, but for our purposes it is the first way that is important. Here the powers are modeled by making the original position a case of pure procedural justice. The representatives are neither bound by, nor are their decisions measured against, any preexisting principle of right or justice (*PL* 73). In the original position, then, representatives are free to pursue the citizen's interest, within the constraints of being symmetrically situated and being behind the veil of ignorance.

The significance of this is that by analogy the same holds for states in the new original position of "The Law of Peoples." Apparently states are modeled as self-authenticating sources of valid claims. And most certainly the construction is a case of pure procedural justice. This implies that representatives of states are in no way bound to serve, or to represent, the interests of the citizens of states. The voices of persons taken to be citizens are simply muffled behind the voting of representatives pursuing the interests of states. Nothing could be farther from the traditional liberal conception of the relationship between the interests of individuals and those of the state. Therefore, even at the first step of the first stage of the construction, before representatives of hierarchical states are included, liberals have grounds for rejecting the procedure.

Because the interests of persons are inappropriately suppressed behind those of the states, it is quite easy for Rawls simply to assume that individuals in hierarchical states will accept the law of peoples that legitimizes those states. On this point at least, Ackerman characterizes the problem quite well:

The fact is that none of Rawls's "well-ordered" hierarchies will be free of natives who are themselves inspired by liberal ideas of liberty and equality. There is no Islamic nation without a woman who insists on equal rights; no Confucian society without a man who denies the need for deference. Sometimes these liberals will be in a minority in their native lands; but given the way Rawls defines a "well-ordered" hierarchy, it is even possible that native liberals might be a majority.[11]

The failure of this new original position to model the interests of persons is the reason that Rawls has no argument for the inclusion of principle (7). Human rights, indeed individual rights in general, cannot be secured by a procedure of construction that does not represent the interests of persons. The construction of *Political Liberalism* derives a fully adequate scheme of equal basic liberties because the parties pursue the interests of *persons* within the constraints of being symmetrically situated and being behind the veil of ignorance.

In "The Law of Peoples," Rawls asserts that basic human rights are minimum standards for well-ordered political institutions (57 [herein 441]). This is a revision of the account of being well-ordered given in *Political Liberalism*. In *Political Liberalism* the requirements for a society being counted as well-ordered include only the general acceptance of the same principles of justice, and general knowledge of that general acceptance; public knowledge of, or reasonable belief in, the satisfaction of the principles of justice by the society's basic structure; and finally a citizenry in compliance with society's basic institutions because they are just (*PL* 35). According to the criteria of *Political Liberalism*, a theocracy with a citizenry sharing a common conception of the good and with a constitution brutally intolerant of other conceptions could be well-ordered. In "The Law of Peoples" the concept of a well-ordered society, with its inclusion of a human rights requirement, has spread onto liberal territory. To qualify as well-ordered in "The Law of Peoples" a state must be proto-liberal.

None of what Rawls has to say about the relationship between being well-ordered and respecting rights amounts to a justification for the inclusion of principle (7). Furthermore, although Rawls claims that well-ordered hierarchical regimes uphold "a certain liberty of conscience" (57 [herein 441]) this must certainly be a considerably weaker version of this liberty than is commonly invoked as a fundamental right since Rawls's hierarchical state is organized around a conception of the good, and places duties and obligations on its members on the basis of this conception (51 [herein 436]).

Establishing the claims that Rawls's modeling of the interests of states is inappropriate, and that he has no adequate justification of human rights, does not constitute full proof that my modeling of the interests of persons taken to be the citizens of states is appropriate. As I have noted, Rawls asserts that a set of principles like mine must be principles of a comprehensive liberalism. He finds it troublesome to treat all persons, regardless of their society and culture, as individuals who are free and equal, and reasonable and rational (55 [herein 439]). Rawls might in fact contend that doing so involves employing a metaphysical conception of personhood.

My procedure involves modeling all persons, whether or not they are citizens from a liberal democratic tradition, as free and equal, and reasonable and rational. The main reason against doing this seems to be that, in many cases, this does not correspond with how citizens of particular states are viewed in their own tradition. But an appeal to empirical conceptions of personhood and citizenship does not fit well into this discussion. In *Political Liberalism*, Rawls is careful to distinguish three different points of view (*PL* 28). These are the points of view of the parties in the original position, of the citizens in a well-ordered society, and of us. The first is an artificial psychology that serves as a device for constructing justice. The second is an ideal that might be (but is not yet) realized in the world. The third is the perspective (our perspective) from which the results of the construction are to be assessed. The point of modeling is not to represent individuals' actual self-conceptions, or the metaphysical conception of the self that is affirmed by the tradition to which they belong, but to model the values that are implicit in the functioning of liberal democracies.[12]

An exposition of a political conception of justice has two stages. The first sets out the conception as a freestanding view. The second concerns an account of the conception's stability, which account involves appealing to an overlapping consensus (*PL* 64).[13] A concern that not all of us, that is not all of the people of the world, will positively assess the result of the construction because it is the result of modeling values that we do not all share is a concern appropriate to the second stage. That many may not positively assess the principles does not impugn the legitimacy of the construction at the first stage. Furthermore, the stability that is generated by overlapping consensus requires a political conception of justice that coheres with political conceptions of citizenship and society under ideal conditions, not necessarily conceptions currently held.

In *Political Liberalism,* Rawls recognizes that not every citizen of the state in the liberal democratic tradition will accept the two principles of justice that are constructed from the original position. Many will not do so because they are unreasonable. Such citizens desire to impose their own comprehensive doctrines on others, or the comprehensive doctrine that these citizens follow is unreasonable and does not overlap enough with the principles to allow the citizens to affirm both. In any case, parties to the original position of *Political Liberalism* would be all the more concerned with securing such features of the two principles of justice as the full scheme of liberties, if they knew that there were to be unreasonable people who might try to subvert individual liberties (*PL* 64-65). Therefore, concerns appropriate to stage two do not affect the construction at stage one.

Even though it makes no difference to the question of the appropriateness of the construction, it is interesting to speculate about how much agreement on principles (1) through (9) we might currently find. Although Rawls simply asserts that many people would not assent to principles similar to (8) and (9), the percentage of those who would so decline may be lower than he admits. National economies, for example, decrease in importance as the world market increases via dramatic moves toward international free trade.[14] Few will deny that we live in a system of global cooperation in the production and consumption of goods and services. This reinforces notions of world citizenship that have been around for some time. Even in the eighteenth century Kant was well aware of these notions:

> Since the narrower or wider community of the peoples of the earth has developed so far that a violation of rights in one place is felt throughout the world, the idea of a law of world citizenship is no high-flown exaggerated notion. It is a supplement to the unwritten code of the civil and international law, indispensable for the maintenance of human rights and hence to perpetual peace.[15]

In our time there is a growing body of international law and convention that recognizes the importance of liberal democratic and egalitarian values. At the Copenhagen Meeting of the Conference of Security and Cooperation in Europe in 1990, participating states passed resolutions, among others, reaffirming that democracy is an inherent element of the rule of law, securing the rights to freedom of thought, conscience, and religion, and reaffirming the importance of economic, social, and cultural rights.[16] These resolutions were agreed to by states from Western Europe and North America with long democratic traditions but also by the post-Communist states of Eastern Europe. Even if the leaders of less democratic states would be less inclined to sign on to such principles, this tell us precious little about what the citizens of those states think.

Still it is conceivable that more people would agree to Rawls's seven principles than my nine. Determining whether or not this possible narrower base of agreement is a significant defect of the principles I propose requires further examination of the value of the breadth of an agreement.

## 5

Rawls's concern that a theory of international justice should not be excessively narrow might be interpreted as a worry about the stability of such an agreement. In this section I shall argue that greater stability is not generated by merely wider agreement; stability is instead generated by a certain kind of agreement that has nothing to do with its breadth.

One might believe that a reason to choose a wider agreement is the greater stability of the international order that would rest upon it. For one might suppose that a wider agreement about less would produce a more stable international order than a narrower one about more. In "The Law of Peoples," Rawls is concerned to see a certain kind of agreement arise, one that is stable in the right way. To be stable in the right way, the agreement must be about institutions and practice that more or less satisfy the principles of justice, and the principles must be honored by all because they are just and beneficial to all (48-49 [herein 433]). This sort of agreement is called an overlapping consensus in *Political Liberalism*. The object of an overlapping consensus is a moral conception, and the conception is affirmed on moral grounds (*PL* 147). It is precisely because an overlapping consensus involves a moral affirmation that it is stable. On this account stability is generated not by width of agreement, but by the kind of agreement.

Rawls's use of the concept of overlapping consensus appears to be motivated primarily by a concern to show how a liberal regime can be legitimately stable (*PL* 136–37). He wants to show how a moral, and not just a prudential, obligation to the principles of justice is possible. Participants in an overlapping consensus, as opposed to a modus vivendi, are bound by more than a mere calculation of their rational self-interests. Thus, certain destabilizing problems for a modus vivendi, such as assurance problems, do not arise in an overlapping consensus.[17] If a person's commitment to the principles is moral and not merely prudential, then presumably she will adhere to them regardless of whether she can be assured that others will do the same. This ensures the stability of the order organized around the principles.

Greater stability does not result from a wide agreement about principles of conduct, if the agreement cannot be characterized as an overlapping consensus, which requires that the agreement's basis be a moral commitment to the principles. Ironically, Rawls would be defeating the purpose of trying to establish a stable international order, if the principles on which it was founded were selected because of their apparent capacity for generating wide agreement. Agreements to adhere to such principles would be prudential not moral, and therefore subject to assurance problems.

On grounds of stability alone there is no reason to prefer a wider agreement. The choice between an agreement based on liberal democratic and egalitarian principles, such as (1) through (9), and a wider agreement on principles, such as (1) through (7), is in fact a choice between a narrow overlapping consensus and a wider modus vivendi. The latter is a modus vivendi because it would require liberal democratic egalitarian regimes to recognize illegitimate regimes.

Furthermore, whatever stability a wider agreement generated would be less desirable because the value of an agreement is a function of the principles themselves. In *Political Liberalism*, Rawls is concerned to show that stable agreement is possible about principles that organize a liberal democratic egalitarian society. One finds no great concern to stabilize every existing order, nor should one. There is no reason to mourn the destruction of unjust social and political orders.

## 6

Another interpretation of the concern about narrowness is to understand it as a worry about a lack of toleration. A liberal theory of international justice ought to incorporate the liberal value of toleration. Rawls claims that a requirement that regimes be liberal would violate this (37 [herein 422]). This seems to me to be a misunderstanding of what tolerance requires. In any case, it stands in contradiction to the account of what tolerance demands that is developed in *Political Liberalism*. Rawls's claim about the demands of tolerance in "The Law of Peoples" is wrong, but explicable by the analogy between states and individuals on which he relies.

In *Political Liberalism*, tolerance requires a freestanding political conception of justice that is not justified by reference to any particular comprehensive conception of the good. This is required because there are a variety of reasonable comprehensive conceptions of the good, not all of which can be true (*PL* 60). "Thus, it is not in general unreasonable to affirm any one of a number of reasonable comprehensive doctrines. We recognize that our own doctrine has, and can have, for people generally no special claims on them beyond their own view of its merits" (*PL* 60). It would be unreasonable for the state to endorse any one particular comprehensive conception of the good life, since this would suggest that all of the others were false, and since there are no final noncontroversial grounds upon which to base such truth claims. If the state were to endorse any particular comprehensive doctrine, it could not maintain this without being oppressive, that is without placing unreasonable demands on those who adhere to other comprehensive doctrines (*PL* 37). Reason, then, demands state tolerance—lack of endorsement—of any particular comprehensive doctrine. What is required is a set of principles of justice that do not require for their justification any one comprehensive philosophical conception of the good exclusively and which can be affirmed from within any reasonable comprehensive doctrine (*PL* 10, 154). But reason does not demand equal treatment for unreasonable comprehensive doctrines. In cases where such doctrines lead to injustices, the doctrines themselves may have to be denied (*PL* 152). With respect to individual actions, justice defines the limits of tolerance.

A line of reasoning analogous to this is developed by Will Kymlicka in a discussion of the value of culture. He argues that liberals should value culture far more highly than they have thus far because culture provides the context in which choices between a variety of conceptions of the good life take on meaning.[18] Kymlicka argues that respect for an individual's culture is important to liberals just insofar as that culture contributes to that individual's capacity for freely choosing and pursuing her conception of the good life. Respect for culture does not, however, entail respect for those activities, practices, or institutions of a culture that restrict this capacity of individuals. By analogy there are many activities, practices, and institutions that liberals should not tolerate, specifically those which violate the principles of justice. The point is that the limits of tolerance with regard to activities, practices, and institutions are set by the principles of justice.

In "The Law of Peoples," Rawls asks the following question: "What form does the toleration of nonliberal societies take?" (37 [herein 421f]). The answer he offers is that the limits of tolerance extend to well-ordered hierarchical societies (66 [herein 449]). The principles of international justice must be such that they can include well-ordered hierarchical societies in addition to liberal ones. This he takes as important because he associates intolerance with imposing foreign, Western ideals on other cultures. He wishes to avoid resting the law of peoples on a theory that "many if not most hierarchical societies might reject as liberal or democratic or else in some way distinctive of Western tradition and prejudicial to other cultures" (57 [herein 441]).

To establish principle (7), Rawls needs to ground a respect for human rights in some theory other than one that will be seen as an intolerant Western imposition. To do this he puts the notion of a well-ordered society to work. He claims that overlapping consensus about respect for human rights can exist only if the societies in consensus are well-ordered. He imagines well-ordered hierarchical states in which no religions are persecuted or denied the civic and social conditions that permit their practice in peace and without fear (53 [herein 437]).

Unless there are many such nonliberal societies (which on empirical grounds seem doubtful), it is not at all clear that such a principle of tolerance broadens the basis of agreement much beyond liberal societies. Furthermore, as already noted, since being well-ordered now requires respecting human rights, which places a state somewhat along the way to being liberal, those suspicious of the imposition of Western values might also suspect the concepts of well-orderedness and human rights as "distinctive of the Western tradition and prejudicial to other cultures." The one example of a well-ordered hierarchical society respecting human rights that Rawls gives, namely Hegel's *Philosophy of Right*, would not mitigate this concern.

The more important problem, for liberal theory at least, is that Rawls's suggested limits included regimes which are organized around comprehensive conceptions of the good. These regimes are, then, internally unreasonable, intolerant, and oppressive by the standards of *Political Liberalism.* To be "tolerant" of such regimes is akin to being "tolerant" of unjust actions or oppressive cultural practices. In short, there are no good reasons for being so. In fact just as institutionalizing an arrangement that permitted individuals to be unjust could be seen as being complicit in the injustice, so institutionalizing principles of international conduct that licensed oppression could be seen as being complicit in the oppression.

Rawls finds his way into this problem because he views state interests as analogous to human interests. This allows him to assert that just as there are many reasonable individual comprehensive moral doctrines that should be tolerated, so there are many state ideologies that should be tolerated (66, especially note 55 [herein 449, esp. 460, n. 56]). Once again, we find the interests of individuals being suppressed behind the interests of the state—a matter that no liberal should tolerate.

One other element of a concern about tolerance might be about the sort of interventions justified against noncomplying states. This is a concern of nonideal theory. I turn now to brief discussion of nonideal theory.

## 7

Rawls notes two problems that nonideal theory must address. These are the existence of states in unfavorable conditions for justice due to the lack of material and cultural resources, and the relations between states that comply with the law of peoples and those that do not. There are other problems that are equally important, but in response to Rawls in this section I shall briefly outline how my principles and their procedure of construction might be applied to matters that concern him.[19]

Even in unfavorable circumstances, for example due to material scarcity, Rawls sees no case for international resource redistribution. This is because he sees such a principle as constructed by a procedure that is not appropriate for the subject-matter of international justice (63 [herein 447]). Since the publication of *A Theory of Justice,* several people have argued that from the original position described in that work the difference principle would be chosen to apply across states and not merely within them.[20] Such a claim might be rejected by

Rawls as supposing the original position included representatives of all of the individuals of the world. He would reject such an original position because it does not fulfill his minimum standard of realism, for it might call into question the international system of states.[21] On the construction that I propose, representatives of citizens of states would be in a position to discuss principles of international redistribution of resources. Such principles would be of concern to them because they have no idea in which state the citizens whom they represent reside and because they aim to pursue the rational advantage of those citizens. Therefore, there is a prima facie case for an international redistributive principle, and this case results from a procedure that does not call into question the international system of states.

Another problem of nonideal theory is that of relations between compliant and noncompliant states. Assume these latter to be states that do not honor some one or some combination of principles (7), (8), or (9). Some might fear that my account is susceptible to legitimizing imperialist or illiberal interventions against such states.

This fear is unfounded. I have argued that principles (7) through (9) (the liberal democratic and egalitarian principles) are individually necessary and collectively sufficient for including principles (3) and (4) (principles of nonintervention). Although the nonobservance of one of principles (7), (8), and (9) is sufficient for negating a general prohibition against interventions, there is nonetheless room for other conditions that must be met in order to justify a particular intervention. Perhaps confusion about the difference between negating a general prohibition against interventions and justifying a particular intervention motivates a concern about interventions into the affairs of non-Western states.

Liberals should rightly worry about imposing a liberal order. Any order that is not wanted by its citizenry, whether professing liberal goals or not, would seem required to resort to oppressive measures eventually to remain in existence. In such cases, if the imposition itself is not unjust, the resulting order may quickly become unjust. This model of intervention may be motivating Rawls's worry about intolerance. The negation of a general prohibition against intervention in the absence of a liberal democratic egalitarian order does not amount to license to intervene forcefully to establish such an order in all states in which that order does not already exist.

In order to clarify matters, two distinctions need to be drawn. The first distinguishes between forceful interventions (including military and material aid to oppositionists, espionage, embargos, etc.) and peaceful interventions (including persuasion, encouragement, and positive incentives). The second distinguishes between those conditions that warrant forceful intervention and other conditions.

I agree with Rawls that a goal of the application of nonideal liberal international theory should be to bring all societies eventually to honor the ideal liberal theory (61 [herein 445]), but there are a range of methods available. Different ones are applicable under different conditions. What is required to make the case for a particular forceful intervention is not merely the nonobservance of principles (7) through (9), but the fulfillment of some justified criteria that specify under which conditions forceful interventions are permissible. The above comments suggest that one such criterion must be that there is some large percentage of people who uphold liberal democratic egalitarian values. Additional criteria requiring a reasonable belief that the intervening force will in fact remedy the nonobservance of the relevant principle and not commit some other greater injustice are also appropriate. Still, a full set of criteria remains to be established. Both the establishment of such a set and a full account of the range of peaceful interventions are required by an adequate liberal theory of international justice.

Including principles (8) and (9), each as necessary conditions for the prohibition of the use of force, does not increase the likelihood of imperialist interventions. What is needed, with or without their inclusion, is greater clarity on the kinds of interventions and their justifying conditions. Furthermore, including (8) at least, would bring the law of peoples more into line with what is, on Thomas Franck's interpretation, the general direction of current international law.

> It is no longer arguable that the United Nations cannot exert pressure against governments that oppress their own peoples by egregious racism, denials of self-determination and suppression of freedom of expression. That litany is being augmented by new sins: refusals to permit demonstrably free elections or to implement their results.[22]

## 8

In sum, Rawls's justification of the law of peoples appears ill-founded. The procedure relies too heavily on an analogy between states and individuals, which analogy does not permit the conclusion that he would like to draw about the relationship between limiting internal and external sovereignty. This, however, does not impugn the constructivist project either in general or with regard to this particular subject-matter. An alternative construction procedure is viable; and this procedure derives a political conception of international justice.

The implication of this argument is significant for both ideal and nonideal liberal international theory. Principles (1) through (9) should be viewed as the ideal liberal theory of international justice, instead of merely (1) through (7) as Rawls maintains. Not only are Rawls's seven principles insufficiently sensitive to the situation of individuals within a state, but the omission of principles ensuring liberal democratic and egalitarian principles appears ad hoc. If a concern for human rights is admitted as limiting what can be done in the name of sovereignty, other liberal democratic egalitarian concerns about the treatment of individuals should count as limiting sovereignty as well.

For nonideal theory an implication is that where any one of the three principles, (7) through (9), is not observed, then there is a prima facie case for other states not to comply with principles (3) and (4). Although a concern to prevent the imposition of democratic functioning and egalitarian principles of justice in states may be warranted, such a concern need not lead to a general prohibition against interventions; it can be met by a set of criteria stipulating when particular forceful interventions are permissible and a full account of the range of available peaceful interventions. Those criteria and that account remain to be developed.

## NOTES

1. Much of the time required to write this paper was made possible by the NEH through its Summer Seminar program. I would like to thank the NEH for its support. I am also in debt to Harry Brighouse for the several very helpful discussions, to Allen Buchanan for his comments on an earlier draft, and to Sharon Lloyd for a helpful discussion.

2. References in parentheses are to be understood as follows: If only numbers appear, they refer to the page numbers of "The Law of Peoples," *Critical*

*Inquiry* 20:1 (autumn 1993): 36–68 [the original version from which *Critical Inquiry* excerpted is reprinted herein 421–60]; if numbers follow the letters *PL*, they refer to page numbers in *Political Liberalism* (New York: Columbia University Press, 1993); if the numbers follow the letters *TJ*, they refer to page numbers in *A Theory of Justice* (Cambridge: Harvard University Press, 1971).

3. Bruce Ackerman, "Political Liberalisms," *Journal of Philosophy* XCI, no. 7 (July 1994): 364–86. See especially, pp. 377–85.

4. Michael Walzer's theory of the justice of war trades on such an analogy. See *Just and Unjust Wars* (New York: Basic Books, 1977) p. 55.

5. Onora O'Neill also thinks that the political constructivist procedure is unable to arrive at principles which are binding for nonliberal societies. Cf. *Constructions of Reason* (Cambridge: Cambridge University Press, 1994), pp. 206–18.

6. Already in *A Theory of Justice*, p. 378, Rawls presents the legislators in the original position who lay down the principles of international justice as representatives of "nations," by which he clearly means states, not individuals.

7. More recently, Rawls's use of the term "peoples" has been ambiguous between nations and states. He claims, "I sometimes use the term 'peoples' to mean much the same as nations, especially when I want to contrast peoples with states and a state apparatus." "50 years after Hiroshima," *Dissent* (summer 1995): 327 n. 1. But in the same paper he makes the following inference: "A decent democratic society is fighting against a state that is not democratic. This follows from the fact that democratic people do not wage war against each other," Ibid., p. 323. The inference is plainly unintelligible unless "democratic people" means democratic states.

Furthermore, although nations may possess certain properties, it would be bizarre to attribute democratic to, say, the French. Still, it may be perfectly appropriate to attribute it to their state apparatus. Despite what Rawls claims in the note, it is this second meaning that he seems to employ consistently in this paper.

8. Immanuel Kant, *Perpetual Peace*, ed. Lewis White Beck, Library of the Liberal Arts (Indianapolis: Bobbs-Merrill, 1957), 37.

9. This is consistent with Rawls's view that the principles of justice should be chosen as if reasonably favorable conditions for their acceptance exist. If such conditions, in fact, do not exist, then the principles are not altered, rather long-term political reform is required. Cf. John Rawls, "Reply to Habermas," *Journal of Philosophy* XCII, no. 3 (March 1995): 152.

10. I shall not argue it here, but this construction might be taken as replacing the construction of domestic justice, rather than following upon it. This would be consistent with Henry Shue's contention that "it is impossible to settle the magnitude of one's duties in justice (if any) toward the fellow members of one's nation-state—or whatever one's domestic society—prior to and independent of settling the magnitude of one's duties in justice (if any)

toward non-members." "The Burdens of Justice," *Journal of Philosophy* LXXX, no. 10 (October 1983): 603.

11. Ackerman, pp. 382–83.

12. Charles Beitz points out that even if the conceptions of person in the original position are more congenial to the self-conceptions of citizens of liberal democracies, the conceptions themselves may still have universal application. Charles Beitz, "Cosmopolitan Ideals and National Sentiment," *Journal of Philosophy* LXXX, no. 10 (October 1983): 596 [reprinted in *Global Ethics: Seminal Essays*, 107–17, at 111f].

13. More recently Rawls has argued that there are three kinds of justification of the political conception of justice in political liberalism. These are *pro tanto* justification, full justification and public justification. Cf. "Reply to Habermas," pp. 142–44.

14. Cf. E. J. Hobsbawm, *Nations and Nationalism Since 1780* (Cambridge: Cambridge University Press, 1992), pp. 181–83; and Charles Beitz, *Political Theory and International Relations* (Princeton: Princeton University Press, 1979), 144–49 [cf. herein 32-34].

15. Kant, p. 23.

16. 29 I. L. M. 1305 (1990).

17. Cf. Thomas W. Pogge, *Realizing Rawls* (Ithaca: Cornell University Press, 1989), pp. 213–14, for a somewhat different account of the way in which an overlapping consensus solves assurance problems.

18. Will Kymlicka, *Liberalism, Community, and Culture* (Oxford: Clarendon Press, 1989), chapter 8.

19. Another very important matter for nonideal theory, especially given the ideal theory that I set out, is the conduct between states both of which do not uphold some one, or all, of principles (7) through (9). Furthermore, I don't attempt here the difficult task of determining what the appropriate principle of international distributive justice should be.

20. See for example Brian Barry, *The Liberal Theory of Justice* (Oxford: Clarendon Press, 1973), pp. 128–33; Brian Barry, *Theories of Justice* (Berkeley: University of California Press, 1989), p. 189; and Beitz, *Political Theory and International Relations*, pp. 150–53; R. G. Peffer, *Marxism, Morality, and Social Justice* (Princeton: Princeton University Press, 1990), pp. 404-12; and Pogge, *Realizing Rawls*, chapter 21.

21. Thomas Pogge argues that an international redistributive mechanism can be derived from the original position Rawls presents in "The Law of Peoples." Cf. Thomas Pogge, "An Egalitarian Law of Peoples," *Philosophy and Public Affairs* 23:3 (summer 1994) [reprinted herein 461–93].

22. Thomas Franck, "The Emerging Right to Democratic Governance," *American Journal of International Law* 86 (1992): 46, 85.

# 19. ALLEN BUCHANAN

Buchanan draws a distinction between two normative questions about secession, which he claims require different answers: 1. Under what conditions does a group have a moral right to secede? 2. Under what conditions should a group be recognized as having a right to secede as a matter of international *institutional* morality, including a morally defensible system of international law? He begins his inquiry by surveying a range of theories of secession, distinguishing between theories that present secession as a primary right, and those that see it as a remedial right, available if and only if the group has been subjected to certain injustices. Primary Right Theories hold that no such injustice is required as a precondition to just secession, and are further divided into Ascriptive Group Theories and Associative Group Theories. According to the former, it is groups whose members together share an ascriptive characteristic such as ethnicity, or being a member of a nation or people, that have the right to secede; the latter class of theories, by contrast, require nothing more of the group than a common desire to form their own state. Buchanan then proceeds to lay out his reasons for concluding that Remedial Right Only Theories are superior to Primary Right Theories of either kind.

## Theories of Secession

*First published in* Philosophy and Public Affairs *26: 1 (winter 1997): 31–61.*

After a long period of neglect, political philosophers have turned their attention to secession. A growing number of positions on the justification for, and scope of, the right to secede are being staked out. Yet, so far there has been no systematic account of the *types* of normative theories of secession. Nor has there been a systematic assessment of the comparative strengths and weaknesses of the theoretical options.

Indeed, as I shall argue, there is even considerable confusion about what sorts of considerations ought to count for or against a theory of the right to secede. Although some writers pay lip service to the distinction between arguments to justify a moral right to secede and arguments to justify prescriptions for how international law should deal with secession, they have not appreciated how great the gulf is between their moral justifications and any useful guidance for international law. This article begins the task of remedying these deficiencies.

## I. THE INSTITUTIONAL QUESTION

Most existing theories either fail to distinguish between two quite different normative questions about secession, or fail to appreciate that the two questions require quite different answers.

1. Under what conditions does a group have a moral right to secede, independently of any questions of *institutional* morality, and in particular apart from any consideration of international legal institutions and their relationship to moral principles?

2. Under what conditions should a group be recognized as having a right to secede as a matter of international *institutional* morality, including a morally defensible system of international law?

Both are *ethical* questions. The first is posed in an institutional vacuum and, even if answerable, may tell us little about what institutional responses are (ethically) appropriate. The second is a question about how international institutions, and especially international legal institutions, ought (ethically) to respond to secession.

Those who offer answers to the first question assume that answering it will provide valuable guidance for reforming international institutions. Whether this is the case, however, will depend upon whether the attractive features of noninstitutional theories remain attractive when attempts are made to institutionalize them. I shall argue that they do not: Otherwise appealing accounts of the right to secede are seen to be poor guides to institutional reform once it is appreciated that attempts to incorporate them into international institutions would create perverse incentives. In addition, I shall argue that moral theorizing about secession can provide significant guidance for international legal reform only if it coheres with and builds upon the most morally defensible elements of existing law, but that noninstitutional moral theories fail to satisfy this condition. I contend that unless institutional considerations are taken into account from the beginning in developing a normative theory of secession, the result is unlikely to be of much value for the task of providing moral guidance for institutional reform.

Which question one is trying to answer makes a difference, because different considerations can count for or against a theory of the right to secede. Because I believe that the more urgent and significant task for political philosophy at this time is to answer the second question, I will concentrate on theories of the right to secede understood as answers to it.[1]

The chief reason for believing that the institutional question is the more urgent one is that secession crises tend to have international consequences that call for international responses. If these international responses are to be consistent and morally progressive, they must build upon and contribute to the development of more effective and morally defensible international institutions, including the most formal of these, the international legal system.

Because secessionist attempts are usually resisted with deadly force by the state, human rights violations are common in secession. Often, the conflicts, as well as the refugees fleeing from them, spill across international borders. Recent events in the former Yugoslavia demonstrate both the deficiencies of international legal responses and the lack of consensus on sound ethical principles to undergird them.[2]

Some, perhaps most, recent writers offering accounts of the right to secede do not even state whether, or if so how, their proposals are intended to be incorporated into international legal regimes.[3] They refer only to "the right" to secede, without making it clear whether this means a noninstitutional ("natural") moral right or a proposed international legal right. Others signal that they are proposing changes in the way in which the international community responds to secession crises, and this presumably includes international legal responses, but they appear unaware of the gap between their arguments concerning the justification and scope of a moral right to secede and the requirements of a sound proposal for reforming international law.[4] Finally, some analysts acknowledge this gap and cautiously note that their theories are only intended to provide general guidance for the latter enterprise, but provide no clues as to how the gap might be bridged.[5] None of these three groups has articulated or even implicitly recognized the constraints that are imposed on accounts of the right to secede, once it is clearly understood that what is being proposed is an international legal right.

Keeping the institutional question in the foreground, I will first distinguish between two basic types of theories of the right to secede: *Remedial Right Only Theories* and *Primary Right Theories*. All normative theories of secession can be classified under these two headings. In addition, I will distinguish between two types of Primary Right Theories, according to what sorts of characteristics a group must possess to have a Primary Right to secede: *Ascriptive Group Theories* and *Associative Group Theories*.

Then I will articulate a set of criteria that ought to be satisfied by any moral theory of the right to secede capable of providing valuable guidance for determining what the international legal response to secession should be, and explain the rationale for each criterion.

Finally, after articulating the main features of what I take to be the most plausible instances of Remedial Right Only Theories and Primary Right Theories of secession, I will employ the aforementioned criteria in their comparative evaluation. The chief conclusion of this comparison will be that Remedial Right Theories are superior. Whatever cogency Primary Right Theories have they possess only when viewed in an institutional vacuum. They are of little use for developing an international institutional response to problems of secession.

## II. TWO TYPES OF NORMATIVE THEORIES OF SECESSION

All theories of the right to secede either understand the right as a *remedial* right only or also recognize a *primary* right to secede. By a right in this context is meant a *general*, not a *special*, right (one generated through promising, contract, or some special relationship). Remedial Right Only Theories assert that a group has a general right to secede if and only if it has suffered certain injustices, for which secession is the appropriate remedy of last resort.[6] Different Remedial Right Only Theories identify different injustices as warranting the remedy of secession.

Primary Right Theories, in contrast, assert that certain groups can have a (general) right to secede in the absence of any injustice. They do not limit legitimate secession to being a means of remedying an injustice. Different Primary Right Theories pick out different conditions that groups must satisfy to have a right to secede in the absence of injustices.

*Remedial Right Only Theories.* According to this first type of theory, the (general) right to secede is in important respects similar to the right to revolution, as the latter is understood in what may be called the mainstream of normative theories of revolution. The latter are typified by John Locke's theory, according to which the people have the right to overthrow the government if and only if their fundamental rights are violated, and more peaceful means have been to no avail.[7]

The chief difference between the right to secede and the right to revolution, according to Remedial Right Only Theories, is that the right to secede accrues to a portion of the citizenry, concentrated in a part of the territory of the state. The object of the exercise of the right to secede is not to overthrow the government, but only to sever the government's control over that portion of the territory.

The recognition of a remedial right to secede can be seen as supplementing Locke's theory of revolution and theories like it. Locke tends to focus on cases where the government perpetrates injustices against "the people," not a particular group within the state, and seems to assume that the issue of revolution arises usually only when there has been a persistent pattern of abuses affecting large numbers of people throughout the state. This picture of legitimate revolution is conveniently simple: When the people suffer prolonged and serious injustices, the people will rise.

In some cases, however, the grosser injustices are perpetrated, not against the citizenry at large, but against a particular group, concentrated in a region of the state. (Consider, for example, Iraq's genocidal policies against Kurds in northern Iraq.) Secession may be justified, and may be feasible, as a response to selective tyranny, when revolution is not a practical prospect.

If the only effective remedy against selective tyranny is to oppose the government, then a strategy of opposition that stops short of attempting to overthrow the government (revolution), but merely seeks to remove one's group and the territory it occupies from the control of the state (secession), seems both morally unexceptionable and, relatively speaking, moderate. For this reason, a Remedial Right Only approach to the right to secede can be seen as a valuable complement to the Lockean approach to the right to revolution understood as a remedial right. In both the case of revolution and that of secession, the right is understood as the right of persons subject to a political authority to defend themselves from serious injustices, as a remedy of last resort.

It was noted earlier that Remedial Right Only Theories hold that the *general* right to secession exists only where the group in question has suffered injustices. This qualification is critical. Remedial Right Only Theories allow that there can be *special* rights to secede if (1) the state grants a right to secede (as with the secession of Norway from Sweden in 1905), or if (2) the constitution of the state includes a right to secede (as does the 1993 Ethiopian Constitution), or perhaps if (3) the agreement by which the state was initially created out of previously independent political units included the implicit or explicit assumption that secession at a later point was permissible (as some American Southerners argued was true of the states of the Union). If any of these three conditions obtain, we can speak of a *special* right to secede. The point of Remedial Right Only Theories is not to deny that there can be special rights to secede in the absence of injustices. Rather, it is to deny that there is a *general* right to secede that is not a remedial right.

Because they allow for special rights to secede, Remedial Right Only Theories are not as restrictive as they might first appear. They do *not* limit permissible secession to cases where the seceding group has suffered injustices. They *do* restrict the general (as opposed to special) right to secede to such cases.

Depending upon which injustices they recognize as grievances sufficient to justify secession, Remedial Right Theories may be more liberal or more restrictive. What all Remedial Right Only Theories have in common is the thesis that there is no (general) right to secede from a just state.

*A Remedial Right Only Theory.* For purposes of comparison with the other basic type of theory, Primary Right Theories, I will take as a representative of Remedial Right Only Theories the particular version of this latter type of theory that I have argued for at length elsewhere.[8] According to this version, a group has a right to secede only if:

1. The physical survival of its members is threatened by actions of the state (as with the policy of the Iraqi government toward Kurds in Iraq) or it suffers violations of other basic human rights (as with the East Pakistanis who seceded to create Bangladesh in 1970), *or*

2.    Its previously sovereign territory was unjustly taken by the state (as with the Baltic Republics).

I have also argued that other conditions ought to be satisfied if a group that suffers any of these injustices is to be recognized through international law or international political practice as having the right to secede.[9] Chief among these is that there be credible guarantees that the new state will respect the human rights of all of its citizens and that it will cooperate in the project of securing other *just terms* of secession.[10] (In addition to the protection of minority and human rights, the just terms of secession include a fair division of the national debt; a negotiated determination of new boundaries; arrangements for continuing, renegotiating, or terminating treaty obligations; and provisions for defense and security.) This bare sketch of the theory will suffice for the comparisons that follow.

*Primary Right Theories.* Primary Right Theories fall into two main classes: *Ascriptive Group Theories* and *Associative Group Theories.* Theories that include the Nationalist Principle (according to which every nation or people is entitled to its own state) fall under the first heading. Those that confer the right to secede on groups that can muster a majority in favor of independence in a plebiscite fall under the second.

*Ascriptive Group Theories.* According to Ascriptive Group versions of Primary Right Theories, it is groups whose memberships are defined by what are sometimes called ascriptive characteristics that have the right to secede (even in the absence of injustices). Ascriptive characteristics exist independently of any actual political association that the members of the group may have forged. In other words, according to Ascriptive Group Theories of secession, it is first and foremost certain *nonpolitical* characteristics of groups that ground the group's right to an independent political association.

Being a nation or people is an ascriptive characteristic. What makes a group a nation or people is the fact that it has a common culture, history, language, a sense of its own distinctiveness, and perhaps a shared aspiration for constituting its own political unit. No actual political organization of the group, nor any actual collective choice to form a political association, is necessary for the group to be a nation or people.

Thus Margalit and Raz appear to embrace the Nationalist Principle when they ascribe the right to secede to what they call "encompassing cultures," defined as large-scale, anonymous (rather than small-scale, face-to-face) groups that have a common culture and character that encompasses many important aspects of life and which marks the character of the life of its members, where membership in the group is in part a matter of mutual recognition and is important for one's self-identification and is a matter of belonging, not of achievement.[11]

*Associative Group Theories.* In contrast, Associative Group versions of Primary Right Theories do not require that a group have any ascriptive characteristic in common such as ethnicity or an encompassing culture, even as a necessary condition for having a right to secede. The members of the group need not even believe that they share any characteristics other than the desire to have their own state. Instead, Associative Group Theorists focus on the *voluntary political choice* of the members of a group (or the majority of them), their decision to form their own independent political unit. Any group, no matter how heterogeneous, can qualify for the right to secede. Nor need the secessionists have any common connection, historical or imagined, to the territory they wish to make into their own state. All that matters is that the members of the group voluntarily choose to associate together in an independent political unit of their own. Associative Group Theories, then, assert that there is a right to secede that is, or is an instance of, *the right of political association.*

The simplest version of Associative Group Primary Right Theory is what I have referred to elsewhere as the *pure plebiscite theory* of the right to secede.[12] According to this theory, any group that can constitute a majority (or, on some accounts, a "substantial" majority) in favor of secession within a portion of the state has the right to secede. It is difficult to find unambiguous instances of the pure plebiscite theory, but there are several accounts that begin with the plebiscite condition and then add weaker or stronger *provisos.*

One such variant is offered by Harry Beran.[13] On his account, any group is justified in seceding if (1) it constitutes a substantial majority in its portion of the state, wishes to secede, and (2) will be able to marshal the resources necessary for a viable independent state.[14] Beran grounds his theory of the right to secede in a *consent theory of political obligation.* According to Beran, actual (not "hypothetical" or "ideal contractarian") consent of the governed is a necessary condition for political obligation, and consent cannot be assured unless those who wish to secede are allowed to do so.

Christopher Wellman has more recently advanced another variant of plebiscite theory.[15] According to his theory, there is a primary right of political association, or, as he also calls it, of political self-determination. Like Beran's right, it is primary in the sense that it is not a remedial right, derived from the violation of other, independently characterizable rights. Wellman's right of political association is the right of any group that resides in a territory to form its own state if (1) that group constitutes a majority in that territory; if (2) the state it forms will be able to carry out effectively what was referred to earlier as the legitimating functions of a state (preeminently the provision of justice and security); and if (3) its severing the territory from the existing state will not impair the latter's ability to carry out effectively those same legitimating functions.

Like Beran's theory, Wellman's is an Associative Group, rather than an Ascriptive Group variant of Primary Right Theory, because any group that satisfies these three criteria, not just those with ascriptive properties (such as nations, peoples, ethnic groups, cultural groups, or encompassing groups) is said to have the right to secede. Both Beran and Wellman acknowledge that there can also be a right to secede grounded in the need to remedy injustices, but both are chiefly concerned to argue for a Primary Right, and thus to argue *against* all Remedial Right Only Theories.

According to Primary Right Theories, a group can have a (general) right to secede even if it suffers no injustices, and hence it may have a (general) right to secede from a perfectly just state. Ascriptive characteristics, such as being a people or nation, do not imply that the groups in question have suffered injustices. Similarly, according to Associative Group Theories, what confers the right to secede on a group is the voluntary choice of members of the group to form an independent state; no grievances are necessary.

Indeed, as we shall see, existing Primary Right Theories go so far as to recognize a right to secede even under conditions in which the state is effectively, indeed flawlessly, performing all of what are usually taken to be the *legitimating functions* of the state. As noted above in the description of Wellman's view, these functions consist chiefly, if not exclusively, in the provision of justice (the establishment and protection of rights) and of security.

Notice that in the statement that Primary Right Theories recognize a right to secede from perfectly just states, the term "just" must be understood in what might be called the uncontroversial or standard or theory-neutral sense. In other words, a perfectly just state here is one that does not violate relatively uncontroversial individual moral rights, including above all human rights, and that does not engage in uncontroversially discriminatory policies toward minorities. This conception of justice is a neutral or relatively uncontroversial one in this sense: We may assume that it is acknowledged both by Remedial Right Only Theorists and Primary Right Only Theorists—that both types of theorists recognize these sorts of actions as injustices, though they may disagree in other ways as to the scope of justice. In contrast, to understand the term "just" here in such a fashion that a state is assumed to be *unjust* simply because it contains a minority people or nation (which lacks its own state) or simply because it includes a majority that seeks to secede but has not been permitted to do so, would be to employ a conception of the justice that begs the question in this context, because it includes elements that are denied by one of the parties to the debate, namely Remedial Right Only Theorists. To repeat: The point is that Primary Right Theories are committed to the view that there is a right to secede even from a state that is perfectly just in the standard and uncontroversial, and hence theory-neutral sense.[16]

## III. CRITERIA FOR EVALUATING PROPOSALS FOR AN INTERNATIONAL LEGAL RIGHT TO SECEDE

With this classification of types of theories of the right to secede in mind, we can now proceed to their comparative evaluation. Special attention will be given to considerations that loom large, once we look to these theories for guidance in formulating proposals for a practical and morally progressive international legal approach to dealing with secession crises. The following criteria for the comparative assessment of competing proposals for how international law ought to understand the right to secede are not offered as exhaustive. They will suffice, however, to establish two significant conclusions. First, theories of the moral right to secede that might initially appear reasonable are seen to be seriously deficient when viewed as elements of an institutional morality articulated in a system of international law. Second, some current theories of the right to secede are much more promising candidates for providing guidance for international law than others. Others fail to take into account some of the most critical considerations relevant to the project of providing a moral foundation for an international institutional response to secession crises.

1. *Minimal Realism.* A proposal for an international legal right to secede ought to be morally progressive, yet at the same time at least minimally realistic. A *morally progressive* proposal is one that, if implemented with a reasonable degree of success, would better serve basic values than the status quo. Preeminent among these values is the protection of human rights.

A proposal satisfies the requirement of *minimal realism* if it has a significant prospect of eventually being adopted in the foreseeable future, through the processes by which international law is actually made. As we shall see, it is important to keep in mind one crucial feature of this process: International law is made by existing states (that are recognized to be legitimate by the international community).[17]

Minimal realism is not slavish deference to current political feasibility. The task of the political philosopher concerned to provide principles for an international legal response to secession crises is in part to set moral targets—to make a persuasive case for trying to transcend the current limits of political feasibility in pursuit of moral progress. Nevertheless, moral targets should not be so distant that efforts to reach them are not only doomed to failure, but unlikely to produce any valuable results at all.

To summarize: A theory is morally progressive and minimally realistic if and only if its implementation would better serve basic values than the status quo and if it has some significant prospect of eventually being implemented through the actual processes by which international law is made and applied.

2. *Consistency with Well-Entrenched, Morally Progressive Principles of International Law.* A proposal should build upon, or at least not squarely contradict, the more morally acceptable principles of existing international law, when these principles are interpreted in a morally progressive way. If at all possible, acceptance and implementation of a new principle should not come at the price of calling into question the validity of a well-entrenched, morally progressive principle.

3. *Absence of Perverse Incentives.* At least when generally accepted and effectively implemented under reasonably favorable circumstances, a proposal should not create perverse incentives. In other words, acceptance of the proposal, and recognition that it is an element of the system of international institutional conflict resolution, should not encourage behavior that undermines morally sound principles of international law or of morality, nor should it hinder the pursuit of morally progressive

strategies for conflict resolution, or the attainment of desirable outcomes such as greater efficiency in government or greater protection for individual liberty. (For example, an international legal principle concerning secession whose acceptance encouraged groups to engage in ethnic cleansing, or that encouraged states to pursue repressive immigration policies, or discriminatory development policies, would fail to meet this criterion.)

The chief way in which acceptance as a principle of international law creates incentives is by conferring *legitimacy* on certain types of actions. By doing so, international law reduces the costs of performing them and increases the cost of resisting them. (These costs consist not only of the risk of tangible economic or military sanctions, but also the stigma of condemnation and adverse public opinion, both domestic and international.) Hence, by conferring legitimacy on a certain type of action, international law gives those who have an interest in preventing those actions from occurring an incentive to act strategically to prevent the conditions for performing the actions from coming into existence.

To illustrate this crucial legitimating function of international law and the incentives to which it can give rise, suppose that a principle of international law were to emerge that recognized the legitimacy of secession by any federal unit following a majority plebiscite in that unit in favor of independence. Such a principle, or rather *its acceptance* as a valid principle of international law, would create an incentive for a state that wishes to avoid fragmentation to resist efforts at federalization. For if the state remains centralized, then it will not face the possibility of a secessionist plebiscite, nor have to contend with international support for secession if the plebiscite is successful. As we shall see, some theories of secession create just such an incentive. The incentive is perverse, insofar as it disposes states to act in ways that preclude potentially beneficial decentralization.

Among the various benefits of decentralization (which include greater efficiency in administration and a check on concentrations of power that can endanger liberty) is the fact that it can provide meaningful autonomy for territorially concentrated minorities without dismembering the state. In some cases, federalization rather than secession may be the best response to legitimate demands for autonomy by groups within the state. Thus a theory of secession whose general acceptance would create incentives to block this alternative is defective, other things being equal.

4. *Moral Accessibility*. A proposal for reforming international law should be morally accessible to a broad international audience. It should not require acceptance of a particular religious ethic or of ethical principles that are not shared by a wide range of secular and religious viewpoints. The *justifications* offered in support of the proposal should incorporate ethical principles and styles of argument that have broad, cross-cultural appeal and motivational power, and whose cogency is already acknowledged in the justifications given for well-established, morally sound principles of international law. This fourth criterion derives its force from the fact that international law, more so than domestic law, depends for its efficacy upon voluntary compliance.

Although these four criteria are relatively commonsensical and unexceptionable, together they impose significant constraints on what counts as an acceptable proposal for an international legal right to secede. They will enable us to gauge the comparative strengths of various accounts of the moral right to secede, at least so far as these are supposed to provide guidance for international institutional responses to secessionist crises.

## IV. COMPARING THE TWO TYPES OF THEORIES

Remedial Right Only Theories have several substantial attractions. First, a Remedial Right Only Theory places significant constraints on the right to secede, while not ruling out secession entirely. No group has a (general) right to secede unless that group suffers what are uncontroversially regarded as injustices and has no reasonable prospect of relief short of secession. Given that the majority of secessions have resulted in considerable violence, with attendant large-scale violations of human rights and massive destruction of resources, common sense urges that secession should not be taken lightly.

Furthermore, there is good reason to believe that secession may in fact exacerbate the ethnic conflicts which often give rise to secessionist movements, for two reasons. First, in the real world, though not perhaps in the world of some normative theorists, many, perhaps most, secessions are by ethnic minorities. But when an ethnic minority secedes, the result is often that another ethnic group becomes a minority within the new state. All too often, the formerly persecuted become the persecutors. Second, in most cases, not all members of the seceding group lie within the seceding area, and the result is that those who do not become an even smaller minority and hence even more vulnerable to the discrimination and persecution that fueled the drive for secession in the first place.[18] Requiring serious grievances as a condition for legitimate secession creates a significant hurdle that reflects the gravity of state-breaking in our world and the fact that secession often does perpetuate and sometimes exacerbate the ethnic conflicts that give rise to it.

*Minimal Realism.* Remedial Right Only Theories score much better on the condition of minimal realism than Primary Right Theories. Other things being equal, proposals for international institutional responses to secessionist claims that do not pose pervasive threats to the territorial integrity of existing states are more likely to be adopted by the primary makers of international law—that is, states—than those which do.

Primary Right theories are not likely to be adopted by the makers of international law because they authorize the dismemberment of states even when those states are perfectly performing what are generally recognized as the legitimating functions of states. Thus Primary Right Theories represent a direct and profound threat to the territorial integrity of states—even just states. Because Remedial Right Only Theories advance a much more restricted right to secede, they are less of a threat to the territorial integrity of existing states; hence, other things being equal, they are more likely to be incorporated into international law.

At this point it might be objected that the fact that states would be unlikely to incorporate Primary Right Theories into international law is of little significance, because their interest in resisting such a change is itself not morally legitimate. Of course, states will not be eager to endanger their own existence. Similarly, the fact that a ruling class of slaveholders would be unlikely to enact a law abolishing slavery would not be a very telling objection to a moral theory that says people have the right not to be enslaved.[19]

This objection would sap some of the force of the charge that Primary Right Theories score badly on the minimal realism requirement *if* states had no morally legitimate interest in resisting dismemberment. However, it is not just the self-interest of states that encourages them to reject theories of the right to secede that makes their control over territory much more fragile. States have a *morally legitimate interest* in maintaining their territorial integrity. The qualifier "morally legitimate" is crucial here. The nature of this morally legitimate interest will become clearer as we apply the next criterion to our comparative evaluation of the two types of theories.

*Consistency with Well-Entrenched, Morally Progressive Principles of International Law.* Unlike Primary Right Theories, Remedial Right Only Theories are consistent with, rather than in direct opposition to, a morally progressive interpretation of what is generally regarded as the single most fundamental principle of international law: the principle of the territorial integrity of existing states.

It is a mistake to view this principle simply as a monument to the self-interest of states in their own survival. Instead, I shall argue, it is a principle that serves some of the most basic morally legitimate interests of *individuals*.

The interest that existing states have in continuing to support the principle of territorial integrity is a morally legitimate interest because the recognition of that principle in international law and political practice promotes two morally important goals: (1) the protection of individuals' physical security, the preservation of their rights, and the stability of their expectations; and (2) an incentive structure in which it is reasonable for individuals and groups to invest themselves in participating in the fundamental processes of government in a conscientious and cooperative fashion over time. Each of these benefits of the maintenance of the principle of territorial integrity warrants explanation in detail.

Individuals' rights, the stability of individuals' expectations, and ultimately their physical security depend upon the effective enforcement of a legal order. Effective enforcement requires effective *jurisdiction*, and this in turn requires a clearly bounded territory that is recognized to be the domain of an identified political authority. Even if political authority strictly speaking is exercised only over persons, not land, the effective exercise of political authority over persons depends ultimately upon the establishment and maintenance of jurisdiction in the territorial sense. This fact rests upon an obvious but deep truth about human beings: They have bodies that occupy space, and the materials for living upon which they depend do so as well. Furthermore, if an effective legal order is to be possible, both the boundaries that define the jurisdiction and the identified political authority whose jurisdiction it is must persist over time.

So by making effective jurisdiction possible, observance of the principle of territorial integrity facilitates the functioning of a legal order and the creation of the benefits that only a legal order can bring. Compliance with the principle of territorial integrity, then, does not merely serve the self-interest of states in ensuring their own survival;

it furthers the most basic morally legitimate interests of the individuals and groups that states are empowered to serve, their interest in the preservation of their rights, the security of their persons, and the stability of their expectations.

For this reason, states have a morally legitimate interest in maintaining the principle of territorial integrity. Indeed, that is to indulge in understatement: States, so far as their authority rests on their ability to serve the basic interests of individuals, have an *obligatory* interest in maintaining territorial integrity.

The principle of territorial integrity not only contributes to the possibility of maintaining an enforceable legal order and all the benefits that depend on it; it also gives citizens an incentive to invest themselves sincerely and cooperatively in the existing political processes. Where the principle of territorial integrity is supported, citizens can generally proceed on the assumption that they and their children and perhaps their children's children will be subject to laws that are made through the same processes to which they are now subject—and whose quality they can influence by the character of their participation.

For it to be reasonable for individuals and groups to so invest themselves in participating in political processes there must be considerable stability both in the effective jurisdiction of the laws that the processes create and in the membership of the state. Recognition of the principle of the territorial integrity of existing states contributes to both.

In Albert Hirschman's celebrated terminology, where exit is too easy, there is little incentive for voice—for sincere and constructive criticism and, more generally, for committed and conscientious political participation.[20] Citizens can exit the domain of the existing political authority in different ways. To take an example pertinent to our investigation of secession, if a minority could escape the authority of laws whose enactment it did not support by unilaterally redrawing political boundaries, it would have little incentive to submit to the majority's will or to reason with the majority to change its mind.[21]

Of course, there are other ways to escape the reach of a political authority, emigration being the most obvious. But emigration is usually not a feasible option for minority groups and even where feasible is not likely to be attractive, since it will only involve trading minority status in one state for minority status in another. Staying where one is and attempting to transfer control over where one is to another, more congenial political authority is a much more attractive alternative, if one can manage it.

Moreover, in order to subvert democratic processes it is not even necessary that a group actually exit when the majority decision goes against it. All that may be needed is to issue a credible threat of exit, which can serve as a de facto minority veto.[22] However, in a system of states in which the principle of territorial integrity is given significant weight, the costs of exit are thereby increased, and the ability to use the threat of exit as a strategic bargaining tool is correspondingly decreased.

In addition, the ability of representative institutions to approximate the ideal of deliberative democracy, in which citizens strive together in the ongoing articulation of a conception of the public interest, also depends, in part, upon stable control over a definite territory, and thereby the effective exercise of political authority over those within it. This stability is essential if it is to be reasonable for citizens to invest themselves in cultivating and practicing the demanding virtues of deliberative democracy.

All citizens have a morally legitimate interest in the integrity of political participation. To the extent that the principle of territorial integrity helps to support the integrity of political participation, the legitimacy of this second interest adds moral weight to the principle.

To summarize: Adherence to the principle of territorial integrity serves two fundamental morally legitimate interests: the interest in the protection of individual security, rights, and expectations, and the interest in the integrity of political participation.

We can now see that this point is extremely significant for our earlier application of the criterion of minimal realism to the comparison of the two types of theories of secession. If the sole source of support for the principle of territorial integrity—and hence the sole source of states' resistance to implementing Primary Right Theories in international law—were the selfish or evil motives of states, then the fact that such theories have scant prospect of being incorporated into international law would be of little significance. For in that case the Primary Right Theorist could simply reply that the criterion of minimal realism gives undue weight to the interests of states in their own preservation.

That reply, however, rests on a misunderstanding of my argument. My point is that it is a strike against Primary Right Theories that they have little prospect of implementation even when states are motivated solely or primarily by interests that are among the most morally legitimate interests that states' can have. Thus my application of the minimal realism requirement cannot be countered by objecting that it gives undue weight to the interests of states in their own preservation.

Before turning to the application of the third criterion, my argument that the principle of the territorial integrity of existing states serves morally legitimate interests requires an important qualification. That principle can be abused; it has often been invoked to shore up a morally defective status quo. However, some interpretations of the principle of territorial integrity are less likely to be misused to perpetuate injustices and more likely to promote moral progress, however.

*The Morally Progressive Interpretation of the Principle of Territorial Integrity.* What might be called the absolutist interpretation of the principle of the territorial integrity of existing states makes no distinction between legitimate and illegitimate states, extending protection to all existing states. *Any* theory that recognizes a (general) right to secede, whether remedial only, or primary as well as remedial, is inconsistent with the absolutist interpretation, since any such theory permits the nonconsensual breakup of existing states under certain conditions. This first, absolutist interpretation has little to recommend it, however. For it is inconsistent with there being *any* circumstances in which other states, whether acting alone or collectively, may rightly intervene in the affairs of an existing state, even for the purpose of preventing the most serious human-rights abuses, including genocide.

According to the *progressive* interpretation, the principle that the territorial integrity of existing states is not to be violated applies only to *legitimate* states—and not all existing states are legitimate. There is, of course, room for disagreement about how stringent the relevant notion of legitimacy is. However, recent international law provides some guidance: States are *not* legitimate if they (1) threaten the lives of significant portions of their populations by a policy of ethnic or religious persecution, or if they (2) exhibit institutional racism that deprives a substantial proportion of the population of basic economic and political rights.

The most obvious case in which the organs of international law have treated an existing state as illegitimate was that of Apartheid South Africa (which satisfied condition [2]). The United Nations as well as various member states signaled this lack of legitimacy not only by various economic sanctions, but by refusing even to use the phrase "The Republic of South Africa" in public documents and pronouncements. More recently, the Iraqi government's genocidal actions toward Kurds within its borders (condition [1]) was accepted as a justification for infringing Iraq's territorial sovereignty in order to establish a "safe zone" in the North for the Kurds. To the extent that the injustices cited by a Remedial Right Only Theory are of the sort that international law regards as depriving a state of legitimacy, the right to secede is consistent with the principle of the territorial integrity of existing (legitimate) states.

Here, too, it is important to emphasize that the relevance of actual international law is conditional upon the moral legitimacy of the interests that the law, or in this case, changes in the law, serves. The key point is that the shift in international law away from the absolutist interpretation of the principle of territorial integrity toward the progressive interpretation serves morally legitimate interests and reflects a superior normative stance. So it is not mere conformity to existing law, but consonance with morally progressive developments in law, which speaks here in favor of Remedial Right Only Theories. Moreover, as I argued earlier, the principle that is undergoing a progressive interpretation, the principle of territorial integrity, is one that serves basic moral interests of individuals and groups, not just the interests of states.

In contrast, any theory of secession that recognizes a primary right to secede for any group within a state in the absence of injustices that serve to delegitimize the state, directly contradicts the principle of the territorial integrity of existing states, *on its progressive interpretation*.[23] Accordingly, Remedial Right Only Theories have a singular advantage: Unlike Primary Right Theories, they are consistent with, rather than in direct opposition to, one of the most deeply entrenched principles of international law on its morally progressive interpretation. This point strengthens our contention that according to our second criterion Remedial Right Only Theories are superior to Primary Right Theories.

So far, the comparisons drawn have not relied upon the particulars of the various versions of the two types of theories. This has been intentional, since my main project is to compare the two basic *types* of theories. Further assessments become possible, as we examine the details of various Primary Right Theories.

## V. PRIMARY RIGHT THEORIES

*Avoiding Perverse Incentives.* Remedial Right Only Theories also enjoy a third advantage: If incorporated into international law, they would create laudable incentives, while Primary Right Theories would engender very destructive ones (criterion 3).

A regime of international law that limits the right to secede to groups that suffer serious and persistent injustices at the hands of the state, when no other recourse is available to them, would provide protection and support to just states by unambiguously sheltering them under the umbrella of the principle of the territorial integrity of existing (legitimate) states. States, therefore, would have an incentive to improve their records concerning the relevant injustices in order to reap the protection from dismemberment that they would enjoy as legitimate, rights-respecting states. States that persisted in treating groups of their citizens unjustly would suffer the consequences of international disapprobation and possibly more tangible sanctions as well. Furthermore, such states would be unable to appeal to international law to support them in attempts to preserve their territories intact.

In contrast, a regime of international law that recognized a right to secede in the absence of any injustices would encourage even just states to act in ways that would prevent groups from becoming claimants to the right to secede, and this might lead to the perpetration of injustices. For example, according to Wellman's version of Primary Right Theory, any group that becomes capable of having a functioning state of its own in the territory it occupies is a potential subject of the right to secede. Clearly, any state that seeks to avoid its own dissolution would have an incentive to implement policies designed to prevent groups from becoming prosperous enough and politically well-organized enough to satisfy this condition.

In other words, states would have an incentive to prevent regions within their borders from developing economic and political institutions that might eventually become capable of performing the legitimating functions of a state. In short, Wellman's version of Primary Right Theory gives the state incentives for fostering economic and political dependency. Notice that here, too, one need not attribute evil motives to states to generate the problem of perverse incentives. That problem arises even if states act only from the morally legitimate interest in preserving their territories.

In addition, a theory such as Wellman's, if used as a guide for international legal reform, would run directly contrary to what many view as the most promising response to the problems that can result in secessionist conflicts. I refer here to the proposal, alluded to earlier and increasingly endorsed by international legal experts, that every effort be made to accommodate aspirations for autonomy of groups *within* the state, by exploring the possibilities for various forms of decentralization, including federalism.

Wellman might reply that the fact that the implementation of his theory would hinder efforts at decentralization is no objection, since on his account there is no reason to believe that decentralization is superior to secession. There are two reasons, however, why this reply is inadequate.

First, as we saw earlier, decentralization can be the best way to promote morally legitimate interests (in more efficient administration, and in avoiding excessive concentrations of power) in many contexts in which secession is not even an issue. Hence, any theory of secession whose general acceptance and institutionalization would inhibit decentralization is deficient, other things being equal. Second, and more important, according to our second criterion for evaluating proposals for international legal reform, other things being equal, a theory is superior if it is consonant with the most well-entrenched, fundamental principles of international law on their morally progressive interpretations. The principle of territorial integrity, understood as conferring protection on legitimate states (roughly, those that respect basic rights) fits that description, and that principle favors first attempting to address groups' demands for autonomy by decentralization, since this is compatible with maintaining the territorial integrity of existing states. It follows that the Primary Right Theorists cannot reply that the presumption in favor of decentralization as opposed to secession gives too much moral weight to the interests *of states* and that there is no reason to prefer decentralization to secession. The point, rather, is that decentralization has its own moral attractions and in addition is favored by a well-entrenched, fundamental principle of international law that serves basic, morally legitimate interests of individuals (and groups).

Even if Wellman's view were never formally incorporated into international law, but merely endorsed and supported by major powers such as the United States, the predictable result would be to make centralized states even less responsive to demands for autonomy within them than they are now. Allowing groups within the state to develop their own local institutions of government and to achieve a degree of control over regional economic resources would run the risk of transforming them into successful claimants for the right to secede. Beran's version of Primary Right Theory suffers the same flaw, because it too gives states incentives to avoid decentralization in order to prevent secessionist majorities from forming in viable regions.

If either Wellman's or Beran's theories were implemented, the incentives regarding *immigration* would be equally perverse. States wishing to preserve their territory would have incentives to prevent potential secessionist majorities from concentrating in economically viable regions. The predictable result would be restrictions designed to prevent ethnic, cultural, or political groups who might become local majorities from moving into such regions, whether from other parts of the state or from other states. Similarly, groups that wished to create their own states would have an incentive to try to concentrate in economically viable regions in which they can *become* majorities—and to displace members of other groups from those regions.

There is a general lesson here. Theories according to which majorities in regions of the state are automatically legitimate candidates for a right to secede (in the absence of having suffered injustices) look more plausible if one assumes that populations are fixed. Once it is seen that acceptance of these theories would create incentives for population shifts and for the state to attempt to prevent them, they look much less plausible.

The same objections just noted in regard to the Primary Right Theories of Wellman and Beran also afflict that of Margalit and Raz, although it is an Ascriptive Group, rather than an Associative Group, variant. On Margalit and Raz's view, it is "encompassing groups" that have the right to secede.

Like the other Primary Right Theories already discussed, this one scores badly on the criteria of minimal realism and consistency with deeply entrenched, morally progressive principles of international law. Also, if incorporated in international law, it would create perverse incentives.

First, it is clear that no principle that identifies all "encompassing groups" as bearers of the right of self-determination, where this is understood to include the right to secede from any existing state, would have much of a chance of being accepted in international law, even when states' actions were determined primarily by the pursuit of morally legitimate interests. The reason is straightforward: Most, if not all, existing states include two or more encompassing groups; hence acceptance of Margalit and Raz's principle would authorize their own dismemberment. Second, the right to independent statehood, as Margalit and Raz understand it, is possessed by every encompassing group even in the absence of any injustices. Consequently, it too runs directly contrary to the principle of the territorial integrity of existing states on its most progressive interpretation (according to which just states are entitled to the protection the principle provides).

Third, if accepted as a matter of international law, the right endorsed by Margalit and Raz would give states incentives to embark on (or continue) all-too-familiar "nation-building" programs designed to obliterate minority group identities—to eliminate all "encompassing groups," within their borders save the one they favor for constituting "the nation" and to prevent new "encompassing groups" from emerging. Instead of encouraging states to support ethnic and cultural pluralism within their borders, Margalit and Raz's proposal would feed the reaction against pluralism.

*Moral Accessibility.* The last of the four criteria for assessment, moral accessibility, is perhaps the most difficult to apply. None of the accounts of the right to secede under consideration (with the possible exception of the Nationalist Principle in its cruder formulations) clearly fails the test of moral accessibility. Therefore, it may be that the comparative assessment of the rival theories must focus mainly on the other criteria, as I have done.

Nevertheless, it can be argued that Remedial Right Only Theories have a significant advantage, so far as moral accessibility is concerned. They restrict the right to secede to cases in which the most serious and widely recognized sorts of moral wrongs have been perpetrated against a group, namely violations of human rights and the unjust conquest of a sovereign state. That these are injustices is widely recognized. Hence if anything can justify secession, surely these injustices can. Whether *other* conditions also justify secession is more controversial, across the wide spectrum of moral and political views.

Recall that according to all Primary Right Theories, a group has the right to form its own state from a part of an existing state, even if the state is flawlessly performing what are generally taken to be the legitimating functions of states—even if perfect justice to all citizens and perfect security for all prevail. Presumably the intuitive moral appeal of this proposition is somewhat less than that of the thesis that the most serious injustices can justify secession.

## VI. POLITICAL LIBERTY, THE HARM PRINCIPLE, AND THE CONSTRAINTS OF INSTITUTIONAL MORALITY

The Primary Right Theories advanced by Beran, Wellman, and Margalit and Raz share a fundamental feature. Each of these analysts begins with what might be called the *liberal presumption in favor of political liberty* (or freedom of political association). In other words, each develops a position on the right to secede that takes as its point of departure something very like the familiar liberal principle for *individuals*, which is so prominent in Mill's *On Liberty* and which Joel Feinberg has labeled "The Harm Principle."

According to the Harm Principle in its simplest formulation, individuals (at least those possessed of normal decision-making capacity) ought to enjoy liberty of action so long as their actions do not harm the legitimate interests of others. Wellman is most explicit in his application of the Harm Principle to the justification of secession:

> We begin with liberalism's presumption upon individual liberty, which provides a *prima facie* case *against* the government's coercion and for the permissibility of secession.... [T]his presumption in favor of secession... is outweighed by the negative consequences of the exercise of such liberty. But if this is so, then the case for liberty is defeated only in those circumstances in which its exercise would lead to harmful conditions. And because harmful conditions would occur in only those cases in which either the seceding region or the remainder state is unable to perform its political function of protecting rights, secession is permissible in any case in which this peril would be avoided.[24]

Margalit and Raz similarly note that harmful consequences of the exercise of the right to secede can override the right, when they caution that the right must be exercised in such a way as to avoid actions that fundamentally endanger the interests either of the people of other countries or the inhabitants of the seceding region.[25] And Beran at one point complicates his theory by acknowledging that the right to secede by plebiscite is limited by the obligation to prevent harm to the state from which the group is seceding, as when the seceding region "occupies an area which is culturally, economically, or militarily essential to the existing state."[26]

What these theorists have failed to appreciate is that even if the Harm Principle is a valuable principle to *guide* the design of institutions (if they are to be liberal institutions), it cannot itself serve as an overriding principle *of* institutional ethics. An example unrelated to the controversy over the right to secede will illustrate this basic point.

Suppose that one is a physician contemplating whether to administer a lethal injection to end the life of a permanently unconscious patient whose autonomic functions are intact and who will continue to breathe unassisted for an indefinite period of time. Suppose that after careful consideration one correctly concludes that giving the injection will produce no harm to the patient (since the patient has no interests that would suffer a "setback" as a result of ending his permanent vegetative existence) or to the family or anyone else. As a matter of the morality of this individual decision—apart from any consideration of what might be an appropriate set of principles of institutional ethics, it may be permissible to administer the injection.

However, it is a quite different question as to whether the principles of the institution within which the action is to occur, whether as a matter of law or in some less formal way, ought to permit physicians to exercise their judgment as to whether to administer lethal injections to permanently unconscious patients. For one thing, a consideration of what would be the appropriate institutional principles requires that we look, not just at the harmful consequences *of this particular action*, but at the harmful consequences *of legitimizing actions of this sort*. The first, most obvious worry is that by legitimizing acts of active nonvoluntary euthanasia when no harm is expected to result, we may encourage killings in situations that are in fact relevantly unlike the ideal case described above. For example, there may be factors (such as pressures of cost containment or bias against certain ethnic groups or against the aged) that will lead some physicians to engage in active nonvoluntary euthanasia under circumstances in which a net harm to the patient or to others will result. Second, legitimizing the practice of physician-administered nonvoluntary euthanasia may encourage some individuals to engage in *other* acts that have bad consequences. For example, if it became expected that physicians would administer lethal injections to elderly patients when their quality of life was very poor, a significant number of physicians might shun the practice of geriatric medicine, either because they have moral scruples against killing or because geriatric practice would come to be regarded as having a lower professional status. The result might be that geriatric medicine would either not attract a sufficient number of physicians or would attract the wrong type of individuals. Whether or not such consequences would occur and, if they would occur, how much moral weight they should be accorded is controversial. The point, however, is that they are relevant considerations for determining whether, as a matter of institutional morality, physicians ought to be empowered to engage in nonvoluntary active euthanasia.

Similarly, one cannot argue straightaway from hypothetical or actual cases in which secession harms no one's legitimate interests to the conclusion that, as a matter of international law, or even of informal political practice, we should recognize a right to secede whenever no harm to legitimate interests can be expected to result from the exercise of the putative right in the particular case. And we certainly cannot argue, as Beran and Wellman do, that the only legitimate interests to be considered are those of the two parties directly involved. (Margalit and Raz, at least, recognize that the legitimate interests of the inhabitants of all countries are relevant to determining the scope and limits of the right to secede, whereas Beran considers only the legitimate interests of the remainder state and Wellman only the legitimate interests of the people of the remainder state and those of the members of the seceding group.)

The most fundamental problem, however, is not that these theorists have failed to consider all the harmful effects of the particular exercise of the putative right to secede. Rather, it is that they have failed to understand that the institutionalization of an otherwise unexceptionable ethical principle that recognizes a right can create a situation in which unacceptable harms will result, even if these harms do not result from any particular exercise of the putative right. Unacceptable harms may result, not from exercises of the putative right, but rather from strategic reactions on the part of states that have an interest in preventing the conditions for exercising the putative right from coming about.

The chief mechanism by which this occurs, in the case of legal institutions, is by the encouragement to harmful behavior that can result from *legitimizing* certain actions. As I emphasized above, when a type of action is legitimized by international law, the costs of performing it are, other things being equal, lowered. But, for this very reason, those whose interests will be threatened by the performance of these actions have an incentive to prevent others from being in a position to satisfy the conditions that make performance of the actions legitimate.

For example, as was shown earlier, serious harms may occur as states apprehensive of their own dissolution take measures to prevent regions within them from developing the economic and political resources for independent statehood, or to prevent minorities from developing "encompassing cultures," or to bar groups from immigrating into an area where they might become a secessionist majority. In each case, the harms that would result from the incorporation of the putative right to secede into international law would *not* be caused by a particular group of secessionists who exercised the right so described. Instead, the harms would result from the actions of states reacting to incentives that would be created by the acceptance of this conception of the right as a principle for the international institutional order.

## VII. IDEAL VERSUS NONIDEAL THEORY

I have argued that Primary Right Theorists have not appreciated some of the most significant sorts of considerations that are relevant to making a case that a proposed principle of rightful secession ought to be recognized as such in the international system. Because of a lack of *institutional* focus, Primary Right Theories fail to appreciate the importance of states, both practically and morally. Once we focus squarely on institutions, and hence on the importance of states, we see that Primary Right Theories (1) are deficient according to the criterion of minimal realism (because they neglect the role of states as the makers of international law), (2) are not consistent with morally progressive principles of international law (because they contradict the principle of the territorial integrity even when it is restricted to the protection of morally legitimate states), and (3) create perverse incentives (because their proposed international principles would encourage morally regressive behavior by states in their domestic affairs). My contention has been that by failing to take institutional considerations seriously in attempting to formulate a right to secede, these analysts have produced normative theories that have little value as guides to developing more humane and effective international responses to secessionist conflicts.

Before concluding, I will consider one final reply which those whose views I have criticized might make. The Primary Right Theorists might maintain that they and I are simply engaged in two different enterprises: I am offering a *nonideal* institutional theory of the right to secede; they are offering an *ideal*, but nonetheless, institutional theory. They are thinking institutionally, they would protest, but they are thinking about what international law concerning secession would look like under ideal conditions, where there is perfect compliance with all relevant principles of justice.[27] Thus, from the fact that in *our* imperfect world attempts to implement their principles would create perverse incentives or would be rejected by states genuinely concerned to prevent violations of human rights that might arise from making state borders much less resistant to change is quite irrelevant. None of these adverse consequences would occur under conditions of perfect compliance in (all) valid principles of justice.

This criticism raises complex issues about the distinction between ideal and nonideal political theory that I cannot hope to tackle here. However, I will conclude by noting that this strategy for rebutting the objections I have raised to Primary Right Theories comes at an exorbitant price: If such theories are only defensible under the assumption of perfect compliance with all relevant principles of justice, then they are even less useful for our world than my criticisms heretofore suggest—especially in the absence of a complete set of principles of justice for domestic and international relations.

International legal institutions are designed to deal with the problems of our world. A moral theory of international legal institutions for dealing with secessionist conflicts in our world must respond to the problems that make secessionist conflicts a matter of moral concern for us, the residents of *this* world. A moral theory of institutions for a world that is so radically different from our world, not only as it is, but as it is likely ever to be, cannot provide valuable guidance for improving *our* institutions. The gap between that kind of "ideal" institutional theory and our nonideal situation is simply too great.[28] Moreover, unless the full ideal theory of justice is produced or at least sketched, it is unilluminating to deflect objections by declaring that they would not arise if there were complete compliance with all principles of justice.

This is not to say, however, that there is no room for ideal theory of any sort. The Remedial Right Only Theory that I endorse is in a straightforward sense an ideal theory: It sets a moral target that can only be achieved through quite fundamental changes in international legal institutions and doctrine. (If I am right, this target is morally progressive, but not disastrously utopian.) My skepticism, rather is directed only to theories that are so "ideal" that they fail to engage the very problems that lead us to seek institutional reform in the first place.

# NOTES

I am deeply indebted to Thomas Christiano for his detailed comments on a draft of this article. It was Christiano's paper "Secession, Democracy, and Distributive Justice" (*Arizona Law Review* 37, no. 1 [1995]: 65–72) that encouraged me to take a more institutional approach to secession. I am also very grateful to the editors of *Philosophy & Public Affairs* for stimulating me to strengthen several key arguments. I also received helpful comments from Richard Bolin, Harry Brighouse, Wayne Norman, David Schmidtz, Christopher Wellman, and Clark Wolf.

1. There is another question that a comprehensive normative theory of secession ought to answer: Under what conditions, if any, ought a constitution include a right to secede, and what form should such a right take? See Allen Buchanan, *Secession: The Morality of Political Divorce from Fort Sumter to Lithuania and Quebec* (Boulder, CO: Westview Press, 1991), pp. 127–49.

2. International law recognizes a "right of all peoples to self-determination," which includes the right to choose independent statehood. However, international legal practice has interpreted the right narrowly, restricting it to the most unambiguous cases of decolonization. The consensus among legal scholars at this time is that international law does not recognize a right to secede in other circumstances, but that it does not unequivocally prohibit it either. Hurst Hannum, *Autonomy, Sovereignty, and Self-Determination: The Accommodation of Conflicting Rights* (Philadelphia: University of Pennsylvania Press, 1990), pp. 27–39; W. Ofuatey-Kodjoe, *The Principle of Self-Determination in International Law* (New York: Nellen Publishing, 1977); Christian Tomuschat, ed., *Modern Law of Self-Determination* (Dordrecht: Martinus Nijhoff Publishers, 1993).

3. Harry Beran, *The Consent Theory of Political Obligation* (London: Croom Helm, 1987); David Copp, "Do Nations Have a Right of Self-Determination?" in Stanley G. French, ed., *Philosophers Look at Canadian Confederation* (Montreal: Canadian Philosophical Association, 1979), pp. 71–95; David Gauthier, "Breaking Up: An Essay on Secession," *Canadian Journal of Philosophy* 24, no. 3 (1994): 357-72.

4. Daniel Philpott, "In Defense of Self-Determination," *Ethics* 105 (January 1995): 352–85; David Gauthier, "Breaking Up: An Essay on Secession," *Canadian Journal of Philosophy* 24, no. 3 (1994): 357–72; Michael Walzer, "The New Tribalism," *Dissent* 39, no. 2 (spring 1992): 165–69.

5. Avishai Margalit and Joseph Raz, "National Self-Determination," *Journal of Philosophy* 87, no. 9 (1990): 439-61 [reprinted in *Global Ethics: Seminal Essays*,181–206]. Christopher Wellman, "A Defense of Secession and Political Self-Determination," *Philosophy & Public Affairs* 24, no. 2 (Spring 1995): 357–72.

6. Some versions of Remedial Right Only Theory, including the one considered below, add another necessary condition: the *proviso* that the new state makes credible guarantees that it will respect the human rights of all those who reside in it.

7. John Locke, *Second Treatise of Civil Government* (Hackett Publishing, 1980), pp. 100–124. Strictly speaking, it may be incorrect to say that Locke affirms a right to revolution if by revolution is meant an attempt to overthrow

the existing political authority. Locke's point is that if the government acts in ways that are not within the scope of the authority granted to it by the people's consent, then governmental authority ceases to exist. In that sense, instead of a Lockean right to revolution, it would be more accurate to speak of the right of the people to constitute a new governmental authority.

8. Allen Buchanan, *Secession*, pp. 27–80.

9. Allen Buchanan, "Self-Determination, Secession, and the Rule of International Law," in *The Morality of Nationalism*, ed. Robert McKim and Jeffrey McMahan (Oxford: Oxford University Press, 1997), pp. 301–23.

10. This proviso warrants elaboration. For one thing, virtually no existing state is without some infringements of human rights. Therefore, requiring credible guarantees that a new state will avoid *all* infringements of human rights seems excessive. Some might argue, instead, that the new state must simply do a better job of respecting human rights than the state from which it secedes. It can be argued, however, that the international community has a legitimate interest in requiring somewhat higher standards for recognizing new states as legitimate members of the system of states.

11. Avishai Margalit and Joseph Raz, "National Self-Determination," pp. 445–47 [*GESE* 187–90].

12. Allen Buchanan, "Self-Determination, Secession, and the Rule of International Law."

13. Harry Beran, *The Consent Theory of Political Obligation*, p. 42.

14. Beran, ibid., adds another condition: that the secession not harm the remainder state's essential military, economic, or cultural interests.

15. Christopher Wellman, "A Defense of Secession and Self-Determination," p. 161.

16. It is advisable at this point to forestall a misunderstanding about the contrast between the two types of theories. Remedial Right Only Theories, as the name implies, recognize a (general) right to secede only as a remedy for injustice, but Primary Right Theories need not, and usually do not, deny that there is a remedial right to secede. They only deny that the right to secede is only a remedial right. Thus a Primary Right Theory is not necessarily a Primary Right Only Theory.

17. The statement that it is states that make international law requires a qualification: non-governmental organizations (NGOs) are coming to exert more influence in the international legal arena. However, their impact is limited compared to that of states.

18. Donald Horowitz, "Self-Determination: Politics, Philosophy, and Law," in Ian Shapiro and Will Kymlicka, eds., *NOMOS XXXIX Ethnicity and Group Rights* (New York: New York University Press, 1997), pp. 421–63.

19. This example is drawn from Christopher Wellman, "Political Self-Determination," unpublished manuscript.

20. Albert O. Hirschman, *Exit, Voice, and Loyalty* (Cambridge, MA: Harvard University Press, 1970).

21. Cass R. Sunstein, "Constitutionalism and Secession," *University of Chicago Law Review* 58 (1991): 633–70.

22. Allen Buchanan, *Secession*, pp. 98–100.

23. Here it is important to repeat a qualification noted earlier: The progressive interpretation of the principle of territorial integrity operates within the limits of what I have called the relatively uncontroversial, standard, or theory-neutral conception of justice, as applied to the threshold condition that states must be minimally just in order to be legitimate and so to fall within the scope of the principle of territorial integrity. Therefore, it will not do for the Primary Right Theorist to reply that his theory is compatible with the progressive interpretation of the principle of territorial integrity because on his view a state that does not allow peoples or nations to secede or does not allow the secession of majorities that desire independent statehood *is* unjust. The problem with this reply is that it operates with a conception of justice that goes far beyond the normative basis of the progressive interpretation and in such a way as to beg the question by employing an understanding of the rights of groups that is not acknowledged by both parties to the theoretical debate.

24. Christopher Wellman, "A Defense of Secession and Self-Determination," p. 163.

25. Avishai Margalit and Joseph Raz, "National Self-Determination," pp. 459–60 [*GESE* 202f].

26. Harry Beran, *The Consent Theory of Political Obligation*, p. 42.

27. For a valuable discussion of the distinction between ideal and nonideal theory and for the beginning of a normative account of secession from the standpoint of domestic institutions (including constitutional provisions for secession), see Wayne Norman, "Domesticating Secession," in Stephen Macedo and Allen Buchanan, eds., *NOMOS XLV, Secession and Self-Determination* (New York: New York University Press, 2003), pp. 193–237. For a discussion of the idea of a constitutional right to secede, see Allen Buchanan, *Secession*, pp. 127–49.

28. I am indebted to Harry Brighouse for his suggestion that the sort of ideal theory which would have to be assumed by Primary Right Theorists in order to escape my objections is so extreme as to be practically irrelevant.

# 20. KOK-CHOR TAN

In his Oxford Amnesty Lecture "The Law of Peoples," John Rawls argues that certain nonliberal societies are analogous to nonliberal domestic groups united by reasonable comprehensive doctrines and therefore qualify for liberal toleration. Tan criticizes this argument for sidelining important differences between nonliberal societies and nonliberal views held within a liberal society. He goes on to develop the diagnosis that this problem in Rawls's global theory is not due to a faulty application of political liberalism to the global context but rather is symptomatic of a fundamental problem with political liberalism's idea of toleration.

## Liberal Toleration in Rawls's Law of Peoples

*First published in* Ethics *108: 2 (January 1998): 276–95.*

How should a liberal state respond to nonliberal ones? Should it refrain from challenging their nonconformity with liberal principles? Or should it criticize and even challenge their nonliberal political institutions and practices? In "The Law of Peoples,"[1] John Rawls argues that while tyrannical regimes, namely, states which are warlike and/or abusive of the basic rights of their own citizens, do not fall within the limits of liberal toleration, nonliberal but peaceful and well-ordered states, what he refers to as "well-ordered hierarchical societies" (WHSs), meet the conditions for liberal toleration. That tyrannical regimes are not to be tolerated is uncontentious enough for most liberals; what is more contentious in Rawls's thesis is his claim that WHSs are to be tolerated. It is this claim that I wish to examine in this article.[2]

# TOLERATION IN POLITICAL LIBERALISM

The law of peoples is the "globalized" version of Rawls's domestically conceived political liberalism, and so I shall begin by quickly reviewing some of the basic ideas of political liberalism, especially that of toleration. In *Political Liberalism,* Rawls tells us that one of the main challenges facing a liberal-democratic society is the problem of maintaining legitimate stability in the face of deep and irreconcilable moral, religious, and philosophical diversity found in most contemporary states.[3] Authoritarian suppression of differences is, of course, not a legitimate option here. But neither is state imposition of liberal values across all areas of society legitimate because, Rawls argues, not all individuals accept the values of liberalism—for example, the idea of individual autonomy—as applicable to every aspect of their lives. To members of some religious communities, the notion that one can reevaluate and revise her religion-based conception of the good life is a foreign and incomprehensible one. Given that reasonable persons can have "reasonable disagreements" over religious, moral, or philosophical comprehensive doctrines, it would be, therefore, unreasonable for the state to insist that they adopt the liberal idea of autonomy in all areas of their lives.[4] The state would in this case be acting on a contentious comprehensive view, a view not everyone can reasonably be asked to accept, and so would be illegitimate in the eyes of some.

Because of the facts of diverse comprehensive doctrines and reasonable disagreement, Rawls thinks that legitimate stability can be attained only if liberalism itself is detached from its own contentious comprehensive moral doctrine and its application consequently restricted to the political realm. The liberal idea of autonomy is, in this view, applicable only to individuals qua citizens, pertaining only to their *public* rights and duties; it is not regarded as a value necessarily applicable in nonpolitical associations like the home, the church, or cultural associations. As Rawls tells us, "political virtues must be distinguished from the virtues that characterized ways of life belonging to comprehensive religious and philosophical doctrines, as well as from the virtues falling under various associational ideals (the ideals of churches and universities, occupations and vocations, clubs and teams) and those appropriate to roles in family life and to the relations between individuals."[5] This move away from liberalism as a philosophy to govern all of life—that is, comprehensive liberalism—to liberalism as a philosophy to govern only political life is the project of political liberalism. When liberalism is thus confined to the political sphere of a pluralistic liberal society, it is no longer a contentious doctrine but can become the subject of an overlapping consensus between different (including nonliberal) comprehensive views. When this overlapping consensus is in place, liberalism attains what Rawls calls a "freestanding" status; at this point it does not depend on any particular comprehensive philosophical foundation (e.g., Kantian or Millian) for support, but is a political philosophy founded on "neutral ground" and can be equally supported by the different comprehensive doctrines present in society.[6]

None of the above presupposes that all comprehensive doctrines present in a pluralistic liberal-democratic society will endorse political liberalism. Some will simply be intolerant of different comprehensive doctrines; others may violate the public political rights their own members qua liberal citizens are entitled to (e.g., the right to vote in public elections, to exit and form or join new associations, to employment, and to a basic public education). These comprehensive doctrines are what Rawls refers to as "unreasonable" and are to be criticized and even challenged by the liberal state.[7] Were political liberalism compromised or tailored accordingly to gain the allegiance of all existing comprehensive views, it would be "political in the wrong way, . . . in the sense of merely specifying a workable compromise between known and existing interests."[8] The overlapping consensus would, in this case, be more properly a modus vivendi than a real consensus around liberal ideals. So, Rawls's restriction of liberal principles to the political realm must not be read as a compromise of liberal ideas but as a requirement of liberal toleration itself; and unreasonable views are views which fail to meet the conditions for liberal toleration.

The overlapping consensus is more precisely, then, a consensus between *reasonable* comprehensive views (i.e., views which are tolerant of other views and which do not violate the public political rights of their own adherents). Nonetheless, and very importantly for Rawls, a comprehensive view need not be "internally" liberal as well in order to meet the conditions of "reasonableness." That is to say, the practices and traditions internal to a particular comprehensive view need not accord with liberal principles before we can expect it to be tolerant of other doctrines and respectful of the public rights of its own members. There are several examples of associations which hold nonliberal but reasonable comprehensive views: the church and the (traditional male-dominated) family are two cases, to use Rawls's own examples from the previously quoted passage, of associations which can be internally nonliberal yet reasonable on Rawls's terms.[9] The internal arrangements of these associations cannot by themselves be the criteria for reasonableness because, given the fact of reasonable disagreement, there is no legitimate basis for questioning the truths of their affiliated comprehensive views. As such, "political liberalism does not attack or criticize any reasonable view,"[10] not even if these views are internally nonliberal. As long as a comprehensive view accepts liberal principles as binding in the public political sphere (as expressed in its dealings with other views and in its regard for the public political rights of its members), it lies within the limits of liberal toleration.[11]

## GLOBALIZING POLITICAL LIBERALISM

The law of peoples extends this understanding of liberal toleration to guide the relations between states. This short passage in the opening of "The Law of Peoples" sums up the extension project neatly: "Just as a citizen in a liberal society must respect other person's comprehensive religious, philosophical, and moral doctrines provided they are pursued in accordance with a reasonable political conception of justice, so a liberal society must respect other societies organized by comprehensive doctrines, provided their political and social institutions meet certain conditions that lead the society to adhere to a reasonable law of peoples" (p. 43 [herein 422]). Rawls wants his global toleration to be, as in the domestic case, a liberal ideal and not one derived from the need to compromise liberal principles in the face of global diversity. To proceed thus, a reasonable law of peoples is first conceived of, and only after is it asked whether nonliberal regimes can also freely endorse this law.

So, in the first step of the extension, Rawls envisions representatives of liberal states participating in a global "original position" deliberation in order to arrive at the global principles of justice.[12] As with the domestic original position, the parties to the global original position are deprived of certain contingent or morally irrelevant facts by imagining them to be deliberating behind "the veil of ignorance." They do not know "the size of the territory, or the population, or the relative strength of the people whose fundamental interests they represent. . . . They do not know the extent of their natural resources, or level of their economic development, or any such related information" (p. 54 [herein 430]). Under this hypothetical fair and equal state, Rawls believes that liberal delegates would agree to the following global principles:

1.  Peoples are free and equal, and their freedoms are to be respected by other peoples.

2.  Peoples are equal and parties to their own agreements.

3.  Peoples have the right to self-defense but not to wage war.

4.  Peoples are to observe the duty of nonintervention.

5.  Peoples are to observe treaties.

6.  Peoples are to observe justice in war.

7.  Peoples are to honor basic human rights. (p. 55 [herein 431])

The next crucial step of this globalization project is to see whether representatives of nonliberal states too would freely assent to these principles. Obviously, representatives of tyrannical states, namely, states which are warlike and/or are abusive of the basic rights of their citizens, will not endorse these global principles. But rather than alter the global principles to accommodate these "outlaw regimes," as Rawls calls them, which would be a blatant instance of a modus vivendi, or making liberalism political and stable in the wrong way, Rawls notes that these regimes are to be publicly criticized in international forums, "contained" and even forcibly challenged in extreme cases (pp. 73–74 [herein 445–46]). Rawls's stance in this "nonideal" case of outlaw regimes is relatively uncontentious (for liberals) and need not detain us further here. It is with regard to a class of nonliberal states, the class of "well-ordered hierarchical societies," that Rawls makes a more contentious claim: Liberal states must tolerate these nonliberal societies.

Well-ordered hierarchical societies are states that meet these three necessary conditions: They are peaceful, they are organized around a common good conception of justice and (consequently) are legitimate in the eyes of their own peoples, and they honor basic human rights (pp. 60–62 [herein 435–37]).[13] The second condition shows that WHSs are not liberal states (for no liberal state can be organized around a common good conception of justice).[14] Moreover, while WHSs are expected to respect the basic human rights of their citizens (the third condition), these basic rights do not include quintessential liberal rights like the rights of free speech (p. 62 [herein 436f], democracy (pp. 69-71 [herein 441–43]), and equal freedom of conscience (p. 63 [herein 437]). Yet, Rawls argues, these two conditions together with the condition that a WHS be peaceful are sufficient to ensure that representatives of WHSs will also endorse the global principles agreed on by his liberal representatives. They would, for example, respect the principle of nonintervention and aggression, honor basic human rights, and ensure that their citizens receive their share of duties and rights as dictated by the conceptions of justice peculiar to their societies.[15]

Because they are in compliance with these global principles, WHSs qualify as states in "good standing" and therefore "there would be no political case [on the part of liberal states] to attack these nonliberal societies militarily, or to bring economic or other sanctions against them to revise their institutions" (p. 81 [herein 451]). While "critical commentary [against WHSs] *in liberal societies* would be fully consistent with the civil liberties and integrity of those societies" (p. 81 [herein 451], my emphasis), *public* criticism by liberal representatives in international political forums like the United Nations, the European Union, and other similar international political bodies is ruled out.[16] Rawls treats WHSs as the global analog of domestic reasonable but nonliberal comprehensive doctrines; and so as the liberal state ought to tolerate reasonable nonliberal comprehensive doctrines, so too should the liberal global society tolerate WHSs. Given reasonable disagreement, it would be contrary to liberal toleration to expect all well-ordered societies to be domestically liberal and to endorse all the essential liberal individual rights. A liberal global order, in Rawls's view, must have the conceptual space for certain nonliberal societies; in other words, it must be able to accommodate WHSs, not as a matter of compromise, but as a matter of (liberal) principle.

## COMPREHENSIVE VIEWS AND NONLIBERAL POLITICAL SOCIETIES

But why would/should liberal delegates be content with the list of global principles Rawls presents? Would they not want a more demanding list of global principles (one which, for one, demands the respect of all the essential liberal rights) and hence be less willing to count WHSs as reasonable regimes or regimes in good standing? Liberals, after all, are concerned ultimately with individual well-being; why should they, then, tolerate regimes whose institutions sustain domestic inequality and are antithetical to any liberal aspiration citizens of these regimes may have? Indeed, we may ask whether these global principles are the ones citizens of WHSs themselves would accept were we to postulate a single-stage "all-inclusive [global] original position with representatives of all the individual persons of the world" (p. 65 [herein 439]) instead of the two-stage procedure Rawls favors where only delegates of societies are represented in the second and global stage.

As we have seen, Rawls holds tolerating WHSs to be analogous to tolerating reasonable nonliberal comprehensive views within liberal society. But this is a deeply flawed analogy. There are important differences between comprehensive views and state regimes, which Rawls forgives. First, in the case of comprehensive doctrines, what is permitted are moral, religious, or philosophical differences, not political ones. As we have seen, while it would be unreasonable for a liberal state to enforce a vision of the good based on a moral, philosophical, or religious comprehensive doctrine, it would not hesitate to criticize (and even attack if necessary) comprehensive views which advocate nonliberal politics. These views would be denounced as "unreasonable" views. The reason why a liberal state cannot condone nonliberal political views is obvious: A political philosophy cannot accommodate another competing political philosophy without undermining itself. As Ronald Dworkin tells us, any political theory must "claim truth for itself, and therefore must claim the falsity of any theory that contradicts it. It must itself occupy ... all the logical space that its content requires."[17] A political philosophy, for reasons of consistency, must take a stance against competing political philosophies.[18] Rawls himself accepts this; he admits that when it comes to the crunch, when political liberalism itself is challenged, we may have no choice but to invoke some of liberalism's comprehensive views (thereby doing that which "we had hoped to avoid") to justify putting down the challenge.[19]

But at the international level, Rawls advocates tolerating regimes with nonliberal *political* institutions. He says that "whenever the scope of toleration is extended... the criteria of reasonableness is relaxed" (p. 78 [herein 449]), and so nonliberal politics, unreasonable in the domestic context, becomes reasonable in the international context. Accordingly, certain views not permitted in domestic liberal society are deemed permissible if expressed in foreign societies. It seems that while Rawls would say that a liberal state should criticize a domestic comprehensive view that forbids its members from exercising their public rights (like the right to vote in public elections), this same state should not criticize a WHS that denies some of its citizens this same right. This seems blatantly inconsistent to me. Why does Rawls hold this position?

Rawls does not provide a satisfactory answer here. He points out that although domestic liberalism begins from a political conception of the person as free and equal and rooted in a liberal public culture, to begin from similar assumptions in the international case would make the basis of justice "too narrow" (pp. 65–66 [herein 439]). This is one of Rawls's expressed reasons for employing a two-stage original position procedure.[20] But why avoid this "too narrow" basis for a law of peoples? Is it because liberal toleration requires that we do? Or is it because Rawls worries that WHSs would not endorse the law of peoples otherwise? It can't be the former reason. As I mentioned, liberal toleration in the domestic context does not require toleration of nonliberal politics; indeed it must demand otherwise. Yet Rawls has given us no principled reason why it should be any different in the global context other than the diversity of political cultures. Absent a good justification, it appears that Rawls has simply relaxed the limits of toleration in order to accommodate representatives of WHSs, to ensure that his law of peoples can be endorsed by some nonliberal states as well.

This modifying of political liberalism to satisfy international conditions is, Fernando Teson points out, a serious error of "The Law of Peoples." He says, "A political theory cannot survive if one keeps amending its assumptions at every turn to reach results that do not seem to match the theory in its original form. This is simply a way of immunizing the theory against (moral) falsification."[21] The seriousness of Teson's objection is appreciated once we recall one of Rawls's motivations for extending political liberalism to cover international relations: "In the *absence of this extension* to the law of peoples, a liberal conception of political justice would appear to be *historicist* and to *apply only* to societies whose political institutions and culture are liberal. In making the case for justice as fairness, and for similar more general liberal conceptions, it is *essential to show that this is not so*" (p. 44 [herein 423], my emphasis). That is, it is important for Rawls that political liberalism can be demonstrated to have global scope, that its basic ideas can be freely endorsed by (some) nonliberal societies as well. But if this endorsement is accomplished only by modifying some of the basic tenets of political liberalism in a seemingly ad hoc manner (namely, by relaxing the limits of toleration without good reason), then Rawls has not succeeded in demonstrating the global applicability of his theory on his own terms.

It seems then that, his claim not withstanding, Rawls's international project is beneath it all a project of modus vivendi, of seeking a compromise between liberal and nonliberal regimes, rather than that of achieving stability with respect to liberal justice.[22] To accommodate WHSs, Rawls had his liberal delegates agree on a global theory of justice that is overly generalized and less demanding than a real liberal global theory would be.

Now, one may argue that there is nothing counterintuitive or obviously inconsistent about responding differently to domestic and international nonliberal practices. A liberal state, as a matter of practice or strategy, cannot always react in the same way to similar kinds of domestic and international violations of liberties given the different conditions of domestic and international societies. One obvious instance of this difference is that there is no established enforcement body in global society to enforce judgments that a liberal state may make against nonliberal states. A liberal state cannot pass enforceable laws criminalizing, say, female genital mutilation in another country the way it can within its own borders.[23] Thus, it cannot help but tolerate certain abuses overseas that it would not condone at home.

But this objection neglects the distinction between making a judgment and acting on that judgment.[24] The fact that we may be (genuinely) compelled to act differently between similar cases does not necessarily entail that we have or ought to have judged these cases differently. That we may be forced to put up with certain illiberal practices overseas because of practical constraints does not mean that we need to judge them morally acceptable. We still judge them unacceptable as we do similar domestic abuses even though we may not be able to act on these judgments the way we can in the domestic context. But the normative implication of this distinction between judgment and acting on judgment is significant: If we admit that we are unable to act on a judgment because of practical constraints, then we should be ready to act on this judgment once the constraints are lifted. Indeed, one can say that we are morally obliged, at the very least, to work toward the lifting of these constraints as an immediate objective. So, overlooking the judgment/acting distinction—and thereby mistakenly claiming (as does the above objection) that we tolerate some foreign illiberal practices, when we are actually compelled to put up with them—misses this important implication.[25]

A second important difference between reasonable nonliberal comprehensive doctrines and WHSs that Rawls overlooks is that in the case of the former, individual members have recourse to democracy in the political sphere. They are citizens of a liberal-democratic state besides being members of particular (nondemocratic) communities. So, even if the internal practices of their communities are undemocratic in nature, members of these communities are still able to exercise their democratic rights in their other capacity as citizens.[26] In this way, they are, to a degree, able to influence public policies that may have some positive effects on the practices of their communities. (I shall say more later on how public policies can affect communal practices.)

On the other hand, ordinary citizens of WHSs do not have this recourse. Unlike members of nonliberal private associations who are nonetheless free and equal citizens of a larger democratic society, citizens of WHSs are not citizens of any democratic order. They do not, for example, enjoy democratic global citizenship which may help rectify their lack of democratic rights in their own countries. Therefore, unlike members of nonliberal associations, citizens of WHSs do not have the opportunity to democratically influence external (i.e., global) policies that may help reform and democratize the institutions of their own societies.

The fact that WHSs are undemocratic seriously undermines Rawls's proposed two-stage original position. Recall that in the second stage, in the global original position where the principles of global justice are to be fleshed out, it is representatives of *societies* and not of *individuals* who are the parties to the hypothetical deliberation. But if the representatives of WHSs are not democratically elected by their own peoples, it is very unlikely that they can meet Rawls's own stipulation that "the peoples they represent are represented reasonably" (p. 54 [herein 430]). Accordingly, the two-stage procedure cannot merely be a methodological preference with possibly no consequential differences, as Rawls seems to suggest at one point.[27] On the contrary, whether we opt for a two-stage procedure or a single global procedure (which will provide a "device of representation" for all individuals of the world, as opposed to societies) has obvious implications for the kinds of global principles we will arrive at. It is clear, for example, that individuals reasonably represented behind the veil of ignorance will reject global principles that condone the kinds of institutional arrangements associated with WHSs. After all, individuals (unlike state delegates) know that they could find themselves as lowly placed members of a hierarchical society when the veil is lifted; so, why would they accept global principles that would sanction their possible subordinate status in their own countries?

Indeed, the two-stage procedure is especially objectionable if we remember that WHSs are not expected to envisage a domestic original position for determining their domestic principles of justice. Consequently, not only is there no guarantee of the fairness of these domestic principles, but by allowing only delegates of these societies (who tend to be the ones benefiting from their domestic arrangements anyway) to be represented at the second-stage deliberation, these delegates are able to settle on global principles that accept their domestic arrangements as beyond rebuke.

Now, Rawls asserts that it is not implausible for a people organized hierarchically in their own country to endorse global principles which treat all well-ordered societies with equal concern and toleration: "A people sincerely affirming a nonliberal conception of justice may still think their society should be treated equally in a just law of peoples, even though its members accept basic inequalities among themselves. Though a society lacks basic equality, it is not unreasonable for that society to insist on equality in making claims other societies" (p. 65 [herein 439]). But this depends entirely on *who* speaks for the people. This point is especially crucial because we cannot expect all citizens of a WHS to share a common conception of the public good. Even if we grant the assumption that each state represents a national or cultural entity (i.e., a people), we can still expect there to be internal disagreement over existing political arrangements and even over interpretations of cultural and traditional practices. Surely, it is not unrealistic to believe that members of castes or classes at the lower rungs of a hierarchical society would oppose the dominant values and traditions and the established institutional practices of their society were they empowered to do so. Given that Rawls allows nondemocratically appointed delegates to speak for citizens of WHSs, we must be very suspicious of the kinds of global principles these delegates will endorse, especially if these principles call for equal toleration between states at the expense of equality between citizens within states.

At this point, some comments concerning Rawls's second condition for a WHS, that it "meet[s] the essentials of legitimacy in the eyes of its own people" (p. 79 [herein 449]), are in order. Now, Rawls does not mean by this that there can be no dissent at all in a WHS; in fact, he explicitly allows for the "possibility of dissent" here. He says, however, that the opportunity for expressing any such dissent is "not, to be sure, in a way allowed by democratic institutions, but appropriately in view of the religious and philosophical values of the society in question" (p. 62 [herein 436]).

The crucial question here, then, is whether there can be disagreements in a WHS regarding the (restricted) procedures by which differences can be voiced. Rawls is not explicit on this, but it seems to me that he must allow for disagreements at this basic level for the following reasons. First, given his own "fact of oppression" (i.e., the fact "that only the oppressive use of state power can maintain a continuing common affirmation of one comprehensive religious, philosophical, or moral doctrine"),[28] Rawls must concede that unless a regime organized around a common good conception of justice is successfully tyrannical (thus not a WHS but an outlaw regime), there will prevail certain fundamental disagreements over its basic institutional arrangements or structure, including over how dissent can be voiced.[29] Second, it is quite implausible that members of, say, a caste society objecting to their caste status and the restrictions that follow it will accept, nonetheless, the caste-bound procedures by which their objections may be raised. Opposition to the one entails opposition to the other. As such, in accepting the possibility of dissent in a WHS, Rawls must also accept that there will also be disagreements over how dissent can be expressed.

If there must be fundamental disagreements among citizens in a WHS, then the legitimacy condition, that a WHS "meet[s] the essentials of legitimacy in the eyes of its own people," cannot be understood literally to mean that all citizens of a WHS actually accept its basic structure as just. "People" here does not refer to individual persons of a society but refers, more precisely, to an embodiment of a collective way of life or to a nation. In other words, a political society meets the essentials of legitimacy for Rawls when its basic structure is organized in accordance with its own history, conventions, and traditions. This "communitarian" reading of the legitimacy condition fits neatly with Rawls's elaboration of this condition: A WHS is a society organized around a comprehensive view, it has a common good conception of justice, and its basic institutions are structured "appropriately in view of [its] religious and philosophical values" (pp. 61–62, 64–65, 69–70 [herein 435–37, 438f, 441f]).[30] But as mentioned, the fact that a society is structured according to its own history, culture, and tradition does not rule out dissension over its basic institutional arrangements.[31]

To sum up the points made in this section, the main flaw in Rawls's global thesis is his belief that the global overlapping consensus between different political societies is morally equivalent to a domestic overlapping consensus between different comprehensive views.[32] This is a seriously flawed belief because, as pointed out, comprehensive views are unlike political societies in two important ways: The former does not insist on political diversity and, moreover, it operates within a larger liberal-democratic framework. The global overlapping consensus Rawls presents in "The Law of Peoples" is more a political compromise worked out between liberal and nonliberal state delegates than a consensus around genuinely liberal values.

## THE PROBLEM OF TOLERATION IN POLITICAL LIBERALISM

The idea of tolerating nonliberal regimes is therefore objectionable. Is this a problem of application (that is, a problem arising from a mistaken application of basically sound ideas to the international case, in which case what is to be done is not to reject the teachings of political liberalism but to reapply them correctly)? Or does this in fact highlight a fundamental flaw with political liberalism itself, in which case what we are required to do is to jettison the theory and seek out alternatives?

I argue that the toleration problem in the law of peoples is not a problem of application but an accentuation of a problem inherent in political liberalism itself. The idea of toleration is, of course, shared by all liberals. It is a central liberal belief that the state ought not to discriminate between individuals' genuinely private conceptions of the good life. But individuals are not the only subject of liberal toleration. Most liberals today also believe that the state ought to tolerate different group-based ways of life (for example, of religious or cultural communities), not because these ways matter in themselves but because of their moral significance to members of these groups.[33]

But what is the limit of this group-based toleration? For many liberals, groups whose practices and traditions are antithetical to the liberal aspirations of their own members are not to be tolerated. So, a group that does not permit its members the right and freedom to reevaluate and revise the internal practices and traditions of the group falls outside the bounds of liberal toleration.[34] But, as we have seen, political liberals want to extend group toleration to groups that are internally nonliberal. This is important, Rawls claims, because liberals should not expect all individuals to have liberal aspirations and therefore we ought not to challenge reasonable ways of life that are not liberal in character. But this extension of toleration to nonliberal views is problematic once we recognize that within any association there are always internal minorities or dissenters. It is one thing *not* to *expect* individuals to be liberals (in their private lives), it is quite another *not* to *support* whatever liberal aspirations they may have against oppressive group traditions. Surely as a liberal, Rawls cannot remain indifferent if the aspirations of (some) members of nonliberal reasonable groups to reevaluate and revise their conceptions of the good, and their corresponding group practices and institutions, are thwarted by their own groups. But because of his reluctance to criticize the internal practices of reasonable groups, he seems to have reneged on his liberal commitment to these individual dissenters. There is, therefore, a serious tension within political liberalism between its toleration of nonliberal reasonable groups and its commitment to the individual liberty of (dissenting) members of these groups.

Now, one could argue that in the case of domestic political liberalism, this tension is fortuitously alleviated by two important features of a liberal-democratic society, features which I shall show to be lacking in the international context. The state enforced right of exit and the "liberalizing effects" of liberal public policies on nonliberal ways of life, it could be argued, allow the political liberal to have it both ways, that is, to tolerate nonliberal groups without forgoing her commitment to individual liberty. Let me quickly explain how these two mitigating features operate in domestic society.

The first of these features is straightforward: Private associations must permit their members the right to leave and join other associations should they so desire. To deny members this basic right is unreasonable in the Rawlsian sense; denying members the right to leave and join different associations would be contrary to the political idea of citizens as free and equal. As Rawls says, "In the case of ecclesiastical power, since apostasy and heresy are not legal offenses, those who are no longer able to recognize a church's authority may cease being members without running afoul of state power."[35] So, while the state need not insist that reasonable private doctrines organize themselves internally according to liberal ideals, it must secure for members the right to leave their associations should they so desire. This is one way the political liberal hopes to escape the tension between its dual commitments to group toleration and individual liberty.

The second feature is a little more complicated and invokes the idea of liberal neutrality. Political liberalism, or liberalism for that matter, does not pretend to be neutral in its effect as Rawls points out. What liberalism is neutral about is in the way policies are justified; they are not to be justified on grounds that some (reasonable) ways of life are intrinsically superior to others and hence more worthy of state support, or that some are intrinsically inferior and hence ought to be done away with. But this does not mean that neutrally justified policies cannot have repercussions on the private arrangements of reasonable groups. Neutrality of consequence or effect is impossible to attain as Rawls himself notes.[36] To use one common example, the liberal emphasis on civic education, which (for the political liberal) is justified solely on neutral political grounds (namely, the cultivation of traits and character necessary for equal and free citizenship), can have "liberalizing" consequences beyond the political sphere. As Rawls writes, "It may be objected that requiring children to understand the political conception in these ways is in effect, though not in intention, to educate them to a comprehensive liberal conception. ... It must be granted that this may indeed happen in the case of some…[but the] unavoidable consequences of reasonable requirements for children's education may have to be accepted, often with regret."[37] This indirect "liberalization" of nonliberal private practices does not entail a rejection of their affiliated comprehensive views. For the political liberal, this liberalizing effect is an unintended side effect of a neutrally justified public policy. It is just a "regrettable" fact that public policies impartial about the internal arrangements of reasonable groups can have nonetheless nonneutral (liberalizing) effects on these arrangements. However, the fact that neutrally justified policies are not neutral in consequences allows the political liberal state to indirectly reform the internal arrangements of reasonable nonliberal groups, thereby protecting and promoting individual liberty (the liberal aspiration), without explicitly rejecting these group arrangements as inadmissible (the political liberal aspiration).

Thus, we can see how Rawls, at the domestic level, can hope to maintain his toleration for nonliberal reasonable groups without forfeiting his liberal commitment to liberal dissenters within these groups. The trickle-down effects of liberal public policies will eventually win the day for them; but in the meantime, should these dissenters find their internal oppression unbearable, they have the state-protected right to leave their associations.

Now, some commentators have asked whether the right of exit and the liberalizing tendencies of liberal public policies can resolve this tension in political liberalism entirely. They point out that a formal right of exit is of little solace for most people, and that the liberalizing effects of liberal public policies are limited in their reach.[38] I agree with these criticisms, but for now I only want to show that as far as the international setting goes, these two alleviating features are conspicuously absent.

First, is there a meaningful and substantial right of exit in the international context? The social unit that this right is demanded against in this case would be one's country. Is there such a right in international society? It is true that Rawls insists that well-ordered societies must recognize the right of emigration as a basic human right (p. 68 [herein 441]). But what is the point of this demand if it is not reinforced by the demand that states also be obliged to accept immigrants?[39] Most liberals, and this includes Rawls, are reluctant to insist on the right to *immigrate to* even though they may support the right to *emigrate from*.[40] Indeed, there is no mention in "The Law of Peoples" of any duty on the part of a people to accept immigrants. A right to emigrate from a country without a corresponding right to immigrate to a country is a facile right. In the domestic setting, when one leaves one's private association, one is able to join another, even if it is the default community, as when one leaves the church and joins the secular community. In international society, on the other hand, one cannot leave one's country unless also adopted by another country.

Moreover, apart from the issue of whether the right to emigrate is meaningful without the corresponding right to immigrate, there is also the question of individual capacity: Is it reasonable to expect an individual to leave one's country of birth if the political institutions of that country are unbearably oppressive? Or, to put it differently, is giving one the right to leave one's country a real choice? Oddly enough, on this matter, Rawls himself notes that "normally leaving one's country is a grave step: it involves leaving the society and culture in which we have been raised, the society and culture whose language we use in speech and thought to express and understand ourselves, our aims, our goals, our values."[41] Whether it is true that it is harder to leave one's country than one's religion as Rawls appears to be implying is not the issue here.

What is relevant is that given Rawls's acknowledgment that leaving one's country is more of a wrenching experience than renouncing one's comprehensive doctrine, he must admit that the right of exit is especially weak and empty in the international context, that the right of individuals to leave their country if they find their continuing membership in it too unbearable is very small comfort (even if this right were supplemented by the right to enter another country). On Rawls's own terms, the right of exit does not mitigate the tension between tolerating nonliberal groups and protecting individual liberty in the global case.[42]

Is there any global liberalizing effect on nonliberal regimes? Does Rawls's law of peoples include this provision? It is not clear if it does, at least in any substantive sense. What kinds of global policies would have liberalizing effects on the domestic institutions of WHSs? Obviously, the one policy Rawls refers to in his domestic theory, that of a liberal public education, is not available in the international scene—there is no global educational policy, no global public schools all the children of the world are expected to attend. Likewise, some liberals argue that public policies aimed at improving gender equality can have positive effects in the homes and private associations (e.g., equal career opportunity in the public sphere can result in greater equality in the private sphere, some liberals argue); yet there is clearly no global equivalent here.[43] Moreover, because Rawls insists that the internal arrangements of WHSs are off-limits to political criticism and economic sanctions (pp. 80-81 [herein 450–51]), liberal states cannot insist on any link between liberalization and trade or developmental aid, which is one important liberalizing tool available to liberal states against nonliberal states.

The one possible liberalizing tendency I can think of in the global setting would be the effects of cultural exchanges. Films, books, intellectual exchanges, and art play an important role in educating and raising public awareness and in informing individuals of the world of different possibilities and options. But Rawls would have no qualms about permitting the governments of WHSs the right to censor ideas contradictory to their "common" good conceptions of justice. As we may recall, freedom of expression or speech is not a necessary condition for a WHS; to demand this right as universal would make the law of peoples too "sectarian," according to Rawls.[44] But more relevantly, the issue here is not whether individuals themselves can come to appreciate and acquire liberal values, but whether we should support those who already hold liberal aspirations. More so than with public policies in the domestic case, it is unlikely that global practices and policies can eventually turn the tide against oppressive traditions in favor of these dissenters within a reasonable time span, especially if these are state-sanctioned oppressions. Thus, Rawls's reluctance to take a stance against WHSs in the clear absence of any significant global liberalizing effect and a de facto right of exit belies his liberal commitment to individual liberty.

## CONCLUSION

Political liberalism faces a tension between tolerating reasonable nonliberal comprehensive views and supporting individual liberal aspirations. This tension is most vividly exposed and left entirely unremedied in the globalized version of the theory because of the special conditions of the international realm. In extending his domestically conceived theory to cover international relations, Rawls, inadvertently and very ironically, has rendered more visible this fundamental problem with political liberalism. The problem of toleration in "The Law of Peoples" is not so much a problem of application as an accentuation of an inherent theoretical problem. Political liberalism's emphasis on toleration conflicts with its other liberal commitments, which in the domestic context is fortuitously (and only to a degree I stress again) alleviated. But a sound political theory cannot wait to be saved from internal tensions by fortuitous and contingent social circumstances—there is no guarantee that these circumstances will always be obtained, as they have not at the global level.[45]

## NOTES

I am grateful to the reviewers and editors of *Ethics*, Jean Baillargeon, Frank Cunningham, Karen Detlefsen, and David Dyzenhaus for their helpful comments, advice, and suggestions. Remaining errors are, of course, my own responsibility.

1. John Rawls, "The Law of Peoples," in *On Human Rights*, ed. Stephen Shute and Susan Hurley (New York: Basic Books, 1993), pp. 41–82 [220–230, reprinted herein 421–60]. References to this work will hereafter be cited in parenthesis in the text.

2. Before beginning, I should note that Rawls makes two fundamental assumptions in "The Law of Peoples," which I grant for the purpose of this

discussion. Rawls assumes that (a) there are clear and well-delineated peoples whose communal boundaries coincide with the boundaries of their political communities (i.e., he assumes a state is more or less representative of a nation or people), and (b) these boundaries are morally beyond challenge and how they were arrived at morally irrelevant. As some commentators have pointed out, these assumptions, even for an "ideal" global theory, are highly problematic. See Thomas Pogge, "An Egalitarian Law of Peoples," *Philosophy and Public Affairs* 23 (1994): 195–224, pp. 197–99 [reprinted herein 461–93, at 464–66]; and esp. Stanley Hoffmann, "Dreams of a Just World," *New York Review of Books* 42 (November 2, 1995): 52–57, p. 53.

3. John Rawls, *Political Liberalism* (New York: Columbia University Press, 1993), pp. xvi–xviii.

4. We can expect "reasonable disagreements" because of the "many hazards involved in the correct (and conscientious) exercise of our powers of reason and judgment in the ordinary course of political life." These hazards arise because of (a) the fact of conflicting evidence, (b) disagreements over the weight given to pieces of evidence, (c) the indeterminacy of our concepts and principles, (d) different individual "total experience," which in turn affects the interpretations and considerations we give similar pieces of evidence, (e) the difficulty with assessing normative claims, and (f) the difficulty with setting priority for all possible cases of conflicts. Rawls calls these hazards the "burdens of reason." John Rawls, "The Domain of the Political and Overlapping Consensus," in *The Idea of Democracy*, ed. David Copp, Jean Hampton, and John E. Roemer (Cambridge: Cambridge University Press. 1993), pp. 245–69, p. 248 (hereafter cited as "Overlapping Consensus").

5. Rawls, *Political Liberalism*, p. 195.

6. Ibid., pp. 144, 155. As Rawls puts it, for its justification, political liberalism "seeks common ground—or if one prefers, neutral ground—given the fact of pluralism" (p. 192).

7. Rawls, *Political Liberalism*, pp. xvi–xvii, and "'Overlapping Consensus," p. 253.

8. Rawls, "Overlapping Consensus," p. 259.

9. Witness, for example, the prohibition against women or homosexuals from holding offices in certain religious communities; or witness also, more persuasively, the traditional male-dominant family within which female members are accorded a subordinate role.

10. Rawls, *Political Liberalism*, pp. xix–xx.

11. Some liberals question Rawls's claim that an internally nonliberal doctrine can accept liberalism as a political ideal. For example, Will Kymlicka thinks it is not obvious "why anyone would accept the ideal of autonomy in political contexts unless they also accept it more generally [in their nonpolitical lives as well]." Will Kymlicka. *Multicultural Citizenship: A Liberal Theory of Minority Rights* (Oxford: Oxford University Press. 1995), p. 160. The coherence of the political liberal project rests on the tenability of this "moral dualism" of Rawls.

I leave this discussion aside and shall examine instead, albeit concentrating on the international case, whether liberals should even entertain the idea of tolerating nonliberal views.

12. The original position, as we may recall, is "a device of representation" where representatives of rational but reasonable individuals deliberate on the appropriate principles of justice for the basic structure of their society. See, for example, Rawls, *Political Liberalism*, pp. 22–28. To ensure that this hypothetical deliberation is fair and equal, parties deliberate behind a "veil of ignorance." That is, they are asked to imagine that they do not know their actual status and stations in society. In this way, no one party could insist on terms biased in her favor according to her own social standing. The important difference, the significance of which shall be discussed in due course, with the global original position is that it is now a device of representation where peoples or societies and not individuals are represented: "As before the parties [to the original position] are representatives, but now they are representatives of *peoples*" (p. 48 [herein 426]; my emphasis). Or, to put it more perspicuously (as suggested by Pogge, p. 206n. [herein 491 note 15]), it is delegates of societies, and not individuals of the world, who are hypothetically represented at the global original position.

13. The kinds of basic rights Rawls has in mind are rather minimal. They cover the rights to subsistence and security (the right to life), to liberty (e.g., freedom from slavery or forced occupation) and personal property, to formal equality before the law (in the sense that similar cases be treated similarly), to a limited liberty of conscience, and to emigrate (pp. 62, 68 [herein 437, 441]).

14. Some would argue, to the contrary, that a liberal state can indeed be organized around a common-good conception of justice. See, for example, Charles Taylor, "The Politics of Recognition," in *Multiculturalism*, ed. Amy Gutmann (Princeton, NJ: Princeton University Press, 1992), 25–73, at pp. 56–61. Also, Xiaorong Li claims that "[if] Rawls's 'hierarchical society' could respect all these rights, such a society would hardly differ from a contemporary liberal democratic society." Li, "A Critique of Rawls's 'Freestanding' Justice," *Journal of Applied Philosophy* 12 (1995): 263–71, at p. 269. I think the above claims are disputable but I shall not challenge them here. For further discussion, see Will Kymlicka, *Liberalism, Community and Culture* (Oxford: Oxford University Press, 1989), esp. chapter 5.

15. So a caste society that accords different rights and duties to members of different castes can be well-ordered if this unequal distribution of rights and duties is in accordance with the traditions and rules of the caste system and not arbitrarily enforced as when similar castes are treated differently.

16. As Fernando Teson rightly points out, "Rawls's international law principles do not even authorize representatives of liberal societies to publicly (that is, in an international forum such as the United Nations) *criticize* the nonliberal practices [in WHSs]. . . . For in Rawls's international system, liberals

could derive no argument from international law to make such a [public] criticism. They could do so only if the hierarchical societies failed to observe what Rawls calls 'basic' human rights, such as if they arbitrarily killed or tortured people or if public officials violated their own conceptions of justice" (Teson, "The Rawlsian Theory of International Law," *Ethics and International Affairs* 9 [1995]: 79–99, 88–89). For Rawls, this distinction between passing judgments against WHSs as private citizens and associations within liberal societies on the one hand, and passing judgments as official delegates of liberal societies in international forums on the other, parallels his stance in his domestic theory that while individuals and associations may question nonliberal comprehensive views in their private capacities, the liberal state (and individuals in their public capacities) may not. See, e.g., Rawls, "The Law of Peoples," p. 81 [herein 451], and *Political Liberalism*, pp. 215–16.

17. Ronald Dworkin, *A Matter of Principle* (Cambridge, MA: Harvard University Press, 1985), p. 361.

18. We must get clear, therefore, as to what liberalism claims to be neutral about. Liberalism claims to be *ethically neutral* in the sense that it aims to be impartial between different private conceptions of the good life. But it (because of this) cannot claim to be *politically neutral* in the sense of being indifferent about how society is to be organized politically. This is obvious: A commitment to ethical neutrality necessarily entails a commitment to a particular type of political arrangement, one which, for one, allows for the pursuit of different private conceptions of the good.

19. Rawls writes, "Nevertheless, in affirming a political conception of justice we may eventually have to assert at least certain aspects of our own comprehensive religious or philosophical doctrine (by no means necessarily fully comprehensive). This will happen whenever someone insists, for example, that certain questions are so fundamental that to insure their being rightly settled justifies civil strife.... At this point we may have no alternative but to deny this, or to imply its denial and hence to maintain the kind of thing we had hoped to avoid" (Rawls, *Political Liberalism*, pp. 152, 153, 250–51). Under this extreme situation, the "freestanding" aspiration of political liberalism is suspended.

20. Rawls writes, "The difficulty with an all-inclusive, or global, original position is that its use of liberal ideals is much more troublesome, for in this case we are treating all persons, regardless of their society or culture, as individuals who are free and equal, and as reasonable and rational, and so according to liberal conceptions. This makes the basis of the law of peoples too narrow" (p. 66 [herein 439]). His other reason for using the two-stage procedure is that this is a methodological preference, with possibly no consequential difference (p. 50 [herein 427f]). I shall examine this other reason in due course.

21. Teson, p. 85. The falsification in question being the fact that not all societies value freedom, human rights, and democracy as do liberal societies.

22. This observation has been made by Hoffman, who points out that the motivation of the law of peoples is "implicit but clear enough: this 'overlapping consensus' is really just a modus vivendi among quite different models of society" (Hoffmann, p. 54).

23. Nor, indeed, can international society enact enforceable global laws given the lack of any international law enforcement body. At present, international law is, as we commonly hear, "toothless."

24. This distinction was recently pointed out in Kymlicka, *Multicultural Citizenship*, pp. 164–66. Kymlicka's point in making this distinction is to show that judging the practices of certain minority groups to be illiberal does not entail that the liberal state is therefore "drawn down the path of interference." Similarly, Joseph Raz points out that while oppressive cultural practices should be criticized, we should exercise "restraint and consideration in thinking of the means by which [these practices are]... to be countered" (Raz, *Ethics in the Public Domain* [Oxford: Oxford University Press. 1994], p. 170).

25. As a matter of fact, Rawls would dissociate himself from the above objection because it treats toleration of WHSs to be a matter of strategy or a modus vivendi. But this is not Rawls's understanding of toleration. Remember that for Rawls, tolerating WHSs is required as a matter of liberal justice and not because of the lack of means of enforcing liberal views globally. In his view, liberal states ought to tolerate WHSs regardless of their capacities for acting or the fact of international conditions. Rawls is not simply claiming that we are unable to act on our judgments against WHSs and therefore we need to accommodate them; his point is that these judgments would be illegitimate in the first place.

26. Rawls takes this to be one of the reasons why nonliberal comprehensive views are permissible within a liberal-democratic state: Private associations are permitted "to offer different terms to its members . . . depending on the worth of their potential contribution to society as a whole." This is "because in their case the prospective or continuing members are already guaranteed the status of free and equal citizens, and the institutions of background justice in society assure that other alternatives are open to them" (Rawls, *Political Liberalism*, p. 42).

27. As he writes, "I think there is no clear initial answer to this question [whether to have a two-stage or one-stage original position]. We should try various alternatives and weigh their pluses and minuses. Since in working out justice as fairness I begin with domestic society, I shall continue from there as if what has been done so far is more or less sound" (p. 50 [herein 427]).

28. Rawls, "Overlapping Consensus," p. 246.

29. I owe this observation to an editor of *Ethics*.

30. Teson interprets this legitimacy condition in a similar way: "On [Rawls's] view, we look to tradition and history; they, and not the government or the majority, establish the limits of freedom" (Teson, p. 88). This "communitar-

ian" understanding of WHSs mirrors Michael Walzer's account of the state as a "historic community" where citizens "express their inherited culture through political forms worked out among themselves." Walzer, "The Moral Standing of States," *Philosophy and Public Affairs* 9 (1980): 209–29, p. 211 [reprinted in *Global Ethics: Seminal Essays*, 51–71, at 53].

31. The discussion in the above three paragraphs has benefited from different helpful comments by Frank Cunningham and the reviewers and editors of *Ethics*.

32. Hoffmann, p. 54.

33. This group-based toleration is justified on the grounds that an individual's well-being is intimately tied to the "prosperity" of her community. As Kymlicka puts it, one's cultural membership provides "the context of choice" which gives meaning to one's conception of the good. Thus, liberals have good individualistic reasons for respecting (and even supporting when necessary) group-based diverse ways of life (Kymlicka, *Liberalism, Community and Culture*, chapter 8). See also Raz, chapter 5, esp. pp. 113–17.

34. Sec Kymlicka, *Multicultural Citizenship*, chapter 8; and Raz, chapter 7, esp. pp. 169–74.

35. Rawls, *Political Liberalism*, p. 221.

36. Ibid., pp. 192–94.

37. Ibid., pp. 199–200.

38. On the small consolation of the right of exit in domestic cases, see Leslie Green, "Internal Minorities and Their Rights," in *Group Rights*, ed. Judith Baker (Toronto: University of Toronto Press, 1994), pp. 101–17. He argues that "the mere existence of exit does not suffice to make it a reasonable option. It is risky, wrenching, and disorienting to have to tear oneself from one's religion or culture" (Green, p. 111). On the limits of the liberalizing effects of liberal public policies on private arrangements (of the family in particular), see John Exdell, "Feminism, Fundamentalism, and Liberal Legitimacy," *Canadian Journal of Philosophy* 24 (1994): 441–64, 461; and Susan Moller Okin, "*Political Liberalism*, Justice and Gender," *Ethics* 105 (1994): 23–43, 32. Indeed, it seems that Rawls must admit that neutrally justified public policies cannot have liberalizing effects in all areas of society. For if this were not the case, why would he expect political liberalism to be better able than comprehensive liberalism to secure the basis for legitimate stability? That is, if the consequences of these two kinds of liberalism on the internal practices of nonliberal reasonable groups are ultimately the same, why would either of these liberal theories be any more acceptable than the other to individuals holding diverse views? The only difference between political and comprehensive liberalism in this case would be in the way each justifies liberal public policies: Comprehensive liberals would say that the objective of, say, liberal education is "to foster the values of autonomy and individuality as ideals to govern much if not all of life," whereas the political liberal, to repeat, justifies this policy solely on political (i.e., neutral) grounds

(Rawls, *Political Liberalism*, p. 199). But adherents of nonliberal comprehensive views worry about the actual effects of liberal policies on their ways of life and not just about how these policies are justified to them. So, in order for political liberalism to be a plausible alternative to comprehensive liberalism in the first place, Rawls must concede that the liberalizing tendencies of neutrally justified policies are limited in reach (see Exdell, pp. 453–55). But if this is so, then political liberalism does not avoid entirely the tension between toleration and individual liberty even in the domestic context.

39. While it could be argued that liberal states have the duty to accept political refugees, it would seem that Rawls cannot classify political dissenters of WHSs as prospective political refugees; to do so would imply critical judgments of the political institutions of the WHSs in question. See Teson, p. 90.

40. Kymlicka, *Multicultural Citizenship*, pp. 124–26.

41. Rawls, *Political Liberalism*, p. 222.

42. Concerning individual capacity, besides the psychological costs discussed above, there are also economic ones. Ironically, individuals who may have the strongest reason to leave their country are often also the ones most badly exploited and hence least able to muster the financial resources necessary for travel, documentation, and other immigration-related expenses. I owe this point to David Dyzenhaus.

43. Of course, other liberals object to this line of argument; see Exdell; and Okin. The point here is that this is an argument the political liberal can at least attempt in the domestic setting.

44. See his list on p. 62 [herein 437]. Just to recall, Rawls says that what is demandable universally are the rights to security and subsistence, to liberty and property, to exit, and for formal equality before the law.

45. I call these circumstances (1) contingent because, as I pointed out, the significance of a formal right of exit is contingent on other conditions being in place, there being somewhere else to go to for one, and (2) fortuitous because (for the political liberal) the liberalizing effects of liberal policies on nonliberal reasonable associations are unintended and fortuitous side effects.

# 21. HILLEL STEINER

Following John Locke, Steiner argues that all persons possess equal rights to self-ownership and to natural resources. The aggregate value of the world's natural resources constitutes a global dividend to which all persons have a valid claim to an equal share. The claim that each person has an equal share of this dividend requires that those who occupy or possess more than an equal share pay taxes into a global fund as restitution to everyone else. From this fund all persons are entitled to draw an equal share, not on grounds of need but on grounds of their valid claim to an equal share of the world's natural resources.

## Just Taxation and International Redistribution

*First published in* Nomos XLI: Global Justice, *ed. Ian Shapiro and Lea Brilmayer (New York: New York University Press, 1999), 171–91.*

### I. COMPOSSIBLE RIGHTS

What should we provide to other persons, and what do we morally owe them? Most people, I think, would agree that these two questions are not equivalent and that we can make little headway toward understanding the demands of justice unless we see the various items sought in the second question as forming only a subset of those sought in the first. There are many things—goods and services, including services of forbearance—that we ought to provide to others and that we would therefore do wrong to withhold from them. Their flourishing, their autonomy, their liberty, often their very survival, vitally depend on such provision. Yet only some of these things can be said to be owed to them. Only some of these correlate to rights in those persons. Only some of them are concerns of justice. Which ones?

Evidently, answers to this question vary substantially from one conception of justice to another: Memberships in the set of owed things are notoriously contested, though some are more contested than others. Among the less controversial are those items that we owe as restitution; that is, no theory of justice that I know of treats the deprivation consequent on a rights violation simply as a regrettable piece of misfortune occasioning no claim in its victim.[1] Thus, the owed status of those items is due to their (sometimes imperfect) capacity to substitute for other owed things and to compensate for our failures to provide them.

A second type of owed thing—at least as uncontroversial as restitutions—consists of those items that we contractually undertake to provide.[2] Even so meager a conception of justice as Hobbes's seems to underwrite their inclusion. Hobbes's account of the matter also serves to remind us how problematic even contractual duties can be, how contracts can fail to be worth the actual or hypothetical paper they are written on. My contractual undertaking to supply you with the Brooklyn Bridge fails to vest me with a duty to do so (and fails to vest you with the right correlative to that duty) if I have already given such an undertaking to someone else or, more generally, if the Brooklyn Bridge is not mine to supply.

For what is true of both restitutional and contractual duties to provide is that they unavoidably presuppose rights on the part of the putative providers. They presuppose their antecedent rights to whatever it is that they owe. Thus we might usefully characterize these presupposed rights as *prior rights* and the rights doing the presupposing—the rights correlatively entailed by restitutional and contractual duties—as *posterior rights*.[3]

Even if what I owe you is (merely?) a forbearance, it is clear that others' noninterference with its provision is a necessary condition of my being able to provide it and, thus, of my having a duty to do so.[4] If, contrarily, others do interfere and, moreover, are at liberty, empowered, or even duty bound to do so, then the set of rules sustaining my forbearance duty and their liberty (power, duty) is incoherent. It generates a set of incompossible rights, and such sets imply contradictory judgments about the permissibility of particular actions.[5]

So if the set of restitutionally and contractually owed things is to be a possible set, if none of these duties to provide is to be deemed invalid because it cannot be fulfilled, it must be embedded in a larger set of owed things: a set that therefore includes *non*posteriorly owed things. As Hobbes correctly perceived, I cannot have a duty to forbear from blocking your exit if others, who have a right "even to my own body," install it permanently in the doorway. Nor can I owe you the corn I contracted to deliver if others, lacking a duty not to deprive me of it, do so.

This key feature of the logic of compossible rights is succinctly captured in Locke's remark that "where there is no property, there is no injustice."[6] Injustices, we are presuming, consist at least of nonfulfillments of restitutional and contractual duties. For such injustice to be possible, for such duties to exist, they must be fulfillable. A set of jointly fulfillable posterior duties presupposes a further set of duties that are thus nonposterior and that protect the domains—the action spaces—in which posterior duties can be fulfilled free from anyone's permissible interference.[7] And of course, those nonposterior, domain-protecting duties must themselves be jointly fulfillable ones. Hence and as Locke's remark suggests, it requires no great conceptual strain to see these domains—these zones of noninterference—as consisting of property rights.

## II. THE GLOBAL FUND

If the set of owed things must include a core subset of forbearances—prior negative duties not to encroach on others' domains—what are the contents of those domains? The immediate answer is that these are bewilderingly variable. Who owns what or, conversely, who owes whom forbearance from interference with what activities, is plainly not a question that can be interestingly answered in the abstract. The contents of respective domains vary enormously both temporally and interpersonally, for the simple reason that domain owners have—and tend continuously to exercise—protected liberties to engage in multifarious activities amounting to transformations of those contents and/or transferences of them to the domains of others.

What can be answered in the abstract is what sort of rule can justly constrain the initial formation of those domains. Given their highly variegated contents and the corresponding variety of forbearances correlatively owed to their several owners, what sort of rule appropriately determines the initial conditions from which all this variegating activity then generates permissible departures? In short, what must persons' initial domains be like to be just?

It is a sufficiently agreed feature of justice that however varied and complex its complete set of distributive demands may be seen to be under different theories, there is some foundational level at which equality is the appropriate norm. Precisely what must be distributed equally and, consequently, what sorts of thing may be distributed unequally remain a matter of philosophical dispute. But that something requires equal interpersonal distribution seems to be an intrinsic feature of justice, however it is construed.[8]

According to the view being developed here from the requirements of rights compossibility, the items to be justly equalized are persons' initial domains: the ultimately antecedent or prior rights that they have and successively transform and transfer to create posterior rights and duties for themselves and others. So those ultimately prior rights look like being ones to *un*transformed and *un*transferred things. Others' ultimately prior duties are to refrain from interfering with the varying dispositional choices that each makes in respect of those things. If each person is justly vested with an equal initial domain, it follows that each is justly bound by correlative duties of equal initial forbearance. What things, then, can count as untransformed and untransferred?

Here we could do worse than again to follow Locke's general guidance and construe such things as being of two basic types: our bodies and raw natural resources.[9] To say that persons have the initial rights to their own bodies is not to deny that they are at liberty to transform or transfer parts of those bodies or those bodies' labor—or, more generally, to invest those things in pursuit of their several ends—and thereby successively to modify those initial rights. It is to imply only that others' initial forbearance duties include not interfering with their doing so. These various duties of equal initial forbearance—this foundational bundle of entirely negative duties—can thus be compendiously construed as correlating to the initial rights of self-ownership vested in each person, initial rights against any form of enslavement or lesser servitude.

But if equal initial domains—equal initial action spaces—give us each titles to our bodies, they must also give us titles to things external to our bodies, since unimpeded access to such things is a necessary condition for the occurrence of any action. And this is where raw natural resources come to figure as the other constituents of those domains. Part of our foundational set of duties of equal initial forbearance are duties to acquire no more than an equal portion of such resources, leaving (as Locke put it) "enough and as good for others."[10]

What if some persons acquire more than this, leaving others with less? Then presumably the former, having defaulted on their duties of initial forbearance to the latter, owe them restitution. This compensation, whatever form it may take, must be equivalent to the value of what has been overacquired. So here we have a case of noncontractual but nonetheless positive duties to provide goods: duties that, though noncontractual, are clearly in the owed category and correlate to rights vested in those to whom they are owed. These are not what Brian Barry aptly characterized as "duties of humanity," and indeed, their validity is in no way predicated on their beneficiaries being in a state of need.[11] These duties are ones of justice and they arise, posteriorily, as straightforward restitutional implications of the overacquirers' failure to comply with their prior negative duties of forbearance.

It is not hard to see how this line of thinking begins to approach the issue of just international redistribution. The world's raw natural resources are compendiously describable as constituting a set of territorial sites, and the value of any such site is the sum of the values of all the sub- and supraterranean resources, as well as the surface areas, it comprises.[12] The aggregate global value of these sites thus constitutes the *dividend* in the Lockean computation of what "enough and as good for others" amounts to. No doubt this aggregate global value fluctuates over time, as does the magnitude of the Lockean *divisor*, that is, the number of others that there are. Whatever these fluctuations may be, each person's initial domain includes a right to the *quotient:* a right to an equal portion of the aggregate global value of territorial sites.

Elsewhere, I have suggested that we can conveniently conceive of the rights and duties implied by this argument as jointly constituting a global fund.[13] Liabilities to pay into the fund accrue to owners of territorial sites and are equal to the value of the sites they own, and claims to equal shares of that fund are vested in everyone. The global fund is thus a mechanism for ensuring that each person enjoys the equivalent of enough and as good natural resources.[14]

An essential characteristic of nations is that they are actual or aspiring claimants of territorial sites. The scope of their jurisdictional claims extends not only to sections of the global surface but also to the resources found below them and the airspace, portions of the electromagnetic spectrum, and so forth located above them. Private persons and state agencies who control the use of these things usually have a fairly shrewd idea of what they are worth. They know that an acre on the Bangladeshi coast is worth less than an acre in the center of Tokyo. Accordingly, the global fund's levy on the ownership of the latter will be greater than on the ownership of the former.[15]

Of course, within the limits of what justice permits, nations are presumably licensed to determine their own domestic objectives and to deploy the range of redistributive measures appropriate to those ends. But what justice clearly does not permit is their determining the distributive entitlements of persons outside their respective jurisdictions. Thus, although the full value of that Tokyo acre is justly owed to the global fund, whether liability for its payment should fall exclusively on its owner or should be financed in some other way may be a matter for decision by Japanese political-choice processes. What cannot justly be a matter for such political choices is the amount owed to the global fund for Japanese territorial sites.

The core idea here, that just redistribution is to be funded by an egalitarian allocation of natural resource values, is not a novel one. Nor should its Lockean origins be allowed to obscure the fact that it has more recently come to figure—in one form or another—in a wide variety of conceptions of justice, many of which are distinctly un-Lockean in provenance. Indeed, several of these accounts have similarly extended this idea to the international plane. It is on the two most developed such accounts that I wish now to focus, since, in my view, their lack of Lockean foundations seriously impairs the coherence of that extension.

## III. AGAINST BEITZ

Charles Beitz has advanced what must count as one of the first sustained attempts to derive an argument for international redistribution from a more general theory of justice.[16] His claim is that Rawlsian theory can underwrite the extension of the difference principle to the international plane in two ways. As is familiar, Rawls sees this principle as determining a fair distribution of the benefits and burdens produced by social cooperation. Rawls's mistake, in Beitz's view, is to assume that the boundaries of the cooperative schemes to which this principle applies are given by the notion of a self-contained national community. For the facts of contemporary international relations—in particular, the interdependence resulting from international investment and trade—indicate that the world is not made up of self-contained nations but imply the existence of a global scheme of social cooperation.[17]

But Beitz wants to go further and to privilege one kind of international redistribution by liberating the case for it from any reliance on these contingent facts of contemporary international relations. Accordingly, he argues that even if we counterfactually suspend the assumption of such functioning schemes of social cooperation and interdependence, the veiled parties to a set of Rawlsian international contractual deliberations would nonetheless know that natural resources are distributed unevenly over the earth's surface. Hence they "would view this distribution of resources much as Rawls says the parties to the domestic original-position deliberations view the distribution of natural talents."[18] That is, these contracting parties—each appropriately ignorant of their comparative territorial circumstances—would regard this natural resource distribution as a morally arbitrary fact and, consequently, the benefits derived from these resources as justly subject to redistribution.

Beitz is not slow to acknowledge the problematic aspects of Rawls's view that the natural talent distribution is morally arbitrary. These problems have been well rehearsed in the literature and include such considerations as the fact that

> natural capacities are parts of the self, in the development of which a person might take a special kind of pride. A person's decision to develop one talent, not to develop another, as well as his or her choice as to how the talent is to be formed, and the uses to which it is to be put, are likely to be important elements of the effort to shape an identity. The complex of developed talents might even be said to constitute the self.[19]

Because talents are tied to persons as identity-constituting elements, their location and consequent relative interpersonal distribution do not seem best described as morally arbitrary. Indeed, it is plausibly suggested that persons' claims to their talents are protected by considerations of personal liberty, that is, by Rawls's lexically prior first principle.[20]

Moreover, this line of reasoning suggests another important respect, unremarked by Beitz, in which differential talent distribution may be an unlikely candidate for moral arbitrariness. For even if—at some cost to the standard interpretation of his principles—Rawls were thus to concede nonarbitrariness to the distribution of self-developed talents, he might still wish to insist on the arbitrariness of the distribution of pre-self-developed ones. Indeed, it is precisely this distinction that is underwriting his attribution of arbitrariness to talent differentials, in his insistent imputation of those differentials to individuals' differential genetic endowments and background social circumstances.

Yet even this concession would not suffice to sustain his thereby modified arbitrariness claim. For if my talent's being constitutive of my self is conceded to be a matter of moral relevance, the fact that its initial development occurred at the hands of others—notably, my parents—rather than my own, does not obviously deprive it of that relevance. Parents typically choose whether to attach considerable value to, and invest considerable sacrifice in, the development of their children's talents or, more generally, their capacities.[21] Consequently, it is misleading to characterize the level of talent we possess when we arrive at the threshold of adulthood and moral agency as fully imputable to chance contingencies, insofar as this is suggested by a phrase like "background social circumstances," a phrase that implausibly leaves delinquent parents morally blameless.[22]

In any case, Beitz argues—and however problematic may thus be Rawls's construal of talent differentials as arbitrary—no such difficulty attends the claim that nations' natural resource differentials are similarly arbitrary. "The natural distribution of resources is a purer case of something being 'arbitrary from a moral point of view' than the distribution of talents."[23] The two cases are said to be importantly *dis*analogous and for two reasons. First, and unlike talents, natural resources cannot be understood as constitutive of selves. Hence the denial that they are tied to persons in morally relevant ways does not engender the sorts of problem associated with the corresponding denial in regard to talents. Second, and unlike talent acquisition, natural resource appropriation is a rivalrous affair: "The appropriation of scarce resources by some requires a justification against the competing claims of others."[24] There must be principled reasons that the latter should bear the opportunity cost of refraining from the beneficial use of resources that are no one's product and of which the former's appropriation deprives them. The only plausible such reason for that forbearance appears to be that, by so doing, forbearers become entitled to a share of those benefits.

Consistent as this conclusion is with the Lockean one advanced previously, two serious difficulties beset Beitz's manner of reaching it.

In the first place, it is unclear that postulating the competing claims of others, as a warrant for the presence of Rawlsian distributive concerns, is consistent with his counterfactual suspension of the assumption that the world is not made up of self-contained nations and that international relations therefore exhibit functioning schemes of social cooperation and interdependence. For situations in which some persons' appropriative claims compete with those of others and these groups are each (members of) different nations, are unmistakably situations in which the nations involved cannot be described as "self-contained." One group's self-denying respect for the claims of the other, whose otherwise unattainable level of prosperity thereby depends on that forbearance, would surely be an instance of what Rawls often refers to as the "burdens of cooperation."[25] This implies the presence, not the absence, of international cooperation and interdependence.

Equally significantly, it is unclear that Beitz is correct to claim that natural resources lack the identity-constituting quality of natural talents. It would be patently absurd to think of them as constitutive of individuals' selves: A resource's owner is fully identifiable without any reference to that resource. But within the Rawlsian framework, that is not the relevant point of comparison. Nor, therefore, does it support Beitz's disanalogy claim. For on his own reading of it, the Rawlsian forum for fashioning principles of international justice is a second original position: one that, unlike the first, is populated not by individuals but, rather, by nations.[26] And it would be difficult, to say the least, to think of any single feature—or combination of them—that is less controversially constitutive of a nation's identity than its territorial site.[27]

So I am driven to conclude that Beitz is unsuccessful in his attempt to use the Rawlsian framework to underwrite the international redistribution of natural resource differentials. The charge of distributional arbitrariness, which is what usually occasions redistribution in Rawlsian theory, is not made to stick. And since the special case—for privileging the redistribution of those differentials as noncontingently just—is one that relies on the inconsistently sustained heuristic assumption of noninterdependent nations, that case also fails.

## IV. AGAINST POGGE

More recently, Thomas Pogge has been similarly engaged in constructing an international extension of Rawlsian principles for just redistribution.[28] But his enterprise begins with an explicit caveat on what Rawls actually says about the basis for that extension, although it is a caveat that Pogge sees as amply warranted by more fundamental Rawlsian commitments. Rawls, as was noted, conceives of the principles of international justice as chosen in a second original position, the parties to which are nations, not individuals. Pogge—persuasively in my view—argues that the arrangements that would emerge from such a situation "would be incompatible with Rawls's individualistic conviction that in matters of social justice only *persons* are to be viewed as ultimate units of (equal) moral concern."[29] In support of this claim about Rawlsian justice and individualism, he quotes a passage that might well have come straight out of Nozick's *Anarchy, State and Utopia* but that, in fact, is Rawls's own methodological statement that

> we want to account for the social values, for the intrinsic good of institutional, community, and associative activities, by a conception of justice that in its theoretical basis is individualistic. For reasons of clarity among others, we do not want to rely on an undefined concept of community, or to suppose that society is an organic whole with a life of its own distinct from and superior to that of all its members in their relations with one another. ...From this conception, however individualistic it may seem, we must eventually explain the value of community.[30]

A person's nationality, Pogge suggests, is just one more deep contingency (like genetic endowment, race, gender, and social class) that is present from birth and operates as a morally arbitrary factor in generating interpersonal inequalities. Accordingly, it is more consonant with the individualistic spirit of the Rawlsian project that parties to the second original position be persons, not nations—and even more consonant that there be only a single (person-populated) original position that generates a single set of norms for global application.[31]

All this seems to be going in the right direction as far as the Lockean view, advanced previously, is concerned. Leaving aside their deep differences over the foundationalism of contracts,[32] both the Lockean and Poggean positions conceive just principles as generating a set of egalitarian individual redistributive entitlements of global scope. Moreover, Pogge, too, sees natural resource values as especially eligible to fund these entitlements. My complaint, as with Beitz's argument, is that the case for this eligibility is not convincingly made out—though for different reasons.

Pogge's mechanism for this egalitarian redistribution is one that he dubs the *Global Resources Tax* (GRT).[33] Like Beitz, his claim for its privileged plausibility rests on its alleged nonreliance on several highly defensible theoretical and empirical assumptions that would lend it even greater support. Specifically, he believes the case for it can be made even if we accept (1) that the forum for choosing international principles is to be a second original position populated only by nations; (2) that each of these nations is a "people," that is, is a linguistically, ethnically, culturally, and historically homogeneous unit; and (3) that no injustice has attended the emergence of current national borders. Although Pogge himself accepts none of these propositions—ones that he finds present in Rawls[34]—his project is to vindicate GRT despite this "self-imposed triple handicap."[35]

So what, then, is GRT?

> The basic idea is that, while each people owns and fully controls all resources within its national territory, it must pay a tax on any resources it chooses to extract. The Saudi people, for example, would not be required to extract crude oil or to allow others to do so. But if they chose to do so nonetheless, they would be required to pay a proportional tax on any crude extracted, whether it be for their own use or for sale abroad. This tax could be extended, along the same lines, to reusable resources: to land used in agriculture and ranching, for example, and, especially, to air and water used for the discharging of pollutants.[36]

Pogge argues that although the incidence of such a tax would fall exclusively on resource owners, its burdens would not, inasmuch as it would raise prices for consumer goods and services in proportion to their natural resource content, that is, in proportion to "how much value they take from our planet." The cost of gasoline would contain a higher proportion of GRT than would the cost of a museum ticket.

In another passage, Pogge suggests that the theoretical appeal of this tax ought to be very wide indeed:

> The GRT can therefore be motivated not only forward-lookingly, in consequentialist and contractualist terms, but also backward-lookingly: as a proviso on unilateral appropriation, which requires

compensation to those excluded thereby. Nations (or persons) may appropriate and use resources, but humankind at large still retains a kind of minority stake, which, somewhat like preferred stock, confers no control but a share of the material benefits. In this picture, my proposal can be presented as a global resources dividend, which operates as a modern Lockean proviso. It differs from Locke's own proviso by giving up the vague and unwieldy condition of "leaving enough and as good for others." One may use unlimited amounts, but one must share some of the economic benefit. It is nevertheless similar enough to the original so that even such notoriously anti-egalitarian thinkers as Locke and Nozick might find it plausible.[37]

Pogge then offers a perceptive discussion of the moral, political, and economic problems of both setting the Rawlsian-optimal rate of GRT and ensuring the intended redistribution of its proceeds. Some of these problems are indeed ones facing any redistributive global tax. However, the issue I wish to address is the prior one of whether GRT, as described, actually does possess the broad theoretical appeal Pogge attributes to it.

Clearly, and leaving aside the disputable claims about Locke's anti-egalitarianism and the vagueness and unwieldiness of his own proviso, GRT at first glance appears to come very close to the Lockean-inspired global fund proposal advanced earlier. It, too, sponsors a global resources dividend by entitling everyone to a share of the benefits from natural resources that only some unilaterally control. The difference—and it is one of the utmost theoretical relevance here—lies in their respective identifications of the tax base to be used.

In Pogge's account, that base is the aggregate value of only *used* resources, with only some proportion of that value to be taxed. Whereas for the global fund (and, I think, for Beitz), that base is the aggregate value of *owned* resources—whether used or not—with that value to be taxed at a rate of 100 percent.

To see the significance of this difference, let's return to Pogge's example of Saudi oil. Suppose there is a large oil deposit located beneath the Ka'aba mosque in Mecca. If, as Pogge is heuristically assuming, each nation is to be taken as a fully homogeneous unit; if it owns and fully controls all resources in its territory and is not required to extract, or to allow others to extract, any of these resources; and if it is required to pay GRT on only those resources that it does choose to extract, then we can be reasonably certain that the Ka'aba oil will not be extracted. Nor, therefore, will it be GRT taxed, whereas the ownership of that site, like any other, would be global fund taxed to the full extent of its natural resource value. This does not imply that under the global fund, the Saudis would be required to defile that sacred site and sink wells to extract the oil it contains. It implies only, in Pogge's own terms, that in unilaterally appropriating that site, they must compensate those thereby excluded. What they choose to do with that site is justly up to them.

The more general theoretical point here is simply this: If nations are presumed to be homogeneous in the way Pogge is counterfactually stipulating and if they are to be fully sovereign over the natural resources in their territorial sites, then some set of what Pogge calls "collective values and preferences"—some common conception of the good—will inform the domestic rules regulating the use of those resources. For some nations, these regulations will be far less restrictive and will allow far more extraction or varieties of use than are permitted by other nations' value sets. Rules regulating the extraction of American oil will, we might assume, be less restrictive than their counterparts in some other places. And one question thus is: Who should justly bear the costs of each nation's value set? For of any two nations with equal resource endowments, the more restrictive one will contribute less GRT than its counterpart does. Yet other things being equal, both will receive the same share of the total revenue thereby yielded. From an egalitarian perspective, from a global fund perspective—perhaps from *any* perspective—it looks as though the value set of the former is being subsidized by the latter. And this seems sufficient grounds to eliminate at least Lockeans and Nozickians from Pogge's list of theoretical constituencies who will find GRT attractive.

It is true that the question for Pogge is not directly the one just posed: Who should justly bear the costs of each nation's value set? Rather, it is, What natural resource tax would the nations, which are the veiled parties to the second and international original position, rationally choose? This is how that former, more direct question must be couched in the broad Rawlsian contractualist framework that Pogge embraces. More specifically, would they choose GRT or the global fund?

How should we approach the answer to this question? I assume that each nation's being veiled in ignorance means that it is crucially unaware of two things. It does not know whether and to what extent it is resource rich or resource poor, that is, above or below average in its resource endowment. Similarly, it is ignorant of the content of its value set, that is, whether and to what extent it is use restrictive or use permissive with regard to natural resources. With these two variables in play, all that each nation can know is that when the veil is lifted, it will find that it occupies one of four positions: (1) it is resource rich and use restrictive; (2) it is resource rich and use permissive; (3) it is resource poor and use permissive; or (4) it is resource poor and use restrictive. Being use restrictive lowers one's liability to GRT but not to the global fund, whereas being resource rich raises one's liability to the global fund but not to GRT. Thus, as we have seen, under GRT but not the global fund, a resource-rich nation whose value set is strongly informed by, say, "green" concerns or location-based religious ones, will contribute less to international redistribution than will an equally resource-rich nation whose value set assigns less prominence to such restrictive concerns.

In general, the global fund promises a higher tax yield for this redistribution than does GRT, for two reasons. The first is that it taxes owned resources rather than used resources and the latter are only a subset of the former. Second, in taxing only use, GRT rate setters must consider the disincentive effects of setting that tax rate too high. Whereas the global fund rate is invariable at 100 percent, the GRT rate must not be so high as to discourage the use of those (fewer) resources that are not subject to use restrictions. It is, of course, a matter of empirical investigation as to what higher tax rate will deliver a lower total tax yield than some lower tax rate. But we know almost certainly that a GRT rate of 100 percent on what is in any case a lower maximum tax base will strongly discourage the use of all those resources. So compared with the global fund, GRT labors under a double handicap in seeking to maximize funds for global redistribution and is bound to deliver less. And this seems sufficient grounds to eliminate consequentialists, as well, from Pogge's list of theoretical constituencies who will find it attractive.

Can GRT retain some appeal for, at least, Rawlsians? Would rational choosers behind their veil of ignorance prefer it to the global fund? I think that although there are strong reasons to suppose otherwise, nevertheless and under Pogge's heuristic assumptions, the answer is ultimately yes—but at a significant cost. Let us first look at those strong reasons against it.

From a Rawlsian perspective, the global fund also labors under a redistributive handicap, namely, that it must distribute its proceeds equally to all and cannot target them to the worst off. Although an equal share of global fund proceeds is bound to be greater than an equal share of GRT proceeds, Rawlsian *maximin* does not require such proceeds to be distributed equally. Hence whether it would be GRT or the global fund that maximizes the receipts of the worst off would depend entirely on the aggregate yield of GRT, which in turn depends on both the proportion of global resources that are not subject to domestic use restriction and the optimal tax rate that can be levied on them. In some circumstances, it would be GRT that maximins; in others, it would be the global fund. However, a resource tax that would invariably trump both of these in the maximinning stakes would be one that imposes the global fund's levies but discards its equal distribution of them in favor of a maximinning one. So on the face of it, GRT should have no appeal for Rawlsians, either. Fortunately for Pogge's argument—though unfortunately for the worst off—this is not true. Why not?

As we have seen, the global fund is no respecter of nations' value sets: It taxes all their resources indiscriminately and regardless of whether or not domestic value sets permit their use. Now a plausible suggestion is that the relation between nations and their value sets is not unlike the relation that Beitz previously found between individuals and their talents: that is, that its value set is constitutive of a nation's identity.

I myself have no definite view on this suggestion. But if we take it to be true—and it is not made less plausible by Pogge's heuristic assumption that nations are each completely homogeneous entities—then it looks like the liberty-protecting apparatus of Rawls's first principle must again swing into play in an original position populated, as Pogge also heuristically assumes, by nations and not by individuals. For as Beitz noted, the possession of identity-constituting items is not appropriately viewed as an instance of moral arbitrariness and is protected by lexically prior considerations of liberty. Accordingly, to tax use-restrictive nations as heavily as equally resource-endowed nations whose value sets are use permissive—as the global fund would do—is akin to taxing talented individuals purely for having those talents and regardless of whether or not they use them to secure benefits. The Rawlsian first principle clearly prohibits this: It does not penalize potentially successful neurosurgeons for becoming mediocre poets instead. Hence, citing Rawls's remark that "greater natural talents are not a collective asset in the sense that society should compel those who have them to put them to work for the less favored," Pogge himself observes that "this much is enshrined in Rawls's first principle"[38] and insists that

> Rawls simply takes for granted [that] persons have their natural endowments in a thick, constitutive sense and are fully entitled to (exercise control over) them. There is no question that Genius's talents must not be destroyed or tampered with or taxed and that she must not be coerced to develop or exercise them.[39]

So GRT, despite its lower maximinning capacity, looks like the best resource tax that the worst off can hope for. Ironically perhaps, it thus appears that what Pogge described as self-imposed handicaps on his argument for GRT—namely, the heuristic assumptions of national homogeneity and a nation-populated second original position—turn out to be key supports for that argument.

This is not the end of the matter, however. For since Pogge himself offers convincing reasons for rejecting those assumptions, an obvious question is how the case for GRT would fare in that event. What if—consonant with the individualism that he finds at the core of Rawlsian theory, though not in Rawls's own international extensions of it—the contract situation were instead Pogge's favored single global original position populated by individuals rather than nations and, moreover, individuals whose nationality is simply one more of those nonconstitutive deep contingencies that are hidden from them behind the veil of ignorance? Would these choosers still prefer the resource-use base of GRT, or would they opt for the resource-ownership base of the global fund? The latter but not the former would exact the value of their oil deposit from whoever chose to acquire the ownership of the Ka'aba mosque site. But it would also yield a greater maximin. Which would be chosen?

Here we need only recall that a defining feature of Rawlsian contractors is their ignorance of the contents of their value sets. Moreover, individuals' respective conceptions of the good, being revisable without a loss of personal identity, are nonconstitutive of them. In Rawls's famous phrase, "the self is prior to the ends which are affirmed by it."[40] These contractors are similarly ignorant of their respective natural resource holdings, which are similarly nonconstitutive of them. So individuals, unlike nations, are not constrained by the first principle's lexical priority in their choice of resource tax. Hence the same risk-averse reasoning that leads them to prefer maximin distribution ought to induce a preference for the global fund's tax base over that of GRT.

If this is indeed the warranted conclusion for Rawlsians, it nonetheless remains an open question as to whether Rawlsian maximin or Lockean equality is the appropriate norm for distributing the proceeds of that tax. Elsewhere I have argued that a comprehensive understanding of what counts as natural resources—along with consistently factored culpabilities, and the corresponding redress, for individuals' adversities—imply that those who remain worse off under Lockean resource equality do so because of their own choices.[41] But since that is another whole story in itself and one that raises much larger issues about the foundations of these two conceptions of justice, it is probably best left unaddressed here.[42]

## NOTES

1. This is not to deny either that many restitutional claims are difficult to substantiate or that even if sufficiently substantiated, fulfilling them may be undesirable from the perspective of values other than justice.

2. At least, under appropriate conditions of voluntariness—with these being variously implied by the different conceptions of justice in question.

3. And hence their respective correlatives as *prior* and *posterior* duties.

4. On the principle that "ought implies can." That is, another person's preventing my doing the dutiful action A is a sufficient condition for denying any delinquency on my part. The same is true with regard to preventing my doing B, when the latter is (1) permissible and (2) a necessary condition of my doing A.

5. See Hillel Steiner, *An Essay on Rights* (Oxford: Blackwell, 1994), pp. 74–101.

6. John Locke, *An Essay Concerning Human Understanding,* ed. Peter Nidditch (Oxford: Oxford University Press, 1975), p. 549. Similarly, Hobbes: "It is consequent also to the same condition [that is, the absence of the possibility of injustice], that there be no propriety, no dominion, no *mine* and *thine* distinct" *(Leviathan,* ed. Michael Oakeshott [Oxford: Blackwell, 1946], p. 83).

7. That is, they protect these domains or action spaces in the normative sense of precluding permissible encroachment on them—not in the empirical sense of precluding actual encroachment.

8. See Amartya Sen, *Inequality Reexamined* (Oxford: Oxford University Press, 1992), p. ix: "A common characteristic of virtually all the approaches to the ethics of social arrangements that have stood the test of time is to want equality of *something*. . . . They are all 'egalitarians' in some essential way. . . . To see the battle as one between those 'in favor of' and those 'against' equality (as the problem is often posed in the literature) is to miss something central to the subject" (italics in original).

9. Locke himself believes that our bodies are owned not by ourselves but by God. Cf. John Locke, *Two Treatises of Government*, ed. Peter Laslett (Cambridge: Cambridge University Press, 1967), pp. 289, 302.

10. I interpret this as a duty that, like all correlative duties, can be owed to only those who share some element of contemporaneity with us. For an argument as to why future generations lack rights against present ones, see Steiner, *An Essay on Rights*, pp. 259–61. It is also argued (pp. 250–58, 273) that symmetrically, past generations lack rights against present ones and that accordingly, the estates of the dead are subject to this same egalitarian distributive norm.

11. See Brian Barry, "Humanity and Justice in Global Perspective," in J. Roland Pennock and John W. Chapman, eds., *NOMOS XXIV: Ethics, Economics and the Law* (New York: New York University Press, 1982) [reprinted herein 179–209].

12. That is, the value of a territorial site is equal to the difference between the aggregate market value of all its contents and the aggregate market value of those of its contents that constitute improvements made to it by human activity.

13. See Steiner, *An Essay on Rights*, chapter 8.

14. In this sense, the global fund is a source of what is currently called "unconditional basic income."

15. Too many accounts of natural resource values continue to take an unduly "geological-cum-biological" view of their subject and fail to appreciate—as persons in real estate markets do not—that portions of sheer (surface and aboveground) space also possess value.

16. Charles Beitz, *Political Theory and International Relations* (Princeton, NJ: Princeton University Press, 1979). [Part 3 of Beitz's book, in which the referenced pages are, is based on his essay "Justice and International Relations," first published in *Philosophy and Public Affairs* 4: 4 (summer 1975): 360–89, reprinted herein 21-48.]

17. Ibid., pp. 143–53 [cf. herein 32–40].

18. Ibid., p. 137 [cf. herein 27].

19. Ibid., p. 138 [cf. herein 28].

20. Ibid., p. 139 [cf. herein 28].

21. Such investment strongly reflects parental ambitions. And theories denying its moral relevance thereby lack what Dworkin aptly labeled "ambition sensitivity" in his argument that just distributions are ambition sensitive

and endowment insensitive. See Ronald Dworkin, "What Is Equality? Part 1: Equality of Welfare, and Part 2: Equality of Resources," *Philosophy & Public Affairs* 10 (1981): 185–246, 283–345.

22. To impute it to chance contingencies is problematically to imply that our identities are invariant with respect to the identities of our parents. It is true that what is more adequately so characterized is the factor of our talents that is supplied by their genetic endowments. In *An Essay on Rights*, pp. 237–49 and 273–80, I suggest how and why that factor may be construed as an element of natural resources without impairing self-ownership and what the just redistributive implications of this are. On the just liabilities of delinquent parents, see also my "Choice and Circumstance," *Ratio* 10 (1997): 296–312.

23. Beitz, *Political Theory and International Relations*, p. 140 [cf. herein 29].

24. Ibid., p. 141 [cf. herein 30].

25. There are many degrees of cooperation. In Hobbesian states of nature, to refrain from predatory activity is to be a cooperator. Any denial that such scenarios constitute the relevant baseline for identifying cooperation itself presupposes an alternative precontractual baseline that must consist of a distributive norm prescribing a set of inviolable domains whose owners' interactions would then count as cooperation.

26. Ibid., pp. 133–34 [cf. herein 24-25]. See John Rawls, *A Theory of Justice* (Oxford: Oxford University Press, 1972), p. 378.

27. It is under the description *territorial site*—rather than in terms of "$x$ gallons of crude oil, $y$ hectares of arable land, etc."—that nations designate the object of their jurisdictional claims. That is, not just any old $x$ gallons and $y$ hectares will do.

28. See Thomas Pogge, *Realizing Rawls* (Ithaca, NY: Cornell University Press, 1989), and "An Egalitarian Law of Peoples," *Philosophy & Public Affairs* 23 (1994): 195-224 [reprinted herein 461–93].

29. Pogge, *Realizing Rawls*, p. 247 (italics in original).

30. Rawls, *A Theory of Justice*, pp. 264–65; cf. Pogge, *Realizing Rawls*, p. 247.

31. Pogge, *Realizing Rawls*, pp. 246ff.

32. As suggested previously, the core of one argument against foundational contractualism is simply that a necessary condition of the joint performability—the possibility—of the set of contractually undertaken duties is the joint exercisability of the liberties they presuppose: an exercisability that is guaranteed only by a set of prior (compossible) rights. For recent debate on locating the foundations of justice in contracts, see the exchanges among Brian Barry, Neil MacCormick, and myself in "Brian Barry's *Justice as Impartiality*: A Symposium," *Political Studies* 44 (1996): 303–42.

33. Pogge, "An Egalitarian Law of Peoples," p. 199 [herein 466, note: GRD (Global Resources Dividend) replaces GRT (Global Resources Tax)].

34. See John Rawls, "The Law of Peoples," in Stephen Shute and Susan Hurley, eds., *On Human Rights* (New York: Basic Books, 1993) [41–82, 220–230, reprinted herein 421–60].

35. Pogge, "An Egalitarian Law of Peoples," p. 199 [herein 466].

36. Ibid., p. 200 [herein 467].

37. Ibid., pp. 200–201 [herein 467–68].

38. Pogge, *Realizing Rawls*, p. 64.

39. Ibid., p. 79.

40. Rawls, *A Theory of Justice*, p. 560.

41. See Steiner, *An Essay on Rights*, and "Choice and Circumstance." That their adversities are self-incurred certainly does not imply any absence of duties to relieve them. It implies only that such duties are ones of humanity rather than justice and hence are not justly enforceable.

42. This chapter has greatly benefited from comments and criticisms supplied by Jerry Cohen, Katrin Flikschuh, Ian Shapiro, and Andrew Williams.

# 22. MICHAEL BLAKE

Blake considers whether liberals, consistent with moral egalitarianism, may apply principles of distributive justice in a manner that discriminates between compatriots and foreigners. His approach does not invoke special duties toward compatriots, but seeks to show that general duties have distinct implications in domestic and international contexts. Because a state subjects only its own nationals to its coercive legal system, it has special duties of justification toward those individuals. These duties can explain, consistent with moral egalitarianism, why the application of principles of distributive justice is limited by national borders.

## Distributive Justice, State Coercion, and Autonomy

*First published in* Philosophy and Public Affairs *30: 3 (summer 2001): 257–96.*

Liberalism has difficulty with the fact of state borders. Liberals are, on the one hand, committed to moral equality, so that the simple fact of humanity is sufficient to motivate a demand for equal concern and respect. Liberal principles, on the other hand, are traditionally applied only within the context of the territorial state, which seems to place an arbitrary limit on the range within which liberal guarantees will apply. This difficulty is particularly stark in the context of distributive justice; state boundaries, after all, often divide not simply one jurisdiction from another, but the rich from the poor as well. Allowing these boundaries to determine distributive shares seems to place an almost feudal notion of birthright privilege back into the heart of liberal theory.[1]

This difficulty has led many philosophers to argue that some revision of liberal theory is necessary. These proposals frequently involve either the demand that liberalism focus on previously neglected particularistic commitments, or the demand that it abandon such local concerns and endorse a cosmopolitan vision of distributive justice. What I want to do in this article is identify a different way in which liberalism might deal with the worries created by the fact of state borders. My argument is that a globally impartial liberal theory is not incompatible with distinct principles of distributive justice applicable only within the national context. This is true, however, not because we care more about our fellow countrymen than we do about outsiders, but because the political and legal institutions we share at the national level create a need for distinct forms of justification. A concern with relative economic shares, I argue, is a plausible interpretation of liberal principles only when those principles are applied to individuals who share liability to the coercive network of state governance. Such a concern is not demanded by liberal principles when individuals do not share such links of citizenship. What a principle demands changes depending upon the context in which it is applied; that we owe distinct things to fellow nationals need indicate not partiality toward those nationals, but rather a more sophisticated understanding of what impartiality really demands.

In making this argument, I appeal both to John Rawls's theory of justice and to a principle of autonomy I believe underlies contractarian theories such as Rawls's. I do not think that the usefulness of what I say here depends upon the wholehearted acceptance of either of these; I use Rawls's theory as an egalitarian one amenable to the approach I defend, but nothing in my strategy prevents its use by those more opposed to Rawlsian theorizing. The strategy I employ seeks to endorse the idea that we can defend principles of sufficiency abroad and principles of distributive equality at home—because these principles can be understood as distinct implications of impartial principles in distinct institutional contexts. That is, the solution of the difficulty noted above is to be found not in a search for justified partiality, but in the interpretation of impartiality itself. Or so, at any rate, I argue. As a way of introducing my argument to this effect, I will introduce three distinctions.

## I. THREE PRELIMINARY DISTINCTIONS

### RELATIVE AND ABSOLUTE DEPRIVATION

We can begin by noting that there are two quite different ways of evaluating the moral status of someone's bundle of resource holdings. We could, in the first case, look simply at that bundle in isolation from those held by others. In some situations, this sort of analysis seems sufficient to demonstrate that something morally problematic has occurred. If someone faces a situation of drastic poverty and deprivation, and we are confident that her situation is created or remediable by human agency, then it seems we might be able to articulate a moral duty toward that person—without yet looking at how her bundle stacks up to those of others. The moral shortfall of her situation is found simply in how little she has, not in how much less she has than others.

The analysis of poverty often takes this form. We can understand such an analysis of a bundle of resources as the analysis of absolute deprivation. It seems plausible to me that much international poverty can be condemned in terms of *absolute deprivation*. There is, I think, a threshold to decent human functioning, beneath which the possibility of autonomous human agency is removed. It seems to be a matter of moral gravity whenever we might prevent someone from falling below that line and fail to do so. The moral problem here, however, does not seem to make any appeal to the holdings of others. That other individuals have more is not, I think, an essential part of the moral claim; it is, at best, a signal that the deprivation in question could be remedied.

The idea of absolute deprivation, however, does not account for all cases in which we want to condemn as inappropriate someone's bundle of holdings. Sometimes, that is, we seem to look precisely to the difference between individual bundles for the source of our moral concern. In many liberal theories, liberal principles give rise not simply to principles condemning poverty but to principles mandating some degree of economic equality. This analysis looks to the gap between rich and poor, and not simply to the fact of poverty itself. Such cases involve a concern not simply with absolute deprivation, but with *relative deprivation* as well. When relative deprivation is morally illegitimate, the moral gravity of the case might be thought to increase as the gap between rich and poor widens. The holdings of the better situated are not simply a signal that poverty might be avoided; they are an integral part of our moral condemnation of the distribution.

What I want to establish in this article, to use this terminology, is that liberalism can concern itself with absolute deprivation abroad, and reserve a concern for relative deprivation for the local arena. Liberal principles can condemn some forms of poverty regardless of institutional relationship; some forms of poverty deny the very possibility of autonomous agency, and so can be condemned by an impartial liberalism committed to the autonomous agency of all. But a concern for relative deprivation becomes an implication of liberal thought only when individuals share more than common humanity. An impartial liberalism will condemn some disparities in the holdings of goods as unjustifiable to those who share liability to a coercive system of political and legal institutions. Shared citizenship, that is, gives rise to a concern with relative deprivation that is absent in the international realm. Thus, what looks like partiality is in fact the implication of an impartial principle under a different set of circumstances.

## PARTIAL AND IMPARTIAL JUSTIFICATORY STRATEGIES

This last idea might be made more plausible with the introduction of another distinction: one between partial and impartial justificatory strategies. If what we are trying to do is justify an apparent deviation from impartial treatment, there are two distinct methods of accomplishing our ends. The first is to give some reason why partiality is, in this case, appropriate. The second is to demonstrate that the apparent deviation is illusory. What looks like unequal treatment is, in fact, what equality demands.

The first strategy is, I think, the more common in the literature on international poverty. Frequently, those who seek to justify the limitation of distributive guarantees to the local realm seek some set of reasons why preference or priority for the local community is appropriate.[2] The debate between the partialist and the cosmopolitan thus turns on the legitimacy of preferring one's own—a debate, I think, that tends to turn more than it should upon the choice of metaphor: the cosmopolitans interpreting nationality as a morally arbitrary fact of persons, which is akin to race, and the partialists interpreting nationality as more akin to familial relationships.

The second strategy, however, would be to abandon this attempt to find a legitimate source of partiality. This strategy would, instead, seek to explain the apparent inequality as a valid implication of an impartial principle. We could note, here, that the specific guarantees and protections created by a principle can vary depending upon the context within which it is applied. To modify an example from Aristotle: A trainer might give Milo the wrestler six pounds of food per day, and his wispy assistant only one.[3] The trainer could try to justify this with reference to a legitimate preference for Milo's interests and needs; perhaps Milo shares something with the trainer that permits that trainer to abandon the attempt to treat Milo and his assistant equally. The trainer might, instead, say that he is not in fact abandoning impartiality in treating his two charges in this way. What is an apparent inequality in treatment is, in fact, a perfectly impartial application of a principle by which the trainer is commanded (in this case) to give his charges just that amount of food they require. What looks like a case of favoritism is in fact a case in which impartiality has more complicated implications than we had expected.[4]

The strategy of the present article, then, is to begin with a principle that is globally impartial—which does not prefer the local to the foreign—and see whether the demands of that principle become more complex as circumstances become more complex. In particular, as I have mentioned above, I argue that this will imply the moral relevance of relative deprivation within the domestic context but not within the international context.

All of this, however, assumes that states, much as we know them today—with a limited territorial reach and a limited set of persons over which their coercive power is exercised—will continue to exist. Justifying this assumption is our next task.

## INSTITUTIONAL AND NONINSTITUTIONAL THEORY

A theorist might take a variety of attitudes toward the political institutions we find in the world today. One attitude would involve abstracting away from the institutions we currently have, and asking what sorts of institutions we would endorse if we were starting from scratch. This approach—which we might call noninstitutional theory—would not privilege those institutions we have over others we might have developed. What borders would look like—and, for that matter, whether things like states with things like borders ought to exist—would be perfectly valid questions for the theorist to ask.

Another sort of attitude would prompt one to ask not what institutions we ought to have, but what the institutions we currently have would have to do to be justified. This sort of theory—which I call institutional theory—would take much more of the world as a pretheoretical given for purposes of analysis. It would include, I think, both the fact of state power and the division of territorial jurisdiction found in the world today. It would ask not whether we ought to have developed such a world, but what the various states we have now must do for their powers to be justifiable.

These two forms of theory are best regarded as ideal types—we might well develop forms of theory that mix both institutional and noninstitutional forms of analysis. In this article, however, I will engage in a very institutional form of theorizing. This is not, I should emphasize, to say that noninstitutional theory is not useful. Noninstitutional theory is well equipped to answer certain sorts of questions, just as institutional theory is well equipped to answer others. The questions that are most pressing in the current international arena, however, seem to require an institutional approach to theorizing. If we want to ask what states as we know them owe to their own citizens and to others, we ought to begin with states as they are currently situated—both in terms of the powers they possess and in terms of the territory over which they have authority.

There are some advantages to beginning with such an approach. The division of the world into distinct political units is likely to continue for the foreseeable future, and a theory that accepts this fact can provide us with more present-day guidance than one that cannot. In the real world, too, alteration of political units and redrawing of political lines is never without cost, and this fact is kept more in view by a theory that acknowledges political institutions than by one that does not. There are, of course, disadvantages to such an approach; in taking much of the world for granted, there are some questions it is unable to address. Such a theory is not well equipped to answer questions of legitimate secession and territorial change, since institutional theorizing treats matters of borders as pretheoretical givens for the purposes of analysis.[5] This only shows, however, that no single approach to theorizing can answer all questions we need to address. For the questions I address here, however, I am convinced an institutional approach is best.

Institutional theory can, I think, keep our attention directed toward the fact that persons can be situated in more than one institutional context, and that therefore the content of our liberal principles can perhaps vary depending upon the context within which they are applied. That is, it is well-positioned to acknowledge both an impartial principle and the distinct implications of that principle in distinct institutional contexts. In this, I think, we might preserve our sense both that liberalism must apply itself to the global arena, and our sense that shared liability toward the state might affect the content of what liberalism demands. As Appiah has it:

> States, on the other hand, matter morally intrinsically. They matter not because people care about them, but because they regulate our lives through forms of coercion that will always require moral justification. State institutions matter because they are both necessary to so many modern human purposes and because they have so great a potential for abuse.[6]

Appiah's sentiment here is emblematic of institutional theory, and reflects the desire that our theories do abstract away from aspects of the world that stand in need of philosophical analysis and justification—including the tremendous coercive powers of the state.[7]

One question that immediately arises, however, is that of the conservative bias of such an approach. Is it unduly conservative to demand that we bracket the consideration of state powers and state borders in the present inquiry? I do not think so, once the nature of this sort of theorizing is made clear. A commitment to institutional theory is not a commitment to an acceptance of the policies and actions of the states of the world today. Admitting that states exist, and provisionally taking their borders to be the ones we see today, does not commit us to accepting as gospel what governments say about their own powers. We seek, instead, to derive principles by which the exercise of state power might be justified to all those who are subject to such power. If that project is successful, we might have developed an account by which each state might justify its exercise of political authority. There does not seem to be anything unduly conservative about such an account.

I want to sum up this section by recapping the ways in which I have classified my own approach. I have drawn three distinctions that, I hope, will go some way toward clarifying the approach I choose to take. My approach is institutional in that it accepts the political institutions of sovereign states to be such as they currently are in the world, and asks not what institutions ought to exist but what our institutions might do to be justifiable to all. It accepts that the duties owed to strangers and the duties owed to fellow citizens are distinct, but distinguishes them in an impartial, rather than a partial, manner; it is not that we care more about our fellow countrymen, but that an impartial principle will give rise to distinct burdens of justification between individuals who share liability to the coercive power of the state. And, in the area of distributive justice, this approach will accept the conclusion that liberal principles will condemn certain forms of relative deprivation within the domestic arena, while the same liberal principles will demand a respect only for certain sorts of absolute deprivation in the international arena. It is only because they are required for the justification of coercive force to all those who face it, I argue, that a moral concern with relative deprivation is implied by a liberalism committed to autonomy, and therefore a concern for specifically economic egalitarianism is only morally required within the context of a domestic legal system.

If all this is correct, then I think we may have a means by which to dissolve the problem with which we began. The principle of autonomy I will identify demands that such coercive practices and institutions be either justified or eliminated; since the institution of the state is not likely to disappear at any point soon, and because some form of political coercion seems necessary for autonomous functioning, I think we must instead seek principles by which state coercion could be justified. Only in this search for the justification of state coercion, I argue, does egalitarian distributive justice become relevant.

In the international arena, by contrast, no institution comparable to the state exists. No matter how substantive the links of trade, diplomacy, or international agreement, the institutions present at the international level do not engage in the same sort of coercive practices against individual moral agents. This is not to say that coercion does not exist in forms other than state coercion. Indeed, international practices can indeed be coercive—we might understand certain sorts of exploitative trade relationships under this heading, and so a theory concerned with autonomy must condemn such relationships or seek to justify them. What I do say, however, is that only the relationship of common citizenship is a relationship potentially justifiable through a concern for equality in distributive shares. The Rawlsian theory of justice, I think, is best interpreted in this way—as a demonstration of what must be the case, in the context of basic liberties and in distributive shares, before coercive institutions are to be justifiable to individuals entitled to be the circumstances of autonomy. In this, I suggest, we will arrive at a principled division between citizen and stranger, and a way of situating liberalism's concern for domestic distributive shares within its global concern for the autonomy of all human agents. Thereby, the tension within liberalism identified at the beginning of this article might be dissolved.

I have, in this section, mentioned the principle of autonomy without properly introducing it; I have hardly explained what this term means, let alone explained what it would mandate in the international arena. I will, in the next section, try to make good on the former defect and will reserve a discussion of the latter topic for another occasion. The structure of my argument will be as follows: I begin by examining some implications of the principle of autonomy; I then proceed to the forms of justification that might legitimate otherwise impermissible violations of autonomy; I demonstrate that the appropriate forms of justification will mandate a concern for distributive shares only within the confines of a domestic state; and I conclude the account with a brief fable designed to illustrate the applicability of the liberal principle of autonomy in the international arena. I will, then, assume for the purposes of the present article that autonomy is something we do and ought to care about in all human beings, and will proceed to examine the argument along the lines given above. The topic of the next section, accordingly, becomes: What, exactly, do we mean when we speak of autonomy?[8]

## II. LIBERALISM AND AUTONOMY

Autonomy has a long pedigree within liberal political philosophy. It is found, most prominently, in political theories taking off from Kantian premises, but a concern for autonomy is found within a wide variety of approaches to political justification.[9] A liberalism committed to the global protection of individual autonomy, I think, stands as a plausible candidate for a defensible and internally coherent liberalism. Such a principle makes no arbitrary differentiation between citizen and stranger but respects equally the autonomy of all individuals—although, as I have suggested, what constraints on action this will entail differ depending upon institutional context. We might therefore begin our inquiry by taking liberalism to demand the protection of individual autonomy, and see what results this assumption will have in the contexts of international and domestic distributive justice. I will not, in the present context, offer a defense of the moral relevance of autonomy; for the moment, I hope that the principle of autonomy as used here may simply be shown to produce plausible and attractive results in the arenas of domestic and international justice. The principle I use in this exercise, therefore, will be the following: All human beings have the moral entitlement to exist as autonomous agents, and therefore have entitlements to those circumstances and conditions under which this is possible. This principle reflects the liberal commitment to autonomy as a basic value, and the belief that the autonomous agency of a foreigner and that of a citizen are alike in moral importance.

Taking autonomy as a value, however, does not determine which variant of autonomy will be defended. In the present section, I outline the liberal principle I defend. I would begin this presentation by introducing Joseph Raz's notion of autonomy, in which autonomous agents are understood to be part authors of their own lives; the autonomous person is able to develop and pursue self-chosen goals and relationships. There are, naturally, certain preconditions that exist before a human agent could be understood as autonomous. Raz identifies three. First, there must be the appropriate mental abilities: The individual in question must have the abilities to form the complex intentions required of an autonomous planning agent, and must have the forms of rationality sufficient to follow through on what those intentions require. I would emphasize that these abilities might be divided into two forms: the mental skills required to act as an agent, and the appropriate attitudes toward one's own life necessary to see one's self as an agent. The latter abilities, since they are subject to at least some control from political institutions, seem to be an appropriate focus of justice. The former abilities, however, seem to be largely beyond the reach of politics, and so I will not focus on this requirement in what follows.[10] The second requirement is that the set of options in question must be adequate; the mental faculties of choice must be presented with options between which choice is possible. What this demands, of course, is a famously difficult problem, but—with Raz—we might argue in the present context that no general theory of adequacy is required; it is, perhaps, easier to identify certain circumstances or conditions as inadequate than it is to develop a general approach to what adequate sets of options might share. And, finally, autonomy is incompatible with the existence of coercion. Coercion and manipulation, as Raz notes, reduces the will of one person to the will of another; they are marked as violations of autonomy not simply in virtue of that fact, but because of the symbolic gesture this fact represents. In subjecting the will of one otherwise autonomous agent to the will of another, coercion demonstrates an attitude of disrespect, of infantilization of a sort inconsistent with respect for human agents as autonomous, self-creating creatures.[11] Coercion, both in itself and because it demonstrates contempt for the individual coerced, is forbidden by a liberal principle that demands respect for the conditions of autonomy.

It is, I think, worthwhile to examine some aspects of this concern for autonomy. The first is that the form of autonomy I defend here, while it reflects a Kantian respect for individual agency, is not Kant's own; it reflects, rather than a monistic picture of human autonomy in which the moral law is equivalent in all rational agents, a pluralistic picture of human agency in which there are a multiplicity of valuable options and ways of life. Autonomy, on this latter construal, is a matter of respect for human creatures as agents able to develop specific plans, attachments and interests; as such, it is committed to a pluralism about the specific ways of life to which this autonomous pursuit might be directed.

The second aspect of autonomy I would emphasize is that respect for autonomy is not satisfied by the mere exercise of practical reason. What we demand is not simply the existence of a faculty of choice, or even the mere existence of some options within which this faculty is to be active. Even the most solitary prisoner, after all, can still make decisions, even if they are such minor ones as whether to read the book by his bedside or to go to sleep. The notion of autonomy, reflecting as it does respect for the conditions of partial authorship of one's own life, has a more determinate moral content than this. The idea of autonomy reflects an image of individual human agents as creating value by their creative engagement with the world; their allegiances, choices, and relationships constitute sources of value. This creation of value can be destroyed or respected by institutions in the world. The principle of autonomy, that is, relies upon a normative conception of human agents as entities who can take part not simply in practical reasoning about what actions to undertake, but in reflective deliberation about what values and ideals to endorse and pursue. The principle, therefore, demands more than the simple exercise of practical reasoning. It demands that the set of options provide adequate materials within which to construct a plan of life that can be understood as chosen rather than as forced upon us from without.

The third aspect of autonomy I would explore in the present context is that autonomy does not seem to demand the maximization of the number of options open to us. Indeed, it seems plausible that past a certain point, having further options may actually reduce our ability to make sense of and organize our lives in accordance with our plans.[12] Autonomy, it seems, does not depend upon the sheer number of options available, at least above a certain baseline of adequacy. This fact, I think, will have significant implications in the study of distributive justice. If holdings of goods are relevant for the options they open up to us—as well as, perhaps, the ways in which they make access easier to options we already possess—then it does not seem that we necessarily gain any additional autonomy as our holdings increase past a certain level. However much those additional holdings might increase our hedonic tone, a theory premised upon respect for autonomy will not regard these holdings as increasing the morally primary aspect of persons upon which liberal theory is premised. We cannot, therefore, read off autonomy simply by looking at either holdings of goods or at number of options realistically open to us. Above a certain baseline, neither becomes morally important from the standpoint of liberal justice. This fact is, I think, important since it points the way to a conclusion about distributive justice and relative deprivation in the international arena.

The fourth, and final aspect of the picture of autonomy I wish to highlight is that even if the above account is true—even if, that is, nothing of any great moral importance hinges upon the number of options open to individuals, above the baseline of adequacy—then it is nonetheless true that certain ways of acting so as to change the options open to us do seem to be relevant. On the account I defend here, that is, there is a world of difference between becoming a doctor because it seems the best option realistically open to me, and becoming a doctor because someone else has made it the best option open to me by making other choices difficult or impossible to pursue. The former reflects simply rational choice among an otherwise acceptable set of alternatives; if I would have preferred to live my life as a crime-fighting superhero, but the circumstances of my society rule that out as a realistic option, it does not seem that my autonomy is invaded by the absence of the superhero option from my set of attainable lives. All sets of options, after all, include constraints on what we can realistically do or be; the mere fact of a limited set of options, as above, hardly seems to matter from the standpoint of the principle I have introduced. But the latter alternative—in which my own free choice from among alternatives is vitiated by another's deliberate agency denying my ability to choose for myself—seems quite different in its moral gravity. In removing otherwise acceptable options—perhaps I could, and would, have become an attorney—the coercer denies my ability to live my own life from the inside, and to create value for myself in the world. What matters here, as above, is not simply what things I may realistically do or be; it is why that set of things looks the way it does, and whether or not it reflects a conscious human attempt to manipulate it so as to subsume my will under another's.

The picture of autonomy I have discussed here is not uncommon within political philosophy. I think a similar concern for autonomy is found in Rawls's own conception of rational autonomy, which is concerned with the capacity of individuals to "form, to revise, and to pursue a conception of the good, and to deliberate in accordance with it."[13] The notion of rational autonomy reflects a concern with the Rawlsian idea of the two moral powers, the power to act in accordance with a conception of justice and to form and pursue a conception of the good. Individuals, conceived of as free and equal in their moral powers, are understood here as self-authenticating sources of value, able to give value to plans and allegiances through the free exercise of their moral abilities. Rawls's notion of rational autonomy, I think, can be interpreted and defended in accordance with the discussion given above. What I want to do in the rest of this article is to show what such a principle might require in the international arena, and demonstrate that Rawls's own theory of justice might profitably be viewed as a theory by which the coercive force of the state might be justified to free and equal persons who have a prima facie moral entitlement to be free from all coercion. For now, I would note simply that the global defense of the conditions of autonomous functioning seems at the very least to be a plausible starting point for an analysis of a global liberal theory.

The principle I defend, therefore, mandates the following: that all individuals, regardless of institutional context, ought to have access to those goods and circumstances under which they are able to live as rationally autonomous agents, capable of selecting and pursuing plans of life in accordance with individual conceptions of the good. There are, I think, several methods by which people might be denied the circumstances of autonomy; famine, extreme poverty, crippling social norms such as caste hierarchies—all of these structures seem comprehensible as violations of a liberal principle devoted to the defense of the circumstances of autonomy, although I cannot here defend these claims in detail. It is enough in the present context to notice that a consistent liberal must be as concerned with poverty abroad as that at home, since borders provide no insulation from the demands of a morality based upon the worth of all autonomous human beings.

There is much more to be said in the above context, but I want now to turn to the issue of coercion. People can be denied their autonomy by being starved, deeply impoverished, or subjected to oppressive and marginalizing norms, but they can also face a denial of autonomy that results from outright coercion. I will refrain from offering a complete theory of coercion in the present context;[14] I will only note that, as I have insisted upon throughout this exercise, whether an individual faces a denial of autonomy resulting from coercion cannot be read off simply from the number of options open to her. Coercion is not simply a matter of what options are available; it has to do with the reasons the set of options is as constrained as it is. Coercion is an intentional action, designed to replace the chosen option with the choice of another. Coercion, we might therefore say, expresses a relationship of domination, violating the autonomy of the individual by replacing that individual's chosen plans and pursuits with those of another. Let us say, therefore, that coercive proposals violate the autonomy of those against whom they are employed; they act so as to replace our own agency with the agency of another.

Perhaps the most obvious form of coercion we might examine is that of state punishment. Coercion by criminal penalties, writes Joseph Raz, is a global invasion of autonomy; incarceration, after all, removes "almost all autonomous pursuits" from the prisoner.[15] This is not to say that such punishment cannot sometimes be justified—very few people think that all criminal punishment is, by its very nature, morally prohibited—but it is to say that it is necessarily an affront to autonomy, and as such something standing in need of justification. Coercive acts and practices are prima facie prohibited by the liberal principle of autonomy.

This, however, gives rise to a new topic—the issue of justification. Sometimes, after all, actions that the above analysis would tell us are condemned by our principle seem nonetheless morally justifiable. Some cases of coercion, we tend to think, are at least in certain circumstances justifiable invasions of individual autonomy. A question therefore arises about the appropriate forms of justification, by which an otherwise impermissible invasion of autonomy might be legitimated. The next section, accordingly, will examine the issue of coercion in greater detail, by analyzing what might divide legitimate and illegitimate forms of coercion; my particular focus will be on the imposition of state punishment.

## III. JUSTIFICATION AND COERCION, ONE: THE CRIMINAL LAW

Some forms of coercion—including some aspects of state coercion—seem morally acceptable; we would not want to endorse a liberal principle that told us that state coercion was never morally appropriate. The question therefore arises: What sorts of considerations could justify what would otherwise be an impermissible violation of autonomy? Note, first of all, that states of affairs that are open to human control are, morally speaking, distinct from those that are not. Before a state of affairs can be condemned by the liberal principle of autonomy, it must be in some sense amenable to control by human agency. To return to the case of famine, we might note that if the world simply did not have the resources necessary to keep any of its citizens alive, then the loss of autonomy felt by those individuals could not be charged as a moral failing to any agent or group of agents; no individual or group could be charged with a violation of the liberal principle of autonomy. The circumstances of the world, in this case, would render hunger inevitable, and human will could not hope to reduce or prevent such suffering. That hunger in the modern world is not like this—that the world actually does have the ability to maintain its inhabitants—indicates that a morally problematic situation, rather than a tragic one, has arisen.

But let us take the case of coercion clearly engaged in by human agents against other human agents. Justification for such coercion can sometimes arise as a result of consent. In law, if I consent to a potential harm being done to me, then no legally cognizable harm has taken place—in lawyers' Latin, *volenti non fit injuria*. In morality, similarly, if I consent to remove from myself the means of autonomous action in some area of life—say, by voluntarily allowing myself to be coerced (imagine a case in which I give you permission to swat me if you catch me drinking)—then the moral harm of coercion no longer seems to exist. Using one's agency to consent to the elimination of previously held options does not, as a rule, violate the principle of autonomy. Not all such contracts are compatible with the principle of autonomy—voluntary slavery, since it abdicates the entire field of autonomous planning for the duration of life, might be excluded—but as a rule, consent is a possible way to justify what would otherwise be prohibited.

We have, in these ideas, the beginning of a method by which we might understand the potential justification of state punishment—and, from there, return to the issue of relative deprivation and just distributive shares. To see this, however, we must note what form the justification of punishment would have to take. It cannot, of course, be explicit consent—in attempting to justify the imposition of incarceration for manslaughter, for instance, we do not ask the prisoner in the dock what sorts of punishments are those to which he would consent. We phrase our request for justification, rather, in terms of hypothetical consent—not what is consented to, at present, but what would be consented to, ex ante, under some appropriate method of modeling rational consent. This approach to criminal punishment reflects the retributivist tradition, on which we can say that criminal's punishment is legitimated not because his punishment will be useful for others, but because he himself, as a rational agent, can be understood under the appropriate hypothetical circumstances as having willed it.[16]

We might, therefore, try to find justification in a variant of Thomas Scanlon's notion of reasonable rejection—if the prisoner in the dock could not reasonably reject a coercive rule licensing incarceration for his offense, then we may take him as having consented, as a reasonable agent, to the imposition of that coercive legal rule in the first place.[17] This tool, I think, will allow us to understand what sorts of coercion might be justifiable, and, in the end, will help us understand how coercive state institutions are the institutional prerequisite for the relevance of egalitarian distributive justice.

Let us therefore return to the analysis of state punishment, and ask what the notion of hypothetical consent can tell us in this context. Let us begin by reiterating that coercive punishment is, on this approach, presumptively forbidden as a violation of autonomy. We seek to justify these punishments against this presumption by finding ways in which the punishment might be understood as one to which we could not reasonably withhold our consent. This approach would, I think, nicely correspond with our sense that punishment—the deliberate imposition of judicial harm—is always an evil; a necessary evil, sometimes, but still something extraordinary that stands in need of special justification. Most of us, then, think that some punishments are legitimate, and that some are not; the constitutional notion of "cruel and unusual punishment" might be taken to reflect our latter sense, that some punishments are not justifiable invasions of the principle of autonomy. Indeed, U.S. Supreme Court jurisprudence in this area can be plausibly reconstructed to reflect this way of seeing the issue. The essence of cruel and unusual punishment, in the United States, is not to be found in some essential feature of the punishment itself, but in a proportionality between the degree of punishment and the seriousness of the offense. Thus, capital punishment for the crime of murder is not necessarily cruel and unusual punishment;[18] capital punishment for the crime of rape, by contrast, is proportionately too severe to be justifiable ex ante to the one facing the punishment.[19] These cases can be explained on the autonomy approach given above; while capital punishment always infringes upon autonomy in a particularly stark and immediate way, in some cases this putative violation can be justified by means of the hypothetical consent of all those potentially facing the punishment. In some cases of murder, we would be forced (the Court supposes) to accept that it is a legitimate moral response to a deliberate taking of life. In the crime of rape, however, we are not so forced. Whatever one may think of the content of the Court's reasoning, the pattern of argument seems to correspond with our analysis of the principle given above,[20] particularly in view of the Court's declaration that the core idea of the prohibition on cruel and unusual punishments is the protection of human dignity.[21] This approach would, finally, also explain our conviction that some punishments are abhorrent enough to be ruled out as responses to virtually any crime imaginable. Violations of autonomy, we have already noted, admit of degrees, and if punishment always stands in prima facie tension with autonomy, it still exists in a variety of strengths; some punishment is so unmaking of individual autonomy as to be ruled out as a response to any crime.[22]

In this section, I have limited my focus to the function of the state in administering the criminal law. There are, however, forms of legal administration other than that seen in criminal law. Although the focus of philosophers of law has been more squarely centered on criminal law than on these other forms—including, among others, the law of property, torts, contracts, and taxation—these forms of legal adjudication deserve independent attention from within liberal political theory. In the next section of this article, I focus on these forms of law; I will try to establish that they involve coercive state action, and that they are therefore demand justification in exactly the same way as the imposition of criminal punishments. I will, finally, try to demonstrate that only in this demand for justification does a concern for relative deprivation become relevant—and, therefore, that only between people who share the coercive mechanisms of a state does a concern for specifically economic egalitarian justice become appropriate.

# IV. JUSTIFICATION AND COERCION, TWO: THE CIVIL LAW

Coercion is certainly presented in the law in its most stark form in the institution of criminal punishment. But it seems that even private law—the law of contracts, property, and torts—is rife with coercion as well. Contract law is often analyzed as a limited grant of (coercive) legislative power by which individuals are empowered to make legal rules determining ownership that all must be compelled to obey.[23] Property law, too, has a basis in coercion; it is, as Jeremy Waldron notes, a commitment to using collective force against certain persons should they attempt to exercise control over certain goods. Taxation law, too, although not technically a part of private law, seems to involve implicit threats of coercive state action as well. In all these areas of law, the adjudication of disputes will issue in a coercive transfer of legal rights. Whenever a civil judgment is made, for instance, the legal rights transferred from the defeated party to the victor are ones that are ultimately enforced with coercive measures. If we refuse to go along with the transfer in question, we risk imprisonment for contempt. All of these sanctions are built into the structure of the private law. Such practices are, it seems, every bit as coercive, if not as dramatic, as punishment in the criminal law, and stand in a similar need for justification. A civil judgment gives us a choice between surrendering goods or freedom in much the same way as a gunman's threat; while the former is at least potentially justifiable, and the latter generally inexcusable, the conditions under which the former may be justified require an inquiry into hypothetical justification in precisely the same manner as punishment. Although the purposes of the coercive sanctions differ between private law and criminal law, the fact of coercion is necessarily found within all areas of legal rules:

> Every decision [judges] make imposes their will on other human beings. When a judge sentences a defendant to prison, the judge's decision takes away the defendant's liberty. When a judge finds contractual liability, the decision forces one party to compensate the other. Every word, then, masks a deed. And the deed, ultimately, is one of power and coercion.[24]

Such an analysis seems to find echoes in Supreme Court jurisprudence as well. In *Shelley v. Kraemer*, the Court noted that the enforcement of a restrictive covenant was as much a matter of state action as incarceration, and that the same principles of constitutional analysis would therefore apply.[25] Enforcing a contract, after all, is ultimately legitimating the use of force; and that, we must agree, is something that stands in need of justification from within a liberal theory premised upon autonomy.

Political philosophy has rarely addressed the conditions of moral legitimacy of the private law in any explicit way. The private law, however, stands in as much need of theoretical justification as the practice of punishment. Anthony Kronman has noted, for instance, that the rules governing contract law stand in need of defense from within liberal political philosophy. The law allows certain forms of advantage-taking—such as superior knowledge or intelligence—to influence contractual outcomes and prohibits the use of other forms, such as physical intimidation. There is nothing natural or obvious in this way of developing contract law; surely, the agreements that will be protected by the use of state power stand in as much need of moral defense as any aspect of state punishment.[26] All the forms of legal rules we use are ultimately backed up with coercive measures that implicate the liberal principle of autonomy. The law of taxation, for instance, is clearly coercive. Federal income taxation plainly involves the taking away of previously earned resources from individuals. As above, this form of law seems properly regarded as a putative violation of the liberal principle of autonomy; it gives us, in essence, a choice between surrendering our goods or our lives. This is not to say that such taxation is not justified—if there are to be legal systems at all, coercive means of providing for their upkeep seem required. But it does mean that such taxation is presumptively wrong until justified through the giving of reasons that could not be reasonably rejected by those who face the taxation. What I would conclude here, at any rate, is that law is a web of coercion in which both private and criminal law are understandable as prima facie in violation of the principle of autonomy, and in which both private and criminal law therefore stand in need of theoretical justification. As Robert Cover had it, every judicial act is an act of implicit violence, whether that act is the imprisonment of a criminal or the adjudication or a property dispute;[27] it is up to political philosophy to decide whether such implicit state violence is legitimate.[28]

There is one final aspect of this picture of legal coercion worth noticing. Law is not an isolated parcel of unrelated legal rules; it is, if it is to have the force of law at all, unified into a legal *system*. What this means, as a matter of jurisprudence, is that rules must meet certain formal requirements before they can be understood as legal rules; they must be capable of being followed, they must not conflict, they must be available for public knowledge, and so on. These constraints mean that legal rules in a constitutional regime form a unified system of laws, and we might take it as the task of domestic political philosophy to justify the commands of that legal system as a whole to those who live within its coercive grasp. Rawls, for instance, appears to take this as the task of political philosophy; he describes the attributes of a legal system in a way that makes it sound very much like the basic structure he wishes to analyze, and in *A Theory of Justice* appears to identify the legal system with the basic structure—an equation made much more clear and explicit in *Political Liberalism*. This focus has sometimes been taken as arbitrary.[29] In fact, I think it might be reread as reflecting a consistent concern with the circumstances under which a coercive legal system could be justified to all those who live within it. The fact of a legal system, and the need for justification this creates, makes concerns of relative deprivation relevant at the domestic level.

Is there really no equivalent to such a coercive network of law at the international level? Coercion can, after all, occur both between nations as well as within them. What I think is true, however, is that only the sorts of coercion practiced by the state are likely to be justified through an appeal to distributive shares. Only the state is both coercive of individuals and required for individuals to live autonomous lives. Without some sort of state coercion, the very ability to autonomously pursue our projects and plans seems impossible; settled rules of coercive adjudication seem necessary for the settled expectations without which autonomy is denied. International legal institutions, in contrast, do not engage in coercive practices against individual human agents. Other forms of coercion in the international arena, by contrast, are generally indefensible—or, if they are defensible, do not find their justification in a consideration of their distributive consequences. At present, I want only to point out the difference between domestic and international legal institutions; only the former engage in direct coercion against individuals, of the sort discussed above in connection with the criminal and civil law. There is no ongoing coercion of the sort observed in the domestic arena in the international legal arena.[30] It is, I have suggested, only this form of coercion that makes a concern for relative deprivation relevant for a liberal political theory. What I want to do now is give some reasons in support of this claim. Given that state legal systems involve coercion both in the private law and in criminal law, how might we justify the former sort of coercion to comport with the liberal principle of autonomy?

We are trying, in this inquiry, to determine a means by which legitimate coercion might be distinguished from illegitimate coercion. Some patterns of coercive law, that is, seem acceptable to us, and some do not. Let us take as our aim the development of principles by which the two might be distinguished. The idea of hypothetical consent we have examined demands that we be given reasons for our coercion that we could not reasonably reject. Let us bracket the notion of reasonableness for a moment and look at those criteria that would be relevant to the giving or withholding of consent. What criteria would be morally appropriate for the justification of the forms of coercion found in the private law? We have already examined this idea in connection with legal punishment in the criminal law. The seriousness of the offense was the primary criterion on which we would premise our giving or withholding of consent. But private law is not quite the same in focus as criminal law. Private law is directed at the protection of private entitlements, not the prevention of public harms; whereas a crime is conceptualized as an offense against the body politic, the law of contracts, torts, and property aims at the definition and protection of private holdings and entitlements. These laws define, collectively, what sorts of entitlements will exist in our society; they determine what shall count as property, what sorts of private agreements will receive public enforcement, and—in the law of taxation—what sorts of otherwise private resources must be turned over for public purposes. This pattern of laws, then, defines how we may hold, transfer, and enjoy our property and our entitlements.[31] In so doing, I think, these laws create a pattern of entitlements; the state, through the noncriminal aspect of its legal system, defines how property will be understood and held, and what sorts of activities will produce what sorts of economic holding. Consent can be, I think, partially based upon these consequences of various ways of allocating and protecting entitlements. The principles we seek will mandate or constrain certain ways of allocating entitlements, and the consequences these principles have for holdings of property seem a relevant criterion on which consent might be given or withheld.

To briefly summarize my argument so far: Individuals who share a legal system also share liability to a coercive legal system. The legal system is coercive, and thus stands in prima facie conflict with the liberal principle of autonomy. Since we cannot eliminate the state, given the (paradoxical) importance of government for the protection of autonomy, we seek instead a means by which the content of that legal system might be justified through hypothetical consent to all those who live lives the dimensions of which are defined within that system. The legal system coercively defines what resources flow to which activities; the latter fact seems to provide one relevant criterion on which consent might be given or withheld.[32]

There is nothing here, of course, that yet discusses the issue of *relative* holdings of goods. This will change, I think, as we examine more closely the fact that the coercive laws we are discussing apply not simply to an individual but to an entire society. Justification through hypothetical consent, here, is owed to every individual facing consent; the liberal principle of autonomy is concerned equally with all the autonomy of all human beings, so that a coercive scheme enmeshing a wide set of individuals must be justified to each and every one of those so coerced. The idea of consent we employ here, I think, must reflect this fact. It must, that is, model the circumstances of all those facing legal coercion, to ensure that the consent of each such individual is ensured. We seek a device, then, that prevents special pleading—that prevents the justification of principles that benefit some, but that could be reasonably rejected by some other segment of society. A device must therefore be derived that allows us to develop principles that could not be reasonably rejected by any individual faced with social coercion. Such a device would have to abstract away from morally arbitrary aspects of the individuals considered since principles resting upon such morally arbitrary aspects of people could obviously be reasonably rejected by those disfavored.

This presentation has intentionally been both brief and familiar. It is meant to introduce Rawls's own conception of the original position, and to suggest that the device of the original position is plausibly understood as a way of modeling those conditions under which we might develop principles of justice to which we could not reasonably withhold our consent—but, further, my analysis here is meant to suggest that the original position is only a useful device in the context of the justification of certain forms of coercion. The conditions of the original position, further, lead to a principle constraining relative deprivation; this is expressed in *A Theory of Justice* by means of an analysis of rational choice under uncertainty, but I think the analysis of the original position given here can allow us to see that the real purpose of the difference principle is to justify coercion to all those coerced, including the least advantaged. We have to give all individuals within the web of coercion, including those who do most poorly, reasons to consent to the principles grounding their situation by giving them reasons they could not reasonably reject—a process that will result in the material egalitarianism of the form expressed in the difference principle, since justifying our coercive scheme to those least favored by it will require that we demonstrate that no alternative principle could have made them any better off. A principle that would allow material inequality greater than that of the difference principle, on this reading of Rawls, would be a principle that some members of society could reasonably reject; such principles would inevitably involve the reduction of life chances for the worst off, as compared with those experienced under the difference principle, in a way that the worst off could reasonably reject. I will not reproduce the entirety of Rawls's arguments for this conclusion here; I trust they are relatively familiar, and at any rate doing them justice would require more space than I presently have. What I will insist on here is that a liberal theory that begins with a concern for autonomy may properly develop a concern for relative deprivation as a way of justifying state coercion. We may read the conditions of Rawls's original position as a way of modeling the appropriate conditions of hypothetical consent by which the moral harm of coercion might be nullified. The liberal principle of autonomy requires that coercion be justified through hypothetical consent, and that the conditions of this consent in the arena of private law may require—as Rawls argues they do—considerations of relative deprivation and material equality. It is not the case, therefore, that liberalism is committed to an equality of material shares in the global arena. Material equality becomes relevant only in the context of certain forms of coercion, forms not found outside the domestic arena.

As I have said before, I do not think that my argument depends upon accepting Rawls's own arguments. I have assumed, for the present purposes, that his argument from the original position to his principles of justice is correct. If someone is not convinced by Rawls's own argument to the effect that this justification must take the form of the difference principle, I think I am still able to maintain that such a justification requires the hypothetical consent of all members of society, in a way that will inevitably produce a principle constraining acceptable forms of relative deprivation. Those who share liability to a coercive government, after all, must have relatively equal abilities to influence that government's policies under any plausible theory of liberal justice; relative deprivation seems, therefore, an important implication of liberalism domestically for reasons that fail to hold internationally. The liberal principle of autonomy will, between people who share a coercive legal web of private law, make *some* considerations of relative holdings of goods relevant in the context of the justification of that coercion, given the need to arrive at conditions by which we might model hypothetical consent. The necessity of justifying the coercive practices of the private law to all those who are coerced requires us to look at the material effects of the coercion from the standpoint of all those who are coerced, and requires us to obtain the consent of all those so coerced. This process will, I think, inevitably constrain the forms of material inequality permissible within the confines of the state, given the need to justify coercion to the least favored members of society. This seems to hold true even if some other principle of material deprivation is taken to emerge from the appropriate conditions of hypothetical consent.

For the committed Rawlsian, of course, I think my approach can serve a valuable role in defending Rawls's concern with coercion. The next section of this article focuses upon Rawls, and will offer an interpretation of his work within which this focus upon coercion is a consistent and justifiable aspect of his theory as a whole. I will close the present section by saying that what I hope to have proved in the article up to now is that an impartial liberalism can consistently differentiate the content of what is owed to fellow citizens from what is owed to human beings considered simply as such. Liberalism need not choose between partiality for our fellows and a global disregard for political institutions; liberal impartiality, properly understood, does not condemn distinct duties to fellow countrymen, but rather implies their existence. What we share with one another necessarily alters what our impartial liberal principles demand.

## V. RAWLS AND COERCION

What I want to do in the present section is to give, very briefly, a reading of Rawls that demonstrates his compatibility with the approach taken here. I disagree with Rawls, obviously, on the implications of his own theory in the international arena;[33] but I think the approach I describe here can be plausibly viewed as a rational reconstruction of Rawls's method that avoids some problems inherent in his international extension of his theory. What I say here, then, is perhaps not what Rawls himself would agree with, but it is certainly open to me to argue that—given his writings—it is what he should have argued all along.

Rawls's concern for coercion is made more explicit in his later writings, although it is present in his earlier work as well.[34] I would begin by noting that Rawls takes the coercive nature of legal institutions as a basic fact in need of justification: "Political power," argues Rawls, "is always coercive power backed by the government's use of sanctions, for government alone has the authority to use force in upholding its laws."[35] Rawls then argues that it is this sort of power—the coercive power of the state—that stands in need of justification. Both Rawls and I, in this, take the existence of the state as a pretheoretical given.[36] He accepts the account of states that makes reference to their ability to use coercion in determining what action will be permitted within the state's territory. What Rawls seeks to justify is the use of that authority, by appeal to the norms of public reason which respect autonomy:

> [W]e ask: when may citizens by their vote properly exercise their coercive political power over one another when fundamental questions are at stake? Or in the light of what principles and ideals must we exercise that power if our doing so is to be justifiable to others as free and equal? To this question political liberalism replies: our exercise of political power is proper and hence justifiable only when it is exercised in accordance with a constitution the essentials of which all citizens may reasonably be expected to endorse in the light of principles and ideals acceptable to them as rational and reasonable. This is the liberal principle of legitimacy.[37]

Rawls's account of liberal theory, then, begins with the fact of state coercion and seeks to find a way by which this coercion might be justifiable. Rawls argues that coercive power can be justified only if it is power that can be legitimately understood as a use of power by which citizens of a democratic regime coerce *themselves*. Hence, for Rawls, political power must be exercised in accordance with a constitution that respects the status of individual citizens as autonomous agents—that is, literally, as agents ruled by laws they give to themselves.[38] Thus, the laws of a society—or, more precisely, the constitutional essentials and questions of basic justice that will guide subsequent political deliberation—must be justifiable through the use of public reason to all those individuals who are to be bound by those laws. To coerce people in ways that they could not reasonably accept—to, for example, use the coercive power of the state to enforce one particular view of the good life—is to treat people as less than free and equal participants in the project of self-rule:

> [C]itizens as free and equal have an equal share in the corporate political and coercive power, and all are equally subject to the burdens of judgment. There is no reason, then, why any citizen, or association of citizens, should have the rights to use the state's police power to decide constitutional essentials or basic question of justice as that person's, or that association's, comprehensive doctrine directs. This can be expressed by saying that when equally represented in the original position, no citizen's representative could grant to any other person, or association of persons, the political authority to do that. Such authority is without grounds in public reason.[39]

This account of Rawls's methodology makes it clear that Rawls intends his principles of justice to hold only within a set of individuals who share coercive political institutions, since those institutions stand in need of justification through the use of public reason. In this, I suggest, state coercion has been recognized by Rawls as the precondition for a legitimate concern with relative distributive shares.

On this reading of Rawls, the state has to offer different guarantees to different persons, not because it cares more about one set or the other, but because it is doing different things to some—things that stand in need of justification. To insiders, the state says: Yes, we coerce you, but we do so in accordance with principles you could not reasonably reject. To outsiders, it says: We do not coerce you, and therefore do not apply our principles of liberal justice to you—although you do have an entitlement to the preconditions of autonomous functioning, and we will ensure that these are provided to you if you do not have them now. Both of these, however, reflect a common concern with the liberal principle of autonomy, understood here as a liberal principle global in its reach.

This approach seems to make sense of Rawls's own description of his theory, much attacked by the cosmopolitan reading of Rawls. As Rawls notes, his theory does not seek to apply each time there is a division of something advantageous or disadvantageous; churches and universities, for example, distribute goods to their members, but Rawlsian principles of justice do not apply to such institutions. Rawls therefore notes that libertarianism, since it has no public coercive law applying equally to all persons, has no place for a basic structure.[40] Similarly, Rawls is explicit that no basic structure is available for analysis in the international arena.[41] Rawls limits his attention to the state, since the state can do something churches and universities cannot—directly and coercively determine the sorts of returns flowing to various positions, through coercive private law measures ultimately backed (as Rawls notes) by force. My account can, I think, explain why Rawls maintains this focus. Coercion, unlike the simple division of a good, implicates the ability of individual agents to live their lives according to their own plans; it demands justification, specifically justification by which we can legitimately understand ourselves as the author of our own coercion. The liberal principle of legitimacy can now be linked to a more general duty, that of respect for autonomy, which exists both within and beyond the borders of the state. Rawls focuses upon the domestic situation, but I think his otherwise inexplicable break between the domestic and international spheres can be explained by adding my own theory to his.

I think, finally, that this approach can help solve a problem that has much exercised critics of Rawls in recent years. Many theorists have argued that Rawls's discussion of society as a cooperative venture for mutual advantage is deeply problematic since it would imply that the severely disabled—those who are not able to cooperate in any economically viable way—ought to be expelled from society; this is a problematic conclusion, given that such persons seem more in need of the guarantees of justice than most of us.[42] On the approach given here, this objection is mistaken—it confuses the criteria of *membership* with the criteria of *justification*. The criteria for membership within the group of people entitled to justification through principles of liberal justice, on my account, is membership as citizen within the territorial state. This first stage determines the class of people to whom justification is owed;

the fact of coercion is what mandates the provision of such justification. Only then, in a second stage, is justification offered, and it is at this stage that the normative idea of society as a scheme of cooperation enters. The use of this idea is legitimated here because we seek, in justification, to get principles by which the coercive legal system might be legitimated to everyone by which they could be understood to voluntarily consent—by which, that is, they might be understood as if they were autonomous agents, freely coming together to develop principles of cooperation. It is not that society is a cooperative venture for mutual advantage; the existence of the severely disabled within society, offered as rebuttal of this ideal, is sufficient to demonstrate that. But it is also true that a society whose membership is defined through its legal system might nonetheless employ this notion to justify the coercive legal system to its own citizens.

In many ways, this last objection to Rawls is similar to the misreading of Rawls made by the cosmopolitans. Their argument that the states of the world form a cooperative enterprise is now comprehensible as theoretically misguided, in addition to counterintuitive in results. Coercion, not cooperation, is the sine qua non of distributive justice, making relevant principles of relative deprivation. As a final way of discussing this, I finish with a brief fable that goes some way toward making these conclusions palatable.

## VI. A TALE OF TWO STATES: BORDURIA AND SYLDAVIA

I would like to conclude this article with a more concrete example of the way in which the version of liberalism I defend here would defend itself against a cosmopolitan critic. For this task, we might imagine two societies and see how the liberal principle of autonomy would defend the importance of material equality within, but not without, the boundaries of the state. Begin with a hypothetical case of two autarkic nations.[43] Citizens in each have heard tales of the people beyond the mountains, but there are no links established between the two nations of any sort. In one nation—call it Borduria—advanced techniques of farming and relatively better soil lead to a lush form of life, and soon the nation finds itself with time enough to develop an advanced literature, good universities, and excellent entertainment. In the other nation—call it Syldavia—natural conditions and a lack of technical know-how produce a less abundant crop each year. Syldavia suffers accordingly, given the sheer amount of exertion needed to extract food from the earth. However, no one in Syldavia suffers to any great degree—all have enough food to live a normal and productive life, and no one is in imminent danger of falling into starvation or objectionable poverty. However, their holdings of goods and resources are markedly inferior to those of the inhabitants of Borduria. One day, a party of Syldavians decides to go exploring, and crosses the mountains into the unexpectedly lush fields of Borduria. After a few days of getting to know their hosts, the Syldavians begin to complain. Why, they argue, is it fair that you have more than we do? Surely, the fact that we were born on the other side of the mountain is an accident of fate, and should not be used to justify the fact of an inequality. The Syldavians then suggest that the Bordurians and Syldavians create an international panel charged with maximizing the worst-off representative citizen in the set of individuals who are citizens of either country—whose first recommendation, they expect, will be the introduction of transfer payments from Borduria to Syldavia.

Are the Bordurians bound by the logic of liberalism to accept the demands of the Syldavians? I think not. The Bordurians can perfectly consistently reply that they are concerned with the protection of autonomy, and that this has led them to be concerned with the relative material inequality of those who are coerced through Bordurian private law by the Bordurian government. Otherwise, they explain, some Bordurians would face an ongoing coercive threat that could not be justified to them with reasons they could not reasonably reject. However, since the Syldavians are not bound by the legal web binding Bordurians—they are not threatened with imprisonment if they fail to pay taxes to the Bordurian government, nor do they find themselves threatened with coercive judgments in the Bordurian courts—the situation as regards the relative deprivation of the Syldavians is a little different. Since the Syldavians are simply less well-off than the Bordurians, rather than below the threshold of autonomous functioning, the Bordurians might quite consistently hold their ground against the Syldavian demands. The Bordurians might be altruistic or decent enough to give some of their wealth to the Syldavians, but that seems to be a matter more of supererogation than of obligation. No obligation exists, on the account given here, to concern ourselves with relative deprivations in the absence of a shared coercive legal system.

This is, of course, a fanciful example, and few have endorsed the idea that simply sharing a world is enough to give rise to egalitarian duties such as a Rawlsian would endorse domestically.[44] The more relevant case, of course, is what happens once widespread links of trade and diplomacy begin to take place between the two nations. Charles Beitz and Thomas Pogge have both argued that a sufficient degree of such links comprises a cooperative scheme for mutual benefit of the sort appropriate for analysis through Rawlsian methods.[45] Let us imagine, therefore, that the Bordurians and the Syldavians have begun to trade with one another, and that after a certain point in the relationship a similar party of Syldavians approach the Bordurian capital with a list of demands. The trade, they note, has advantages to both parties, but the advantages to the Bordurians are larger than the advantages to the Syldavians. After ten years of trading, perhaps, the situation of the Syldavian peasants has improved only slightly relative to the situation of autarky, but that of the Bordurian peasants is much greater than it was in autarky. Surely, the Syldavians argue, this cannot be right. After all, from within the original position, we would not know whether we were Bordurians or Syldavians, and we ought therefore to condemn the current social institutions of trade and diplomacy if they allow this degree of material inequality.

The Bordurians, I think, would be quite right to resist this appeal. The original position, they could explain patiently, is not a device to be used every time there is a division of a good—it is designed to demonstrate what sorts of justification could be given for certain forms of coercion by representing the circumstances under which hypothetical consent might be judged. In the present case, there seems to be no coercion going on at all. The Bordurians were under no obligation to begin trading with the Syldavians—indeed, they were under no obligation to do anything with or for them at all, given their morally acceptable situation in autarky. Trade, the Bordurians could note, is a matter here of offers, not of threats. The Bordurians' offer of regular trading routes was not a coercive offer; it did not take away any entitlement from the Syldavians. And the Syldavians' situation before the offer was—ex hypothesi—a morally acceptable one, given that it did not involve poverty of the sort likely to violate the principle of autonomy. There was no presumptively wrongful proposal in the Bordurian offer to trade. Neither, I think, are the Bordurians under any obligation to continue trading with the Syldavians since the situation of the Syldavians without trade was morally acceptable. (This is, of course, assuming that the Syldavians have not adjusted their internal economy to render a threshold level of physical functioning impossible to achieve without foreign trade. This might well be a false assumption, in which case things are that much more complex.) All of this, I think, demonstrates that no is coercion present in the international trading relationship here that would require the use of the original position for justification. Brian Barry similarly notes that no degree of economic interaction can form the moral equivalent of the relational web between citizens of a modern state.[46] Barry is not explicit about what sorts of relationships he thinks exist in the state, or about how they are morally different from mere trade. The above account can, however, give an explanation for Barry's intuition. What is present within the state, but not without it, is the fact of ongoing coercion. Barry's intuition is, I think, quite correct, and the Bordurians have no reason to give into the Syldavian claims.

Suppose the Syldavians have one final try. Surely, they argue, what matters morally is individual welfare—which we might understand as the number of things we are able realistically to do and to be—and Bordunian laws, inasmuch as they eventually affect what sorts of goods make it to the international market and at what price, affect what options are open to us as surely as that of any individual Bordurian. Why, therefore, do we not deserve a justification in terms we couldn't reasonably reject for the laws of Bordunia? Why do the Bordurians have a say when we do not?

In response, I think, the Bordurian government need only return to the liberal principle of autonomy, and emphasize that relative well-being and relative sets of available options are not necessarily implicated in this form of liberal egalitarianism. We are under no obligation to maximize the world's welfare—or the welfare of any one part of it, for that matter—but we *are* under an obligation to avoid denying the conditions of autonomy to all human beings. We coerce our own citizens, the Bordurians might say, in ways we don't coerce you; that deserves a justification, which we provide by ensuring that Bordurians have the right to political participation and to fair equality of opportunity, and by ensuring a relatively stringent principle of equality among Bordurians. The fact of coercion, and not the effect on welfare, deserves the justification. An analogy might help. When the laws of Borduria imprison a man for stealing, it undoubtedly affects the welfare both of the man and of (let us say) his friends, who will miss his companionship. But the man deserves a different sort of justification from us, since we are carrying through on a threat to remove his ability to pursue his own plans and projects in an autonomous way. The man is affected in a different way than his friends—and it isn't simply a matter of degree, but one of kind. The man is coerced, and if he cannot be given a reason for that fact that he could not reasonably accept, then what is done to him is wrong. The man's friends face no equivalent violation of autonomy, and are therefore not entitled to the same form of justification. The coercive nature of the laws, and not simply their effects upon welfare, make them a matter requiring justification.

At this point in the story, it seems that my theory would endorse a largely laissez-faire attitude toward global economic relationships. This appearance is, I think, misleading. The implications of a defense of individual autonomy would, I think, mandate a surprising degree of international reorganization and reform, given the current degree of economic destitution at work in the world.[47] While the existence of a coercive network of law is a precondition of a concern with relative deprivation, a concern with absolute deprivation seems not to have any such institutional precondition. If famine and deprivation are remediable, those political institutions that are able to remedy them have an obligation to do so—given the ways in which famine and deprivation deprive individuals of the exercise of their capacities for autonomy. The defense of autonomy would, I think, commit consistent liberals to the defense of a wide variety of other forms of human rights, including rights to be free from some of the more crippling systems of caste hierarchy, and perhaps the right to democratic governance. The precise articulation of what human rights would follow from this conception of autonomy, however, cannot be addressed in the present context. I am convinced, however, that whatever does follow is unlikely to be satisfied by the world we have today.

## VII. CONCLUSIONS

What I hope I have established is that the appearance of inconsistency identified at the beginning of this article is largely illusory. Liberalism can consistently limit its concern for relative deprivation to the domestic arena, and be concerned only with absolute deprivation in the international arena. A liberalism committed to the moral equality of all persons, and to the equal protection of the autonomy of all human beings, may nonetheless treat citizen and stranger differently based upon relevant differences in institutional relationship. The precise metric of egalitarian justice—the way, that is, in which our equal respect for autonomy is manifested—varies depending upon institutional context. A concern for domestic economic equality and international economic sufficiency reflects, I think, a consistent and thoroughgoing concern for the liberal principle of autonomy.

I will close this article with an analogy I hope will prove useful. The denial of the vote in an American election to an American citizen, let us say, would be something the principle I have identified here would condemn; it would be objectionable both through the symbolic insult and stigmatization it involves, and also through the lack of autonomy inherent in facing coercive laws one cannot help create.[48] The denial of the right to vote in American elections to a French citizen living in France, by contrast, has neither of these morally problematic effects.[49] The mere fact of material inequality greater than that allowed by the difference principle, I think, has now been shown to be morally equivalent to the denial of the vote: Between people who share a state it is morally prohibited, but it is not a valid implication of liberal equality for those who do not—a conclusion that holds true even if one's citizenship is the result of facts that are, in themselves, morally arbitrary. Material inequality is therefore more like a denial of suffrage than most liberal theorists have previously thought. Both are morally wrong in the context of shared citizenship, but not in themselves of moral concern when they occur between individuals not so situated. Indeed, they are of a piece: Both are justificatory strategies by which the coercive legal system might be justified to individuals. This approach can, I conclude, answer the cosmopolitan challenge given above; it can explain that the borders of the state, while perhaps arbitrary, are not morally *irrelevant*. Rather than putting a feudal privilege back into liberal theory, the limitation of our concern with relative deprivation to the domestic arena reflects the fact that those within face the fact of state coercion in a way that those without do not. We have, I think, arrived at a good way of understanding what we owe both to our fellow citizens and to the world. Work remains to be done on precisely what is owed to the foreign citizens and to the world, but I leave this for another time.

## NOTES

I would like to thank the following for their helpful comments on previous drafts of this article: Chris Bobonich, Ronald Dworkin, Lori Gruen, Frances Kamm, Jon Kaplan, Christine Korsgaard, Steve Macedo, Don Moon, Thomas Nagel, Susan Okin, Alan Patten, Jim Pryor, Tim Scanlon, the Editors of *Philosophy & Public Affairs*, and an anonymous reviewer for this journal. Special thanks are due to Debra Satz for her guidance and mentoring throughout this project.

1. This image is borrowed from Joseph Carens, "Aliens and Citizens: The Case for Open Borders," in Will Kymlicka, ed., *The Rights of Minority Cultures* (Oxford: Oxford University Press, 1995), p. 332 [first published in *The Review of Politics* 49: 2 (spring 1987): 241–73, reprinted herein 211–33, at 212].

2. Ronald Dworkin's idea of "associative obligations," as well as Richard Miller's idea of legitimate patriotic concern, take this form. See Dworkin, *Law's Empire* (Cambridge: Harvard University Press, 1986), pp. 195–205; and Miller, "Cosmopolitan Respect and Patriotic Concern," *Philosophy & Public Affairs* 27, no. 3 (1998): 202–24.

3. See Aristotle, *Nicomachean Ethics*, book II, chapter 6 (1106a36-b7). See also Amartya Sen, *Inequality Re-Examined* (New York: Russell Sage, 1992).

4. I would note, as a further complication, that many—if not most—attempts to justify a deviation from an impartial principle end up justifying that partiality based upon some other impartial principle. See, for example, Robert Goodin, "What Is So Special About Our Fellow Countrymen?" *Ethics* 98 (July 1988): 663–86 [reprinted herein 255–84], which justifies a local preference based upon the globally beneficial consequences of such a preference.

5. I should note, however, that although these borders are taken for granted in this stage of the inquiry, we can still ask two further questions about the division of the world into states: First, what conditions would have to obtain such that this division into states could be justifiable to all? Second, what principles of nonideal theory would have to be developed to govern the use of secession as a remedy for certain forms of injustice? An account of secession might therefore be developed from some considerations introduced in this article. Principles dealing with immigration might be developed in a like manner. For an sketch of what such an account of immigration might look like, see my entry on "Immigration," in R. G. Frey and Christopher Heath Wellman, eds., *A Companion to Applied Ethics* (Blackwell Companions to Philosophy) (Oxford: Blackwell Publishers, 2005), pp. 224–37.

6. Anthony Appiah, "Constitutional Patriots," in Joshua Cohen, ed., *For Love of Country* (Boston: Beacon Press, 1996), pp. 21–29.

7. I would also insist, further, that both noninstitutional and institutional forms of ideal theory exist; the mere fact of accepting political institutions does not render a theory nonideal. All theorizing requires us to accept some aspects of the world as theoretical premises for analysis; the assumptions can

be as thin as the fact of moderate scarcity, or as substantive as the assumption of distributed sovereignty. But the question of what principles constrain state action assuming full compliance and an absence of catastrophic resource shortfall is quite distinct from the question of how to guide state action when human wills or natural conditions fall radically short. I would reserve the term "nonideal theory" for the latter sort of question, and insist that it is possible to do ideal theory of an institutional sort. Indeed, I think ideal theory of such a sort is the most likely to give us guidance in the real world; it does this not by accepting nonideal conditions, but by showing us how our institutions might be justified under ideal circumstances.

8. I would also close this section by noting that I assume, for purposes of the present article, that the set of people bound under the territorial reach of a state's laws and the set of that state's citizens are equivalent. They are not, of course, and I hope to examine elsewhere the consequences of dropping this assumption. For the present, however, I will use this assumption for reasons of explanatory ease.

9. John Stuart Mill, for instance, grounds a concern for autonomy in utilitarian premises, whereas such thinkers as Martha Nussbaum derive this concern from Aristotelian grounds. See John Stuart Mill, *On Liberty* (1859) (Indianapolis: Hackett Publishing, 1978), and Martha Nussbaum, "Non-Relative Virtues: An Aristotelian Approach," in Martha Nussbaum and Amartya Sen, eds., *The Quality of Life* (Oxford: Oxford University Press, 1993), pp. 224–69.

10. I do not say that they are totally beyond the reach of political life; the approach given here might argue for certain programs of education required to bring otherwise disabled persons up to autonomous functioning, for example. I am grateful to Debra Satz for pointing out the implications of such disabilities in the present context.

11. See Joseph Raz, *The Morality of Freedom* (Oxford: Clarendon Press, 1986), pp. 376–78; see also Thomas Scanlon, "The Significance of Choice," in Stephen Darwall, ed., *Equal Freedom* (Ann Arbor: The University of Michigan Press, 1995), pp. 39–104.

12. Gerald Dworkin, "Is More Choice Better than Less?" *Midwest Studies in Philosophy* 7 (1982): 47–61; and Scanlon, "The Significance of Choice."

13. John Rawls, *Political Liberalism* (New York: Columbia University Press, 1993), p. 72. Rawls differentiates rational autonomy from full autonomy, by which the citizens of a political society are able to act from principles of justice that would be agreed to by rationally autonomous individuals. Since I want to concentrate for the moment on the demands of autonomy in the absence of political society, I will not discuss full autonomy in the present context. I would note also that although Rawls develops a political liberalism unconnected to any comprehensive doctrine, and Raz develops a comprehensive perfectionism based upon his respect for autonomy, they are in agreement on autonomy as a basic value. I view Raz's perfectionism as separable from his defense of

autonomy, and Rawls's principles ultimately rest upon an extremely similar notion of human autonomy, even if this latter is derived (in Rawls's later writings) from ideals implicit in the popular culture. I regret that I do not have time to explore these matters in any greater detail at present.

14. My approach to coercion is heavily influenced by Alan Wertheimer, *Coercion* (Princeton: Princeton University Press, 1987). See also Raz, *The Morality of Freedom*, p. 148.

15. Raz, *The Morality of Freedom*, p. 419.

16. See Herbert Morris, "Persons and Punishment," *The Monist* 52 (October 1986): 475–501; Jeffrie Murphy, "Marxism and Retribution," *Philosophy & Public Affairs* 2, no. 3 (1973): 217–43.

17. See Thomas Scanlon, "Contractarianism and Utilitarianism," in Amartya Sen and Bernard Williams, eds., *Utilitarianism and Beyond* (Cambridge: Cambridge University Press, 1982), pp. 103–28. See also Scanlon, *What We Owe to Each Other* (Cambridge: Harvard University Press, 1999).

18. *Gregg v. Georgia*, 428 U.S. 153 (1976).

19. *Coker v. Georgia*, 433 U.S. 584 (1977).

20. It may also explain the conviction of some theorists of punishment that purely deterrent punishment is never justified, although I will not explore this idea here. See Murphy, "Marxism and Retribution," for a good account of this line of argumentation.

21. *Trop v. Dulles*, 356 U.S. 86, 100 (1958).

22. I would note, in passing, that I am not saying that a more "cruel" form of punishment—in the ordinary sense of a more painful or humiliating form of punishment—is necessarily a greater violation of autonomy than a less "cruel" form. I am saying that one way of understanding the Supreme Court's vision of cruel and unusual punishment is with reference to the idea of autonomy. Those forms of punishment that cannot be justified to citizens understood as autonomous agents are comprehensible as cruel and unusual in this latter sense. Thus, an unduly painful form of execution might constitute a violation of autonomy, but not because it is "cruel" in the ordinary sense of the word, but rather because this particular form of punishment could not be justified to free and equal citizens. I am grateful to an anonymous editor at *Philosophy & Public Affairs* for urging me to be clearer on this matter.

23. See H. L. A. Hart, *The Concept of Law* (Oxford: Clarendon Press, 1961), pp. 28–29.

24. Michael D. Danekan, "Moral Reasoning and the Quest for Legitimacy," 43 *American University Law Review* (1993): 49.

25. *Shelley v. Kraemer*, 334 U.S. 1 (1948).

26. Anthony Kronman, "Contract Law and Distributive Justice," 89 *Yale Law Journal* (1980): 472. I disagree with Kronman on one central point; he argues that the forms of justification open to a liberal are limited to notions such as fairness and economic egalitarianism. I think, in contrast, that we

ought to begin with our more minimal idea of autonomy; this inquiry will end up with an economically egalitarian content in some contexts, but such an outcome will be the result of our moral inquiry, rather than (as Kronman has it) the beginning.

27. Robert M. Cover, "Violence and the Word," 95 *Yale Law Journal* (1986): 1601. Cover notes that law is always played on a field of violence and death; if this is most apparent in the criminal law, "all law which concerns property, its use and its protection, has a similarly violent base" (n.16).

28. This way of looking at the private law may remind some readers too much of John Austin, whose coercion-based philosophy of law was convincingly disputed by H. L. A. Hart. I would note here only that Austin's question and my own differ to such a degree that my use of coercion may not be susceptible to the same criticisms as his own. See H. L. A. Hart, *The Concept of Law*, and John Austin, *The Province of Jurisprudence Determined*, 5th ed. (1885), ed. Wilfred E. Rumble (Cambridge: Cambridge University Press, 1995).

29. See, for example, G. A. Cohen, "Where the Action Is: On the Site of Distributive Justice," *Philosophy & Public Affairs* 26, no. 1 (1997): 3–30.

30. J. Donald Moon and others have pressed on me the objection that the entire international system might be based upon coercion—seen, for instance, in the coercive exclusion of would-be immigrants at the border. This may be correct, but it is important to remember that each distinct form of coercion requires a distinct form of justification. The refusal of entry to a would-be member may or may not be justifiable; the form such justification would take, however, would be significantly different from that offered to a present member for the web of legal coercion within which she currently lives. The mere fact that exclusion is coercive does not erase the distinction between prospective and current membership. Only the latter, I argue, gives rise to a legitimate concern for relative deprivation.

31. It is worthwhile to note, in this connection, that real property in the United States must be—in theory, if not in legal practice—traced back to an original grant from the sovereign for it to be legally cognizable as property.

32. We may notice, now, that I have begun to talk directly about property and entitlements, which seems a more expansive set of concerns than I was earlier willing to allow in the context of autonomy. There is, I think, a good reason for this. Our earlier consideration was the identification of a given situation as violating or respecting autonomy. In this, we noted, there was no necessary concern—above a certain baseline—for the size of our holdings of goods or the number of options realistically open to us. Our present focus, however, is on the justification of a situation already identified as coercive, and therefore as violative of the liberal principle of autonomy. In this focus, I think, more expansive criteria may be employed; we can give and withhold our consent based on considerations that, in themselves, are not necessarily implicated in every discussion of autonomy. In deciding whether to accept a

coercive regime defining returns to various positions, that is, we might well examine that proposal in terms of its effects on our resources and economic holdings. The private law is coercive, and it has consequences for the allocation of goods; the former fact makes the private law stand in need of justification, while the latter provides the means by which our consent—the method of our justification—might be given or withheld.

33. See John Rawls, *The Law of Peoples* (Cambridge: Harvard University Press, 1999), for Rawls's own views of the implications of contractualism abroad.

34. See, for instance, John Rawls, *A Theory of Justice* (Cambridge: Harvard University Press, 1971), p. 343: "It is generally agreed that extorted promises are void ab initio. But similarly, unjust social arrangements are themselves a kind of extortion, even violence, and consent to them does not bind. The reason for this condition is that the parties in the original position would insist upon it." Rawls is here, of course, not explicit about the fact that domestic law is coercive—this is, however, the interpretation he gives to his earlier account by the time of *Political Liberalism*.

35. Rawls, *Political Liberalism*, p. 136.

36. John Rawls, "The Law of Peoples," in *On Human Rights*, ed. Stephen Shute et al. (New York: Basic Books, 1993), pp. 41–82 [220–30, reprinted herein 421–60]. See also Rawls, *The Law of Peoples*.

37. Rawls, *Political Liberalism*, p. 217.

38. Ibid., p. 77.

39. Ibid., pp. 61–62.

40. Ibid., p. 264.

41. Rawls, "The Law of Peoples," 220–21, n. 2 [herein 452–53].

42. See Robert Goodin, "What Is So Special about Our Fellow Country-men?" [reprinted herein 255–84].

43. The story here is borrowed in part from James Buchanan, "A Two-country Parable," in Warren F. Schwartz, ed., *Justice in Immigration* (Cambridge: Cambridge University Press, 1995), pp. 63–66.

44. But see Charles Beitz, "Cosmopolitan Ideals and National Sentiment," *Journal of Philosophy* 80 (October 1983): 591–600 [reprinted in *Global Ethics: Seminal Essays*, 107–17].

45. See Charles Beitz, *Political Theory and International Relations* (Princeton: Princeton University Press, 1979, and Thomas Pogge, *Realizing Rawls* (Ithaca: Cornell University Press, 1989).

46. Brian Barry, "Humanity and Justice in Global Perspective," *Nomos 24: Ethics, Economics and the Law*, ed. J. R. Pennock and J. W Chapman (New York: New York University Press, 1982), p. 233 [reprinted herein 179–209, at 191–92]: "Trade, if freely undertaken... is not, it seems to me, the kind of relationship that gives rise to duties of fair play.... Trade in pottery, ornamenta-tion, and weapons can be traced back to prehistoric times, but we would hardly feel inclined to think of, say, the Beaker Folk as forming a single cooperative

enterprise with their trading partners. No more did the spice trade unite east and west."

47. Barbara Crossette, "Half the World Lacks Sanitation, Says UNICEF," *New York Times* (July 23, 1997), A9.

48. The denial of the vote in this way, I think, might well be understood as a practice of marginalization—a symbolic statement that the individual denied is not worthy of autonomous deliberation and must accept the values and principles of others in an uncritical way. This notion of the symbolic importance of the vote is discussed in greater detail in Judith Shklar, *American Citizenship* (Cambridge: Harvard University Press, 1991).

49. A similar idea is expressed by Jeremy Waldron, "Special Ties and Natural Duties," *Philosophy & Public Affairs* 22, no. 1 (1993): 3–30 [reprinted herein 391–419]. Waldron introduces an idea of range-limited duties as implications of natural duties—as, for example, citizens have distinct duties toward only their own state, which result from a general and natural duty to support just institutions. This dovetails nicely with my own idea that an impartial principle can have distinct implications in distinct contexts. Where Waldron and I differ is primarily in theoretical focus. His focus is on the obligation of the citizen toward the state while mine is on what the state must do toward the citizen—and the noncitizen—for its exercise of coercive power to be justified.

# COMMON INDEX

References in Roman numerals (i, ii, iii…) are to the Common Preface. References in Arabic numerals (1, 2, 3…) are to *Global Justice: Seminal Essays*. References in italic Arabic numerals (*1, 2, 3…*) are to *Global Ethics: Seminal Essays*. This index was composed by Matt Peterson.